American Literary Scholarship 1991

American Literary Scholarship

An Annual 1991

Edited by David J. Nordloh

Essays by David M. Robinson, Frederick Newberry, Benjamin Franklin Fisher IV, John Wenke, Gary Lee Stonum, Robert Sattelmeyer, Sarah B. Daugherty, George Kearns, Cleo McNelly Kearns, Alexander J. Marshall, III, Susan F. Beegel, William J. Scheick, Gary Scharnhorst, Jo Ann Middleton, Charlotte Hadella, Jerome Klinkowitz, Richard J. Calhoun, Peter A. Davis, Michael Fischer, F. Lyra, Rolf Meyn, Algerina Neri, Keiko Beppu, Jan Nordby Gretlund, Elisabeth Herion-Sarafidis, and Hans Skei

Duke University Press Durham and London 1993

LC 65-19450 ISBN 0-8223-1315-4

Printed in the United States of America

on acid-free paper ∞

Contents

Foreword

J. Albert Robbins, co-editor of this series for more than 20 years, died on 4 March 1992 at the age of 77. Production of last year's volume was so far advanced when this news arrived that the only acknowledgment of the fact and of his contribution to *American Literary Scholarship* was the inscription "In memory of J. Albert Robbins" facing the title page. Al Robbins might have approved the brevity of that, so modest and self-effacing a man was he, so completely dedicated to the work of American literature through his many and constant bibliographical activities. He recorded his departure from *ALS* in the foreword to the 1988 volume with characteristic understatement: "*ALS 1987* marks the last number edited by James Woodress, and this volume the last edited by J. Albert Robbins." But we who knew him and worked with him over the years know that his service to the profession was significant and lasting, and we mourn his loss.

Louis Owens, who prepared last year's volume as the newly designated co-editor of *ALS,* alternating with David J. Nordloh, has chosen to resign the position to devote more time to his teaching responsibilities, to other research, and to his fiction-writing. His place will be taken by Gary Scharnhorst, University of New Mexico, who is represented in the current volume by the chapter on "19th-Century Literature." Because Professor Scharnhorst was already committed to a teaching exchange taking him out of the United States for part of 1992, he was not able to take over the preparation of the volume following this one. Instead, David Nordloh has agreed to edit two in a row, and so is responsible for *ALS 1992.* Authors are invited to direct review copies of books and articles to him at the Department of English, Indiana University, Bloomington, IN 47405.

The roster of chapter contributors has changed as well. Gary Lee

Stonum has taken over the "Whitman and Dickinson" chapter from John Carlos Rowe; Alexander J. Marshall, III replaces longtime contributor M. Thomas Inge in preparing the "Faulkner" chapter; and Keiko Beppu takes a turn at "Japanese Contributions" in the "Foreign Scholarship" chapter, alternating with Hiroko Sato. The section on "East European Contributions" for 1990, prepared by F. Lyra, and that on "German Contributions" for the same period, prepared by Rolf Meyn, arrived too late for inclusion in last year's volume; they appear this time side by side with the 1991 essays. Michel Gresset has resigned "French Contributions," and no one has been found to replace him this year.

Next year's volume will see further changes in authorship. Leland S. Person will take over the "Hawthorne" chapter from Frederick Newberry; Tom Quirk will replace Robert Sattelmeyer at the helm of the "Mark Twain"; Richard A. Hocks will return to the "Henry James," which Sarah B. Daugherty did so capably during his *ALS* sabbatical; Albert J. DeFazio III will replace Susan F. Beegel in the "Fitzgerald and Hemingway" chapter; Catherine Calloway will take over for Charlotte Hadella in "Fiction: The 1930s to the 1960s"; and Alicia Kae Koger will replace Peter A. Davis in covering "Drama." In the "Foreign Contributions" chapter it will be Hiroko Sato's turn at "Japanese Contributions." A warm welcome to the new contributors, and warmest thanks to departing colleagues for hard work and judicious prose.

I want to acknowledge general administrative support from Indiana University in the preparation of this volume, and the cooperation of Terence Ford, Director, and his staff at the Center for Bibliographic Services, MLA, in supplying a preprint of relevant portions of the *International Bibliography* for use by *ALS* contributors. More special to me have been the capable assistance of Nancy May-Scott, my secretary in the Graduate Program in American Studies at Indiana, and the vigilance and good humor of Bob Mirandon and Pam Morrison of Duke University Press. Some sins of mine these friends forgive; most they hide from public view with their own good works.

David J. Nordloh
Indiana University

Key to Abbreviations

Festschriften, Essay Collections, and Books Discussed in More Than One Chapter

The Aching Hearth / Sara Munson Deats and Lagretta Tallent Lenker, eds., *The Aching Hearth: Family Violence in Life and Literature* (Plenum)

The Aesthetics of Murder / Joel Black, *The Aesthetics of Murder: A Study in Romantic Literature and Contemporary Culture* (Hopkins)

African American Writers / Valerie Smith, ed., *African American Writers* (Scribner's)

Americana & Hungarica / Charlotte Kretzoi, ed., *Americana & Hungarica* (Budapest: Department of English, L. Eötvös University, 1989)

American Autobiography / Paul John Eakin, ed., *American Autobiography: Retrospect and Prospect* (Wisconsin)

American Designs / Jeanne Campbell Reesman, *American Designs: The Late Novels of James and Faulkner* (Penn.)

An American Empire / Serge Ricard, ed., *An American Empire: Expansionist Cultures and Politics, 1881–1917* (Aix-en-Provence: Université de Provence, 1990)

The American Ideal / Peter Carafiol, *The American Ideal: Literary History as a Worldly Activity* (Oxford)

American Literature and the Destruction of Knowledge / Ronald E. Martin, *American Literature and the Destruction of Knowledge: Innovative Writing in the Age of Epistemology* (Duke)

The American Scene / Stuart Hutchinson, *The American Scene: Essays on Nineteenth-Century American Literature* (St. Martin's)

American Writing Today / Richard Kostelanetz, ed., *American Writing Today* (Whitston)

The Artist and His Masks / Agostino Lombardo, ed., *The Artist and His Masks: William Faulkner's Metafiction* (Bulzoni)

Authorship and Audience / Stephen Railton, *Authorship and Audience: Literary Performance in the American Renaissance* (Princeton)

Beautiful Machine / John Seelye, *Beautiful Machine: Rivers and the Republican Plan, 1755–1825* (Oxford)

Between Worlds / Amy Ling, *Between Worlds: Women Writers of Chinese Ancestry* (Pergamon, 1990)

By the Law of Nature / Howard Horwitz, *By the Law of Nature: Form and Value in Nineteenth-Century America* (Oxford)

Claiming the Heritage / Missy Dehn Kubitschek, *Claiming the Heritage: African-American Women Novelists and History* (Miss.)

Classics of Civil War Fiction / David Madden and Peggy Bach, eds., *Classics of Civil War Fiction* (Miss.)

The Columbia History of the American Novel / Emory Elliott et al., eds., *The Columbia History of the American Novel: New Views* (Columbia)

Comparative American Identities / Hortense J. Spillers, ed., *Comparative American Identities: Race, Sex, and Nationality in the Modern Text* (Routledge)

Conflicting Stories / Elizabeth Ammons, *Conflicting Stories: American Women Writers at the Turn into the Twentieth Century* (Oxford)

Consumption and American Culture / David E. Nye and Carol Pederson, eds., *Consumption and American Culture* (Netherlands: Free Univ. Press)

Contexts for Hawthorne / Milton R. Stern, *Contexts for Hawthorne*: The Marble Faun *and the Politics of Openness and Closure in American Literature* (Illinois)

Cultural Power/Cultural Literacy / Bonnie Braendlin, ed., *Cultural Power / Cultural Literacy: Selected Papers from the Fourteenth Annual Florida State University Conference on Literature and Film* (Florida State)

Curtain Calls / Mary Anne Schofield and Cecilia Macheski, eds., *Curtain Calls: British and American Women in the Theater, 1660–1820* (Ohio)

Daughters, Fathers, and the Novel / Lynda Marie Zwinger, *Daughters, Fathers, and the Novel: The Sentimental Romance of Heterosexuality* (Wisconsin)

Detective Fiction and Literature / Martin Priestman, *Detective Fiction and Literature: The Figure on the Carpet* (St. Martin's)

Discourse and Character / Wojciech Kalaga and Tadeusz Slawek, eds., *Discourse and Character* (Katowice [Poland]: Uniwersytet Slaski, 1990)

Discourses/Texts/Contexts / Wojciech Kalaga and Tadeusz Slawek, eds., *Discourses/Texts/Contexts* (Katowice [Poland]: Uniwersytet Slaski, 1990)

Diverse Voices / Harriet Devine Jump, ed., *Diverse Voices: Essays on Twentieth-Century Women Writers in English* (St. Martin's)

Domestic Individualism / Gillian Brown, *Domestic Individualism: Imagining Self in Nineteenth-Century America* (Calif., 1990)

Dwelling in the Text / Marilyn R. Chandler, *Dwelling in the Text: Houses in American Fiction* (Calif.)

The Ends of Rhetoric / John Bender and David E. Wellbery, eds., *The*

Ends of Rhetoric: History, Theory, Practice (Stanford, 1990)
Faulkner and Religion / Doreen Fowler and Ann J. Abadie, eds., *Faulkner and Religion: Faulkner and Yoknapatawpha, 1989* (Miss.)
The Feminist Companion to Literature in English / Virginia Blain et al., *The Feminist Companion to Literature in English: Women Writers from the Middle Ages to the Present* (Yale)
Free Women / Kate Fullbrook, *Free Women: Ethics and Aesthetics in Twentieth-Century Women's Fiction* (Temple, 1990)
Freud, Religion, and the Roaring Twenties / Henry Idema III, *Freud, Religion, and the Roaring Twenties: A Psychoanalytic Theory of Secularization in Three Novelists: Anderson, Hemingway, and Fitzgerald* (Rowan & Littlefield, 1990)
From Harlem to Paris / Michel Fabre, *From Harlem to Paris: Black American Writers in France, 1840–1980* (Illinois)
Haunting the House of Fiction / Lynette Carpenter and Wendy K. Kolmar, eds., *Haunting the House of Fiction: Feminist Perspectives on Ghost Stories by American Women* (Tennessee)
Home Ground / J. Bill Berry, ed., *Home Ground: Southern Autobiography* (Missouri)
The Idea of Wilderness / Max Oelschlaeger, *The Idea of Wilderness: From Prehistory to the Age of Ecology* (Yale)
Imagined Places / Michael Pearson, *Imagined Places: Journeys into Literary America* (Miss.)
Influence and Intertextuality / Jay Clayton and Eric Rothstein, eds., *Influence and Intertextuality in Literary History* (Wisconsin)
In Respect to Egotism / Joel Porte, *In Respect to Egotism: Studies in American Romantic Writing* (Cambridge)
Labor into Art / David Sprague Herreshoff, *Labor into Art: the Theme of Work in Nineteenth-Century American Literature* (Wayne State)
Lesbian Texts and Contexts / Karla Jay et al., eds., *Lesbian Texts and Contexts: Radical Revisions* (NYU, 1990)
Liberating Visions / Robert Michael Franklin, *Liberating Visions: Human Fulfillment and Social Justice in African-American Thought* (Fortress, 1990)
Liberating Voices / Gayl Jones, *Liberating Voices: Oral Tradition in African American Literature* (Harvard)
Lyric Contingencies / Margaret Dickie, *Lyric Contingencies: Emily Dickinson and Wallace Stevens* (Penn.)
Macropolitics of Nineteenth-Century Literature / Jonathan Arac and Harriet Ritvo, eds., *Macropolitics of Nineteenth-Century Literature: Nationalism, Exoticism, Imperialism* (Penn.)
Marvelous Possessions / Stephen Greenblatt, *Marvelous Possessions: The Wonder of the New World* (Chicago)
The Mockingbird in the Gum Tree / Louis D. Rubin, Jr., *The Mockingbird in the Gum Tree: A Literary Gallimaufry* (LSU)
The Modern American Urban Novel / Arnold L. Goldsmith, *The Modern*

American Urban Novel: Nature as "Interior Structure" (Wayne State)
The Modernist in History / Ronald Bush, ed., *T. S. Eliot: The Modernist in History* (Cambridge)
Natural Right and the American Imagination / Catherine H. Zuckert, *Natural Right and the American Imagination: Political Philosophy in Novel Form* (Rowan & Littlefield)
New Readings of the American Novel / Peter Messent, *New Readings of the American Novel: Narrative Theory and Its Application* (St. Martin's, 1990)
Novel Frames / Joseph R. Urgo, *Novel Frames: Literature as Guide to Race, Sex, and History in American Culture* (Miss.)
Occidental Ideographs / Franklin R. Rogers, *Occidental Ideographs: Image, Sequence, and Literary History* (Bucknell)
Order in Variety / R. W. Crump, ed., *Order in Variety: Essays and Poems in Honor of Donald E. Stanford* (Delaware)
The Poetics of Appalachian Space / Parks Lanier, Jr., *The Poetics of Appalachian Space* (Tennessee)
The Poetics of Imperialism / Eric Cheyfitz, *The Poetics of Imperialism: Translation and Colonization from* The Tempest *to* Tarzan (Oxford)
Politics in the African-American Novel / Richard Kostelanetz, *Politics in the African-American Novel: James Weldon Johnson, W. E. B. Du Bois, Richard Wright, and Ralph Ellison* (Greenwood)
The Politics of Voice / Malini Johar Schueller, *The Politics of Voice: Liberalism and Social Criticism from Franklin to Kingston* (SUNY)
Praise Disjoined / William P. Shaw, ed., *Praise Disjoined: Changing Patterns of Salvation in 17th-Century English Literature* (Lang)
Reading Black, Reading Feminist / Henry Louis Gates, Jr., ed., *Reading Black, Reading Feminist: A Critical Anthology* (Meridian, 1990)
Redefining Autobiography / Janice Morgan and Colette T. Hall, eds., *Redefining Autobiography in Twentieth-Century Women's Fiction: An Essay Collection* (Garland)
Removals / Lucy Maddox, *Removals: Nineteenth-Century American Literature and the Politics of Indian Affairs* (Oxford)
Representing Modernist Texts / George Bornstein, ed., *Representing Modernist Texts: Editing as Interpretation* (Michigan)
The Role of the Mythic West / Jan Bakker, *The Role of the Mythic West in Some Representative Examples of Classic and Modern American Literature: The Shaping Force of the American Frontier* (Mellen)
Romantic Revolutions / Kenneth R. Johnston et al., eds., *Romantic Revolutions: Criticism and Theory* (Indiana, 1990)
Rough Justice / M. L. Friedland, ed., *Rough Justice: Essays on Crime in Literature* (Toronto)
Savage Eye / Christopher Sten, ed., *Savage Eye: Melville and the Visual Arts* (Kent State)
Sentimental Modernism / Suzanne

Clark, *Sentimental Modernism: Women Writers and the Revolution of the Word* (Indiana)

Sister's Choice / Elaine Showalter, *Sister's Choice: Tradition and Change in American Women's Writing* (Oxford)

The Spectator and the City / Dana Brand, *The Spectator and the City in Nineteenth-Century American Literature* (Cambridge)

Sporting with the Gods / Michael Oriard, *Sporting with the Gods: The Rhetoric of Play and Game in American Culture* (Cambridge)

Theater Enough / Jeffrey H. Richards, *Theater Enough: American Culture and the Metaphor of the World Stage, 1607–1789* (Duke)

Theorizing American Literature / Bainard Cowan and Joseph G. Kronick, eds., *Theorizing American Literature: Hegel, the Sign, and History* (LSU)

Tradition and the Talents of Women / Florence Howe, ed., *Tradition and the Talents of Women* (Illinois)

The True and Only Heaven / Christopher Lasch, *The True and Only Heaven: Progress and Its Critics* (Norton)

The United States South / Valeria Gennaro Lerda and Tjebbe Westendorp, eds., *The United States South: Regionalism and Identity* (Bulzoni)

Using Lacan, Reading Fiction / James M. Mellard, *Using Lacan, Reading Fiction* (Illinois)

The Vanderbilt Tradition / Mark Royden Winchell, ed., *The Vanderbilt Tradition: Essays in Honor of Thomas Daniel Young* (LSU)

A Voice of Their Own / Martha M. Solomon, ed., *A Voice of Their Own: The Woman Suffrage Press, 1840–1910* (Alabama)

Waking Giants / Herbert N. Schneidau, *Waking Giants: The Presence of the Past in Modernism* (Oxford)

"We Are All Indians" / Wojciech Kalaga and Tadeusz Slawek, eds., *"We Are All Indians": Violence Intolerance Literature* (Katowice [Poland]: Uniwersytet Slaski, 1990)

The Workings of the Spirit / Houston A. Baker, Jr., *The Workings of the Spirit: The Poetics of Afro-American Women's Writing* (Chicago)

Writing in the New Nation / Larzer Ziff, *Writing in the New Nation: Prose, Print, and Politics in the Early United States* (Yale)

Periodicals, Annuals, and Series

AL / *American Literature*

ALR / *American Literary Realism, 1870–1910*

American History Illustrated

American Journal of Psychoanalysis

American Periodicals

AmerS / *American Studies*

AmerSS / *American Studies in Scandinavia*

AmLH / *American Literary History*

Amst / *Amerikastudien*

ANQ: A Quarterly Journal of Short Articles, Notes, and Reviews

AQ / *American Quarterly*

ArAA / *Arbeiten aus Anglistik und Amerikanistik*

Arcadia: Zeitschrift für Vergleichende Literaturwissenschaft

ArQ / *Arizona Quarterly*
ASch / *American Scholar*
ATQ / *American Transcendental Quarterly*
BALF / *Black American Literature Forum*
BB / *Bulletin of Bibliography*
Bête Noir
Biography / *Biography: An Interdisciplinary Quarterly*
Border States
Boundary 2
BSJ / *The Baker Street Journal: An Irregular Quarterly of Sherlockiana*
BSWWS / Boise State University Western Writers Series
ByronJ / *The Byron Journal*
C&L / *Christianity and Literature*
The Californians
Callaloo: A Black South Journal of Arts and Letters
CanL / *Canadian Literature*
CCTEP / *Conference of College Teachers of English Studies*
CEA / *CEA Critic*
Chapter & Verse
ChH / *Church History*
ChLB / *Charles Lamb Bulletin*
CJAS / *Canadian Journal of African Studies / Revue Canadienne des Etudes Africaines*
CLAJ / *College Language Association Journal*
ClioI / *CLIO: A Journal of Literature, History, and the Philosophy of History*
CLQ / *Colby Library Quarterly*
Clues: A Journal of Detection
CMC / *Crosscurrents / Modern Critiques*
CML / *Classical and Modern Literature*
CollL / *College Literature*
ConL / *Contemporary Literature*
Constructions
Contemporanea
CRevAS / *Canadian Review of American Studies*
Crit / *Critique: Studies in Modern Fiction*
CritI / *Critical Inquiry*
Criticism: A Quarterly for Literature and the Arts
Cultural Critique
Diaspora
DicS / *Dickinson Studies: Emily Dickinson (1830–86), U.S. Poet*
DLB / *Dictionary of Literary Biography*
DNR / *Dime Novel Roundup*
DQR / *Dutch Quarterly Review of Anglo-American Letters*
DR / *Dalhousie Review*
DUJ / *Durham University Journal*
DWF / *DonnaWomanFemme* (Rome)
EAL / *Early American Literature*
EAS / *Essays in Arts and Sciences*
ECent / *The Eighteenth Century: Theory and Interpretation*
ECLife / *Eighteenth-Century Life*
Edda: Nordisk Tidsskrift for Literaturforskning / Scandinavian Journal of Literary Research
EdWR / *Edith Wharton Review* [formerly *Edith Wharton Newsletter*]
EIC / *Essays in Criticism* (Oxford, England)
EigoS / *Eigo Seinen* (Tokyo)
EIHC / *Essex Institute Historical Collections*
ELH [formerly *Journal of English Literary History*]
ELN / *English Language Notes*

ELWIU / *Essays in Literature* (Western Ill. Univ.)
ESC / *English Studies in Canada*
ESQ: A Journal of the American Renaissance
Expl / *Explicator*
Faulkner Studies
FJ / *Faulkner Journal*
GettR / *Gettysburg Review*
GPQ / *Great Plains Quarterly*
Gulf Coast
HJR / *Henry James Review*
HN / *Hemingway Review*
HSE / *Hungarian Studies in English* (Debrecen)
HTR / *Harvard Theological Review*
HUSL / *Hebrew University Studies in Literature and the Arts*
Ideas '92
IFR / *International Fiction Review*
Il Ponte
ISh / *The Independent Shavian*
JAC / *Journal of American Culture*
JADT / *Journal of American Drama and Theatre*
JAH / *Journal of American History*
JAmS / *Journal of American Studies*
JASAT / *Journal of the American Studies Assn. of Texas*
JDN / *James Dickey Newsletter*
JDTC / *Journal of Dramatic Theory and Criticism*
JEP / *Journal of Evolutionary Psychology*
JER / *Journal of the Early Republic*
JML / *Journal of Modern Literature*
JNT / *Journal of Narrative Technique*
Journal of Homosexuality
Journal of Mississippi History
Journal of Psychohistory
JSSE / *Journal of the Short Story in English* (Angers, France)
KR / *Kenyon Review*
LAmer / *Letterature d'America: Rivista Trimestale*
Legacy: A Journal of Nineteenth-Century American Women Writers
LHY / *Literary Half-Yearly*
Lingue e letterature
LIT / *Literature Interpretation Theory*
LJHum / *Lamar Journal of Humanities*
Malavoglia
MD / *Modern Drama*
MELUS: The Journal of the Society for the Study of Multi-Ethnic Literature of the United States
Menckeniana: A Quarterly Review
MFS / *Modern Fiction Studies*
Mississippi Review
MissQ / *Mississippi Quarterly*
MLR / *Modern Language Review*
MLS / *Modern Language Studies*
MMisc / *Midwestern Miscellany*
MOR / *Mount Olive Review*
Mosaic: A Journal for the Interdisciplinary Study of Literature
MQ / *Midwest Quarterly: A Journal of Contemporary Thought* (Pittsburg, Kans.)
MR / *Massachusetts Review*
MSEx / *Melville Society Extracts*
MStrR / *Mickle Street Review*
MTJ / *Mark Twain Journal*
Names: Journal of the American Name Society
N&Q / *Notes and Queries*
Natural History
NCF / *Nineteenth-Century Literature*
NConL / *Notes on Contemporary Literature*
NCP / *Nineteenth Century Prose*
NCTR / *Nineteenth Century Theatre*
NDQ / *North Dakota Quarterly*

Neohelicon: Acta Comparationis Litterarum Universarum
NEQ / *New England Quarterly*
NewC / *The New Criterion*
NHR / *Nathaniel Hawthorne Review*
NietzscheS / *Nietzsche Studien*
NLH / *New Literary History: A Journal of Theory and Interpretation*
NMHR / *New Mexico Humanities Review*
NYH / *New York History*
OL / *Orbis Litterarum: International Review of Literary Studies*
OLR / *Oxford Literary Review*
ON / *Old Northwest: A Journal of Regional Life and Letters*
Oregon English Journal
Paideuma: A Journal Devoted to Ezra Pound Scholarship
P&L / *Philosophy and Literature*
PennH / *Pennsylvania History*
PLL / *Papers on Language and Literature*
PMLA: Publications of the Modern Language Assn.
PNotes / *Pynchon Notes*
PoeS / *Poe Studies*
Poesia
POMPA / *Publications of the Mississippi Philological Association*
PQ / *Philological Quarterly*
Professional Geographer
Prospects: An Annual Journal of American Cultural Studies
PSt / *Prose Studies*
PULC / *Princeton University Library Chronicle*
PUUHS / *Proceedings of the Unitarian Universalist Historical Society*
PVR / *Platte Valley Review*
RALS / *Resources for American Literary Study*
Raritan, A Quarterly Review
RCF / *Review of Contemporary Fiction*
Renascence: Essays on Value in Literature
Representations
RES / *Review of English Studies*
RFEA / *Revue Française d'Etudes Américaines*
Rhetoric Review
Rivista di Studi Anglo-Americani
RMR / *Rocky Mountain Review of Language and Literature*
Robert Frost Review
RSAJ / *RSA Journal: Rivista di Studi Nord-Americani*
RSQ / *Rhetoric Society Quarterly*
SAF / *Studies in American Fiction*
Sagetrieb: A Journal Devoted to Poets in the Pound-H.D.-Williams Tradition
SAIL / *Studies in American Indian Literature*
SAJL / *Studies in American Jewish Literature*
SALit / *Chu-Shikoku Studies in American Literature*
SAQ / *South Atlantic Quarterly*
SAR / *Studies in the American Renaissance*
SCR / *South Carolina Review*
SCRev / *South Central Review: The Journal of the South Central Modern Language Assn.*
SDR / *South Dakota Review*
SECC / *Studies in Eighteenth-Century Culture*
SELit / *Studies in English Literature* (Tokyo)
Shenandoah
SHR / *Southern Humanities Review*
SIR / *Studies in Romanticism*
SJS / *San Jose Studies*
SLJ / *Southern Literary Journal*

SN / *Studia Neophilologica*
SNNTS / *Studies in the Novel* (North Texas State Univ.)
SoAR / *South Atlantic Review*
SoQ / *Southern Quarterly*
SoR / *Southern Review*
SoSt / *Southern Studies*
Soundings: An Interdisciplinary Journal
SPAS / *Studies in Puritan American Spirituality*
SR / *Sewanee Review*
SSF / *Studies in Short Fiction*
StAH / *Studies in American Humor*
StHum / *Studies in the Humanities* (Indiana, Pa.)
Storia Nordamericana
StQ / *Steinbeck Quarterly*
Style
SWR / *Southwest Review*
TCL / *Twentieth-Century Literature*
TexP / *Textual Practice*
Text: Transactions of the Society for Textual Scholarship
Thalia: Studies in Literary Humor
Theatre Topics
Thought: A Review of Culture and Idea
THStud / *Theatre History Studies*
TJ / *Theatre Journal*
TS / *Theatre Survey*
TSLL / *Texas Studies in Language and Literature*
TSWL / *Tulsa Studies in Women's Literature*
TUSAS / Twayne's United States Authors Series
UDR / *University of Dayton Review*
UMSE / *University of Mississippi Studies in English*
Utopian Studies
VMHB / *Virginia Magazine of History and Biography*
VQR / *Virginia Quarterly Review*
W&I / *Word and Image: A Journal of Verbal / Visual Enquiry* (London, England)
WAL / *Western American Literature*
WCPMN / *Willa Cather Pioneer Memorial Newsletter*
WHR / *Western Humanities Review*
WMQ / *William and Mary Quarterly*
Women's Studies Quarterly
WS / *Women's Studies*
WVUPP / *West Virginia University Philological Papers*
WWR / *Walt Whitman Quarterly Review*
YER / *Yeats Eliot Review*
YJC / *The Yale Journal of Criticism: Interpretation in the Humanities*

Publishers

Aarhus / Aarhus, Denmark: Universitetsforlag
Alabama / Tuscaloosa: Univ. of Alabama Press
Allyn and Bacon / Boston: Allyn and Bacon
Almqvist and Wiksell / Stockholm: Almqvist and Wiksell
AMS Press / New York: AMS Press, Inc.
Apt / New York: Apt Books
Archon / Hamden, Conn.: Archon Books
Ball State / Muncie, Ind.: Ball State University
Bantam / New York: Bantam Books
Beacon / Boston: Beacon Press, Inc.
Blackwell / Oxford: Basil Blackwell, Ltd.
Borgo / San Bernardino, Calif.: Borgo Press
Bowling Green / Bowling Green,

Ohio: Bowling Green State Univ. Popular Press
Bucknell / Lewisburg, Pa.: Bucknell Univ. Press (dist. by Associated Univ. Presses)
Bulzoni / Rome: Bulzoni Editore
Bunkashobo Hakubunsha (Toyko)
BYU / Provo, Utah: Brigham Young Univ. Press
Calif. / Berkeley: Univ. of California Press
Cambridge / New York: Cambridge Univ. Press
Carcanet / Manchester, England: Carcanet Books
Central Florida / Orlando: Univ. of Central Florida Press (dist. by Univ. Presses of Florida)
Chelsea / New York: Chelsea House Publishers (div. of Main Line Book Co.)
Chicago / Chicago: Univ. of Chicago Press
Clarendon / Oxford: Clarendon Press
Colorado / Niwot, Col.: Univ. Press of Colorado
Columbia / New York: Columbia Univ. Press
Continuum / New York: Continuum Publishing Co. (dist. by Harper & Row Pubs., Inc.)
Cornell / Ithaca, N.Y.: Cornell Univ. Press
Crescent / New York: Crescent Books
CSU-Fresno / Fresno, Calif.: Press at California State Univ.
CSU-Long Beach / Long Beach, Calif.: California State University, Long Beach (dist. by University Publishing Associates)
Dalkey Archive / Elmwood Park, Ill.: Dalkey Archive Press
Dangaroo / Sydney, N.S.W.: Dangaroo Press
Delaware / Newark: Univ. of Delaware Press (dist. by Associated Univ. Presses)
Doubleday / New York: Doubleday & Co., Inc. (div. of Bantam Doubleday Dell Publishing Group, Inc.)
Duke / Durham, N.C.: Duke Univ. Press
Eerdmans / Grand Rapids, Mich.: W. B. Eerdmans
Facts on File / New York: Facts on File, Inc.
Fairleigh Dickinson / Teaneck, N.J.: Fairleigh Dickinson Univ. Press (dist. by Associated Univ. Presses)
Farrar / New York: Farrar, Straus & Giroux, Inc.
Feminist Press / Feminist Press of the City University of New York
Florida / Gainesville: Univ. of Florida Press
Florida State / Tallahassee: Florida State Univ. Press
Fordham / New York: Fordham Univ. Press
Fortress / Minneapolis, Minn.: Fortress Press
Garland / New York: Garland Publishing, Inc.
Georgia / Athens: Univ. of Georgia Press
Greenwood / Westport, Conn.: Greenwood Press, Inc.
Grove / New York: Grove Press (dist. by Random House, Inc.)
Guilford / New York: Guilford Press
Gunter Narr / Tübingen: Gunter Narr Verlag

Hall / Boston: G. K. Hall & Co. (div. of Macmillan Publishing Co.)

Harper / New York: Harper & Row Publishers, Inc.

Harvard / Cambridge: Harvard Univ. Press

Heyday / Berkeley, Calif.: Heyday Books

Hopkins / Baltimore: Johns Hopkins Univ. Press

Houghton Mifflin / Boston: Houghton Mifflin Co.

Idaho / Moscow: Univ. of Idaho Press

Illinois / Champaign: Univ. of Illinois Press

Indiana / Bloomington: Indiana Univ. Press

Iowa / Iowa City: Univ. of Iowa Press

I.U.O. / Naples: Istituto Universitario Orientale

Kent State / Kent, Ohio: Kent State Univ. Press

Kentucky / Lexington: Univ. Press of Kentucky

Knopf / New York: Alfred A. Knopf, Inc. (subs. of Random House, Inc.)

Kukusho Kankokai (Tokyo)

Lawrence Hill / Chicago, Ill.: Lawrence Hill Books

Liber / Tokyo: Liber Press

Library of America / New York: Library of America (dist. by Viking Penguin, Inc.)

Library Research Associates (Monroe, N.Y.)

Limelight / New York: Limelight Editions

Locust Hill / West Cornwall, Conn.: Locust Hill Press

Longman / White Plains, N.Y.: Longman, Inc.

LSU / Baton Rouge: Louisiana State Univ. Press

McFarland / Jefferson, No. Car.: McFarland & Co., Inc.

Macmillan / London: Macmillan Publishers, Ltd.

Maisonneuve / Washington, D.C.: Maisonneuve Press (div. of Institute for Advanced Cultural Studies)

Marburg / Marburg, Germany: Universitätsbibliothek Marburg

Mass. / Amherst: Univ. of Massachusetts Press

Meckler / Westport, Conn.: Meckler Publishing Corp.

Mellen / Lewiston, N.Y.: Edwin Mellen Press

Mercer / Macon, Ga.: Mercer Univ. Press

Meridian / Utica, N.Y.: Meridian Publications

Michigan / Ann Arbor: Univ. of Michigan Press

Minnesota / Minneapolis: Univ. of Minnesota Press

Miss. / Jackson: Univ. Press of Mississippi

NCTE / Urbana, Ill.: National Council of Teachers of English

NCUP / Formerly College & University Press

Nebraska / Lincoln: Univ. of Nebraska Press

Negative Capability / Mobile, Ala.: Negative Capability Press

New Mexico / Albuquerque: Univ. of New Mexico Press

No. Car. / Chapel Hill: Univ. of North Carolina Press

Northeastern / Boston: Northeastern Univ. Press

North Texas: Denton: Univ. of North Texas Press
Northwestern / Evanston, Ill.: Northwestern Univ. Press
Norton / New York: W. W. Norton & Co., Inc.
NYU / New York: New York Univ. Press
Ohio / Athens: Ohio Univ. Press
Ohio State / Columbus: Ohio State Univ. Press
Okla. / Norman: Univ. of Oklahoma Press
Omnigraphics (Detroit, Mich.)
Oxford / New York: Oxford Univ. Press, Inc.
Pandora (London)
Paragon / New York: Paragon House Publishers
Penguin / New York: Penguin Books
Penn. / Philadelphia: Univ. of Pennsylvania Press
Penn. State / University Park: Pennsylvania State Univ. Press
Pergamon / Tarrytown, N.Y.: Pergamon Press
Perm' / Perm', Russia: Gosudarstvennyi Universitet Imeni A. M. Gor'kogo
Persea / New York: Persea Books
Peter Lang / New York: Peter Lang Publishing, Inc. (subs. of Verlag Peter Lang AG [Switzerland])
Plenum / New York: Plenum Publishing Corp.
Praeger / New York: Praeger Publishers
Pratt / Baltimore, Md.: Enoch Pratt Free Library
Princeton / Princeton, N.J.: Princeton Univ. Press
Prometheus / Buffalo, N.Y.: Prometheus Books
Purdue / West Lafayette, Ind.: Purdue Univ. Press
Random House / New York: Random House, Inc.
Rodopi / Amsterdam: Editions Rodopi BV
Routledge / New York: Routledge, Chapman & Hall, Inc.
Rowan & Littlefield / Savage, Md.: Rowan & Littlefield
Rutgers / New Brunswick, N.J.: Rutgers Univ. Press
St. James / Chicago: St. James Press
St. Martin's / New York: St. Martin's Press, Inc. (subs. of Macmillan Publishing Co.)
Sairyusha (Tokyo)
Scarecrow / Metuchen, N.J.: Scarecrow Press, Inc. (subs. of Grolier Educational Corp.)
Schirmer / New York: Schirmer Books
Scribner's / New York: Charles Scribner's Sons
Sierra Club / San Francisco: Sierra Club Books (dist. by Random House, Inc.)
Smithsonian / Washington, D.C.: Smithsonian Institution Press
So. Car. / Columbia: Univ. of South Carolina Press
So. Ill. / Carbondale: Southern Illinois Univ. Press
Stanford / Stanford, Calif.: Stanford Univ. Press
Steinbeck Society / Muncie, Ind.: Steinbeck Research Institute, Dept. of English, Ball State Univ.
Story Line / Santa Cruz, Calif.: Story Line Press

Sugden / Peru, Ill.: Sherwood Sugden
SUNY / Albany: State Univ. of New York Press
Susquehanna / Selinsgrove, Pa.: Susquehanna Univ. Press (dist. by Associated Univ. Presses)
Syracuse / Syracuse, N.Y.: Syracuse Univ. Press
Temple / Philadelphia: Temple Univ. Press
Tennessee / Knoxville: Univ. of Tennessee Press
Texas / Austin: Univ. of Texas Press
Texas A & M / College Station: Texas A & M Univ. Press
Thunder's Mouth: New York: Thunder's Mouth Press
Toronto / Toronto: Univ. of Toronto Press
Twayne / Boston: Twayne Publishers (imprint of G. K. Hall & Co., div. of Macmillan Publishing Co.)
UCA / Conway, Ark.: UCA Press
Univ. Press / Lanham, Md.: University Press of America
Viking / New York: Viking Penguin, Inc.
Vintage / Healdsburg, Calif.: Vintage Publications
Virginia / Charlottesville: Univ. Press of Virginia
Wayne State / Detroit: Wayne State Univ. Press
Whitston / Troy, N.Y.: Whitston Publishing Co.
Wisconsin / Madison: Univ. of Wisconsin Press
Yale / New Haven, Conn.: Yale Univ. Press
York / Fredericton, N.B., Can.: York Press

Part I

1 Emerson, Thoreau, and Transcendentalism

David M. Robinson

New editions of primary material, including Emerson's letters and sermons, Thoreau's journal, and Fuller's dispatches from Europe, led a very active year in Transcendentalist studies. This work was complemented by renewed attention to the place of Transcendentalism in American intellectual development and by important interpretive work on Emerson's major addresses of the late 1830s.

i Scholarly Editions and Source Material

Eleanor M. Tilton's edition of volume 8 of *The Letters of Ralph Waldo Emerson* (Columbia) includes letters from 1845 through 1859, with information on Emerson's English tour of 1847–48, his lecture schedule in the 1850s, and his preparation of the Margaret Fuller *Memoirs.* Of particular interest are letters to Caroline Sturgis, including a description of *Leaves of Grass* written a few days before the famous letter of congratulation to Whitman. I continue to appreciate Tilton's restoring to this edition letters printed in scattered sources that Rusk only listed. In addition to Tilton's volume, Melanie L. Bauer adds six letters on Emerson's lecture engagements in "Emerson's Acquaintance with Abijah Metcalf Ide, Jr.: Six Unpublished Emerson Letters" (*RALS* 17:258–62), and Kent P. Ljungquist reprints Emerson's response to a critique of his theory of the impersonality of God ("Emerson Responds to a Critic: An Uncollected Letter," *AN&Q* n.s. 4:125–29). Ronald A. Bosco's edition of volume 3 of *The Complete Sermons of Ralph Waldo Emerson* (Missouri) includes sermons from 10 October 1830 through 20 November 1831, encompassing the period of Ellen Tucker Emerson's death in February 1831. Emerson's public response to the death, Sermon CVII, avers that "Christian faith removes the dread from the grave" from both "those who die" and "those who survive," but Bosco reminds us that the sermons overlay "the turmoil in Emerson's private life" at this period. Despite his grief, or perhaps because of it, these sermons record spiritual perseverance and intellectual growth, a merging of the oldest New England piety with a growing sense of Romantic empowerment, captured in a sentence from Sermon CIX (5 March 1831): "If God is infinite (and we can find no bound) we who are his children have part in his infinity also." The volume includes extensive textual notes and a detailed chronology.

The third volume of Thoreau's *Journal* (Princeton), ed. Robert Sattelmeyer, Mark R. Patterson, and William Rossi covers 1848 through 1851, a period that marks "the beginning of a gradual shift in his journalizing practice." Thoreau here ceased to think of the Journal as a workbook for other projects and began the more systematic chronicle of his observations and perceptions that suggests his conception of it as a work with its own integrity. Even though the Journal of these years was significant in the formulation and reformulation of *Walden* and contains early versions of many memorable passages, I was struck by its different voice. In place of the confident and purposive narrator of *Walden,* we find a delicate and vulnerable man, whose deep but unfocused yearning makes up one of the Journal's important strands. Part of Thoreau's vulnerability comes from his growing sense of isolation; in his "Historical Introduction," Rossi discusses the "crisis in his relationship with Emerson" (see also *ALS 1989,* pp. 12–13, for Sattelmeyer's earlier essay on this topic). The journals of this period include several remarkable descriptions of moonlight walks in the summer of 1851 (I judge this the most impressive writing in the volume) and comments on his engagement with contemporary science.

Larry J. Reynolds and Susan Belasco Smith have provided an important resource for the study of Fuller in *"These Sad But Glorious Days": Dispatches from Europe, 1846–1850* (Yale), the complete text of all of Fuller's articles from Europe for the *New-York Tribune.* Reynolds and Smith call the dispatches "arguably Fuller's finest literary achievement," and it is clear that she adapted the epistolary form brilliantly for public use. The editors remind us too that Fuller was a vital conduit of information about the 1848 revolutions in Europe. The dispatches are gauges of Fuller's sensibility and perceptions, but they also record her capability to submerge her personality in the European events that she saw as so crucial. Smith's introduction to a new edition of Fuller's *Summer on the Lakes, in 1843* (Illinois) includes a cogent discussion of the work as an "internal journey of self-exploration" which "occupies a pivotal position in Margaret Fuller's development as a writer, a Transcendentalist, and a feminist." The excerpts from the journal of one of Fuller's pupils included in Laraine R. Fergenson's "Margaret Fuller as a Teacher in Providence: The School Journal of Ann Brown" (*SAR*, pp. 59–118) add to our knowledge of her experiment in teaching in 1837–38, a time when Fuller was deeply engaged in work on Goethe and beginning to test the "progressive and feminist pedagogy" that marked her later "Conversations" in Boston.

In "The Record of a Friendship: The Letters of Convers Francis to Frederic Henry Hedge in Bangor and Providence, 1835–1850" (*SAR*, pp. 1–57), Guy R. Woodall offers an interesting, well-annotated collection of 18 letters which illuminate the complicated position of Transcendentalists who remained committed to institutions such as the Unitarian denomination and Harvard College. Francis's letters aimed to keep Hedge apprised of developments in Cambridge, and they include his sympathetic account of Emerson's Divinity School Address and the controversy that followed: "the fluid of malignity had been collecting a good while,—& needed but a slight point of attraction to draw it down on E's head." Francis B. Dedmond's "The Selected Letters of William Ellery Channing The Younger (Part Three)" (*SAR*, pp. 257–343) includes letters from 1859–64 with valuable annotations. Channing felt himself to be a literary failure—"Mediocre poetry is worse than nothing & mine is not even mediocre"—but his personality is fascinating and his friendships, at the edge of Emerson's Concord circle, of interest. What other Transcendentalist could have referred to Emerson as "the happy Dante of New England" who writes of "his seven heavens"? Sterling F. Delano reprints "Christopher Pearse Cranch's *Address Delivered Before the Harvard Musical Association* (28 August 1845)" (*RALS* 17:239–53), in which Cranch calls music "the finest expression of life . . . the soul's effort to speak its mother tongue in a strange land."

ii Transcendentalism and American Intellectual History

The recent disintegration of any consensus on American intellectual continuity is stimulating new attempts to establish more localized narratives of influence and succession, in which Transcendentalism plays a varied part. Americanists have long needed a comprehensive history of Fourierism in America, a movement which was fueled by the reformist spirit of Transcendentalism and which influenced it in turn. Carl J. Guarneri's richly informative *The Utopian Alternative: Fourierism in Nineteenth-Century America* (Cornell) answers that need, tracing the movement from its European origins to its fading into a "sect" in America in the 1850s. Despite its "awkward vocabulary and fantastic claims," Fourierism rose rapidly in popularity, drawing many Americans from the artisan and agrarian ranks with its promise that "unfettered individual effort and a communal ethos could be reconciled in a perfect social order." Guarneri argues that this very appeal eventually constituted the ideological failure of the movement—its "utopian creed . . . promised too much and required too little." But his evidence also reveals cases of practical failures, many of them involving poor decisions in land acquisition. Fourierism can in this sense be seen as a series of experiments, each with a particular history. Guarneri successfully integrates those discrete narratives into a coherent account of the movement's rise and fall. Christopher Lasch's *The True and Only Heaven* associates Emerson and Brownson with an alternative political tradition defined by its commitment to the laboring producer and its skepticism of the dogma of social progress. Lasch casts a wide net in defining what is arguably less a tradition than a pieced-together version of a usable past, but in the process he offers some stimulating readings of 19th-century thinkers. Scholars of Transcendentalism will want to consult his portrait of Brownson as a social critic (pp. 184–97) and his quite original depiction of a "populist" Emerson (pp. 243–79), who endorsed the "sacrifice [of] some of the 'conveniences' of civilization to the moral culture conferred by farming or a craft."

In *Sporting with the Gods* (pp. 368–406) Michael Oriard perceptively describes Transcendentalism as a movement in which "an ideal of holy play competed with a contradictory insistence on purposeful striving," a division that reflects a fundamental and still unresolved tension in American culture. For Emerson, play represented "spontaneous, instinctual," and present-oriented experience ("My life is a May game"), an early emphasis that was increasingly hedged in and qualified. For Thoreau, a "dialectic of *earnest play*," typified in his account of the saunterer, held the poles of play and work in productive tension. This analysis yields an effective reading of *Walden,* a text informed by "the paradox that work must be play." Oriard describes the transmission of this ideology in liberal theology and sentimental fiction, arguing convincingly that the antinomian emphasis on play in Transcendentalism "prefigured the later cultural revolutionaries of play, the bohemians of the 1910s and the Beats of the 1950s." Russell B. Goodman's *American Philosophy and the Romantic Tradition* (Cambridge) extends the effort of Stanley Cavell and others to include Emerson in an American philosophical tradition that includes William James and John Dewey, declaring the end of an era in which "James and Dewey could not be regarded seriously as philosophers, or Emerson regarded as a philosopher at all." He is less inclined to call Emerson a pragmatist, however, than to read James and Dewey through Romantic categories, explaining how their projects were enabled by Emerson's view of the "shaping power of the individual mind" and his rejection of a narrow empiricism. In *By the Law of Nature* (pp. 57–84) Howard Horwitz locates several parallels between the discourse of Transcendentalist ethics and that of economic protectionism. Horwitz suggests that Transcendentalism adapted a "logic of critique circulating widely" in America which established nature as a standard of value.

In *The American Ideal* Peter Carafiol argues that the movement was "less an event in the world than an event in the minds of American scholars," rooted in the essentially professional need of Americanists to define "the uniquely American character of a distinct literary tradition." In his survey of Transcendentalist scholarship Carafiol finds little evidence of a coherent definition of the field, but much evidence of the need among scholars for the existence of such a field. He cites Emerson's "The Transcendentalist" as a text that "defuses all attempts" to pin "Transcendentalism down for scrutiny," and he discusses Thoreau's *A Week* as an example of the enactment of "the temporality, which is to say the textuality, of the self in relation to its own history"—a recognition that Carafiol feels is required in future Transcendentalist scholarship. Richard A. Grusin's *Transcendentalist Hermeneutics: Institutional Authority and the Higher Criticism of the Bible* (Duke) explores the impact of biblical higher criticism on "the Transcendentalist understanding of the historical authority of institutionalized religion," attempting to revise the movement's reputation as anti-institutional. In Grusin's analysis Emerson's resignation from his pulpit was "a continuation of the goals of his ministry," and Parker's appeal to the authority of the heart was less the rejection of historical institutions than the sanctioning of a different social institution, "the authority of the mother." Even Thoreau's concerns with "the interpretive and historical issues raised by his wide readings" led him to "an understanding of mythological interpretation" that is related to the higher criticism. Louis P. Masur's " 'Age of the First Person Singular': The Vocabulary of the Self in New England, 1780–1850" (*JAmS* 25:189–211) notes the recent emphasis on "the self as historically situated and socially constructed" and charts from that perspective the evolution of a cluster of related terms—self-denial, self-improvement, and self-reliance—that are rooted in post-Revolutionary discourse on self-government. These terms evolved into markers of broader cultural values through such texts as Channing's *Discourses* and *Self-Culture* and Emerson's "Self-Reliance."

iii Emerson

"The American Scholar" and the Divinity School *Address* were the focus of the most substantial Emerson criticism this year, with several essays reopening the addresses as performative or cultural events and extending our knowledge of their theological background. Robert Milder's perceptive reading of " 'The American Scholar' as Cultural Event" (*Prospects* 16:119–47) situates it in "the tradition of the Unitarian man of letters consecrated by Buckminster" and proposes that Emerson, like Buckminster, "but with a radically different politics," invoked the figure of the scholar as an agent of cultural salvation. Emerson redefined the "literary and commercial" as "competing vocabularies and systems of value," an appropriation of the vocabulary of the Unitarian clerisy that formed the basis of his attempt to redefine his age "as a moment of cultural opportunity." Milder's view of Emerson's appropriation of Unitarian discourse in "The American Scholar" is consonant with Stephen Railton's depiction of Emerson's "need as a visionary performer to bring the world of his audience round *to him*" (*Authorship and Audience,* pp. 23–49). Railton sees the Divinity School *Address* as Emerson's long-postponed shaking off of his Unitarian past (see also Colacurcio, below), but he stresses Emerson's "attempt to co-opt instead of confront the Unitarians' convictions." This attempt "meant redefining his listeners' vocabulary covertly," the experimentation with stable uses of words that so frustrated Andrews Norton. Emerson's failure to win his audience completely, as signified by the controversy that followed, "chilled his hopes for an instant 'conversion of the world' " and forced him, in "Self-Reliance" and after, into the paradoxical stance of "the prophet as performer," seeking continually to renew his visionary bond with the audience. But as Michael J. Colacurcio effectively shows in " 'Pleasing God': The Lucid Strife of Emerson's

'Address' " (*ESQ* 37:141–212), the *Address* can be seen as a breakthrough text. Colacurcio describes how the initial empowerment of Channing's emphasis on the "internal" evidences of Christianity (see also Wesley T. Mott's recent analysis: *ALS 1989*, p. 5), with its "ambiguous and partial internalization of the burden of revelation," eventually pushed Emerson beyond Channing's emphasis on the centrality of Jesus. Taking Channing's 1821 Dudleian lecture as its essential precursor, the *Address* was a somewhat belated culmination of Emerson's efforts "to redo, perhaps outdo, the higher logic of Channing's rather special treatment of the Christian evidences"; its essential claim, one which subsequently shaped American literature, is that "the Age of Revelation remains entirely open." In a related consideration of Emerson's Christology, "Young Emerson and the Mantle of Biography" (*ATQ* n.s. 5:151–68), Susan L. Roberson argues that Emerson's use of heroic models began to change in the late 1830s, giving way to a hero "whose main resource is his own self-trust." Roberson stresses the interplay between the developing heroic self and the figure of Jesus, a process that included "a simultaneous humanizing of Jesus and deifying of man." Elisabeth Hurth identifies Jakob Böhme as another important influence on the *Address* in "The Uses of a Mystic Prophet: Emerson and Boehme" (*PQ* 70:219–36), one who provided Emerson "with a remarkable source of stimulus and corroboration for his own criticism of the Unitarian church and historical Christianity."

These explorations are complemented by Joel Porte's insightful description of Emerson's transition from orator to essayist (*In Respect to Egotism*, pp. 106–23). In adopting the essay as his form Emerson undertook "a public display of his own uncertainties," a challenge he answered in part through his depiction of the creative energy of the poet. Porte describes "Experience," which records the most crucial challenge of self-revelation, as Emerson's demonstration of "the spirit's recuperative powers." David Jacobson's important new reading of "Self-Reliance," "Vision's Imperative: 'Self-Reliance' and the Command to See Things as They Are" (*SIR* 29 [1990]:555–70), proposes that Emerson's skepticism does not result in "a prolific indeterminacy," but entails his belief in "the phenomenological causality of the individual." Revising Cavell's reading of Emerson as one which "disposes the individual in an essentially alien world," Jacobson describes Emerson's early thought as "the recognition of one's causality in nature, one's coincidence with the directionality, the onward appearance of nature, and thus one's manifestation of the universal sense of nature." In "From Wordsworth to Emerson" (*Romantic Revolutions*, pp. 202–18) David Bromwich notes Wordsworth's impact on the composition of "Self-Reliance," observing that Emerson's reading "recovers a revolutionary idea of Wordsworth's aims." In *Towards Reading Freud: Self-Creation in Milton, Wordsworth, Emerson, and Sigmund Freud* (Princeton, 1990) Mark Edmundson reads the transparent eyeball passage as a retreat from the achievement of "a renovated self" caused by Emerson's failure "to figure the antagonist against which he contends," grief for the loss of his wife and brother. Edmundson finds in "Threnody" a more profound confrontation with grief, which anticipates Freud's analysis of the work of mourning.

Other contributions to the ever-growing literature on Emerson's influence and reputation include two essays on Hawthorne's resistance to Emerson. Larry J. Reynolds's fascinating account of "Hawthorne and Emerson in 'The Old Manse'" (*SNNTS* 23:60–81) contends that "the move to Concord obviously forced Hawthorne to contend directly with the force of Emerson's personality and influence." Emerson's philosophical idealism interposed itself between Hawthorne and the Concord countryside, and, more disturbingly, Emerson's presence seemed to interpose itself between Hawthorne and his Transcendentalist wife Sophia. The resulting rivalry subtly shaped "The Old Manse" and later works. David Hicks also discusses this tension between Hawthorne and Emerson in "'Seeker for He Knows Now What': Hawthorne's Criticism of Emerson in the Summer of 1842" (*NHR* 17, i:1, 3–4), locating in Hawthorne's jealousy of Sophia's worship of Emerson the source of several derogatory journal comments on Emerson in 1842. Hicks notes that Hawthorne ceased his spiteful comments about Emerson as Sophia's fascination with him cooled, and that he replaced them with philosophical criticism of Emersonianism in his fiction. The thesis of John B. Williams's *White Fire: The Influence of Emerson on Melville* (CSU—Long Beach) is that "Emerson was Melville's most immediate and probably his most evocative source." The first part of his study explores Emerson's impact on Melville in the late 1840s, stressing Emerson's lectures on "Mind and Manners of the Nineteenth Century" and the newspaper accounts of them as important to Melville's development. The second part is an overview of Melville's fiction as a response to Emerson, with *Moby-Dick* described as a merging of the influences of Emerson and Hawthorne. Occasionally, Williams is inclined to press his thesis too hard, but his work on the Emerson lectures is illuminating, and he offers a number of parallels between the work of Melville and Emerson. In "Beyond Deconstruction: America, Style and the Romantic Synthesis in Emerson" (*CRevAS* 22:61–82) J. Trevor McNeely notes the continuing "revaluation of Emerson" and argues that Emerson must be reclaimed through a recovery of the Romantic concepts of the imagination and polarity. In "Nietzsche's Antinomianism" (*NietzscheS* 20:109–33) George J. Stack proposes that Nietzsche's often misunderstood appeal to act "beyond good and evil" has important origins in Emerson's search for an "affirmative ethics of 'self-existence' " with its implicit rejection of conventional moral strictures. Stack's "Emerson and Nietzsche: Fate and Existence" (*NCP* 19:1–14) emphasizes Nietzsche's Emersonian belief "that freedom is found in our self-conscious recognition of our powers."

Although I regard Emerson's political legacy as decidedly progressive, that is by no means a unanimous view, as several recent essays suggest. In "Emerson's Corporate Individualism" (*AmLH* 3:657–84) Christopher J. Newfield reads the competing "Herbertian" and "Orphic" voices of the "Prospects" chapter of *Nature* as a reflection of Emerson's situation "midway between secular individualism and a quasi-socialism authorized in part by his anachronistic Neoplatonic metaphysics." Approaching Emerson's theory of the self in the context of discourse about the legal corporation, he argues that the "powerful individualism" represented by the Orphic poet is available only through an eradication of "private individuality." Newfield's reading of "Friendship" and "Love" in "Loving Bondage: Emerson's Ideal Relationships" (*ATQ* n.s. 5:183–93) analyzes Emerson's depictions of the politics of relationships. Male-male relationships "rest on a vexed conjunction of rivalry and detachment" that preserves the autonomy of the participants, but forces them into a role of "domination or submission." Male-female relationships are marked by a subtle form of patriarchal domination—"hegemonic rather than tyrannical" coercion—the dynamic of which is the imagination of "a union that overcomes rivalry and even the individual identities of the participants." In "Rethinking Resistance: Nature Opposed to Power in Emerson and Melville" (*WVUPP* 37:39–51) Peter Quigley finds in *Nature* "a political philosophy of expansion, an environmental position of domination, and a narcissistic aesthetic practice," limits that Melville exposes in depicting Ahab and Ishmael as versions of the Emersonian self.

iv Thoreau

Criticism of Thoreau centered on his process of self-constitution in life and art and the related question of his theory of perception, resulting in several varied critical and biographical portraits. The most significant contributions were two illuminating explorations of his antagonistic relationship with his Concord neighbors: Stephen Railton's *Authorship and Audience* (pp. 50–73) and Robert Milder's "An 'Errand to Mankind': Thoreau's Problem of Vocation" (*ESQ* 37:91–139). Railton's well-crafted essay argues that "*Walden* was built around Thoreau's sense of himself as beleaguered by his audience," which was always, for him, Concord: "Wherever he walked in the village he felt compelled to wear the epithets 'idler' and 'loafer' pinned to him like Hester's *A* by his neighbors' judgment." Noting perceptively that his published works "are all based on the comparatively brief time he spent away from his parents' house," Railton locates Thoreau's insecurity in an intense need to resecure his family's—particularly his mother's—love. His enactment of this insecurity in *Walden* encompassed both aggression toward his readers and a larger attempt "to be reunited" with them. Milder is in accordance with Railton in approaching Thoreau's works as "transmutations of long-standing personal conflicts" rooted in psychic insecurity. By identifying "the transcendentalist injunction to self-culture" with the process of making "his life his vocation," Thoreau came to associate "heroism with resistance to society," specifically that of his Concord neighbors. His resulting "consciousness of addressing a refractory audience" fundamentally shaped *Walden* and *A Week,* and it accounts for *Walden*'s " 'rhetoric of ascent' through which he undertakes to awaken his sleepwalking readers and lead them from one plane of being to another." In "Democratic Ideology and Autobiographical Personae in American Renaissance Writing" (*Amst* 35:267–80) Lawrence Buell argues that American democracy authorized various forms of autobiographical personae, thus producing a "dissonant array of autobiographical discourses" that lacked any consistent correlation with democratic ideology. This cultural situation problematized the construction of an exemplary self, the work that was central to Thoreau, Hawthorne, Harriet A. Jacobs, and Whitman. Taking *Walden* as an example, Buell shows how the encounter with John Field generates "uneasiness and self-division" in Thoreau's persona, the result of "arrogating to himself the status of exemplum." The antagonistic and self-divided figure described in these studies is consonant in some respects with the restless, energetic, and self-originating Thoreau of Joel Porte's *In Respect to Egotism* (pp. 164–88), although Porte more heavily accentuates Thoreau's positive artistic purpose: to replace the myth of the Fall that had imbued itself into the New England landscape with "a more comprehensive fable of rebirth." Thoreau's work presents us with "a perpetually resurrecting self," difficult to tame or domesticate, who even after his return from Walden "never intended to relinquish his marginal existence."

Thoreau's difficulties in sustaining a social identity can be related to his attempt to be "at home in the world," the central theme of Frederick Garber's *Thoreau's Fable of Inscribing* (Princeton). In Garber's view, "home making in the world stands as a kind of metadiscourse that comments on all others and seems finally to hold them together." Thoreau's "proto-Heideggerean recognition of the relations of being, dwelling, and location" enabled him to conceive his texts as "a way to *be* in the world" rather than "a way to *meet* the world," and they should thus be read as acts of "mapping" or "self-location." Such charting will be, like language itself, necessarily "incomplete, imperfect, open-ended, unresolved," and in this sense Garber has proposed a new set of terms for comprehending the Thoreauvian quest. Garber's Thoreau is a more self-contained and strongly centered man than the one described by Milder or Railton, closer to the home-builder of Marilyn R. Chandler's *Dwelling in the Text,* pp. 23–45. Chandler stresses the "three-point analogy" of Thoreau's building the cabin, writing the book, and forming his life, describing the Walden cabin as indicative of the enlarged sense of "stewardship" that Thoreau proposes "as a significant aspect of moral responsibility." In *What Thoreau Said: Walden and the Unsayable* (Idaho) William C. Johnson, Jr., offers an insightful reading of *Walden* that emphasizes Thoreau's attempt to forge an integrative polarity from the duality of perception, stressing Thoreau's concept of "fact as the spiritual potential of matter." Johnson sees Thoreau's principal struggle as epistemological, but he also recognizes its fundamentally ethical character, rooted in a "respect for the sacred nuances of being itself." The studies of Garber, Chandler, and Johnson can be read profitably in the context of Douglas Anderson's recent analysis of Thoreau's often overlooked domesticity (see *ALS 1990,* p. 12), and Johnson's detailed readings of passages in *Walden* extend the recent work of Peck, Golemba, and Boudreau (*ALS 1990,* pp. 10–11).

Thoreau's concern for "home" is, as Garber shows, an expression of his desire for a fulfilling life in the natural world. His articulation of this desire was an enabling factor in the tradition of nature writing, a growing area of interest in Thoreau studies. In "Better Mythology: Perception and Emergence in Thoreau's Journal" (*NDQ* 59:33–44) H. Daniel Peck finds Thoreau's influence less a "legacy of specific ideas about nature" than a "fundamental shift in 'perception'" centered on the "phenomenon," an "integral, composite" event of perception that transcends both subjectivity and scientific empiricism. Thoreau understood the phenomenon as "a reciprocity between nature's emergent reality and the perceiving mind," a concept with important implications for the contemporary nature writer's search for "a literary form that somehow could enact the *process* of the self engaging the natural world." I recommend this special issue of the *North Dakota Quarterly* devoted to "Nature Writers/Writing," edited by Sherman Paul and Don Scheese. Peck's and Johnson's accounts of Thoreau's attempt to construct an essentially integrative epistemology is countered by Robert E. Abrams's "Image, Object, and Perception in Thoreau's Landscapes: The Development of Anti-Geography" (*NCF* 46:245–62), which stresses Thoreau's "scrutiny of sights and scenes that disrupt categorization and blur ostensible ontological boundaries." Abrams describes Thoreau's exploration of "the limits of stable schemata of perception" and the resulting confrontation with a "more immediate, more volatile world." Thoreau thus relinquishes "settled objective truth for accumulating, even paradoxical profiles of 'where we are.'" In *The Idea of Wilderness,* pp. 133–71, Max Oelschlaeger interprets Thoreau's purpose, especially at Walden, as an attempt to recover a "Paleolithic" consciousness that centers on an awareness of humanity's rootedness in and dependence on natural processes. Oelschlaeger stresses Thoreau's "lifetime of primary experiences" in nature as the basis of his idea of the wilderness, and he identifies "A Winter Walk," *Walden,* and "Ktaadn" as principal Thoreauvian texts. In making a case for the primal Thoreau, Oelschlaeger is inclined to denigrate Emerson too severely as "a disembodied transcendental spectator who brings with him abstract principles to impose on nature." Jeffrey E. Simpson's perceptive "Thoreau: The Walking Muse" (*ESQ* 37:1–33) focuses on "Walking" and the Journal to illustrate how the walk "allows for a correspondence of spirit and body that overcomes dualistic separations," demanding "a dynamic, organic, creative adaptation to the land." Simpson connects the "total responsiveness" required in a walk with "Heidegger's 'primordial' thinking," noting that "Thoreau often sounds . . . like a protophenomenologist when he describes his walks." David C. Smith's "Walking as Spiritual Discipline: Henry Thoreau and the Inward Journey" (*Soundings* 74:129–40) also discusses sauntering as "a form of walking which led to self-discovery and spiritual renewal."

In "Thoreau's Sexuality" (*Journal of Homosexuality* 21, iii:23–45) Walter Harding contends that "Thoreau's heterosexual drive was very low, indeed almost nonexistent," and that "his actions and words, consciously and/or subconsciously, indicate a specific sexual interest in members of his own sex." To substantiate his case, Harding explains Thoreau's seeming lack of erotic interest in women, amasses a catalog of his responses to male physical appearance, and describes his reading in literature with homosexual themes. He finds it unlikely that Thoreau had any homosexual experience, and he argues that his desire was sublimated into a love for nature. In a related discussion of the erotic in Thoreau, Michael Warner situates "*Walden*'s Erotic Economy," pp. 157–74 in *Comparative American Identities,* in the larger context of the transformations of personal identity under capitalism, arguing that "Thoreau wants what Marcuse would call a transformed libido." Warner relates Thoreau's "posture of a Narcissus" at Walden Pond to his conflicting psychic economies of asceticism and utopian eroticism. Thoreau's "ascetic wish for purification is also a wish to reenable sensual self-relation," a division that exemplifies the condition of modern self-alienation.

In "Did Henry Thoreau Write 'Conflict of Laws'?" (*NEQ* 64:433–44) Linck C. Johnson reexamines Gary Scharnhorst's attribution of "Conflict of Laws" to Thoreau (see *ALS 1988,* p. 7), arguing that the essay by "H. T." can be more closely aligned to the Christian nonresistance movement led by Adin Ballou. While both Scharnhorst and Johnson argue from internal and contextual evidence, Johnson's case against attribution seems to me the more persuasive. These articles call our attention to the rich context of political argument underlying Thoreau's "Civil Disobedience."

v Fuller and Other Transcendentalists

Fritz Fleischmann presents a very solid overview of Fuller's development in "Margaret Fuller," pp. 39–68 in *Classics in Cultural Criticism,* volume 2, *USA,* ed. Hartmut Heuermann (Peter Lang, 1990). Reading Fuller's lifelong effort of "self-creation" as an important act of cultural criticism, Fleischmann describes her unusual awareness of "her own alienation" as a woman committed to self-culture in a society that did not authorize it. "Her most radical work" as a cultural critic "starts from transcendentalist premises of self-fashioning," eventually becoming a "call to action" premised on a reconception of gender roles that defined " 'male' and 'female' as interdependent metaphorical principles." In Italy, far enough removed from the American scene, Fuller completed her "self-fashioning": "Self-authorized, she urges her country to re-form as well." Fuller's struggle against cultural restraints for self-expression is also the subject of Christina Zwarg's "Womanizing Margaret Fuller: Theorizing a Lover's Discourse" (*Cultural Critique* 16 [1990]:161–91), which centers on Fuller's letters to James Nathan, published in 1903 as the *Love-Letters of Margaret Fuller.* Zwarg approaches the text as "an epistolary frame" which reveals Fuller's maneuvers "through a series of subject-positions in order to deliver herself from cultural and psychological constraints." Commenting perceptively on the conflicting reactions to Fuller's work and example, Zwarg analyzes the motives behind the eventual publication of the letters, including Julia Ward Howe's introduction to them. Elaine Showalter's "Miranda and Cassandra: The Discourse of the Feminist Intellectual," pp. 311–27 in *Tradition and the Talents of Women,* describes a "revisionist exploration of the myths of female knowledge" in Fuller and Florence Nightingale, and it places Fuller's depiction of Miranda at the head of "an influential tradition of the American feminist intellectual—as motherless and isolated from other women." Eve Kornfeld and Melissa Marks's "Margaret Fuller: Minerva and the Muse" (*JAC* 13, iii[1990]:47–59) offers a reinterpretation of Fuller which "mediates" between her historical identity as a Transcendentalist and her reputation as a feminist and political activist. Kornfeld and Marks emphasize Fuller's early attainment of a spiritual vision of "organic unity" and "intuition" as keys to her development, and they describe her intellectual career as an attempt to harmonize the conflicting demands "of thought and action, of poetic vision and social reform, and of individuality and community." Paula Kopacz's "Feminist at the Tribune: Margaret Fuller as Professional Writer" (*SAR,* pp. 119–39) makes a strong case for the centrality of Fuller's *Tribune* writings, particularly during her overlooked New York period. Kopacz describes Fuller's stance there as that of a "feminist transcendentalist" and emphasizes her acute awareness of social ills. Madeleine B. Stern has issued a revised second edition of *The Life of Margaret Fuller* (Greenwood) with a survey of books on Fuller, 1942–1990. Carolyn Feleppa Balducci's *Margaret Fuller: A Life of Passion and Defiance* (Bantam/Barnard Biography Series) offers an overview of Fuller's life aimed at a general readership.

Fuller's travel writings also drew attention. Susan Belasco Smith augmented her edition of *Summer on the Lakes* (see above) with an interpretive essay, "*Summer on the Lakes:* Margaret Fuller and the British" (*RALS* 17:191–207). Smith characterizes *Summer* as "a book that responds directly to British travelogues," a process through which Fuller arrived at "a world view that unites the actual and the potential," thus forming the basis of her later work on feminism and politics. William W. Stowe's "Conventions and Voices in Margaret Fuller's Travel Writing" (*AL* 63:242–62) proposes that the "polyvocal travel-writing tradition" helped establish Fuller as a writer through its capacity to serve "as a meeting place for various narrative voices, literary styles, levels of speech, and kinds of subjects." Stowe adduces examples of Fuller's polyvocal practice in *Summer on the Lakes* and her letters to the *Tribune.*

In "The Ann Sisters: Elizabeth Peabody's Millennial Historicism" (*AmLH* 3:27–45), an impressive essay of historical revision, Nina Baym argues that Peabody's historical reputation as a Transcendentalist "ignores the Christian overtext of her work and makes her, as it were, marginal to herself." Baym focuses on Peabody's entirely overlooked historical work, finding there a "powerfully gendered" version of millennialism adopted from her mother. Reading Friedrich Froebel's theories of early childhood education in 1859, Peabody formed a constructive response to the national crisis and found, only then, a basis for the strong advocacy of women's rights. Helen R. Deese has chronicled "A New England Women's Network: Elizabeth Palmer Peabody, Caroline Healey Dall, and Delia S. Bacon" (*Legacy* 8:77–91), describing how these women, though holding differing views on the movement for women's rights, provided crucial support to the intellectual work of others. Peabody exerted "an enormously formative influence" on Dall, and both became involved with the career of the "brilliant, unbalanced, and strangely persuasive" Bacon.

John Beer's "William Ellery Channing Visits the Lake Poets" (*RES* 42:212–226) describes Dr. Channing's contacts in 1822–23 with Coleridge, Southey, and Wordsworth, and includes new material on Wordsworth from Channing's journal of his tour. In "The Transient and Permanent in Theodore Parker's Christianity, 1832–1841" (*PUUHS* 22, part 1:1–18) Dean Grodzins places Parker's controversial sermon in the context of his theological development, explaining that Parker's waning belief in the historical certainty of the Bible came into conflict with an emotional need to affirm the historical Jesus. Influenced in part by David Strauss's conception of the genius of Jesus, Parker identified "the words of Jesus," as opposed to the miracles or other elements of the supernatural, as "the Permanent element in Christianity," a positive emphasis overlooked by most of his contemporaries. Arthur Versluis offers a useful account of Samuel Johnson's "Oriental Religions" series in "From Transcendentalism to Universal Religion: Samuel Johnson's Orientalism" (*ATQ* n.s. 5:109–23), seeing the works as an important attempt to assert the fundamental identity of the world's religions and thus prophesy "the coming Universal Religion."

Oregon State University

2 Hawthorne

Frederick Newberry

Not counting a Hawthorne encyclopedia and a biography of Rose Hawthorne Lathrop, a record 11 books were published on Hawthorne in 1991. In addition, both *Studies in the Novel* and *Essex Institute Historical Collections* devoted entire issues to him; G. K. Hall issued a collection of essays on the short stories; and St. Martin's issued the text of *The Scarlet Letter* together with five essays in demonstration of a promising new critical apparatus for undergraduates. By my reckoning, the overall quality of the books and essays marks a banner year—no mean feat, since the critical enterprise gets tougher and trickier with each passing year. Of course, some of the scholars discussed here, like too many in recent years, have fallen shy of carefully researching the critical record—a few egregiously so. Still, in this my last year of writing this chapter, I am pleased to conclude on a more or less high note. Though there remain few "experts" on Hawthorne, the burgeoning number of people writing on him suggests that his importance continues without serious challenge.

i Bibliography, Biography, and Reference Guides

The January issue of *Essex Institute Historical Collections* (vol. 127) contains admirably informed essays by Rita K. Gollin (*Scarlet Letter*), John L. Idol (*Seven Gables*), Melinda M. Ponder (*Blithedale*), and David B. Kesterson (*Marble Faun*), who remind us of the influences exerted on texts by visual and tactile designs of publication. In an effort to gauge the reception of the novels by successive generations of readers, they describe and analyze significant editions, from the original imprints to more recent lurid paperbacks and scholarly publications, paying special attention to methods by which publishers have presented the texts through bindings, illustrations, type fonts, and scholarly introductions or afterwords. Underscoring their interests, numerous illustrations are included. The last item in the *EIHC* issue is Susan R. Murray's valuable checklist, a bibliographical description of every item mentioned in the four essays.

Veterans and novices will profit from *A Nathaniel Hawthorne Encyclopedia* (Greenwood) by Robert L. Gale, who successfully duplicates his laudable encyclopedia on Henry James. Included are biographical sketches of Hawthorne's kin, friends and acquaintances, correspondents, and historical figures mentioned in his works; descriptions of all the novels, tales, sketches, poems, and miscellaneous pieces; and identifications of characters and others appearing in his works. Limited but helpful cross references are part of Gale's apparatus. Of nine appendixes, the most useful is a compendium of Hawthorne's writings. I noticed only one identification missing—that of Joseph Moody, who is mentioned in a footnote to "The Minister's Black Veil"; and one error—Ellen Fuller's marrying William Henry Channing, cited in the Margaret Fuller entry (but Gale gets it right in the William Ellery Channing entry).

Edwin Haviland Miller's biography, *Salem Is My Dwelling Place: A Life of Nathaniel Hawthorne* (Iowa), adds occasional new evidence to the record of Hawthorne's outer life but assumes that the veiled, insoluble mystery of Hawthorne dwells within the conflicted psyche of a boy who lost his father at the age of four and never recovered. His mother not only failed to take charge of him in a household crowded with aunts and uncles but also declined the affection he needed, increasingly withdrawing into widowhood and forsaking the world. Miller relentlessly pursues these questionable perspectives through direct and indirect analogies to the fiction, notebooks, and correspondence. Everywhere he finds Hawthorne searching for a father or Great Mother, and everywhere he diminishes him to the level of a little boy—an Ilbrahim or Owen Warland. Ineffectual husbands and fathers in the fiction reflect Hawthorne's relations with Sophia and his children. In moments of need or crisis, Hawthorne breaks down like a Tobias Pearson, Reuben Bourne, or Dimmesdale. Predictably, Hawthorne's sexual identity is unstable, which poses quite a problem for the Manse years; but here Miller's tactical use of evasion and slippery associations are especially glaring, most demonstrably in his treatment of Hawthorne's relations with Margaret Fuller. Yet in the potentially homoerotic relations of Hawthorne and Melville, Miller writes more carefully, sensitively, and even movingly. The best chapter in the book is "President Pierce's 'Prime Minister.' " But overall, Miller's opposition to the importance of history and ideas in Hawthorne's mental life results in a narrow portrait. And one might wish that, rather than having presented a Hawthorne determined by infantile experiences, Miller had fully approached his project with his own admonition on Mark Van Doren's excoriation of Zenobia and Coverdale in mind: "Maybe so, although one could, and in modesty should, assume that Hawthorne knew what he was about."

Unlike Miller's book, Patricia Dunlavy Valenti's *To Myself a Stranger: A Biography of Rose Hawthorne Lathrop* (LSU) has no overriding thesis to argue and thus shies away from speculation, perhaps too much so. Nevertheless, it is a welcome study of Hawthorne's youngest daughter, well-researched and written in a style of simple elegance no longer fashionable, yet for all that the more appealing. Valenti presents young Rose's grief over not becoming close to her preoccupied and increasingly ailing father, and she patiently traces the financially strapped condition of the Hawthornes after the death of "papa." Thereafter come the subsequent quarrels between all three children following Sophia's death, the marriage of Rose to George Parsons Lathrop, and her postpartum bout with insanity. Surprises are in store for most readers. When Rose was scarcely 10 years old, Hawthorne forbade her from ever writing stories. And contrary to legendary gossip, her marriage was marked by love, mutual support of each spouse's work as author, and a spiritual affinity exemplified in their scandalous conversion to Roman Catholicism. Steadily clarifying itself in Valenti's account is the fitful process by which Rose ultimately separated from Lathrop and became Mother Sister Mary Alphonsa of the Sisters of Charity who devoted the last two decades of her life to founding Free Home in New York City, where she treated patients with incurable cancer. Besides *Memories of Hawthorne,* Rose wrote many stories and poems; and Valenti devotes one chapter to a general description of them; evidently, she does not think they reveal much about Rose's inner life.

Would that Edwin Haviland Miller could have taken a lesson from the delicately modulated essay of Leland S. Person, Jr., "Inscribing Paternity: Nathaniel Hawthorne as a Nineteenth-Century Father" (*SAR,* pp. 225–44). Drawing from several Hawthorne texts and challenging the scant scholarship, Person analyzes Hawthorne's initial confusion over his biological and authorial fatherhood and argues for his finally coming to terms with himself as a father-provider who could balance the claims of family and work. Between these two poles, Person locates Hawthorne's struggle to give his children, especially Una and Julian, the sustained and playful attention they needed. The struggle became acute in the case of Una, as reflected in *The Scarlet Letter,* wherein Hawthorne records fears expressed elsewhere about children being pre- and postnatally influenced by the thoughts and emotional condition not only of mothers but also of fathers. Person contextualizes these fears in the 19th century at large through Henry Clarke Wright's *Marriage and Parentage* (1854). The essay seems to me an indispensable contribution.

Bill Ellis's "Hawthorne's Last Day at the Consulate: 'To Think of Doing Good' " (*SAR,* 245–56) presents a new document in Hawthorne's hand: a testimony of a sailor charging a third mate with the unaccountable physical abuse of another sailor that probably caused his death. Ellis, who probably knows more than anybody about Hawthorne's consular experience, takes the anomalous fact that Hawthorne himself wrote this testimony in his last moment of office as evidence not of his heretofore supposed quietism during his final months as consul but of his continuing commitment to do something about the horrendous cruelty aboard the U.S. merchant fleet. Moreover, Ellis surmises that this event puts the lie to Hawthorne's reiterated belief in effective social change coming in God's own good time.

Condensing familiar details from biographical records, David Hicks's " 'Seeker for He Knows No[t] What': Hawthorne's Criticism of Emerson in the Summer of 1842" (*NHR* 17, i:1, 3–4) modestly argues that Hawthorne's petty notebook jibes at Emerson during the early Manse period resulted from Emerson's having "cast a shadow on three of the most important aspects of Hawthorne's life: the admiration of his wife, his literary success, and his new house."

ii Critical Books

A contender for the year's best book is Sacvan Bercovitch's *The Office of* The Scarlet Letter (Hopkins). Two of the four chapters appeared previously (see *ALS 88,* pp. 22–23). In all four Bercovitch historicizes anew how the novel performs "cultural work" in terms of practical criticism ("ethnography of literary context") and an anthropological sense of ideology ("reciprocities between social construction and textual creation"). The novel's central event is Hester's return to America, where she accommodates her former radical independence to what becomes the inherently liberal process of American consensus politics. All of the characters' stated and unstated urges against revolution or the status quo are mediated by Hester's return, an act of reconciliation congruent with her adopting the prophetic role of a gradualist. So reaching and gripping is Bercovitch's consensus thesis that it becomes a Norris-like octopus, incorporating Hawthorne's ironies and paradoxes, issues of dissent and rebellion, national disruptions like the English Civil War, the American Revolution (along with adultery, the "novel's fundamental donnée"), and European revolutions at mid-19th century. Bercovitch's achievement is obviously brilliant. Behind the effort, of course, lies his ongoing quarrel with Perry Miller, waged against the Hawthornean agency of Michael Colacurcio. One also senses the strain of accommodating too many pluralist energies under the American political umbrella. It will surprise some readers, for instance, to learn that Jonathan Pue fought on the side of American patriots. And it may trouble some readers to discover that Bercovitch fails to address the problem of Hester's becoming an underground artist after her return, just as he fails to confront the implications of Pearl's having been lost to America. That loss may well be Hester's revenge, the results of which Hester returns to America to witness, thus making her far less the prophetic exemplum of a gradualist liberal telos than Bercovitch allows.

Also vying for best book of the year is Lauren Berlant's *The Anatomy of National Fantasy: Hawthorne, Utopia, and Everyday Life* (Chicago). Despite the burdensome demands of its style, the book richly examines Hawthorne from New Historicist perspectives, with a chapter on "Alice Doane's Appeal" (see *ALS 89*, pp. 32–33), and three chapters on *The Scarlet Letter.* Berlant explores the ways individual identity converges with and veers away from collective political fantasies that represent and serve the successful ideology of a nation. She finds Hawthorne in an uneasy relationship with the cluster of juridical, territorial, genetic, and experiential politics of America, the entangled constituents of the "National Symbolic." Choosing to become a citizen of somewhere else, Hawthorne understands that citizenship requires acculturation to "national symbols, spaces, narratives, and rituals," and that the price one pays for national identity is "self-ablation." He repudiates not only the law's definition of his citizenship but the process by which the National Symbolic regulates the production of a citizen's national fantasy. Quizzing and resisting efforts of political orthodoxy to instill a monolithic American identity, Hawthorne opposes "an official technology of memory" and insists on "the productive indeterminacy of national, personal, juridical, and political identity." He therefore rejects the law's hegemonic habit of abstracting the self either from the body or from local identity in the name of a stabilized symbolic order. His antihegemonic stance extends to his treatment of women, who "emerge as uncanny, paradoxical, politically unintelligible: as fantasy projections of patriarchal fear about the imminent end of male hegemony within the political public sphere, as occasions for serious critiques of that same patriarchal culture, and as eroticized subjects who speculate that other forms of collective life might be imaginable, even in America." Accordingly, unlike Bercovitch, Berlant discovers in Hawthorne an advocate for creating new self-identities by divorcing the self's attachment to abstract political fulfillment. The book dazzles with brilliance.

Another candidate for best book is Milton R. Stern's *Contexts for Hawthorne:* The Marble Faun *and the Politics of Openness and Closure in American Literature* (Illinois). Only two of the five chapters directly focus on *Faun;* others contextualize it and Hawthorne's more important fiction in exemplary association with major writers (Poe, Emerson, Melville, Whitman) who struggled with traditional conflicts embedded in Classicist-Romanticist polarities. These conflicts are political both in cultural and literary ways. By "openness," therefore, Stern means to suggest regnant traits of Romanticism: "revolutionary, future-facing, and explosive repudiation of past and present states"; and he scientifically associates these with the expanding, limitless world of the Big Bang. By contrast, "Closure" signifies a Classical, conservative preference for the past and present, "tight control and gravitational centralization, compacted time and space." States of being suggested by these opposed terms in the Classic-Romantic dichotomy depend on one another for their existence. Hawthorne turns out to have a failure of nerve in fully pursuing the Romantic-utopian energies that lead him to resist the chauvinistic national ideologies of his contemporary marketplace. Though desiring to be a citizen of somewhere else, he inveterately sought to belong to the very American present his fiction resists. The care and craft by which Stern argues, his sensitivity to the tonalities of language, and his abiding intelligence and equability result in a mature, sometimes brooding study that will surely be a reliable guide to Hawthorne (indeed, to the American Renaissance, generally) for years to come.

Less reliable, mostly unoriginal, and sometimes vapid, Charles Swann's *Nathaniel Hawthorne: Tradition and Revolution* (Cambridge) works through several tales and the novels in order to herald the undiminished power of Hawthorne in creating *Septimius Felton* as an unfortunately abbreviated capstone to the novelist's historical project. Arguing (usually silently and unfairly) against Colacurcio, Bercovitch, and me, Swann reads Hawthorne's attitudes toward the American Revolution in the same way as do Michael Davitt Bell, John P. McWilliams, and George Dekker: a necessary tragedy that, God be praised, the American patriots won. In his defense of a tough-minded Hawthorne who endorses Puritan revolution and the tragic birth of the nation, Swann never considers the valuable question that Colacurcio has provocatively urged us to ask about Hawthorne's treatment of historical outcomes: what if events had not turned out the way they did? Immune to Hawthorne's ironies on revolution, Swann is not oblivious to similar ironies on 19th-century America; but, unlike Stern, he fails to see a connection between source and product, fails to see a betrayal of revolutionary idealism. Failures in scholarship also mar the study. For example, the chapter on "Alice Doane's Appeal" is compromised by its unawareness of Lauren Berlant's article (see above); and when he ridicules Colacurcio for his treatment of Hester, Swann is obviously ignorant of Colacurcio's essay " 'The Woman's Own Choice' " (see *ALS 1985*, p. 32).

Joel Pfister's *The Production of Personal Life: Class, Gender, and the Psychological in Hawthorne's Fiction* (Stanford) also ignores a wealth of germane scholarship on the tales and novels. Yet Pfister amasses a huge bibliography of cultural studies from which to construct the contexts specified in his title. Uninterested in psychoanalysis ("psychobabble"), he locates Hawthorne in a mid-19th-century, middle-class America having successfully and smugly privatized the family life of hearth/home and defined domestic gender roles, to which ideological activity he both conforms and rebels. Though his fictions are implicated in the processes of industry and commercial life, "Hawthorne often proves critical of the ideological role that his writing plays in these processes. He is a product, agent, and critic of an emerging middle-class interiority, and is aware that his participation in reproducing the forms of subjectivity of his class is political." Though his second point seems overstated, Pfister writes lucidly, grounds his views in history, and produces an important study of the production of intersubjective social consciousness. His readings of Hawthorne's women (the "disturbing influence") are particularly splendid.

Of the 189 pages in J. Hillis Miller's *Hawthorne and History: Defacing It* (Blackwell), only 87 of them pursue the relationship of theory and reading as applied to "The Minister's Black Veil." Opposed to previous (or future) interpretations that claim authoritative primacy on any basis other than rhetoric, Miller shows Hawthorne's anticipating both Derrida and de Man. Fresh readings of the tale abound, including the extrapolated significance of word definitions drawn from Greek and Roman origins. Miller is especially astute in working with the trope prosopopoeia in its application to Hooper's effort to hide his face: "If Hooper's face behind the veil, like that of all his neighbours, is yet another veil, then it can be said that the real face too is not a valid sign but another de-facement. The face de-faces . . . it [Miller's ellipses]." A central thesis statement may be instructive: "A preternatural horror is interwoven with the threads of Hooper's veil, at least to Hooper's sense of it. This makes the veil, so it seems, an example of what Hawthorne has been seeking unsuccessfully in all his writing: the material embodiment of a spiritual or allegorical meaning. The 'horror' woven into the physical threads of the crape, however, is the horror of the inaccessibility of what is behind the veil. It is the preternatural horror of unveiling the possibility of the impossibility of unveiling, even within or beyond the grave." What Miller finally claims is that the tale exemplifies the undecidability of the difference between allegory and realism, fiction and history. Indeed, as a performative act, the tale is a history pushing beyond the historical present of its writing and the interpretative history of the past it invokes.

Balanced in argument and graceful in style, *Prophetic Pictures: Nathaniel Hawthorne's Knowledge and Uses of the Visual Arts* (Greenwood) by Rita K. Gollin and John L. Idol, Jr., is the fullest study of their title's subjects, beginning with Hawthorne's earliest days in Salem and concluding with his frequent and sometimes frustrating experiences in the galleries of Rome. Gollin and Idol carefully expose the relationship between the visual arts and authorship in Hawthorne's earliest tales, Sophia's influence on his acquiring a cultivated appreciation of art after their marriage, his preferring the realism of the early Dutch masters while in England, and his valiant though somewhat vain—because belated—"crash course" on the visual arts in Rome, largely exploited in *Faun.* After this study, no one should wonder about the pictorial origins of Hawthorne's fiction. Featured late in the book are 29 black-and-white photographic reproductions of paintings and sculptures that Hawthorne saw while abroad, along with responses to their originals from his notebooks and fiction.

For a book comprising 201 pages, E. Michael Jones's *The Angel and the*

Machine: The Rational Psychology of Nathaniel Hawthorne (Sugden) contextualizes with a vengeance, for not until page 119 does he begin brief analyses of "Sights from a Steeple," "The Birth-mark," and the four major novels. Up to that point, Jones argues for the imagistic and philosophical importance of the two nouns in his main title, not simply for Hawthorne but for Victorian America at large. His basic argument is that, through Carlyle, Fichte, Schelling, and others, American Romantics were culturally and philosophically trapped in advocating a scientific-mechanistic world that would free them from concerns about the body in order to release the soul, the sentimental angel so common in the rhetoric of Poe, Hawthorne, Emerson, and Melville. "The angel was the way out of the machine, which for the popular mind meant the grim realities of life in an increasingly industrial society, but unfortunately it was the way out of the world—the only real world—as well." Hawthorne himself "never gave up the angel-machine dichotomy: at first he unconsciously accepted it; then he attacked it, and finally he capitulated to it." Were the scholarship on Hawthorne as searching as that on the unsuccessful Romantic effort to solve the dualism of matter and spirit, Jones's study would be more worthwhile than it is.

Anyone hoping to find a luminous thought or two in Peter Buitenhuis's The House of the Seven Gables: *Severing Family and Colonial Ties* (Twayne) will search in vain. Perhaps this undistinguished study by a fairly distinguished critic was overly fettered by requirements in Twayne's "Masterwork Studies" series. Whatever the case, it would take a good deal of academic cynicism to imagine its usefulness, even for undergraduates. A wearisome number of duly entitled sections—mostly composed of radically distilled and thus distorted banalities from the critical canon—substitute for an active, informed engagement with the text. Neither recent nor old journal articles find their way into the notes or bibliography. Factual errors also mar the book. Worst of all, the promise of the subtitle is scarcely broached.

There may be an undergraduate out there in the republic of letters who can profit from Klaus P. Hansen's *Sin and Sympathy: Nathaniel Hawthorne's Sentimental Religion* (Peter Lang), but everyone else will deserve my "I told you so" for wasting time in consulting it. A nightmare of categories, the book divides into four sections (Theology, Sentimentalism, History, and Art), within which appear sub- and sub-subdivisions. As for the content, Hansen depends entirely on selected previous criticism, which he somehow manages to unsophisticate. An example of his critical acumen will serve as my final warning: Colacurcio's *The Province of Piety: Moral History in Hawthorne's Early Tales* "impresses us by its vast knowledge about the beginnings of New England, but its interpretations of Hawthorne's tales are often absurd. Colacurcio sees Hawthorne as a precursor of Perry Miller, who was only interested in the past for its own sake and knew everything about it. With this approach Hawthorne's tales become unrelated pieces of historiography with no moral or philosophical interest."

iii General Essays

Though brief, Klaus P. Stich's "Hawthorne's Intimations of Alchemy" (*ATQ* n.s. 5:15–30), an excellent achievement in scholarship, intertextual cross-referencing, and interpretation, should not be missed; Stich recovers the religious and psychological meanings of alchemy known to or suspected by Hawthorne—even anticipating Jung's deep and broad interest in the subject—and he reveals their crucial importance to "The Great Carbuncle," "Ethan Brand," *Scarlet Letter, Faun,* and the unfinished romances. Nothing less than the romancer's project as a concoctionist, an alchemical amalgamist, is at stake, and on the sexual level such blending distills into androgyny. The scarlet *A* may indeed stand for Alchemy, just as Hester's name, through a series of etymologies, finally evokes the Virgin Mary, Isis, and Venus, who relate to the mystical Sophia of the alchemists. Yes, Hawthorne's very marriage is at stake. Stich might well consider enlarging this piece into a monograph, but it already amounts to a self-perpetuating elixir.

Beginning with seasoned reflections on the differences between Emerson and Hawthorne, Joel Porte's "Hawthorne: 'The Obscurist Man of Letters in America,'" in *In Respect to Egotism,* pp. 124–63, views "The Old Manse" as a veiled, face-to-face confrontation with Emerson's *Nature* and its transparent eyeball. Indeed, Hawthorne sees the biblical problem of veils persisting in modern times, prohibiting an original relation to the universe and God. Instead of searching for the spirit behind masking appearances, Hawthorne focuses on objects themselves, not with respect to his own egotism but rather in common with us all, which makes him neither a theorist nor an explainer but a describer: "The *condition* of men and women—the forms and gestures of the body, movements, expressions, nervous tics, choices of clothing, habits of posture and speech, outbursts, cadences, and silences—these are the signs of the self that Hawthorne never tired of recording." Porte works through "The Minister's Black Veil," "The Birth-mark," and *Scarlet Letter,* less remarkably on the last.

A pair of keen observations are worked out well in Gillian Brown's "Hawthorne, Inheritance, and Women's Property" (*SNNTS* 23:107–18). First, "according to Hawthorne, family inheritance, an endowment both economic and moral, links persons to real property as well as to physical properties and characteristics, placing persons under the power of their legacies." Thus the inheritance plot in *Gables* "recapitulates the 'mad scientist' plots of the tales, but with the crucial difference that the conditions of victimage dissolve in a happy, healthy, and prosperous ending for the inheritors." Second, it is no happenstance that Hester's *A* changes meanings, because "a woman's transformation of her status as adulteress is the medium through which Hawthorne imagines the cancellation of moral debts and resolution of social conflict." It may be unnecessary to add that Brown does not so imagine them.

In an exceedingly smart theoretical essay, "Romance and the Prose of the World: Hegelian Reflections on Hawthorne and America," in *Theorizing American Literature,* pp. 163–93, Joseph G. Kronick relates the self-reflexivity of Hawthorne and *all* American literature with that of the nation itself, examining more particularly how self-reflexivity entails problems of representation, reference, allegory, mimesis, and romance—and how in turn these conform to Hegel's concept of prosaism, which bears on the issues of art, history, and the state. Within his massive *Sporting with the Gods,* Michael Oriard often deals with Hawthorne but most fully where he views Hawthorne in skeptical opposition to sentimental and Transcendental attitudes toward children and play (pp. 385–92). Except in *Faun,* wherein occurs a balance of play in the face of life's tragedy, Hawthorne's treatment of play virtually always "connotes the state of childhood and prelapsarian innocence, but life demands something more." Completely overlooking Hawthorne's frequent advice to frolic, Oriard's treatment seems unbalanced.

Rita K. Gollin writes a salutary and jocular review of Hawthorne's attitudes toward bodily needs and functions in "Nathaniel Hawthorne: The Flesh and the Spirit; or, 'Gratifying Your Coarsest Animal Needs' " (*SNNTS* 23:82–95). Gleaning comments on food, bodily torments from insects, urination, and defecation, she finds both a temperate and an indulgent Hawthorne, one opposed to "unmitigated sensuality" and yet one not above scatological humor, and she concludes that in "reading

Hawthorne's letters and notebooks along with the fiction, one of the biggest surprises is the extensiveness, the explicitness, and (on the whole) the good humor of his confrontation with what we would call the facts of life."

Judy Schaaf Anhorn finds Hawthorne's consciousness of his dwindling imaginative powers central to his last and terribly neglected book, in "Literary Reputation and the Essays of *Our Old Home*" (*SNNTS* 23:152–66). "Up the Thames," for example, describes the Thames tunnel with scarcely concealed broodings on his future loss of reputation. And in "Lichfield and Uttoxeter," Hawthorne recognizes that because the scene of Johnson's celebrated penance had receded too dimly in time, it merely amounted to "a romancer's dream." "As sentimental pilgrim, Hawthorne has been searching for clues in the actual to defend an idea about romance, to corroborate the imagination's evidence that, because invention springs from actuality, life will bear supporting witness to memory, or even to imagination. Such a hope is, of course, destined to fail." Clearly opposed to Woodson (below), Anhorn presents small evidence from a big book in support of this thesis.

More reliable and written by someone who probably knows as much about Hawthorne as anybody ever has, Thomas Woodson's " 'Hawthornesque Shapes': The Picturesque and the Romance" (*SNNTS* 23:167–82) avows that Hawthorne preferred the romance over the novel *because* he did not have to sacrifice either quotidian detail or contemporary reality. Woodson believes that Hawthorne and Alexander Pope address novelistic realities better than does Thackeray. "Generally, Hawthorne's contexts suggest that most often 'novels' are undistinguished objects of material culture, not provoked by studious ideas, fit to be consumed on railroads or observed as Kenyon and Donatello do in the market stalls of Perugia." Hawthorne uses the picturesque inherited from Scott and others to suggest " 'that odd state of mind wherein we fitfully and teasingly remember some previous scene or incident,' mysteriously familiar because it unveils the deeper truth fit for the romance form." Somewhat in opposition, Gayle L. Smith's "The Light of Reflection: Hawthorne and the Luminist Sublime" (*Prospects* 16:117–204) argues that Hawthorne's pictorial language bears less resemblance to the picturesque mode of the past and his own time than to the luminist movement of the future. Smith does not dogmatize, preferring to explore and suggest how several Hawthorne sketches anticipate the luminist concerns of Martin Johnson Heade and John Frederick Kensett. Supported by an impressive gallery of art historians, she writes compellingly on Hawthorne's critique of the "stereotyped aesthetic formulas" of his contemporaries in his probe of the "psychological processes involved in experiencing the sublime."

A superior model of research in historical and genealogical records, Margaret B. Moore's "Hawthorne, the Tories, and Benjamin Lynde Oliver, Jr." (*SAR*, pp. 213–24), discovers additional influences on Hawthorne's sympathetic treatment of Royalists during and following the Revolutionary War. Many of these sources involve the Oliver family, resident in Salem for more than a century. Perhaps most influential was Benjamin, Jr., who tutored Hawthorne in 1820 and 1821 and who later wrote widely on political moderation. From him and informed Salemites, Hawthorne may well have heard stories of the Oliver family's mistreatment, dispossession, and disgrace at the hands of patriot enthusiasts.

In "Soul Murder and Other Crimes of the Heart: Familial Abuse in Nathaniel Hawthorne's Fictional Psychodramas," in *The Aching Hearth*, pp. 119–34, Maryhelen C. Harmon selects examples of psychic damage usually inflicted on women victims by men and society, all within a traditional context of the obligation borne by literature to provide a corrective moral for human failings. Among Harmon's readings, Hester's *A* stands for Abused. Alfred H. Marks tries again to pin down the tale of Tieck's that Hawthorne was reading at the Manse in 1843, on this occasion drawing resonant parallels between the works, in "*The Scarlet Letter* and Tieck's 'The Elves' " (*NHR* 17, ii:1, 3–5).

Frequently confusing Hawthorne the man with the voice(s) in his works, Lucy Maddox tortuously essays to equate Hawthorne's attitudes toward Indians and women, in "Saving the Family: Hawthorne, Child, and Sedgwick," in *Removals*, pp. 89–130. Maddox may be correct in saying that Hawthorne viewed the extinction or removal of Indians from New England as a settled affair, but it does not follow that he endorsed it. And she may be correct in saying that Hester capitulates to white patriarchal power, but it does not follow that she gives up the wild (Indian) side of herself in order to protect herself and Pearl, as if they were the last of the Mohicans.

Readers can avoid Catherine H. Zuckert's "Hawthorne's Politics of Passion," in *Natural Right and the American Imagination*, pp. 63–98, which is at best half-informed in the relevant scholarship and which offers such gems as this on the social contract in *The Scarlet Letter:* "The foundation of political union should . . . be understood more like the compact underlying a middle-class marriage: as an expression of a joint desire to live together, based on the free choice of the parties, in light not only of their individual failings but also of their complementary strengths and talents."

iv Essays on the Novels

a. *The Scarlet Letter* Ross C. Murfin edits *Nathaniel Hawthorne:* The Scarlet Letter (St. Martin's), a volume in the series Case Studies in Contemporary Criticism, obviously intended as a postmodernist alternative to the Norton Critical Edition. Murfin's journeyman introduction offers nothing new and, worse, both confuses facts and attributes original discoveries in Hawthorne scholarship to critics already indebted to unacknowledged others. Appearing chronologically are a reprinting of the Centenary Edition of the novel; a spotty section on critical background; brief but helpful introductions to five critical approaches, followed in each instance by an essay demonstrating the approach; and a glossary of terminology. Four of the five essays are revised (basically shorter) versions of journal articles: Joanne Feit Diehl on psychoanalytic criticism, David Leverenz on reader-response, Michael Ragusis on deconstruction, and Sacvan Bercovitch on New Historicism. Shari Benstock writes a new piece in the mode of feminist criticism, "*The Scarlet Letter* (a)dorée, or the Female Body Embroidered," pp. 288–303. Touching on several issues raised by uncited predecessors, Benstock asks whether the feminine bears "the same relation to storytelling as it does to embroidery or the female body to sin." The answer: the powerful feminine dimension of the novel "works not to exploit oppositional structures of sexual-textual difference but rather to expose the fictional nature of these modes, revealing absolute sexual difference as a fantasy of patriarchal oppositional and hierarchical logic."

Informed and intelligent, Douglas Anderson's "Jefferson, Hawthorne, and 'The Custom-House'" (*NCF* 46:309–26) initially yokes the language and circumstances of Hawthorne's preface to the second edition with those of Jefferson in the Declaration of Independence, largely over the issue of altering or expunging suggested in references to adulteration in "Custom-House" and *Scarlet Letter.* Douglas is most insightful on the relation of Hawthorne's representation of the adulterations suffered by Salem to those of Jefferson's Declaration, concluding that "Salem itself is a part of the larger political and moral adulteration that is expressed in its national government, in the formative documents of that government, and in the character of the founders. Strong traits of their nature, too, Hawthorne seems to suggest, have intertwined themselves with our own, and if the results are indeterminate, . . . then it is an indeterminacy that springs from the textual condition of Jefferson's indeterminate Declaration."

In " 'To Open an Intercourse with the World': Hawthorne's *Scarlet Letter,*" in *Authorship and Audience,* pp. 105–31, Stephen Railton applies more pressure than have Nina Baym, Kenneth Dauber, Edgar Dryden, and Gordon Hutner to the issue of Hawthorne's relation to his audience. Railton claims that Hawthorne's rhetorical strategies are more exemplary than those of Emerson, Melville, Thoreau, and Whitman because, eschewing a relationship with nature, he sought a sympathetic union within a social or domestic milieu. Like these other writers, Hawthorne confronted "the grotesque failure of American society as potential audience," but he resorted to rhetorical strategies whereby he could decorously lure his audience into a subversion of its pieties about human nature. The Puritan spectators in the novel "are essentially a group of Victorian readers disguised by their historical costumes. What they lack—self-knowledge and sympathy—defines [the novel's] 'apostolic errand,' " permitting Hawthorne "to introduce his genteel audience to the morally intricate truth about themselves."

Apparently a prolegomenon to a future study, Emily Miller Budick's "Hester's Skepticism, Hawthorne's Faith; or, What Does a Woman Doubt?: Instituting the American Romance Tradition" (*NLH* 22:199–211) is too brief to untangle the snarls in the title, let alone much else. On the one hand, Hawthorne is sensitive to women, challenging the patrilineal control and heritage of the Puritan fathers; on the other, Budick insupportably charges that his maleness "may be even more invidious than feminist critics have yet portrayed it." Hawthorne's Custom-House confinement parallels Hester's jail term; and thus Pearl's birth coincides with Hawthorne's rebirth, and ergo Hawthorne is Pearl, whose desire to know her father equates with Hawthorne's inheriting Surveyor Pue. But Hawthorne also wants to know his mother and accordingly becomes Hester. All of these identifications emerge from scantily explained contexts of history and romance tradition, further vexed by sexual associations of the scarlet letter with those of Poe's purloined letter, and further yet by the philosophical imbroglio involving subjectivity and otherness.

Boldly declaring that Hawthorne's is not the language of discourse but of visual images, Franklin R. Rogers's "Lost in a Moral Wilderness: Hawthorne, *The Scarlet Letter*," in *Occidental Ideographs*, pp. 76–99, recalls some early work on the novel by Leland S. Schubert and Roy Male but catapults beyond them, concentrating on the coherent-making associations of verbal pictures that comprise the openings and closures in the novel's structure as well as on the lives of the central characters and the Puritan community. Rogers lucidly comments on veils and revelations, the structural relationship between preface and novel, and the almost perfectly duplicated structures of the first and second halves.

Though unacquainted with recent work on Hawthorne's attitudes toward slavery, Deborah L. Madsen's " 'A for Abolition': Hawthorne's Bond-Servant and the Shadow of Slavery" (*JAmS* 25:255–59) cogently links the historical outlook on black slavery in "Chiefly about War-Matters" with white bondage in *Scarlet Letter*, claiming that these forms of commodification sully the credentials of the Founding Fathers. Compatible in subject matter, Jennifer Fleischner's "Hawthorne and the Politics of Slavery" (*SNNTS* 23:96–106) unconvincingly argues that in "the relationship between Hawthorne's own political situation in 1850 and *The Scarlet Letter* is a prototype of the displaced connections among the nation's political situation with regard to slavery in 1850, Hawthorne's own political allegiances, the politics of *The Scarlet Letter*, and the politics of his 'political' writings." Fleischner reads the conclusion of the novel (à la Jonathan Arac but sans Hester) as if it allegorizes the national slavery debate. More peculiarly, she never really addresses in a conjunctive way the subjects of her title.

Amid scholarly errors, misnamings, and misidentifications, Eileen Dreyer's " 'Confession' in *The Scarlet Letter*" (*JAmS* 25:78–81) suggests that Dimmesdale's refusal to confess to an earthly confessor may depend on Hawthorne's potential knowledge of the contrition/attrition controversy involving William Chillingworth, available to him in Thomas Fuller's *The Worthies of England* and Thomas Broughton's *An Historical Dictionary of All Religions*. Woefully ignorant of contemporary criticism, Stuart Hutchinson's "Hawthorne: *The Scarlet Letter (1850)*," in *The American Scene*, pp. 37–56, reads like a gentlemanly man-of-letters overview from the 1940s in its magisterial tone, its borrowings, and its cursory connections of Hawthorne with a panoply of Western writers.

b. *The House of the Seven Gables* Aligning the novel with the 1848 presidential campaign, Charles Swann, "*The House of the Seven Gables:*

Hawthorne's Modern Novel of 1848" (*MLR* 86:1–18), examines the text's conflicted attitudes toward technological and social progress in relation to mid-century cultural optimism. Swann best summarizes his thesis: "Hawthorne's novel . . . suggests that the dominant mode of representation is still (historical) writing, and the history of the naming of new ways of communication supports the notion that this was, at some level, recognized as the master code. (It is no accident that the tele*graph,* the photo*graph*—even the daguerro*type*—are so named.) If that is so, then however much the radical ruptures with the past are (temporarily) desired by Hawthorne's hero of the summer of 1848, they remain subordinated to the syntax and grammar of a particular kind of historical sentence and narrative: one which emphasizes continuity and development . . . rather than discontinuity and new beginnings, while at the same time recognizing the tragedy of the irredeemable losses of the past." An example of excellent research that deserves special mention is Swann's limning Hawthorne's reference to "gutta perch."

A fascinating demonstration of how "the metaphorical identity of body and house" in *Gables* "functions as a means of examining the representation of reality by narrative language," Charles Campbell's "Representing Representation: Body as Figure, Frame, and Text" in *The House of the Seven Gables* (*ArQ* 47, iv:1–26) seems to argue a tautology: that the novel's failure "is its failure to provide for any stable or permanent framing, producing instead a framework of multiple frames continually exceeded by figures which appear, transform, and vanish too quickly to be definable—bodies made fluid metamorphosing into types, images, metaphors, portraits, figurines, pastry, and sex symbols: a mad, unframeable, unassimilable fiction."

Attempting to show how the novel's happy, conservative ending comports with theme and structure, Teresa Goddu's "The Circulation of Women in *The House of the Seven Gables*" (*SNNTS* 23:119–27) grafts Edward Everett's call for a democratic redistribution of wealth with Gayle Rubin's idea on "traffic in women." Hepzibah's association with incest reveals her failure to circulate; Alice Pyncheon's link to forced exchange (unlawful rape) reveals the failure of unregulated circulation; while Phoebe's successful business and extrafamilial marriage clears up the historically persistent traffic jam. Counterpointing Goddu's and others' happy reading of the novel, in an essay of wry bite and laudable phrasing, Claudia D. Johnson's "Unsettling Accounts in *The House of the Seven Gables*" (*ATQ* n.s. 5:83–94) argues that Hawthorne's "guile in the

Preface" diverts "the reader from the sordid vengeance at hand." Undercutting his own ostensible moral on the futility of vengeance, Hawthorne continues in *Gables* where he left off in "The Custom-House," immolating Salemites for his loss of the surveyorship. As a result, this "vengeance brings both author and reader to a darkness at the center of that 'sunniest' of novels"—a darkness highlighted by frequent appearances of the word "nothing" in the novel's midsection. Johnson smartly correlates nothingness with the corpses of the Judge and the one evoked in "The Scowl and the Smile" chapter.

c. *The Blithedale Romance* Dana Brand's "*The Blithedale Romance* and the Culture of Modernity," in *The Spectator and the City,* pp. 122–55, provocatively serves a double-course thesis. First, better than anybody else of his generation, Hawthorne reflects the incipient urban world of Baudelaire, one of novelty and excitement passively experienced by masses of people from around the world. Despite implicit dangers in modern urban life, Hawthorne prefers the city over the country, evident in his satire on the antiurban social experiment. Second, the novel "is the culmination of Hawthorne's critique of the culture of modernity" whose "representative subjectivity is that of the flaneur": someone like Coverdale or Westervelt whose reserve and spectatorship represent an invidious form of individualism that reduces complexity to simple images and seeks to exert power over others.

d. *The Marble Faun* Writing perhaps the year's best essay, T. Walter Herbert, Jr., masterfully illuminates the novel's psycho-social-sexual dynamics in "The Erotics of Purity: *The Marble Faun* and the Victorian Construction of Sexuality" (*Representations* 33:114–32). Beginning with the Victorian misreading of Spenser's Una and the lion by way of John Bell's statue *Purity,* Herbert outlines the complexities of "purity asserted and purity assailed" in Dr. Franco's efforts to seduce the tutor of the Hawthornes' children, Ada Shepard. Engaged to an American to whom she spells out the details of Franco's passionate advances, she prevails but at a cost typifying Victorian compromises: "Shepard enacts her fitness for a middle-class marriage by soliciting the passion that she sublimates, and she is encouraged by the ethos of purity to do so, since a woman can hardly appear transcendently pure to a man not sexually aroused by her." Herbert connects the implications of this case with Victorian misreadings of Hiram Powers's *The Greek Slave.* All of these *texts* are in turn related to the gender and sexuality texts of *Faun,* wherein Hawthorne is "intuitively aware of the dialectical process by which erotic solicitation and its denial sustain and incite each other, as do the denial and cultivation of womanly aggression, and his narrative dwells obsessively on the resultant paradoxes." Like Shepard, Hilda maintains her purity but at a cost of knowing the other side of herself (Miriam) whom she spurns; and between the two Hawthorne creates an unbridgeable abyss.

Claiming that Hawthorne anticipates the importance to psychology of modern-day research in kinesis, John L. Idol's "'A Linked Circle of Three' Plus One: Nonverbal Communication in *The Marble Faun*" (*SNNTS* 23:139–51) nicely elucidates the ways Hawthorne observes and dramatizes the function of body language and tones of voice "to provide information, regulate interaction, express intimacy, exercise social control, and facilitate service to others." One reads this uncommonly sensitive essay with the impression that, for a man who allegedly hated to be touched, Hawthorne was extraordinarily attuned to the expressive power of the human body, especially hands.

If John Dolis's "Hawthorne's Gentle Reader: (The Hen) House of (Family) Romance" (*ArQ* 47, i:29–47) is read as a parody of de Manian, Lacanian, and Derridean criticism, most readers will find it an amusing examination of *Faun*'s anatomy—its head (penis and ears) and tail (tale), which in their enfolded origins (phallic power), however small (according to the Greeks, the greater the number of folds in the penis, the greater the erection), are convertible. But I suspect no parody here. Dolis does point out salient links between Donatello and Pearl. Charging Hawthorne at the start with an anti-Semitism interlaced with sexual anxiety over the otherness represented by the beautiful Jewish woman in the *English Notebooks,* after whom Miriam ostensibly is modeled, Elissa Greenwald's "Hawthorne and Judaism: Otherness and Identity in *The Marble Faun*" (*SNNTS* 23:128–38) rather implausibly winds up declaring that, beyond Miriam's Jewishness as a source of her mysterious difference, Hawthorne perceives how this source "ties her more strongly to the humanity which confronts such mysteries in every religion and culture."

v Essays on Tales and Sketches

Albert J. von Frank edits and writes a well-researched Introduction to *Critical Essays on Hawthorne's Short Stories* (Hall). Along with eight selections from 19th-century commentary, von Frank includes 10 essays from the 1950s through the early 1980s that focus on particular issues or tales, and three new essays. Synoptically smart, Teresa Toulouse's "Seeing Through 'Paul Pry': Hawthorne's Early Sketches and the Problem of Audience," pp. 203–18, would have acquired even more gravity were it aware of Mary M. Van Tassel's work (see *ALS 88,* p. 34). Toulouse places the narrator-audience relations of Hawthorne's sketches in oppositional dialogue with those of Addison and Steele's *Spectator* papers and Irving's *Sketch Book.* "Many of [Hawthorne's] sketches present a narrator who threatens, undermines, or changes traditionally accepted relations between being seen and being seen through. Far from consistently projecting some unified audience that participates in a shared play of perspectives or feelings, this narrator invariably belies the assumption that transparency can be achieved or maintained—or, insofar as it is a product of older social assumptions, that it is indeed still desirable." Hawthorne cannot use the ideal of Addison, Steele, or Irving because the fluctuations in contemporaneous American culture prevent him from assuming their "concrete social reality and stable history." Credibly speculating on Goodman Brown's past and its similarity with Dimmesdale's, Jerome Loving's "Pretty in Pink: 'Young Goodman Brown' and New-World Dreams," pp. 219–31, argues that "both Dimmesdale and Brown deny the significance of their sexual past and thus commit a version of Hawthorne's 'unpardonable sin' in their teleological rejection of the idea that 'evil'—the sexual act—'is the nature of mankind.' In rejecting it, they deny their connection with the Old World and, hence, the necessity of their inevitable fall in the New World." Even more cogent and felicitous, Loving claims that Brown is responsible for deflowering his own faith: "Before he had Faith, he *had* faith in the power of the future, but ever afterward the sexual act becomes allegorized into a dreamlike ceremony about a past that is perennial." Rife with problems, Allan Lloyd-Smith's "Hawthorne's Gothic Tales," pp. 232–43, relies on Fredric Jameson for acculturizing the Gothic mode in early 19th-century America but proceeds diffusely through a series of tales to insinuate various psychosexual displacements belonging to Hawthorne. Making his best general point, Smith says that in "Hawthorne's hands, the Gothic is 'performed': it is not allowed to direct the form of the narrative but is instead manipulated and distorted ironically for purposes that include a recognition of its origins in destabilized personal and political situations."

In "Fideism vs. Allegory in 'Rappaccini's Daughter' " (*NCF* 46:223–44) John N. Miller, exploring biographical applications to fiction somewhat more cautiously than does Edwin Haviland Miller, submits Sophia and Hawthorne's mother and sisters as real-life, allegorized models for the confused portrait of Beatrice. Miller opposes—without rejecting—the criticism that would construe the tale as a test in epistemology failed by Giovanni. Indeed, Giovanni's bewilderment over how to view Beatrice stems as much from the tale's obvious contradictions as from anything else; and these contradictions, says Miller, may well result from Hawthorne's ambivalent feelings about family relations in the edenic realm of Raymond, Maine. Giovanni's *fancy* can certainly be impugned, but neither his faith nor his reason can be legitimately faulted.

An amusing hoax that may divert investigators, "On 'Rappaccini's Son': A Note on a Twice-Told Tale" (*NHR* 17, i:5–8), by Herbert S. Bailey, Jr., compares Bailey's bogus story with the bona fide tale.

"Doing Cultural Work: 'My Kinsman, Major Molineux' and the Construction of the Self-Made Man" (*SNNTS* 23:20–27), by T. Walter Herbert, Jr., submits three models of emergent manhood from de Tocqueville's observations on contradictions in American middle-class attitudes toward democracy and aristocracy. Impinging on Robin and thus on the reader in experiencing the social and psychological work advanced by the tale is this lucid point: "The filial revolt required of the democratic individual may free him from the entanglements of deferential dependence, but it also strikes a blow against the source of his own identity: to trample on an old man's heart is to defile one's own." More sensitive yet, Herbert argues that the reader does not have to conform to the ostensible cultural work recommended by a text: "cultural work still takes place when we become resisting readers, when we seek to consolidate our own identities over-against what the work solicits. If we find that a text tells us who we are and what our world is like better than we can otherwise tell ourselves, we then accord it a consummate value."

Contextualizing "The May-pole of Merry Mount" within a nonprivileging yet critical demand for a distinctively provincial praxis, Michael J. Colacurcio's "Cosmopolitan and Provincial: Hawthorne and the Reference of American Studies" (*SNNTS* 23:3–19) argues with familiar wit and acumen that, despite its extracultural, universal referentiality in Miltonic texts, the tale nevertheless depends on specific local circumstances that Hawthorne recovered in specific texts on American experience for its particular—that is, American—meanings. Endicott's and Blackstone's appearances tell us nothing about Hawthorne's indebtedness to Milton but lead us instead to Hawthorne's historical sources, a decidedly American Studies project. Initially endorsing that project, my own "Fantasy, Reality, and Audience in 'Drowne's Wooden Image'" (*SNNTS* 23:28–45) establishes the latter stage of the French and Indian War as the historical setting of the tale and hypothesizes John Singleton Copley's function as that of a colonial artist too often stifled, as is Drowne, by the public demand for a mimetic form of art. I immodestly argue that all previous critics have misread the tale by duplicating this demand, thus refusing to accept the tale's invitation to indulge in the make-believe world of fantasy and hence failing to recognize that Drowne has no real-life model for his work of art.

Profitably read in tandem with Stich's piece (above), most notably concerning androgyny and Sophia, Leland S. Person, Jr.'s "Hawthorne's Bliss of Paternity: Sophia's Absence from 'The Old Manse'" (*SNNTS* 23:46–59) compares the preface with the notebooks and applies the biographical results to a brief reading of "The Artist of the Beautiful." Person may overemphasize Hawthorne's anxiety as a writer and father, but his thesis is intriguing: "exploring the possibility of autogenesis enables Hawthorne to replicate his own single parentage (by his mother) in the only way available to him as a man—by projecting himself as a bachelor father. He compensates for the absence of a father in his life by being mother and father—an autogenetic father—in his art. And to veil or obscure that rootedness—the origins of real as well as literary 'children'—Hawthorne disassociates his writing in the Preface from the marital relationship that, ironically, made possible his own natural 'bliss of paternity.'"

Also concerned with Sophia but in different ways, Larry J. Reynolds's "Hawthorne and Emerson in 'The Old Manse'" (*SNNTS* 23:60–81) claims that Hawthorne engaged in a detrimental, imaginative struggle against Emerson, whom he saw as his double and a father figure, in order to acquire the kind of power, the "mesmeric victimization," over Sophia fictionalized in "Rappaccini's Daughter" and "Ethan Brand." Hawthorne's protracted delay in completing the preface and his inability to write it as a tale resulted from this struggle. The argument and main readings seem to me farfetched, but doubtless others will find them fetching.

Though not so fully aware of the criticism as it should be, Dean Wentworth Bethea's "Heat, Light, and the Darkening World: Hawthorne's 'The Artist of the Beautiful'" (*SoAR* 56, iv:23–35) respectably posits a mediating position between familiar dichotomies: "interlaced with the social reality he ultimately faces, Warland's creative process evinces an amalgam of artistic insight, practical experience, and rational cognition that is centrally concerned with the relationship between art and society." Most valuably, however, Bethea sees the devaluation of Owen's miniaturized art as analogous to the demeaning of the short story by lovers of the novel; and he skillfully reads Owen's engraved box as a rendition of Keats's "Ode on a Grecian Urn." Near the beginning of his "Void in the Narrative: The Seduction of the Reader in Nathaniel Hawthorne's 'Alice Doane's Appeal' " (*ATQ* n.s. 5:73–82), R. McClure Smith suggests that his approach will not provide a new interpretation so much as an interpretation of the critical responses to the tale; yet because Smith is unfamiliar with the leading criticism on the story, his aim is short-circuited from the start.

Providing the best corrective yet, Richard Toby Widdicombe's "Hawthorne's 'Celestial Rail-road' and Transcendentalism: Apologia or Caricature?" (*NHR* 17, ii:5–9) demonstrates that Transcendentalism amounts to a minor target of the tale's satire. Instead, "the *major* element in the story involves the narrator's drawing a heavily ironized and bitterly satirical portrait of mid-nineteenth-century American society, one which shows him to be radically critical of materialism, unquestioned progress, spiritual complacency, and widespread ignorance—all of which evils he casts at the door of America's economic prosperity and individual might."

In the best and fullest reading of Hawthorne's last short story, Monika M. Elbert's "Hawthorne's 'Hollow' Men: Fabricating Masculinity in 'Feathertop' " (*ATQ* n.s. 5:169–82) spins from the demasculinized theme in T. S. Eliot's poem to 19th-century problems of manly identity brought on by capitalism and the cult of domesticity. Among other rich summary points, Elbert says, "The character of Feathertop embodies all the contradictory and self-limiting poses of the gentleman in search of selfhood in the marketplace. Hawthorne attempts to subvert the mid-nineteenth-century definition of successful entrepreneurial manhood as well as of Old World gentility; more specifically, he unveils the anxieties emanating from man's pursuit of a vocation in an ever-technologizing society."

Duquesne University

3 Poe

Benjamin Franklin Fisher IV

This year's work impresses on us the necessity for not attempting to compartmentalize Poe's writings or the secondary materials into overly rigid categories. Thus, for example, although several items surveyed below might ostensibly invite treatment as detective fiction critiques, they just as appropriately bring into play far wider considerations. As has been usual lately, Poe's tales draw repeated commentary, and the poems but little. *Pym* and *Eureka,* too, elicit scant attention. Nonetheless, Poe continues to thrive amid diversity, and therefore our first item to notice is Diane Johnson's "Dreams of E. A. Poe" (*NY* 18 July: 7–8, 10), in which the author in his times and our times comes to us in biographical and analytical terms. Johnson highlights Poe's awareness of the world of his day and the literary uses to which it could be adapted; thus, his modulations on the double and on death, for example, have altogether understandable, and not weird, foundations. Johnson's is a balanced overview.

i Bibliographic, Textual Studies

Jana L. Argersinger and Steven Gregg's "Subject Index to 'International Poe Bibliography': Poe Scholarship and Criticism, 1983–1988" (*PoeS* 24:1–48) supplements similar earlier retrieval lists for the journal. Two of Poe's own texts are made available by Burton R. Pollin in "*The Living Writers of America:* A Manuscript by Edgar Allan Poe" (*SAR,* pp. 151–211). Pollin edits and annotates the manuscripts of "The Living Writers," which Poe calculated as part of a critical survey of American literary culture, and a review of Eugene Sue's popular novel, *The Wandering Jew;* the manuscripts are in the Morgan and Huntington libraries. These pieces shed light on Poe's critical outlooks, his projected magazines, and the "Longfellow War." The second document may also add to our knowledge of Poe's and Sue's common literary sources in Pückler-Muskau. Pollin's "Frances Sargent Osgood and *Saroni's Musical Times:* Documents Linking Poe, Osgood, and Griswold" (*PoeS* 23 [1990]:27–36) exposes another of Griswold's specious presentations of "evidence" concerning Poe. Mrs. Osgood's poem, "A Dirge," and her "Reminiscences of Poe" originally appeared in *Saroni's,* although Griswold implied that they were of a later date. Another relationship involving Poe and one of his well-known, if not well-liked, contemporaries is charted by W. T. Bandy in "Poe and Tasistro" (*PoeS* 23 [1990]:37–40), in which the laudatory review of *Tales of the Grotesque and Arabesque* in the 28 December 1839 *New-York Mirror,* presumably (Poe thought) the work of "Count" Louis Fitzgerald Tasistro, is set off against the Tasistro's deviousness and plagiarisms.

ii General Studies

No doubt the most eagerly awaited book in Poe studies for this year is Kenneth Silverman's *Edgar A. Poe* (Harper Collins). This biography, it was hoped, would supersede A. H. Quinn's account that has long been considered the "standard." Silverman has missed no bit of biographical material, however minor, that has surfaced in the half-century since Quinn's book appeared (Silverman's use of major Poe repositories is evident), and his expression is generally engaging. What may surprise readers, however, are the heavily Freudian approaches to many of the works, much in the vein of Marie Bonaparte, and the shying away from many of the good critical studies of Poe's writings. Although Silverman brings the personalities of those associated with Poe to life, his attitude toward the principal figure seems remote, as if he wished to remain detached from his subject. In addition, if Silverman's drift is toward proposing Poe himself as "Outis" (pp. 250–53, 490n), I, for one, desire stronger evidence (see in this regard Pollin, "Living Writers," above).

A provocative chapter on Poe in Stephen Railton's *Authorship and Audience* should appeal to academic and nonacademic readers. A sense of performance, Railton submits, underlies every work by Poe, who never left off trying to control his audience in order to assert "control over his own mind." Thus, his narrators and protagonists are often essential to each other, exemplified here by the Dupin tales, "The Gold-Bug," and "Usher." The last tale appears in this context as a marvelous subversion of Gothic formulas, and Roderick's outburst of "Madman!" at its conclusion simultaneously reveals one of Poe's deepest personal fears (i.e., his separateness) and intimates how the reader has been duped by ready acceptance of the narrator's assumptions. The Poe who "complicated and reinvigorated the clichés of Gothic fiction" worked thus through the double-edged technique of sobriety and literary hoax. Here is convincing criticism of the poles of rationality and irrationality.

In the *Columbia History of the American Novel,* Poe receives significant comment in three chapters. Predictably, Michael T. Gilmore (pp. 61–62, 66–67) discusses Poe's disaffection with the American literary marketplace. Gilmore cites "Usher," "The Poetic Principle," and the poor sales of *Eureka* as examples of Poe's negativism and "disinterestedness." Poe on the imagination, writes Terence Martin (pp. 79–83), contrasts markedly with Hawthorne and Melville. Martin emphasizes the mordant humor in Poe's fiction, and he analyzes the preoccupation of all three authors with revenge and its ramifications. Joan Dayan (pp. 93–104) charts Poe's racial attitudes, especially as they appear in "Murders," *Pym,* and "Hop-Frog." Her postulate that Poe's women characters may emerge from racial issues is intriguing. Dayan's unqualified acceptance of Poe's authorship of the much-disputed Paulding-Drayton review, which she terms his "most disturbing, because most authentic 'love poem,'" will not convince all readers and thus diminishes the general usefulness of her critique.

In *Abyss of Reason: Cultural Movements, Revelations, and Betrayals* (Oxford), Daniel Cottom's scattered, terse comments about Poe in a matrix of spiritualism-surrealism, particularly as he figures into the verse of Lizzie Doten, are interesting in themselves, although what they suggest might be pursued in a full-dress study of Poe among the spiritualists.

iii Poems

The image of Poe as displaced figure, especially in his role as spokesperson for his culture, occupies Joseph N. Riddell in "Thresholds of the Sign: Reflections on 'American' Poetics" (*Theorizing American Literature,* pp. 53–82). Poe "is disfigured by his own figurations," as are other American poets, particularly Hart Crane, who in *The Bridge* "gives himself up as modern poet/poem/word to the disfigurement and displacement of Poe ('The Tunnel') or the marginality [of others] in a capitalist culture." Interesting technical similarities—"the overinsistent reiteration of negatives [that] keep faith with the insistence of mourning in the face of the desire to escape"—in Bradstreet and Poe are pointed out by Mitchell Breitweiser in another essay in the same book ("Early American Antigone," pp. 125–61). In "Edgar Allan Poe's Control of Readers: Formal Pressures in Poe's Dream Poems" (*ELWIU* 18:68–75) James Postema puts together tight analyses of Poe's methods to force readers to suspend logic as they enter worlds of "Fairy-Land" and "Dream-Land." The second poem has less accessible structures of apparently endless journeying.

iv *Pym,* Sea Tales, *Eureka*

William E. Lenz's "Poe's *Arthur Gordon Pym* and the Narrative Techniques of Antarctic Gothic" (*CEA* 53, iii:30–38) ought to be required reading for anyone interested in Poe's book. Lenz convincingly demonstrates how Poe inverted many 19th-century notions of and expectations about the Antarctic; in so doing, he created an Antarctica that embodied the wellsprings of "symbol, supposition, and superstition," its primary force being the great white figure, representing "the unknown itself," who blocks Pym's way. Lenz is another who reminds us of Poe's sensitivity to and repeated uses of his age's literary conventions and cultural scene (features in his work which are often forgotten at present), as evinced notably in *Pym* and "MS. Found." These works anticipate others such as *The Sea Lions, Moby-Dick,* and *V.* To be read in tandem with Lenz is Huafu Paul Bao's "The Emancipation of the Ego: An Archetypal Reading of Two Sea Tales by Poe" (*POMPA,* pp. 12–17). Bao sees "MS. Found" and "A Descent" as emblematic of the ego's encounter with the Great Mother (the sea) and the consequent transformations of the hero (the narrator in each).

Kindred concerns are analyzed by Rosella Mamoli Zorzi, who in "The Text as City: The Representation of Venice in Two Tales by Irving and Poe and a Novel by Cooper" (*Rivista di Studi Anglo-Americani* 6 [1990]:285–300) links "The Assignation" (originally "The Visionary") to Irving's "The Adventure of the Mysterious Stranger" (from *Tales of a Traveller*) and Cooper's *The Bravo* as expressive of the city of Venice as intertext. Within recognized conventions of early 19th-century literature, this trio brought to the fore Venice as part of Gothic tradition, an imaginative rather than literally geographic creation. Shades of Mrs. Radcliffe, Heinrich Zschokke, William Dunlap, and M. G. Lewis loom in the background.

Like Lenz, Susan Welsh turns to Poe's contemporaneous horizons, in this case as he composed his last full-length book, in "The Value of Analogical Evidence: Poe's *Eureka* in the Context of a Scientific Debate" (*MLS* 21, iv:3–15). Her estimate is that two types of scientific writing underlie the book, "natural theology writing, and the more secular and largely synthetic surveys of scientific theory or information as it stood in the 1840s." Welsh's ideas on how a wide scientific context ties into Poe's theories of analogy and his satire on academic methods and rhetoric are arresting. The bibliography—objectively encompassing relevant materials from Poe's own day and from later analytic studies—attests Welsh's authority over her subject. Her article should be kept close to Lenz's on the "must-have" Poe shelf.

v Tales

a. Neglected Tales Katrina Bachinger interprets "Hop-Frog" as Menippean satire on "Napoleonic challenges to monarchic rule," in which Poe drew on Byron, Moore, Lamb, and Shelley to portray a coded figure of George IV. Bachinger's knowledgeable analysis of these writers—"Together (or Not Together) against Tyranny: Poe, Byron, and Napoleon Upside Down in 'Hop-Frog' " (*TSLL* 33:373–402)—loses force because of her attempt at very broad coverage within a fairly brief compass. Mary Lucas explains how Poe tellingly employs techniques commonly associated with plays in his fiction: "Poe's Theatre: 'King Pest' and 'Hop Frog' " (*JSSE* 14 [1990]:25–40). Detailing Poe's knowledge of the contemporary milieu of the drama and of more general dramatic traditions, Lucas indicates his subtle manipulations of dramatic form in the three-act structuring of "King Pest" and of masque, anti-masque, and revenge tragedy in "Hop-Frog." She also reminds us that Disraeli's popular novel, *Vivian Grey,* may have loomed in the backgrounds of both pieces. Thus, she supplements studies by Ruth Leigh Hudson, Alexander Hammond, Burton R. Pollin, and E. Kate Stewart, just as she makes us aware implicitly of the particular benefits to be derived from a solid study of Poe and Renaissance drama. With Poe's fictional techniques in mind, we might turn to Jerome D. Denuccio's "Fact, Fiction, Fatality: Poe's 'The Thousand-and-Second Tale of Scheherazade' " (*SSF* 27 [1990]:365–70). Often dismissed as frothy satire, this tale actually "represents Poe's investigation of both the nature of fiction and the relation between author and reader." Thus, Scheherazade's movement to closure obstructs the self-generation inherent in a fiction that ensures its survival. Denuccio's position challenges Evan Carton's in *The Rhetoric of the American Romance* (1985). Poe on the nature of creativity through language also informs Joseph A. Dupras's "Mystery and Meaning in Poe's 'X-ing a Paragrab'" (*SSF* 27 [1990]:489–94), which reveals how readers are generally baffled when language does not promptly supply a meaning.

b. "The Gold-Bug," Later Tales Consciously removing it from beneath the umbrella of "Poe's ratiocinative tales," James W. Mathews in "Legrand's Golden Vision: Meaning in 'The Gold Bug' [*sic*]" (*CEA* 53:23–29) alerts us to mythical, mystical texture in the tale, marshaling clues that Legrand's quest is like that of many another mythological protagonist and that he seeks and ultimately discovers the roots of "his ultimate imperishable self, his supreme imaginative powers, which have been buried. . . ." Mathews's evaluations of the relevant secondary bibliography, to which his study makes a good addition, are worth consulting. The self of Legrand (and, evolving from him, Sherlock Holmes) also occupies Alastair Fowler, who adopts a slightly different viewpoint in "Sherlock Holmes and the Adventure of the Dancing Men and Women" (*Addressing Frank Kermode: Essays in Criticism and Interpretation,* ed. Margaret Tudeau-Clayton and Martin Warner [Illinois], pp. 154–68). Here, Poe's tale is revealed as a subtext for Conan Doyle's; in both tales, the sleuth's reaction to the cipher is one of "mixing arrogance with patronising encouragement." For "Poe's landscape of horror [Doyle] substitutes the ordinary wasteland of Norfolk"—and does not mock his predecessor. Related ideas are articulated in Jeanne M. Malloy's "Apocalyptic Imagery and the Fragmentation of the Psyche: 'The Pit and the Pendulum'" (*NCF* 46:82–95). Human separation from the divine and the ensuing redemption through "suffering and [the acquirement of] self-knowledge" place this tale, for me, in the same emotional rank as "The Gold-Bug."

"The Cask of Amontillado" remains a perennial quarry among Poe's critics. In a thoughtfully considered, exciting study, Richard P. Benton, "Poe's 'The Cask' and the 'White Webwork Which Gleams'" (*SSF* 28:183–94), draws on his own professional scientific knowledge and on relevant literary criticism to buttress a convincing reading of text and intertext as they converge in implications of the word "nitre" and in the subtle wordplay. Benton also adds to our knowledge of implications in the Montresor motto, which has engaged so many other readers, and, drawing on Catholic and Masonic lore, to innuendo in the famous concluding line. Instead of being treated to yet another example of Poe's familiarity with the pseudosciences of his day, we are impressed with his awareness of the hard varieties.

Another tale that has attracted increasing attention provides the basis for Monika M. Elbert's " 'The Man of the Crowd' and the Man Outside the Crowd: Poe's Narrator and the Democratic Reader" (*MLS* 21, iv:16–30), an essay that makes good reading alongside Benton's. Diverging from earlier critics (e.g., Edmund Wilson), Elbert places Poe as indeed a political animal of his times, one who embraced both Whig and Democratic principles, and one who registered the uneasinesses that occurred because of such a transitional attitude. For Elbert, neither the narrator of "The Man of the Crowd," who seems to manifest happiness, nor Roderick Usher, the man outside the crowd, attains satisfaction with life. The former reveals that we may readily fall prey to the "crime" of losing our individuality; the latter reveals the disasters inherent in too assertive an individuality.

Thence we move naturally to Dana Brand's chapter on Poe in *The Spectator and the City* (pp. 79–105). Poe appears here in a framework of Americans who employed the flaneur character, i.e., a detached observer of the urban scene. Poe's nearest model was perhaps N. P. Willis, although Poe altered the original type (as found, say, in Dickens) into one who could read and interpret the spectacle and language of urban import. "The Man of the Crowd" prepares the way for the Dupin tales, in which the sleuth penetrates the essences of what to others are obscurities. His abilities make him "a panoramic interpreter of interpretations." Sound thinking about Poe's conscious conception of detective-story methodology as hoax deftly concludes this discussion.

c. Ratiocinative Tales Joel Black in *The Aesthetics of Murder* offers scattered remarks on this branch of Poe's accomplishments. Most significant among them was the shifting of the center of interest from the criminal hero found in antecedent crime fiction to the sleuth as "artist-hero," a characteristic maintained by subsequent writers in this mode. Countering one line of thought, Black argues for differences rather than similarities between the sleuth and his/her quarry, and he reminds us, following in the footsteps of Stefano Tani in *The Doomed Detective* (1984), that Poe's criminals, instead of being taken to jail, are depicted as "irrational agents who must be controlled" or "caged" like the ape in

"Murders." Broader claims mark Martin Priestman's *Detective Fiction and Literature,* which posits that in detective fiction popular and established literary art are so fully interrelated as to grow well-nigh indistinguishable. Poe is credited not only for modifying Gothic tradition into ratiocinative tale but for having "virtually invented the English short story itself" and providing significant models and theories for what bore fruit as early modernism. Poe's influence on the English short story in the 1890s—that era of ferment and change in so many cultural forces and, notably, one in which criminal and creative impulses were often held up as near relatives—is also given special notice. Priestman persuasively defines the expectations created by a growing magazine readership for ever more specialized literature and the links between those expectations and "sensationalism."

We are not far afield in turning to Erich H. Ritter's "Ratiocination about an Ape: A Poeto-Logical Investigation of a Murderer" (*OL* 46:65–86). Using Kierkegaardian theories, Ritter posits that Dupin is an aristocrat ruined by the French Revolution, one who is, moreover, an aesthete for whom the orangutan (a nonhuman) would be perfect perpetrator of atrocities, as a human being would not. Dupin represents, "in speculative terms, an idealistic possibility, an investigation in a typological character who contradicts essential Romantic characteristics (through rationality) as much as he emphasizes them (through imagination)." In this context "Usher" presents an opposition wherein Poe's subversion of Gothic horror "deals contemporary reading expectations" a "powerful yet covert blow" (see also Kopley, below).

vi Sources, Influences, Affinities

J. Lasley Dameron's "More Analogues and Resources for Poe's Fiction and Poems" (*UMSE* n.s. 9:154–66) offers much to stimulate follow-ups. Audrey Lavin's brief and sensible "A Birder's Rereading of Poe's 'Romance,'" in the same journal (pp. 199–204) brackets Poe's poem with Audubon's graphics on California condors and South Carolina paroquets. In "'The Sombre Madness of Sex': Byron's First and Last Gift to Poe" (*ByronJ* 19:128–40), Katrina Bachinger argues zealously that sources for "Oh Tempora! Oh, Mores!"—in which Poe satirizes his contemporary, King Pitts—lie in Byron's *The Age of Bronze* and *Waltz.* Bachinger also reads "Usher" as an exploration of sexuality, notably in what might have been thought to be perversions, as derivative from Byron. She seems, however, to overlook other assessments of Poe's knowledge of scientific lore by David E. E. Sloane, George R. Uba, and David W. Butler (see *ALS 1989,* p. 47). Overall, the factuality here is defused by attempts to include a Foucauldian analysis of Byron and a propensity to try to cover too much. Thus, rambling blunts the study's impact. We find, in the main, more reasonable cultural connections marshaled in Richard Kopley's *Edgar Allan Poe and "The Philadelphia Saturday News"* (Pratt, for the Poe Society). Kopley argues for the influence of the newspaper, which ran from July 1836 to early January 1839, on Poe's creative imagination, particularly as that imagination went to work on "The Murders in the Rue Morgue." Thus, Poe's death-dealing orangutan accrues an enlarged ancestry, one in which racial outlooks figure large. Germane contemporaneous notice of *Pym* is also considered. Some other parallels seem less likely; as regards "Ligeia," red wine flowed freely in the pages of countless literary works besides those printed in the *Saturday News,* and the connection with "Usher" might as feasibly work for "Cask." Nonetheless, we gain heightened senses of the mosaic work in "Murders."

Probably the most provocative study of Poe's influence appears in Bruce Michelson's *Wilbur's Poetry: Music in a Scattering Time* (Mass.), where Poe's known impact is seen in varied new lights. Correspondences between Poe's and Richard Wilbur's writings, whether in Wilbur's case they devolve from smooth or "quarrelsome" thoughts, as Michelson interprets them, are especially illuminating. "A Note on Willa Cather's Use of Edgar Allan Poe's 'The Pit and the Pendulum' in *The Professor's House*" (*MFS* 36 [1990]:57–60) presents Thomas Strychacz's thoughts on how Cather's novel envelops "her enduring fascination with this master of the Gothic tale." The fates of the protagonists in each work are vastly different. Another influence—which elicited comments in early issues of *Poe Studies* (1970, 1972) in regard to sources in "Cask"—comes to us from a different angle in Barbara Burch's "Nabokov and the Detective" (*Clues* 12:101–21). Nabokov's V., Humbert Humbert, and Charles Kinpote descend from Dupin and Sherlock Holmes. John T. Irwin also addresses the impact of Poe's ratiocinative fiction in "The Journey to the South: Poe, Borges, and Faulkner" (*VQR* 67:416–32). Borges in several works of fiction and a 1970 autobiographical essay probably identified with Poe as a southerner confronting the northern literary establishment and felt affinities with Poe's conceptions of doubling. Borges's fondness for Poe was also "probably mediated and reenforced by . . . William Faulkner . . . in terms of a dual military/literary tradition." Irwin again addresses affiliations between Poe and the Argentinean as writers of detective fiction in "A Clew to a Clue: Locked Rooms and Labyrinths in Poe and Borges" (*Raritan* 10, iv:40–57). No "mere" influence study, this one presents the interrelated sophistication of these writers' play with elements of detection inherent in language itself, specifically in thematics of clues and labyrinths. Irwin also notes Poe's comic propensities, notably those of ironic insinuation. This ingenious critique should not be overlooked. R. F. Fleissner calls our attention to continuances of the Poesque as he surveys possibilities for origins of the names of Sherlock Holmes and (what may have influenced Holmes's creator) that of C. Auguste Dupin: "Poe's C. Auguste Dupin and Sherlock Holmes's Initial Again" (*BSJ* 41:226–29).

Myles Raymond Hurd plausibly indicates how another renowned Poe tale contributes significantly to the plot element—Sherman McCoy's downfall—in a contemporary novel: " 'The Masque of the Red Death' in Wolfe's *The Bonfire of the Vanities*" (*NConL* 20.3 [1990]:4–5). Like Irwin, Hurd offers sensible comments regarding literary artistry. Tom Wolfe is not the only recent writer to draw on "Masque"; witness Edith Skom's detective novel, *The Mark Twain Murders* (1989), and Stephen King's horror novel, *The Shining* (1977).

The subject of Poe and madness rears its head time and again, generally as a part of some larger issue. One such study, which does not minimize Poe in pursuing its topic, is John Cleman's "Irresistible Impulses: Edgar Allan Poe and the Insanity Defense" (*AL* 63:623–40). Cleman demonstrates that in his crime tales, specifically "The Black Cat," "The Tell-Tale Heart," and "The Imp of the Perverse," Poe by no means avoids moral issues, as has been frequently charged. Instead, he draws on aspects of the insanity defense, which became an increasingly important feature of criminal trials of the early 1840s, to undergird psychological explorations in his fiction. Two studies of another Romantic writer might illuminate this subject. Carolyn Misenheimer's "Charles Lamb and Robert Southey: Longevity of Friendship and Its Disruption of Ideals" (*ChLB* 75:73–84) indicates that both men feared insanity and that these anxieties showed up in their writings under guises of dreams and fantasy. Poe might well have read and identified with such thoughts.

Equally valuable ideas are to be found in Uttara Natarajan's " 'A Soul Set Apart': Lamb and the Border-Land of Imaginative Experience" (*ChLB* 75:85–92), in which Lamb's ponderings of the workings of imagination and his delineations of feelings of emotional isolation might well be matched with Poe's. The notes in both essays invite further exploration.

University of Mississippi

4 Melville

John Wenke

i Editions

Hennig Cohen's facsimile of the second printing of *Israel Potter: His Fifty Years of Exile* (Fordham) appears with a critical essay and annotations. Identifying the novel as Melville's last "popular success," Cohen evaluates this "serious but unpretentious book, [as] at times funny and sad and sly." Cohen analyzes the table of contents as "a synopsis and a prefiguration" and then examines Melville's sources and multiple genres. In an impressive work of lucid scholarship Cohen's discursive annotations do not simply gloss specific items in *Israel Potter;* rather, he ranges through Melville's life and work. The "Jaffa" entry, for example, illuminates kindred materials from *Mardi,* Bayle's *Dictionary, Moby-Dick,* and the *Journals.* Of special interest are brilliant entries on Potter's "change of garments" and Benjamin Franklin's "hive of a head."

The definitive *Clarel: A Poem and a Pilgrimage in the Holy Land,* ed. Harrison Hayford, Alma A. MacDougall, Hershel Parker, and G. Thomas Tanselle, appears as volume 12 of the Northwestern-Newberry edition and makes readily available Melville's massive and mysterious poem. This edition presents a mildly emended version of the Putnam 1876 copy-text. The "principal sources for emendation were Melville's annotated copy and the editors' close reading of the text." The editors reprint Walter Bezanson's ground-breaking introduction to the 1960 Hendricks House *Clarel.* Bezanson makes good the following claim: "the poem is labyrinthine, but it is no morass. . . . a great chunk of [Melville's] life is better examined here than anywhere else." Besides discussing plot, structure, poetics, characters, recurrent images, representations of the self, and historical and literary contexts, Bezanson treats *Clarel* as a diffused, oblique autobiographical poem containing such authorial self-projections as Rolfe and Ungar. Hershel Parker's equally indispensable "Historical Supplement" follows and updates Bezanson. Unfortunately, the editors require the reader to flip back and forth between the two items, a nuisance that discourages narrative continuity and scatters information. The editorial apparatus includes "Discussions" and the "List of Emendations" and such related documents as "Melville's Annotated Copy of *Clarel*" and "Parallel Passages in *Clarel* and Melville's 1856–57 *Journal*." The year's foremost addition to Melville scholarship, *Clarel* is a model of precision and thoroughness.

ii Biographical Contexts

Designed to reach a popular audience, Hershel Parker's "Herman Melville" (*American History Illustrated* 26, iv:28–47) draws on recent discoveries and provides a lively, engaging, generously illustrated biographical essay. Parker's prodigious knowledge of Melville's life finds an outlet in this gracefully compressed biographical essay. Parker extends the province of documentary evidence into often prescient summations. As a boy, Melville emanated "a chronic restlessness that his mother and others often perceived as impatience and rudeness"; late in life, he "possessed a thronging, vast sense of world history in which his random and purposeful reading through the decades had become inextricably fused with his early personal experiences and his reflections upon those adventures." Parker publishes for the first time an arresting photograph (circa 1858) of Elizabeth Melville and daughters Bessie and Frances. Janet Galligani Casey in "New Letters of Gansevoort Melville: 1845–1846" (*SAR*, pp. 141–50) prints letters written to Henry Ellsworth, chargé d'affaires to Norway and Sweden, while Gansevoort was secretary of the legation in London. She contends that these letters will serve scholars interested in "Herman's prose style and diction." The letters illustrate Gansevoort's "political and social acumen."

In "The Judge Dragged to the Bar: Melville, Shaw, and the Webster Murder Trial" (*MSEx* 84:1–8) Tom Quirk illuminates the relationship between the notorious 1850 trial and Chief Justice Shaw and his family. Quirk summarizes events surrounding the case. Even Shaw's instructions to the jury sparked controversy, and he was pilloried with tabloidesque frenzy. While marshaling "no concrete evidence that Melville concerned himself much about the case," Quirk does cite related passages from *Moby-Dick*. Quirk's strongest contribution resides in his consideration of

Melville's abiding interest in "the sorts of difficult questions" raised by the case, especially how "malice" and "judgment" inform the content of Captain Vere's drumhead court speech. James C. Wilson's *The Hawthorne and Melville Friendship: An Annotated Bibliography, Biographical and Critical Essays, and Correspondence Between the Two* (McFarland) ably fulfills the multifarious mission announced in the title. Wilson summarizes the biographical and literary dimension of the relationship: "Hawthorne . . . found in Melville precisely what Melville found in him: an intellect capable of diving beneath the surface of contemporary American life." Wilson makes the often overlooked point that Hawthorne did not suddenly flee the Berkshires in distress over Melville's importunate attentions. If anything precipitated the departure, it was Hawthorne's dispute with his landlord over fruit trees. In "An Essay in Bibliography" Wilson cogently considers biography, mutual influences, literary expressions of the relationship, parallel figures, and generic and theoretical approaches. Basem Ra'ad in "D.D. Revealed?" (*MSEx* 86:10–11) speculates on the identity of "D.D.," a book specified in an undated letter by Melville to Evert Duyckinck. Ra'ad nominates Amelia Opie's *Detraction Displayed* (1828) and makes a solid case for dating the letter between 1849 and 1853.

iii General

Situating Melville within canon and history continues to excite disagreement. In "The Price of Diversity: An Ambivalent Minority Report on the American Literary Canon" (*CollL* 18, iii:15–29) Hershel Parker denounces the Heath *Anthology of American Literature* for attempting to package Melville according to the so-called politically correct standards of late-20th-century multiculturalism. Parker argues for retaining a communal core of American classics and decries the elevation of political ideology over literary valuation. Parker's critics, of course, would claim that any valuation is inherently ideological. *The Columbia History of the American Novel* shies away from placing Melville within canonical hierarchies. Instead, his works serve as exemplars within market, generic, and sociological contexts. In "The Book Marketplace I" (pp. 46–71) Michael T. Gilmore contends that Melville's work reflects a "distancing from the domestic zone" and considers Melville's tempestuous "quarrel with the marketplace." Terence Martin's "The Romance" (pp. 72–88) identifies Promethean Ahab as reflective of the Romance, a "fiction of intensity that feeds on caricature and seeks to confront the absolute." The "latitude of the romance" permits Melville to displace the quotidian in favor of Gothic revenge (in "Benito Cereno") and ideational fable (in *Billy Budd*). In "Fiction and the Science of Society" (pp. 189–215) Susan Mizruchi makes the dubious claim that *Billy Budd*'s "overriding concern . . . is social transformation." Once again, *Billy Budd* becomes a game preserve for tendentious hypotheticals: "Had Billy not killed Claggart, Captain Vere would have had to find some other reason for his demise."

Christopher Sten's generously illustrated *Savage Eye: Melville and the Visual Arts* collects 14 original essays that consider Melville's knowledge of painting, graphics, sculpture, and architecture as it impinges on his work. The appendixes list pertinent books owned or borrowed and a checklist of criticism. In his judicious "Melville and the Visual Arts: An Overview" (pp. 1–39) Sten offers a chronological survey, a critical assay, and a prolegomenon to the succeeding pieces: "Melville approached the subject of art as an American *naif* or 'savage,' with no formal training and few preconceptions, but a powerful imagination and an easy self-assurance." Sten elaborates on Melville's "strong visual sensibility . . . and powerful visual memory." Of special note is Sten's discussion of how Melville saw art as evoking mystery, a tendency that informs his aesthetic and philosophical concerns.

As a whole and in most of its parts, *Savage Eye* makes a major contribution to Melville studies. With customary prescience, Sanford E. Marovitz in "Melville's Temples" (pp. 77–103) illustrates how Melville's fascination with temples appears not only in "The Two Temples" but centers much of his work from *Moby-Dick* on. Melville uses these structures—and attending associations with "height, depth, and penetration imagery with variations in light and architectural reference"—to explore the presence and absence of spirituality. Frequently, temples are associated with staging, with theatrics-in-life. Marovitz's illuminating study of *Clarel* culminates with Mar Saba as Melville's "vastest, grandest stage." Bryan C. Short's excellent " 'Like bed of asparagus': Melville and Architecture" (pp. 104–16) complements and extends Marovitz's concerns. According to Short, "Melville's responses to architecture reveal an imagination at war with itself, a visionary sensibility in conflict with the evidence of vision." Melville develops an "anti-architecture" theory of writing as the "dumb stones"—architectural product—give way to endless revision—art as incomplete process.

In "Toning Down the Green: Melville's Picturesque" (pp. 145–61) John Bryant finds that the picturesque provides "a critical vocabulary of being and creation . . . a dynamic chiaroscuro that empowered him to 'fuse' both bright and dark sides of his vision into what Hawthorne . . . had called 'the moral picturesque.'" Bryant convincingly links "Melville's moral chiaroscuro" to principles of "fusion and repose." What Bryant calls an "aesthetics of repose 'softens' the sublime; it places limits on chaos, confines self-indulgence, and restrains dark groping speculation." Basem L. Ra'ad in "Melville's Art: Overtures from the Journal of 1856–57" (pp. 200–217) claims that this journal "constitutes in its totality . . . a treatise of substantial proportions" on a "range of natural and man-made structures." Ra'ad locates Melville as a "conscious aesthetician . . . a theorist of structure, and a post-Romantic precursor of the iconography of the modern wasteland." Ra'ad justifiably attempts to rehabilitate the image of Melville as a depressed and morbid traveler, but with his strong-armed imposition of collateral citations and theories he schematizes Melville's often inchoate impressions out of proportion. For example, Melville's terse commentary on his 1856 beach walk with Hawthorne is deemed "revolutionary in the sense that it subsumes wildness and desolation." The words "Sands & grass" do not describe the dreary locale; rather, they stand "as coexistent symbols of mind and civilization."

Two important works respectively chart Melville's epistemology and his vexed relation to his audience. Ronald E. Martin in *American Literature and the Destruction of Knowledge,* pp. 31–50, finds that Melville (and Dickinson) replaced conventional formulations with "an individual self-biased metaphor system" that provided the only resource for epistemological activity and psychological therapy. Martin convincingly argues that Melville respected factual knowledge and had a "complex fascination-distrust" for his culture's explorations of moral, theological, and philosophical issues. Martin brilliantly considers Melville's engagement with the problematics of knowing, especially the degree to which direct experience reveals both the fallibility of preconception and the difficulty (or impossibility) of forging solutions that adequately contend with infinitude. In *Moby-Dick, Pierre,* and *The Confidence-Man,* Melville attacks "the linguistic order of the world and the possibility of higher truth." Stephen Railton in " 'You Must Have Plenty of Sea-Room to Tell the Truth In': Melville's *Moby-Dick*" (*Authorship and Audience,* pp. 152–89) offers a fresh, penetrating approach to Melville's troubled attempts to forge a relationship with his reader. Ishmael's predicament is symptomatic; his direct addresses to the reader counterpoint the implications of his name: "It shows Melville's desire to enter into a personal relationship with his audience while reserving the right to his own estranged identity." After discussing Tommo's narrative stance in *Typee* as oscillating between "deference to and disdain for the reader's position," Railton tracks Melville's divided feeling for his audience in *Mardi* and *Pierre.* With his "divisive uncertainty about the response he wanted" and its sources in "his own conflicted narcissism," Melville blamed his readers for not loving him on his own terms.

If Martin and Railton successfully illuminate Melville's work through its burden of psychological agitation, Zan Dale Robinson in *A Semiotic and Psychological Interpretation of Herman Melville's Fiction* (Mellen) takes egregious liberties in purporting to read Melville's life and work through a hodgepodge psychosemiotic gestalt. Robinson announces, "I found that Melville obviously chose his subjects and objects consciously, but that his unconscious striving determined the direction his expressions followed." Having dispensed with surface and intentionality, Robinson thus licenses his claim that "all of Melville's fictional writings were expressions of his deep-rooted cannibalistic and incestuous desires." In Robinson's scheme, the "pattern of wood and stone was a semiotic sign, or literary signature, of Melville's unconscious self." Frequently, a dubious summation—"I found that fantasies of cannibalism, incestuous desires, guilt, and castration anxieties are common to all men"—provides his a priori premise: "In essence, Melville's penning of *Typee* was a form of displacement for his desire to mate with the mother and to replace the father." Metonomy becomes another self-licensing device for constructing cartoon cuts of Melville's unconscious. Are Tommo and Toby running out of food and trying to stretch their fare? Certainly not: "The separation of the bread was a totemic device that symbolically permitted Melville to ingest the father, and simultaneously and psychologically, to scatter and displace him. That was the manner in which Melville structured his text and characters." This argument often reads like a jargon-ridden parody. The intrepid reader will confront turgid prose, elliptical organization, and preposterous allegations.

Melville's medical condition is much better served by Richard Dean Smith's *Melville's Complaint: Doctors and Medicine in the Art of Herman Melville* (Garland). Himself a physician, Smith delivers a topical analysis of medical matters. The book is packed with odd, arresting observations:

what works in fiction would not find its way into a pathology report. Bartleby could not have walked to the last wall and died of starvation without first having spent days in a coma. Billy Budd's "blow to Claggart's forehead may have caused unconsciousness and serious brain injury, but not instantaneous death." On occasion, Smith conflates Melville and his narrators—plausible in *Omoo,* not so in *Mardi.* Kevin J. Hayes and Hershel Parker, eds., in *Checklist of Melville Reviews* (Northwestern) revise the 1975 Steven Mailloux and Hershel Parker *Checklist.* The new volume "incorporates the discoveries of the last decade and a half." With bibliographies and index, Hayes-Parker will aid the important work of understanding Melville's various audiences.

iv Source, Influence, Affinity

Savage Eye contains a number of valuable source and influence studies. In "Melville's Reading in the Visual Arts" (pp. 40–54) Douglas Robillard reports that the range of Melville's "concerns went beyond painting and sculpture to such peripheral areas as the craft of engraving, book illustrations, flower arrangements, pottery and ceramics, and gems." Robillard greatly advances our understanding of Melville's relation to Madame de Staël, Edmund Burke, Sir Joshua Reynolds, John Ruskin, and James Jackson Jarves. Robillard evidences a particularly deft touch in specifying Melville's debt to literary pictorialism. Robert K. Wallace's "Bulkington, J. M. W. Turner, and 'The Lee Shore' " (pp. 55–76) discounts Harrison Hayford's theory that Bulkington is a vestigial figure from an earlier stage of composition and asserts "that Melville added [Bulkington] as a deliberate augmentation of the mature story. . . . Bulkington is one of the many tributes in *Moby-Dick,* none of them explicit, to the life and the art of the painter J. M. W. Turner." In making a genetic argument, Wallace imagines a skein of "probable" and "likely" contingencies: "Had [Melville] been able to accept a December invitation to spend Christmas at the home of C. R. Leslie, this might have happened." If Melville made so many allusions to Turner, why did he not mention the painter by name? Melville figured that "any reader familiar" with Turner would recognize "the Turneresque essence of Bulkington." John M. J. Gretchko's "The White Mountain, Thomas Cole, and 'Tartarus': The Sublime, the Subliminal, and the Sublimated" (pp. 127–44) is an informative, closely argued (and sometimes gnarled) piece of literary and topographical sleuthing. Gretchko contends plausibly that Cole's painting "The Notch of the White Mountains" directly influenced Melville's "serious burlesque of the sublime" in "The Tartarus of Maids." In "Melville and Dutch Genre Painting" (pp. 218–45) Dennis Berthold argues for the centrality of this 17th-century school not only in "Daniel Orme" but in many other works. With its treatment of ordinary life, especially domesticity and geniality, Dutch genre painting counterpoints and qualifies Melville's engagement with more ponderous philosophical concerns: "This tendency is not just aesthetic: it is moral, political, and eventually deeply personal." According to Berthold, the realistic nature of Dutch art was suited for an American democratic audience. In a beautifully written essay that deftly integrates biographical, literary, and pictorial resources, Berthold makes his case by citing allusions in *Typee, Mardi,* and *White-Jacket* and examining scenes and themes in *Redburn, Pierre,* "The Fiddler," and "The Piazza."

John B. Williams in *White Fire: The Influence of Emerson on Melville* (CSU, Long Beach) seeks to demonstrate that Emerson provided Melville's central influence. Drawing on contemporary periodicals, unpublished lectures, and published essays, he asserts that Melville was deeply interested in Emerson even before he heard Emerson speak in 1849. Emerson's influence takes the form of "patterned responses" to materials in the 1849 lecture, especially references to "cracked human nature, life as an angle of vision, identity of the self and nature, and the shipwreck of the soul." Even though all of these complexes appear in Melville's work before the Emerson lecture, Williams insists on reading Melville's works as constituting continuing responses to Emersonian tropes. His argument for Emerson's indirect influence on *Mardi* is a particularly untenable New Historicist patchwork. *White Fire* is overly determined and reductive, especially in the distorting priority that Williams gives to "transactual relationships" or the "creative community" among living writers. Everything is seen through the Emersonian lens; thus, even when Melville knew little of Emerson, he "had certain natural affinities for Emersonian ideas."

Alan Golding in "Pursuing Olson Pursuing Melville: The Beginnings of *Call Me Ishmael*" (*MSEx* 86:1–6) insightfully considers the creative foreground and genesis of Charles Olson's quirky, declamatory, classic study of Melville. In "Harris's Cross-Cultural Dialogue with Melville" (*Wilson Harris: The Uncompromising Imagination,* ed. Hena Maes-Jelinek [Dangaroo], pp. 83–91), Joyce Sparer Adler examines the provocative ways in which the Caribbean novelist reads and reinvents Melville's works. In Harris's *Carnival,* Bartleby undergoes an amusing transsexual redaction as Alice Bartleby. Adler also discusses Harris's responses to *Moby-Dick,* "Benito Cereno," *The Confidence-Man,* and *Billy Budd.* In "Sendak on Melville: An Interview" (*MSEx* 87:1–6), Richard Kopley has a highly interesting conversation with the great author and illustrator of children's books. Kopley draws Sendak out on how Melville "crowds my life in extraordinary ways." In *Enter Isabel: The Herman Melville Correspondence of Clare Spark and Paul Metcalf,* ed. Paul Metcalf (New Mexico), one will find little that is new. The volume is mostly tiresome, especially Spark's self-advertisement and surly putdowns of "Melville Society types," her only prospective audience. Metcalf, Melville's great grandson, reveals himself as a patient, generous correspondent; he offers illuminating insights into Eleanor Melville Metcalf, Charles Olson, and Henry A. Murry.

v Early Works

John Bryant in "Melville's *Typee* Manuscript and the Limits of Historicism" (*MLS* 21, ii:3–10) considers "how manuscript study, a largely textual matter, can illuminate the potentials and problems of historicism, a decidedly contextual approach." Bryant disputes the New Historicist contention that social forces are primary agents in literary acts; he proposes, as a first principle, that writers are "prime movers" of the text. While "imaginative texts are the product of a discourse between a writer and history," it makes sense, Bryant argues by way of the *Typee* manuscript fragment, to "learn how writers forge ideologies out of the contingencies of their lives and creativity itself." Melville's deletion of a conventional Sunday school image shows him to have been a discriminating rewriter. To have retained the "Little Henry" allusion would have undermined his antimissionary stance. In consciously rejecting a cultural shibboleth, Melville advanced a subversive agenda. Keyed to the Northwestern-Newberry volume, Larry Edward Wegener's *A Concordance of Herman Melville's Mardi; and a Voyage Thither* (Garland) offers a two-volume contextual concordance and five appendixes. Included is an illustrated map of the Mardi archipelago and a rhapsodic manifesto in the form of a critical introduction: "each island nation cuts itself off from one or more of the time markers for past, present, and future." Wegener also discusses as self-evident constructs what he calls "the three angels of *Mardi* in relation to this unity of time."

Jonathan L. Hall in " 'Every Man of Them Almost Was a Volume of Voyages': Writing the Self in Melville's *Redburn*" (*ATQ* n.s. 5:259–71) insightfully considers Melville's fictions of identity, arguing that the critical concern over the formal discontinuity between the young Redburn (the actor) and the older Redburn (the narrator) has been a way of worrying "about something more substantial: Melville's unorthodox conception of the self." The narrator's failure to impose "continuity" derives from his decentered being: "the narrator constantly shrinks from examining what is unresolved and unresolvable in the text of his past experience and his ongoing conception of himself." Not everyone will agree that this narrator is "stuck in an extended adolescence." Ernest S. Bernard's "Spontaneous Combustion in *Redburn:* Redburn's Ultimate Guidebook?" (*SNNTS* 23:348–56) explores the pertinence of a sailor's "apparent spontaneous combustion." In rejecting the notion that Melville would use "gratuitous" violence "as a means to sell books," Bernard views the incident as a means of saving "the faith of his protagonist." In "*White-Jacket*'s Classical Oration" (*SNNTS* 23:237–44) Kathleen E. Kier plausibly argues that Melville modeled some of his chapter-clusters on the seven-part classical oration, primarily the Ciceronian form. Melville uses such an "outmoded . . . restrictive formula" to advance (and make acceptable) subversive polemical purposes.

vi Moby-Dick

Ahab attracted considerable attention. Joel Porte in "Melville: Romantic Cock-and-Bull; or, The Great Art of Telling the Truth" (*In Respect to Egotism*, pp. 189–212) finds that "Cock-A-Doodle-Doo!" bears structural and thematic resemblances to *Moby-Dick.* In a valuable discussion that touches on *Mardi* and *The Confidence-Man,* Porte explores Melville's critique of self-promoting inflations of manhood. Porte makes a strong case for seeing Ahab's soliloquies as rhetorical bombast. Ahab becomes a noisy braggart, whose rage distracts him from the nothingness lurking behind the "pasteboard masks." Among this year's most interesting essays is John W. Rathbun's brief "*Moby-Dick:* Ishmael's Fiction of Ahab's Romantic Insurgency" (*MLS* 21, iii:3–9). According to Rathbun, Melville's first five books depict narrative conflicts between chronicle and "imaginative" invention. In *Moby-Dick,* Melville "carries this strategy about as far as it can go when he develops two separate kinds of fictions, one embedded in the other." Ishmael's "chronicle of the whaling voyage" contains his "deliberate authorial intrusion . . . [into a] wholly imagined, self-contained 'story.'" Rathbun argues that Father Mapple's reference to "Jonah's slouched hat and the self-correcting cabin lamp" delineate the "limits within which Ahab is made to act." Ishmael rejects Ahab's romantic, self-dramatizing insurgency in favor of "philosophical uncertainties." Wai-chee Dimock in "Ahab's Manifest Destiny" (*Macropolitics of Nineteenth-Century Literature*, pp. 184–212) offers a slippery (occasionally cryptic) meditation on the multiforms of freedom as they apply to Melville as "imperial" author, the White Whale as transcendent self-referent and dominating, destructive agent, and Ahab as embodying Melville's allegorical "battle for sovereignty" and "revenge on the reader." Dimock concentrates on Ahab's individualism, his freedom as paradoxically expressed within his "doomed" linearity of purpose. Ahab's allegorical relation to Native Americans evokes a host of political repressions in the antebellum United States. In *Ahab* (Chelsea) Harold Bloom reprints numerous critical extracts and 10 critical essays that engage the nature of Ahab's character. Bloom's pithy and incisive introduction "centers upon Ahab as a Gnostic quester." In "Following Ahab to Doom or 'Goberning de Shark': *Moby-Dick* as Democratic Reflection" (*CMC* 40:256–64) Nancy Klenk Hill converts the novel into a bland, distressed sermonette reflecting our contemporary democratic crisis: "we, the people as crew, watch passively and lament our 'fate' as our ship careens on a Nantucket sleigh-ride toward disaster."

John F. Birk in "Unsealing the Sphinx: The *Pequod*'s Egyptian Pantheon" (*ATQ* n.s. 5:283–99) makes a well-researched and surprisingly plausible case for Melville's conscious adaptation of ancient Egyptian deities to *Moby-Dick:* "the cruise of the *Pequod* . . . is nothing less than a modern-day analogue of the journey of the Egyptian god-peopled 'cosmic ship.'" In "The Divided Body: Topographical Dualism in *Moby-Dick*" (*ATQ* n.s. 5:31–40) Clark Davis reads Rabelais's influence on *Moby-Dick* by means of Bakhtin's analysis of Rabelais, a piece that focuses on the division between "upward" and "downward" as reflecting heaven and earth. Once the paradigm is asserted, Rabelais stands in tangential, if not gratuitous, relation to the discussion. Davis offers more a cogent exegesis of a key image-complex than a case for influence. Peter Quigley's "Rethinking Resistance: Nature Opposed to Power in Emerson and Melville" (*WVUPP* 37:39–51) positions Ishmael and Ahab in relation to a poststructuralist pastiche of theoretical observations. Quigley's intention is to use Emerson and Melville to expose "the intellectual and political heritage of today's environmental movement." His environmental focus seems slighted in favor of scattershot speculations amid a profusion of quotations. In "Melville: *Moby-Dick*" (*The American Scene,* pp. 57–72), Stuart Hutchinson discusses self and New World themes.

David Sprague Herreshoff's "The Floating Factory Sinks" (*Labor into Art,* pp. 28–68) elaborates on the workaday intensities of the *Pequod*'s crew and their search for whales as opposed to Ahab's "single combat" approach to slaying Moby Dick. Herreshoff gives special attention to the ship's racial-political-power configuration, especially Ishmael's "transcendence of racism." Herreshoff does not attempt to situate his argument in relation to other scholarship. Also working in a self-imposed critical vacuum is Robert Martin in "Sleeping with a Savage: Deculturation in *Moby-Dick*" (*ATQ* n.s. 5:195–203). Except for propping up Leslie Fiedler as a straw man, Martin cites three of his own pieces and no work by any other Melville scholar. Martin sees *Moby-Dick* as a fictive world riddled with sexual signs and signification, but with grim conviction he consistently overworks his case. Far more provocative is Camille Paglia's location of Melville among the American Decadents in her megahit, *Sexual Personae: Art and Decadence from Nefertiti to Emily Dickinson* (1990; rpt. Vintage, pp. 584–95). Paglia views *Moby-Dick* in terms of a projected dramatization of sexual mythologies: "The novel subtly hermaphroditizes the great whale without genuinely diluting his masculinity." It is curiously appropriate that Melville is indexed between Medusa and menstruation: Paglia sees Melville's "archetypal vision of the great squid. . . . [as] the snaky Medusa-head of nature, swampy and inert. . . . The squid is faceless, but is it sexless? We will see this 'pulpy mass' again in Melville's story *The Paradise of Bachelors and the Tartarus of Maids,* where it represents woman's nonstop fertility." Paglia's contribution is vital and incandescent.

Two critics identify *Moby-Dick*'s influence on specific contemporary artistic contexts. Robert K. Wallace in "Sightings of the White Whale" (*Contemporanea* 24:60–67) deftly explores how Frank Stella's "metallic creations" as well as his silk screens from *The Waves* recast Melvillean motifs. Wallace links Melville and Stella through their social and ecological preoccupations and in their depictions of Ahab's "bandaged soul." In "Modern Theatre and Melville's *Moby-Dick:* Writing and Sounding the Whale" (*MD* 34:107–17) Anthony Kubiak is more interesting than convincing. He sees *Moby-Dick* as expressing " 'avante-garde' impulses" that reveal a "profound sensitivity to the problematic phenomenology of the stage." He makes the odd generic contention that the novel is emblematic of an " 'alternative' theoretical and experimental tradition in American theatre."

vii *Pierre* to *The Confidence-Man*

Nancy Fredericks in "Melville and the Woman's Story" (*SAF* 19:41–54) incisively explores "the increasing involvement of women in reading, writing, and publishing" as reflected in Melville's fiction from 1852 to 1856. After *Moby-Dick,* Fredericks argues, Melville moved away from "a bastion of masculinist aesthetics" toward confronting "the challenge that the female community presented to male writers." Fredericks demonstrates how Melville's gender-specific sense of audience finds issue in a proliferation of female artist-figures. She makes her case for Melville's "feminism" by associating his works with "the darker side of women's political powerlessness." In " 'Nature, and but nature': Skeletons in Melville's Bowers" (*ATQ* n.s. 5:273–81) Judith R. Hiltner considers the implications attending Melville's "recurring images of fertile greenery blanketing the petrified remains of human endeavor." During the 1853–56 period such images, Hiltner contends, "rarely function to reinforce a sense of regeneration." Rather, "Melville's skeptical qualifications . . . undermine any sense of harmony between the natural and the human." In Hiltner's finely realized piece, the effusions of nature mask the ineluctable decay that awaits all human beings and their endeavors.

Gillian Brown's *Domestic Individualism* devotes "Part Three: Melville's Misanthropy" to two essays. "Anti-sentimentalism and Authorship in *Pierre*" (pp. 135–69) charges the novel with containing "perhaps the nineteenth century's most negative portrayal of domestic values." Pierre's individualism develops through his assault on the domestic sphere and its sentimental depiction in the literary marketplace. Brown is less persuasive in the strange account of how genius becomes validated as the readers cannibalize—that is, consume—a text: "Melville's exemplary moment in literary relations retains the ambitions of the writer, in a culture of consumption, to be consumed." In "The Empire of Agoraphobia" (pp. 170–95) Brown views "Bartleby" as "a tale of the marketplace," reflecting "the American iconography of stillness featuring invalidism, woman, and home . . . as predominant figures of restfulness." At times, Brown descends into cloying deconstructive play on mobility as stasis—for instance, "how walls move" and "the circularity of the stationary."

One wonders how asocial, nonhistorical, cadaverous Bartleby could represent the hysterical woman: "women signified the stability of the private sphere which Bartleby's wall-like stance exhibits, the standard of self-containment which the hysteric melodramatized." Brown then links Gilman's "The Yellow Wall-paper" and "Bartleby" as "key moments in and representations of the mobilization of immobility."

Basem Ra'ad in " 'The Encantadas' and 'The Isle of the Cross': Melvillean Dubieties, 1853–54" (*AL* 63:316–23) takes issue with Hershel Parker's argument that *The Isle of the Cross* was a book-length treatment of the "Agatha" materials, which Melville completed but was "prevented from publishing" (see *ALS 1990*, p. 67). Ra'ad asserts that *Isle* was not a book at all but Sketch Eighth of "The Encantadas." Although Ra'ad does not refute Parker's well-founded chronology and conjecture, he does reveal that Melville made collateral use of the "Agatha" story. Wyn Kelley's "Melville and John Vanderlyn: Ruin and Historical Fate from 'Bartleby' to *Israel Potter*" (*Savage Eye*, pp. 117–26) connects John Vanderlyn and his painting "Caius Marius Amidst the Ruins of Carthage" with the themes of "ruin and historical fate" in the short fiction and *Israel Potter*. Kelley makes a plausible case for linking Vanderlyn to Melville's "conception of the failed hero." Her life-parallels between Vanderlyn and Melville seem less convincing. Among the year's more discerning (and enjoyable) essays is Philip Young's "The Machine in Tartarus: Melville's Inferno" (*AL* 63:208–24). After dismissing "The Paradise of Bachelors" as a diminutive exercise, Young praises "The Tartarus of Maids" as an "extraordinary, underrated performance," especially as it reflects "scarcely explored levels of classical myth and Christian allegory." The story is "proto-modernist" Melville: the "wintry landscape . . . hints of the reckless inner landscape" of the narrator, a "voyeur in the mill" of virginity, alienated from the forces of gestation. Young derides what he takes to be nonsense—the sociological reading of the oppressed female worker—in favor of viewing the tale as a mythic excursion into a Dantesque underworld, the "frozen circle" of the *Inferno*. The maids are Dante's nonverbal "shades." The story "is an unapologetic testament of fruitless anger at the 'metallic necessity' that governs the reproduction of the species." The readings of Young and Paglia (*Sexual Personae*, pp. 590–92; see above) are complementary. With its "genital topography," her "Tartarus" depicts "a descent into a sexual underworld, both inferno and Venusberg."

In " 'Why Talk of Jaffa?': Melville's *Israel Potter*, Baron Gros, Zummo, and the Plague" (*Savage Eye,* pp. 162–78), Hennig Cohen discusses the biblical Jonah as resource for *Israel Potter* and considers Melville's response to Gros's painting *Napoleon Visiting the Plague Hospital at Jaffa.* Cohen explores Melville's interest in the plague motif. Perhaps responding to G. G. Zummo's realistic wax sculptures, Melville was drawn to, and produced, exemplifications of human dissolution. Jan Bakker in *The Role of the Mythic West,* pp. 65–86, reads *Israel Potter* as Melville's most "Western" and political novel. Clark Davis in "The Body Deferred: *Israel Potter* and the Search for the Hearth" (*SAF* 19:175–87) associates *Israel Potter* with the "muted echo" of the "Ishmaelean strain in Melville's fiction, a commitment to physical comfort and metaphysical acceptance, to play and the restless search for genial warmth." In tracking Potter's abiding search for home and hearth Davis illuminates the implications of Potter's physicality, especially as manifesting his interrupted "search for fullness."

Gloria Horsley-Meacham's "Bull of the Nile: Symbol, History, and Racial Myth in 'Benito Cereno'" (*NEQ* 64:225–42) argues that the narrative is ostensibly racist. Horsley-Meacham looks "for any signs of hidden dissent" from invidious stereotyping and finds Melville interpolating "symbols of African grandeur, like the 'bull of the Nile.'" Such evocations constitute thematic counterpoints to Captain Delano's blind, beneficent self-justifications: "the Nilotic motif exemplifies the finest in Melville's truth-telling, for it signals not only what is clearly egalitarian and humane in an otherwise equivocal tale but also what is patiently subversive." She carefully considers Melville's curious transformations of Delano's *Narrative.* Horsley-Meacham, however, offers as narrator a monistic "Melville" and thus might have cast her fine argument in relation to the subtleties of the problematical narrative voice in "Benito Cereno." To expose "Melville's clever subterfuge" at the level of image does not resolve how "Melville" orchestrates his competing points of view. Darryl Hattenhauer in "'Follow Your Leader': Knowing One's Place in *Benito Cereno*" (*RMR* 45:7–17) applies (without explaining the pertinence of) Yi-Fu Tuan's method of spatial analysis to "Benito Cereno." The paradigm seems tangential if not irrelevant to an argument which primarily reveals how Melville's narrator blurs distinctions among apparent polarities. In "Daumier's Robert Macaire and Melville's Confidence Man" (*Savage Eye,* pp. 179–99) Helen P. Trimpi makes a plausible and informative case for believing Melville's confidence man was influenced by Daumier's series of lithographs of Robert Macaire, a fictive trickster, the creation of French actor Frédérick Lemaître. Between the 1830s and 1860, the Macaire figure was a popular presence on the French, English, and American stage. Trimpi explores "two versions of a fictional character-type who engages in constant role-playing and deceit as a means of getting ahead in society."

viii Late Works

George Monteiro in "Melville and the Question of Camões" (*UMSE* n.s. 8 [1990]:1–21) reviews the scholarship on Camões's influence on Melville. In a series of finely argued explications Monteiro takes up the question of how the Portuguese epic poet not only "served Herman Melville the poet," but also "became increasingly emblematic" of Melville's own life in his last decades. In "The Old Sailor's Lament: Recontextualizing Melville's Reflections on the Sinking of 'The Stone Fleet' " (*NEQ* 64:633–42) Mary Malloy discusses "The Stone Fleet" as Melville's most "poignant and personalized" poem in *Battle Pieces.* Malloy examines the poem's relation to the December 1861 *New York Times* nostalgia piece on the Union navy's sinking of 16 stone-filled whaleships to blockade the Charleston harbor. Dennis Loyd in " 'All is Hushed at Shiloh': A Reminiscence" (*Border States* 8:7–14) places Melville's "Shiloh" poem in relation to the great battle itself and other aesthetic reenactments.

James Duban's illuminating "From Bethlehem to Tahiti: Transcultural 'Hope' in *Clarel*" (*PQ* 70:475–83) links the upbeat strains of the "Epilogue" to *Clarel* to a "Hawaiian expression for hope—'manaolana,' " a word that translates as "swimming thought." Melville's evocation of "a swimmer rising from the deep" conflates a quester's difficult passage with the embrace of faith and hope. Furthermore, Duban argues that "manaolana" situates Polynesian elements of the poem within a "governing context of recollection that unites Melville's romantic and primitivistic thinking." Douglas Robillard in "Wrestling with the Angel: Melville's Use of the Visual Arts in *Timoleon*" (*Savage Eye,* pp. 246–56) examines Melville's "literary pictorialism." Robillard usefully applies Marianna Torgovnick's schemata for the deployment of the visual arts in literary works, elaborating on "the decorative, the biographical, the ideological, and the interpretive" modes.

Two important essays engage the relation of *Billy Budd* to ancient resources. In "Classical Iconography in the Aesthetics of *Billy Budd, Sailor*" (*Savage Eye,* pp. 257–76) Gail Coffler deftly argues that "the

Apollo and the *Antinous*" are "key icons" in *Billy Budd* and reflect "the Greek idea of perfect male beauty." Coffler discusses the conflict between Greek and Roman iconography: "Rome and Greece express a political and aesthetic dichotomy. [Melville] admires . . . the idealism associated with Greece—the independent, humanistic spirit of her democracy" and he associates the Classicist values of "structure, order, and tradition" with Rome. Gloria Horsley-Meacham in "The First Budd: Melville and Mythic Origin" (*ESQ* 37:57–70) argues that the black handsome sailor in *Billy Budd* reveals Melville's preoccupation with "myth and human origin." In distinction to Billy, who is associated with Hellenic gods, the "black Pagod" is related to "the dark idols of 'Old Orienda,'" especially Buddha. Horsley-Meacham explores 18th- and 19th-century works on ancient mythology to consider how Melville applied the concept of "Black Buddha as mythic progenitor." Finally, John M. Budd in "Law and Morality in *Billy Budd* and *The Ox-Bow Incident*" (*CLAJ* 35:185–97) offers a comparison/contrast exercise on Melville's and Clark's treatments of justice and morality with the purpose of presenting "alternative insights into human nature." Budd on *Budd* produces a disappointing rehearsal of old problems.

Salisbury State University

5 Whitman and Dickinson

Gary Lee Stonum

Those who read both halves of this chapter may notice several broad similarities in the work on Whitman and Dickinson. Both bodies of scholarship share a strong interest in gender and sexuality, especially same-sex relations and desires. The interest can be seen even in some of the textual and bibliographic work, and it is certainly visible in other forms of historical research. The main complement to gender studies as a motivating force would seem to be the various forms of rhetorical criticism, that is, questions about how style, genre, and other formal matters intersect with the actual disposition that readers and writers bear toward one another.

On the other hand, the Whitman and the Dickinson portrayed by this similarly motivated scholarship have about as much in common with one another as Pythagoras and Confucius, another pair of contemporaries who plied the same trade. Rather than revealing links between the poets, these works testify to a widely shared intellectual climate. Little in the shared concerns even particularly singles out Whitman scholars and Dickinson scholars, two groups that may now have less overlap in membership than ever before. The representative Dickinson critic, for example, more than likely looks first to other women writers for points of comparison, whereas not so long ago such a scholar might have looked to Whitman, to Emerson as Whitman and Dickinson's common ancestor, and to similar concerns of the Old Criticism and History.

i Walt Whitman

a. Bibliography, Editing In "Whitman: A Current Bibliography" (*WWR* 9:45–53, 111–14) Ed Folsom continues to produce one of the best

My thanks to Sarah Turner for help in the research toward this essay.

continuing bibliographies in the profession: complete, up-to-date, and usefully annotated. Two other well-documented pieces by Folsom add to our understanding of how Whitman's writings were actually circulated during his lifetime. In " 'Affording the Rising Generation an Adequate Notion': Whitman in 19th-century Textbooks, Handbooks, and Anthologies" (*SAR*:345–75) he contests a lingering belief that Whitman was unpopular with the literary establishment of his time. In addition, he challenges the more recent view, identified with Nina Baym, that postbellum cultural arbiters established a narrowly New England- and Puritan-centered version of American literary culture, thereby Whiggishly vaunting their own genteel literature as the culmination of America's one valid tradition. Folsom argues that 19-century textbooks and anthologies were more diverse than such a view would allow, and more specifically that such documents regularly included substantial coverage of ungenteel and un-Bostonian Whitman. (Unanswered by Folsom's rejoinder are the broader issues of just when, how, and with what degree of success a New England cultural hegemony took hold of American literary history.)

Folsom admits, however, that the Whitman who appeared most prominently in respectable 19th-century venues was often much tamer than the one visible in any full edition of *Leaves of Grass.* Moreover, despite protestations, Whitman acquiesced at times to the selective presentation of his work, as Folsom argues more directly in *"Leaves of Grass, Junior:* Whitman's Compromise with Discriminating Tastes" (*AL* 63:641–63). At the same time Whitman was proclaiming the inviolable integrity of his enterprise, he permitted others to excerpt, anthologize, and (arguably) bowdlerize him. Folsom's evidence makes for a mild claim, it should be noted, less that Whitman directly cooperated with the anthologizers than that he neglected genuine opportunities to halt them. Nevertheless, even silence and inaction undermine any simple contrast between the poet's principled nobility and the publishing industry's opportunism.

b. Biography Despite the centrality of old and new historical methods in much current work on Whitman, very little directly biographical writing appeared this year. William Homer's "New Light on Thomas Eakins and Walt Whitman in Camden" (*MStrR* 12 [1990]:74–82) draws on Horace Traubel's unpublished diaries to document more fully Eakins's visits with Whitman in early 1891. And in *Whitman in His Own*

Time (Omnigraphics), a volume designed for the reserve-room shelf, Joel Myerson collects 35 accounts of the poet by friends and associates.

c. Criticism: General The most original study of Whitman this year is Dana Brand's long chapter in *The Spectator and the City*. Brand asks the unusual question of how, in looking at urban crowds, Whitman differs from Hawthorne's Miles Coverdale. His answer is that Whitman increasingly gazes at people and things as if he were viewing a photograph. The magnetic fascination of the urban scene is then the same that Whitman (embryonically, in an 1846 newspaper article) and Roland Barthes (magisterially, in *Camera Lucida*) describe as distinctive to photography's allure. Human faces appear as if they were faces of the dead, viewable from across an unbreachable gulf of space and time and yet powerfully soliciting the viewer's compassion. Brand accordingly argues that in "Crossing Brooklyn Ferry," the poem in which Whitman first fully develops a discourse of urban spectatorship, the poet "replaces the spectatorship of the *flaneur* with the indiscriminating gaze of a camera endowed with an ability to love what it cannot gain access to." Moreover, the poet also imagines himself as if photographically visible to future generations, at once subject and object, living and dead.

A second, even more far-reaching claim of Brand's phenomenology is that Whitman directly links the cameralike gaze to homoerotic love. Brand argues that adhesive love in "Calamus" is characteristically experienced as an act of silently gazing into the eyes of a stranger with whom one is mysteriously and magnetically intimate. Furthermore, because this gaze presupposes distance or absence (by contrast to the unfallen corporeality of amative presence in "Children of Adam"), it has an inherently "spiritual" significance and can therefore serve as the basis of a political theory. Whitman's utopian vision of democratic comradeship in effect multiplies the interlocked gazes of adhesive strangers. Alternatively, it imagines the adhering couple arm in arm, looking not at one another this time but gazing out on the photographable world from a shared perspective.

Brand's methods differ sharply from Michael Moon's in *Disseminating Whitman: Revision and Corporeality in* Leaves of Grass (Harvard), although Moon's study shares with Brand's a belief that the literary, the political, and the sexual are as inextricable as Whitman always claimed they were. Moon is chock-full of fascinating, often flamboyant, and notably diverse claims, but as he notices, his arguments work more by assertion than demonstration.

By revision, Moon means not stylistic tinkering but global changes in aim, especially from the 1855 to the 1860 editions. (Moon also examines the 1867 edition, offering an impressive, primarily psychoanalytic interpretation of Whitman's Civil War poems; but the argument strikes me as functionally independent of his main claims about revision.) The 1855 *Leaves of Grass* is said to depend centrally on "fluidity," a collective or composite form of selfhood which Moon equates with male homosexuality and indeed contrasts to the "solidity" of female identity and/or sexuality. (Surprisingly, Moon understands the latter as chiefly or even essentially heterosexual.) Thanks to such fluidity, author and reader can mirror one another bodily and thus directly identify with one another's experiences. However, the 1856 edition adds an antithetical concern with the unbridgeable distinctions among persons, genders, generations, and eras that persist despite Whitman's efforts. The concern marks the arrival of the oedipal in Whitman's world, for unbridgeable—that is to say, categorical—distinctions presuppose the oedipal logic of castration. (All negation derives from *"le 'non' du pére,"* the power of which depends in turn on the fear of castration.) By 1860, Whitman's new claim to a scriptural and specifically typological authority reconceives the self as still fluid but no longer so plastic. Moreover, it links historical typology to typography. It would seem that the technology of print, in contrast to touch or voice, allows for "returning impressions indifferently" and that such multiplication of impressions circumvents the oedipal demarcation of categorical difference. At least I think so; I found this third phase the most elusive part of Moon's schema.

Baldly summarized, Moon's account of the sequence of editions may appear reductive in his so sharply distinguishing editions that also obviously retain a good bit of continuity. Actually, the account functions more as a pretext or an abandoned scaffolding than a Procrustean thesis, as if the urgent interest in sexual bodies overtook an earlier plan. As a result, intriguing claims about how and why Whitman revised successive editions remain undeveloped. The same could be said about Moon's eclectic methodology, which in adroitly deploying Lacanian psychoanalysis, historical materialism, and a broadly Foucauldian concern with sexual discourse rarely works one method out fully or clarifies its congruency with the others.

On the other hand, Moon maintains a persistent and thorough commitment to gay studies as a key to Whitman. Not only is his Whitman almost exclusively homosexual, but Moon maintains that a "literal 'sexual' level must never be discounted" in interpreting Whitman. Thus, whereas Brand somewhat squeamishly emphasizes the visuality of adhesive love, Moon celebrates the carnality of various phallic, anal, and oral acts. More important, he makes such identificatory celebration a central basis for reading Whitman, implying that if one is not aroused by the poems then one has not attained the corporeal presence Whitman regularly proclaimed as the aim of his work. No sex in the head for Moon, in other words, not even the convenient euphemisms of sublimation. He does not, for example, shrink from the possibility that women cannot read Whitman as Whitman would be read, although he does regret that possibility as an ideological shortcoming in the poet.

Sexuality is also the topic of William Schurr's "Walt Whitman's *Leaves of Grass:* The Making of a Sexual Revolution" (*Soundings* 74:101–27), which portrays Whitman as prophet of 1960s-style sexual liberation. Schurr's overly simplified picture of a Victorian America's repressiveness is nicely countered by Kenneth Price's "Walt Whitman, Free Love, and *The Social Revolutionist*" (*American Periodicals* 1:70–82), which among other things confirms that the terms of Whitman's sexual vocabulary could be found in antebellum free-love journals. Price documents Whitman's interest in one such journal, a copy of which was found among his papers 40 years later. Another perspective on Whitman's sexuality is found in a brief but trenchant section of David Bergman's *Gaiety Transfigured* (Wisconsin). Under the rubric of "choosing our fathers," that is, constructing a specifically gay literary tradition, Bergman ponders the difference between Whitman's frequently boastful stance and the egolessness that Bergman argues is characteristic of later writers.

The year's other major study, Mark Bauerlein's *Whitman and the American Idiom* (LSU), shares with Moon an attempt to chart Whitman's career as an allegorical progress through successive editions of *Leaves of Grass.* For Bauerlein, however, Whitman's revisions all stem from a single, fundamental impasse: the incompatibility of representation, especially verbal representation, with Whitman's goal of unmediated presence. Accordingly, Bauerlein depicts Whitman's career as the various phases of a resistance to "theory," where theory is understood in the DeManian sense as the knowledge that language is always already fallen. The result may be the most unpolemically devastating full-length study of Whitman ever written, for although Bauerlein ostensibly does not come to bury the poet, he portrays Whitman as time after time attempting to accomplish ends that theory knows to be naive. Whitman knows, too, according to Bauerlein, for the poet's linguistic researches and the sheer activity of writing keep bringing him up against the truth. The stages of that knowledge and Whitman's differingly futile attempts to deny or circumvent it mark the discrete stages of his poetics. He first seeks to transcend the problem by writing self-reflexive poetry, such as the 1855 version of "Song of Myself," which relentlessly both asserts and questions its own status, contradicting itself precisely in order to contain multitudes. The poetry's self-referential thematization of its own composition persists in later editions, but in 1856 it gets supplemented with an explicit attention to guiding the reader's response. (Like Brand, Bauerlein sees the novelty of "Crossing Brooklyn Ferry" in its concern with how the poet will appear to futurity—in other words, to his readers.) However, interpretation can no more be made natural or organic than composition, so in 1860 Whitman finally becomes a literal reviser, not just adding to *Leaves of Grass* to make it more and more clearly what it already is, but changing it to make it accord better with what must be its as yet unrealized vision. The maneuver effectively gives up the game, for it acknowledges a structural gap between intention and text. Words fall short of hopes and desires; no poem ever quite allows us to possess the origin of all poems. The key sequence is the "Sea Drift" cluster, which Bauerlein reads persuasively as a confession that Whitman's language experiment—the attempt to create an organic, transparent, and visionary poetry—has failed.

Such recognition is not for Bauerlein a breakthrough to wisdom but the end of Whitman as a poet worth reading. For although Bauerlein acknowledges concerns other than the semiotic themes he foregrounds—namely politics, sex, and religion—he asserts that if you "take away the linguistic dilemmas framing those thematic conflicts," you are left with "notoriously dull" poetry.

Kathryne V. Lindberg's "Whitman's 'Convertible Terms': America, Self, Ideology" (*Theorizing American Literature,* pp. 233–68) expresses a similar impatience—and doubts Whitman's ideological rectitude to boot—in the course of a faintly Derridean examination of Whitman's relation to Hegelianism. I suspect the topic will bear further, more assiduous looking into.

d. Criticism: Individual Works Mark Maslan's "Whitman's 'Strange Hand': Body as Text in *Drum-Taps*" (*ELH* 58:935–55) transposes the usual links that Whitman criticism draws between corporeality and writing by interpreting the latter as handwriting. Maslan argues that, rather than insisting on the body's unassailable, literally incarnate presence, and identifying such presence with the self, Whitman turns his own body into a mere sign or representation of selfhood. The method (Michael Fried out of Elaine Scarry) is novel, and the arguments daring, but they depend greatly on some troublesome claims. For example, Maslan insists on the referential identity of the dead soldiers in "Vigil Strange" and "Come Up from the Fields Father." Nevertheless, the article interestingly challenges some entrenched ideas about bodily presence, and it brings to bear a critical method that is likely to be of further use.

Kenneth M. Price and Cynthia G. Bernstein's "Whitman's Sign of Parting: 'So long!' as *l'envoi*" (*WWR* 9:65–76) begins by proposing a speech-act definition of the *envoi* as it develops from Chaucer to Longfellow. Price and Bernstein then offer a detailed stylistic analysis of how "So long!" fits this definition and of how the poem functions in the 1860 *Leaves of Grass.* Their arguments possess the virtue of posing a limited, well-defined question and answering it comprehensively. A. James Wohlpart's less original "From the Outsetting Bard to Mature Poet: Whitman's 'Out of the Cradle' and the *Sea-Drift* Cluster" (*WWR* 9:77–90) stresses the difference between the outsetting boy-poet and the "uniter of here and hereafter." The point of this claim is to give structural primacy to the entire sequence of poems, rather than to "Out of the Cradle Endlessly Rocking" seen in isolation.

e. Affinities and Influences Several essays derive from a 1989 conference exploring Whitman's relation to the visual arts. Of most interest to Whitman scholars is Ruth Bowan's " 'The Gathering of the Forces': Walt Whitman and the Visual Arts, 1844–55" (*MStrR* 12 [1990]:10–30), which usefully surveys Whitman's interest in painting and photography in the 1840s and 1850s, focusing on his friendship with the photographer Gabriel Harrison and his involvement with the short-lived Brooklyn Art Union. Two essays by art historians compare Whitman to French painters. However, Laura Meixner's " 'The Best of Democracy': Walt Whitman, Jean-François Millet, and Popular Culture in Post-Civil War America" (*MStrR* 12 [1990]:31–48) and Albert Boime's "Courbet and

Whitman: A Case Study in International Rebellion" (*MStrR* 12 [1990]: 49–74) tell us more about the painter in each case than the poet.

Admirers of Angus Fletcher's criticism should be warned that his "Whitman and Longfellow: Two Types of the American Poet" (*Raritan* 10, iv:131–45) has little to say about Whitman beyond truisms one might announce to an audience unfamiliar with the poet.

ii Emily Dickinson

a. Bibliography and Editing Barbara Kelly's "Checklist (mostly 1990)" (*DicS* 78:34–43) remains the only annual bibliography of secondary works. Despite good coverage of book reviews and useful, brief annotations on many items, it does not purport to be complete or comprehensive. A few detailed descriptions appear in the "New Publications" section of the *Bulletin* of the Emily Dickinson International Society (3, i:8–11 and 3, ii:8–11), but otherwise researchers and students are pretty much left to the increasingly beleaguered MLA bibliography.

Despite several anecdotal references to Dickinson's manuscripts, Martha Nell Smith's "Gender Issues in Textual Editing of Emily Dickinson" (*Women's Studies Quarterly* 19, iii–iv:78–111) deals less with textual scholarship than with biography. Like a number of recent scholars, Smith wonders whether Susan Gilbert Dickinson was not central to the poetry of her friend and later sister-in-law. However, although Smith is clearly inclined to nominate Susan as both lover and contributing editor, her claims are more tentative and diffuse than those of Sue's other recent champions. The article's most original contribution to Dickinson studies may be in questioning a simple division between homosexual and heterosexual desire and in doubting the frequently supposed chastity of fond relations between women in 19th-century America.

A more conclusive, albeit narrowly focused examination of the same territory appears in Ellen Louise Hart's "The Encoding of Homoerotic Desire: Emily Dickinson's Letters and Poems to Susan Dickinson, 1850–1886" (*TSWL* 9 [1990]:251–72), which directly counters the widely held view that Susan and Emily were no longer close after the 1850s. Hart bases her case on the text which Johnson prints as Letter 912, but which Hart convincingly demonstrates to be verse. This 1884 letter-poem imagines for Susan and Emily a postmortem reunion of the sort that numerous other poems represent as heterosexual (or as uncertainly gendered). The argument's importance is that it refutes what had been proposed both as a categorical distinction in Dickinson's poetry between love of women and love of men and as a clear sign of the latter's greater importance to her.

b. Biography Susan Gilbert Dickinson is also central to this year's one biographical monograph, but as the Susan who survived Emily, not the one deemed to have been her closest literary confidante. Except for the sensational but oddly half-hearted insinuation that Emily Dickinson committed suicide, John Evangelist Walsh's *This Brief Tragedy: Unraveling the Todd-Dickinson Affair* (Grove Weidenfeld) has little to say about the poet's life or work. Walsh writes best as a partisan in the war between the houses, arguing that the unflattering picture of Susan conveyed by Whicher, Sewall, and Longsworth derives primarily from Mabel Loomis Todd, Susan's rival for the affections of Austin Dickinson. In addition, Walsh argues persuasively that Todd's editorial devotion to Emily came only after the unexpected success of the 1890 volume of poems, to which Todd had attended only desultorily.

Two psychiatric studies address Dickinson from essentially clinical perspectives. Norbert Hirschhorn in "A Bandaged Secret: Emily Dickinson and Incest" (*Journal of Psychohistory* 18:251–81) sensitively but inconclusively compares the modern "incest-family profile" to what we know or surmise about the poet and her family. Susan Kavaler-Adler's "Emily Dickinson and the Subject of Seclusion" (*American Journal of Psychoanalysis* 51:21–38) uses object-relations theory to update an old claim, namely, that Dickinson's withdrawal from the world was indeed a pathological symptom, not the witting or fruitful choice that literary scholarship has more recently been willing to deem it. The disdain for our often "protective reverence" is refreshing, but Kavaler-Adler relies more on analytic dogma than accurate information, at one point even attributing Thomas Wentworth Higginson's poem "Decoration" to Dickinson. Moreover, although the author is a practicing analyst, her use of Melanie Klein and D. W. Winnicott seems wooden by comparison to the lay analysis of such critics as Cynthia Griffin Wolff.

c. Criticism: General The year's two most important studies both propose to extend and revise earlier feminist views of Dickinson, in particular those views that in seeing Dickinson preeminently as a woman poet have supposed such an identity unproblematic or stable. Mary

Loeffelholz's *Dickinson and the Boundaries of Feminist Theory* (Illinois) is the more polemical; in effect, she uses a number of Dickinson's poems to test feminist claims put forth in the dozen years since Gilbert and Gubar's *Madwoman in the Attic.* Loeffelholz herself primarily endorses the Lacanian and semiotic concerns of poststructuralist feminism, although she also briefly bows toward materialist notions of history and even proposes to mediate between historicist and textualist claims.

Loeffelholz is most suspicious of sentimental or celebratory essentialism: notions of gender or authorship that minimize difficulties and misgivings in order to privilege female achievement. For example, Loeffelholz argues that the developing tradition of women's writing in the 19th century offered Dickinson less a cheering resource than a set of problems, contradictions, and ambivalences, most of them linked to a thematics of internal violence. Similarly, she criticizes Wolff's emphasis on the dyadic relation of mother to infant as a model for object relations in Dickinson, insisting that Wolff underestimates the importance of male objects and overlooks the triangular (that is, oedipal) structures underlying ostensibly dyadic, face-to-face encounters.

Rather than exalting a woman's sphere or promoting a women's language that might supplement the otherwise male language of poetic authority, Loeffelholz's Dickinson seeks out the differences within male language itself. Accordingly, Loeffelholz focuses on several poems that engage but also challenge Bloomian notions of the (male) poet's errand into (female) nature. For similar reasons she is interested in poems that replace the quintessentially Emersonian link of "I" and "eye" with the triad of "ear," "hear," and "here." It is both a strength and a weakness of Loeffelholz's study that it is so tied to thorough readings of a few Dickinson poems. The strength is that, in the mode of deconstruction generally, she counters easy generalizations with a tough and subtle attention to detail. The weakness is that her broader arguments have a disturbingly ad hoc quality. Even as a gadfly to the more systematic arguments of Wolff, Margaret Homans, and Joanne Feit Diehl, however, Loeffelholz offers sophisticated, sometimes dazzling readings that genuinely challenge the boundaries of both Dickinson criticism and poststructuralist feminism.

Margaret Dickie's *Lyric Contingencies: Emily Dickinson and Wallace Stevens* (Penn.) approaches the two poets through genre, specifically through what Dickie posits as a categorical distinction between lyricism and the essentially narrative base of all other modes. Modern lyric is for her preeminently the mode of contingent experience, that which cannot be easily fitted to some coherent story, that which cannot be easily subsumed to the experience of a stable, continuous self, and that which cannot otherwise be easily taken as representative or universal.

Dickie's treatment of Dickinson is relatively brief, fewer than 50 pages, which creates a problem for the primarily negative definition of lyric contingency. For example, to demonstrate that Dickinson's "lyric speakers have no narrative continuity, no social viability, [and] no steadfast identity" would seem logically to require examining a good many speakers in a good many poems. Dickie works instead by pointing out (often convincingly) the shortcomings in various critics' claims to the contrary. The result is necessarily more suggestive than conclusive. Rather than fully synthesizing a rival portrait of Dickinson as Rortyesque heroine, making herself up anew out of every changing circumstance or divergent inflection, Dickie largely contents herself with noticing the gaps in extant claims for the poet's consistency and coherence.

The two most important such claims are Emersonian and feminist. The first measures Dickinson's aims against Emerson's demand that the poet be a representative man; for Dickie, this view must either devalue Dickinson as incoherent or fail to understand the discontinuous, incommensurable moments of individuality actually present in the poetry. The second viewpoint similarly misunderstands Dickinson's individuality, assimilating it to a gender-based theory of identity and fitting it to a narrative of repression, subversion, or struggle. Both views limit the radical nature of the poet's imaginative resources to "prose models of character."

Bryan C. Short's "Stowe, Dickinson, and the Rhetoric of Modernism" (*ArQ* 47, iii:1–16) proposes a series of breathtaking claims about rhetoric and literary history. Addressing some of the same concerns as Loeffelholz, Short proposes to correlate Dickinson's figures of thought and speech with a revised, nonsexist version of Harold Bloom's theories. He argues that Bloom's exemplary attention to poetic voice, understood as the interlacing of style and ethics, is the baby to save as we throw out the bathwater of his militant, male High Romanticism. From that theoretical base, with nods to Homans and Alicia Ostriker, Short proposes that Dickinson replaces "figures of progress, struggle, and redemption with those of polyvocal stillness, of echo and expectation." One part of the claim is that Dickinson is not haunted by belatedness; another is that her figurative language bursts the bounds established by Bloom's tropology.

Little of this can be definitively established in a brief essay, of course, and Short's fondness for sweeping generalization will not sway skeptics. Nevertheless, his are claims to be reckoned with, and they may ultimately mark a way of advancing beyond what others have said about Dickinson's rhetoricity.

Joan Kirkby's *Emily Dickinson* (St. Martin's), which seems meant as a brief introduction, explicates poems under the thematic rubrics of language, fictiveness, gender, gothicism, and nature. The necessarily compressed, somewhat tendentious explications portray a consistently feminist Dickinson. More unusually, they portray a proto-structuralist Dickinson, someone who heeds the primacy of the symbolic order far more assiduously than other critics have supposed. Kirkby relies frequently on dictionaries of symbol and myth to read Dickinson's imagery, and she believes that one can peremptorily hack a path through biographical thickets by relying on the letter of Dickinson's letters.

Jane Donahue Eberwein in " 'Graphicer for Grace': Emily Dickinson's Calvinist Language" (*SPAS* 1 [1990]:170–201) proposes no innovative view of Dickinson, but she does provide an unusually sure and succinct perspective on Dickinson's religious concerns. The article draws on substantial research into Congregationalism, but rather than an argument about environment or historical context Eberwein refreshingly bases her case on the poet's language. In other words, rather than mainly reconstructing the beliefs and debates to which Dickinson would have been exposed and to which she might have responded, Eberwein fastens on the theological terminology in Dickinson's writings and compares Dickinson's usage to established uses and beliefs. The conclusion, that Dickinson's imagination gravitated toward the bright side of her religious heritage, thus seems more careful and judicious than earlier, often more sweeping studies of Dickinson's religiosity. The article can thus be recommended as an unusually handy, one-stop introduction to Dickinson's Calvinist heritage. On the other hand, perhaps as the necessary price for her method, Eberwein assumes that the language of Calvinist theology is the necessary center or point of departure for all imaginable religious usages. Her Dickinson makes spiritual analogies from otherwise secular terms but never the reverse.

Two other articles interpret the poetry from a religious perspective. Eberwein's "Emily Dickinson and the Bumble Bee's Religion" (*DicS* 77:23–33) extends her claim about the poet's comparatively sunny views by examining bee imagery in letters and poems. Even when circumstances might dictate an alternative, Dickinson reads the bee as emblem of summer's bounty rather than its brevity. Diane Gabrielson Scholl's "Emily Dickinson's Conversion Narratives: A Study of the Fascicles" (*SPAS* 1 [1990]:202–24) inconclusively examines several fascicles for evidence of a Calvinist conversion narrative.

d. Criticism: Individual Works Two essays in Temma Berg, ed., *Engendering the Word: Feminist Essays in Psychosexual Politics* (Illinois, 1989) deserve belated notice. Anna Shannon Elfenbein in "Unsexing Language: Pronominal Protest in Emily Dickinson's 'Lay this Laurel' " (pp. 208–23) impressively examines how the elegy for Edward Dickinson both invokes and challenges patriarchal traditions through the play of gender in its pronouns and referents. Leigh Gilmore in "The Gaze of the Other Woman: Beholding and Begetting in Dickinson, Moore, and Rich" (pp. 81–102) also considers but a single Dickinson poem, "I think I was enchanted," but she does so with far-reaching consequences for the psychology of literary empowerment. Gilmore argues that the poem's inscription of Elizabeth Barrett Browning fits it to a pattern of relations between women that escapes the predominantly oedipal or family-romance model of literary influence.

e. Affinities and Influences Rowena Revis Jones's "Edwards, Dickinson, and the Sacramentality of Nature" (*SPAS* 1 [1990]:225–53) compares the imagery in several of Dickinson's poems to the sacramental view of nature articulated by Jonathan Edwards. However, it is unclear what is at stake in the comparison, since she proposes nothing especially pointed about Edwards, Dickinson, or the relation between them.

Case Western Reserve University

6 Mark Twain

Robert Sattelmeyer

The recovered manuscript of the first half of *Adventures of Huckleberry Finn* continued to overshadow other developments in Mark Twain studies this year. A session at MLA offered a preview of the manuscript's riches, and a few months later arrangements became final to return it to the Buffalo and Erie County Public Library where, it is to be hoped, it will soon be accessible to scholars. The year also saw notable studies by Victor Doyno on the writing of *Huckleberry Finn* and by Jeffrey Steinbrink on the early years of Twain's career in the East. Perhaps still profiting from the renewed interest generated by its centennial in 1989, *Connecticut Yankee* was the subject of a half-dozen substantial articles, while *Pudd'nhead Wilson,* all the rage the last few years, slipped noticeably.

i Editions

The only noteworthy edition this year was John Cooley's *Mark Twain's Aquarium: The Samuel Clemens Angelfish Correspondence, 1905–1910* (Georgia), which prints 300 letters between Twain and his schoolgirl friends during the last five years of his life, along with related documents such as notebook entries and sections from the autobiographical dictations. The letters are carefully annotated, and the introduction and headnotes provide useful and accurate context. The significance of these relationships has been much debated, of course, and Cooley's balanced and responsible editing job—bringing together virtually all of the extant evidence—provides an invaluable resource for biographers and critics.

The letters themselves do nothing to undermine Cooley's position "that there is no evidence to suggest real impropriety or scandal in connection with any of the angelfish," although if there ever were such evidence in the correspondence it is not likely to have survived. Cooley believes that Twain's fascination (obsession?) with young girls stems from both his lifelong dream of a "platonic sweetheart" and his yearning for grandchildren. But he also notes that Twain dropped his friendship with the girls when they crossed the threshold of sexual maturity and that he expressed jealousy and anger toward the boyfriend of his last "angelfish," Helen Allen. In the largest context, Cooley argues, these friendships "suggest an effort on Clemens's part to create a counterforce, albeit fragile and threatened, against the awesome forces of despair that overpowered his view of the human condition" during his last years. Cooley makes the same points in "Mark Twain's Aquarium: Editing the Samuel Clemens–Angelfish Correspondence" (*MTJ* 27, i[1989]:18–24), in which he tells in more detail the story of how he became involved in this project (one of the angelfish, Marjorie Breckenridge, was his cousin).

ii Biography

Guy Cardwell's *The Man Who Was Mark Twain: Images and Ideologies* (Yale) is a sort of retro *The Ordeal of Mark Twain* for the 1990s. Like many before him, Cardwell is disturbed by the tendency of Americans both to mythologize Mark Twain and to regard him as representative of the best of American culture, so he sets out "to undermine superstitiously devised memorial statues that have been cherished as acceptable likenesses." His analysis rests largely on the cultural criticism of the Howells/Brooks/De Voto/Wecter eras, however, and culminates, for all intents and purposes, with Hamlin Hill's 1973 *Mark Twain: God's Fool.* Thus, he operates without reference to recent cultural critics, New Historicists, and "social constructionists" whose work might support his views. To the extent that earlier critics *were* partly responsible for the erroneous images of Mark Twain that pervade popular culture, his emphasis is understandable. But it gives the book a somewhat dated feel, particularly since Cardwell himself, for all his criticism of Van Wyck Brooks, falls back on a reductionist Freudian trashing of Twain's personality. Relying mainly on Alexander Jones's 1956 analysis of Twain's sexuality, Cardwell focuses on topics that he considers not to have been sufficiently explored by critics: namely, "purity in several of its aspects; masturbation; impotence; and pedophilia." The predictable results are a gaggle of neuroses that disqualify Twain from status as American Hero, but, as tends to be the case in amateur literary psychoanalysis, the writer and the writings are submerged if not lost altogether. Sections of the book are valuable for their synopsis of the earlier critical debate on Mark Twain's "wound," but *The Man Who Was Mark Twain* is mainly a book for those who like their idols crumbled.

Jeffrey Steinbrink's *Getting to Be Mark Twain* (Calif.), on the other hand, demonstrates that despite the innumerable biographies and "character" studies of Samuel Clemens/Mark Twain, there is still a wealth of unexplored territory, particularly if the writer allows primary documents to speak for themselves and is not compelled to concoct a tortuous psychiatric workup of the victim. The book focuses on 1868–71, a period marked by Twain's return from the *Quaker City* excursion and his writing of *The Innocents Abroad,* his courtship of Olivia Langdon (with its concomitant period of moral reform), his marriage, his efforts to establish himself as a newspaper editor and magazine writer with the Buffalo *Express* and the *Galaxy,* the writing of *Roughing It,* and, finally, his rejection of a career in journalism and his establishment in Hartford as a successful writer of books. It is Steinbrink's contention that during this period Twain's "life took the shape it was essentially to hold from then until its close," its patterns emerging from the competing pressures and ambitions of his nascent literary career and the profound changes in his personal life. In particular, "Mark Twain" was retooled and refined during this time, as Twain carefully adapted his western literary persona to the requirements of the eastern literary establishment, curbing some of the coarseness and inelegancies of his frontier humor and adding a component of social and moral criticism to his character.

The transformation was not easy. The reason Twain produced so little memorable writing during his year of "reform" while he was courting Olivia was "very likely his alienation from the imaginative resources embodied in Mark Twain"; nevertheless, "person and persona" were eventually reconciled. In this context, Steinbrink treats more fully and sympathetically than earlier biographers Twain's relationship with Olivia's family, especially her father, Jervis Langdon. While not downplaying the potentially repressive and stifling nature of the obligations under which he placed his son-in-law, Steinbrink emphasizes Langdon's philanthropy and generosity and says that he "reaffirmed Clemens's faith in the efficacy of virtue and by so doing heightened his indignation at the hypocrisy that characterizes what Clemens himself came to call the Gilded Age." Given the current critical climate, perhaps the most noteworthy aspect of this thoughtful and informative study (besides reminding us that Mark Twain came perilously close to settling down in Cleveland in 1869) is that the writer who emerges is not a psychological cripple but someone productively poised to exploit not only the literary climate of Hartford but the more important imaginative territory of the Mississippi Valley of his youth.

Thanks mainly to *MTJ,* there were a number of briefer biographical studies. The entire Fall 1989 number (27, ii[issued in 1991]) is devoted to "Hero in a Fool's Paradise: Twain's Cousin James J. Lampton and Colonel Sellers," by Lucius M. Lampton (a descendant), who provides a wealth of genealogical information and family anecdotes about the man who was the model for Colonel Sellers in *The Gilded Age* and other works. Among other biographical articles, in "Macfarlane, 'Boarding House,' and 'Bugs': Mark Twain's Cincinnati Apprenticeship" (*MTJ* 27, i[1989]:14–17), Wesley A. Britton attempts to reestablish the importance of the Scotsman and fellow printer named "Macfarlane" or "MacFarland" with whom Twain boarded in Cincinnati in 1856–57. He cites the attributed "Cincinnati Boarding House Sketch" of 1856 and a letter to Annie Taylor of the same year as evidence that the portrait of Macfarlane's deterministic philosophy in Twain's *Autobiography* and Paine's biography is probably accurate.

The archaeological background of Twain's visit to Ephesus on the *Quaker City* tour in 1867 is filled in by David Roessel's "Mark Twain at Ephesus" (*MTJ* 27, i[1989]:27–31), and in the same issue Craig S. Smith and Kevin Coots describe "Virginia City's Joke on Twain" (pp. 32–33), reprinting an 1879 article from a Longmont, Colorado, newspaper recounting a practical joke played on Twain after a lecture in 1866.

Finally, Dennis Welland's *The Life and Times of Mark Twain* (Crescent) is a coffee-table book that offers a conventional account of Twain's life and career—of the sort Cardwell would object to—amid a welter of 250 illustrations, some misidentified and many of only tangential relevance.

iii General Interpretations

This category was remarkably thin in book-length studies this year, with only John E. Bassett's *"A Heart of Ideality in My Realism" and Other Essays on Howells and Twain* (Locust Hill) making a significant contribution. Bassett's subject is the problem of literary authority for American writers after the Civil War; he focuses on Howells and Twain because they were the first postwar writers to succeed "along the lines of the new entrepreneurial model." Unlike Howells, who sought to efface himself within an aesthetic of representation, Twain flaunted his persona and achieved authority through the power of performance. There are rewarding readings of *Roughing It, The Gilded Age, Life on the Mississippi, Huckleberry Finn, The Prince and the Pauper, A Tramp Abroad,* and *Connecticut Yankee,* and the essays are up-to-date in their concern for such things as "self-fashioning." Twain emerges, perhaps not surprisingly in this context, as a thoroughly modern writer's writer, one who, more than even Faulkner, "put writing at the center of his writing—as theme and as phenomenon. The authority of the writer and the power of the performer tie together his prose as much as any particular social value does." Patricia M. Mandia's *Comedic Pathos: Black Humor in Twain's Fiction* (McFarland) is a monograph that suffers the fate of most attempts to retrofit a modern mode to works of an earlier period: its energy is dissipated in rehearsing how this or that work evinces characteristics of "black humor," though to what purpose is not entirely clear. The analysis runs mainly to plot summary, and there is little illumination of what the differences might be between the putative "black humor" of Twain and any other kind of humor or comedy that appears in his works.

Race and religion rear their familiar heads, though not as frequently as in the recent past. Shelley Fisher Fishkin's "False Starts, Fragments, and Fumbles: Mark Twain's Unpublished Writing on Race" (*EAS* 20:17–31) treats its subject briefly but provocatively, arguing that Twain never completed or published several manuscripts with racial themes in part because he was unwilling to face the public consequences of fully exposing his beliefs on the subject as his friend George Washington Cable had done to his discomfiture. These fragments, then, are of a piece with *Huck Finn* and *Pudd'nhead Wilson,* in which "Twain limns a subversive indictment of racism . . . only to abandon its implications before he's two-thirds of the way through." Everett Emerson traces "Mark Twain's Quarrel With God" (*Order in Variety,* pp. 32–48). His aim is not to break new ground but to summarize the development of Twain's religious view from his fundamentalist childhood to his old age when he "heartily despised" the God of the Old Testament but "profoundly misunderstood Christianity." Emerson seems somewhat surprised, at this late date, by some of Twain's religious views. "Did Samuel Clemens really believe *that?*" he asks after quoting a particularly virulent indictment of the deity, but concludes that he probably did.

A refreshingly unjaundiced and balanced overview of "Mark Twain and the Idea of American Superiority at the End of the Nineteenth Century" is offered by Manfred Pütz (*An American Empire,* pp. 215–36). Pütz traces Twain's nationalism through fairly well-defined stages: debunker of European superiority (*The Innocents Abroad*), missionary (when he took it upon himself to attack foreign critics and promote American institutions, as in *Connecticut Yankee*), and finally crusader against the unwarranted exporting of Western ideology in the form of imperialism. But Twain managed "to hold on to the idea of American superiority while, at the same time, quarrelling with the evidence for it in the sphere of international politics." Ironically, his earlier advocacy of American superiority eventually "helped pave the way for the very forces he would later learn to detest."

Michael Oriard's *Sporting with the Gods* is a serious study that follows its subject from the Puritans to New Agers and treats Twain in the context of an uneasy Victorian frame of mind that endorsed play as a means of satirizing dominant values while covertly embracing those very ideals. "In *Tom Sawyer, The Prince and the Pauper,* and *Joan of Arc,* Twain subscribed to the conventional sentimentalizing of childhood play, reserving adulthood for seriousness and work. In *Huckleberry Finn,* on the other hand, Twain challenged such conventions, but here he was defeated by an inability to wed his fantasy of freedom to his sense of necessity and limitation." A thought-provoking study, it suggests a somewhat wider playing field for the subject of play (as opposed to humor) in Twain. Humor gets its due, however, in St. George Tucker Arnold, Jr.'s "Mark Twain's Birds and Joel Chandler Harris's Rabbit: Two Modes of Projection of Authorial Personality in Comic Critters" (*Thalia* 11, i:34–41), an engaging article that is much less solemn than its title might suggest. Arnold examines the different strains of animal humor in southern and southwestern oral traditions and shows how Twain adapted and improved on his sources in such characters as Tom Sawyer's cat Peter and Jim Baker's Blue Jay. The creature that Twain most identified with was the bird, and Arnold finds that the most important version of this totemic animal is the Indian Crow described in *Following the Equator* that "has been a gambler, a low comedian, a dissolute priest, a fussy woman, a blackguard, a scoffer, a liar, a thief, a spy . . . a lecturer."

The old issue of Twain's "southernness" or lack thereof gets rehashed in Tjebbe Westendorp's "Mark Twain's Southern Strategy" (*The United States South: Regionalism and Identity,* ed. Valeria Gennaro Lerda and Tjebbe Westendorp [Bulzoni], pp. 93–103). The question posed is of a dubious either/or kind: "did he evade the issue of his Southern identity or was it his Missouri background that was responsible for his moral stand against some of the evils of this time?" The answer arrived at (through a discussion of "The Private History of a Campaign that Failed," mostly) is, in the best tradition of the hair-ball oracle, partly yes and partly no. Finally, an essay that investigates a similar moral concern is Daniel L. Wright's "Flawed Communities and the Problem of Moral Choice in the Fiction of Mark Twain" (*SLJ* 24, i:88–97). It advances the familiar neo-Emersonian argument that in Twain's fiction (specifically *Huck Finn, Pudd'nhead Wilson,* and *The Mysterious Stranger*) society is everywhere in a conspiracy against the individual's innate goodness. Amazingly, articles such as this one still blithely cite the corrupt 1916 Paine-Duneka text of *The Mysterious Stranger.*

iv Individual Works Before 1885

The early years of Twain's career—except for Steinbrink's *Getting to Be Mark Twain*—were relatively neglected this year. No significant articles on *The Innocents Abroad, Roughing It,* or *The Gilded Age* appeared, although Lawrence I. Berkove's "Mark Twain and Horace Greeley: Penpals" (*Thalia* 11, ii[1990]:3–11) takes off from the bogus Greeley letter in chapter 70 of *Roughing It* to explore Twain's relationship with Greeley and the long-term effects in the popular press of his good-natured satire on Greeley's penmanship.

Tom Sawyer elicited a few brief articles. An interesting note by Edgar J. Burde, "Slavery and the Boys: *Tom Sawyer* and the Germ of *Huck Finn*" (*ALR* 24, i:86–91), argues that a revision in the manuscript shows Twain adding "moral depth and seriousness" to Huck's character in the earlier novel by having him describe his relation to the slave Uncle Jake. Neither Tom Sawyer nor Twain, at the time, was capable of grasping the significance of Huck's character with respect to slavery. Allison R. Ensor's "'Mightier than the Sword': An Undetected Obscenity in the First Edition of *Tom Sawyer*" (*MTJ* 27, i[1989]:25–26) points out that in the "Examination Evening" illustration the saying "The Pen Is Mightier than the Sword" appears on the schoolroom wall, with an almost imperceptible space between the second and third word. Ensor believes this was intentional on the part of the illustrator, True Williams, and that Twain noticed the joke and was amused by it, since he later used the same wordplay in his burlesque poem "AGE—a *Rubáiyát*" and in "The

Mammoth Cod." It may well be that Twain borrowed the joke later, but, given his reaction to the anatomically correct alteration of Uncle Silas that almost got into *Huckleberry Finn,* it is difficult to image him being amused. Finally, Earl F. Briden offers a plausible new source for chapter 17, where the boys return to listen to their own funeral eulogies, in "Tom Sawyer's Funeral—Shades of Charley Warner" (*AN&Q* n.s. 4:75–78); Charles Dudley Warner, with whom Twain had recently collaborated on *The Gilded Age,* has a story in his *Back-Log Studies* (1873) in which a youth dreams that he has died and attends his own funeral as a spirit.

Beverly R. David produced an interesting piece of art-historical detective work in "Tragedy and Travesty: Edward Whymper's *Scrambles Amongst the Alps* and Mark Twain's *A Tramp Abroad*" (*MTJ* 27, i[1989]:2–8), showing the extent of Twain's unacknowledged borrowings of both pictures and text from Whymper's well-known account of a mountain-climbing accident in 1865. She concludes—accurately, it would seem—that "the Matterhorn chapter in *A Tramp Abroad* is, unfortunately, a poor pastiche of borrowed and abridged text, indirect piracy of prints, and alterations of famous illustrations."

Two essays focused on *Life on the Mississippi.* The first, Marilyn Lancaster's "Twain's Search for Reality in *Life on the Mississippi*" (*MQ* 33:210–21), tautologically argues that the book "is a novel [*sic*] whose structure is generated through the redefinition of experience—a structure consistent with a writing process that reexamines meanings, producing in the wake of the reexamination its own evolutionary structure." Lawrence Howe's "Transcending the Limits of Experience: Mark Twain's *Life on the Mississippi*" (*AL* 63:420–39), on the other hand, is a sophisticated reading of Twain's efforts to achieve "representativity" in the book, of how he attempted, in the face of his lack of Civil War service, to turn that very lack of experience to his advantage and become a personal embodiment of the idea of America. Employing Freudian and Bakhtinian theories judiciously, Howe argues that Twain accomplishes this end by subverting various authority figures, such as the pilot Brown, Isaiah Sellers, and Sir Walter Scott, and by "redistributing value from actual to textual experience."

v Adventures of Huckleberry Finn

Victor A. Doyno's *Writing Huck Finn: Mark Twain's Creative Process* (Penn.) extends the work of scholars—especially Walter Blair and Victor

Fischer in recent years—on the contexts and composition of the novel. Doyno closely analyzes Twain's revisions in the manuscript of the second half of the novel (he was unable to do more than briefly glance at the newly recovered manuscript of the first half). The first six chapters focus on matters of "Stylistics," studying the effect of Twain's often minute and nuanced revisions on tone, character, humor, imagery, and plot. In the second and third sections ("Thematics" and "The Question of Unity") Doyno widens his focus to consider important contexts as well as the evidence of the text itself. Some of these subjects are familiar ("Christianity in Conflict with Morality," for example), but others offer interesting new implications for the contemporary frame of reference. This is particularly true of the chapter on "Literacy, Copyright, and Books," in which Doyno reinterprets Tom Sawyer's enslavement to romance fiction in terms of Twain's concern during the 1880s with the problem of international copyright. The "Sir Walter disease" was not simply a problem of the antebellum South, for the breakdown of "trade courtesy" after the Civil War meant that the American market was once again flooded with cheap pirated editions of European fiction which left American writers economically disadvantaged. If all that the average American had access to were these foreign novels, then the national character and imagination would suffer. The Phelps plantation section of the novel, Doyno believes, is not merely an overlong burlesque of Tom Sawyer's fondness for "authorities," but a critique of a contemporary cultural problem. Although Twain's revisions have been much cited and studied by earlier critics going back to De Voto, and although it is regrettable that Doyno was not able to incorporate evidence from the first half of the manuscript, *Writing Huck Finn* manages to break new ground and invites further exploration in several areas, particularly when the manuscript of the novel's first half becomes accessible to scholars.

The Critical Response to Mark Twain's "Huckleberry Finn," ed. Laurie Champion (Greenwood), obviously has plenty of company as a collection of criticism on the novel, but it is a useful volume, particularly for undergraduate libraries. Divided into "Early Response," "Criticism 1930–1959," "Criticism 1960–1985," "Centennial Celebration," and "Contemporary Criticism," the essays provide a fair summary of critical reaction; the volume also includes a selective bibliography. The book might have been stronger if the editor's principles for inclusion and exclusion were stated—it is curious, for instance, that neither Van Wyck Brooks nor Bernard De Voto is represented—and if the original publication data for the pieces chosen were listed somewhere other than on the copyright page.

Gregg Camfield's "Sentimental Liberalism and the Problem of Race in *Huckleberry Finn*" (*NCF* 46:96–113) manages to shed new light on a shopworn subject. Camfield explores the intellectual backgrounds of 19th-century sentimentalism, particularly its roots in 18th-century philosophical and psychological theories, and he shows that while Twain is generally thought of as a debunker of sentimentality, he used its traditions to further his own ends. Abolitionists had traditionally employed sentimental conventions to inculcate the common humanity of blacks, and Camfield shows that in *Huck Finn* "the book's advocacy of racial equality, though buried in irony, is almost completely sentimental."

The Phelps farm refuses to stay put. Sherwood Cummings is the latest to take a crack at nailing it down in "Mark Twain's Moveable Farm and the Evasion" (*AL* 63:440–58). He summarizes the recent conjectures of Michael Miller, Gerald Hoag, and Walter Blair and Victor Fischer, and offers his own opinion that it belongs near Pointe Coupee, Louisiana. He also suggests that Twain himself is responsible for the confusion; after clearly setting the farm in Louisiana in the novel itself, Twain vacillated (as part of the general vacillation of the evasion section) and "declined to make the setting signify, and later moved it to [the presumably less signifying] Arkansas." A larger issue that refuses to die is the nature of the ending. In "Overreaching: Critical Agenda and the Ending of *Adventures of Huckleberry Finn*" (*TSLL* 33:492–513) Richard Hill takes on the evasion "industry," which he attempts "to sort and classify, with the particular aim of rebutting the negative readings and examining the various agendas that inspire them." It is finally wrong, he concludes, to apply "sophisticated aesthetic, intellectual, or ideological" agendas to the novel, which all of us really "know in our hearts . . . was written for children." This strikes me as both at odds with the facts and unnecessarily condescending—as if one could answer objections to the moral vision of the ending by saying it was only for children after all.

Henry B. Wonham's "The Disembodied Yarnspinner and the Reader of *Adventures of Huckleberry Finn*" (*ALR* 24, i:2–22) is an engaging essay that reminds us how much the complex issue of Huck's place in his culture depends on Twain's sophisticated adaptation of his deadpan mode of storytelling. Huck, on the fringes of the community, longs for "membership in an interpretive community," but he is doomed to failure by his role in a novel where the tacit compact is between implied author and reader, a novel employing "dramatic irony as a way of engaging its reader's interpretive participation according to the pattern of tall tale performance and response." Like "the boys" in the story of Jim Blaine's grandfather's ram, we are in on the joke, while Huck, like the hapless narrator of that tale, is not.

The title of Nadine Schoenburg's "Huck Finn's 'Floating Family' as a Paradigm of American Society" (*Neohelicon* 18:239–56) pretty well summarizes its familiar contention—here improbably updated by reference to Allan Bloom—that Huck and Jim form an alternative family on the raft that epitomizes both positive and negative aspects of American culture. The family and domestic life are surely subjects that deserve more thoughtful treatment in *Huck Finn* and elsewhere in Twain's writings.

Source studies on the novel were few and tended to the obscene or the farfetched. In the more interesting category, James Ellis elaborated on "The Bawdy Humor of THE KING'S CAMELOPARD or THE ROYAL NONESUCH" (*AL* 63:729–35). It appears that the performance was more sublimely off-color even than Wallace Graves maintained in his 1968 article alleging that the skit's original title "The Burning Shame" referred to a lighted candle protruding from the performer's posterior; Eric Partridge's *Dictionary of Slang and Unconventional English* glosses this expression as denoting "a lighted candle stuck into the private parts of a woman," and Ellis argues that the "King's Camelopard" further suggests that the King was equipped "with a gargantuan phallus, perhaps one that could be made to rise and fall in enacting . . . a phallic pantomime that was directed toward an invisible woman's vagina." This hypothesis would certainly account for Huck's reluctance to describe the "capers" and "*shines* that old idiot cut" (and perhaps for the fact that it was a tragedy), but in any event it appears that no one was hiding his light under a bushel. Kelly Anspaugh's "Huck Finn Meets an Old Master" (*MTJ* 27, i[1989]:9–13) is more interesting for its delineation of Twain's burlesque "Titian's Moses" frontispiece in *A Tramp Abroad* than for its claim that Twain revised Huck's "All right, I'll go to Hell" speech with an eye to Giorgione's *Trial of Moses.* E. W. Pitcher's "Huck Finn as Sarah Williams: A Precedent for the Discovery Trick" (*N&Q* 38:324) offers a most tenuous possible source for the gender-discovery trick in chapter 11 in a 1786 (!) Charleston newspaper story about a farmer who unmasks potential thieves dressed as women by tossing objects in their laps. He says "this might have been reprinted years later and come to Twain's attention."

vi Individual Works After 1885

It was a good year for *Connecticut Yankee,* after several years of its playing second fiddle to *Pudd'nhead Wilson.* Martha Banta's "The Boys and the Bosses: Twain's Double Take on Work, Play, and the Democratic Ideal" (*AmLH* 3:487–520) is an essay in the best sense of the word, trying out various ideas (most helpfully, Thorstein Veblen's) about the differences between boys and bosses, primitive and advanced capitalism, the idyllic past and the Taylorized industrial future, all as epitomized by Hank Morgan (although with many a backward glance at *Roughing It* and *Life on the Mississippi*). Twain's own conflicted interests in being both boy and boss make him the natural medium through which to investigate some of these transitions in late-19th-century American society and to interrogate their consequences in our own times. Another fine essay, Bruce Michaelson's "Realism, Romance, and Dynamite: The Quarrel of *A Connecticut Yankee in King Arthur's Court*" (*NEQ* 64:609–32) bypasses the novel's lack of a coherent narrative voice to focus instead on its more constantly present elements; Michaelson finds that in its all-out attack on "every conceivable enemy of personal integrity," the novel is finally at odds with "the demands of narrative as well as with life in any human society." The very inconsistency of the narrative voice is a positive feature, however (its changefulness is interesting, Michaelson aptly observes), and points us toward recognizing the incompatibility that is dramatized between the yearning for complete freedom and the inevitability of determinedness. This incompatibility only finds its release in "one of the most disturbing leitmotifs" in the novel, namely, the presence of gigantic explosions everywhere.

Two essays explore the implications of the novel's representation of radically different ways of perceiving reality in the Middle Ages and the late 19th century. Thomas D. Zlatic's "Language Technologies in *A Connecticut Yankee*" (*NCF* 45:453–77) profitably examines the differences between the "literate mentality" that Hank Morgan embodies to revolutionize King Arthur's Britain and the mainly oral culture that he finds there. The confrontation that ensues had a deep relevance for Twain himself, who was a product of the "oral Midwest" at the same time that he had an early exposure to and eventually a lifelong commitment to print technology. As the novel demonstrates, "neither oral nor literate thinking can capture all the plenitude of reality; each reveals and thematizes certain ways of being in the world while obscuring others." What Zlatic emphasizes is dramatized in a different medium—maps—according to Roger George's " 'The Road Lieth Not Straight': Maps and Mental Models in *A Connecticut Yankee in King Arthur's Court*" (*ATQ* n.s. 5:57–67). George observes that the impossibility of giving or (for Hank) understanding directions in Camelot reveals a split between two ways of viewing the world—the 6th-century Britons have a viewpoint characterized by aimlessness and submissiveness to authority, while Hank embodies the modern, progressive, cause-and-effect model aptly represented by the strip map. He fails to change the 6th-century paradigm, of course, but Twain's own understanding of the "aimlessness" of narrative might seem to ally him with the Arthurians' point of view more than we suspect.

A source-and-theme study that also touches on "language technology" and, incidentally, argues for the artistic coherence of the novel, a point of view rarely taken these days, is Lawrence I. Berkove's "The Gospel According to Hank Morgan's Newspaper" (*EAS* 20:32–42). Berkove uncovers a multitude of references to the Gospel stories of the birth of Christ in the account of the birth of the newspaper—which Hank is the creator of—and sees this underlying imagery as part of Twain's careful exposure of "the changes that transform Hank from a democrat to a despot who would write his own gospel." A final technological twist is given to this year's studies of the novel by Kevin J. Harty's "Camelot Twice Removed: *Knightriders* and the Film Versions of *A Connecticut Yankee in King Arthur's Court*," in a collection edited by Harty, *Cinema Arthuriana: Essays on Arthurian Film* (Garland, pp. 105–20). He provides a survey of early (1920, 1931, 1949) and contemporary film knockoffs, before turning to George Romero's *Knightriders*, a 1981 movie about neo-Arthurian bikers, which resembles Twain's novel only in its dark vision.

The moral instruction offered by "The Man That Corrupted Hadleyburg" was the subject of two articles. Earl F. Briden's "Twainian Pedagogy and the No-Account Lessons of 'Hadleyburg' " (*SSF* 28:125–34) places the story in the context of other works of the period and searches out "the author's meaning" (à la E. D. Hirsch), which is that the townspeople are unable to learn an authentic morality from either theory or practice. A more breathtaking interpretive leap is taken by Joseph Church, in

"Twain's 'The Man That Corrupted Hadleyburg'" (*Expl* 49:94–97), who says that because the 160-pound bag of gold in the story "is approximately the weight of an average man, Twain seems interested in figuratively connecting the stranger and his bag, this latter, I believe, serving as a synecdoche, a part representing the whole man. And because a man's sack, either as a figure or as a part of his figure, signifies his testes, Twain appears jokingly to insinuate that Hadleyburg is sterile."

Pudd'nhead Wilson, after relentless dissection over the last few years for its portrayal of racial themes, received no sustained treatments in 1991. In a wide-ranging discussion of consanguineous and figural kinship in American culture, Marc Shell's "Those Extraordinary Twins" (*ArQ* 47:29–75) inevitably concludes that the Siamese twins and the identical twins in the novel and *Those Extraordinary Twins* "explore the philosophical and grammatical—and eventually also biological and racial—complexities of a binary dialectic involving kind and kin." It takes a long time to crack this nut, though, and the essay is given to rather mystifying leaps of analogical assertion ("What the idea of Jesus' Umbilical Cord is to Christianity the fact of Siamese twins is to Christendom"); still, it is held down by 165 endnotes.

One of the best essays on the late fiction was "Mark Twain's View of the Universe" by Thomas D. Zlatic (*PLL* 27:338–55), which is anything but the sophomoric overview its title might lead one to expect. The "view" in the title is meant to be taken literally, for Zlatic shows how a variety of 19th-century scientific theories that Twain absorbed fostered a privileging of the visual as a means of understanding and presenting reality. The preeminence of vision "harmonizes with a spatialization of time that pictures life as a meaningless unfolding of pre-determined and eternally-existing patterns of physical states that are totally controlled by physical mechanics." Zlatic argues convincingly that this deadening model virtually overwhelmed Twain's late fiction in the form of a naive scientific literalism that "objectifies, quantifies, reifies, and spatializes time and mental process so that acts become invariable in size and importance; time is reduced to points in a line; novelty and originality are made impossible; and becoming is defined as an illusion."

Other treatments of late works include "Mark Twain's Eden/Flood Parable: 'The Autobiography of Eve'" (*ALR* 24, i:23–38), an ambitious effort by Howard G. Baetzhold, Joseph B. McCullough, and Donald Malcolm to reconstruct the working manuscripts of the "Autobiography of Eve," which was misdated and imperfectly edited by Bernard De Voto as "Papers of the Adam Family" in *Letters from the Earth.* The reconstructed text foregrounds Twain's intention to construct a parable of his own times, and the authors conclude that "ultimately a recognition of the original form of the 'Autobiography of Eve' is mandatory for a complete assessment of the development of these materials. The original concept, presented as a textual 'variant,' has literary merit in its own right and represents Mark Twain's most ambitious attempt to use a feminine first-person narrator." Fleda Brown Jackson's "Reconciliation and Optimism in Twain's 'Mysterious Stranger' Manuscripts" (*CLAJ* 35:57–71) continues a trend of recent years of detecting positive elements in Twain's last major work of fiction. She traces changes in image patterns in the three versions of the story and finds a movement toward the reconciliation of some obdurate opposites in "No. 44," where the protagonist is able to transcend inherited polarities through the act of creation and where productive human relationships are possible. In "The Fantastic Record of a Maniac: 'King Leopold's Soliloquy' Revisited" (*An American Empire,* pp. 237–43), Daniel Royot sketches the historical background and artistic techniques of Twain's most scathing piece of anti-imperialist satire. Finally, Jim Zwick addresses a minor but important textual problem in "Who Wrote the Couplet? Textual Variants in Mark Twain's 'Salutation to the Twentieth Century' " (*MTJ* 27, i[1989]:34–39), concluding that Twain did play a role in the publication of the "Salutation" as a printed card distributed by the New England Anti-Imperialist League, and probably did write the couplet which appears separately on the bottom of the card: "Give her the glass; it may from error free her/When she shall see herself as others see her."

Georgia State University

7 Henry James

Sarah B. Daugherty

My predecessor in writing this chapter, Richard A. Hocks, provides me with an excellent point of departure. In "The Several Canons of Henry James" (*ALR* 23, iii:68–81) he outlines the basic patterns of James criticism since the early 1980s, when James became the object of postmodern theory. Significant trends include the deemphasis of formalist masterworks, a new interest in the problem novels, revisionist readings of familiar texts (notably *The Wings of the Dove* and *The Golden Bowl*), and increased attention to nonfictional writings. I would add that *The Portrait of a Lady* and *The Ambassadors,* which initially failed to attract the theorists, are now being "rebaptized" into the new dispensation. Moreover, even after a decade of revisionism there is still a lively debate between the traditionalists and the critics of Hocks's "second wave." The former (R. W. B. Lewis, Millicent Bell) draw on the insights of the revisionists but ultimately regard James as an embattled defender of selfhood; the latter (Ross Posnock, Jeanne Reesman) view him as a postmodern precursor, a challenger of centered subjectivity and the politics of single design. For critics of both camps, and for would-be mediators (Susan Griffin), William James continues to be a key figure: a source of Henry's ideas, yet his personal and intellectual rival. "The Turn of the Screw," however, is less often treated as the key Jamesian text—a development for which many of us are grateful. A number of essays focus instead on the tales of male protagonists, the "poor gentlemen" who may be projections of their creator or perhaps the targets of his irony.

i Reference Works, Biographical Studies

Judith E. Funston's *Henry James: A Reference Guide, 1975–1987* (Hall) will be welcomed as a companion to the earlier bibliographies by Linda

Taylor (covering criticism from 1866 through 1916), Kristin McColgan (1917–59), and Dorothy Scura (1960–74). Funston indexes more than 2,300 items, including dissertations, essays in periodicals omitted by MLA, and significant book reviews (such as those of Leon Edel's biography and his *Selected Letters*). The descriptive annotations are helpful and generally accurate, despite occasional misprints.

Teachers of James's fiction will be aided by three short books addressed primarily to undergraduates and nonspecialists. George Bishop's *Henry James: Life, Work, and Criticism* (York) includes a carefully selected bibliography of secondary sources. Judith Woolf's *Henry James: The Major Novels* (Cambridge) offers dogmatic but witty commentary in the tradition of F. R. Leavis. A contemporary introduction, designed for instructors who highlight the controversies provoked by James's fiction, is David Kirby's The Portrait of a Lady *and* The Turn of the Screw: *Henry James and Melodrama* (Macmillan Education). As his subtitle indicates, Kirby favors the views of Jacques Barzun and Peter Brooks; but he does justice to the New Critics and their postmodern successors, directing students to the most important participants in "the critics' debate."

The major biographical study of the year is R. W. B. Lewis's *The Jameses: A Family Narrative* (Farrar). This lengthy but readable history draws on a variety of sources: biographies from F. O. Matthiessen's *The James Family* through Jean Strouse's *Alice James,* unpublished material in the archives at Houghton Library, and interviews with the family's descendants (whose fortunes are chronicled in an appendix). Although Lewis details the problems besetting his subjects—the bouts of depression and hypochondria suffered by William and Henry, Alice's long decline, Wilky's financial woes, and Bob's descent into alcoholism—he is diffident in offering psychological interpretations; and specialist readers may prefer a more analytical approach. Yet Lewis's account corrects and modifies the Freudian readings of Leon Edel. Mary Walsh James may well have been "the healthiest member of the family," not the prototype of the devouring mothers often portrayed in Henry's fiction. And in comparison with his siblings, Henry himself emerges as a successful, and relatively sane, professional writer.

As do many recent scholars, Lewis highlights the parallels between Henry and William, especially in relation to Henry Senior. Early in their careers, the sons asserted the importance of will as a protest against the paternal ideal of self-surrender; yet *The Wings of the Dove* and *The*

Varieties of Religious Experience are belated tributes to the father's spirituality. But whereas Henry was generous in his acknowledgment of William, William was beset by jealousy of the brother whom he wrongly characterized as "shallower and vainer."

Several essays detail further chapters of Jamesian biography. In "Henry James, Sr., in the Late 1830s" (*NEQ* 64:46–81) Alfred Habegger documents the father's adherence to the doctrines of Robert Sandeman, whose belief in justification by faith afforded escape from the "strenuous quest for righteousness." Hence the paradox that later influenced the novelist son: "only that which is secular and nonreligious can put forth any claim to be truly spiritual." Bonney MacDonald's "'Sympathetic Exaggerations of Fact': Henry James's Early Years" (*HJR* 12:175–80) explores the writer's self-fashioning in the 1870s, relating this process to Burton Bledstein's paradigms in *The Culture of Professionalism.* Carole Kessner in "The Emma Lazarus-Henry James Connection: Eight Letters" (*AmLH* 3:46–62) reproduces correspondence from the 1880s, demonstrating that James was far more sympathetic with Jews of his own social class than with the arriviste immigrants. Beverly Haviland in "Civilization and Its Contents: Henry James's Return to New York, 1904" (*HJR* 12:166–74) offers photographs of monuments referred to in *The American Scene,* either as exemplars of "false signs" or as illustrations of the vital connection between art and culture. Alan G. James's "A Memorable Naturalization: How Henry James Became a British Subject and Lost His United States Citizenship" (*HJR* 12:55–68) includes a photocopy of the novelist's "humble memorial" to the British government.

ii Sources, Influences, Parallels

The leading scholar of James's sources, Adeline R. Tintner, has published yet another book, *The Cosmopolitan World of Henry James: An Intertextual Study* (LSU). It focuses on James's response to writers at the turn of the century, such as Oscar Wilde, Alphonse Daudet, and Gabriele D'Annunzio—sophisticates whose jaded outlook was hostile to his own dream of a more generous, spiritualized cosmopolitanism. In particular, he deplored their preoccupation with concealed sexual attachments; hence, for example, *The Sacred Fount* parodies fashionable "houseparty novels" instead of merely exemplifying the genre. Tintner's introduction notes the limits of her methodology: given James's transmutations of his material, the quest for particular sources is not always fruitful. And with some exceptions, James's minor stories contain more direct allusions to their sources than do the major texts.

Two essays document James's enduring fascination with Shakespeare. Adrian Poole in "Henry James, War and Witchcraft" (*EIC* 41:291–307) argues for the influence of contemporary performances of *Othello,* a play to which James often alluded in connection with issues of manliness. He was intrigued by the figure of the soldier charming spectators through his physical presence and the power of his bewitching tales. In "The Master Lesson: James Reading Shakespeare" (*HJR* 12:69–83) Nina Schwartz presents a Lacanian analysis of the novelist's 1907 essay on *The Tempest.* For James and his characters, Shakespeare's lesson was that a secret invests its bearer with authorial control—but only if the "master" accepts the determining power of mystery and the absence of final authority.

iii Critical Books

Four major studies offer differing perspectives on a central issue for Jamesians. Is the author best understood as a champion of the free individual, a defender of "the liberty of the subject" against environmentalist theories of character? Or did James challenge the idealists' belief in selfhood, thus anticipating the "politics of nonidentity" practiced by today's cultural materialists? The former view is strongly presented in Millicent Bell's *Meaning in Henry James* (Harvard). As Bell explains, James could hardly escape the influence of Balzac and Zola; hence *The Bostonians* and *The Princess Casamassima* exemplify "the determinate plot," and hence even Milly Theale bears some uncomfortable resemblances to her rival Kate Croy, the heir of the naturalist tradition. Nonetheless, argues Bell, "James's deepest sympathies lay with those characters who resisted entrapment by cultural expectations—his idealistic spirits like Isabel, his marriage renouncers like Fleda Vetch, his largely silent and detached witnesses to life like Strether and the generous Maisie." Indeed, adds Bell, "the explosive principle" within James's fiction, which is responsible for the indeterminacy so often admired by postmodern critics, arises from the resistance of these characters to the design of conventional plots. Bell also notes the price James paid for his aesthetic, in that his figures often fail to achieve the "definition which character gains from its manifestation in choice." These arguments are familiar; yet in my view Bell's account of James's intentions—his probable readings of texts and contexts—remains more persuasive than the revisionists' efforts to portray him as a member of their own school.

Those who disagree will turn to Ross Posnock's *The Trial of Curiosity: Henry James, William James, and the Challenge of Modernity* (Oxford). And even traditionalists will welcome a new interpretation of James supported by wide-ranging, original scholarship. Like Bell, Posnock regards James as a rebel against convention—yet one who preferred "immersion" to idealism, who believed that "the self is not itself alone but defined by what is outside it," and who created such characters as Strether "less to legitimate and authorize centered subjectivity than to reveal its compromised status and obliviousness to its own solipsism." Bell's James looks backward to the Romantics; Posnock's looks forward to the modernists, affiliating himself "with the new century and its endless possibilities."

The advantage of Posnock's approach is that it does, as he maintains, disclose the intellectual writer often obscured by the canonizers. Because Posnock takes James seriously as a cultural critic, he stresses the continuity between *The American Scene* and the fiction, treating the period from 1904 through 1916 as a second "major phase" of critique and autobiography. Posnock also draws connections between James and the modernists who preceded and followed him: Walt Whitman, George Santayana, Henri Bergson, John Dewey, Walter Benjamin, Theodor Adorno, Richard Rorty, and many others with whom the novelist is seldom compared. As for William James, Posnock regards him as a more conservative, and less healthy-minded, critic than Henry. The younger brother reveled in curiosity, whereas the elder suffered from an "abiding psychic rigidity." William was too much the philosopher *of* will to appreciate Henry's vision of freedom *from* will.

James's modernist context is also the subject of Jeanne Campbell Reesman's *American Designs: The Late Novels of James and Faulkner.* Granted, says Reesman, the protagonists of these narratives are powerful individualists tempted to commit "the sin of design" on others; yet the novels themselves demand a "community of interpretations," thus anticipating the hermeneutics of Richard Rorty and Mikhail Bakhtin. *The Ambassadors,* on this view, becomes the narrative of Strether's rejection of "certainty of vision" in favor of "dialogic knowledge," while *The Golden Bowl* celebrates Maggie's attainment of intersubjectivity. Reesman herself admits that these readings may provoke skepticism. Maria Gostrey, after all, better embodies "communal values" than does the solitary Strether, and the end of *The Golden Bowl* presents a powerful image of the gap between the Prince and the Princess, even as they embrace. Skeptics may also note the contrasts between James, the deracinated expatriate, and the lifelong resident of Oxford, Mississippi, for whom "community" was more than an ideal. But Reesman draws some illuminating parallels, showing how the narrative techniques of both James and Faulkner require collaboration from readers.

Susan M. Griffin's *The Historical Eye: The Texture of the Visual in Late James* (Northeastern) is the most specialized of this year's James books. But Griffin's topic—the connection between Henry's fiction and William's functionalist psychology—affords her a critical vantage point on the larger issue of the Jameses and selfhood. For the functionalists, the self was neither a fixed entity (as the associationists had argued) nor a tabula rasa at the mercy of its environment. Rather, the functionalists believed in an active, reciprocal relationship between self and world, the remnants of free will being "located in moments of attentive perception." Whereas to Reesman the word "interest" has a negative connotation (it "usually leads to tampering with someone else's freedom"), Griffin discerns the more positive results of Strether's power to shape his world "through active, interested seeing." In addition to analyses of *The Ambassadors* and *The Golden Bowl*, Griffin's book offers chapters on *The American Scene*, "Winchelsea, Rye, and 'Denis Duval,'" and "Within the Rim." The later James was less fortunate than Strether or Maggie in that his identity was threatened by historical changes making it increasingly difficult for him to construct "bridges between past and present." Ultimately, as the dying James confused himself with Napoleon, his sense of boundaries dissolved. Griffin reminds us, then, of the tragedy of nonidentity—a tragedy downplayed by Posnock as he celebrates the advent of modernity.

iv Criticism: General Essays

Three major essays outline James's strategies for defining and defending his ambiguous masculinity. In "The Feminine Orphan and the Emergent Master: Self-Realization in Henry James" (*HJR* 12:20–54) William Veeder shows that the novelist adopted twin personae—the orphan and the American girl—as a defense against his fear of castration by a hostile family and an equally hostile culture. *The Portrait of a Lady*, says Veeder, is a work of disguised autobiography, flawed because its "manifest commitment to life is subverted by a latent espousal of orphanhood." But *The Ambassadors* marks the end of "the therapy phase"; *The Wings of the Dove* and *The Golden Bowl* both manifest James's determination not to escape into "his cherished position of negated safety." Finally, in the autobiographical volumes, "the orphan figure of fantasy steps forth undisguised as Isabel or Strether or Densher," though James "stops short of full understanding."

David McWhirter in "Restaging the Hurt: Henry James and the Artist as Masochist" (*TSLL* 33:464–91) demonstrates that *The Tragic Muse* is likewise autobiographical. The passive-aggressive behavior of Nick Dormer resembles that of his creator, for whom "the liberation of and into aesthetic desire [was] effected by a castrating father." But McWhirter agrees with Veeder that James achieved at least partial self-awareness, to the point that his later novels no longer reenact his oedipal drama.

"Henry James, George Sand, and the Suspense of Masculinity" (*PMLA* 106:515–28) by Leland S. Person, Jr., argues that the ambiguously gendered French writer posed a threat to James but also suggested a means of countering the threat. Inspired by her example, James experimented with "a pluralized masculinity"—notably in *The Ambassadors*—and thus outflanked the feminists. (As Strether, his manhood newly defined, pities the sobbing Madame de Vionnet, James puts women in their place.)

Several critics offer divergent views of James's authorial role, especially in the prefaces to the New York Edition. To Sara Blair in "Henry James and the Paradox of Literary Mastery" (*P&L* 15:89–102) the prefaces illustrate James's investment in "coercive forms of power," since they rely on the metaphysics of presence often undercut by the fiction. But David McWhirter's "(Re)Presenting Henry James: Authority and Intertextuality in the New York Edition" (*HJR* 12:137–41) argues that James brought together a number of " 'voices' (the original texts, the revisions, the prefaces, the frontispieces, even, perhaps, the eloquent silence of the excluded novels and tales) . . . without insisting that they converge in any architectural or monumental completeness." In "The Seeds of James's Grand Monument: Or, When Growing Becomes Building" (*HJR* 12:255–70) O. Alan Weltzien notes the conflict between inorganic metaphors of architecture and organic metaphors of growth in the prefaces, suggesting that James was more aware of contradiction than were such later formalist critics as R. P. Blackmur.

Amy Clampitt in "A Poet's Henry James" (*SWR* 76:9–21) explains why the author's example is still important to contemporary writers: the stillness at the center of his works results from his awareness of complexity, an awareness counter to the simplifying tendencies of American life.

v Criticism: Individual Novels

For several critics, *Roderick Hudson* is a key to James's early philosophy and biography. Chris Brown in "The Discourse of the Alps in *Roderick Hudson*" (*ELWIU* 18:235–42) notes that James undermined his culture's faith in environmental cures. His skepticism may have been influenced by John Ruskin's *Modern Painters,* with its chapters on "The Mountain Gloom" as well as "The Mountain Glory." Linda M. Lohn's " 'An Abyss of Abysses': Will, Morality, and Artistic Imagination in James's *Roderick Hudson*" (*HJR* 12:93–100) reminds us once again of the importance of William James. Though William disliked the novel, it illustrates his theory that an "explosive will"—one that ceases to relate to the world of outside objects—dooms the sufferer to self-absorption and eventual collapse. In "Henry James's *Roderick Hudson:* A Convergence of Family Stories" (*HJR* 12:199–211) Brad S. Born shows how the novelist distanced himself from his rival and older brother by drawing on their father's fables of "promising youth ending badly." The fictional Roderick reenacts William's early abandonment of an artistic career—a choice that "facilitated Henry's individuation." Sheila Teahan's "Hawthorne, James, and the Fall of Allegory in *Roderick Hudson*" (*HJR* 12:158–62) demonstrates that the elder romancer was yet another rival. Roderick, as allegorist, plays out the role of James's doomed precursor; but since this "fall" is staged in allegorical terms, James inevitably imitates Hawthorne and underscores his own belatedness.

The Portrait of a Lady has also received attention from critics, chiefly from those concerned with the interplay of self-determination and social determination. Robert Shulman's chapter "Realism" in the *Columbia History of the American Novel* (pp. 160–88) treats *Portrait* as an exemplary text: "James reveals that the market society has infiltrated the deepest recesses of the self." *Portrait* is likewise the subject of a chapter in Marilyn R. Chandler's *Dwelling in the Text.* For Chandler, the central irony is that Isabel's physical and social confinement increases even as her worldly vision widens; with only the simple American home as the basis for comparison, she has no means of judging the estates that are offered to her. "James's Pyrotechnic Display: The Book in Isabel's Portrait" (*HJR* 12:146–53) by Sharon Baris focuses on the equivocal image of Isabel holding a book yet gazing away from its pages. On one view, she is a self-reliant interpreter, or even a theorist disregarding the existence of a text; yet she also resembles the Madonna of Italian paintings, "a Lady whose text has been so famously and authoritatively given." A second essay by Baris, "Gender, Judgment, and Presumptuous Readers: The Role of Daniel in *The Portrait of a Lady*" (*HJR* 12:212–30), notes that Isabel (like Shakespeare's heroines) insists on being her own judge. But since she betrays herself in the process, she learns to question the myth of judgment and control. Emily Miller Budick in "James's Portrait of Female Skepticism" (*HJR* 12:154–58) contends that Isabel, like Hawthorne's Hester, perceives the injustice of patriarchal society while signaling her acceptance of life through her return to the daughter figure, Pansy. Yet James also follows Hawthorne, says Budick, by casting his heroine's skepticism "in decidedly male terms."

James's own lack of political commitment is the topic of Carola Kaplan's "The Spectre of Nationality in Henry James' *The Bostonians* and Joseph Conrad's *Under Western Eyes*," pp. 37–54 in David Bevan, ed., *Literature and Exile* (Rodopi, 1990). To justify their expatriation, James and Conrad portrayed their revolutionaries as insincere neurotics, in the process rejecting "the idea of radical social transformation brought about by the efforts of women."

Linda M. Lohn's "The Neurasthenic Dilemma: Mental Dis-ease and Epistemology in James's *The Princess Casamassima*" (*ATQ* n.s. 5:125–35) focuses on the figure of the invalid Rose Muniment—a character partly based on Alice James. But once again, the novelist's revision of reality suggests his masculine bias; whereas the real Alice tried to "balance the social with the solipsistic," the fictional Rose suffers from "contractions in the field of consciousness" (another diagnosis courtesy of William James).

Several studies of the later novels focus on the problematic relationship between language and value. "The Word and the Self in *The Ambassadors*" (*Style* 25:89–103) by Michael Wutz traces Strether's evolving conception of the written word. As editor of the *Woollett Review*, he uses it to encode his identity; but when his experience reveals the deceptive nature of writing, he acknowledges "the insufficiency of such a purely textual definition of selfhood."

An essay by Onno Oerlemans, "Literary Value and *The Wings of the*

Dove" (*ESC* 17:177–96), offers a revisionist reading of the novel—one in which Kate Croy becomes the "exemplary character," able to balance her own intrinsic worth and the shifting values of the marketplace.

John Alberti's "The Economics of Love: The Production of Value in *The Golden Bowl*" (*HJR* 12:9–19) takes issue with conventional readings based on an assumed dichotomy between love and money. For James, as for Clifford Geertz, says Alberti, the important point is "to understand how value systems are human creations"—a lesson Maggie learns as she becomes an active negotiator. Cheryl B. Torsney's "Specula(riza)tion in *The Golden Bowl*" (*HJR* 12:141–46) draws on the theories of Luce Irigaray to analyze the roles played by Maggie. Initially she is "the speculum of her father's desire" for Amerigo; but she becomes a speculator, disrupting the "homosocial exchange" between Adam and the Prince and consigning Charlotte to the specular position.

vi Criticism: Tales

In "Henry James's 'De Grey': The Gothic as Camouflage of the Medical" (*MLS* 21, ii:36–44) Gerard M. Sweeney suggests that the story concerns a sexually transmitted disease, probably syphilis. (Readers may recall Carol Bensick's similar explication of Hawthorne's "Rappaccini's Daughter.")

Lynn Wardley's "Reassembling Daisy Miller" (*AmLH* 3:232–54) examines the cultural context of the tale and explains why Daisy is so threatening to Winterbourne. Nineteenth-century psychologists such as Stanley Hall regarded female adolescence as a "neo-atavistic stage," one in which masculine and feminine tendencies "struggle for prepotency." ("You're a queer mixture," he tells her.) "Daisy Miller's Parasol" (*SSF* 27 [1990]:591–601) by Philip Page notes that this object is an emblem not only of plot but of narrative form, since readers are denied access to Daisy's consciousness.

As mentioned, the stories with male protagonists—especially writers and artists—have received considerable attention. A good general study is Peter Barry's "Embarrassments and Predicaments: Patterns of Interaction in James's Writer-Tales" (*OL* 46:87–104). Applying structuralist methodology to such texts as "The Author of Beltraffio," "The Middle Years," "The Death of the Lion," and "The Figure in the Carpet," Barry concludes that James affirms the value of friendship, challenging the notion that some secret endows narratives with formal perfection. For

James and his acolyte-narrators, "there is always something outside the text." In "The Dangers of Fiction: Henry James's 'The Lesson of the Master' " (*SSF* 27 [1990]:81–88) Craig A. Milliman reaches a parallel conclusion. According to this ironic reading, Paul Overt is not the artist-hero but "the bewildered aesthete" whom St. George manipulates and baffles.

Another ironic interpretation is offered by Bruce Henricksen in " 'The Real Thing': Criticism and the Ethical Turn" (*PLL* 27:473–95). Although this tale "deconstructs the opposition between culture and society," its "ethically crippled narrator" fails to critique his own potboilers; and his "uncritical reading of the Monarchs as the real thing illustrates Roland Barthes's notion that social myths exist as 'alibis' that cause the cultural to appear to be natural." Susan Bazargan in "Representation and Ideology in 'The Real Thing' " (*HJR* 12:133–37) also posits a distance between James and the artist-narrator, adding that the story adumbrates the postmodern "crisis of representation" described by Fredric Jameson.

The homoerotic subtext of "The Pupil" is a topic of Michael Moon's "A Small Boy and Others: Sexual Disorientation in Henry James, Kenneth Anger, and David Lynch" (*Comparative American Identities,* pp. 140–56). This essay among others raises the issue of how far critics should proceed in their quest for "perverse energies." When Mrs. Moreen draws on her "soiled suede gloves," does she invite Pemberton (even subliminally) to handle a "dirty undressed kid"?

"A Medical Source for *The Turn of the Screw*" (*SAF* 19:217–20) by William J. Scheick suggests that the Jameses were probably familiar with the theories of Andrew Combe, especially given their concern over Alice's mental health. Combe's popular textbooks emphasized women's susceptibility to hallucinations. Two linguistic studies demonstrate why "The Turn of the Screw" remains undecidable: "Possible-Worlds Semantics, Frame Text, Insert Text, and Unreliable Narration: The Case of *The Turn of the Screw*" (*Style* 25:42–70) by José Antonio Álvarez Amorós; and "Ghostly Ambiguity: Presuppositional Constructions in *The Turn of the Screw*" (*Style* 25:71–88) by Helen Aristar Dry and Susan Kucinkas.

For psychological critics, "The Beast in the Jungle" has become a crucial text. William James makes yet another appearance in H. Lewis Ulman's "A Possible Lair: 'The Tigers in India' and 'The Beast in the Jungle' " (HJR 12:1–8). In an 1894 essay William had distinguished between our "intuitive knowledge" of objects encountered directly and our "representative knowledge" of absent objects. Since Marcher's mental images obscure his "vision" of the present world, Henry James not only dramatizes his brother's theories but explores complications that William had neglected.

"The Beast in the Jungle" is also the subject of a chapter in James M. Mellard's *Using Lacan, Reading Fiction* (Illinois). Throughout most of his life Marcher repeats the structure of Lacan's mirror stage, with May playing the role of the other—or mother—who constitutes his identity. But when he encounters the stranger at May's tomb, he belatedly faces Symbolic authority. Fortunately, Mellard's persuasive reading is more accessible than the theoretical discussion preceding it. A comparatively sympathetic view of Marcher is taken by Herbert Perluck in "The Dramatics of the Unspoken and Unspeakable in James's 'The Beast in the Jungle' " (*HJR* 12:231–54). If we attend to the narrative's silences and contradictions, argues Perluck, we may perceive Marcher not as an allegorical figure but as a tragic character who questions his right to love and to ask for love in return.

Esther Rashkin's "A Spectacle of Haunting: James's *The Jolly Corner*" (*OLR* 12 [1990]:69–100) presents another revisionist reading notable for its ingenuity. According to Rashkin, Brydon is not merely a divided consciousness but a character under occupation by several ghostly identities—especially that of his cuckolded grandfather, who shrinks from the sight of his illegitimate heir. Once more, skeptics may be reluctant to accompany the critic on her search for subtexts. (That the usurper is Brydon's uncle, says Rashkin, can be inferred from his wearing a monocle—a pun on *mon oncle.*)

"Revising Henry James: Reading the Spaces of *The Aspern Papers*" (*AL* 63:263–78) by Ellen Brown examines not only the preface and frontispiece to the New York Edition but also the changes made by James in the text of the novella (first published in 1888). Overall, James's revisions increase his authorial control, though in his preface he "refuses to give us too much guidance on the thematics of his fiction."

vii Conference Proceedings

The spring issue of *The Henry James Review* (12, ii) is largely devoted to papers presented at recent conferences and special events: the 1988 Dallas premiere of Dominick Argento's opera *The Aspern Papers* and the 1989 and 1990 James Society sessions at the MLA conventions in Washington, D.C., and Chicago. I have summarized the most important of these papers under the appropriate headings. Given the vitality of James scholarship, we may look forward to the sesquicentennial events in 1993.

Wichita State University

8 Pound and Eliot

George Kearns and Cleo McNelly Kearns

A number of outstanding full-length studies of Pound appeared in 1991—those by Miyake, Rainey, Redman, and Dasenbrock, noted below—as well as articles based on new information concerning sources and affinities. No one will be surprised to hear that Pound's ideology, especially his fascism overt or covert, is an overriding concern. With the exception of Alexander Schmitz's marvelous piece on the *Cantos* as music, there is little interest in poetics per se or in readings of the poetry apart from sources and ideology (if there is an "apart"). The question of whether the *Cantos* have unity is revived, however. If the year was particularly rich for Pound, it was somewhat less so for Eliot. A significant work that gives equal treatment to the two poets is Michael North's *The Political Aesthetic of Yeats, Eliot, and Pound.* Other notable books on Eliot include J. P. Riquelme's intelligent *Harmony of Dissonance,* Steve Ellis's fresh and provocative *The English Eliot,* and Paul Murray's solid and informed *Eliot and Mysticism.* An anthology, ed. Ronald Bush, collects essays presented in 1988 as conference papers. The notes on Pound are by G.K., those on Eliot by C.M.K.

i Pound

a. Text, Biography, and Bibliography An unpublished essay by Pound, "Affirmations VI: The 'Image' and the Japanese Classical Stage," appears in the *Princeton University Library Chronicle* (53:17–29). The piece appears to have been intended for the "Affirmations" series in *The New Age* in 1915. The typescript is one of 17 items composing an important collection of papers now at Princeton. Most are drafts and notebooks by Pound and/or Fenollosa relating to Japanese nō, but one is described as

10 pages of holograph notes that look "like a draft of a portion of a *Cantos*-like poem." There is an introductory note on the acquisition by A. Walton Litz (pp. 9–11), as well as a note and briefly annotated checklist by Earl Miner (pp. 12–16).

Volker Bischoff has compiled an extraordinarily thorough bibliography (5,390 entries) of *Ezra Pound Criticism, 1905–1985: A Chronological Listing of Publications in English* (Marburg). Dissertations are included, as are some fairly ephemeral reviews, memoirs, letters to the editor, in fact almost any publication that discusses Pound, even where the title might not suggest a text including references to the poet. Entries are alphabetical by year; books and even book reviews are accompanied by a list of the reviews and comments they occasioned. Bischoff invites readers to send him additions and corrections for a projected second edition to include a detailed subject index.

There is not much in the way of biography per se, although there is much about Pound's intellectual biography in the books and articles discussed below. Of some interest is Jerome Kavka, M.D., "Ezra Pound's Personal History: A Transcript, 1946" (*Paideuma* 20, i–ii:143–85). Kavka, the young psychiatrist to whom Pound was assigned as patient in late 1945, provides transcripts of four interviews from January 1946. They are painful reading: the semiorganized, at times extremely paratactic thoughts of an abject, confused, deeply fatigued man who "burst a mainspring in Pisa," yet who can still call himself an "incurable optimist." The transcripts are accompanied by psychiatric interpretations unlikely to increase regard for that science. At one point, for example, Pound mentions birds he hears chirping outside. Shortly after, he expresses a wish to be moved from the ward in which he was first placed. The doctor's view: "He referred to the birds and to his wish to get out of the confined ward to a freer area. This, to some extent, was a reflection of a regressed state of grandiosity. . . . Was this similar to the grandiosity of Leonardo da Vinci, who in the marketplace purchased caged birds and set them free?"

In "Letters From the 'Foreign Correspondent': Ezra Pound to Alice Corbin Henderson" (*Paideuma* 20, i–ii:187–92) Ira B. Nadel succinctly describes the extensive correspondence between Pound and the assistant editor of *Poetry,* herself an avant-garde poet whose work Pound critiqued and published. Most of the letters, almost all from Pound to Henderson, date from 1912–17, but they continue through 1949. They are valuable not only for details of his career, but because his respect for Henderson, "the only intelligent element (in that frying pan) [of *Poetry*]," invoked what Nadel describes as "a style unflagging in its intensity and strength," dealing with a wide range of subjects.

b. General Studies Reed Way Dasenbrock's *Imitating the Italians: Wyatt, Spenser, Synge, Pound, Joyce* (Hopkins) is an imaginatively researched study, with endnotes often as interesting as the text. Dasenbrock argues that the Victorian understanding of Italy for Pound has been overestimated, as has an aestheticized image "emphasizing [Pound's] interest in Italian art over his interest in Italian politics and social thought." A better understanding of Pound's "Italy" can help us understand his turn toward Italian Fascism. Three chapters focus on Pound's affinities with Leopardi, Machiavelli, and Dante. The interest in Leopardi, which was to diminish in time, is seen in parallels between the Italian poet's cry for a "resorgiamento" and Pound's early calls for an American Renaissance; Leopardi's collections, first *Canzoni,* later *Canti,* suggest formal imitation deeper than the coincidence of titles, *Canti/Cantos.* Chapter 8, "Pound's Machiavellian Moment," drawing on the work of J. G. A. Pocock, explores political themes in Renaissance humanism and the relations between Machiavelli's *Discorsi* and the "free-floating, ideologically eclectic nature of Pound's political thinking." The chapter is of particular interest in regard to Pound's readings of Jefferson and John Adams, and of the *Cantos'* turn from the former to the latter. Chapter 9, "Ezra Pound, the Last Ghibelline," reminds us that Dante was the author of *De Monarchia* and other political writings. Of contrasting theories of imitation—transformation and replication—Pound knew well, Dasenbrock suggests, that transformation was needed in his use of the *Commedia;* but he did not see the folly of following the alternative humanist theory—replication—in politics. Mussolini, in short, was no Dantescan emperor.

Pound as an eclectic, somewhat unstable Ghibelline is recognized as well in Tim Redman's admirably thorough account of his economic-political career, *Ezra Pound and Italian Fascism* (Cambridge). Indeed, in one of the many quotations from unpublished archival sources that Redman offers, Pound calls *Jefferson and/or Mussolini* "MY de Monarchia." Redman's title does not suggest his book's extensive exposition and historicization of the economic proposals that lead into and accompany Pound's involvement with Mussolini. Three chapters provide—to my knowledge—the best treatments we have of what Pound took from his associations with Orage and the *New Age,* Douglas, and, later, Gesell.

The remaining chapters chronologically cover his relations with Italian Fascism through the '30s, the war, and the final phase, "The Republic of Salò and Left-Wing Fascism." The index provides a useful list of references to the *Cantos.* Redman is aware of the range of judgments surrounding Pound's economics and politics; his account is nuanced and historically situated. Interpretive comments are generally measured and just, although inevitably they will be controversial. ("The theoretical bases for Pound's ideas about economics [are] on the whole sound, despite their at times eccentric formulation.") This is as complete a *record* as we are likely to have.

Complete, of course, is never complete. Additional traces of Fascist-related ideology in the *Cantos* are uncovered by the ingenious Lawrence S. Rainey in *Ezra Pound and the Monument of Culture: Text, History, and the Malatesta Cantos* (Chicago). A brilliant book: the most *divertente* work on Pound since *The Pound Era* and equally resistant to adequate characterization in a brief comment. It is two books in one, although the two are intertwined. This is Rainey's theoretical argument—a contribution to current debates in textual criticism—in behalf of "transmission" (of documents, "fact," image, ideology) as the missing ingredient in most criticism, which emphasizes production and reception. I shall not comment here on the theory, stimulating as it is. Rainey, however, has little use for theory in the abstract, preferring to work through "thick description," in this case of the transmissions that surround the production and reception of the Malatesta cantos. Through his prodigious research we may see them as overdetermined within a curious three-dimensional maze of Renaissance, 19th-century, and present-day falsification, credulity, misquotation, and mistranslation, as well as willful, interested, careless, unconscious, or creative lapses of attention. Quite an indictment of ways in which students of Pound, including the present writer, have replicated assumptions as if they were historical verities. How and why was Malatesta's Tempio constructed (not by Sigismondo) as a *tempio d'amore* to Isotta? Why has it so often been said that his wife, Polissena, was murdered by him—and how did an ideology of vitalism make Pound decide that she simply "died"? Why have the intertwined letters "I" and "S" been read not as an emblem of Sigismundo alone, but as a sign of eternal romantic union? "Here the sign takes on extraordinary weight, epitomizing the entire project of *The Cantos*—to discern and write the counter-history of secular vitalist spirituality, as well as to place that spirituality at the core of a new ethical culture in the twentieth century." An appendix includes the principal source of Canto 73.

While extended essays on Pound in recent years have seldom neglected the political dimensions of his poetics, or vice versa, no study has been more complex and nuanced than Michael North's *The Political Aesthetic of Yeats, Eliot, and Pound* (Cambridge). Where Redman's book on Pound and Italian Fascism is more a thorough chronicle, North's is more theoretical; indeed, his text bristles with such names as Adorno, de Man, Dilthey, Hegel, Gadamer, and Lukács. North's project, successfully managed, is to avoid "the either-or . . . where aesthetic modernism touches modern politics in general." Neither apologist nor prosecutor, North, following Raymond Williams, sees modernism's attack on industrial capitalism and liberal democracy, whether conservative or Marxist, as sharing a common enemy in liberalism. Debates over the nature of historiography and poetics are thoroughly explored. "Just as Eliot and Yeats were . . . too conservative to become fascists, Pound became one precisely because he was a modernist and because he needed a system that promised to back modernism with a strong set of eternal values that would somehow leave modernism untouched." Yet "Pound could not remain interested in any program because his politics were essentially anti-programmatic." When there have been so many reductive treatments of Pound's politics, or merely self-congratulatory rhetoric, North's rigor and complexity are welcome. This is now the first work to which I would send a student interested in Poundian politics—indeed, in modernism and politics in general.

"A love affair comprehends exasperation along with exaltation," says Donald Davie in a foreword to *Studies in Ezra Pound* (Carcanet). The collection includes the seminal *Poet as Sculptor* (1964) and 16 articles, notes, and reviews through a final (?) "More on the Muddle of *Thrones*" (1990)—all or most of Davie's writings on Pound, with the exception of the 1975 volume in the Modern Masters series. Here is the record of a greatly intelligent poet-critic's blessedly unpredictable, always compelling engagement with texts that both fascinate and irritate him. Here, too, are his acerbic skirmishes with other readers, especially assorted Lacanians and post-structuralists. As Davie looks back over the matter, he finds that his interest in the *Cantos* increasingly corresponded to an interest in historiography. "So far as thinking as many do that the failure [of the *Cantos*] was predetermined from the first, because wrongly conceived, I offer a reading of the poem which suggests on the contrary that the crucial failure came late; and came because of a misunderstanding about historiography." As students of Pound know, or should, one cannot read two pages of Davie without finding instruction and surprise. Wisdom here is never sedation.

Ronald Bush's "Excavating the Ideological Faultlines of Modernism: Editing Ezra Pound's *Cantos*" is a contribution to a larger project on the theory of editing, George Bornstein's well-selected and introduced *Representing Modernist Texts.* Bush is working on an edition of the manuscripts of the Pisan sequence, and he calls, as do most scholars, for a complete edition of the *Cantos.* The present essay indicates how interesting such an edition might be. Arguing against ideologically totalizing or reductive readings of the poem, he wants to "credit the *Cantos* as a site of real ideological competition," as an inclination toward mythic closure in dialogue with "a genuine commitment to radical openness of a kind now commonly associated with postmodernism." Bush draws telling examples from a comparison between the 1919 and 1925 versions of Canto 6 (showing both feminist and antifeminist/patriarchal impulses); and from a study of the evolving production of Cantos 74 and 83, the Na Khi material in *Thrones,* and Cantos 110, 115, and the formerly—it has been repositioned in later printings—problematically positioned and titled "120" of *Drafts and Fragments.* I confess difficulty in hearing an "authoritative tone" in the famous "I have tried to write Paradise" lines—and isn't the authority for their inclusion and placement in 1972 very much in question, anyway? Yet Bush takes them as an indication of Pound's "thirty year habit of resisting his poem's antiauthoritarianism," a habit not strong enough to erase a "continuing and vigorous conflict of ideologies."

In a Derridean mode Kathryne V. Lindberg makes a high-spirited attack on ideologically closed or polarized ways of reading in "A Battle of Puns and the Extra Pound: Joyce and Pound Over Shakespeare's Authorizing 'Will' " (*Boundary 2* 18, i:157–73). As one would expect from the author of *Reading Pound Reading,* Lindberg delights in the heterogeneous energies of Pound's texts, which disrupt his own "search for a stable truth on which to base political and poetic authority." "Signatures" of other writers circulate unpredictably through Poundian texts, complicating and undermining authorship/authority. Shakespeare's punning play on his "authorizing" signature is traced through the trumping play on all those Will's by Stephen and Joyce in *Ulysses,* then crosses, through Sonnet 135's "*Will* in over-plus," into the Cavalcanti translation of Canto 36.

c. Relation to Other Writers Although Pound makes only a few references to Swedenborg, there is reason to believe him more important than has been suspected, especially if we give credence to Pound's remark in an unpublished letter of 1956 about trying to "hook" Dante to Swedenborg, "as I have done for 50 years." *Paideuma* 20, iii, has three linked articles on Pound and the Swedish visionary theologian. Demetres Tryphonopoulas in "Ezra Pound and Emanuel Swedenborg" (pp. 7–15) explores Swedenborg as a shared interest between Pound and Yeats in the Stone Cottage years, and he suggests that Pound may have contemplated his projected long poem "as an occult system like the one found in Swedenborg's visionary works." In a densely argued "Yeats, Pound, and Nietzsche" (pp. 17–30), Leon Surette notes Pound's well-established interest in Swedenborg before he met Yeats. Yeats's synopticism allowed him to bring together Swedenborg, the occult, and Nietzsche, and then Pound and Nietzsche, in *A Vision.* Yeats wanted to see the *Cantos* and *A Vision* as works of "historical and noumenal prophecy," and he may have hoped, through *A Vision,* to guide the increasingly political Pound away from his "apostasy" from the wisdom and insight they had earlier shared. Andrezej Sosnowski in "Pound's Imagism and Emanuel Swedenborg" (pp. 31–38) continues the discussion with some remarkable quotations from Swedenborg which suggest an influence on—certainly an affinity with—the esoteric aspects of Imagism and, perhaps, "the core of the method" of the *Cantos.*

In " 'Amplius in Coitu Phantasia': Pound's 'Cavalanti' and Avicenna's *De Almahad*" (*Paideuma* 20, i–ii:63–90) Matthew Little and Robert Babcock present interesting research on Pound and the Arabic philosopher, and they illuminate scattered references to Avicenna (Ibn Sīnā) and Islam in the "Cavalcanti" essay and in the *Cantos.* The piece is of interest in regard to Pound's sense of Paradise; its most direct bearing is on his concept of sex in relation to physical and intellectual love as rendered in the translation of Cavalcanti's "Donna mi Prega."

Keith Tuma draws on unpublished letters from Basil Bunting to Pound for a concise review of relations between the two poets in "Pound,

Eliot, Yeats, Auden and Basil Bunting in the Thirties" (*Sagetrieb* 10, i–ii:99–121). Tuma explores in particular the influence of "Propertius" on "Chomei at Toyama" and Bunting's "increasing dismay" at Pound's economic-political propaganda and his anti-Semitism, leading to an angry break in 1938.

A fascinating account of poetic influence, comic and ironic misprision, and the adroitness of poets and critics at performing contortions to rationalize their activities under authoritarian pressures is found in " 'Misunderstanding' Western Modernism: The *Menglong* Movement in Post-Mao China," by Xiaomei Chen (*Representations* 35:143–63). The *menglong* poets flourished from 1978 to 1983, attempting "a poetic quality detached from clear-cut political messages"; at first attacked as obscure and "unfaithful to socialist realism," *menglong* was eventually accepted by the ruling ideology. It is a story of curious twists in which Pound's modernist poetics (about which the Chinese knew very little) "rescued the *menglong* movement [and] sanctioned Chinese classical traditions now recognized as 'positive' and 'historically progressive.' " Chinese poetry, as it were, could return to itself *through* Pound's "understanding" of Chinese tradition.

d. The Shorter Poems and Translations Geoffrey Hill's "Envoi (1919)" is a revised version of one of the Clark Lectures of 1986, now gathered as *The Enemy's Country: Words, Contexture, and Other Circumstances of Language* (Stanford). Although it does not attempt to answer some of the more direct questions asked of the poem, this is a learned and subtle essay—so subtle in fact that its point may have escaped me. Hill appears to be ambivalent about the poem's outburst of affirmation and lyricism within *Mauberley.* "The strength and weakness of 'Envoi (1919)' is that we are given a not wholly satisfactory process in the guise of a satisfyingly finished piece." A reader of *Mauberley* might profit from considering this meditation, yet not be faulted for not having done so.

Working largely with the Pound-Margaret Cravens correspondence, Robert Spoo explores a complex surrounding Pound's early work on the Cavalcanti translations in "Pound's Cavalcanti and Cravens' Carducci" (*Paideuma* 20, iii:77–88). "Pound's letters to Cravens contain a veritable running account of his work on *Guido.*" Spoo finds that "in Pound's comments on Carducci . . . and in his preface to *Guido,* Cravens' voice can be faintly heard suggesting, debating, and moderating ideas. What has remained a silent partnership for so long is just now audible."

e. The Cantos I have admired Akiko Miyake's contributions to *Paideuma,* and *Ezra Pound and the Mysteries of Love: A Plan for* The Cantos (Duke) fulfills the promise of her intricately researched articles. Whether one agrees with its individual judgments and astute critique of philosophical-historical fault lines in the poem, the book is a thesaurus of information. The focus is on esoteric dimensions of the *Cantos,* dimensions that may broadly be indicated by the "light from Eleusis," other "mysteries of love," and a syncretism of Dante-Plotinus-Confucius. Miyake argues that while the *Cantos'* ideograms "tend to open the text rather than to provide a sense of overall unity," Pound intended a "stricter kind of coherence . . . one based on Gabriele Rossetti's *Il mistero dell' amor platonico del medio evo* (1840)." Indeed, Miyake's report on Rossetti is convincing: her ideas are like a snowball, gathering everything to it as it rolls through the *Cantos.* Miyake's method is to follow the poetry chronologically, first through Pound's "earlier attempts at ascension," then through the *Cantos,* offering a reconstruction of the poem's intentions by way of sources and backgrounds, reasonable interpretation, close scrutiny of Chinese ideograms, and so on. This approach produces at times a somewhat tighter, more coherent narrative than recent critics have sought or welcomed. Following her sympathetic explication, Miyake offers fresh, sharp, at times exasperated critiques of Pound's methods, especially as his selective, visionary interpretations—of Confucianism, for example—run up against actualities in history. Her central objection is to the influence of Esoteric Buddhism, passing through Fenollosa to the ideogramic method at large, becoming, as Pound mixed it with Neoplatonism, "an intellectual blind alley." In effect, it allows one to "suggest and create any complex idea, whether celestial, political, or philosophical, through joining images and evoking visions . . . and one cannot make mistakes. The existence of this black hole, hidden in Fenollosa's irrationalism . . . proved to be more serious as Pound's *Cantos* came to include complicated events of history, for the poet had lost the way to criticize his own judgments." What may be convincing as poetry is not convincing "as a description of truth and justice." Miyake is good at making philosophical distinctions often glossed over by critics. Her book is probably the most valuable in many years for reading the *Cantos.*

Where Miyake claims only an intention of coherence in the *Cantos,* Stephen Sicari in *Pound's Epic Ambition: Dante and the Modern World* (SUNY), although aware of counterarguments, "renews the dominant focus of Pound's early commentators in looking for a structural or formal principle that organizes the poem's heteroclite material." That unifying principle is "the theme of the wandering hero." Compared with the sophisticated approaches to the *Cantos* of recent years, the book is a rather plain walk-through of the poem; the Dantesque-Odyssean wanderer as unifying form seems to me at best a positive way of seeing what Pound, in his old age, viewed more pejoratively—that the wanderer had collected a "rag-bag."

Massimo Bacigalupo's "Ezra Pound's Cantos 72 and 73: An Annotated Translation" (*Paideuma* 20, iii:9–41) is essential for anyone who does not read Italian, and the very full annotations are essential even for those who do. He gives a detailed "Background and Foreground" to the Italian cantos, as well as to annotated translations of Italian notes and drafts of Cantos 74 and 75, and a transcription of a brief English draft related to the Italian notes. It would be superfluous to point out the importance of Bacigalupo's work in this area. In "A Musical Allusion in Ezra Pound's Canto 83" (*N&Q* 38:345–46), Bacigalupo has discovered the source of "soll deine Liebe sein" in a sentimental concert song by Carl Bohm.

Eva Hesse's "Why Lucifer 'Fell' in N. Carolina: An Alternative View" (*Paideuma* 20, iii:91–93) offers a most ingenious suggestion for a famously difficult line in Canto 74, finding a source in the career of "Charlie Sung [Soong]." John Glendening's essay on Pound and Blake (*Paideuma* 20, iii:95–106) strikes me as overinterpretation, yet it may be of interest in regard to Blake's appearance in Canto 16. An intelligent, brief note by Ethan Lewis, "The ABC of Ending: Pound's 'Addendum for C'" (*Paideuma* 20, i–ii:63–66), might well be read in conjunction with Ronald Bush's essay noted above. The "Addendum," Lewis suggests, may be seen "as Pound's didactic, ornery ending" of the *Cantos,* countervailing the more confessional and humble tones of 116, the last completed canto, and the final fragments in "CXVII et seq."

Finally, I come to a delightful but by no means lightweight piece, Alexander Schmitz's "Ideogram-Audiogram" (*Paideuma* 20, iii:43–62). Schmitz's improvisatory essay on reading the *Cantos* as music is a fresh and liberating approach to the poem: I cannot imagine myself teaching the *Cantos* without drawing on his suggestions. "It's music," Pound said in 1968, "musical themes that meet each other." His own concept of the poem's music, like that of critics who have found musical analogies, was probably based in the Western classical tradition of theme, countersubject, fugue, etc. But Schmitz asks us to listen to the poem as jazz, especially (for Schmitz, apparently the pinnacle) bebop. There is much here about Pound and music, and some technical discussion of chords which I must take on faith, but I am convinced. Pound wanted Ethel Merman to sing his opera, *Villon.* Wouldn't it have pleased him to hear his own "brilliant jazzy scat" performed, as Schmitz suggests, by Bobby McFerrin?

ii Eliot

a. Text, Biography, and Bibliography "Viv and Tom: The Eliots as Ether Addict and Co-Dependent" (*YER* 11:33–36) by Anthony E. Fathman, a medical doctor, provides a diagnosis which should increase the compassion and stem the rush to judgment of those who wish to comment on Eliot's difficult first marriage. "Eliot and Women" (*The Modernist in History,* pp. 9–22) is biographer Lyndall Gordon's capsule summary of her research on Eliot's relationships with his first wife, his close friend Mary Trevelyan, and especially Emily Hale, the great love of his early and again of his middle years. For the later period Paul Horgan's reminiscence of Eliot in old age (*ASch* 60:407–13) includes a vivid account of one of the poet's performances on the lecture circuit: a 1958 reading before some 12,000 people at the University of Texas, Austin. Horgan's description of Eliot's command of the audience is electrifying, and his sketch of the poet in old age, happy at last, offers pathos as well as pleasure.

Those interested in Eliot's life and times will especially wish to note Noel Annan's *Our Age: English Intellectuals Between the World Wars—A Group Portrait* (Random House), a book of a kind uncommon in the United States, which takes up the task of evaluating events and figures contemporary with his own life from the informed perspective of one who was, like Eliot, active and engaged in several arenas. Annan has not forgotten how hard it was in the heat of the moment to call every shot correctly, and he gives full accounts of the discussions of state and university policy and of public and private attitudes toward war, sexuality, education, class, and culture that informed England during Eliot's most active years. Annan also offers a brief but moving testimony to the effect on many members of his generation of living in the shadow of a great poet with Eliot's capacity for invention and self-renewal.

b. General Studies J. P. Riquelme's *Harmony of Dissonance* (Hopkins) is a complex study of Eliot's poetics, informed by scrupulous attention both to postmodern theory and to Eliot's own voices and practices. The result is a book primarily for specialists concerned with the intersections of romanticism and modernism, but the text is full of insights and readings strong enough to be valuable beyond its purview. Riquelme argues convincingly for a continuum between romanticism and Eliot's work, although he gives due weight to the strength of Eliot's revision of that tradition. I especially like his analysis of Eliot's attraction to fragmentary texts from lost worlds and his recognition that much of the wisdom of *Four Quartets,* in spite of its elegaic voice, is counterintuitive.

More apparently recherché and making in a sense an opposite point is Steve Ellis's *The English Eliot* (Routledge), which examines Eliot's classicism—a neglected issue—and seeks to establish its parallels in contemporary architecture, landscape painting, religion, and politics. Ellis places Eliot in the context of a broad general discourse about abstraction and internationalism current in England from the late '20s through the early '40s. That discourse, Ellis argues, is classical in a sense variously understood and variously defined by its participants, but always stressing the need for abstraction, form, and restraint. Ellis mines Eliot's work on *The Criterion* to good effect, making clear the parameters of many positions otherwise difficult to understand, and he reads Eliot's poetry, especially *Four Quartets,* with due attention to its formal and structural as well as thematic properties.

One other general book is worth noting: Astradur Eyssteinsson's *The Concept of Modernism* (Cornell), an informed, lucid, and well-considered study of the evolution of an important literary term. Eyssteinsson sketches Eliot's contributions to this concept without the anxious over-elaboration that haunts much criticism on this matter.

Several works this year on Eliot's religion include Narsingh Srivastava's *The Poetry of T. S. Eliot: A Study in Religious Sensibility* (Apt) and A. V. C. Schmidt's "The Integrity of Eliot" (*EIC* 41 [1991]:222–39). More significant is Joseph Schwartz's "T. S. Eliot's Idea of the Christian Poet" (*Renascence* 43:215–27), which seeks to understand how Eliot's views developed. Schwartz finds interesting evidence for a pronounced mechanistic strain of thought in Eliot's early years, and he is able to articulate the difficulties inherent in Eliot's later attempts to define the relationship between poetry and belief.

The popular impression that Eliot was a kind of mystic is closely examined in two works, Donald Childs's "T. S. Eliot's Rhapsody of

Matter and Memory" (*AL* 63:474–88) and Paul Murray's *T. S. Eliot and Mysticism: The Secret History of* Four Quartets (St. Martin's). Childs devotes most of his attention to the early poetry and makes good use of both recent criticism and primary texts. Among other things, he understands and explicates Eliot's intoxication with and then recovery from an early exposure to Bergson and its implications for the issue of logocentrism raised by the application of postmodern theory to Eliot's work. Like Murray, whose longer study is discussed below, Childs is well aware of Eliot's philosophical ambivalence about mystical discourse and his marked restraint toward mystical rhetoric and mystical truth claims, a restraint which makes their carefully considered appearance in his poetry all the more powerful.

Murray's study is a full-length examination of Eliot's sources for mystical theory and practice, of his gingerly and critical attitude toward them, and of the qualified way in which he appropriates them in his own work. Murray has a thorough grasp of the theological issues and traditions at stake with respect to mysticism, and he is broadly knowledgable about Eliot's philosophical and cultural interests. Among other things, he makes a case, based in part on references and reviews in *The Criterion,* for Søren Kierkegaard's influence on Eliot's thought and sensibility. His discussion of the concept of incarnation is excellent, and his chapter on Eliot's "spiritual patriotism"—a useful and original critical term—illuminates a little-understood aspect of Eliot's sensibility.

Only two essays on the still problematic question of gender in Eliot's poetry seem to have appeared this year, Nancy Gish's comparison with Marianne Moore, reviewed below, and Carol Christ's "Gender, Voice, and Figuration in Eliot's Early Poetry" (*The Modernist in History,* pp. 23–37). Christ argues that in his early poetry Eliot "constructs a drama whereby he separates himself from a [19th-century] feminized poetic idiom at the same time that he appropriates its effects through the ventriloquized voice." Christ's essay not only is free from tendentious argument but also treats the issue of gender in relation to specifically literary values.

c. Relation to Other Writers In an article in the *Southwest Review* (76:550–63) both hard to read and hard to classify, Jeffrey Perl, a major Eliot critic, begins with a provocative estimation of *The Waste Land* ("didactic, moralistic, more than a little comic, and so public in intention that it is virtually a piece of journalism") and proceeds to a consideration of Eliot and Beckett. This comparison entails an attempt—elliptical in the extreme—to situate both writers in terms of modernism's response to 20th-century disasters, of which the Holocaust is the paradigm. In spite of making the valid point that early modernist writers saw themselves as therapists to a culture in breakdown, this somewhat experimental essay in criticism does not quite come off.

Richard Poirier, another distinguished critic, contributes to the collection of essays *Addressing Frank Kermode: Essays in Criticism and Interpretation,* ed. Margaret Tudeau-Clayton and Martin Warner (Illinois). "The Pater of Joyce and Eliot" (pp. 169–89) lauds Pater both for the emphasis he placed on complex and intense experience in the reception of art and for his stress on skepticism and discipline as a scaffold for that experience. Tendentiously rebuked here for his "trashing" of Pater and his attempt to "suppress" a noble precursor, Eliot had an ambivalent relation to Pater and to aestheticism—in part the relation of a practicing poet to an academic critic—which remains largely unexplored.

The influence of classical Greek literature and philosophy on Eliot is canvassed by several critics. Kenneth J. Reckford's "Eliot's *Cocktail Party* and Plato's *Symposium*" (*CML* 11:303–13) argues a case for Eliot's debt to Plato. Reckford begins with striking parallels between *The Symposium* and the play, including ones between the figures of Harcourt-Reilly and Socrates. Reckford also is sensitive to the curious mélange of Christian, primitive, and private poetic allusion that creates the play's texture. Nothing wooden here, and much that would contribute to good teaching. Elsie Leach's case for the importance of Aeschylus, "*Agamemnon* as a Source of *Murder in the Cathedral*" (*YER* 11:14–18), makes an interesting coda.

Virginia Phelan discusses the literary relationship between Charles Williams and Eliot in her "Unidentified but Invited: Charles Williams at *The Cocktail Party*" (*YER* 11:29–32)—as does Paul Murray in passing—and she argues for the influence of Williams's curious theology of romantic love on Eliot's consideration of the marriage theme and his construction of the play. Jewel Spears Brooker's "From Epithalamium to Rhapsody: Mind and World in Wordsworth and Eliot" (*YER* 11:37–39) explores the perennial issue of Eliot's relationship to romanticism and argues skillfully for a shift from Wordsworth's sense of a potential paradisical union between mind and world to Eliot's sense of an uneasy rupture between the two.

Nancy Gish in "Eliot and Marianne Moore: Modernism and Difference" (*YER* 11:40–43) treats the admiring but reticent relationship between the two poets as an occasion for examining several issues in Eliot and feminist criticism. Using a critical concept of *femmage* (meaning a kind of collage which respects the integrity of the materials—particularly "feminine" materials—of which it is composed) to define the elusive difference between Eliot's and Moore's use of quotation, Gish seeks to show more generally why Moore's work resists Eliot's way of construing the relationship between tradition and the individual talent.

Shyamal Bagchee's analysis of the literary relations between Eliot and Hopkins ("Subtle Souls and Dry Bones: Hopkins and Eliot," *YER* 11:48–54) notes that Eliot relegated Hopkins firmly to the back benches of poetry. Bagchee seeks to show why this negative response represents both a resistance and a failure of sensibility on Eliot's part. He provides many close readings, and each poet emerges from the comparison with new strengths as well as familiar weaknesses. E. D. Lloyd-Kimbrel ("A Condition of Complete Simplicity: Poetic Returns and Robert Frost's 'Directive,'" *Robert Frost Review* 4:7–17) finds many echoes of "Little Gidding" (1942) in Frost's fine poem "Directive" (1946), reopening a discussion of the mutual influence between these two poets that has perhaps been too little pursued.

Finally, A. Walton Litz in "The Allusive Poet: Eliot and His Sources" (*The Modernist in History*, pp. 137–52) returns to the perpetual enigma of Eliot's pervasive employment of allusion, offering new examples and making a working distinction between conscious and subliminal echoes, while also noting that the distinction between them cannot be based exclusively on Eliot's statements of intention in the matter.

d. Poems and Plays Eliot's poetry is the focus of several essays in *The Modernist in History*. In "*Ara Vos Prec:* Eliot's Negotiation of Satire and Suffering" (pp. 41–66) James Longenbach discusses *Ara Vos Prec* with his customary learning and willingness to risk literary judgment. He notes, among other things, that the French poems of Eliot's early career are "a kind of misplaced exorcism." John T. Mayer, "*The Waste Land* and Eliot's Poetry Notebook" (pp. 67–90), traces the evolution of *The Waste Land* along lines laid down in Mayer's 1989 book, with careful attention to unpublished sources. (It is easy to play the "should have read" game, but both these essays seem to me to suffer from lack of exposure to Robert

Crawford's *The Savage and the City* [1987].) I did not find Alan Williamson's return to "spatial criticism" and to the study of archetypes persuasive ("Forms of Simultaneity in *The Waste Land* and *Burnt Norton*," pp. 153–66), but I did admire the candor and clarity of his defense of this neo-Jungian endeavor. Lawrence Rainey's meticulous reconstruction of the circumstances of publication of *The Waste Land* and his analysis of the precise place of the literary journals and media involved in the literary and commercial culture of the period ("The Price of Modernism: Publishing *The Waste Land*," pp. 67–90) is a fascinating piece of literary history. Ronald Bush's own contribution to the collection, "T. S. Eliot and Modernism at the Present Time: A Provocation" (pp. 191–204), also deals with the reception of Eliot's work. Both Bush and Rainey seek to tie their discoveries to current issues in criticism. Both also find the heritage of modernism ambiguous (by which they seem to mean not *necessarily* fascist!), and both seek to give it a fuller context in the past and a renewed justification in the present. The project is laudable, but as executed here it seems curiously retrenched.

Most of the other articles on particular works in the Eliot canon examined for this review seemed weak. Robin Schulze's "The Trope of the Police Force in T. S. Eliot's Cambridge Prologue" (*YER* 11:19–23) must stand as typical of many. It argues that some lines involving low-life brawls that Eliot dropped from *The Waste Land* were excised, "stylistic considerations aside," as "an act of self policing." Here as elsewhere the issue of literary judgment is dismissed with an airy wave of the hand, when in fact it is of the essence. We are given instead a recapitulation of the one-dimensional view that Eliot's every exercise of discrimination was an act of criminal repression. "Stylistic considerations aside," Mrs. Lincoln, how did you like the play?

Speaking of plays, Eliot's drama fares slightly better than his poetry and criticism this year. Besides the studies by Reckford and Phelan, there is Linda Wyman's "'Where Words are Valid': The Language of Eliot's Drama" (*YER* 11:44–54), which provides an introduction to the defining characteristics of Eliot's drama, informed by a solid but unobtrusive sense of the genre and language issues involved. Armin Paul Frank's "Ghosts from What Might Have Been: T. S. Eliot's Plays of Antinaturalistic Analysis" (*YER* 11:7–13) explores a comparison between Eliot and Ibsen that yields more fruit than one might expect, including the perception that while Eliot's protagonists always have a choice, it is not unconditioned.

e. Criticism Among the few entries of note on Eliot's criticism this year are a book and an essay by Michael North, "Eliot, Lukács, and the Politics of Modernism" (*The Modernist in History,* pp. 169–89) and *The Political Aesthetic of Yeats, Eliot, and Pound* (Cambridge). North is working within the parameters of the same literary project as Bush and Rainey, although less tentatively and perhaps to better effect. In his essay he makes use of what appears a very tangential and fleeting intersection between Lukács and Eliot to establish a fuller and more illuminating parallel between them. North's comparison of Lukács's rather willed leap of faith into the arms of the Communist party with Eliot's equally willed jump into those of the institutional church recognizes a time when Marxism and Christianity seemed serious alternatives, two modes of opposition—although with very different valences—to an intolerable status quo.

Rutgers University
New Jersey Institute of Technology

9 Faulkner

Alexander J. Marshall, III

In "Faulkner and His Critics: Moving into the 90s" (*ArQ* 47:117–35) Deborah Clarke asks the unavoidable question: "Is it possible to say something new and interesting about Faulkner?" As Clarke points out, the exigencies of the profession keep us trying, and the siren song of theory is always tempting us into treacherous waters where "Faulkner's fiction is in danger of getting lost behind the theory." Indeed, some of the 11 book-length studies and 70 essays reviewed here could be described as either threadbare or fanciful; a few could even make us wonder how they ever made it into print. But by and large this year's scholarship reveals sincere attempts to come to terms with Faulkner—in every sense of that phrase. Thus, critics are challenged to find new metaphors to explain the tensions, ambiguities, and paradoxes at the heart of Faulkner's artistic vision—and, perhaps, to accommodate a dead white male to the contemporary ideological climate. That Faulkner remains a major literary subject even through times of canon reformation and political correctness is evidenced not only by the number of works focusing on his life and his art, but by articles such as John N. Duvall's "Doe Hunting and Masculinity: *Song of Solomon* and *Go Down, Moses*" (*ArQ* 47:95–115), Anthony Hilfer's "Critical Indeterminacies in Toni Morrison's Fiction: An Introduction" (*TSLL* 33:91–95), Nehama Aschkenasy's "Yehoshua's 'Sound and Fury': *A Late Divorce* and Its Faulknerian Model" (*MLS* 21, ii:92–104), and John T. Irwin's "The Journey to the South: Poe, Borges, and Faulkner" (*VQR* 67:416–32), essays showing how Faulkner's influence endures and how studying Faulkner can both illuminate writers from a variety of backgrounds and continue to enrich our understanding

Preparation of this chapter was made possible by a grant from the Walter Williams Craigie Faculty Endowment of Randolph-Macon College.

of the human condition. As Gene M. Moore's "Ethnicity and the Faulkner Canon" (*DQR* 21:4–19) points out, Faulkner criticism has averaged almost 140 articles per year during the past decade and has "value[d] most highly those works in which identity is most problematic." While this year's numbers have fallen off, the interest in indeterminacy and identity remains at the forefront, thanks largely to the special double issue of the *Faulkner Journal* (Fall 1988/Spring 1989; published Fall 1991) devoted to "Faulkner and Feminisms."

i Bibliography, Editions, and Manuscripts

While we have no new "corrected texts" this year, we do have Noel Polk's interesting account of some of the problems he encountered in preparing one. In "Where the Comma Goes: Editing William Faulkner" (*Representing Modernist Texts,* pp. 241–58), Polk also offers his insights into the editing process in general and the implications of that process for the canon. The Garland Faulkner Annotation Series (Garland) published two works this year: *Flags in the Dust,* annotated by Linda Elkins McDaniel, and *Absalom, Absalom!,* annotated by David Paul Ragan. Both are useful.

I am pleased to note that the extensive Faulkner Collection at the University of Virginia has become even more comprehensive: Joan St. C. Crane reports the acquisition of a 26-page carbon typescript of "Vision in Spring" containing "textual variants that distinctly differentiate it" from the version Judith L. Sensibar used in 1984 (see *ALS 1984,* p. 159). Crane lists other "Faulkner Major Book Acquisitions" (*Chapter & Verse,* May, pp. 13–16) from Carl Petersen's collection: various first editions of *Soldier's Pay* and *The Sound and the Fury,* a second variant binding of *Sartoris,* and a sizable treasury of foreign translations and editions.

ii Biography

This year may prove very important in Faulkner biography. With new documents, letters, and studies coming to light, a successor to Joseph Blotner's work becomes more and more likely. In "Carvel Collins's Faulkner: A Newly Opened Archive" (*MissQ* 44:257–72) James G. Watson reviews the history and the contents of the massive Collins Collection of Faulkneriana at the Harry Ransom Humanities Research Center, the University of Texas. Since restrictions on the collection were removed at Collins's death in 1989, his "jealously guarded" secrets may yield "that something" which will lead to a "reconceptualize[d]" Faulkner. Karl F. Zender prints "Two Unpublished Letters from William Faulkner to Helen Baird" (*AL* 63:535–38). And Susan Snell's *Phil Stone of Oxford: A Vicarious Life* (Georgia) is a fascinating biography of Faulkner's friend and literary mentor that illuminates the true extent of the literary debt. Snell points out the "great irony" that "while so self-consciously engaged as Faulkner's 'Muse,' . . . Stone, almost unwittingly, served American literature more significantly as one of the fictionist's principal character studies—and mirrors." Faulkner apparently "ransacked Stone's genealogy" for character types as well as plots. The Gavin Stevens connection has long been obvious, but the book surprised me in some interesting ways (the conflation of Stone's gambling stories with his great uncles Amodeus and Theophilus led to the creation of "Was," and Stone's first sexual experience was with a woman named Dewey Dell, just to name a few). Snell suggests that "perhaps Faulkner has conditioned us to regard the particulars of Stone's character and ethos as typically 'Southern' because William Faulkner defined 'Southern' to us (as to himself) in the guise of Phil Stone," who himself "tirelessly refined his own mythology to fit that of a communal Southern mold or ideal." Another of Faulkner's Oxford friends is the subject of "The Great Author, the Great Scholar, and the Small-Town Reporter" (*Journal of Mississippi History* 53:115–29) in which R. D. Mullen sets the record—and especially Frederick Karl—straight about his brother Phil "Moon" Mullen's relationship with the Oxford *Eagle,* William Faulkner, and Faulkner's reputation. That Oxford has changed its opinion about Faulkner is certainly an understatement. Michael Pearson's "The Sound of the Past: Faulkner's Mississippi" (*Imagined Places,* pp. 65–124) describes contemporary Oxford and Faulkner's place in it. Interesting information about Faulkner and Oxford may also be found in various items in *The Faulkner Newsletter.*

iii Criticism: General

Our perennial fascination with language was again coupled with our need to relate Faulkner to real life. M. E. Bradford's general essay, "A Refined Myopia: Faulkner and the New Literary History" (*SR* 99:77–85), will be of some interest to students of Faulkner's later works but is mostly an appeal for criticism to reconnect texts with human nature and social reality. Sanford Pinsker does just that—but with a twist—in "William Faulkner and My Middle East Problem" (*VQR* 67:397–415), "a humanistic application of [Faulkner's] vision to circumstances at once radically different and ineluctably the same"; and certainly Jim Cox is exemplary in "Beneath My Father's Name" (*SR* 99:412–33), an essay offering some critical insights into both Faulkner and Richard Wright but probably most notable for Cox's personal reminiscences and observations about what it is to be Southern and about the "South in every American."

Christopher Waldrep's study of "William Faulkner, Robert Penn Warren, and the Law" (*SoSt* n.s. 2:39–50) contrasts two views of American justice, the "rational," represented by Faulkner, that believes justice is almost always served in the end, and the "irrational," represented by Warren, that does not: "According to Faulkner, justice was both a cosmic force and popular will." (Michael Millgate takes a very different view, as we shall see below.) Lothar Honnighausen's "On the Uses of the Term 'Regionalism' for the Study of Faulkner" (*The United States South*, pp. 41–53) looks at the realistic and metaphorical implications of Faulkner's "own little postage stamp of native soil." Some particularly interesting aspects of Don H. Doyle's "The Mississippi Frontier in Faulkner's Fiction and in Fact" (*SoQ* 29, iv:145–60) are his account of Chickasaw history, from "an unconquered people" through "the days of doom and dispossession," and the comparison of Lafayette County's Alexander Pegues to Yoknapatawpha's Thomas Sutpen. In another background study, "Gavin Stevens: Faulkner's Favorite" (*AN&Q* n.s. 4:21–24), M. C. Flannery and John G. Cawelti note that Phil Stone is "the usual model" for the Jefferson lawyer who "is certainly more a spokesman for Faulkner than any other character in the Yoknapatawpha saga"; however, the authors suggest that Stevens may be the literary descendant of Ephraim Tutt, the detective/lawyer popularized in the '20s by Arthur Train.

The critic's position between author and reader is the subject of Carol M. Andrews's "Cleanth Brooks on Faulkner: Yoknapatawpha and the Vanderbilt Tradition" (*The Vanderbilt Tradition*, pp. 189–96). Andrews warns that Brooks's "very authority can pose a problem for the reader trying to understand the complexities of Faulkner's fiction; it can be difficult to separate Brooks's own critical precepts from the fictional world he makes so accessible to the reader." Another prominent southernist and Faulknerian, Louis D. Rubin, Jr., has collected many of his fine essays on southern literature in *The Mockingbird in the Gum Tree,* and naturally Faulkner figures in many of them. Of particular interest are "The Dixie Special: William Faulkner and the Southern Literary Renascence" (see *ALS 1982,* p. 152) and "The High Sheriff of Yoknapatawpha County: A Study in the Genius of Place" (*ALS 1990,* p. 155), two of Rubin's essays from the Faulkner conferences at Oxford.

The 1989 conference proceedings were published this year. *Faulkner and Religion* presents a range of essays attempting to understand the role of religion in Faulkner's life and art. (Articles on specific works will be taken up in the appropriate sections below.) Charles Reagan Wilson's "William Faulkner and the Southern Religious Culture" (pp. 21–43) examines the actual denominational characteristics of the South—more Methodist and Baptist than Calvinist—and the "Southern civil religion that saw religious significance in the Confederate experience." Alfred Kazin cites the influence of regional and familial decline in "William Faulkner and Religion: Determinism, Compassion, and the God of Defeat" (pp. 3–20). Richard King finds the cultural sources of "World-Rejection in Faulkner's Fiction" (pp. 65–84) in early Christian and Gnostic traditions, and King notes that while Faulkner often "neutralizes or counteracts the impulse toward rejection of the world by thematic and structural oppositions," he also presents "the pervasive scene of emptiness, loss, and nothingness in his work"; nevertheless, this bleakness drives the modernist's creative impulse and belief in the redemptive and reparative powers of art. Evans Harrington's " 'A Passion Week of the Heart': Religion and Faulkner's Art" (pp. 157–76) finds a "beatific vision" of love, sorrow, and suffering in Faulkner's works. And I examine the difficulties of expressing a vision of perfection in "The Dream Deferred: William Faulkner's Metaphysics of Absence" (pp. 177–92), arguing that Faulkner used indirection, suggestion, and evocation to "transcend the limits of verbal discourse . . . by taking advantage of the very contingencies that problematize and undermine language."

Given this interest, it is not surprising that I was particularly impressed by Judith Lockyer's *Ordered by Words: Language and Narration in the Novels of William Faulkner* (So. Ill.), a Bakhtinian study of various avatars of Horace Benbow, "men of words" in whom "Faulkner locates his own anxieties about the possibilities and limitations in language." Lockyer examines 12 major works, from *Sartoris* to *A Fable,* to show how "novel writing . . . allowed Faulkner to confront the terrible element of imprecision in language, the limits of its authority, and to put that up against his belief in the power of the word to assert the self and to constitute order and meaning in the world."

iv Criticism: Special Studies

The double issue of *The Faulkner Journal* (4 [1988–89]) offers some engaging and provocative essays on "Faulkner and Feminisms." Frann Michel opens the issue with what must be the most provocative title in the history of Faulkner criticism: "William Faulkner as a Lesbian Author" (4:5–20). Michel's examination of "male feminization" focuses largely on *Mosquitoes* and argues that "Faulkner's literary career began in an era when the destabilization of gender relations was particularly visible, and his works, especially his early works, reveal a preoccupation with male feminization, both authorial and characterological." Michel suggests that what she refers to as "Faulkner's 'lesbianism' consists in a doubling of a version or versions of the feminine generated by a masculine ideology characterized by gynophobia, misogyny, and male gender anxiety." Diane Roberts examines the social and political as well as the emotional and physical implications of "Ravished Belles: Stories of Rape and Resistance in *Flags in the Dust* and *Sanctuary*" (4:21–35). In "Feminism and Faulkner: Second Thoughts or, What's a radical feminist doing with a canonical male text anyway?" (4:55–65) Minrose C. Gwin notes that since "the politics of Faulkner criticism is male politics [and] the discourse of Faulkner criticism is male discourse," feminists readers have been, like Rosa Coldfield, "positioned outside the dominant discourse of the community"; wondering whether "feminist readers benefit from reading Faulkner," Gwin finds that "what he does so well is to show the *process* of women's silencing, the appropriative gesture of male dominance—the naturalization of systems of oppression." Drawing largely on the psychoanalytic theory of Nancy Chodorow, Gail L. Mortimer finds "The 'Masculinity' of Faulkner's Thought" (4:67–81) to be a "way of viewing the self-in-the-world in which the illusion of control of otherness seems to be basic." John N. Duvall's "Authentic Ghost Stories: *Uncle Tom's Cabin, Absalom, Absalom!,* and *Beloved*" (4:83–97) looks at the ways these novels "raise questions about the abuse of patriarchal authority." A more uneven application of feminist theory is Richard Pearce's examination of *The Politics of Narration: James Joyce, William*

Faulkner, and Virginia Woolf (Rutgers), a mixture of insight and oversight making questionable assertions about authority in the major novels—especially *The Sound and the Fury.* William J. Sowder's *Existential-Phenomenological Readings on Faulkner* (UCA) is exactly what the title describes. This collection of previously published essays provides interesting analyses of the perceptions of and the choices made by a range of Faulkner characters, though the argument for existential phenomenology as a critical panacea seems a bit overworked.

In *Sporting with the Gods* Michael Oriard examines the cultural history of tropes that both reflect and shape the American views of life-as-game. Not surprisingly, two sections (pp. 258–70, 296–305) deal with Faulkner's playful use and critique of the southern sporting myth, from "cosmic joker" and "prime maniacal risibility" to the many card games and horse trades. Oriard concludes that "fate, chance, and will equally inform Faulkner's metaphysical universe; race, caste, and freedom his historical one. The dialectical understanding that results from the collision of these forces is summed up in Faulkner's portrait of life as a sporting contest." A different kind of play is the subject of "Faulkner and the Detective Story's Double Plot" (*Clues* 12:1–15) by John G. Cawelti. By comparing Faulkner's use of detective structures to those found in Nabokov, Borges, and Pynchon, Cawelti discovers a distinct difference in vision: whereas the postmodernists "believe that the hope of arriving at some clear sense of truth, reason or meaning is a snare and a delusion," Faulkner "portray[s] a meaningful search for truth." That search for truth is examined in Jeanne Campbell Reesman's *American Designs,* a work bringing together very different writers who, nevertheless, both use complex, "open" narrative structures to examine "problems of knowledge," to involve the reader in the act of interpretation, and to subvert the very notion of "design" as a closed, final, monistic system. While Reesman admits that these points are hardly new, her use of Rorty's philosophy and Bakhtin's critical theory presents them in a contemporary vocabulary. Furthermore, she sees "James's and Faulkner's narrative experimentation as part of the same move toward the hermeneutics invoked today in the opening of the canon and the general emphasis on new voices in literary interpretation." One warning, however: most Faulknerians will find the subtitle misleading—Reesman deals with *Absalom, Absalom!* and *Go Down, Moses,* works not generally considered "late."

v Individual Works to 1929

The new *Faulkner Studies,* out of Japan, began publication this year with a special issue on *Mosquitoes.* Judith Bryant Wittenberg opens with a study of "Configurations of the Female and Textual Politic in *Mosquitoes*" (1:1–19), arguing that the text tends to deconstruct gender roles by "call[ing] into question the psycho-social binary structure 'masculine/feminine,' which locates individuals, attitudes, and behaviors on one side or the other of the dichotomy." This stratagem, however, is countered by "male-generated misogynistic statements that . . . return woman to her proper/inferior place," leaving gender questions open. Edwin T. Arnold looks at Housman's influence in "The Last of the Shropshire Lad: David West, Faulkner, and *Mosquitoes*" (*Faulkner Studies* 1:21–41), an analysis of the "recurring 'David' figure" who appears "guileless" and "vulnerable" in early works but will reappear transformed as Harry Wilbourne, Quentin and Benjy Compson, Joe Christmas, Byron Bunch, Gavin Stevens, and possibly Ike Snopes.

The Sound and the Fury continues to receive a great deal of attention. Doreen Fowler's "The Ravished Daughter: Eleusinian Mysteries in *The Sound and the Fury*" (*Faulkner and Religion,* pp. 140–56) argues persuasively that "Caddy Compson and her daughter strike us with such force because they are modern-day representatives of ancient mythic figures," Demeter and Persephone, goddesses of fertility and transformation, acting out "the myth of eternal recurrence." Giles Gunn's analysis of "Faulkner's Heterodoxy: Faith and Family in *The Sound and the Fury*" (*Faulkner and Religion,* pp. 44–64) reveals the deadly cycle of the Compson family: "Committing themselves variously to an abstract image of the family that is intended to soothe their own sense of personal vanity or betrayal, the Compsons deny to each other . . . the love and support they give to the abstraction itself." Moreover, this "idolization of the abstraction itself, in turn deadens them to [all] that might otherwise continue to hold them together." A. E. Elmore's "Faulkner on the Agrarian South: Waste Land or Promised Land?" (*The Vanderbilt Tradition,* pp. 175–88) argues that *The Sound and the Fury* "is both a conscious variation on Eliot's *Waste Land* and an unconscious rebuttal of the Agrarian notion that the South represents a Promised Land by whose manna and light man may escape the desert of modern industrial and urban captivity." In "Time, Space, and Semiotic Discourse in the Feminization/Disintegration of Quentin Compson" (*FJ* 4 [1988–89]:99–111), Marsha Warren draws heavily on Kristevan and Lacanian theory to try to explain Quentin's decline and suicide. What she finds is not the feminization that "Faulkner's patriarchal text and society" might lead us to expect but a struggle between "ordered thought and language (symbolic discourse)" and "the heterogeneous and the irrational (semiotic discourse)": "By denying time and ultimately language through the silence of death and the fragmentation of order, Quentin denies the very organizing principle of gendered identity—male or female." And what Panthea Reid Broughton refers to as "The Economy of Desire: Faulkner's Poetics, From Eroticism to Post-Impressionism" (*FJ* 4 [1988–89]:159–77) is the transformation that took place with the marriage to Estelle and the writing of the fourth section of *The Sound and the Fury:* "if insatiable desire for an unattainable woman was the impelling factor behind his early writing," in the later works "longings were translated into a structural, rather than an erotic, poetic."

vi Individual Works, 1930–1939

As we might expect, *As I Lay Dying* vied with *Absalom, Absalom!* for the critics' choice this year. Two works focused on the language used by the characters. Colleen Donnelly's "The Syntax of Perception in *As I Lay Dying*" (*CEA* 53, ii:54–68) compares manuscript and published text to study the ways in which Vardaman and Darl manipulate forms of "to be" both to explore ontological questions and to deal with Addie's death; and Deborah K. Chappel's "Pa Says: The Rhetoric of Faulkner's Anse Bundren" (*MissQ* 44:273–85) sees Anse as a "master manipulator of words and people" whose rhetoric reveals "imagination, forethought, and a ruthless will." Chappel's Anse is the shrewd force behind the journey to Jefferson, not the victim of Addie's revenge that the novel suggests. In "*As I Lay Dying:* Experience in Passing" (*SAQ* 90:579–632) Patricia McKee argues that the novel is "about redemption and salvation, but of a kind that occurs in time rather than space: a salvation of experience that passes through and endures in different forms." In her extensive reading of the novel, McKee suggests that by "giving experience time" instead of form, Faulkner somehow overcomes time, a "powerful source of human alienation," and "takes the edge off death." In "Matricide and the Mother's Revenge: *As I Lay Dying*" (*FJ* 4 [1988–89]:113–25) Doreen Fowler argues that it is the death of the mother—not the father—that is the Ur myth of Western culture; through the title and the narrative itself

Faulkner alludes to the archetypal death and revenge of Clytemnestra, "rewrites the dominant myth of our culture, the mythic identification of the mother's body with castration and death, and he allows the dead mother to speak." Tim Poland points out the close association between Cash Bundren and his tools in "Faulkner's *As I Lay Dying*" (*Expl* 49:118–20): when the tools are nearly lost in the river, so is Cash's identity; "only with their retrieval is he allowed to return to the text and speak again."

Carlee Lippman compares the evil of the Popeye of *Sanctuary* and Grenouille of *Das Parfum* in "William Faulkner and Patrick Suskind: Speaking about the Unspeakable" (*LHY* 32, ii:73–85), and William J. Schafer finds in "Faulkner's *Sanctuary:* The Blackness of Fairytale" (*DUJ* 83:217–22) "a nightmare journey" that "develops profound cultural criticisms." One of those criticisms, according to Michael Millgate, is of incompetence and corruption in the legal system. His "Undue Process: William Faulkner's *Sanctuary*" (*Rough Justice,* pp. 157–69) argues that justice fails not only in this but in most of Faulkner's novels: "the persistent failure and even perversion of the legal system serves again and again as both symptom and symbol of a profounder malaise within society at large."

Virginia V. James Hlavsa's *Faulkner and the Thoroughly Modern Novel* (Virginia) contains previously published essays plus one from *Faulkner and Religion* attempting to explain what it means to say that Faulkner is a modernist. Taking her cue from M. H. Abrams's distinction between the Neoclassical artistic mind as "perceiving" and the Romantic mind as "projective," Hlavsa calls the modernists "promiscuous," meaning diverse as well as obsessive. She also examines mythical and Christian modes of modernism before applying these preliminary ideas to an extensive reading of *Light in August.* In one of the more interesting and provocative articles of the year, "The Human Heart in Conflict: *Light in August*'s Schizophrenic Narrator" (*SNNTS* 23:452–69), David M. Toomey argues "that Reverend Hightower is paranoid schizophrenic, and that the entire narrative represents his interior monologue." Using Jung as his frame of reference, Toomey meticulously analyzes the narrative as a projection of Hightower's desires, guilt, and suffering—and as a kind of "self-induced therapy." In a look at one of Faulkner's least-studied works, Michael Zeitlin locates "Faulkner's *Pylon:* The City in the Age of Mechanical Reproduction" (*CRevAS* 22:229–40) "among the most savage indictments of the contemporary scene in modern American literature. . . . unique in Faulkner's *oeuvre* in defining the city as a great collecting-place of modernity's oppressive, alien and hostile forces."

Colleen E. Donnelly's "Compelled to Believe: Historiography and Truth in *Absalom, Absalom!*" (*Style* 25:104–22) is a sound reading of the novel's "reassessment of the process of historical reconstruction," and Linda Wagner-Martin's "Rosa Coldfield as Daughter: Another of Faulkner's Lost Children" (*SAF* 19:1–13) astutely points out the patterns of parental neglect in Faulkner and reads *Absalom, Absalom!* as "the tragedy of the misuse of parental authority. . . . , the story of various white males who destroyed families, particularly the women and children of those families, in their rapacious pursuit of what they defined as 'success.'" Jenny Jennings Foerst examines "The Psychic Wholeness and Corrupt Text of Rosa Coldfield, 'Author and Victim Too' of *Absalom, Absalom!*" (*FJ* 4 [1988–89]:37–53), noting that Rosa's story is "the seizable authority at stake" in the novel, an authority that is silenced by the male narrators in the novel and by many critics as well. Haruko Ohmine also points to Rosa's authority in "The Umbilical Cord of Narrative in *Absalom, Absalom!*" (*Faulkner Studies* 1:43–59) but suggests that her "monologic . . . discourse which has full authority and by its nature won't take any other voices and viewpoints into consideration" needs the corrective of Quentin's "dialogic voice" which would "restore the true implications and consequences of the Sutpen story." In a different direction, William D. Lindsey's "Order as Disorder: *Absalom, Absalom!*'s Inversion of the Judaeo-Christian Creation Myth" (*Faulkner and Religion,* pp. 85–102) examines the way Faulkner "sometimes transmutes myths in the process of adapting them." In this case, Sutpen's act of creation does not bring order—as in its biblical type—but disorder because of "a facile assumption of human innocence and of the unambiguous power of human rationality to calculate what is good." The novel, consequently, calls into question a variety of American myths.

The relationship between figurative language and "arguably one of the most sensitive and divisive issues of our day" is the subject of Janet Carey Eldred's "Faulkner's Still Life: Art and Abortion in *The Wild Palms*" (*FJ* 4 [1988–89]:139–58). Eldred argues that the entire narrative movement—and especially the fate of Charlotte, the artist who voices many of Faulkner's own aesthetic concerns—is tied to the literalization of still-life metaphors, and "Neither Faulkner's 'still life' aesthetics, nor the image of abortion that becomes strongly associated with it, can be reconciled to the metaphor of creativity as procreation."

vii Individual Works, 1940–1949

Some of this year's more successful applications of theory involved *The Hamlet* and *Go Down, Moses.* One interesting Bakhtinian reading is Millie M. Kidd's "The Dialogic Perspective in William Faulkner's *The Hamlet*" (*MissQ* 44:309–20). Kidd argues against the temptation to find a single authority in the text; on the contrary, the novel's "meaning is derived from the continual confrontation between the external narrator's generalizing field of vision and the particular view of individual characters who stand in equal and autonomous counterpoint to him and to each other." A confrontation of a different kind is the subject of Karen R. Sass's "Rejection of the Maternal and the Polarization of Gender in *The Hamlet*" (*FJ* 4 [1988–89]:127–38). Sass argues, from a Chodorovian model, that the dynamics of the novel's male-female relationships are characterized by the male's conflict of desire and repulsion of the feminine. Techniques of feminism and deconstruction inform David W. Robinson and Caren J. Town's "'Who Dealt These Cards?': The Excluded Narrators of *Go Down, Moses*" (*TCL* 37:192–206). The subtitle refers to the novel's black and white women, those who "may not always come to voice, but . . . nonetheless influence or even control what gets said." The ascendancy of these marginal voices provides a "profound critique of patriarchy" and indicates "a shift of power away from those who officially hold it toward those traditionally excluded." And deconstructionists will find familiar echoes in "Reading Typologically, For Example, Faulkner" (*AL* 63:693–711), Eleanor Cook's argument that *Go Down, Moses* "makes essential use of specific biblical typology" while simultaneously calling orthodox typology into question.

In a more traditional vein, Harbour Winn's "Lineage and the South: The Unity of Faulkner's *Go Down, Moses*" (*MQ* 32:453–73) examines the "complex lineal relationships juxtaposed in the sequence of the seven stories that portray [Faulkner's] version of the history of the South and comprise his loose novelistic structure."

viii Individual Works, 1950–1962

I was surprised to find only one essay dealing with late Faulkner, an area that most critics have seen as too long neglected and ripe for study. In "'It Aint Funny A-Tall': The Transfigured Tales of *The Town*" (*MissQ* 44:321–36) Theresa M. Towner compares Faulkner's initial versions of

"Centaur in Brass" and "Mule in the Yard" with their interpolated versions in *The Town.* Towner persuasively argues that Faulkner revised the stories in ways that emphasize Flem's ruthlessness and centrality: "As Flem comes to control aspects of life in Jefferson, the distinct episodes, comic or tragic, of *The Town* lose their individual integrity as they are absorbed into the novel's chronicle of his success."

ix The Stories

Partly because of the overshadowing novels, partly because of Faulkner's own deprecating remarks, his short stories have often received short shrift from critics. It is nice to see that situation changing. In a fine effort to illuminate a relatively neglected area of Faulkner studies, James Ferguson examines the periods, themes, and structures of *Faulkner's Short Fiction* (Tennessee). Noting that "it was the storytelling impulse that gave rise to both the short fiction and the novels," Ferguson calls attention to the "close and complex relationship between Faulkner's work in the two genres," and he urges us to study the stories both for their own sake and for access to the author's psychology and the originating ideas of many of his larger works. In a similar vein, many of Patrick Samway's "Intertextual Observations Concerning Faulkner's 'Mistral' " (*JSSE* 16:65–80) deal with this early story in the context of other early stories and sketches (such as "The Priest," "A Return," and "Snow"); but a more interesting observation examines the ways "Mistral" prefigures novels like *The Sound and the Fury, Absalom, Absalom!,* and *A Fable.* John F. Birk presents a close comparison of "A Rose for Emily" and "Ode on a Grecian Urn" in "Tryst Beyond Time: Faulkner's 'Emily' and Keats" (*SSF* 28:203–13). Milinda Schwab's "A Watch for Emily" (*SSF* 28:215–17) examines Emily's attempts to conquer time. In "Faulkner's 'Dry September' " (*Expl* 49:175–77) Brian Sutton seeks to correct Paul Rogalus's "oversimplifie[d]" version of "the nature and source of the accusations leading to the death of Will Mayes" (see *ALS 1990,* p. 164). Sutton correctly points out that Faulkner maintains ambiguity, referring to a rumor, not a specific allegation by Minnie Cooper. Edmond L. Volpe examines sexual ambiguities resulting from "the loss of male innocence" in "A Tale of Ambivalences: Faulkner's 'Divorce in Naples' " (*SSF* 28:41–45). Oliver Billingslea's "Fathers and Sons: The Spiritual Quest in Faulkner's 'Barn Burning' " (*MissQ* 44:287–308) sees the story contrapuntally, "a magnificently ambivalent text" balancing naturalism and romanticism. And in "Faulkner's Mature Narrative Technique: The Example of 'Tomorrow' " (*SCR* 23:129–35) Philip Cohen examines this "excellent but underappreciated . . . synthesis of traditional and modernist narrative conventions" to demonstrate how the later Faulkner "sought to harness non-traditional narrative technique in the service of a greater realism."

Randolph-Macon College

10 Fitzgerald and Hemingway

Susan F. Beegel

I usually begin this chapter by offering apologies for the slender output of Fitzgerald studies when subjected to comparison with a robust Hemingway industry. Not this year. I rejoice to report that with a critical edition of *The Great Gatsby,* five volumes of facsimile manuscripts, and three fine book-length treatments of Fitzgerald's fiction, not to mention an anthology of Zelda Fitzgerald's work and a feminist biography of her life, this has been a banner year. In addition, editor Ruth Prigozy of Hofstra University has produced the first edition of the *F. Scott Fitzgerald Society Newsletter,* an annual compendium of notes, reviews, bibliography, and professional news that promises to help keep Fitzgerald studies lively. If Fitzgerald scholarship shows a single weakness this year, it is too few well-turned essays, and virtually none at all focusing on the merits of a particular work. The field needs more essayists of the caliber of Milton Cohen or Morris Dickstein, and an energetic anthologist as well. Hemingway studies were only modestly productive, with book-length treatments of *A Farewell to Arms, The Old Man and the Sea,* and *A Moveable Feast,* and a superior anthology of new essays. *The Hemingway Review* and several other journals produced a crop of meat-and-potatoes articles. The biographical front was surprisingly quiet, and, perhaps blessedly, no previously unpublished material was exhumed for posthumous parade. I would have to summarize the year, though, by complaining that with a few notable exceptions Fitzgerald and Hemingway studies seem dangerously isolated from the controversial issues and approaches at large in the academy.

i Text and Bibliography

Matthew Bruccoli has once again made vitally important contributions to textual study of Fitzgerald's work. This year he has produced a long-awaited and long-needed critical edition of *The Great Gatsby* (Cambridge). Although I have not been able to examine the volume, which is out of stock and being reprinted as I write, Bruccoli's experience as editor of The Great Gatsby: *A Facsimile of the Manuscript* (1973) and author of the *Apparatus for F. Scott Fitzgerald's* The Great Gatsby (1974) clearly render him qualified to produce a critical edition of the novel, and it is good to see his effort enjoying success. Equally invigorating is Bruccoli's edition of *Zelda Fitzgerald: The Collected Writings* (Scribner's). Gathering the novel *Save Me the Waltz*, the farce *Scandalabra*, and the stories, articles, and letters in a single volume, Bruccoli has supplied a valuable tool for the growing number of scholars interested in Zelda Fitzgerald's writing career. Working in conjunction with associate editor Alan Margolies and consulting editors Alexander P. Clark and Charles Scribner III, he also has given us more volumes in what is to be an 18-volume set of *The F. Scott Fitzgerald Manuscripts* (Garland). Two late 1990 volumes incorporate the Melarkey and Kelley versions of *Tender is the Night;* two 1991 offerings, the Diver version of the same novel; and three final 1991 volumes collect the manuscripts of *The Vegetable,* Fitzgerald's short stories, and his articles. As I noted last year, an introduction, inventory of extant materials, and chronology of composition are provided for each title in the series, together with facsimiles of all known working notes, manuscripts, typescripts, corrected carbons, and galley proofs, arranged in chronological order of composition. Making Fitzgerald's craft as a writer accessible for all, this carefully executed series is a must purchase for college and university libraries.

Sadly, Hemingway studies seems to lack a Matthew Bruccoli, an editor with the right stuff for breaking the critical-edition barrier. Still, textual studies of Hemingway's work are moving in an encouraging direction. Instead of yet another posthumously mutilated version of previously unpublished work, the year produced a book-length study of *A Moveable Feast* and its manuscripts, work that could eventually lead to a critical edition. Jacqueline Tavernier-Courbin's *Ernest Hemingway's* A Moveable Feast: *The Making of Myth* (Northeastern) is a contextual and textual study of Hemingway's posthumously published memoir. In her first five chapters Tavernier-Courbin discusses in detail the evidence supporting Mary Hemingway's controversial claim that *A Moveable Feast* was based on papers retrieved from the Ritz Hotel; the chronology of the book's composition; its lax treatment of settings in Paris, Lyons, and Schruns; its deliberately inaccurate portrayal of various expatriate writers and artists; and its purposeful aggrandizement of the Hemingway persona. The final three chapters discuss, in order, Hemingway's borrowings for *A Moveable Feast* from early manuscripts and discarded material, Hemingway's own revisions to the manuscripts, and finally the book's posthumous editing by Mary Hemingway and others. Despite its lyricism, literary merit, and biographical interest, *A Moveable Feast* has been widely neglected. Tavernier-Courbin's exhaustively researched study, the first book-length consideration of Hemingway's memoir, creates a solid foundation for future critics by delineating precisely where authorial achievement does and does not reside in the heavily edited published text. *The Making of Myth* is flawed, however, by Tavernier-Courbin's failure to appreciate the uses of mythology. Despite acknowledging that Hemingway called *A Moveable Feast* a "fiction" no less than 18 times in the manuscript, she records her dismay at geographical and historical inaccuracies by the dozen. She does not distinguish between unimportant lapses of memory (in a fiction, it scarcely matters whether streets run parallel or intersect) and supremely important inventions (the deliberate distortion of personal relationships holds clues to narrative strategy).

On the bibliographical front, I provided the new *F. Scott Fitzgerald Newsletter* with a modest compilation of 1990 Fitzgerald scholarship. Matters will improve next year, when Albert J. DeFazio, trained at the University of Virginia's Center for Bibliographic Studies, becomes the Fitzgerald Society's bibliographer. DeFazio's carefully compiled and annotated bibliographies of current research in each issue of *The Hemingway Review* (*HN* 10, ii:84–93; 11, i:69–77) are an important service to Hemingway scholarship, and Fitzgerald studies will benefit from a similarly comprehensive effort by DeFazio. "News from the Hemingway Collection" (*HN* 10, ii:73–77; 11, i:62–64) by Megan Floyd Desnoyers and Lisa Middents continues to provide information on recent manuscript acquisitions and openings at the John F. Kennedy Library.

ii Letters and Biography

Edited by Linda Patterson Miller, *Letters from the Lost Generation: Gerald and Sara Murphy and Friends* (Rutgers) has created excitement in both Fitzgerald and Hemingway circles. The volume contains 262 letters to and from the Murphys and famous friends, including F. Scott and Zelda Fitzgerald, Ernest and Pauline Hemingway, Dorothy Parker and Alan Campbell, Archibald and Ada MacLeish, and John and Katy Dos Passos, among others. Miller's editorship is light-handed and exemplary. She divides this extensive correspondence into three parts, roughly corresponding to the youth, middle age, and final years of the participants. A well-written biographical essay introduces each section, familiarizing the reader with events under discussion. Miller allows the correspondents to speak for themselves, providing each letter with a brief headnote explaining its context and obscurities, rather than burdening its text with unwieldy notes. The resulting book is fascinating. No matter how much one may have read about the Hemingways and the Fitzgeralds, there are new insights to be gained here. A letter from Gerald Murphy to Hemingway, urging him to divorce Hadley, and a very lucid letter from Zelda Fitzgerald, musing on Scott's death, are among the surprises. Hemingway's tender relationship with the Murphys' consumptive son Patrick, and Sara Murphy's lifelong exasperation with Fitzgerald's self-centered behavior are also striking. Indeed, Miller's gathering together the relics of so many remarkable individuals enriches our understanding of them all.

Hemingway biography this year is plunged into the near-silence of an examination room before the proctor calls "time up," while Gioia Diliberto, Peter Griffin, James Mellow, and Michael Reynolds work on their respective book-length projects. There is only a single biographical essay to report. In "Who Removed Hemingway's Ruptured Spleen?" (*HN* 11, i:31–33) Peter Hays and Douglas B. Lurie, M.D., prescribe a substantial dose of skepticism to be taken with Hemingway's preposterous exaggerations of his African plane-crash injuries. Hays also contributes an "Interview with Dr. John H. Jones" (*HN* 11, i:34–37), who played tennis with the Hemingway sons when the Hemingways visited Piggott, Arkansas, during the 1930s.

F. Scott Fitzgerald too received only an essay's worth of biographical attention this year, albeit a superb exercise in critical biography by Milton A. Cohen. "Fitzgerald's Third Regret: Intellectual Pretense and the Ghost of Edmund Wilson" (*TSLL* 33:64–88) describes Fitzgerald's intellectual intimidation by the self-righteous and severe "scholar-priest" Edmund Wilson. Cohen builds a convincing case for ascribing the intellectual pretensions of protagonists Amory Blaine, Anthony Patch, and Dick Diver to Fitzgerald's fruitless efforts to deflect Wilson's "unsettling mix of collegial assistance, acute insight, patronizing advice, condescension, and insult."

This year's biographers were more interested in Zelda Fitzgerald than her husband. She received dubious attention in William Wiser's *The*

Great Good Place (Norton), a book treating five women expatriates (Mary Cassatt, Edith Wharton, Caresse Crosby, and Josephine Baker are the others) who passed "the most critical or significant years of their lives" in Paris. The unsympathetic chapter "Zelda Fitzgerald, 1900–1948" (pp. 214–68) is an example of fictionalized biography at its audacious worst, with invented thoughts, dialogue, and "scenes." Far more engaging is *Zelda Fitzgerald and the Failure of the American Dream for Women* (Peter Lang), an impassioned feminist revision of Fitzgerald biography by Koula Svokos Hartnett. Beginning with Zelda's childhood and ending with her death in a hospital fire, Hartnett views her as a threefold victim: first of a culture conditioning women to accept marriage as the most desirable "career," next of an abusive and egotistical husband demeaning her talents and appropriating her work, and finally of psychiatrists endeavoring to enforce her conformity to self-serving masculine ideals of feminine "sanity." There is a good deal wrong with this book, not the least its partisan oversimplification of the intertwining complexities of Scott and Zelda Fitzgerald's mutually destructive marriage. The text could have benefited from a thorough editing to eliminate assorted malapropisms, clichés, grammatical errors, and stylistic infelicities. Yet *Zelda Fitzgerald and the Failure of the American Dream* is a lively and contentious offering, and it raises some important questions. What role did Scott's alcoholism and insolvency play in driving Zelda's belated career mania? Was she herself an alcoholic? What motivated the abortion(s) she underwent in wedlock? Was Zelda schizophrenic as diagnosed, or was her mental illness depression, exacerbated by prolonged incarceration and inappropriate treatment, as Hartnett contends? This book depends too heavily on secondary sources to provide convincing answers, but as the most extended feminist investigation to date of Zelda Fitzgerald's tragedy it should encourage biographers to look again.

iii Influences, Sources, Parallels

The influence of Francis Cugat's original cover art for *The Great Gatsby* on Fitzgerald's revisions of the novel was a hot topic. You will recall that the cover depicts a beautiful woman's weeping, nude-reflecting, disembodied eyes hovering in the night sky over carnival lights. In "Covering a Debt: F. Scott Fitzgerald and Francis Cugat" (*MFS* 37:235–39) D. Mesher argues that Cugat's jacket illustration was "written into the book" as Fitzgerald claimed, but *not* as the eyes of Doctor T. J. Eckleburg, as scholars have long insisted. Rather, Mesher sees the illustration as the source for "I had no girl whose disembodied face floated along the dark cornices and blinding signs," and uses the *Gatsby* manuscript to show Fitzgerald working toward a more accurate depiction of the art. In "Celestial Eyes—from Metamorphosis to Masterpiece," an illustrated brochure designed by Micki L. Katz and published on 24 October 1991 by "MJB, CS III, and PS to celebrate the Critical Edition of *The Great Gatsby,*" Charles Scribner III discusses Fitzgerald's indebtedness to Cugat and Matthew J. Bruccoli's discovery and purchase of eight Cugat sketches for the *Gatsby* jacket.

One Hemingway work of nonfiction and two novels attracted influence studies. In "Hemingway's View of Emerson: A Note on His Reading" (*HN* 11, i:40–45) John Martin looks at Hemingway's growing respect for Emerson during the course of his career, and argues, not very convincingly, that *Green Hills of Africa* shows indebtedness. *The Sun Also Rises* fared better. An elegant essay by Kathleen Morgan, "Between Two Worlds: Hemingway's Brett Ashley and Homer's Helen of Troy" (*CML* 11:169–80), provides a detailed comparison of the two characters and argues that they are similar, not because *The Iliad* influenced *The Sun Also Rises,* but because "expectations about the behavior of men and women are so similar in the two works." I am disposed to applaud Linda Wagner-Martin's unflinching "Racial and Sexual Coding in Hemingway's *The Sun Also Rises*" (*HN* 10, ii:39–41). She views Hemingway's naming a prostitute for gifted lesbian chanteuse Georgette LeBlanc and his anti-Semitic portrayal of Robert Cohn as characteristic attempts to deny his indebtedness to the many Paris lesbians who helped advance his early career, including and especially lesbian and Jewish Gertrude Stein. Joel Hodson's "Robert Jordan Revisited: Hemingway's Debt to T. E. Lawrence" (*HN* 10, ii:2–16) presents a persuasive argument that the character of Robert Jordan is indebted to T. E. Lawrence's self-characterization in *The Seven Pillars of Wisdom,* and the plot of *For Whom the Bell Tolls* to Lawrence's Book VI—"The Raid Upon the Bridges." Finally, Wolfgang Rudat, continuing his loosely Freudian allusion studies of psychosexuality in Hemingway's fiction, has given us two essays—"The Other War in Hemingway's *For Whom the Bell Tolls:* Maria and Miltonic Gender-Role Battles" (*HN* 11, i:8–24) and "Robert Jordan and Hamlet's Conflicts: *For Whom the Bell Tolls* as Family Romance" (*JEP* 12, i–ii:65–78).

iv Criticism

a. Full-Length Studies: Fitzgerald In this unusually bountiful year for Fitzgerald studies we have three book-length works on his fiction. Twayne's "Masterwork Studies," a series designed to provide "reader's companions" to canonical novels, has given us Richard Lehan's The Great Gatsby: *The Limits of Wonder.* Following the format of the series, Lehan gives us a detailed chronology of Fitzgerald's life and work, followed by useful chapters on historical context, "importance," and critical reception of the novel. Of these obligatory exercises, that on historical context is, surprisingly, most interesting. Lehan, with a strong historic bent, enlivens the well-known facts of the Roaring Twenties (disillusionment following World War I, unprecedented wealth, Prohibition, and all that), with some lesser-known statistics about tax rates for the rich and fatal automobile accidents. We arrive next at the portion of the volume giving Lehan most scope for originality. In an 108-page reading of *The Great Gatsby,* he analyzes in clear and engaging prose the novel's plot, themes, characters, and style and unfolds a richly allusive work of literature. Lehan underscores Fitzgerald's use of autobiographical material (e.g., his broken romance with Ginevra King, his intellectual nurture by Shane Leslie), of historical figures (from Buffalo Bill Cody to Arnold Rothstein), and of literary masterpieces (John Keats's "Isabella and the Pot of Basil," Willa Cather's *A Lost Lady,* Eliot's "The Wasteland," and a host of others). Lehan is eloquent on Fitzgerald's own keen sense of history as exhibited in the novel and whetted by historians including Henry Adams, Frederick Jackson Turner, and particularly Oswald Spengler. This critic excels on the novel's stance toward America's burgeoning multicultural diversity in the 1920s. The only disappointment is Lehan's failure to interest himself in the novel's women characters or the tumultuous changes affecting their real-life contemporaries. He falters too in a final required chapter on style and meaning, viewing style almost exclusively as a pattern of meaning formed by the associative power of repeated images. I cannot, however, recommend this study strongly enough to its intended audience—students and other first-time readers seeking a detailed background for understanding *The Great Gatsby.* It is both readable and learned, and in its detailed treatment of history and literary allusion constitutes a crash course very like Fitzgerald's own "College of One."

This year also saw two books on Fitzgerald's short fiction. Bryant Mangum's useful offering is unfortunately titled *A Fortune Yet: Money in the Art of F. Scott Fitzgerald's Short Stories* (Garland), a misnomer leading one to expect a dreary thematic study. Instead, Mangum's book, like his more appropriately titled 1974 doctoral dissertation, is really "a study in literary economics," a significant investigation of the magazine market's impact on Fitzgerald's art. Ambitious in scope, *A Fortune Yet* spans Fitzgerald's career, covering almost all of the 146 stories published during the author's lifetime. Mangum treats the stories in clusters defined by their relationships to Fitzgerald's developing strategies for critical success, his financial need to respect the formulae of the most lucrative magazine markets, and his occasional use of the short stories as trying grounds for the novels. Two appendixes listing the date of composition, date and place of publication, and price received for each story give a valuable overview of the rise and fall of Fitzgerald's marketability. A significant addition to the growing literature on the short fiction, Mangum's study might nevertheless have been enriched by increased attention to the biographical (how intense was Fitzgerald's financial need from year-to-year?) and historical (how did the depression affect the magazine market?) components of "literary economics." A more detailed demographic presentation of specific magazine audiences and an appreciation of the female consumer's vital role in this market would also have improved the book.

John Kuehl's *F. Scott Fitzgerald: A Study of the Short Fiction* necessarily follows the formula of the Twayne "Studies in Short Fiction" series by providing a brief critical overview of Fitzgerald's career from apprentice pieces to posthumous publications. Kuehl's Part I overview of the career is an impressive display of erudition about Fitzgerald's short fiction. The extended essay sparkles with apt quotation and insightful brief interpretations of the stories, and it certainly constitutes, as it is meant to do, an excellent introduction to the subject. However, Kuehl has decided that only eight of Fitzgerald's short stories are *really* important, and by treating these at length he neglects other works that might vie for honors. His choices ("May Day," "The Rich Boy," "The Ice Palace," "Absolution," "Winter Dreams," "Crazy Sunday," "Babylon Revisited," and "The Diamond as Big as the Ritz") are traditional, and so his discussion does little to enlarge or freshen the Fitzgerald canon for the 1990s. Part II, "Scott Fitzgerald's Critical Opinions," is a revised and expanded version of a 1961 essay by Kuehl, a sophisticated review of Fitzgerald's theories on composition and creativity. In Part III, an all-male cast of critics offers opinions on seven of the eight important stories ("The Ice Palace" is omitted). The volume concludes with a 1935 meditation by William Troy on Fitzgerald as moralist.

b. Full-Length Studies: Hemingway Thanks to the Twayne "Masterwork Studies," there were two full-length treatments of novels by Hemingway this year. Robert W. Lewis's A Farewell to Arms: *The War of the Words* succinctly reviews the novel's literary and historical context—the global catastrophe of World War I, the stature of *A Farewell to Arms* as a classic of modernist fiction, the shocked reception of its graphic depiction of war and sexuality by contemporary critics. It goes on to offer a reading of the novel with special attention to the characterization of Frederic Henry and Catherine Barkley and the development of a narrative voice, point of view, and multiplicity of themes. Best of all is the 21-page chapter "The War of the Words," a particularly fine essay on the inability of both public and private language to convey meaning in *A Farewell to Arms.* Lewis's book is an excellent introduction to the novel for students. He summarizes and makes accessible more than 60 years of extensive scholarship on this much-criticized work. His tone is reassuring and teacherly. Lewis takes nothing for granted, and he can provide a humorous reminder that "tenente" is Italian for lieutenant and not Frederic Henry's last name, while at the same time introducing the uninitiated to more complex and controversial matters, including the novel's narrative structure and feminist approaches to Catherine Barkley.

Gerry Brenner's *The Old Man and the Sea: Story of a Common Man* is another kettle of fish. Always readable, Brenner makes short work of the publisher-mandated categories of literary and historical context, and he is particularly interesting on the 1945–55 decade, neglected by Hemingway scholars and recent enough to be mysterious. Brenner's ostensible mission is to overturn critics who disparage Hemingway's novella as "a sanitary text . . . highly suitable for impressionable teenagers" and to justify the Twayne series title by proving *Old Man* "a masterwork" that "speak(s) across historical periods to a broad range of readers" and "engage(s) readers emotionally and intellectually with its complex treatment of recurrent human issues." Here he begins to pound the novella with a perfect battery of contemporary ideological and psychoanalytic approaches that it simply cannot withstand. His Santiago is an ecocriminal who ought to husband the fragile resources of the sea and practice "catch-and-release" fishing. He is a sexist, as evidenced by the misogynistic language he uses to damn poisonous jellyfish. He has "latent, unconscious homosexual feelings toward Manolin that he cannot accept in himself." He is a "passive-aggressive cripple." *Old Man* is tried and found guilty against a 1990s system of values the 1950s could not begin to imagine. The irreverent Brenner also attacks the celebrated Hemingway style, finding it riddled with inappropriate similes, paternalistic slogans, squinting modifiers, and "silly sentences." He concludes that *Old Man* is *not* a "mounted-on-rails" book (the metaphor is drawn from bullfighting, and describes a straight-charging, easy-to-cape bull) but instead deserves "the attention reserved for masterpieces." A tongue-in-cheek study that demonstrates either the novel's irrelevance to contemporary academic discourse or contemporary academic discourse's irrelevance to *Old Man,* this is the most provocative Hemingway study of 1991, and one hopes it will inspire fierce debate both in the classroom and in the literature.

c. Collections: Fitzgerald This is the second year in a row without a collection of essays on Fitzgerald's work.

d. Collections: Hemingway Editor Frank Scafella's *Hemingway: Essays of Reassessment* (Oxford) was the single collection on Hemingway's work this year. It is a fine general anthology with a number of ground-breaking essays and, astonishingly, no real clangers for filler, as is the case with too many such volumes. The book gathers 16 offerings (two reprinted, 14 original) under three headings: "Fiction and the Manuscripts," "Fiction and Biography," and "Fiction and Psychology." Selections are interleaved, à la *In Our Time,* with previously unpublished quotations from the Hemingway Collection of the John F. Kennedy Library. Scafella's brief introduction (pp. 7–13) gives a capsule overview of each essay.

The section on "Fiction and the Manuscripts" begins with Hershel Parker's "Textual Criticism and the Manuscripts" (pp. 17–31). A widely experienced editor and textual scholar, Parker congratulates Hemingway researchers on the rich possibilities presented by numerous available manuscripts, but he cautions against several varieties of flawed thinking afflicting textual studies of the works of other authors. William Balassi's "The Trail to *The Sun Also Rises:* The First Week of Writing" (pp. 33–51) is a narrative describing, session-by-session, how Hemingway at age 26 began to sketch the characters and events of his first novel. In "Roger Davis of *Islands:* What the Manuscript Adds" (pp. 53–60) Robert E. Fleming looks at the holograph manuscript of *Islands in the Stream* and discovers that the hard-boiled character called Roger Davis in the published version evolved from an earlier character named Roger Hancock, "a sensitive, troubled artist" whose "creation is a confessional act that shows much more about the inward terrain of the writer than Hemingway was ever able to reveal in his published works." My own "Ernest Hemingway's 'A Lack of Passion'" (pp. 62–78) follows, offering the first critical and biographical interpretation and a composition history of the short story, posthumously published last year (*HN* 9, ii:49–93). Paul Smith's "The Bloody Typewriter and the Burning Snakes" (pp. 80–90) concludes the section with a startling discovery from the "Now I Lay Me" manuscripts—in an early version of the story Nick is called "Ernie" and has been *helping his mother* clean the basement and burn his father's prized biological specimens.

"Fiction and Biography" begins with Scott Donaldson's "Toward a Definitive Biography" (pp. 93–103), a thought-provoking catalog of problems from the practical (copyright restrictions) to the theoretical (achieving intellectual empathy) that confront all would-be biographers. With "In the Nominal Country of the Bogus: Hemingway's Catholicism and the Biographies" (pp. 105–40), H. R. Stoneback lashes biographers for failure to accept the author's Catholicism and provides compelling evidence that his conversion was genuine. "Shadowboxing in the Hemingway Biographies" (pp. 142–53), by the combative Donald Junkins, accuses Hemingway's biographers of "fail[ure] to perceive that the dark side of Hemingway's psyche was the vital and necessary root house of his creativity, his personality, and his genius." A shared tendency to moralize, according to Junkins, makes his biographers in general, and Kenneth Lynn in particular, "anti-Hemingway." Biographer Michael Reynolds offers "Up Against the Crannied Wall: The Limits of Biography" (pp. 170–78), a meditation on the unknowability of any biographical subject, on the fictionalization of life by memory almost as it happens. The "Fiction and Biography" section also includes a reprinting (pp. 155–68) of Jackson J. Benson's thought-provoking 1989 essay, "The Life as Fiction and the Fiction as Life."

Earl Rovit kicks off the "Fiction and Psychology" section with a fine meditation, "On Psychic Retrenchment in Hemingway" (pp. 181–88).

He views the final 10 sentences of *The Sun Also Rises* as presenting Jake's "establishment of his own isolation . . . as a kind of moral success" and a proof that "exclusion . . . for Hemingway [is] an instinctive psychic response, a social creed, an aesthetic principle." Ben Stoltzfus follows with "*The Old Man and the Sea:* A Lacanian Reading" (pp. 190–99). This controversial piece demonstrates, with diagrams, how Santiago's dreams of Africa and lions, and daydreams about Joe DiMaggio, fighting cocks, and bone spurs, represent his own—and Hemingway's—latent desire to supplant the "law of the father." Mark Spilka's "The Importance of Being Androgynous" (pp. 201–12) is next, reprinted from his 1990 book, *Hemingway's Quarrel with Androgyny* (Nebraska). "The Concept of Voice, the Voices of Frederic Henry, and the Structure of *A Farewell to Arms*" (pp. 214–32) by James Phelan uses contemporary narrative theory to argue that during the course of a novel more carefully structured than many have realized, Frederic's voice "gradually mov[es] closer to the values of the orchestrator of the voices, Hemingway himself." Tony Whitmore's "Gaiety and Psyche: *For Whom the Bell Tolls*" (pp. 234–44) demonstrates how joking in Hemingway's Spanish Civil War novel becomes "emblematic of an attitude, at first called cheerfulness and then gaiety," which in turn becomes "one of the 'fundamental symbols of consciousness.'" Gerry Brenner's "A Lamp on the Anxiety in Hemingway's 'Vital Light'" (pp. 246–56) concludes the anthology. Brenner concedes that Hemingway's work is variously driven "by wounding, by never-reconciled filial problems with his parents, by homoerotic and androgynous tendencies, and by various cultural agents," but he goes on to insist that the author's primary psychic impulse is an "anxiety of misidentification," a fear of being "misconstrued, misread, misunderstood, or mistaken by others."

e. General Essays: Fitzgerald I am able to record just two truly general essays on Fitzgerald. Both strike me as worthwhile. "F. Scott Fitzgerald: From Religious Symbols to Symbols of Affluence," a chapter (pp. 179–221) in Henry Idema III's *Freud, Religion, and the Roaring Twenties,* records the replacement of Catholic symbolism in the Fitzgerald canon by symbols of material yearning. Morris Dickstein's "Fitzgerald's Second Act" (*SAQ* 90:555–78) provides a similarly overarching view of the canon, this time with an eye toward exploring how, after the Crash of '29, Fitzgerald "tried to build a new career by exploring the ways in which he had been over-extended, self-destructive, like America itself during the Boom years . . . mak[ing] his personal plight . . . somehow definitive of the age."

f. General Essays: Hemingway General essays on Hemingway's fiction were more abundant. A number of them treat clusters of short stories. In "You Can Say That Again: Some Encounters with Repetition in *In Our Time*" (*HN* 10, ii:47–55) Don Summerhayes looks at patterns of repetition within *In Our Time* as a whole. He emphasizes dialogue: as different characters from different stories speak the same lines with new spins on meaning, the case for the thematic unity of the collection grows. Paul Strong's "The First Nick Adams Stories" (*SSF* 28:83–91) also looks at the unity of *In Our Time,* focusing on the contrapuntal plot elements of the Nick Adams stories, with special reference to their manuscript versions. Barry Stampfl in "Similes as Thematic Clues in Three Hemingway Short Stories" (*HN* 10, ii:30–38) borrows from psychoanalysis to interpret Hemingway's use of the words "as if," "like," and "evidently" in the short stories "The End of Something," "The Mother of a Queen," and "Hills Like White Elephants." Paul Smith's "The Chronology of *The First Forty-nine Stories*" (*HN* 11, i:2–7) details the actual order in which Hemingway's collected stories were composed, compares it to the fictive order presented in *The First Forty-nine,* and comments on what the discrepancies reveal about the astonishingly rapid rise and fall of the author's skill as a writer of short stories.

Of two other general essays on Hemingway's fiction, one was, predictably, centered on the still-engrossing gender question; another focused, less predictably, on changing attitudes toward religions. J. Gerald Kennedy's "Hemingway's Gender Trouble" (*AL* 63:187–207) is a judicious comparison of attitudes toward gender, sex, and desire in *A Moveable Feast* and *The Garden of Eden.* Kennedy's discovery of an unpublished sketch from *A Moveable Feast* detailing an experiment with androgyny undertaken by Hemingway in 1924 suggests that the memoir's heterosexual posturing is actually underlain by the same troubled attraction toward androgyny made explicit in the novel. Idema's *Freud, Religion, and the Roaring Twenties* contains a chapter titled "Ernest Hemingway: From Religious Communities to the Privatization of Religion" (pp. 135–77), a fine, commonsense study of religion in Hemingway's work. Focusing on selected short stories and the major novels, Idema looks at the erosion of small-town religious practices by various forces of modernism and their replacement by secular rituals, including trout fishing and bullfighting.

g. Essays on Specific Works: Fitzgerald Regretfully, I have nothing to report in this category.

h. Essays on Specific Works: Hemingway A number of often-criticized Hemingway short stories continued to merit individual attention. Paul Robert Lamb's "Fishing for Stories: What 'Big Two-Hearted River' is Really About" (*MFS* 37:161–81) focuses on the story's deleted ending, published posthumously as "On Writing," to demonstrate in some detail that "Big Two-Hearted River" is not about Nick Adams's war wound or his overbearing mother, but about his developing vocation as a writer. Stephen Miko also rejects "the traumatizers" in another essay on "Big Two-Hearted River": "The River, the Iceberg, and the Shit-detector" (*Criticism* 33:503–21). He also rejects the relevance of "On Writing," critical consensus that Nick's actions are "neurotically overcontrolled," and anything else a New Critic might deem imported from "outside" the story. Miko is left with the novel idea that "Big Two-Hearted River" is exclusively about savoring a fishing expedition, a single-minded short story after all. Howard Hannum's " 'Jig Jig to Dirty Ears': White Elephants to Let" (*HN* 11, i:46–54) provides a reading of "Hills Like White Elephants" which considers the male protagonist's evolving worthlessness to his pregnant partner. Lastly, in "Tracking the Wounded Buffalo: Authorial Knowledge and the Shooting of Francis Macomber" (*HN* 11, i:25–30) Kathleen Morgan and Luis Losada examine, with reference to books owned by Hemingway, the technical details of the big game hunting scenes in "The Short Happy Life of Francis Macomber."

Hemingway's sole play was the subject of a single essay, Erik Nakjavani's "Politics, Propaganda, and the Esthetics of Detective Fiction: The Case of Hemingway's *The Fifth Column*" (*JAC* 14, ii:81–90). Nakjavani reads *The Fifth Column* as political propaganda that uses the popular techniques of the detective story to persuade its audience.

Among Hemingway's novels, *A Farewell to Arms* and *The Garden of Eden* were most popular with critics this year, scoring two essays apiece. Scott Donaldson's "Censorship and *A Farewell to Arms*" (*SAF* 19:85–93) gives a thorough and often humorous history of the novel's suppression in serial form by Boston police and its subsequent bowdlerization by

Charles Scribner's Sons. D. Quentin Miller in a brief essay titled " 'In the Late Summer of That Year': The Problem of Time in *A Farewell to Arms*" (*HN* 10, ii:61–64) chronicles references to time in the novel and concludes, not astonishingly, that Frederic's attitude toward time is affected by his fear of dying in war. In "En-Gendered Problems: Characteral Conflict in Hemingway's *Garden*" (*LIT* 3:115–35) Jerry A. Varsava views criticism of *The Garden of Eden* as divided into two camps: a "protextual" school, reading David Bourne as a "code hero" striving to preserve his artistic identity in the teeth of his wife's emasculating madness; and a "contratextual" or feminist faction, privileging Catherine's point of view and demonizing David. Varsava sensibly suggests combining these seemingly incompatible views and recognizing that the "behavioral straitjacket" of gender expectations victimizes both men and women in Hemingway's fiction. K. J. Peters's "The Thematic Integrity of *The Garden of Eden*" (*HN* 10, ii:17–29) provides a pedestrian comparison of the published version with the manuscript and seems unaware of seminal work on this subject by Barbara Solomon and Robert Fleming.

Two other Hemingway novels attracted single essays. "Nice and Pleasant in *The Sun*" (*HN* 10, ii:42–46) by Louise R. Achuff explores how Hemingway uses such apparently vague and neutral words as "nice," "fine," and "pleasant" to carry "what Harry Levin calls 'the heavy load of subjective implication.' " And in "Ringing the Changes: Hemingway's *Bell* Tolls Fifty" (*VQR* 67:1–18) Michael Reynolds argues that the contemporary reader, jaded by World War II, Korea, and Vietnam, is no longer interested in the subject matter and historical context of *For Whom the Bell Tolls.* However, critical attention to its postmodernist values—gender roles, self-referencing, appropriation, multiple framing, narrative guises, and writing about writing—may "rehabilitate" the novel for our time.

i. Miscellaneous Sam B. Girgus's *Desire and the Political Unconscious in American Literature* (St. Martin's, 1990), which I accidentally overlooked last year, includes a fine and sophisticated chapter titled "Love Goddess" (pp. 180–223) that treats Fitzgerald and Hemingway together. Girgus applies psychoanalytic theory to *The Great Gatsby, The Sun Also Rises,* and *A Farewell to Arms* to demonstrate how characters in these novels embody American society in the 1920s when "love, instead of providing security and warmth, engenders division, while culture signals collapse and fear of the future."

Let me conclude by bidding this space a reluctant but firm farewell. When in 1989 I accepted the task of writing an annual review of Hemingway and Fitzgerald scholarship, a favorite mentor warned me to stay no longer than three years. My three-year term is up, and I am bowing out while it is still comparatively safe to slink down the corridors of convention hotels. To fellow laborers in the vineyard of Hemingway and Fitzgerald studies, my apologies for any affronts and my thanks for three years of stimulating reading.

University of West Florida

Part II

11 Literature to 1800

William J. Scheick

"Much reading is an oppression of the mind, and extinguishes the natural candle, which is the reason of so many senseless scholars in the world" (William Penn, 1699). "My inclination towards learning has been so violent and strong that neither the scoldings of other people . . . nor my own reflections . . . have been able to stop me from following this natural impulse that God gave me. He alone must know why" (Juana Inés de la Cruz, 1691).

i Native Americans and the Colonial Imagination

Undertaking a comparative approach to Gaspar Perez de Villagrá and William Bradford in "Reading Against the Grain: Origin Stories and American Literary History" (*AmLH* 3:209–31), Andrew Wiget notes their different use of biblical and classical tradition, of Roman Catholic inclusion or Calvinistic separation, and of policies concerning the conversion of Native Americans. Their divergent writings, however, mutually contrast to Native American regard for a sacred center (rather than for a distant horizon) and for the conjunction of the material and the supernatural. Relatedly, Earl E. Fitz's *Rediscovering the New World: Inter-American Literature in a Comparative Context* (Iowa) concludes that the plots of the narratives written by explorers from four European nations feature a conflict between the individual and nature, and between one culture and another; New World epics, moreover, adhere to literary rather than to folk models.

In *Ideas '92* (6 [1990]:85–92) Norman S. Grabo's "Villagrá: Between a Rock and Other Hard Places" discloses the poet's use of epic manner as a strategy to defend the conquistadores. In the same issue Julie Greer Johnson's "New World Chronicles and Histories: A Self-Evaluation" (pp. 3–12) notes that colonial satire relies on the example of parody; Frank Norris's "Americo Vespucci's First Voyage" (pp. 33–41) indicates that there is no reason to accept the explorer's account of a voyage to continental America in 1499; and Maureen Ahern's "Alarcón on the Colorado River: Communication and Strategies in His *Relatione della Navigatione et Scoperta* (1540)" (pp. 67–76) observes how discursive practices textually re-create the geographical frontier experience of negotiating the gap between the familiar and the strange.

These narratives of negotiation emerge in Stephen Greenblatt's *Marvelous Possessions* as "mimetic capital," a stockpile of images that have been banked (accumulated) in various cultural modes and are withdrawn to be circulated by means of acts of appropriation, whereby anything nouveau is eventually made to reinforce this same capital. Columbus's necessarily binary rhetoric of the "marvelous," for a typical example, functions as a reflector and as an agent of his own and his culture's colonizing/converting imperative; this rhetoric mediates desires and fears, spirituality and carnality, subjective impressions and oblique perceptions. Rhetorical mediation also interests Louis Montrose, whose "The Work of Gender in the Discourse of Discovery" (*Representations* 33:1–41) focuses on the conjunction of the savage and the feminine in the colonial imagination; this association inverts hidden European male intentions toward the New World. That Jesuit narratives were shaped by preconceptions, especially those interpreting Native Americans as a template of spirituality within providential history, is the subject of "L'éloge de I'Indien dans les Relations des Jesuites" (*CanL* 131:26–35) by Denis Lafrenière.

Mary C. Fuller's "Ralegh's Fugitive Gold: Reference and Deferral in *The Discoverie of Guiana*" (*Representations* 33:42–64) notes various colonial acts of metonymic figuration that always failed to reveal the ambiguity of the New World. The marginalization of the lust for gold interests Frederick A. de Armas in "Fashioning a New World: Lope de Vega and Claramonte's *El nuevo rey Gallinato*" (*Critical Essays on the Literatures of Spain and Spanish America*, ed. Luis T. González-del-Valle and Julio Baena [Boulder, Colo.: Soc. of Spanish and Spanish-American Studies], pp. 1–10); in Claramonte's play, de Armas observes, the desire for power is transformed into a fantasy of alchemical union of self and assimilated Other.

Concern with the aboriginal Other also surfaces in Peter Wild's synoptic *Alvar Núñez Cabeza de Vaca* (BSWWS 101) and in Bernard

Bailyn and Philip D. Morgan's anthology, *Strangers within the Realm: Cultural Margins of the First British Empire* (No. Car.). In the latter volume James H. Merrell's " 'The Customes of Our Countrey': Indians and Colonists in Early America" (pp. 117–56) and Philip D. Morgan's "British Encounters with Africans and African Americans, circa 1600–1780" (pp. 157–219) explore the complexities of frontierlike cultural interaction. In "Pilgrims' Paradox" (*Natural History,* 100, xi:22–26) Samuel M. Wilson details the evolution of the Pilgrims as a cultural icon and Thanksgiving as an uncertain commemoration, and especially (following Lynn Ceci's findings) the invention of Squanto to mask both unpleasant colonial relations with and the fate of the Patuxet.

That the largest "Praying Town" established by John Eliot succumbed to disease, war, racism, economics, and environmental change is documented by Daniel Mandell, whose " 'To Live More Like My Christian English Neighbors': Natick Indians in the Eighteenth Century" (*WMQ* 48:552–79) concludes that the inhabitants of this town sold their land at first to prosper, then to survive. "Increase Mather's *De Successu Evangelij Apud Indos in Nova-Anglia Epistola:* A Commentary and Translation" (*RALS* 17:208–19) presents Catherine S. Vellake's edition of a defense of Puritan missionary activity. And David R. Ransome unearths a document that suggests the sincere intention of the Virginia Company to convert Native Americans to Christianity: "Pocahontas and the Mission to the Indians" (*VMHB* 99:81–94).

One prominent member of the Virginia Company is the subject of Kevin J. Hayes's useful annotated bibliography of secondary scholarship, *Captain John Smith: A Reference Guide* (Hall), and of J. A. Leo Lemay's polemical *The American Dream of Captain John Smith* (Virginia). Lemay determines that Smith's promotional literature, its pastoral tinge notwithstanding, is more realistic in manner (particularly in its record of Native American cultures) and more concerned with hard work and environmental impact than was characteristic of the genre at the time. Believing that honest labor was the way to wealth, Lemay reports, Smith attributed diligence as well as courage, perseverance, fairness, learning, skill, and generosity to certain persons in his narratives to indicate his egalitarian vision of individualism. Smith, explains Jeffrey H. Richards in his thorough and rich *Theater Enough,* not only applied the traditional *theatrum mundi* trope to his encounter with the New World but perceived the actual stage as a rival to the global theater in which he was both a dramatist and actor.

ii Early Colonial Poetry

Theatricality of another kind is treated in *The Work of Self-Representation: Lyric Poetry in Colonial New England* (No. Car.), Ivy Schweitzer's reading of the paradigm of conversion in terms of gendered "subjectivity." Puritan culture, Schweitzer contends, represented redeemed subjects as essentially male, yet it also problematically applied metaphors drawn from female subjugation to these subjects. Taken from this book, her "Semiotics of the Sacrament in Edward Taylor's *Preparatory Meditations*" (*Praise Disjoined*, pp. 237–57) argues that the dynamic of redeemed subjectivity (as evident in "Meditation 1.6") permits the poet to express dialectically a masculine sense of himself as a potentially empowered assertive saint and a feminine sense of himself as a disempowered passive recipient of divine grace. Because the devaluation of women was thereby masked as a form of male transcendence, Schweitzer concludes, this typology of regenerate subjectivity (as exemplified in verse by John Fiske and Taylor) was in effect a form of social control that confiscated the actual identity of female passivity to legitimate male authority and creativity. However, this same application of "female images" of faith and faithlessness, argues Amanda Poterfield in "Women's Attraction to Puritanism" (*ChH* 60:196–209), gave women an important role in shaping Puritan culture; these images opened opportunities for influence (particularly in the domestic sphere) by establishing the authority of women as exemplary Christians and by indicating that male dominion was based on female willingness to endorse it.

Schweitzer claims that Anne Bradstreet subtly and deliberately displaced the cultural paradigm for self-representation, despite the fact that she was used by conspiring males in her family to redress the bad reputation of her sister. In *Anne Bradstreet Revisited* (TUSAS 580) Rosamond Rosenmeier highlights the poet's sense of being in the midst of a cosmic change akin to an alchemical transmutation. The palimpsest of Athena in her poem on Queen Elizabeth, Rosenmeier suggests, figures Bradstreet's vision of Wisdom's role in creation, a role emphasizing the feminine aspect of divinity presently operative in an ongoing cosmic reformation. The poet's concern with transition informs "Civil War and Bradstreet's 'Monarchies'" (*EAL* 26:119–44), in which Jane D. Eberwein reads the poet's ambitious commentary on the direction of English political agitation as a veiled work divided between support for parliamentary reform and regard for monarchical stability in guiding England in its millennial mission.

Edward Taylor accommodated the new science to the Puritan mission, despite his uncertainty concerning where his studies would take him, and he accordingly preferred Paracelsian to Galenic medical theory. In her meticulous explication of "Meditation 2.61" (" 'This Brazen Serpent Is a Doctors Shop': Edward Taylor's Medical Vision" [*SPAS* 2:51–75]) Catherine Rainwater further indicates that the poet's desire to harmonize theological doctrine, scientific detail, and poetic expression inspired him to discover correspondences between Paracelsian method and both biblical typology and Augustinian tradition. Looking beyond the limits of medicine, Jeffrey A. Hammond's "The Puritan Elegiac Ritual: From Sinful Silence to Apostolic Voice" (*SPAS* 2:77–106) reports that celebration of the saint, rather than grief for the deceased, was the objective of Puritan elegists; their implied reader is the final site of the elegiac movement from desperate confusion to hopeful anticipation. Not the ills of the mortal body but resentment over colonial minority status interests James T. F. Tanner, whose "Puritan Humor in Seventeenth-Century American Poetry: Sarcasm as Consequence of the Persecution Complex" (*StAH* 6 [1988]:13–29) reports that Puritans projected their discomfort on their religious and political antagonists.

iii Early Colonial Prose

For Simon P. Newman, the wit of one colonial divine reveals a spokesman whose emphasis on a unifying theological and political consensus was generationally out of phase with his contemporaries: "Nathaniel Ward, 1580–1652: An Elizabethan Puritan in a Jacobean World" (*EIHC* 127:313–26). Consensus is also at issue in *Gifts and Works: Post-Conversion Paradigm and Spiritual Controversy in Seventeenth-Century Massachusetts* (Mercer), Michael Schuldiner's interesting argument that the true Calvinists were those who embraced their minority status and pitted themselves against establishment solutions of the kind reflected in Taylor's *Gods Determinations.* Pertinently, Schuldiner notes, Solomon Stoddard indicated that his opponents, not he, had lowered the requirements for admission to the Lord's Supper when they had rejected John Cotton's early emphasis on spiritual illumination rather than on moral performance (preparation and works) as the only evidence of conversion.

Consensus likewise interests Stephen Foster, whose *The Long Argument: English Puritanism and the Shaping of New England Culture, 1570–1700* (Institute) reports that the Puritan movement resists denominational taxonomy because it was a loose, uneasy, and incomplete alliance of progressive Protestants of various social classes who were never sure whether they were the vanguard or the remnant. Puritanism, accordingly, can best be approached in relation to the various cultural resources it employed in its typically bipolar responses—participation/separation; collective cohesion/sectarian autonomy—to various successive challenges.

Bipolarity informs "The Figure of Captivity: The Cultural Work of the Puritan Captivity Narrative" (*AmLH* 3:1–26), in which Tara Fitzpatrick reveals the conflict between the conservative clergy, who tried to use accounts of captivity to maintain the communal status quo, and the radical narrators, who insisted on personal agency (individuality) in the salvational process. Gilles Thérien's "Le topos de la captivité au dix-septième siècle" (*CanL* 131:37–49) contrasts American and New French captivity narratives on the basis of their differences in responding to settlement and to relations with Native Americans. And John T. Shawcross notes another dualism in "The Old or the Unknown Path?: A Dilemma in Colonial American Life" (*SCRev* 8, i:50–56); Puritan writing reflects a fluctuation between passive submission of the elect to divine design (the unknown path) and active performance of works by the entire population to realize divine design (the old path).

Submission and resistance interests Daniel B. Shea, who reports that female autobiographers express themselves from cultural margins and, accordingly, replace the fixed center of male vision with the metaphor of the journey: "The Prehistory of American Autobiography" (*American Autobiography*, pp. 25–46). Autobiographical resistance is likewise featured in "John Wheelwright's Forgotten *Apology:* The Last Word in the Antinomian Controversy" (*NEQ* 64:22–45), Sargent Bush, Jr.'s disclosure of a previously lost work that presents personal details about its author, including an adamant reiteration of his beliefs. Another antagonist is the subject of *Liberty of Conscience: Roger Williams in America* (Eerdmans), in which Edwin S. Gaustad focuses on Williams's advocacy of liberty of conscience rather than religious toleration. Conformist, rather than resistant, spiritual confessions by average and elite church members are presented in Mary Rhinelander McCarl's "Thomas Shepard's Record of Relations of Religious Experience, 1648–1649" (*WMQ* 48:432–66).

The subtle attribution of sainthood to the deceased is the subject of "Resurrecting Life through Rhetorical Ritual: A Buried Value of the Puritan Funeral Sermon" (*EAL* 26:232–50), in which Etta Madden discloses how Puritan ministers comforted their audience by "textually" reading the deceased's past life in a manner similar to interpreting the Bible. The development of Puritan culture as a religio-political process of textual self-identification, mirrored in such culturally authoritative printed words (*figura*) as "progress" and "New Canaan," is discussed in Sacvan Bercovitch's "The Ends of American Puritan Rhetoric" (*The Ends of Rhetoric,* pp. 171–90); whereas in "Investigations of an Americanist" (*JAH* 78:972–87) Bercovitch defends this sort of reading of Puritan culture against David Harlan's complaints in "A People Blinded from Birth: American History according to Sacvan Bercovitch" (*JAH* 78:949–71).

Concern with textual self-identification also emerges in " 'They Shall No Longer Grieve': The Song of Songs and Edward Johnson's *Wonder-Working Providence*" (*EAL* 26:1–20), Jesper Rosenmeier's explanation of how one colonial historian, anxious over the deaths of New England fathers, found inspiration in Canticles, which provided him with a coherent, typological vision of experience. In what ways Johnson and other New England authors corresponded to or differed from their English contemporaries in the use of these biblical types is discussed in N. H. Keeble's *The Literary Culture of Nonconformity in Later Seventeenth-Century England* (Georgia [1987], pp. 263–82).

If, according to Foster in *The Long Argument,* "Increase Mather invented nothing," merely "organized and arranged" various traditions (including typology), his son Cotton Mather, according to Richards in *Theater Enough,* bequeathed a theatrical conception of the self as a defiant actor on the world stage who risks insult from a corrupt audience. Cotton figures in Margaret Olofson Thickstun's "Mothers in Israel: The Puritan Rhetoric of Child-Bearing" (*Praise Disjoined,* pp. 71–87), which draws on the author's *Fictions of the Feminine* (*ALS 1988*) to emphasize the strategies used by clergy who suggested that the postlapsarian curse of childbirth could be a source of maternal consolation. That Mather's ignorance of the London book trade contributed to his lack of literary success is reported in D. N. DeLuna's "Cotton Mather Published Abroad" (*EAL* 26:145–72). Mather, explains David W. Music in "Cotton Mather and Congregational Singing in Puritan New England" (*SPAS* 2:1–30), not only admired the hymns of Isaac Watts and the Bay Psalm Book, but published a complete original Psalter in English. A review of the life of another composer of sacred music is provided by Karl Kroeger in "William Billings and the Puritan Musical Ideal" (*SPAS* 2:31–50).

Other ideals emerge in "John Winthrop's Rite of Passage: The Origins of the 'Christian Charitie' Discourse" (*EAL* 26:219–31), Hugh J. Dawson's exploration of questions concerning the timing and content of the governor's sermon. Evidence pertaining to how local circumstances encouraged Boston publishers to become innovative and experimental, and as a result how their models became the standard for newspapers along the Atlantic seaboard, is provided in Charles E. Clark's "Boston and the Nurturing of Newspapers: Dimensions of the Cradle, 1690–1741" (*NEQ* 64:243–71). And in "Annis Boudinot Stockton and Benjamin Young Prime: A Poetical Correspondence, and More" (*PULC* 52:231–66) Carla Mulford identifies Stockton as the Amelia in Prime's poem, an edition of which is provided.

iv Edwards, the Great Awakening, and the New Divinity

The concept of the deity's eternal desire to communicate holiness informs Edwards's blurring of traditional categories of typology; and for this theologian, Janice Knight further observes in "Learning the Language of God: Jonathan Edwards and the Typology of Nature" (*WMQ* 48:531–51), typological revelation is a temporal process that includes nature, history, current events, and commerce. Relatedly, Mason I. Lowance, Jr., suggests that Edwards's originality existed, in part, in his combining the thought of various thinkers to forge a version of the typological system that synthesizes divine revelation in Scripture and in nature: "Jonathan Edwards and the Platonists: Edwardsean Epistemology and the Influence of Malebranche and Norris" (*SPAS* 2:129–52). For Richard E. Brantley, in "The Common Ground of Wesley and Edwards" (*HTR* 83 [1990]:271–303), Edwards theologizes empiricism by balancing religious piety and scientific detail in a manner that makes experience, even more inclusively than did John Locke, the means of natural and spiritual knowledge. Edwards's orthodox Calvinism, explains Mark Valeri in "The Economic Thought of Jonathan Edwards" (*ChH* 60:37–54), led to his endorsement of a controlled form of commerce instead of a protocapitalist laissez-faire market economy.

Making capital of religious revivals, another minister, by exploiting print, redefined popular religion, according to Frank Lambert's "The Great Awakening as Artifact: George Whitefield and the Construction of

Intercolonial Revival, 1739–1745" (*ChH* 60:223–46); in this way, too, Whitefield empowered the average person by transforming private and local experience into public performance. In response to the changes and conflicts of the day, the New Divinity likewise engaged in a reinterpretation of its heritage and culture, including a reification of the Great Awakening; as a result, Joseph Conforti discloses in "The Invention of the Great Awakening, 1795–1842" (*EAL* 26:99–118), Edwards's writings became canonized, whereas previously they had not been received as representative or central to American evangelical tradition. But in *Seasons of Grace: Colonial New England's Revival Tradition in Its British Context* (Oxford) Michael J. Crawford reads Edwards's *A Faithful Narrative* as a paradigm for how subsequent colonial revival accounts were structured.

A Quaker contemporary of Edwards who resisted tradition appears in Margaret E. Stewart's "John Woolman's 'Kindness beyond Expression': Collective Identity *vs.* Individualism" (*EAL* 26:251–75), which scrutinizes the transformation of individualistic asceticism into an empathy devoid of hypocritical sentimentality. Revision was likewise central to the thinking of the Roman Catholic contemporary featured in Joseph M. McShane's "John Carroll's Controversy with the Philosophes" (*Thought* 66:279–96); Carroll repudiated radical Deism but was liberal enough toward it to speak for a moderate strain of Enlightenment thinking, especially concerning social virtue and tolerance.

Even while Edwards and others were negotiating the theological tension between spiritual immanence and its representation in practice, a new culture was emerging that would displace orality with print. The examples of *Arthur Mervyn* and *Charlotte Temple*, according to Larzar Ziff's tardy and inadequately researched *Writing in the New Nation*, indicate that publication promotes one's ability to create representations, both in fashioning a personal identity and in reshaping nature.

v Franklin, Jefferson, and the Revolution

How Quaker assumptions about the deity influenced the way one naturalist negotiated the conflict of his time between a scientific and a pious reading of both creation and personal identity is the topic of Nina Reid's "Enlightenment and Piety in the Science of John Bartram" (*PennH* 58:124–38). The influence of the biblical hermeneutics of the Joseph Johnson circle on a Deist who strongly advocated tolerance is assessed by

Robert N. Essick, whose "William Blake, Thomas Paine, and the Biblical Revolution" (*SIR* 30:189–212) identifies the mutual thematic matter and verbal elements of *The Marriage of Heaven and Hell* and Paine's writings. In "Authority in Paine's *Common Sense* and *Crisis Papers*" (*StHum* 18:124–34) Edward H. Davidson and I divulge how Paine's subtle reliance on Scripture as well as his claim to represent the ideal expression of human rights are negotiated by means of a self-authorization that confiscates the very monarchical strategies he exposes as fraudulent.

A poet's exposure to Enlightenment arguments on human rights and abolitionist theory, through the agency of the New England clergy, is reported in James A. Levernier's "Phillis Wheatley and the New England Clergy" (*EAL* 26:21–38). This poet's exploitation of the possibilities latent within her culture's traditional controlling metaphors and, accordingly, her creation of a place for herself within its symbolic structures is observed in Helen M. Burke's "The Rhetoric and Politics of Marginality: The Subject of Phillis Wheatley" (*TSWL* 10:31–45).

Writings by the man who said "religion indeed has produced a Phyllis Whately [*sic*]; but it could not produce a poet," are collected in volume 23 (ed. Charles T. Cullen) and volume 24 (ed. John Catanzariti) of *The Papers of Thomas Jefferson* (Princeton). The influence of Jeffersonian agrarianism, Franklinesque work ethic, and Christian duty on a didactic novel, designed as a synthetic model for an emerging new nation, interests Robert Dunne in "Cultivating a Cultural Hybrid: A Consideration of *The Farmer's Friend*" (*UDR* 21:169–75). The influence of the colonial struggle against authority on one person's evolving definitions of self, especially as an honorable gentleman and a Revolutionary hero, is the subject of "Zealous in the Cause of Liberty: Self-Creation and Redemption in the Narrative of Ethan Allen" (*SECC* 19 [1989]:325–47) by Daniel E. Williams. And the influence of Franklin's experience of congenial company and scientific learning in Scotland on his ideal of culture is documented in Richard B. Sher's "An 'Agreeable and Instructive Society': Benjamin Franklin and Scotland" (*ECLife* 15:181–93).

vi The Early National Period

Whereas Jonathan Swift saw clothing as a symbolic covering of human imperfection, explains Caryn Chaden in "Dress and Undress in Brackenridge's *Modern Chivalry*" (*EAL* 26:55–72), Brackenridge saw clothing as an enhancement of the body and worried about the lack of stable conventions as a state of undress that might leave the new republic vulnerable to excesses. Relatedly, Dennis D. Moore unearths new evidence of early national concern over a lack of social and domestic nurture: " 'A Family Divided Indeed': Domesticity and the Golden Age in Crèvecoeur's Unpublished Manuscripts" (*StHum* 18:110–23). That the disjunctive form of Crèvecoeur's *Letters* suggests the crumbling of earthly hopes before new political forces is the thesis of Norman S. Grabo's "Crèvecoeur's American: Beginning the World Anew" (*WMQ* 48:159–72); beneath the fiction of casual disconnectedness lurks the coherent theme of the universal presence of evil, eternally renewed. Likewise, shifts in narrative voice in the middle letters, as evidence of a transition from enthusiasm to disillusionment concerning the Nantucket utopian undertaking, are identified in "The Nantucket Sequence in Crèvecoeur's *Letters from an American Farmer*" (*NEQ* 64:414–32) by Nathaniel Philbreck.

How subversive multiple voices mediate various social and political conflicts is the topic of Constance J. Post's "Revolutionary Dialogues in American Mock-Epic Poetry: Double-Voicing in *M'Fingal, The Anarchiad,* and *The Hasty-Pudding*" (*StAH* 6 [1988]:40–51). Specifically, according to Alan Taylor's "From Father to Friends of the People: Political Personas in the Early Republic" (*JER* 11:465–91), at the end of the 18th century there was a change in the manner of public presentation; the social enactment of the professed values of the newer liberal order (mobility and equality) conflicted with the Federalist persona of genteel authority. That the verse in late 18th-century bilingual periodicals reveals other differing cultural codes and agendas interests Hélène Marcotte in "Contribution à l'étude comparée de poésies canadiennes (1764–1806)" (*CanL* 131:73–82). How the dominant voice of British literary convention was mutated to suit republican ideas is the subject of "Republican Rhymes: Constitutional Controversy and the Democratization of the Verse Satire, 1786–1799" (*StAH* 6 [1988]:30–39) by Judith Yaross Lee. And in "The Fact of Events and the Event of Facts: New World Explorers and the Early Novel" (*ECent* 32:240–55) Lennard J. Davis observes how the influential symbolic productions of early narratives of discovery facilitated such incipient cultural formations as fiction.

Rosemarie Zagarri has reconstructed from three manuscripts *David Humphreys' "Life of General Washington," with George Washington's "Remarks"* (Georgia). Ronald A. Bosco has introduced and edited " '[M]ercy to pardon & grace to help': Ezra Ripley's Ordination Diary, 1778–1836"

(*SPAS* 2:153–92). Joseph Kent McGaughy points to Melancton Smith in "The Authorship of *The Letters from the Federal Farmer,* Revisited" (*NYH* 70 [1989]:153–70). Brandon Brame Fortune describes one painter's ideological adaptation of older modes of portraiture in order to imitate his contemporaries' historicist method of recording facts: "Charles Willson Peale's Portrait Gallery: Persuasion and the Plain Style" (*W&I* 6:308–24). And in "The Origins of the Humor of the Old South" (*SLJ* 23, ii:3–13) J. A. Leo Lemay identifies 10 primary 18th-century colonial works that anticipate the humorists of the Old South.

Throughout the colonies, argues John Seelye, waterways served visionaries, propagandists, and travel writers as cultural symbols of the millennial republican dream of national unity, but at the same time they in fact led to sectional rivalries, including the Civil War. In his detailed and well-documented *Beautiful Machine* Seelye exposes the dark side of the metaphorical appropriation of landscape as agent of "belief," a dark side evident in human and natural resistance to systems of absolute order. (Three parts of this book, first printed in journals, are reported in *ALS 1987* and *ALS 1989*.) The dark side of a naturalist's anxieties is observed by Philip G. Terrie, whose "Tempests and Alligators: The Ambiguous Wilderness of William Bartram" (*NDQ* 59:17–32) overlooks several previous discussions in indicating that violent encounters reveal a feature of nature and humanity that Bartram tries but fails to reconcile with his preferred Edenic reading of creation.

vii Brown and Contemporaries

Whereas Donald A. Ringe addresses the issue of belief in *Charles Brockden Brown: Revised Edition* (TUSAS 98), Seelye (*Beautiful Machine*) emphasizes Brown's paranoiac identification of uncontrolled waterways with French-inspired anarchy and insanity. Clara's incoherence, as evidence of conflicting 18th-century definitions of female identity, is treated in " 'The arm lifted against me': Love, Terror, and the Construction of Gender in *Wieland*" (*EAL* 26:173–94) by Andrew J. Scheiber, who suggests that Clara finally flees a problematic identity contingent on male-centered power structures that would simultaneously subsume and marginalize her. Other patriarchal structures interest Elizabeth Jane Hall Hinds, whose "Private Property: Charles Brockden Brown's Economy of Virtue" (*StHum* 18:165–79) interprets enclosed spaces as cultural tropes for owned property; these tropes, in turn, foster a bourgeois morality based on the association of domestic economics and self-restraint.

Clara's style questions epistemological assumptions, concludes Alfred G. Litton's "The Failure of Rhetoric in Charles Brockden Brown's *Wieland*" (*LJHum* 16, ii[1990]:23–40); unlike others in the romance, she doubts the ability of language to transform reality. But Joel Porte's *In Respect to Egotism* (pp. 40–47) discerns a quasi-Calvinistic understanding of the human condition in *Edgar Huntly*, especially whenever the inscrutable mind betrays the Enlightenment notion of a mechanistic world and a benign deity. An essential inscrutable absence (void) at the center of the milieu, the action, the protagonist, and the author of Hannah Foster's *The Coquette* is exposed in Adam Goldgeier's "The Coquette Composed" (*Constructions* [1990]:1–14).

The subject of identity surfaces in "Mercy Otis Warren's Gendered Melodrama of Revolution" (*SAQ* 90:531–54), in which Nina Baym indicates that the assertion of political views and the composition of history were compatible with the early national "conservative" view of the separate domestic sphere; if Warren's endorsement of the retirement of women from action associates the feminine with a vulnerable body, it also identifies the feminine with mental activity that can contribute to polity through the expression of ideas. A similar thesis about Warren and two other authors appears in Baym's "Between Enlightenment and Victorian: Toward a Narrative of American Women Writers Writing History" (*CritI* 18:22–41); the consignment of women to the domestic sphere led to their appropriation and feminization of writing, especially of history, in which their authority for *mentally* tracking male labor was augmented by rhetoric derived from family, politics, and religion. Their work led to different examples of female national identity.

Identity also interests Blythe Forcey, whose "*Charlotte Temple* and the End of Epistolarity" (*AL* 63:225–41) indicates that Susanna Haswell Rowson intervenes in her narrative as an ideal motherly voice to insure the effective delivery of her message to an audience, whom she could not trust to understand the way epistolary fiction communicates an author's point because of being situated within the unstable culture of the new republic. One of the problems with this culture, according to Dennis Barone in "'My Vile Arts': Male and Female Discourse in *Charlotte Temple*" (*StHum* 18:135–45), is concealed in Rowson's interweaving of the issues of class, gender, power relations, and language; her dystopian novel suggests that untenable linguistic and philosophic structures, including the separation of rhetoric and virtue, support the social hierarchies of her time.

Censure is likewise a concern in Klaus P. Hansen's "The Sentimental Novel and the Feminist Critique" (*EAL* 26:39–54), which unfortunately is inadequately researched, intemperate in tone, and thoroughly anticipated by Fredric Jameson's conclusions about social anxieties lurking as subtexts, at once subversive to and interactive with the status quo of the surface text. At the level of theme, Hansen points out, female authors agree with the social role they experience, whereas at the dramatic level they unwittingly betray certain misgivings about this role. For Madelon Jacoba, however, women authors consciously raised republican issues, especially concerning the nature of women and the need to educate women for independence, within the female domestic ideal: "The Early Novella as Political Message: *The Margaretta Story* by Judith Sargent Murray" (*StHum* 18:146–64).

Murray, among others, appears in *Curtain Calls,* which includes "Susana Rowson: Feminist and Democrat" (pp. 231–46), in which Doreen Alvarez Saar reads *Slaves in Algiers* as an argument for women, as well as the nation, to rebel against authority to avoid a loss of personal liberty and a rape of the spirit; "Mercy Otis Warren: Dramatist of the American Revolution" (pp. 247–59), in which Jean B. Kern discloses how one author spoke for the recognition of women as a vital force in the developing nation; and " 'Quitting the Loom and Distaff': Eighteenth-Century Women Dramatists" (pp. 260–73), in which Mary Anne Schofield provides brief notations about several playwrights who turned to the theater, as an alternative to the domestic sphere, for a forum to test ideas.

My closing thought, drawn from Henry Norwood's 1649 report of his encounter with Native Americans in Virginia, concerns quitting of another kind: "The Indians stayed with us about two hours, and parted not without a new appointment to see us again. . . . *Ha-na Haw* was their parting word, which is 'Farewell,' pointing again at the place where the sun would be at our next meeting. We took leave in their own words, *Ha-na Haw.*"

University of Texas at Austin

12 19th-Century Literature

Gary Scharnhorst

The expansion of the canon has led in recent years to a veritable explosion of new scholarship devoted to the so-called minor writers of the 19th century. This year is no exception, with the publication of some 50 books and a barrelful of articles germane to this chapter. Long past are the days when the booklists of Ticknor & Fields and the Harpers comprised the canon. In the ongoing project of reconstructing American literary history, more and more women and neglected minority writers have been recalled from the periphery, while such traditionally canonical figures as Cooper, Howells, Adams, Crane, and Norris continue to inspire critical debate. Meanwhile, many of the more obscure "dead white males," from Aldrich to Willis, are being consigned to the footnotes.

i General Studies

Only a decade ago in this space, Kermit Vanderbilt lamented the decline he perceived in the number of general literary studies (*ALS 1981,* p. 215). Nowadays, however, as scholars increasingly engage in cultural criticism, as they discuss the "dialectical agency" of texts or how literature performs "cultural work," the situation seems to have reversed: integrative (especially gendered) analyses of related works are popular again. Perhaps the most important new volume in this category in 1991 is Elizabeth Ammons's *Conflicting Stories* (Oxford), a historically and biographically contextualized study of the fiction of 17 "artistically ambitious," turn-of-the-century American women writers, including Charlotte Perkins Gilman's "The Yellow Wall-paper," Frances Ellen Harper's *Iola Leroy,* Sarah Orne Jewett's *The Country of the Pointed Firs,* and Sui Sin Far's *Mrs. Spring Fragrance* stories. Although this emergent generation of "serious" women writers (to distinguish them from the earlier "professionals," whom Hawthorne infamously dubbed the "d——d mob of scribbling women") in no way constitutes a school, Ammons argues, their fiction exhibits an interest in formal experimentation and often focuses on issues of power. Ammons makes much the same point more briefly in "Men of Color, Women, and Uppity Art at the Turn of the Century," the lead essay in a special issue of *ALR* (23, iii:14–24) on canon issues, guest-edited by Tom Quirk. As Ammons eloquently explains, "women and black men can be seen as the majority, not the minority, of the most important authors" in America around the turn of the century, and their work reflects the "fierce debates and fractures within the society."

Two other essays in the same issue of *ALR* expand the notion of realism to include the work of other marginalized women writers. Much as Walter Blair half a century ago detected the roots of realism in the tradition of western humor, Nancy Walker persuasively contends that the satire of such writers as Marietta Holley was closely allied to the realistic impulse in " 'I cant write a book': Women's Humor and the American Realistic Tradition" (23, iii:52–67); and Cheryl Walker pleads the case for the "surprisingly chilling and tough-minded" verse of such neglected poets as Alice and Phoebe Cary, Lucy Larcom, Ina Coolbrith, and Rose Terry Cooke in "Nineteenth-Century Women Poets and Realism" (23, iii:25–41). In her review-essay "Portraits of the Lady: Imagining Women in Nineteenth-Century America" (*AmLH* 3:396–404) Joanne Dobson fairly concludes that only with the "current republication of women's novels, stories, slave narratives, and vernacular texts" are we now able to revise the prescriptive representations of the nature and role of women "in the predominating discourse." Similarly, Susan K. Harris, the author of last year's *19th-Century American Women's Novels* (*ALS 1990*, pp. 209–10), proposes a "process analysis" of writing by noncanonical women, an investigation of the converging historical, rhetorical, and ideological premises of sentimental novels, in " 'But is it any *good?*': Evaluating Nineteenth-Century American Women's Fiction" (*AL* 63:43–61); and Nina Baym challenges the prevailing generalizations about plantation fiction by reviewing several domestic novels by southern women (e.g., Eliza Dupuy's *The Planter's Daughter*) in her historiographical essay, "The Myth of the Myth of Southern Womanhood" (*HUSL* 18:27–47). And in the first two chapters of *Sister's Choice* (pp. 1–41), an edition of her 1989 Clarendon Lectures, Elaine Showalter rehearses the now-familiar rationale for recanonization. Showalter published another version of the second of these chapters, on feminist discourse, particularly among 19th-century intellectuals, under the title "Miranda and Cassandra" in *Tradition and the Talents of Women* (pp. 311–27).

The monumental *Columbia History of the American Novel* epitomizes some of the pitfalls of writing literary history in an age of critical dissensus. Of its 31 chapters, 12 focus in whole or in part on the 19th century. Its roster of specialists ("the country's finest" scholars of literature and culture, most of them "young," as the publisher's blurb brags) includes Terence Martin on "The Romance," Lora Romero on "Domesticity and Fiction," Susan Mizruchi on "Fiction and the Science of Society," Amy Kaplan on "Nation, Region, and Empire," and Elizabeth Ammons on "Gender and Fiction." Such a history as this one implicitly depends upon the reputations of its contributors for its authority, in effect displacing the issue of literary merit from the novel(ist)s that are discussed to the essay(ist)s that discuss them. Predictably, such a collective endeavor is no seamless garment; rather, it sometimes seems to be a crazy quilt of overlapping essays. Stowe's *Uncle Tom's Cabin*, for example, is discussed in chapters entitled "The Book Marketplace," "Fiction and Reform I," and "Fiction and Reform II." Even more problematically, the 820 pages of text contain nary a footnote; instead, the volume concludes with a 25-page "Selected Bibliography of Critical Works" that is, by accident or design, much less helpful or useful than the bibliography appended to the old Spiller *Literary History*, which at least was annotated and keyed to particular chapters. Thus, there is no way of detecting the immediate source of factual misstatements in the *Columbia History*, such as the errors which riddle the thumbnail biographical sketch of Horatio Alger, Jr., on page 754. Still, my own reservations are modest compared to the more extreme objections of Bruce Bawer (*NewC* 10, iv:20–31), who disparages the volume as "unadulterated political propaganda" which "may be the single most frightening document yet to emerge from the Marxist assault on American higher education"—but that may be nothing more than the gross overstatement of an alarmist.

A spate of provocative general studies silhouette issues of class, race, and gender in the literature of the period. In *Labor into Art* David Sprague Herreshoff brings a Marxist perspective to bear on works by several well-established canonical writers (Thoreau, Melville, Dickinson, Whitman) as well as Douglass's *Narrative*. The approach seems curiously old-fashioned, almost passé, certainly less strident or radical (as the selection of texts may indicate) than the polemics of some poststructuralists. Dana Brand's *The Spectator and the City* largely focuses on the role of the flaneur in texts by Poe, Hawthorne, and Whitman, though it briefly mentions works by several other writers, including Washington Irving and N. P. Willis. In *Removals* Lucy Maddox frames her analysis of, among other texts, Catharine Sedgwick's *Hope Leslie,* Lydia Maria Child's *Hobomok,* and Francis Parkman's *The Oregon Trail* and *The Conspiracy of Pontiac* around the public debates on the "Indian question" during the second quarter of the century, specifically the period immediately before and after the passage of the Indian Removal Act in 1830. In their stories, as Maddox explains, both Sedgwick and Child link "the Indians' struggle with Puritan patriarchy and the struggle of white women with nineteenth-century American patriarchy." Such a strategy was doomed, however, because their fanciful alliances between Indians and white women "disintegrate[d] in the face of historical realities." Parkman, on the other hand, aspired to rescue the American past, and the role of Indians in it, from the foolish sentimentalities of poets and novelists, and he scripted a masculinized version of history in which there is no middle course for the Native American between assimilation and extinction. Maddox's method is obviously selective rather than comprehensive, inasmuch as she only samples a few of the approximately 40 American novels published between 1824 and 1834 which appeal to the "cult of the Vanishing American." The book contains only passing reference to Cooper's Leatherstocking series and virtually ignores Robert Montgomery Bird's *Nick of the Woods.* Joel Porte also devotes the second chapter of his new monograph *In Respect to Egotism* (pp. 54–74) to encounters between whites and Indians depicted in novels by Cooper, Bird, and Simms, and in Parkman's histories.

The year also occasions the publication of a pair of first-rate thematic studies. Howard Horwitz's *By the Law of Nature* juxtaposes such texts as W. D. Howells's *A Hazard of New Fortunes* and Frank Norris's *The Pit* with other forms of 19th-century American economic discourse. *A Hazard* "marks Howells's greatest fictional intervention" in the debate over economic order and moral value, Horwitz concludes, and *The Pit* "explores the nation's transformation to a credit culture." Ambitious in scope, if occasionally overwritten, Horwitz's New Historicist study transcends its origins in the dissertation. Michael Oriard's *Sporting with the Gods* is something of a critical tour de force: a detailed yet comprehensive and eminently readable study of sporting metaphors, particularly as they appear in literary works about war, politics, and business, and how the evolution of the trope mirrored changes in the social status quo. However narrow Oriard's lens may first seem, he in fact surveys an astonishingly vast and diverse textual landscape. With Owen Wister's *The Virginian* as a paradigm text, Oriard examines a variety of canonical and noncanonical works for references to shooting contests, games of ninepin, gambling, racing, hunting, and so forth. His theoretically informed and meticulously documented monograph is a model of interdisciplinary research.

Two other interdisciplinary studies merit mention. In *Writing in the New Nation* Larzer Ziff discusses "the diverging values of political democracy and literary culture in the early decades of the republic"—that is, the divergence of liberal politics and the "social conservatism implicit in literary language and conventions"—with particular reference to Irving's "Rip Van Winkle," Cooper's *The Spy,* and Nicholas Biddle's *History of the Expedition Under the Command of Captains Lewis and Clark.* And John Seelye continues his multivolume saga of the river in American culture in *Beautiful Machine.* Seelye, too, discusses "Rip Van Winkle," which he regards as a "proto-Romantic assertion of wilderness sanctity," and the *History of the Expedition* as an Enlightenment epic, though he attributes its authorship to Meriwether Lewis rather than to Biddle, who edited and stylized Lewis's and Clark's journals. Bruce Greenfield, in fact, sifts and weighs the rhetorical modes and cultural contradictions at the heart of this complex text in "The Problems of the Discoverer's Authority in Lewis and Clark's *History*" (*Macropolitics of Nineteenth-Century Literature,* pp. 12–36).

The renewal of scholarly interest in autobiography as a genre has been fueled in good part by the Wisconsin Studies in American Autobiography series under the general editorship of William L. Andrews. The latest volume in that series, *American Autobiography,* includes several general essays relevant to this chapter. Lawrence Buell, in "Autobiography in the American Renaissance" (pp. 47–69), persuasively demonstrates the importance that the autobiographical mode enjoyed during the first two-thirds of the 19th century by citing expected, exceptional texts (e.g., *Walden, Specimen Days*) less often and to less purpose than unexpected, typical ones (e.g., Douglass's *Narrative,* Parkman's *The Oregon Trail,* P. T. Barnum's *Life,* Lydia Sigourney's *Letters of Life,* and John Neal's *Wandering Recollections of a Somewhat Busy Life*). Susanna Egan problematizes the very definition of the genre, albeit without reaching any very fruitful conclusions, in "'Self'-Conscious History: American Autobiography after the Civil War" (pp. 70–94). Arnold Krupat distinguishes between the synecdoche which informs Native American autobiography and the metonymic figure of Western autobiography, using various texts of the 19th-century Pequot and preacher William Apes as a case in point, in "Native American Autobiography and the Synecdochic Self" (pp. 171–94); and Carol Holly specifies "affiliation" with family or friends as the model of identity which structures 19th-century women's autobiographies, as distinct from the personal stories of success or achievement told by male autobiographers, using Catharine Sedgwick's "Recollections of Childhood" and Lucy Larcom's *A New England Girlhood* to illustrate her point, in "Nineteenth-Century Autobiographies of Affiliation" (pp. 216–34). Ironically, Rose Norman classifies Larcom's as a "dynamic" or "developmental" autobiography, in contrast to Laura E. Richards's "static" or "synchronic" text which "subsumes her childhood self within the story of her family," in "New England Girlhoods in Nineteenth-Century Autobiography" (*Legacy* 8:104–17). Holly's and Norman's taxonomies thus seem at odds. Patricia P. Buckler and C. Kay Leeper's "An Antebellum Woman's Scrapbook as Autobiographical Composition" (*JAC* 14, i:1–8) vividly illustrates the extremes to which the new interest in autobiography may be put. What's next? Packing lists? Of related interest: Tabitha Gilman Tenney's 1801 roman à clef *Female Quixotism*, which Cathy Davidson acclaims as "one of the best novels written in America before 1825," is reprinted with an introduction and notes by Jean Nienkamp and Andrea Collins (Oxford).

Studies of African American autobiographical writings, especially those by women, also begin to proliferate this year. In "The Daughter's Departure: Theory, History, and Late-Nineteenth-Century Black Women's Writings," the introductory chapter to his *The Workings of the Spirit* (Chicago, pp. 1–37), Houston A. Baker, Jr., links the emergence of a community of African American women scholars to the distinctive voices of such African American memoirists as Harriet Jacobs, Pauline Hopkins, and Anne Julia Cooper. Citing autobiographical sources, William L. Andrews graphically charts "the rise of the New Woman and the New Negro in the New South" around the turn of the century in "Booker T. Washington, Belle Kearney, and the Southern Patriarchy" (*Home Ground*, pp. 85–97). Two other essays offer more predictable conclusions about life-writings by 19th-century African American women. In "The Girls Who Became the Women" (*Tradition and the Talents of Women*, pp. 105–24) Nellie Y. McKay invokes the example of *Incidents in the Life of a Slave Girl* to argue that Jacobs "resisted aspects of the social expectations of black people in general and of black women in particular"; and in "Black Womanhood in Nineteenth-Century America: Subversion and Self-Construction in Two Women's Autobiographies" (*AQ* 43:199–222) Beth Maclay Doriani juxtaposes Jacobs's slave narrative and Harriet Wilson's autobiographical novel *Our Nig* to map "the limitations placed on black women and the surprisingly similar ways" Jacobs and Wilson overcame them.

Literary historians of every stripe should welcome the founding of *American Periodicals*, an annual published under the auspices of the Research Society for American Periodicals and devoted to research in magazines and newspapers of all periods. The inaugural issue contains four essays germane to this chapter: Janice Simon's "Imaging a New Heaven on a New Earth: *The Crayon* and 19th-Century American Periodical Covers" (1:11–24), on a magazine that pioneered national "aesthetic discourse"; Lawrence I. Berkove's "New Old Additions to the American Canon" (1:25–33), on recent literary discoveries in the morgues of 19th-century newspapers; Cheryl D. Bohde's " 'Magazines as a Powerful Element of Civilization': An Exploration of the Ideology of Literary Magazines, 1830–1850" (1:34–45), on periodicals as arbiters of a genteel cultural ethos; and Robert J. Scholnick's "*Scribner's Monthly* and the 'Pictorial Representation of Life and Truth' in Post-Civil War America" (1:46–69), on the new "visual language" of pictorial realism that the magazine popularized in the 1870s. Similarly, in "Reading the Walls: The Politics of Architecture in *Scribner's Magazine*, 1887–1914" (*ArQ* 47, i:49–79) Annette Larson Benert explains how the editors of the revived turn-of-the-century *Scribner's* taught their readers to interpret new buildings as "props to patriotism, as signs of our emergence from provincial to world status," and endorsed the romantic urban aesthetic of the City Beautiful movement even as they resisted the encroachments of fictional realism. Of related interest is *A Voice of Their Own*, a collection of 11 essays on 19th- and early 20th-century suffragist papers. Of particular moment are the pieces on the *Woman's Journal* by Susan Schultz Huxman (pp. 87–109) and the *Woman's Column* by Marsha L. Vanderford (pp. 129–52).

Finally, I should commend two exemplary review-essays. Richard Slotkin smartly assesses revisionist scholarship on the conflict in " 'What Shall Men Remember?': Recent Work on the Civil War" (*AmLH* 3:120–35); and John C. Hirsh retrieves an unfashionable critical term from the ash heap of deconstruction in "Realism Renewed" (*JAmS* 25:235–43), a lucid commentary on recent monographs by such specialists on the postbellum period as Daniel Borus, Amy Kaplan, and John W. Crowley.

ii Cooper, Irving, and Contemporaries

A hundred and forty years after his death, Cooper seems to be stirring up a fuss again. There is, I believe, no other literary figure of the period about whom the criticism is so divided. On the one hand, the more traditional scholars, apostolic successors to Robert E. Spiller, James Franklin Beard, and the myth-and-symbol school, honor Cooper as an incisive social commentator, historian, artist, and allegorist. Many of them have met periodically since 1978 at conferences organized by George A. Test, and the proceedings of the seventh such meeting, held in 1989, are published this year by the English department at SUNY-Oneonta. *James Fenimore Cooper: His Country and His Art* contains a total of 15 essays, the most noteworthy of them by such distinguished Cooperians as Kay Seymour House, Donald Ringe, and Thomas Philbrick. Some of the essays are marked by a certain and perhaps understandable defensiveness in tone. These critics are, after all, engaged in a sort of rearguard action, a critical back-and-fill project. In "Cooper's Status and Stature Now" (pp. 1–11) House decries the trend in contemporary American literary studies to trivialize Cooper's achievement and concludes that he is "faring better overseas than he is at home. The terms and contexts in which he is discussed abroad indicate that he still has stature as an American and world writer." In "Cooper Today: A Partisan View" (pp. 162–73) Ringe reaches a similar conclusion about the poverty of much of the critical writing on Cooper and surveys his "religious vision and its significance for his novels," a fallow field for future study. Philbrick discusses the novelist's virtual invention of sea fiction, "an experiment of remarkable scope and duration," in "Cooper and the Literary Discovery of the Sea" (pp. 12–20), an essay first printed in the special Cooper issue of *CRevAS* in 1989. William E. Lenz also situates Cooper's sea fiction in a larger literary context in "Narratives of Exploration, Sea Fiction, Mariners' Chronicles, and the Rise of American Nationalism" (*AmerS* 32, ii:41–61). Not coincidentally, two Cooper scholars also appear this year in their roles as textual editors. Thomas and Marianne Philbrick prepare the MLA-approved edition of *The Red Rover* (SUNY); this text is paired with House's definitive edition of *The Pilot* in an attractive Library of America volume designed for general readers.

Gary Williams sensibly introduces and annotates *Notions of the Americans* (SUNY), another volume with the MLA imprimatur issued in the Cooper Edition. In a chapter on the Leatherstocking series in his book *The American Scene* (St. Martin's, pp. 1–20) Stuart Hutchinson emphasizes Cooper's traditionalism and Anglophilism, his "affirmation of America's cultural continuity with Britain." The least satisfactory of these pieces is Leonard Engel's "Space and Enclosure in Cooper and Peckinpah" (*JAC* 14, ii:86–97), a pedantic effort to apply Turner's frontier thesis to *The Prairie, The Deerslayer,* and western films.

The insurgent Cooper scholars have, on the other hand, an altogether different critical agenda, one that is often (for want of a better phrase) Indian-centered. For better or worse, too, this modern "battle of the books" epitomizes the larger culture wars now raging in the academy. Geoffrey Rans explicitly faults earlier scholars, especially H. Daniel Peck in *A World by Itself* (*ALS 1977*, p. 211), for their "critical evasion" of the political and even "potentially inflammatory" implications of the Bumppo saga in *Cooper's Leather-Stocking Series: A Secular Reading* (No. Car.). According to Rans, the series is "a text which faithfully reproduces the conflicts Cooper faced in his present and in the history his novels contemplate," and he reads this text in the order of its composition so as to establish "the importance of property and class structure in the American society Cooper projects" and how he "subjects that society to a damning critique," especially for its dispossession of the Indian. The dilemma Cooper registers throughout the series between Bumppo's "conservative piety" and Marmaduke Temple's "civilized Christian rule of law," Rans argues, could be resolved neither in fiction nor in history—or, more exactly, could not be resolved fictionally precisely because it could not be resolved historically. Forrest G. Robinson, one of the most astute critics of western American literature, makes a similar point about the second Leatherstocking tale in "Uncertain Borders: Race, Sex, and Civilization in *The Last of the Mohicans*" (*ArQ* 47, i:1–28): "the popular success" of the novel "is somehow geared to its denial of what it at the same time painfully suggests about 'the Indian problem.'" That is, Cooper "manages somehow to express guilt and to repress it at the same time," to equivocate "between what may be construed as defenses and indictments of the claims of civilization." In "The Last Real Man in America" (*AmLH* 3:753–81) David Leverenz, author of *Manhood and the American Renaissance* (*ALS 1989*, pp. 22–23 and passim), teases out a number of audacious links among Bumppo, Owen Wister's cowboy hero, the Rough Riders, Tarzan, Batman, and the contemporary men's movement. T. Hugh Crawford undertakes a Foucauldian analysis of Cooper's novel of the Revolution in "Cooper's *Spy* and the Theatre of Honor" (*AL* 63:405–19). As Crawford explains, the novel subverts the "gaze" as a form of self-policing and "charts a complicated cultural shift" by "showing instead the value of selective deception" and pragmatic opportunism in the person of Harvey Birch. As if in oblique response to Crawford, Lora Romero in "Vanishing Americans: Gender, Empire, and New Historicism" (*AL* 63:385–404) uses *The Last of the Mohicans* as an exemplary text "to interrogate the politics of Foucauldian analysis" and the "apparent obliviousness" of New Historicists "to the rhetorical content of what they present as historical facts." Romero contends that narratives "like the one Foucauldian New Historicism has given us," particularly recent scholarship "on the alleged feminization of [antebellum] society," participates "in the imperialist nostalgia of the discourse it analyzes" and has historically "operated to the detriment of both white middle-class women and people of color." Romero thus locates a critical perspective beyond New Historicism. (Her essay was awarded the 1991 Foerster prize, given annually for the outstanding essay in *AL*.)

Irving seems suddenly to have fallen on hard times again despite the critical revival prompted by the publication of the authoritative Irving edition. The focus of the few studies appearing this year is, moreover, on Irving's travelogues. Jonathan C. Glance identifies an obscure allusion to *The Thousand and One Nights* in *Tales of a Traveller* (*Expl* 49:13–14). In "Eighteenth-Century Aesthetic Theory and the Nineteenth-Century Traveler in Trans-Allegheny America" (*AmerS* 32, i:33–48) Kris Lackey explains how the "descriptive taxonomy and vocabulary" of landscape theory shaped the impressions of natural scenery that Irving recorded in *A Tour of the Prairies* and Parkman in *The Oregon Trail.* The Library of America also issues an Irving volume containing the authoritative texts, with notes by Andrew B. Myers, of *Bracebridge Hall, Tales of a Traveller,* and *The Alhambra.*

Meanwhile, Parkman's stock is on the rise, to judge from the books by Maddox and Porte and essays by Buell and Lackey cited earlier as well as a new book and article. Wilbur R. Jacobs writes an excellent, sympathetic literary biography based partly on newly recovered manuscript sources in *Francis Parkman: Historian as Hero* (Texas); and Philip G.

Terrie reviews the textual evidence that Parkman's experience in the West enabled him to recognize, if only to deny, "the profound similarity between himself and the Indians" in "The Other Within: Indianization on *The Oregon Trail*" (*NEQ* 64:376–92). The Library of America also issues an attractive Parkman volume, with notes by William R. Taylor, containing *The Oregon Trail* and *The Conspiracy of Pontiac*.

Three women diarists of the early and mid-19th century receive scholarly attention. Such personal narratives as journals are increasingly regarded as family records, texts written for a wider audience than the diarist alone. Suzanne L. Bunkers edits *The Diary of Caroline Seabury, 1854–1863* (Wisconsin), a document recently discovered in manuscript in the Minnesota Historical Society. Seabury, a Yankee hired to teach in a woman's academy in Mississippi, details the coming and the early months of the war from the perspective of a woman literally caught in the middle. P. A. M. Taylor edits *More Than Common Powers of Perception* (Beacon), selections from the diary kept by the Boston blueblood Elizabeth Rogers Mason Cabot between 1844 and 1906. Charles East edits the unexpurgated *Civil War Diary of Sarah Morgan* (Georgia), first published in an incomplete form in 1913 under the title *A Confederate Girl's Diary*. Clara Juncker's analysis of this early version of the document in "Behind Confederate Lines: Sarah Morgan Dawson" (*SoQ* 30, i:7–18) is thus flawed, deeply if not fundamentally, by the text she selects. Juncker refers, for example, to the "masculine filters" that strained Morgan's words before they reached print and the "silence of the last pages" of her diary—problems addressed by East's edition.

Nina Baym continues her ongoing investigation of hitherto-marginalized American women history writers, a retrieval project analogous to her *Women's Novels* (*ALS 1978*, pp. 208–09), in no less than four articles this year. In "Between Enlightenment and Victorian: Toward a Narrative of American Women Writers Writing History" (*CritI* 18:22–41) Baym traces the cultural shift early in the 19th century from the post-Revolutionary view of women as "teachers of the nation at large" to the Victorian notion of women inhabiting a "separate sphere" from men, enjoying a life of private domesticity distinct from the public arena. By elaborating how "American Enlightenment women seem to have found in logocentrism the key to their literary empowerment," Baym revises the textualist-feminist assertion that the valorization of language necessarily dispossesses women "by identifying them with body." In her review of the published history writings of Deborah Norris Logan, Mercy Otis Warren, and Hannah Adams, Baym brilliantly begins "to recover a different sort of writing woman from the madwoman in the attic." She returns to the second of these women writers in "Mercy Otis Warren's Gendered Melodrama of Revolution" (*SAQ* 90:531–54), which demonstrates that Warren's *History* is "strongly gender-inflected," though "neither a brief for women's emancipation nor a double-voiced, duplicitous women's text." Rather, its plot assumes "the generic shape of melodrama" with eroticized episodes of "rapine and pillage." In "Women and the Republic: Emma Willard's Rhetoric of History" (*AQ* 43:1–23) Baym treats the life and career of another successful educator and writer of gendered history. And in "The Ann Sisters: Elizabeth Peabody's Millennial Historicism" (*AmLH* 3:27–45) she rehabilitates the reputation of an intellectual too often dismissed as a minor Transcendentalist or derided as a "great-man groupie." Baym argues with reason and conviction that Peabody "assimilated a range of nineteenth-century discursive trends" in writing a form of gendered, millennialist history which recognized the chiliastic promise of America.

Several other writers, contemporaries of Cooper and Irving, attract at least passing notice. Beth L. Lueck discusses another Knickerbocker writer's use of the travelogue "to demonstrate America's glory" during the so-called Paper War with England and incidentally "to satirize some of the absurdities and excesses" of the leisure class in "James Kirke Paulding and the Picturesque Tour" (*UMSE* n.s. 9:167–88). Terry Roberts contributes an appreciative essay-review of last year's *Selected Poems of William Gilmore Simms* (*ALS 1990*, p. 216) to *MissQ* (44:203–07). Simms's first novel, the Gothic *Martin Faber*, is reprinted, with a helpful introduction by Glenn M. Reed, in an edition suitable for classroom adoption (NCUP). Todd G. Willy sympathetically assesses the verisimilar treatment of Native Americans in the fiction of a neglected, early 19th-century reformer in "Literary Realism as Anti-Racism: The Case of William Joseph Snelling" (*ON* 15:143–61), while William Boelhower painstakingly analyzes the "cartographic semiosis" or "topotheory" at work in the *Life of Black Hawk* in "Saving Saukenuk: How Black Hawk Won the War and Opened the Way to Ethnic Semiotics" (*JAmS* 25:333–61). Finally, Eugene England publishes only the second, and by far superior, book-length biocritical study of the much-neglected Frederick Goddard Tuckerman in *Beyond Romanticism: Tuckerman's Life and Poetry* (BYU).

iii Popular Writers of Mid-Century

Scholarship on Harriet Beecher Stowe, Frederick Douglass, and Louisa May Alcott continues to dominate this category. Although Stowe was practically ignored until recently, her claim to canonical status is only strengthened by several essays that appear this year. Increasingly, too, her writings other than *Uncle Tom's Cabin* attract critical attention. In "The New England Kitchen Goes Uptown: Domestic Displacements in Harriet Beecher Stowe's New York" (*NEQ* 64:272–91), the outstanding contribution to Stowe scholarship this year and a sequel of sorts to her essay last year on *Uncle Tom's Cabin* (*ALS 1990*, pp. 218–19), Lisa Watt MacFarlane brilliantly interprets the politics of domestic (dis)order in Stowe's fiction, sharply distinguishing between the idealized matriarchal households of her historical New England novels and the fractured spaces of her later romantic comedies set in New York. Richard Boyd in "Models of Power in Harriet Beecher Stowe's *Dred*" (*SAF* 19:15–30), a Girardian analysis of Stowe's second novel, demonstrates that it "fails to offer any pattern of human relations that is free of the coercive force of imitative desire, free of that authoritarian kind of mimeticism shown as fundamental to patriarchal slave-holding society." The eminent Stowe scholar E. Bruce Kirkham also resurrects three lost essays printed in a horticultural magazine in 1841 (*ON* 15:135–41). A trio of intertextual studies underscores the significance of *Uncle Tom's Cabin* for contemporary African American women novelists. Cynthia Griffin Wolff in " 'Margaret Garner': A Cincinnati Story" (*MR* 32:417–40) and Eileen T. Bender in "Repossessing *Uncle Tom's Cabin:* Toni Morrison's *Beloved*" (*Cultural Power/Cultural Literacy*, pp. 129–42) contend, in effect, that Toni Morrison in *Beloved* completed the story of Eliza's escape begun by Stowe in 1851; whereas Charlotte Goodman in "From *Uncle Tom's Cabin* to Vyry's Kitchen: The Black Female Folk Tradition in Margaret Walker's *Jubilee*" (*Tradition and the Talents of Women*, pp. 328–37) critiques "Stowe's failure to depict the lives of characters like Eliza and Aunt Chloe in all their particularity and complexity." In "Uncle Tom: A Hero at Last" (*ATQ* n.s. 5:95–108) Beatrice A. Anderson submits an amicus curiae brief in defense of Stowe's character which at least summarizes the historical case for the novel's significance. Invoking the devices of rhetorical analysis, Bryan C. Short tries to identify an *ethopoeia* or a space common to texts by writers as different as the antislavery novelist and the private poet in "Stowe, Dickinson, and the Rhetoric of Modernism"

(*AQ* 43:1–16). Both writers, according to Short, "turn the language and imagery of religion against aspects of the existing social order by turning against the figurative myths by which that order is rationalized." On the whole, the essay seems jargon-ridden and overlong for the modest point it makes. And in chapter 8 of *In Respect to Egotism* (pp. 213–28) Porte essays the classical and biblical mythologies subtly inscribed in *Uncle Tom's Cabin* and Douglass's *Narrative.*

Douglass studies receive another boost this year with the publication of William S. McFeely's long-awaited, extensively researched, and stylishly written biography of the abolitionist orator and writer (Norton). William L. Andrews edits *Critical Essays on Frederick Douglass* (Hall), a collection of nine reprinted articles by such well-known scholars as Henry Louis Gates, Jr., Houston A. Baker, Jr., Robert B. Stepto, and Eric J. Sundquist, as well as three original essays commissioned for the volume. Deborah E. McDowell interrogates the critical history that has "privileged and mystified" Douglass's *Narrative* in "In the First Place: Making Frederick Douglass and the Afro-American Narrative Tradition" (pp. 192–214), essentially a gynocritical essay-review of scholarship on Douglass's several autobiographies. The two other new articles are more linguistic in orientation. In "Antitheses" (pp. 148–65) Thad Ziolkowski deconstructs Douglass's *Narrative* to reveal its internal dialectic of "the spectacle of violences" and "the acquisition of literacy"; and in "The Antilanguage of Slavery" (pp. 166–91) Ann Kibbey and Michele Stepto extend the insights of Baker and others in arguing for Douglass's "profoundly rhetorical" representation of slave life in the *Narrative.* Similarly, Eric Cheyfitz relates Douglass's escape from slavery to his appropriation of the master('s) language and voice in the *Narrative* in *The Poetics of Imperialism* (Oxford, pp. 33–40 and passim); and Edward J. Dupey emphasizes Douglass's "acute sensitivity to the power of signs," in particular his subversion of the ideology of the southern garden, in "Linguistic Mastery and the Garden of the Chattel in Frederick Douglass' *Narrative*" (*MissQ* 46:23–33). Employing some of the tenets of speech-act theory, Neil Leroux analyzes the rhetorical flourishes of Douglass's 1852 address "What to a Slave is the Fourth of July?" in "Frederick Douglass and the Attention Shift" (*RSQ* 21:36–46).

As in Stowe's case, Alcott scholarship is fast expanding beyond analyses of the single text on which it was centered for so long, though *Little Women* still commands the most attention of any of Alcott's writings. In a chapter of *Daughters, Fathers, and the Novel* (Wisconsin, pp. 46–75)

Lynda Zwinger quarrels with some feminist readings of Alcott's novel which "see the adolescent Jo as rebelling against the father, and therefore, as being on the right track." Zwinger insists the story "valorizes the maternal" and she describes the arc of the plot in terms of Jo's "journey toward fatherly approval through daughterly virtues." On the other hand, Greta Gaard's " 'Self-Denial Was All the Fashion': Repressing Anger in *Little Women*" (*PLL* 27:3–19) takes its cue from the very readings Zwinger disputes. Alcott may overtly urge the virtues of self-sacrifice on her readers, according to Gaard, but she covertly celebrates Jo's resistance, her failure to repress her anger and to conform. Whereas Zwinger avers that Jo aspires to a writing career in order to please her father, Gaard opines that Jo becomes a writer as "an outlet for her anger." Two essays published this year on Alcott's *Work* spin off, albeit in slightly different directions, from Jane Tompkins's defense of sentimental fiction in *Sensational Designs* (*ALS 1985*, pp. 201–02 and passim). In "The Limits of Sympathy: Louisa May Alcott and the Sentimental Novel" (*AmLH* 3:685–706) Glenn Hendler delineates the utopian aspects of Alcott's feminist fantasy, the secular domestic ideology that undergirds the conventional machinery of the novel. Kathleen Margaret Lant and Angela M. Estes read the story more as a feminist parable inscribed in biblical-typological terms in "The Feminist Redeemer: Louisa Alcott's Creation of the Female Christ in *Work*" (*C&L* 40:223–53). While conceding that Alcott often "wrote in apparent support of the Victorian ideal of domesticity," Rena Sanderson contends in "*A Modern Mephistopheles:* Louisa May Alcott's Exorcism of Patriarchy" (*ATQ* n.s. 5:41–55), an essay sensibly moored in the details of biography, that she deviated from the didactic formula in a late, anonymous *Künstlerroman.* Natania Rosenfeld also foregrounds an unfinished, posthumously published roman à clef against the circumstances of Alcott's relations with her father and sister May in "Artists and Daughters in Louisa May Alcott's *Diana and Persis*" (*NEQ* 64:3–21). In addition, Alcott sleuths continue to dredge the channel of her once-murky career and turn up treasures: Daniel Shealy edits and Madeleine B. Stern introduces a collection of six more unknown early Alcott thrillers under the title *Freaks of Genius* (Greenwood); and Sarah Elbert edits and introduces the original version of Alcott's first adult novel *Moods* for the American Women Writers series (Rutgers).

Since the reissue of her novella *Life in the Iron-Mills* by the Feminist Press in 1972, Rebecca Harding Davis has enjoyed a modest revival, culminating this year with Sharon M. Harris's critical biography *Rebecca Harding Davis and American Realism* (Penn.), the first book-length study of her life and career. Harris reconstructs the salient events with skill and perspicacity, and her monograph should serve to inspire more interest in the pioneering realist. Harris reprises the section of the book on Davis's story "In the Market" in *Legacy* (8:118–21). William H. Shurr, author of *The Marriage of Emily Dickinson* (*ALS 1983*, pp. 87–88), speculates that the character Mitchell actually narrates *Life in the Iron-Mills* and that the story dramatizes his conversion to an early form of social gospel. In "Reading 'Life in the Iron-Mills' Contextually" (*Conversations*, ed. Charles Moran and Elizabeth F. Penfield [NCTE (1990), pp. 187–99]), an essay overlooked last year, Jane Atteridge Rose reads the story against the period's domestic ideology to reveal the tension between its realism and feminism. Mark Seltzer draws many of his examples of the "aestheticization of the natural body in market culture" or the "aestheticization of consumption" from Davis's novella in "The Still Life" (*AmLH* 3:455–86), an article in the periphrastic style whose simplicity of title belies its complexity and even opacity of analysis.

Several other mid-century women writers, including Sara Payson Willis ("Fanny Fern") and Susan B. Warner, attract a modicum of attention this year. Lauren Berlant explores the many voices of female sentimental discourse in "The Female Woman: Fanny Fern and the Form of Sentiment" (*AmLH* 3:429–54), a jargonological black hole, weighing many tons to the column-inch, which is liable to absorb all energy that comes within its orbit. Joyce W. Warren disinters the author's second novel, which fictionalizes the circumstances of her second marriage, in "Fanny Fern's *Rose Clark*" (*Legacy* 8:92–103). Warner's best-seller *The Wide, Wide World*, or perhaps more accurately Tompkins's view of it, continues to earn kudos in the critical marketplace. Isabelle White's argument in "Anti-Individualism, Authority, and Identity: Susan Warner's Contradictions in *The Wide, Wide World*" (*AmerS* 31, ii:31–41) that Warner finessed the issues of power and control in the novel is not very different from the canonical reading of its subversive strategies. Grace Ann Hovet and Theodore R. Hovet invoke Carol Gilligan's model of female maturation to conclude in "Identity Development in Susan Warner's *The Wide, Wide World*" (*Legacy* 8:3–16) that "Warner virtually creates a modern feminine self that is as significant as Emerson's creation of the self-reliant man." However prominent a literary figure Warner may be/have been, such a conclusion seems grossly exaggerated, if not utterly preposterous. Erica R. Bauermeister contests the notion that mid-century novels by such women as Maria Cummins, Warner, and Catharine Sedgwick share a common domestic "masterplot" in the exemplary intertextual study "*The Lamplighter, The Wide, Wide World,* and *Hope Leslie:* Reconsidering the Recipes for Nineteenth-Century American Women's Novels" (*Legacy* 8:17–28). Thomas H. Fick attempts to reclaim a neglected work of "protorealism" in "Catharine Sedgwick's 'Cacoethes Scribendi': Romance in Real Life" (*SSF* 27:567–76), and Stacy Alaimo reasonably undertakes a similar project in "Elizabeth Stoddard's *The Morgesons:* A Feminist Dialogue of *Bildung* and Descent" (*Legacy* 8:29–37). Sandra A. Zagarell also profiles Stoddard's life and career for readers of *Legacy* (8:39–49). Three other biographical sketches of women writers appear in the same volume of this journal: Karen Smith on Mary V. H. Terhune (aka "Marion Harland," pp. 51–57); Stacy Spencer on Caroline Kirkland (pp. 133–40); and Sandra Lockhart on Louise A. K. S. Clappe (aka "Dame Shirley," pp. 141–48). A pair of first-rate biographical articles based in part on unpublished manuscript sources also merit mention: Helen R. Deese's "A New England Women's Network" (*Legacy* 8:77–91), on the association "based upon a mutual recognition of intellectual ability, scholarly ambition, and creativity" of Elizabeth Peabody, Caroline Dall, and Delia Bacon; and Thomas Dublin's edition of "The Mill Letters of Emeline Larcom, 1840–1842" (*EIHC* 127:211–39), which supplements the meager evidence about sister Lucy Larcom's early work experiences in Lowell, Massachusetts.

Critical interest runs much higher nowadays in popular women writers than in their male counterparts. But belying this generalization are the first biographies to be published of a gay poet and a Native American poet and journalist, two men who lived in the eddies and backwaters of the literary mainstream. Would but the first of these books had appeared sooner. Roger Austen completed the typescript of *Genteel Pagan: The Double Life of Charles Warren Stoddard* (Mass.) in 1980, four years before he died. Now edited by John W. Crowley, Austen's narrative is a work of historical reconstruction no less remarkable in its way than A. J. A. Symons's *The Quest for Corvo.* Stoddard emerges a sympathetic figure from the biographical blind spot in which he has been so long obscured, a poet of genuine if limited talent who crossed paths with such notables as Bret Harte, Mark Twain, and W. D. Howells. James W. Parins's extensively researched *John Rollin Ridge* (Nebraska) chronicles the life of a Cherokee, "one of the first modern American Indian writers," who is best-known today, if at all, for his sensational novel loosely based on the exploits of California bandit Joaquín Murieta. Nor are the "paleface" New England writers entirely ignored in 1991. Eugene Hollahan's "Intertextual Bondings between 'The Wreck of the Hesperus' and *The Wreck of the Deutschland*" (*TSLL* 33:40–63), an informed, technical study of the influence Longfellow's ballad exerted on G. M. Hopkins's revolutionary poem; Angus Fletcher's "Whitman and Longfellow" (*Raritan* 10, iv:131–45), a formalist comparison of two coexistent types of American bard; and Reinhard Friederich's "Excelsior!" (*GettR* 4:481–92), an explication of one of Longfellow's most popular lyrics which attracted appreciative readers as different as Poe and Nietzsche. Virgil J. Vogel also scans the map for "Placenames from Longfellow's 'Song of Hiawatha' " (*Names* 39:261–68) and finds more than a hundred. Two essays on other Fireside Poets are the stuff of informational footnotes: Thomas K. Tate corrects a trivial error in the criticism of Lowell's "Memoriae Positum" in "James Russell Lowell's Nephews" (*NEQ* 64:127–29), and Michael Vella discusses a public controversy over antinomianism that raged for several weeks in 1881 in "Fire in the Ashes of Puritanism: The Conflict of Discourses Between John Greenleaf Whittier and the Reverend George Ellis" (*ATQ* n.s. 5:301–15). In addition, Paul C. Wermuth excerpts from a neglected collection of letters by a popular mid-century poet and travel writer in " 'My Full, Unreserved Self': Bayard Taylor's Letters to Charles Melancthon Jones" (*RALS* 17:220–38); and Thomas J. Roberts discusses the folk semiotic tradition of blood-and-thunder juvenile fiction in "*Gold Bullet Sport,* a Dime Novel by Buffalo Bill" (*TSLL* 33:403–44). Last and least, John Ernest's "American Profits: Moral Capitalism in Horatio Alger, Jr.'s 'Ragged Dick' " (*DNR* 60:58–64) consists largely of plot synopsis and the tired and tested argument that Alger's juvenile stories "perfectly contain" the rags-to-riches myth—even though Alger was always more a moralist than a mythmaker and he was canonized a saint in the cult of success only after his death and after his books lapsed from print.

iv Humorists

New scholarship in this category reaches a nadir in 1991, with the appearance of only two books and three articles. Orgone energy is the subject of more research. In his chapter on "The Democratic Nonesuch" in *Authorship and Audience* (pp. 90–106) Stephen Railton supplies one reason for the paucity of recent critical interest in the humor of such 19th-century writers as A. B. Longstreet and Joseph G. Baldwin: it was explicitly a genre designed for a masculinized readership. Southwestern humor in particular was, according to Railton, a "counterattack upon the spirit of the times," a "repudiation of the contemporary surge of democratic impulses" which was effectively destroyed by the Civil War. On the other hand, Edward Watts challenges such assertions in "The Changing Critical Placement of Humor of the Old Southwest" (*MissQ* 44:95–103). Watts insists that the antebellum southwestern humorists appealed to a far broader audience than upper-class males. The significant monograph on 19th-century humor this year is David B. Parker's *Alias Bill Arp: Charles Henry Smith and the South's "Goodly Heritage"* (Georgia), an excellent critical biography of the southern satirist and commentator with generous selections from his writings. Kathryn Sport and Bert Hitchcock also edit *De Remnant Truth: The Tales of Jake Mitchell and Robert Wilton Burton* (Alabama), a collection of 36 dialect sketches told by a former slave and preserved by a white writer and amateur ethnologist à la Joel Chandler Harris. Finally, David E. E. Sloane locates a "democratic entrepreneurial spirit" peculiar to both Yankee and Knickerbocker brands of humor in "The Humor of the Old Northeast: Barnum, Burnham, and the Hen Fever" (*StAH* 6 [1988]:154–62). As Sloane vividly suggests, "the cash nexus" in northeastern humor replaced "the coon hunt" of southwestern writings.

v Post-Civil War Women Writers

Scholarship in this category shows no signs of flagging. As usual, much of the work on postwar women writers centers on such figures as Jewett and Freeman, avatars of that regionalism Fred Lewis Pattee once labeled the "terminal moraine of New England Puritanism." What seems initially to be a curious and even unlikely pairing becomes not merely plausible, but brilliantly insightful, in Marilyn Sanders Mobley's *Folk Roots and Mythic Wings in Sarah Orne Jewett and Toni Morrison* (LSU). Both Jewett and Morrison are "cultural archivists" and "redemptive scribes" who reclaim the lore of their respective communities, explains Mobley, who focuses her Jewett chapters on *Deephaven* and *The Country of the Pointed Firs.* Judith Bryant Wittenberg considers the reflexivity of Jewett's first book, its various narratorial strategies and discursive modes, in "*Deephaven:* Sarah Orne Jewett's Exploratory Metafiction" (*SAF* 19:153–63). Joseph

Church makes a similar, if more specific, point about the representation of gender and race in another overlooked tale in "Fathers, Daughters, Slaves: The Haunted Scene of Writing in Jewett's 'In Dark New England Days'" (*ATQ* n.s. 5:205–24). Church contends that, in this story at least, Jewett disturbs the representational field by "refracting her narrative into disjunctive, conflictual *scenes* of writing." Priscilla Leder writes of a more literal haunting, the ghost story of Captain Littlepage, in "Living Ghosts and Women's Religion in Sarah Orne Jewett's *The Country of the Pointed Firs,*" a somewhat discursive essay in *Haunting the House of Fiction* (pp. 26–40). With its lengthy digression through Poe's *Pym,* Leder's analysis seems strained. Still less satisfactory is Max Loges, "A Collection of Great Souls: Sarah Orne Jewett's *The Country of the Pointed Firs*" (*MOR* 5:43–47), a pedestrian summary of the "private religious faith" ostensibly inscribed in the book. And in "Reading Negotiation and Negotiated Reading: A Practice with/in 'A White Heron' and 'The Revolt of "Mother"'" (*CEA* 53, iii:49–65), Elaine Orr compares texts by Jewett and Freeman to illustrate the pattern or structure of moral inquiry by women.

Freeman appears to better advantage this year in *Critical Essays on Mary Wilkins Freeman* (Hall), ed. Shirley Marchalonis, a collection of reviews and critical articles by Howells, F. O. Matthiessen, Susan Allen Toth, Joseph R. McElrath, Jr., Marjorie Pryse, and Elizabeth Meese, among others, as well as five original essays. John Getz draws the parameters rather too narrowly in his intertextual study "'Eglantina': Freeman's Revision of Hawthorne's 'The Birth-Mark'" (pp. 177–84); the essay should at least have noted Freeman's comparable revision of Hawthorne's "Wakefield" in her uncollected 1904 story "The Slip of the Leash." Martha Satz in "Going to an Unknown Home: Redesign in *The Portion of Labor*" (pp. 185–96) and Deborah G. Lambert in "Rereading Mary Wilkins Freeman: Autonomy and Sexuality in *Pembroke*" (pp. 197–206) deftly break new ground on two of Freeman's longer works. Melissa McFarland Pennell, who wrote a splendid essay on Jewett last year (*ALS 1990,* p. 225), returns with "The Liberating Will: Freedom of Choice in the Fiction of Mary Wilkins Freeman" (pp. 207–21), a study of the author's evolving critique of the rigid New England social codes governing the lives of women. Marchalonis tempers modern notions of Freeman's grim realism with a revisionist reading of several late stories in "The Sharp-edged Humor of Mary Wilkins Freeman" (pp. 222–34). Beth Wynne Fisken also revises the critical consensus by analyzing

Freeman's fiction of the supernatural, in which the author gave "oblique expression to disturbing personal issues without fear of exposure," in "The 'Faces of Children That Had Never Been': Ghost Stories by Mary Wilkins Freeman" (*Haunting the House of Fiction,* pp. 41–63). More predictable and perhaps formulaic in its linguistic analysis is "Frontiers of Language: Engendering Discourse in 'The Revolt of "Mother" ' " (*AL* 63:279–91), in which Martha J. Cutter concludes that the story "invents a system of discourse which slips free from the binary system of sexual difference, of patriarchal or non-patriarchal language, of speaking men or silent women, of barn versus home."

The burgeoning Kate Chopin critical industry, once devoted almost entirely to a single text, diversifies slightly this year. To be sure, *The Awakening* continues to receive its share of attention. The most exciting new essay on Chopin this year, to my mind, is Bert Bender's "The Teeth of Desire: *The Awakening* and *The Descent of Man*" (*AL* 63:459–73). Bender demonstrates beyond a reasonable doubt that the stories of courtship Chopin penned in the 1890s in fact implicate the theory of sexual selection if only to deny that men alone may exercise the sexual prerogative and that *The Awakening* contains her "most extensive and explicit" references to Darwin. I heartily recommend Bender's essay to every teacher who assigns the text. It should serve to reorient discussion of the novel in the classroom no less than in the journals. Katherine Kearns's "The Nullification of Edna Pontellier" (*AL* 63:62–88) is almost as provocative. Kearns offers what is in effect an alternative feminist reading of the novel in which the erstwhile heroine "takes to herself the language, the assumptions, the essential misogyny of a thoroughly masculinized vision" and is "awakened to the damning imperatives of a sensuality which repudiates her intellectual, spiritual, and artistic worth." Manfred Malzahn also questions whether Chopin's protagonist is an altogether sympathetic figure, indeed whether she even commits suicide, in "The Strange Demise of Edna Pontellier" (*SLJ* 23, ii:31–39). In "Kate Chopin's Fiction: Order and Disorder in a Stratified Society" (*UMSE* n.s. 9:119–34), Pearl L. Brown speculates that *The Awakening* sparked a critical uproar when it appeared in 1899 not on account of its eroticism but because the rebellious Edna, unlike Chopin's earlier heroines, defied "the very conventions that connected various subcultures and subclasses and held them in place in the social hierarchy." Such an explanation seems woefully inadequate, for its presumes that the source of a literary cause célèbre is somehow to be found wholly within a text without regard to its publishing milieu. Maria Anastasopoulou discusses the novel as a failed female bildungsroman in "Rites of Passage in Kate Chopin's *The Awakening*" (*SLJ* 23, ii:19–30). Cynthia Guidici presumes to apply the sociological concepts of "domains" and "occasions" to *The Awakening* and several stories in "Kate Chopin's 'Occasional' Women" (*CCTEP* 56:25–34), though the advantages of such an approach are not readily apparent. Guidici still devotes an inordinate amount of space to plot synopses. Roslyn Reso Foy also indulges in some crude armchair psychoanalysis of the character Armand in Chopin's story "Désirée's Baby" (*Expl* 49:222–23). James W. Tuttleton largely commends Emily Toth's "massively detailed" biography of Chopin, published last year (*ALS 1990*, p. 227), in "A Solitary Soul: The Career of Kate Chopin" (*NewC* 9, viii:12–17), while Toth announces the rediscovery of two 1898 interviews with the author in "Kate Chopin on Divine Love and Suicide" (*AL* 63:115–21). Toth also edits and introduces *A Vocation and a Voice* (Penguin), a collection of 23 stories by Chopin suitable for classroom adoption.

The Gilmaniacs seem to be gearing up for a bumper harvest next year, the centenary of the publication of "The Yellow Wall-paper." At least two collections of essays are scheduled for publication. Meanwhile, no less than five critical articles on the story appear in 1991. E. Suzanne Owens extracts the Gothic or supernatural tale from "the story of repression and madness we read today"—that is, Owens reads the story much as it was read prior to the Feminist Press edition of 1973—in "The Ghostly Double behind the Wallpaper in Charlotte Perkins Gilman's 'The Yellow Wallpaper'" (*Haunting the House of Fiction*, pp. 64–79). Similarly, Rae Beth Gordon briefly compares Gothic elements in "Interior Decoration in Poe and Gilman" (*LIT* 3:85–99), and Margaret Delashmit and Charles Long note several similarities between Gilman's story and *Jane Eyre* (*Expl* 49:32–33). Conrad Shumaker, who published an earlier essay on the story in *AL* (*ALS 1985*, p. 219), revisits it in "Realism, Reform, and the Audience: Charlotte Perkins Gilman's Unreadable Wallpaper" (*ArQ* 47:81–93) to explain why contemporary readers of the tale were so threatened by it: Gilman led them into unfamiliar terrain beyond realism, a space beyond the commonplace and conventional, where "if read carefully the story would leave women beside themselves." Wai-chee Dimock uses the tale as an exemplary text to interrogate the relationship between two modes of poststructuralism and to deconstruct their too neat binary opposition in "Feminism, New

Historicism, and the Reader" (*AL* 63:601–22). Its technical sophistication notwithstanding, Dimock's argument is neither arcane nor the prose daunting; rather, the essay is surprisingly accessible to those of us who read widely but not too well in theory. The unpublished *Unpunished,* a hardly boiled detective novel about the murder of a male supremacist written in the throes of Gilman's "feminist despair" of the late 1920s, receives a critical nod in Lillian S. Robinson's "Killing Patriarchy: Charlotte Perkins Gilman, the Murder Mystery, and Post-Feminist Propaganda" (*TSWL* 10:273–85). So much for the critical response to Gilman's fiction this year. Surprisingly, her verse is still virtually unknown to scholars, though it was as a poet that she first earned renown. Gilman's nonfiction is winning an ever-larger audience, however. Larry Ceplair edits *Charlotte Perkins Gilman: A Nonfiction Reader* (Columbia), largely excerpted from her theoretical and sociological writings, most of them obscure or otherwise unavailable to modern scholars. This useful casebook should serve to redirect some of the attention now devoted almost exclusively to "Wall-paper." And Ann J. Lane introduces an offset reprinting of the autobiography *The Living of Charlotte Perkins Gilman* (Wisconsin) which at the very least should have included a detailed index rather than merely reproducing the austere one that appeared in the original 1935 edition.

Other women writers of the period remain cottage industries. Two serviceable biographies are worthy of special mention. Emily Wortis Leider's fulsome *California's Daughter: Gertrude Atherton and Her Times* (Stanford), the first major biography of a western writer sometimes compared during her lifetime to Edith Wharton, seems very nearly definitive. Patricia Dunlavy Valenti's life of Rose Hawthorne Lathrop, *To Myself a Stranger* (LSU), revives a poet too long overshadowed by her father, brother, and husband. In addition, R. W. B. Lewis devotes a substantial part of his genealogical saga *The Jameses* (Farrar) to Alice James, likewise the daughter and sister of prominent men of letters and who, as a diarist, deserves to be better known in her own right. The acerbic ruptures and intellectual inhibitions evident in James's diary are, in fact, Claire Kahane's topic in "The Aesthetic Politics of Rage" (*LIT* 3:19–31). F. D. Reeve also commends the little-known pastoral poetry of Celia Thaxter in "Islands, Cities, and Flowers" (*GettR* 4:454–59), while Carole Kessner rehearses "The Emma Lazarus-Henry James Connection" (*AmLH* 3:46–62) and publishes for the first time seven of the eight letters the poet received from the novelist. William J. Scheick deciphers the semiotic code of Frances Harper's first short story, recently enshrined in the *Heath Anthology,* in "Strategic Ellipsis in Harper's 'The Two Offers'" (*SLJ* 23, ii:14–18).

vi The Howells Generation

Scholars seem increasingly drawn to Howells's early years, as I reported last year, though I should qualify the generalization this year given the sudden and unexpected (by me) surge of interest in *The Rise of Silas Lapham.* In 1991 the major book on Howells, if not quite the "big book" Howellsians have been awaiting for years, is Rodney D. Olsen's *Dancing in Chains: The Youth of William Dean Howells* (NYU), an Eriksonian psychobiography that is both different in scope and focus and ultimately less satisfactory than John Crowley's *The Black Heart's Truth* (*ALS 1985,* pp. 221–22). Olsen's account basically ends with Howells's return from Italy in 1865, in the midst of his literary apprenticeship, whereas Crowley's narrative carries him through the celebrated breakdown of 1881. John E. Bassett analyzes a series of formal and epistemological issues Howells addressed in his oeuvre in *"A Heart of Ideality in My Realism" and Other Essays* (Locust Hill), which includes a pair of reprinted articles on *Their Wedding Journey* and Howells's early criticism and new pieces on *A Chance Acquaintance* and *A Foregone Conclusion.* Bassett's approach is refreshingly New Critical. Daniel Rubey poses several provocative questions about the practical effects of copy-text theory and its assumptions about authorial intention—assumptions challenged by recent critical theory—in "Howells's *Venetian Life* as a Vertical Text" (*Text* 5:315–38). Dewey Ganzel turns the equivalent of a triple-axle in "Thoroughly Knit and Perfectly Clear: *A Modern Instance* Reconsidered" (*ALR* 23, ii:2–19). In pleading his case for Howells's "satire of egocentricity" in the novel, Ganzel advances what was once thought next to impossible: a convincing argument for the coherency of the text, including its final chapters. My own "'A Little Scrap of Autobiography': A Lost Speech and Poem by W. D. Howells" (*ANQ* n.s. 4:129–32) continues my grand project of adding to the Howells bibliography in infinitesimal increments. Meanwhile, critical discourse on Howells is dominated, for better or worse, by discussions of his most famous novel. *New Essays on* The Rise of Silas Lapham (Cambridge) contains an introduction/reception history by editor Donald E. Pease (pp. 1–28) and five essays, only four of them actually new. (Wai-chee Dimock published her piece last year with a different subtitle and without endnotes. See *ALS 1990,* pp. 231–32.) Paul Bové challenges the traditional reading of Lapham's moral rise by finding in the novel a banality and deception which mask the violence of capitalism in "Helpless Longing, or, the Lesson of *Silas Lapham*" (pp. 29–45). John Seelye probes in "The Hole in Howells/The Lapse in *Silas Lapham*" (pp. 47–65) a rupture in the narrative which reveals how the novelist's loyalties were torn and divided subtextually between the vulgarity of Mark Twain (the Laphams) and the gentility of Henry James (the Coreys). James M. Cox makes much the same point about the implicit contrast in the novel between Twain's and James's positions and Howells's siding with the Brahmins in subtle embarrassment at the spectacle of the Laphams in "*The Rise of Silas Lapham:* The Business of Morals and Manners" (pp. 107–28). Daniel T. O'Hara ponders the implications of the "ascetic aesthetic" observed by each of the Laphams in this sublimely conflicted text in "Smiling through Pain: The Practice of Self in *The Rise of Silas Lapham*" (pp. 91–105). Two other fine essays on the novel appear this year in *ALR.* In "An Ethic of Responsibility in *The Rise of Silas Lapham*" (23, ii:20–34), Fritz Oehlschlager argues that the text adumbrates not a utilitarianism glossed in Sewall's economy of pain but an ethics of response and responsibility like that formulated later by Reinhold Niebuhr. And in "Compromise and Complicity in *The Rise of Silas Lapham*" (24, i:39–53) Clare Virginia Eby demonstrates how Howells punctured the stereotype of the businessman, how "interpretations of the businessman drawn from preconceptions and filtered through prejudices are inaccurate, if not dangerous." The distinguished biographer and critic Edwin H. Cady strikes an altogether new and welcome note by detecting the first whiffs of literary modernism in Howells's late poems in "Howells in the Modern Tradition" (*NCF* 45:478–94).

A pair of pioneering realists also receive brief but admiring glances this year. Stephen Becker ardently defends the artistry of the first and arguably the best Civil War novel in "On John William De Forest's *Miss Ravenel's Conversion from Secession to Loyalty*" (*Classics of Civil War Fiction,* pp. 23–36). Becker's essay is less a critical analysis than an appreciation which might serve to introduce a reprint of the novel. Harold H. Kolb, Jr., salvages at least some vestige of Bret Harte's sagging reputation, making a case for his mastery of comic understatement in his early *Overland* tales, in "The Outcast of Literary Flat" (*ALR* 23, ii:52–63). Meanwhile, too, critics turn up a few nuggets and pockets of "color" in the works of other regionalists, though for the most part these white males (e.g., Edward Eggleston, Joaquin Miller, James Lane Allen) have slipped ineluctably into what Irving once called the "literary catacomb, where authors, like mummies, are piously entombed." Barbara Ladd tracks down several historical sources George Washington Cable tapped in writing about a defiant slave whose story he inserted into his master-text in " 'An Atmosphere of Hints and Allusions': Bras-Coupé and the Context of Black Insurrection in *The Grandissimes*" (*SoQ* 29, iii:63–76), and Alice Hall Petry reads a late Cable story against the grain to suggest how his mature style betrayed his ambivalence regarding the veracity of language in "The Limits of Truth in Cable's 'Salome Müller' " (*PLL* 27:20–31). Two other items treat minor men of letters best-known, if at all, for their Orientalism: Jonathan Cott's *Wandering Ghost: The Odyssey of Lafcadio Hearn* (Knopf), a workmanlike hagiography for general readers of the journalist and popularizer of Japanese culture; and Brijraj Singh's "Henry Willard French and India" (*NEQ* 64:574–93), a well-intentioned but tedious attempt to resuscitate the corpus of the forgotten author of *Our Boys in India.* Thomas Becknell frames the "hermeneutical gap" at the heart of Harold Frederic's best novel in terms of reader-response to account for its "power of deception" in "Implication Through Reading *The Damnation of Theron Ware*" (*ALR* 24, i:63–71). A couple of postbellum nature writers celebrated by the realists also earn high critical marks this year. In "Clarence King's Sierra Nevada" (*WVUPP* 37:67–76), Armand E. Singer turns an appreciative eye on the minor classic *Mountaineering in the Sierra Nevada;* and in "John Muir and the Poetics of Natural Conversion" (*NDQ* 59:62–79), John Tallmadge proposes to read *My First Summer in the Sierra* as a narrative of conversion akin to those of Paul and Augustine. Muir's essay collection *Our National Parks* is also reissued this year by the Sierra Club with a foreword by Alfred Runte. Two more reprinted novels set during Reconstruction, one by a southern apologist in the plantation tradition and the other by a Radical Republican, appear in the Masterworks of Literature Series (NCUP): Thomas Nelson Page's *Red Rock,* ed. Lucas Carpenter, and Albion Tourgée's *A Fool's Errand,* ed. Theodore L. Gross.

Late-century writers of color continue to fare well, though critical interest in Chesnutt falls off slightly this year. In "Aunts, Uncles, Audience: Gender and Genre in Charles Chesnutt's *The Conjure Woman*" (*BALF* 25:665–88), Eric Selinger uncovers "a strategic structure or over-plot" to the sexual politics of the stories and frames in Chesnutt's first anthology. Charles E. Wilson, Jr., measures the satirical dimensions of another story in "Chesnutt's 'Baxter's "Procrustes"': Cultural Fraud as Link to Cultural Identity" (*Cultural Power/Cultural Literacy,* pp. 120–28). William L. Andrews also admirably edits and introduces the 18 tales in *Collected Stories of Charles W. Chesnutt* (Penguin), a new classroom text. Paul Laurence Dunbar's dialect poem "When Malindy Sings" and his story "The Lynching of Jude Benson" figure prominently in Gayl Jones's *Liberating Voices,* a study of the emergence of the black American literary tradition. Alisa Johnson examines a neglected story by a recently revived African American woman writer which combines "the feminine quest with the heterosexual love motif" in "Writing within the Script: Alice Dunbar-Nelson's 'Ellen Fenton'" (*SAF* 19:165–74). Xiao-Huang Yin's "Between the East and West: Sui Sin Far—the First Chinese-American Woman Writer" (*ArQ* 47:49–84), a fairly straightforward biographical sketch and thematic exposition, rounds out this section.

The utopians are literally nowhere this year, as though they have been translated en masse to the netherworld. The only notable exception: a new edition of Alice Ilgenfritz Jones and Ella Merchant's *Unveiling a Parallel* (Syracuse), ed. Carol Kolmerten.

vii Crane, Norris, Adams, and the Fin de Siècle

The discovery, announced last year (*ALS 1990,* p. 234), that Thomas Beer forged virtually all of the Crane letters cited in his 1923 Crane biography has already begun to resonate in the scholarship. John Clendenning rightly suggests that the book reveals more about the biographer—his identification with his subject, his transference reaction—than it reveals about Crane in "Thomas Beer's *Stephen Crane:* The Eye of His Imagination" (*PSt* 14, i:68–80). Yet another myth that has accreted in Crane studies is punctured by Elizabeth Friedmann in "Cora's Travel Notes, 'Dan Emmonds,' and Stephen Crane's Route to the Greek War" (*SSF* 27:264–65). Stephen was *not* in Cora's company, it seems, when she was almost shipwrecked on the Black Sea, an adventure that inspired his later satirical sketch. Friedmann thus vindicates, ironically enough, R. W. Stallman's version of events in his 1968 biography of Crane. A couple of Crane articles this year in *ALR* also sail against the prevailing winds of critical fashion: In "The Syphilitic World of Crane's *Maggie*" (24, i:79–85) Gerard M. Sweeney marshals evidence that the slums of Rum Alley are pervaded by venereal disease; and in "Frank Norris and Stephen

Crane: Conviction and Uncertainty" (24, i:54–62) Stanley Wertheim compares Norris's evolutionary meliorism with Crane's nihilism. Ronald E. Martin touches on Crane's literary impressionism, his epistemological dramas, in *American Literature and the Destruction of Knowledge* (pp. 121–30), and Jules Zanger suggests in "Stephen Crane's 'Bride' as Countermyth of the West" (*GPQ* 11:157–65) that Crane sought to subvert in the parodic "The Bride Comes to Yellow Sky" the myth of the Wild West (this much a critical commonplace) as well as Theodore Roosevelt's "bourgeois myth" of loyal, patriotic, and ambitious cowboys. Meanwhile, discussions of two other stories, and chestnuts at that—*The Red Badge of Courage* and "The Open Boat"—virtually monopolize the critical discourse on Crane. Both Philip D. Beidler in "Stephen Crane's *The Red Badge of Courage:* Henry Fleming's Courage in Its Contexts" (*ClioI* 20:235–51) and Terry Mulcaire in "Progressive Visions of War in *The Red Badge of Courage* and *The Principles of Scientific Management*" (*AQ* 43:46–72) presume to contextualize their analysis of the novel. Beidler acknowledges the ironic sense in which Crane invoked notions of courage, yet he asserts—without any theoretical underpinning to the point—that the intended reader would have "been able to 'stabilize' the irony within a relatively familiar context of cultural interpretation." The assumption is essential to Beidler's argument, but it remains, alas, sheer assumption. On his part, Mulcaire quarrels with that strain of recent criticism that reinvents the novel so it seems "a demystifying camera lens directed at the ideology of American industrial capitalism" with its unrelenting class conflict. On the contrary, according to Mulcaire's reformulation of the New Historicist argument, such progressive reformers as Frederick Taylor, the advocate of industrial efficiency, shared with Crane an "ideology of industrial systematization." Taylor's industrial realism was first cousin to Crane's literary realism. Paul H. Lorenz speculates, albeit without hard evidence, that Crane modeled the story of Henry's struggles on Hegel's notion of "dialectical definition," if only as he found it refracted through Whitman, in "*The Red Badge of Courage* as an Exercise in Hegelian Dialectic" (*SJS* 17, iii:32–40). James M. Cox emphasizes Crane's originality and stylistic innovation in "*The Red Badge of Courage:* The Purity of War" (*SHR* 25:305–20; rpt. in *Classics of Civil War Fiction,* pp. 44–62). A pair of essays on Crane's story underscore its epistemological implications: Christopher Metress's "From Indifference to Anxiety: Knowledge and the Reader in 'The Open Boat' " (*SSF*

28:47–53), which examines how the problem of knowledge represented in the tale affects the reader; and Sura P. Rath and Mary Neff Shaw's "The Dialogic Narrative of 'The Open Boat'" (*CollL* 18:94–106), which inscribes the same problem in Bakhtinian terms as an example of heteroglossia. Finally, Grace McEntee's "*Deliverance* as James Dickey's Revision of Crane's 'Open Boat'" (*JDN* 7:2–11) is remarkable only for its insights on the Dickey novel.

Scholarly interest in Adams, especially his personal quest for meaning and system, soars in the midst of our own fin de siècle. As Perry Miller averred, it takes one anxious age to know another. In "Henry Adams: The Letters and the Life" (*SHR* 25:105–23), a sympathetic essay-review of the six volumes of Adams's *Letters,* James M. Cox focuses on Adams's unrequited middle-aged (Middle-Aged?) love for Elizabeth Cameron. A severely truncated version of Cox's review also appears in *AmLH* (3:136–52). Clive Bush offers a delightfully iconoclastic intellectual biography of Adams which highlights his anarchism in *Halfway to Revolution* (Yale, pp. 19–127). Somewhat in the manner of Adams, Bush scorns both tortured prose and scholarly poses. William W. Stowe notes the importance to Adams of travel, a "quintessential marginal activity" he turned to account in such intellectual guidebooks as *Mont-Saint-Michel and Chartres,* in "Henry Adams, Traveler" (*NEQ* 64:179–205). Similarly, John Ernest discusses Adams as a self-styled Other, an outsider who assumed a role typified in the anonymous publication of his novel *Democracy,* in "Henry Adams's Double: Recreating the Philosophical Statesman" (*JAC* 14, i:25–35). B. H. Gilley also details the "biographical overtones" of Adams's roman à clef in "*Democracy:* Henry Adams and the Role of Political Leader" (*Biography* 14:349–65). Kim Moreland traces Adams's increasing distaste for photography—and with astonishing dexterity links it to Clover Adams's suicide in 1885—in "The Photo Killeth: Henry Adams on Photography and Painting" (*PLL* 27:356–70). In "Henry Adams' *Annis Mirabilis:* 1900 and the Making of a Modernist" (*AmerS* 32, ii:103–16) Keith R. Burich points to events in a watershed year in Adams's life to explain his willingness to embrace the language of modern science. Predictably, too, Malini Johar Schueller's chapter on Adams's *Education* in *The Politics of Voice* (pp. 67–85) is biographically oriented, though Schueller's overriding point is that the text demonstrates "the impossibility of any language, ideology, or subjectivity being independent of all others or beyond history and context."

The most important Norris studies this year center on *McTeague* to the virtual neglect of his other fiction, much as Crane scholars seem to have built a firebreak around *The Red Badge of Courage.* In "The 'Octopus' in *McTeague:* Frank Norris and Professionalism" (*MFS* 37:677–88) David Heddendorf assesses Norris's profound ambivalence toward the rise of professional associations and licensers and compares McTeague's loss of career to Dyke's loss of job in *The Octopus.* Two other essays on the novel this year in *WAL* qualify its naturalism by reference to Norris's satire and irony: William J. Hug describes the parodic elements in the final chapters, after McTeague has lost his dental practice and reverted to mining, in "McTeague as Metafiction? Frank Norris' Parodies of Bret Harte and the Dime Novel" (26:219–28); and Susan Prothro McFatter argues that the first half of the novel resembles an ironic romance, the second half a tale of Gothic horror, in "Parody and Dark Projections: Medieval Romance and the Gothic in *McTeague*" (26:119–35). A pair of notes on the novel are less substantial: Alfred G. Litton's "The Kinetoscope in *McTeague*" (*SAF* 19:107–12), on the significance of an early motion picture device to which Norris alludes in passing; and Robert M. Myers's "Dreiser's Copy of *McTeague*" (*PLL* 27:260–67), on the possibility that Norris influenced Dreiser, with a list of marginal glosses. The only major essay I have read this year that is not on *McTeague,* ironically, is one I overlooked last year. According to Sherwood Williams in "The Rise of a New Degeneration: Decadence and Atavism in *Vandover and the Brute*" (*ELH* 57 [1990]:709–36), the novel registers a historical shift in conceptualizations of sexual identity. Norris devotees will also want to check the two 1991 numbers of *FNS* for Norris Society news and bibliographical updates.

I end this chapter with Ambrose Bierce who, his alleged misogyny notwithstanding, is fashionable and semicanonical again, if the inclusion of one of his Civil War stories in the *Heath Anthology* is any indication. It is a remarkable feat of revivification, akin to pulling the stake from Dracula's heart. No less a luminary than Ishmael Reed muses on Bierce's *Tales of Soldiers and Civilians* (*Classics of Civil War Fiction,* pp. 37–43) and finds many a "chilling" and "brilliant" antiwar story. William Conlogue adds credence to this view of Bierce by examining the symbology of ravines and valleys—sites of death and graves—in five of the Civil War tales in "A Haunting Memory: Ambrose Bierce and the Ravine of the Dead" (*SSF* 28:21–29). In "Ambrose Bierce's Civil War Stories and the

Critique of the Martial Spirit" (*SAF* 19:221–28), however, Giorgio Mariani takes a different tack by insisting that Bierce's supposedly intense opposition to war was in fact equivocal and mixed, that he failed "to position himself outside the martial discourse of his time." There is still time to dump him from the next edition of the *Heath*.

University of New Mexico

13 Fiction: 1900 to the 1930s

Jo Ann Middleton

As the canon expands to accommodate newly discovered and rediscovered writers, so too does this chapter. In addition to pioneering efforts by feminist and African-American scholars, there was substantial work on Cather, Wharton, and Dreiser as well as several volumes of correspondence.

i Willa Cather

Cather scholars will welcome the news that Elizabeth Shepley Sergeant's *Willa Cather: A Memoir* (Ohio) is once again available. This edition has the advantage of Marilyn Arnold's thoroughly enjoyable and perceptive foreword, which analyzes the Sergeant-Cather relationship and fortunately does not resist the temptation to compare this memoir to Edith Lewis's. In *Willa Cather and Six Writers from the Great War* (Univ. Press) Joseph J. Kirschke provides brief biographies of six promising young writers who could have served as the inspiration for the fictional Tom Outland. The links that Kirschke suggests are tenuous, but the book should provoke further study. Cultural perspectives on war inform Josephine O'Brien Schaefer's comparison of Virginia Woolf's *Jacob's Room* and *Mrs. Dalloway* to *One of Ours* in "The Great War and 'This age of world's experience' in Cather and Woolf" (Mark Hussey, ed., *Virginia Woolf and War: Fiction, Reality, and Myth* [Syracuse, pp. 134–50]). Cather's "enthusiasm for war," reflecting an American cultural attitude toward war and conquest that countenances such acts as the obliteration of history and culture in "the genocide of Native Americans," contrasts dramatically with Woolf's emphasis on the senseless waste of war, a result of her close proximity to "the mud and rats and gas of the trenches." Joseph R. Urgo juxtaposes *A Lost Lady* with the spring 1988 issue of

Overthrow (*Novel Frames,* pp. 189–221) and argues that the novel both raises questions about the power of historical consciousness to objectify the past and provides a critical lens for understanding cultural methods of self-construction.

Two essays examine the sense of place in Cather's novels. William Barillas, "Placelessness Against Place: Willa Cather's Nebraska Novels" (*MMisc* 19:20–28), finds in *O Pioneers!, My Ántonia,* and *A Lost Lady* a tension between a rootedness unique to Nebraska's early homesteaders and "an opposing placelessness pulling them both back in time to origins in Europe and forward into the materialistic modern world." Comparing passages from *The Song of the Lark,* Sinclair Ross's *As for Me and My House* (1941), and Wright Morris's *The Home Place* (1948), Diane Dufva Quantic demonstrates that Cather's use of specific images and symbols, as well as her attitude toward language and values, puts her securely in the Great Plains tradition, "a subset of the plain prose style" ("The Unifying Thread: Connecting Place and Language in Great Plains Literature" [*AmerS* 32, i:67–83]).

Three feminist studies contain chapters on Cather. Kate Fullbrook's *Free Women,* a major examination of the new configurations of moral success or failure, includes Cather, Wharton, and Stein among the 11 novelists who have shifted the "terms in which good for women is defined." Fullbrook pairs Cather with Zora Neale Hurston (pp. 33–55); combining heroic, folkloric, and realist methods with autobiographical material, both writers construct "allegorical moments that provide new starting points for paradigms of moral virtue." Cather confronts the myth of the lawless, irresponsible, and womanless American West with a new myth of interdependence, partnership, rootedness, and "mutual need between men and women." The essays in *Diverse Voices* explore the ways in which women writers have "addressed language, self-hood and society" in the struggle to "wrest the male-determined language to their own ends." Julia Briggs, especially good on *Sapphira and the Slave Girl* and "Old Mrs. Harris," traces the tension between domesticity and creativity, mother and artist, self and family, the provincial hometown and the wider world throughout Cather's work in "Willa Cather: The Woman as Artist" (pp. 32–56). Judith Fetterley's "*My Ántonia,* Jim Burden, and the Dilemma of the Lesbian Writer" (*Lesbian Texts and Contexts,* pp. 145–63) proposes that *My Ántonia* is "a central, if not *the* central Cather text" because it "defines the nature of Cather's situation as an American writer who was also a lesbian writer and it defines the nature of her solution to the inherent contradiction between American and lesbian." Cather's introduction serves to focus attention on the problem of the narrative voice in the text, the inability to speak directly; instead of explaining Jim, "the introduction leaves us wondering who made the attempt."

Several scholars use Cather's work to illustrate critical, historical, or cultural theses. Peter Messent reads *A Lost Lady* with the help of Wolfgang Iser and Steven Mailloux in "The Dynamics of Reading: *A Lost Lady*" (*New Readings of the American Novel*, pp. 130–61). Cather's novel, which foregrounds issues of gender and sexuality, highlights both the usefulness and shortcomings of Iser's model and demonstrates the validity of Mailloux's model for establishing the importance of types of reading conventions in a particular historical community. In *By the Law of Nature* (pp. 218–38) Howard Horwitz offers a superb reading of *O Pioneers!* as "a meditation on the nature of property and on the relation between property and self." Although Cather's novel intersects with both the homesteading and the women's rights movements, neither natural rights nor feminist reform are issues in the text. Horwitz proposes that Cather's refusal to identify property with self was not only the source of Alexandra's "impervious calm," but also of Cather's own attitude toward art, authorship, and her own last will and testament. In " 'A Poor Man Stinks and God Hates Him': Interpreting Willa Cather's *My Mortal Enemy* in Light of Thorstein Veblen's *The Theory of the Leisure Class*" (*CCTEP* 56:68–75) Lady Falls Brown suggests that Cather in her novel shows the destructive effects of poverty and validates the importance of wealth for personal happiness. Drawing on Veblen's theories dealing with wealth and individual worth, Brown convincingly demonstrates that Myra's inexplicable behavior toward Oswald is better understood if we see her as the product of the leisure class, one who values the outward symbols of wealth, engages in conspicuous consumption, and discovers that she needs money, not passion, to make her happy. In a companion piece, Zhongxiu He, writing from within a socialist political and economic system, examines *My Mortal Enemy* as "a drama of capitalist discord" that focuses on class and money, issues which lead to the destruction of Myra's passion for Oswald ("Poverty as Myra's Mortal Enemy" [*WCPMN* 35:29–32]).

The most engaging work of the year is Demaree Peck's important essay, "Thea Kronborg's 'Song of Myself': The Artist's Imaginative Inheritance in *The Song of the Lark*" (*WAL* 26:21–38), which builds on the efforts of both Susan Rosowski and Marilyn Berg Callander (see *ALS 1990,* pp. 242, 243) to read Thea's story as "a fairy-tale, or wish-fulfillment." Not only does Cather give Thea the artist's "omnipotent ego," which can displace all authority, she also gives her alter ego a series of godfathers to help in her quest. Peck's reading of *The Song of the Lark* draws on both Whitman and Wordsworth to elucidate Thea's sense of self and culminates in a fine explanation of how we identify with Thea to "reclaim that unbounded childhood 'feeling of empire' where ego remains supreme." In "Growth and Development of the Artist: Willa Cather's *My Ántonia*" (*MQ* 33:93–107) Muriel Brown argues that Cather did not abandon her concern with creativity and the role of the artist in *My Ántonia,* but that this novel reflects Cather's growing sense of what constitutes art. Book III, in which Ántonia's name is hardly mentioned, is crucial to understanding Jim's recognition of the connections between the raw material of art and art itself. If Jim did not perceive meaning in Ántonia's story and transfer it into words, it would not exist. Patricia Sell's "Marian Forrester's 'Fine Play-Acting'" (*WCPMN* 35:5–8) celebrates the heroic artistry in Marian Forrester's brilliant and necessary "fine play-acting."

The Professor's House inspired three noteworthy items. In "*The Professor's House:* The Sense of an Ending" (*SNNTS* 23:443–51) Michael Leddy elucidates the complexity of the novel's "remarkably modernist" ending. Rejecting a simple dichotomy between St. Peter's childhood and adult lives, Leddy instead points out a number of distinct lives the Professor has already lived—"three of youth (lived in sequence in Michigan, Kansas, and France) and two of adulthood (lived in the alternation of day and night in Hamilton)"—and suggests that St. Peter finds himself constructing yet another adult life at the novel's end. Janis Stout proposes another look at *The Professor's House* as "profoundly autobiographical," arguing that "journeys have a dual significance in the novel, as symbolic actions and as disguised revelations of self" ("Autobiography as Journey in *The Professor's House* [*SAF* 19:203–15]). The book's journey patterns mirror Cather's trips to the Southwest and to Europe, turning points in her life. Marilyn R. Chandler explores Cather's use of architectural metaphors to reflect both the psychological structure of the main character and the structure of the text (*Dwelling in the Text,* pp. 181–216). *The Professor's House* contains "multiple structures that confine and define" St. Peter; old and new homes incorporate "conflicting values and competing ways of life."

The Special Literary Issue of the *Willa Cather Pioneer Memorial Newsletter* (35:11–34) contains a number of fine essays and "The Church in *Archbishop:* A Session from the Santa Fe Seminar," part of which is John J. Murphy's thoughtful "On the Precipice of a Caesura: *Death Comes for the Archbishop* and Vatican II" (pp. 25–29). Murphy surveys church history, reviews contemporary theology, and reads Latour's process of accommodation and discovery in this "prophetic" novel as a pattern for achieving unity and universality in the post-Vatican church. Jane Giltrow and David Strouck detail Cather's use of "echo effect" and two types of cohesion in a linguistic study, "Lyrical Measures: Cohesion and Sentence Endings in Cather's Prose" (pp. 11–15). Clara Thomas studies the interrelatedness of Cather's *The Song of the Lark* and Margaret Laurence's *The Diviners* in "Portrait of the Artist: Thea Kronberg and Margaret Laurence's Morag Gunn" (pp. 15–19). In other articles, George Greene suggests Parkman and Pascal as sources for *Shadows on the Rock,* then explores Cather's narrative strategy to create a text resembling oral history in "A Colloquy with Clio: Willa Cather's *Shadows on the Rock*" (*DR* 70:219–28), and Virgil Albertini adds to his series of articles on sports in Cather's fiction with "Willa Cather and Baseball: Some Personal and Literary Connections" (*PVR* 17 [1989]:16–24) and "Cather's Lucy Gayheart: A Girl in Motion" (*PVR* 19:37–44).

Joining those who have described Cather's modernism, Loretta Wasserman places the short fiction in the "first wave of twentieth-century modernism" in *Willa Cather: A Study of the Short Fiction* (Twayne). In addition to Wasserman's brief discussions of 18 of Cather's "most challenging works," the volume collects seven commentaries by Cather herself, Edith Lewis, interviewers and reviewers, three previously published essays on Cather's short stories by John J. Murphy, Joan Wylie Hall, and Alice Hall Petry, and excerpts from significant book-length studies by Marilyn Arnold and Susan J. Rosowski. Wasserman's book only whets our appetite for more substantial studies in this area.

Cather's early short stories generated two essays. With his usual discernment, Bruce Baker offers an alternative to the usual view of "Peter" as bleak and naturalistic, explaining how Cather transformed the details of Frank Sadilek's suicide into "a commentary on the persistence of art" ("Willa Cather's 'Peter': From Anecdote to Narrative" [*WCPMN* 34:40–41]). Jeane Harris's "Aspects of Athene in Willa Cather's Short Fiction" (*SSF* 28:177–82) examines Cather's use of the goddess in "Tommy the Unsentimental," "Resurrection," "The Treasure of Far Island," and

"Flavia and Her Artists." Athene's dual nature fits Cather's androgynous females, who express Cather's own dissatisfaction with traditional gender roles and categories.

Lastly, *The Willa Cather Yearbook* (Mellen), ed. Debbie A. Hanson, planned as a tribute to the late Mildred Bennett, collects 11 new essays and two previously published studies. New work includes Bennett on Max Westbrook as well as her comparison of Cather and Wendell Berry; John P. Anders, Joan Wylie Hall, and Debbie Hanson on *My Ántonia;* Ronald W. Butler on "Paul's Case"; Lawrence I. Berkove on *A Lost Lady;* Rhoda F. Orme-Johnson on *The Professor's House;* Mary-Anne Martin on music; Marvin D. Jensen on Cather as a drama critic; and Richard C. Harris on order in Cather's fiction.

ii Edith Wharton and Ellen Glasgow

Wharton scholarship thrives; eight books and more than 20 articles attest to its vigor. Back in print, with a fine introduction by Mary Suzanne Schriber, is *A Motor-Flight Through France* (No. Ill.), Wharton's 1908 travelogue. R. W. B. Lewis's new collection of 21 of Wharton's stories attests to their continuing popularity among general readers as well as critics. Lewis's clear and cogent introduction to *The Selected Short Stories of Edith Wharton* (Scribner's) updates his earlier, definitive treatment of her work in the genre. The volume also contains a complete listing of Wharton stories.

In *Edith Wharton: A Study of the Short Fiction* (Twayne) Barbara A. White adopts a contemporary feminist perspective to analyze Wharton's criticism of social conventions and advance the provocative and clearly presented theory that Wharton was a victim of incest, an experience deeply affecting her life and art. Excerpts from the book appeared in two issues of the *Edith Wharton Review* (8, i:3–12; 8, ii:3–10, 32). Conforming to the three-part format of the Twayne "Studies in Short Fiction" series, the book also contains selections by Wharton on writing, and previously published essays by R. W. B. Lewis and Sandra M. Gilbert. David Holbrook's *Edith Wharton and the Unsatisfactory Man* (St. Martin's) is a much less satisfactory work that also attempts to show that Wharton's "weak, undependable, duplicitous, cowardly, ineffective" male characters originate in an incestuous relationship with her father, which Holbrook is careful to label speculative. Holbrook's failure to distinguish between biography and fiction, his reductive—and sometimes inaccurate—reading of Wharton's texts, and a number of jarring sexist comments mar an all-too-tenuous study.

Wharton's ghost stories are the subject of two essays in *Haunting the House of Fiction.* In "Edith Wharton's Haunted Fiction: 'The Lady's Maid's Bell' and *The House of Mirth*" (pp. 80–107) Kathy A. Fedorko suggests that Wharton's Gothic stories, which recall Poe's, provided a way for Wharton to "enact the psychic drama of repressed female language and eroticism that was part of her own experience." Jennice G. Thomas describes the process by which the "spinster" reclaims her powers of self-definition in "Spook or Spinster? Edith Wharton's 'Miss Mary Pask'" (pp. 108–16), concluding that the story culminates in "Wharton's exposure of sisterhood's failure to alleviate the sufferings of single women." In a related article, "The Evolution of Theme and Technique in Selected Tales of Edith Wharton" (*JSSE* 16:41–50), Evelyn E. Fracasso juxtaposes the early "The Lamp of Psyche" with the later "The Letters" to illustrate Wharton's thematic and technical development.

A significant contribution to Wharton scholarship, *Edith Wharton's Letters from the Underground* (No. Car.) by Candace Waid offers splendid readings of Wharton's major novels, stories, and poetry in a well-argued discussion of Wharton's lifelong preoccupation with the place of the American woman writer. Identifying with Persephone, the daughter who leaves the sentimental world of the mother for the "underworld" of experience that includes realism, writing, eroticism, and the lives of men, Wharton reveals in her work "a self-conscious attention to writing and the conditions of art and a deeply ambivalent preoccupation with women and the conditions of female identity." Waid's consistently intelligent analysis makes this book a pleasure. Anja Salmi looks at Wharton's texts with another myth in mind: in *Andromeda and Pegasus: Treatment of the Themes of Entrapment and Escape in Edith Wharton's Novels* (Helsinki: Suomalainen Tiedeakatemia) she explores Wharton's use of the Andromeda image and the theme of entrapment and escape in *The House of Mirth, The Custom of the Country,* and *The Gods Arrive.* Not only are Wharton's characters Andromeda figures, chained to fate and society, but Wharton herself identified with the myth and saw in it a reflection of the whole social class to which she belonged.

Lev Raphael announces that the time has come to reassess Wharton's "forgotten" novels and examines Wharton's fiction from the perspective of Silvan Tomkins's affect theory in *Edith Wharton's Prisoners of Shame: A New Perspective on Her Neglected Fiction* (St. Martin's). Raphael traces the impact of shame, "the most frequent and possibly the most important of emotions," on Wharton from childhood rejection by her mother to adult relationships with Walter Berry and Morton Fullerton. Wharton's legendary haughtiness was "really shyness, a manifestation of shame." Raphael examines 14 of Wharton's novels, incorporating previously published studies (see *ALS 1988* pp. 236–37) with new analyses, and concludes with a final chapter on "Wharton's Classics." Perhaps the most appealing part of the book is the appendix, in which Raphael describes his discovery of Wharton's "little house" in the gardens of Pavillon Colombe.

Beth Kowaleski-Wallace's skillful and compelling essay, "The Reader as Misogynist in *The Custom of the Country*" (*MLS* 21, i:45–53), locates the misogyny associated with the novel in the act of reading, "an act which metaphorically positions the reader as child in relationship to Undine's failed maternity." Kowaleski-Wallace demonstrates that Wharton challenges both male and female readers with a "narrative that elicits misogynist response" and locates narrative details responsible for such a response. Edith Wharton's bond with her readers is the subject of Barbara Hochman's "The Rewards of Representation: Edith Wharton, Lily Bart and the Writer/Reader Interchange" (*Novel* 24:147–61). *The House of Mirth* demonstrates Wharton's "sense of the indeterminacy and spontaneous contract implicit in the writer/reader interchange" as well as her willingness to invest in the idea of a responsive and creative audience that would offer her not only professional recognition or pay, but appreciation and respect. Peter Messent uses Barthes's readerly "collusion/collision" as a point of entry for discussion of sexuality, power, economics, and gender roles in "*The Portrait of a Lady* and *The House of Mirth:* A Barthesian Reading" (*New Readings of the American Novel*, pp. 162–203). In " 'A Moment's Ornament': Wharton's Lily Bart and Art Nouveau" (*Mosaic* 24, ii:73–91) Reginald Abbott draws a nice parallel between Art Nouveau, "a spectacularly vibrant but short-lived decorative school," and Lily Bart to elucidate "the specifically modern conflicts of form versus function, of artistic integrity, and of the decorative roles of women in art and society versus a woman's true identity" in *The House of Mirth.*

The Age of Innocence inspired three essays this year—and director Martin Scorsese, whose filmed version of the novel is scheduled for release in 1993. In "Ironic Structure and Untold Stories in *The Age of Innocence*" (*SNNTS* 23:262–72) Kathy Miller Hadley studies the three plans that Wharton outlined for the novel to prove that her decision to focus on Newland Archer was a strategy which, by leaving the stories of Ellen Olenska and May Welland untold, undermined the structure of the novel and allowed her to write beyond a traditional 19th-century ending. May Welland's strong-willed determination is the topic of a second essay. Evelyn E. Fracasso's "The Transparent Eyes of May Welland in *The Age of Innocence*" (*MLS* 21, iv:43–48) offers a close textual analysis of her physical characteristics, with particular emphasis on Wharton's symbolic treatment of her eyes. In *Dwelling in the Text* (pp. 149–80) Marilyn R. Chandler investigates Wharton's ability to teach us "to read architecture and interior decoration . . . as an intricate network of symbolic systems" that reflect and maintain a fixed social order and prescribed patterns of behavior. In *Free Women* (pp. 11–31) Kate Fullbrook examines Wharton's recognition that "the foundations of social corruption of her time were built on the exploitation of women of both the ruling and working classes, and on the deformed relationships which prevailed between individual members of the sexes"; Fullbrook proposes that the central problem in Wharton's fiction is how to transform society so that women can develop moral autonomy.

Two biographical items prove that fancy is not dead. Part of the "Women Writers" series, Katherine Joslin's *Edith Wharton* (St. Martin's) begins with a whimsical account of Wharton's life, examines *The House of Mirth, The Custom of the Country, The Age of Innocence,* and *The Mother's Recompense* against the male pastoral romance and the female domestic novel, and ends with a review of the criticism. William Wiser, who concludes in *The Great Good Place: American Expatriate Women in Paris* (Norton) that "women, more so than male expatriates, came early to Paris and stayed late," offers a novelistic account of Wharton's Paris life. Others he sketches are Mary Cassatt, Caresse Crosby, Zelda Fitzgerald, and Josephine Baker.

Wharton's letters continue to reveal new insights. A special issue of *Women's Studies* (20, ii), guest-edited by Annette Zilversmit, contains 10 essays presented at the 1988 Edith Wharton Society Conference. Two essays, Gloria Erlich's "The Libertine as Liberator: Morton Fullerton and Edith Wharton" (pp. 97–108) and Susan Goodman's "A Safe Forum: Edith Wharton's Correspondence with Sara Norton" (pp. 109–120), use published and unpublished letters to evaluate Wharton's choice of male and female friends. In "Edith Wharton at War with the Red Cross: The End of *Noblesse Oblige*" (pp. 121–32) Alan Price taps the "especially rich source" of Wharton's unpublished letters during World War I to record her struggles as a volunteer, marveling at her energy and the sheer amount of correspondence she produced in the face of physical exhaustion. Essays on the significance of Wharton's letters in individual novels include Julie Olin-Ammenthorp's "Edith Wharton, Margaret Aubyn, and the Woman Novelist" (pp. 133–40), Kathleen Pfeiffer's "*Summer* and Its Critics' Discomfort" (pp. 141–52), Clare Colquitt's "Succumbing to the 'Literary Style': Arrested Desire in *The House of Mirth*" (pp. 153–62), Jean Frantz Blackall's "The Intrusive Voice: Telegrams in *The House of Mirth* and *The Age of Innocence*" (pp. 163–68), and Denise Witzig's "Letter(s) from an Unknown Woman: Edith Wharton's Correspondence" (pp. 169–76). In a thought-provoking and original essay, "Forbidden Reading and Ghostly Writing: Anxious Power in Wharton's 'Pomegranate Seed' " (pp. 177–93), Carol J. Singley and S. E. Sweeney round out the issue with a masterful analysis that incorporates biography, psychoanalytic theory, reader-response criticism, and feminist theory. Related to these is Elizabeth Lennox Keyser's " 'The Ways in Which the Heart Speaks': Letters in *The Reef*" (*SAF* 19:95–106), which points out that access to Wharton's letters gives modern readers a distinct advantage over all but one (Fullerton!) of her contemporaries.

The *Edith Wharton Review* continues to publish first-rate essays, notices, and occasionally a special supplement such as "Edith Wharton in Paris" (8, i:13–31). Included here are Paul Bouget's introduction to *The House of Mirth* (pp. 19–22) and Wharton's memorial essay, "Memories of Bouget from Across the Sea" (pp. 23–31), both translated by Adeline Tintner, who supplies an introductory essay (pp. 16–18). Also noteworthy are Wendy M. Dubow's examination of Lily Bart and Undine Spragg as career women in "The Businesswoman in Edith Wharton" (*EdWR* 8, ii:11–18) and Scott DeShong's Bakhtinian reading of *The Reef*, "Protagonism in *The Reef*: Wharton's Novelistic Discourse" (*EdWR* 8, ii:19–23, 32).

Three of the five essays on Glasgow this year deal with questions of influence. Ritchie D. Watson, Jr., challenges the extent to which Glasgow's friendship with Allen Tate influenced her work in "Ellen Glasgow, The Nashville Agrarians and the Glasgow-Allen Tate Correspondence" (*MissQ* 44:35–46). Watson provides a close reading of the 33 extant letters and concludes that, although they record a "fast-blooming and mutually stimulating literary friendship," they do not demonstrate influence in either direction. On the other hand, Kathryn Lee Seidel argues that, in spite of her protests, Gail Godwin has been heavily influenced by Glasgow in "Gail Godwin and Ellen Glasgow: Southern Mothers and Daughters" (*TSWL* 10:287–94). Consciously writing within a southern tradition, Godwin finds in Glasgow a creative model and a literary mother. "Visions of Female Community in Ellen Glasgow's Ghost Stories," Lynette Carpenter's contribution to *Haunting the House of Fiction* (pp. 117–41), highlights differences between novels and ghost stories written while Glasgow was contemplating marriage to Henry Anderson, whose influence on both *The Builders* and *One Man in His Time* is clear. These novels and stories contain some of Glasgow's most radical critiques of marriage; only the stories "envision the possible substitution of relationships between women for the conventional resolution of happy marriage." Sympathy, compassion, and sensitivity allow Glasgow's female characters to encounter and respond to the supernatural in stories that allow Glasgow herself to explore "the alternatives of conventional heterosexual romance and female community."

In "On Ellen Glasgow's *The Battle-Ground*" (*Classics of Civil War Fiction,* pp. 63–82) R. H. W. Dillard points out the complexities inherent in Glasgow's Civil War novel. A study of the "deadly illusion of power and order," *The Battle-Ground* contains Glasgow's acute analysis of the position of women in a male-dominated culture and, in its specific references to Sir Walter Scott, appropriates and subverts the literary tradition which requires a historical novel to romanticize and idealize the Old Order. Finally, in "Narration as Pragmatism in Ellen Glasgow's *Barren Ground*" (*AL* 63:664–82) Catherine Rainwater analyzes the structural and tropological features of *Barren Ground* to demonstrate Glasgow's transformation of Jamesian pragmatism into a narrative that "insists upon examination of possible truths within multiple perceptual frameworks."

iii Gertrude Stein and Sherwood Anderson

Stein scholarship this year is notable for its extraordinary clarity. Jane Palatini Bowers's important study *"They Watch Me as They Watch This": Gertrude Stein's Metadrama* (Penn.) takes Stein's plays as its topic. Bowers employs both semiotic and structuralist concepts but successfully avoids abstract theoretical discussion as she teaches us how to read all of Stein's work through clear and chronological readings of the plays that trace Stein's process of discovery. Bowers also examines Stein's differing accounts of playwrighting in "Plays" and *The Geographical History of America,* and, in an epilogue, situates Stein in the history of modern drama and evaluates her influence on postmodern playwrights and poets. Using Hannah Arendt's distinction between *polis* and *societas* as a starting point, Clive Bush proposes that the breakdown of history for Adams, psychology for James, and the language of common sense and narrative structure for Stein was related to "the social and political changes of their time." Making use in his ambitious and impressive *Halfway to Revolution: Investigation and Crisis in the Work of Henry Adams, William James, and Gertrude Stein* (Yale) of "everything that comes to hand," Bush offers perceptive and original readings that interweave social, cultural, and literary insight in clear, jargon-free prose to discover "what is of relevance . . . for our time." The section on Stein is excellent, with a discussion of the meaning of history and the nature of the artist's role in society as these concerned Stein and a fine digression on the relation of language to knowledge. Separate chapters on *How to Write* (interwoven with brief commentaries on *In Eighteen in America: A Play, A Long Grey Book,* and *The Geographical History of America*), *Making of Americans,* and *Wars I Have Seen* follow. Bush displays scholarly virtuosity as he argues for a more "historical" Stein, locating her work in a wide range of contexts. Although he rejects interdisciplinarity as "modish academic behaviour directed towards new strictures of methodology," this fine work is an example of interdisciplinary study at its best.

Foremost among the essays on Stein this year is Bruce Goebel's "'If Nobody Had to Die': The Problem of Mortality in Gertrude Stein's *The Geographical History of America*" (*PQ* 70:237–52). In a competent and clear discussion Goebel traces Stein's concern with identity as well as mortality in the major works, demonstrating the shortcomings of each in resolving her fear of death and mortal limitation and her determination to create a work of art that could satisfactorily transcend death. The agonizing process of writing *The Geographical History of America,* which forced Stein to face human nature and death, finally allowed her some compromise; "while she may never have lost her fear of death, she confronted and came to an understanding of that fear."

Diana Souhami reconstructs the story of "one of the most solid marriages of the century" from letters, memoirs, and the published writings of Stein and Alice B. Toklas in *Gertrude and Alice* (Pandora). Informed by a deep sympathy for Toklas, Souhami's book, which contains 43 photographs, offers little literary analysis. Clare Brant in "Gertrude Stein: 'Some Could Be Different Ones' " (*Diverse Voices*, pp. 2–31) suggests that readers have too willingly used Stein's biography to avoid the "uncompromising difference" in her writing, and she investigates the relationship between writer and biography using feminist linguistic theories to better understand this difference. Kate Fullbrook's chapter on Stein in *Free Women* (pp. 57–80) might be the best in that book—clear prose which makes equally clear her contention that Stein's idiosyncratic writing "constitutes an attempt to embody a democratic ethos in a non-realist mode." Fullbrook provides readings of *Three Lives* and *The Making of Americans* to demonstrate "egalitarian generosity" as the primary characteristic of Stein's moral base and of her writing.

There are two articles of note on *Tender Buttons.* Christopher Knight's "Gertrude Stein, *Tender Buttons,* and the Premises of Classicalism" (*MLS* 21, iii:35–47) places the book at the culmination of the 19th-century classical tradition of the "innocent eye," which stresses the "absolute thereness of reality." Margueritte S. Murphy, contending that Stein "exploits the vocabulary, syntax, rhythms, and cadences of conventional women's prose and talk," borrows Bakhtin's methodology to prove her case in " 'Familiar Strangers': The Household Words of Gertrude Stein's *Tender Buttons*" (*ConL* 32:383–402).

Cyrena Pondrom asks why Edith Sitwell would first acknowledge the influence of Gertrude Stein in her own work, then deny such influence in "Influence? Or Intertextuality?: The Complicated Connection of Edith Sitwell with Gertrude Stein" (pp. 204–18 in *Influence and Intertextuality in Literary History,* ed. Jay Clayton and Eric Rothstein [Wisconsin]). Traditional methods to study influence are deficient, concerned with linear, single-source, and unidirectional relationships, and the Sitwell-Stein interaction proves that we must develop a vocabulary to address the "polymorphous 'sources' that overdetermine the characteristics" of a literary work since both influence and intertextuality are concepts "enriched by attention to the implications of the other." Marianne DeKoven pairs Stein with Joseph Conrad in "Darker and Lower Down: The Eruption of Modernism in 'Melanctha' and *The Nigger of the 'Narcissus,'* " pp. 67–84 in *Rich and Strange: Gender, History, Modernism* (Princeton), her study of the connections between literary modernism and political radicalism. "[R]ace, class, and childbirth figure together in the disruption of traditional form," thus allowing Stein to put into the text "material too subversive to be contained by the detached, cool, fatalistic narrative she is writing." Finally, Linda Wagner-Martin reads *The Sun Also Rises* as "a dialogue with Stein" in "Racial and Sexual Coding in Hemingway's *The Sun Also Rises*" (*HN* 10, ii:39–41). Wagner-Martin skillfully demonstrates that the novel's anti-Semitism and homophobia reveal Hemingway's struggle with his mentor, "the seemingly all-powerful, generous, Jewish and homosexual Gertrude Stein."

The most significant contribution to Anderson studies again this year is a volume of letters, *Sherwood Anderson's Secret Love Letters: For Eleanor, a Letter a Day* (LSU), ed. Ray Lewis White. Collected here are more than 330 of the letters that Anderson wrote daily during 1932, then hid away for Eleanor Copenhaver to find after his death. Reading these brief reflections on courtship, love, family, politics, and marriage, I discovered a far more likable Anderson than the man revealed in last year's edition of the love letters that Copenhaver *did* get to read while Anderson was still alive (see *ALS 1990*, p. 255).

In *Freud, Religion, and the Roaring Twenties* Henry Idema III discusses *Winesburg, Ohio, Beyond Desire,* and *Dark Laughter* (pp. 69–134) to argue that widespread neurosis after World War I had significant links to secularization. Anderson's work portrays the effects of repression and emotional maladjustment in a culture undergoing a shift from religious traditions toward affluence and materialism. Herbert N. Schneidau devotes a chapter in his *Waking Giants* (pp. 136–201) to Anderson's influence on Hemingway, Faulkner, Wolfe, and Fitzgerald, who owe their ability to make their work out of their own youthful experiences to *Winesburg, Ohio* and Anderson's other early stories.

Two items concern the narrator of "Death in the Woods." In "Cold Pastoral: Sherwood Anderson's 'Death in the Woods'" (*ON* 15 [1990]:19–28) Jules Zanger draws parallels to Whitman's "Out of the Cradle Endlessly Rocking" and Keats's "Ode on a Grecian Urn"; Anderson's narrator is "the adult artist recalling the childhood experience that culminates in the reminiscence that is the work before the reader." William V. Miller in "Psychological Stasis or Artistic Process: The Narrator Problem in Sherwood Anderson's 'Death in the Woods'" (*ON* 15 [1990]:29–41) considers the narrator to be the "interpretative crux" of the story, and he shows how the genealogy of the story reveals Anderson's "characteristic technique and his characteristic artistic vision." In his excellent essay "Refashioning Coleridge's Supernatural Trilogy: Sherwood Anderson's 'A Man of Ideas' and 'Respectability'" (*SSF* 27:221–35) Martin Bidney analyzes Coleridgean image and motif patterns in Anderson's stories to demonstrate that Anderson is "no mere copyist of Coleridge, but one of the strongest remakers of that poet's rewarding, troubling legacy." Last, A. R. Coulthard's brief "Anderson's 'I Want to Know Why' " (*Expl* 49:169–70) argues that the troubling world into which the young narrator is initiated is that of his own sexuality, pointing out that the story's central union of boy, horse and trainer "constitutes a virtual *ménage à trois*."

iv Theodore Dreiser, H. L. Mencken, and Sinclair Lewis

A banner year for Dreiser scholarship begins with the Dreiser Edition text of Dreiser's *Newspaper Days* (Penn.), ed. T. D. Nostwich. Complementing *Theodore Dreiser: Journalism, Volume One* (see *ALS 1988*, p. 242), Dreiser's uncut account of his career in journalism between 1890 and 1894 is both a vivid narrative of the Gilded Age and a self-portrait in which we can find the seeds of characters like Carrie Meeber, Jennie Gerhardt, and Clyde Griffiths. Dreiser scholars will certainly applaud the publication of the revised and expanded *Theodore Dreiser: A Primary Bibliography and Reference Guide* (Hall), ed. Donald Pizer et al. Reflecting Dreiser scholarship since the 1975 edition, it is 900 entries longer than its predecessor. Clearly organized and easy to read, this is a valuable scholarly resource.

Proposing that "man's inner nature" was one of Dreiser's primary concerns, Donald Pizer in "Dreiser and the Naturalistic Drama of Consciousness" (*JNT* 21:202–11) refutes the common assumption that "both Dreiser and naturalism in general neglect or inadequately depict the drama of consciousness"; he examines major crises in *Sister Carrie*, *Jennie Gerhardt*, and *An American Tragedy* to demonstrate Dreiser's successful rendering of the struggle between conflicting emotions. In a study of Dreiser's lifelong struggle to know "what man is and how man should live," *The Quest for the Reality of Life: Dreiser's Spiritual and Esthetical Pilgrimage* (Peter Lang), Miyoko Takeda charts Dreiser's spiritual development through three novels: *The "Genius," The Bulwark*, and *The Stoic*.

The Financier provoked a flurry of articles. In "*The Financier:* Dreiser's Marriage of Heaven and Hell" (*SAF* 19:55–69) Stephen C. Brennan reads the novel in conjunction with Blake's *Marriage of Heaven and Hell* to explain Frank Cowperwood, whose greatest significance lies in his humanity as "the central figure in an archetypal drama of fall and redemption." Harold James, "The Literary Financier" (*ASch* 60:255–76), locates *The Financier* in a tradition that includes Friedrich Spielhagen's *Sturmflut* and Anthony Trollope's *The Way We Live Now* and deals with "the use of social contacts and snobbery in business, with privileged information, speculation and eventual disgrace." In *By the Law of Nature* (pp. 192–217) Howard Horwitz explores Dreiser's use of the "logic of the trust" in *The Financier* and *The Titan* as a metaphor for the impossibility of grounding moral convention in the universal, then contrasts Frank Cowperwood with Eugene Debs to illustrate the transformation in notions of self and value at the end of the century.

Sister Carrie continues as Dreiser's most frequently examined novel. Two articles relate the novel to cultural change. In "The Electrification of the Body at the Turn of the Century" (*TexP* 5:303–25) Tim Armstrong reviews the 19th century's fascination with the application of electricity to the human body for medical, scientific, and ultimately legal purposes, then skillfully demonstrates that both *Sister Carrie* and *An American Tragedy* "stand at the threshold of that abstract awareness of body as circuitry and system." Guy Szuberla offers an intertextual study of *Sister Carrie,* George Ade's *More Fables in Slang,* and the once standardized codes of etiquette in "Ladies, Gentlemen, Flirts, Mashers, Snoozers, and the Breaking of Etiquette's Code" (*Prospects* 15 [1990]:169–96). Irene Gammel finds similarities between *Sister Carrie* and Frederick Philip Grove's *Fanny Essler* in "The City's Eye of Power: Panopticism and Specular Prostitution in Dreiser's New York and Grove's Berlin" (*CRevAS* 22:211–27). Both Carrie and Fanny, female protagonist-actresses, are identified with the metropolis; both are objects of desire for a male gazer, at the same time representing the incarnation of desire; and both are allowed "to be" as long as they remain within the framework of a masculine structure "as art object rather than subject." G. T. Lenard's intriguing, well-argued essay, "New Lives, New Names: Dreiser's Carrie" (*MMisc* 19:29–39), suggests that the term "Sister" in Dreiser's title becomes a yardstick by which we measure the various changes that Carrie undergoes in the course of her acting career. In "Tom Wolfe's *Bonfire of the Vanities:* A Dreiser Novel for the 1980s" (*JAC* 14, iii:43–51) James F. Smith finds likenesses between Wolfe and Dreiser as well as between their novels. Smith ably demonstrates that *Bonfire* and *Sister Carrie* share "scene-by-scene construction, a keen sense of the vernacular, the careful (and even overwhelming) use of details, and specific (not necessarily objective) points of view." In another comparative study, "Speaking Her

Own Piece: Emma Goldman and the Discursive Strains of Autobiography" (*American Autobiography*, pp. 235–66), Blanche H. Gelfant calls attention to *Sister Carrie* and Goldman's two-volume autobiography *Living My Life* as examples of "a coalescence of the complex designs of two subversive writers seeking to gain acceptance for their unacceptable social views." Labeling their strategy "rhetorical overdetermination," Gelfant explains that Dreiser and Goldman both counted on rhetorical excess "to obscure and yet reveal their ideological alienation from established social norms," and she suggests that unlike Dreiser, Goldman does not end her story "with a vision of life as a tangle." We can expect to see more on Goldman, who is also the subject of a chapter in Suzanne Clark's *Sentimental Modernism* (pp. 42–66), which describes Goldman's construction of a self that was both progressive and passionate as "taking up the position of the woman in modernism, within the spectacle, rather than removing herself to the impersonal distance of the author." *New Essays on* Sister Carrie, ed. Donald Pizer (Cambridge), features Pizer's substantial introduction detailing the novel's biographical and historical background as well as its critical reputation, and contains studies by Thomas Riggio on Dreiser's own family and experience as the source of Carrie's "blues"; Barbara Hochman on Carrie's acting career as a key to her character; Richard Lehan on the relationship of Dreiser's fundamental beliefs to the novel's naturalistic form; and Alan Trachtenberg on Dreiser's presence in the text as the narrative voice.

A special Dreiser issue of *Papers on Language and Literature* (27, ii), guest-edited by James L. W. West III, contains a wealth of material: the seven previously unpublished chapters of Dreiser's unfinished novel *The Rake*, the winning essay in a contest sponsored by Boni and Liveright in 1926, and nine new essays. Phillip Gerber introduces Albert Lévitt, a Washington and Lee law professor, and his prizewinning essay, a riveting analysis of the legal, moral, and social ramifications of the questions posed by *An American Tragedy* that gets to the heart of the book's ambiguity (214–42). In addition to Kathryn M. Plank's introduction to *The Rake* (pp. 140–44) and her essay on historical facts and details in *An American Tragedy* (pp. 268–87), the issue includes Arthur D. Casciato's analysis of Ruth Epperson Kennall's contribution to Dreiser's Soviet diary (pp. 174–90); Robert Coltrane's reevaluation of *Twelve Men* as an insight into Dreiser's personal and professional relationships (pp. 191–206); a handwriting analysis by Rose Gatti based on several specimens in the Dreiser collection (pp. 207–13); and Robert M. Myers's account of how he discovered Dreiser's personal copy of *McTeague* in the open stacks of the University of Miami library (pp. 260–67). In addition, James H. Hutchinson discusses the textual history of *The Financier* (pp. 243–59); Frederic Rusch uses the publisher's dummy of "The Hand of the Potter" to establish Dreiser's revisions (pp. 288–299); and Thomas Riggio reprints Helen Richardson's unaltered diary entries made during Dreiser's last days, including passages written shortly after his funeral that detail his final hours (pp. 300–304). Finally, *Dreiser Studies* continues as a source of news, scholarly comment, bibliographical information, and commentaries on criticism.

The Impossible Mencken: A Selection of His Best Newspaper Stories (Doubleday), ed. Marion Elizabeth Rodgers, is a welcome addition to Mencken scholarship. The volume contains nearly 200 articles taken from the *Baltimore Herald,* the *Baltimore Sunpapers,* the *Chicago Sunday Tribune,* the *New York Evening Mail,* and the *New York American.* Rodgers includes both reports (informational) and columns (opinion), so that, in addition to most of the classic Mencken essays like "Valentino" and "The Sahara of the Bozart," we also find assembled here for the first time Mencken's dispatches from the Republican and National Democratic conventions as well as those from the Scopes Trial, the Disarmament Conference, Pan American Conference, and London Naval Conference. Rodgers provides helpful notes to establish the historical context and identify unfamiliar names, and connecting passages to ensure coherence.

Menckeniana, in which Vincent Fitzpatrick's "Bibliographic Checklist" (118:14–16, 119:16, 120:12–16) records even brief mentions of Mencken, offers a number of substantive essays. Mayo Dubasky analyzes Mencken's prose as blank verse in "H. L. Mencken, Poetry Hater" (117:7–11) and discovers that Mencken not only knew what poetry is, but put that knowledge into practice. In a search for the beginnings of Mencken's singular style, Anthony J. Lomenzo examines his 1896 "Ode to the Pennant on the Centerfield Pole" in "H. L. Mencken: Before the Four Horsemen" (117:11–13). Richard Lingeman's "Mencken, Dreiser and God" (119:1–9), delivered as the annual Mencken Lecture, discusses "one of the most vital and influential friendships in American Letters." Though the first real rupture over religion was never resolved, Dreiser and Mencken managed to remain friends for nearly 40 years.

Two other essays merit mention. George Levinson reminds us that Mencken wrote the first published book on Shaw in "H. L. Mencken on

G. B. Shaw" (*ISh* 29:46–51), and Louis D. Rubin, Jr., muses on the "enormous gap between certain ingrained attitudes to which [Mencken] consciously subscribed throughout his life, and the very different set of premises in which he clearly conducted his life" ("The Mencken Mystery" [*SR* 99:445–63]). Calling *The Diary of H. L. Mencken* "one of the saddest, most melancholy books ever published by an American author," Rubin concludes his excellent analysis of Mencken's enigmatic and contradictory personality by suggesting that the time has come for a "first-rate biography" written by someone with access to all the papers.

Sinclair Lewis received even less attention than Mencken. In *"Babbitt* in Overalls: Sinclair Lewis' Abandoned Labor Novel" (*SDR* 29, iv:5–22) James M. Hutchisson provides new insights into Lewis's inability to write the labor novel he began at least seven times. Hutchisson carefully documents the false starts and precipitous halts in Lewis's twenty-year attempt, and he offers perceptive and plausible explanations for Lewis's failure to turn his voluminous notes into a novel. *Main Street* prompts the two remaining items. R. D. Macdonald uses *Main Street* as "an external vantage point" from which to read Stephen Leacock's *Sunshine Sketches* ("Measuring Leacock's Mariposa against Lewis's Gopher Prairie: A Question of Monuments" [*DR* 71:83–103], and James R. Shortridge lists *Main Street* among novels (including those of Owen Wister and Zane Grey) that encapsulate and crystallize regional values ("The Concept of the Place-Defining Novel in American Popular Culture" [*Professional Geographer* 43:280–91]). I also include here *Dorothy Thompson and Rose Wilder Lane: Forty Years of Friendship: Letters, 1921–1960,* ed. William Holtz (Missouri), of interest to Lewis scholars since the letters reveal the complexities in the Lewis-Thompson marriage as well as Wilder's judicious opinions of that relationship. This volume of previously unpublished correspondence is valuable in its own right as a record of changing social ideas, political and economic philosophies, and friendship. Holtz provides useful annotations and notes for the 51 letters, as well as introductions for each of the six series and bridge passages where explanation is necessary.

v John Dos Passos, Jack London, and Upton Sinclair

John Dos Passos' Correspondence with Arthur K. McComb, or, "Learn to sing the Carmagnole" (Colorado, 1989), superbly edited and "narrated" by Melvin Landsberg, is an important addition to Dos Passos scholarship.

Respecting Dos Passos's wishes that these letters be published "with their original punctuation, including misplaced and garbled or misspelled words," Landsberg has done a masterful job of discovering and transcribing more than 90 letters, cards, telegrams, notes, and fragments from Dos Passos to McComb and selecting 108 excerpts from McComb's letters to serve as a gloss on those of Dos Passos. The book contains 26 photographs and includes notes to complement the biographical narrative sections. Dos Passos also figures prominently in *Letters from the Lost Generation: Gerald and Sara Murphy and Friends* (Rutgers), ed. Linda Patterson Miller. This "sequential interweaving" of letters, most of them unpublished until now, written by the Murphys and their literary friends (John and Katy Dos Passos, F. Scott and Zelda Fitzgerald, Ernest and Pauline Hemingway, Archibald MacLeish, Dorothy Parker, Alexander Woolcott), is a fascinating account of the '20s and '30s, the "best sort of eavesdropping" on a wonderful array of writers, and a thoroughly scholarly work. Adding to the pleasure of the letters are Miller's fine introductions and 25 photographs. Donald Pizer looks at some of these same writers in "The Sexual Geography of Expatriate Paris" (*TCL* 36 [1990]:173–85) and discusses the "union of creativity and sexuality in a distinctive Paris locale" in works by Hemingway, Stein, Fitzgerald, Henry Miller, Anaïs Nin, and Dos Passos.

The sole critical essay on Dos Passos to appear this year is Arnold L. Goldsmith's competent discussion of *Manhattan Transfer* in *The Modern American Urban Novel* (pp. 17–38). Goldsmith convincingly argues that Dos Passos's impressionistic technique of rapidly changing vignettes involving many characters captures the "restiveness and despair of a whole generation." The numerous scenes, images, and symbols drawn from nature, which both contrast with and complement the thousands of urban images in the novel, reinforce Dos Passos's love-hate relationship with the city and the ambivalence that became the hallmark of the 20th-century novel. George Garrett in "On Mary Johnston's *The Long Roll*" (*Classics of Civil War Fiction*, pp. 83–95) suggests that Dos Passos (as well as Norman Mailer, Truman Capote, E. L. Doctorow, and Horton Foote) can thank Mary Johnston for inventing the novel that combines fact and fiction. Scholars should also be aware that *Brazil on the Move*, Dos Passos's firsthand account of the political, social, and economic upheaval in Brazil in the 1930s is now out as part of the Armchair Traveller Series (Paragon).

Fascinating for their lack of agreement, four articles and a book keep

London's reputation alive until the completion of the three-volume edition of his short stories due out next year. Joan London's *Jack London and His Daughters* (Heyday, 1990) is, as her son suggests in his preface, "a search for personal answers far more than a daughter's public recollections of a famous father." Dealing with the conflicting loyalties within the London family, the book, which includes 11 pages of family photographs, remains uncompleted—the last section is a synopsis. Margaret Guilford-Kardell has compiled and edited sculptor Finn Haakon Frolich's fond account of his friendship with London, beginning in 1912 and lasting until London's death, in "Sea Dog and Sea Wolf at Play in the Valley of the Moon" (*The Californians* 8:14–23). The tone is conversational, the memories anecdotal, and we are treated to eight more photographs. William E. Cain presents a far different London in "Socialism, Power, and the Fate of Style: Jack London in His Letters" (*AmLH* 3:603–13). Admitting to "baffled disgust," Cain charges that London's letters damage his public image as a staunch socialist, demonstrating beyond question his inherent racism, cruelty, and consuming "chase for wealth." In "The Composition of Jack London's Writings" (*ALR* 23, ii:64–86) James Williams uses the Smoke Bellow stories to contradict the assessment that London always wrote solely for money. Intended to provoke discussion about the whole of the canon, this formidable essay lists in chronological order 406 of London's published and unpublished works, then analyzes the sequence of his writings (novels, stories, essays) as he wrote them rather than as they were published, to demonstrate his diversity, his fascination with form, and his productivity. Williams proposes that further research is needed to discover the "binding threads" in London's work. Peter De Ville quotes passages from *The Rainbow* and *White Fang* to demonstrate "a more than casual similarity of imagery and wording" in "In or Out of the Camp Fire: Lawrence and Jack London's Dogs" (*N&Q* 38:339–41).

Interest in Upton Sinclair dwindles; what little there is concerns *The Jungle.* Hugh J. Dawson has unearthed Winston Churchill's unsolicited 1906 review of *The Jungle* and dissects it in "Winston Churchill and Upton Sinclair: An Early Review of *The Jungle*" (*ALR* 24, i:72–78). Louise Carroll Wade looks first at Sinclair's motives for writing *The Jungle,* then compares what he says about the packers, packinghouse products, and immigrant workers and their community with the historical evidence in "The Problem with Classroom Use of Upton Sinclair's *The Jungle*" (*AmerS* 32, ii:79–102). The "problem" is that, far from being the accurate reference work Sinclair claimed it to be, the book is misleading on nearly every count.

vi W. E. B. Du Bois, Nella Larsen, Jean Toomer, and Others

The contradictions in W. E. B. Du Bois's life and writing intrigued several critics. In "The Political Use of Alienation: W. E. B. Du Bois on Politics, Race, and Culture, 1903–1940" (*AQ* 42 [1990]:301–23) Thomas C. Holt argues that to understand Du Bois and his changing approaches to the same themes, we must read his texts against the "gritty backdrop of the organizations that simultaneously engaged him," since his own life was the point of departure for each of his major explorations of race, culture, and politics. Robert Michael Franklin in his *Liberating Visions* (pp. 43–74) ranks Du Bois with Booker T. Washington, Malcolm X, and Martin Luther King, Jr., as men who have developed "distinctive and significant traditions of moral thinking and social criticism." The dualities in Du Bois are seen in his "twoness description," a perceptive diagnosis of the "psychosocial dilemma of black Americans seeking to merge two selves into a truer self," and his idea of the authentically free individual, who combines two prominent features of traditional African-American life: toil and celebration.

With the publication of *Politics in the African-American Novel* Richard Kostelanetz's 20-year-old manuscript finally makes it into print and proves to be as timely in 1991 as it was prescient in the late 1960s. Kostelanetz traces Du Bois's political attitudes over a span of 50 years, demonstrating that in *The Quest of the Silver Fleece* he rejected the possibility of individual African-American independence within the South, in *Dark Princess* he rejected the North as well as the South, and in the *Black Flame* trilogy he advocated expatriation to Africa and alliance with international communism (pp. 27–68). Nellie McKay suggests that Du Bois understood the politics of gender far better than he is usually given credit for in "The Souls of Black Women in the Writings of W. E. B. Du Bois" (*Reading Black, Reading Feminist,* pp. 225–43).

The Autobiography of an Ex-Colored Man and the moral, political, and emotional ambiguities of passing are the focus of Kostelanetz's chapter on James Weldon Johnson (pp. 19–25). Johnson was steeped in the folk blues tradition, and Kostelanetz points out as the book's version of the blues the special disenchantment of being white but black. In the political sense, passing means rejecting one's African-American heritage for the meager satisfaction of material comfort. *Along This Way: The Autobiography of James Weldon Johnson* (Penguin), with an introduction by editor Sondra Kathryn Wilson, chronicles Johnson's careers as songwriter, diplomat, activist, and professor.

In "Birthrights: Passing, History, and African Properties," pp. 90–142 in her solid study, *Claiming the Heritage,* Missy Dehn Kubitschek argues that by constructing passing as a set of attitudes toward the middle class and the past we can discover a continuity between the woman-authored novels of the Harlem Renaissance and a number of works by African-American women in the 1980s. Connecting passing and the tragic mulatta theme, Kubitschek shows that Nella Larsen's *Quicksand* demonstrates the conditions that make passing an either/or choice of heritage; her novel *Passing* shows the consequences of the decision to live ahistorically, "to truncate all relationships with one's heritage"; and Jessie Redmon Fauset's *Plum Bun* retells the sentimental romance plot in terms of the trope of passing. *Plum Bun: A Novel without a Moral* (Beacon) was also reissued this year with a fine introduction by Deborah E. McDowell.

In "Self-Representation as Art in the Novels of Nella Larsen," her substantial contribution to *Redefining Autobiography* (pp. 149–68), Jacquelyn Y. McLendon asserts that, yes, *Quicksand* is autobiographical and that its importance lies in Larsen's revision of narrative strategies that are white and male to express and achieve her own voice. Mark J. Madigan explains the legal, economic, social, and racial entanglements of the marriage between Leonard Kip Rhinelander, heir to the family fortune, and Alice B. Jones, a mulatta chambermaid, to explicate the reference in *Passing* and to demonstrate how complex the issue of passing was during the Harlem Renaissance ("Miscegenation and 'The Dicta of Race and Class': The Rhinelander Case and Nella Larsen's *Passing*" [*MFS* 36 [1990]:523–29]).

Cullen's prose attracted no attention this year, so the publication of *My Soul's High Song: The Collected Writings of Countee Cullen* (Doubleday), ed. Gerald Early, is very good news. In addition to the poetry, the book includes Cullen's prose translation of *Medea,* the entire text of his novel *One Way to Heaven,* several essays, travel pieces, and speeches, and James Baldwin's 1942 interview with Cullen. Early's brilliantly conceived introduction (pp. 3–73) should be required reading for anyone interested in American letters.

Rudolph P. Byrd's *Jean Toomer's Years with Gurdjieff: Portrait of an Artist, 1923–1936* (Georgia, 1990) seeks to expand the range of Toomer scholarship. In this first full-scale examination of the influence of the Russian philosopher and psychologist George Ivan Gurdjieff on Toomer, Byrd discredits the critical assumption that Toomer's work after 1923 represents a total break from the issues and material he used so powerfully in *Cane.* Arguing that there is a distinct thematic unity in the Toomer canon, Byrd begins with *Cane,* examines the unpublished novels "The Gallonwerps" and "Transatlantic," then devotes chapters to drama (*The Sacred Factory: A Religious Drama*) and to verse ("The Blue Meridian") to demonstrate the continuing presence of "a consistent, optimistic faith in human possibility and wholeness." This clearly written study should provoke further evaluations of Toomer's work. So too should Byrd's new edition of Toomer's *Essentials* (Georgia), "one of the most compelling, unified, and original works" of the Gurdijieff period, a collection of "aphorisms and definitions" that puts Toomer in the tradition of American aphoristic writing of Franklin, Emerson, and Thoreau.

Vera M. Kutzinski considers *Cane* and "La flor de la caña" as *"exceptions* within their respective literary and historical settings" in "Unseasonal Flowers: Nature and History in Plácido and Jean Toomer" (*YJC* 3 [1990]:153–79). Both Toomer and Gabriel de la Concepción Valdes (Plácido) "deromanticize and demythify Afro-American (and American) cultures" in texts which comment on the sentimental commodification of "blackness" in the Cuban "período negro" and the Harlem Renaissance. In "Jean Toomer and the 'New Negroes' of Washington" (*AL* 63:682–92) George B. Hutchison corrects the record of Toomer's association with authors in the New Negro Movement before and during the composition of *Cane.*

William Pickens's *Bursting Bonds, Enlarged Edition, The Heir of Slaves: The Autobiography of a "New Negro"* (Indiana), ed. William L. Andrews, is a firsthand account of the New Negro and the Harlem Renaissance from one of the founders of the NAACP. Two related essays deal with the vision behind the New Negro Movement and provoke reflection on the current debate on multiculturalism. In "Cosmopolitanism, Ethnicity and American Identity: Randolph Bourne's 'Trans-National America'" (*JAmS* 25:443–59) Leslie J. Vaughan presents Bourne's concept of "transnationalism" against the discourse of American nationalism by skillfully examining four converging histories: Bourne's personal autobiography, a social history of immigration against a rising tide of nativism, a political history of military preparedness, and a cultural history of modern cosmopolitanism. Everett H. Akam offers a reappraisal of Alain Locke's concept of cosmopolitanism in "Community and Cultural Crisis: The 'Transfiguring Imagination' of Alain Locke" (*AmLH* 3:255–76). Locke recognized that "racism is one manifestation of a fundamental crisis of values," and he saw cosmopolitanism as a moral discourse that should include demands for racial, economic, and political democracy by challenging, rather than affirming, the tradition of liberalism.

vii Western Writers

Peter Wild rescues naturalist John Van Dyke from obscurity this year. "The Handmaiden of Science in the Romance of John C. Van Dyke's *The Desert*" (*NDQ* 59:80–91) examines Van Dyke's seminal use of science to "serve an artistry of heady visual excitements," and " 'My Dear Van Dyke': 'My Dear Brownell': New Perspectives on Our Foremost (and Most Coy) Desert Writer" (*NMHR* 35:131–48) looks at Van Dyke's correspondence with his publisher, William C. Brownell, to provide a fuller sense of his character and a deeper understanding of his aesthetic stance. In "The Preface as Illumination: The Curious (If Not Tricky) Case of John C. Van Dyke's *The Desert*" (*Rhetoric Review* 9:328–39) Wild also collaborates with Zita Ingham on a close reading of Van Dyke's "well-wrought" preface to *The Desert,* carefully constructed to prepare readers both intellectually and emotionally for his text.

J. Bakker's *The Role of the Mythic West* is an ambitious reexamination of the impact of the frontier American West on novelists ranging from James Fenimore Cooper to Larry McMurtry. His chapter on "The Literary Western" (pp. 157–97) confirms that the conception of the romantic West as a place of high hopes and epic achievements stems in large part from Owen Wister's *Virginian;* another (pp. 199–218) establishes Zane Grey's *Riders of the Purple Sage* as the prototype of the popular Western, characterized by violence, revenge, and the thirst for power. Angela Aleiss reminds us that Zane Grey's fiction often depicted Native Americans as victims of white greed in her comparison of his 1922 story and the movie made from it in "*The Vanishing American:* Hollywood's Compromise to Indian Reform" (*JAmS* 25:467–72).

Biographies highlight this year's scholarship on Western women. Emily Wortis Leider's *California's Daughter: Gertrude Atherton and Her Times* (Stanford) is a meticulously researched and well-written study that traces Atherton's turbulent career not only as a prolific and best-selling novelist, but as an outspoken participant in the debate on gender and society. Although Leider argues that Atherton's importance lies not in her literary achievements but in her accuracy as a social historian, this book makes it clear that it is time for a scholarly rereading of the novels. Leider includes a "Bibliographic Note" to facilitate further study and 40 illustrations, many never before reproduced. Amy Ling's chapter on Sui Sin Far and Onoto Watanna, "Pioneers and Paradigms: The Eaton Sisters," pp. 21–55 in her ground-breaking study *Between Worlds,* is a superb introduction to the lives of the first two Asian-American fiction writers, Edith (Sui Sin Far) and Winnifred (Onoto Watanna), and a brilliant critical survey of their work. Most interesting is her speculation on the reasons one sister so totally embraced her Chinese heritage while the other assumed a Japanese identity. *Wind's Trail: The Early Life of Mary Austin* (Santa Fe: Museum of New Mexico, 1990), ed. Shelley Armitage, contains Peggy Pond Church's study of Austin's early life; Austin's own essay, "The Friend in the Wood"; and Armitage's capable introduction and her essay, "Mary Austin: Writing Nature." For comparison, we can read *Earth Horizon* (New Mexico), afterword by Melody Graulich, Austin's 1932 autobiography.

Not since Harold P. Simonson's *Prairies Within: The Tragic Trilogy of Ole Rölvaag* (see *ALS 1987,* p. 250), which expanded on Neil T. Eckstein's notion of "marginality," has a book appeared on Rölvaag. Unfortunately, Eckstein has not included the insights from that book or from any other published in the 25 years since he completed his dissertation, which is now issued as *The Marginal Man as Novelist: The Norwegian-American Writers H. H. Boyesen and O. E. Rölvaag as Critics of American Institutions* (Garland, 1990) and updated only by a foreword which acknowledges that newer scholarship exists. The book's discussion of Rölvaag's social, economic, and political criticism is competent, whatever its other limitations.

viii General Studies and Additional Authors

The ever-expanding canon is reflected in the thematic organization of most general studies. Most exciting this year is Elizabeth Ammons's *Conflicting Stories.* Ammons creates unlikely pairs of writers (Stein/Austin, Cather/Mourning Dove, Wharton/Fauset, among others) then provides lucid and illuminating readings of their juxtaposed works to prove her thesis that "long fiction by women in the United States from the early 1890s through the late 1920s forms a diverse yet unified body of work." The *Columbia History of the American Novel* fulfills its promise of providing "fresh insights into the texts and into the history of which the novels were and remain a part." Nine of its superb thematic chapters include discussions of the authors in this chapter. Narrower in scope, *1915, The Cultural Moment: The New Politics, the New Woman, the New Psychology, the New Art & the New Theater in America* (Rutgers), ed. Adele Heller and Lois Rudnick, collects 18 essays on the forces that created Modernism in American arts and society. In *From Harlem to Paris* Michel Fabre traces the authenticity and the ambiguities in the "love story between black American writers and artists and France," with good chapters on Du Bois, Johnson, Locke, Cullen, McKay, and Fauset. Colleen McDannell's pioneering study, "Catholic Women Fiction Writers, 1840–1920" (*WS* 19:385–405), surveys the fiction of 38 laywomen to clarify their role in the invention of female Catholic culture. *Short Fiction by Black Women, 1900–1920* (Oxford), collected and introduced by Elizabeth Ammons, contains a wealth of fiction culled from the *Colored American Magazine* and the *Crisis.*

Some lesser-known writers got a lion's share of scholarship this year. The mysterious B. Traven is the subject of a biography and, in a literary hat trick, three critical essays by Kenneth Payne. Traven enthusiasts will welcome Karl S. Guthke's painstakingly researched and clearly written *B. Traven: The Life Behind the Legends* (Lawrence Hill), the first biography to be based on complete access to the Traven archives. Guthke identifies Traven as Bavarian revolutionary Ret Marut, then interweaves a very convincing reconstruction of Traven's life with a critical analysis of his contribution to 20th-century literature. The book contains 49 photographs, excellent notes, and a bibliography. Payne examines Traven's study of the psychology of religious dependency in "Superstition and the Miraculous in B. Traven's Short Story of Mexico, 'When the Priest Is Not at Home' " (*NMHR* 34:50–59); identifies "The Night Visitor" as "a short but significant watershed in Traven's thematic course" that demonstrates his shift away from a technological society toward the traditional values of the Mexican Indians in " 'The Night Visitor': B. Traven's Tale of the Mexican Bush Reconsidered" (*$CRev* 8, i:46–58); and locates an implicit antifascist subtext in *"The Rebellion of the Hanged:* B. Traven's Anti-Fascist Novel of the Mexican Revolution" (*IFR* 18:96–107).

Two book-length studies commemorate the 1990 centennial of H. P.

Lovecraft's birth. In *Lovecraft: Disturbing the Universe* (Kentucky, 1990) Donald R. Burleson submits 13 stories and Lovecraft's novella, "The Shadow over Innsmouth," to deconstructive readings. *An Epicure in the Terrible: A Centennial Anthology of Essays in Honor of H. P. Lovecraft* (Fairleigh Dickinson), ed. David E. Schultz and S. T. Joshi, contains three biographical essays, five on style, imagery, and narrative method, four comparative and genre studies, an overview of Lovecraft's dominant themes, and an extensive annotated bibliography. *Lovecraft Studies*, the primary outlet for Lovecraft scholarship, appears twice a year.

Of interest are two unrelated items. Edgar Rice Burroughs's use of the primitive as a source of empowerment is the focus of "Taking Tarzan Seriously," pp. 42–71 in Marianna Torgovnick's *Gone Primitive: Savage Intellects, Modern Lives* (Chicago, 1990). The solitary work on John P. Marquand, Richard Wires's *John P. Marquand and Mr. Moto: Spy Adventures and Detective Films* (Ball State, 1990), studies Marquand's contribution to the contemporary spy story and the alteration of that work to accommodate Hollywood.

Among the women who inspired the year's essays was Dorothy Canfield Fisher. In a fine article, "Crisis, Conflict, and Constituting the Self: A Lacanian Reading of *The Deepening Stream*" (*CLQ* 27:148–82), Joan G. Schroeter proposes that Fisher's novel is "an exposition of modern Freudian theory as to how the individual evolves psychologically throughout life," then clearly and logically explains each point in her argument. This should go a long way toward alleviating what Schroeter perceives as undervaluation of Fisher. Alice Dunbar-Nelson's narrative strategy and use of the romance is Alisa Johnson's topic in "Writing within the Script: Alice Dunbar-Nelson's 'Ellen Fenton' " (*SAF* 19:165–74). Thomas J. Ferraro suggests that Yezierska's novels should be understood as "an inquiry into the contribution of ethnicity to the triumph of the middle class" in " 'Working Ourselves Up' in America: Anzia Yezierska's *Bread Givers*" (*SAQ* 89 [1990]:547–81). Also, *Anzia Yezierska: A Writer's Life* (Rutgers), by the novelist's daughter Louise Levitas Henriksen, is out in paperback. Finally, three essays in *Tradition and the Talents of Women* are pertinent here. In "A Feminist American Success Myth: Jane Addams's *Twenty Years at Hull-House* (pp. 143–67) Lois Rudnick explains that Addams rejects the male-identified "myth of self generation as the essential myth of the American Dream" in favor of "a competing feminist vision" that celebrates community. Nancy Hoffman's "A Journey into Knowing: Agnes Smedley's *Daughter of the Earth*" (pp. 170–82) elucidates Smedley's "novel of education," which forces us to redefine our notions of realism and anticipates questions raised in the new "anthropological, psychological, and economic scholarship about women." And Blanche Gelfant adroitly traces the movement of "the Girl" from silence to speech, from dispossession to empowerment, in " 'Everybody Steals': Language as Theft in Meridel Le Sueur's *The Girl*" (pp. 183–210).

Drew University

14 Fiction: The 1930s to the 1960s

Charlotte Hadella

Publication of several noteworthy books which deal with a number of writers of this period prompts the addition of a General section to this year's essay. As Steinbeck scholarship continues to thrive, rising critical interest in Baldwin and Wright also accounts for the growth in the Proletarian section. Southerners are getting more attention than ever, with some of the best work being done on Zora Neale Hurston. Bellow is the star of the Easterners section this year; and though commentary on Western writers seems to be dwindling, D'Arcy McNickle was the subject of one good essay.

i General

American Writing Today, ed. Richard Kostelanetz, with an introduction by Kostelanetz and a bibliography compiled by Kostelanetz and Jerome Klinkowitz, features 46 essays and conversations by an impressive group of critics and writers. In this ambitious anthology, Kostelanetz has collected Voice of America broadcast transcripts from the 1980s, restoring the essays that were cut by USIA in an earlier two-volume edition available only abroad. Discussed in *American Writing Today* are a number of fiction writers who were publishing in the 1930s–1960s: Edmund Wilson, Gertrude Stein, Vladimir Nabokov, Henry Miller, Bernard Malamud, James Baldwin, Ralph Ellison, Saul Bellow, Jack Kerouac, and others.

In a narrower study, *The Modern American Urban Novel*, Arnold L. Goldsmith analyzes nature in scenes, imagery, and symbolism of seven modern novels: *Manhattan Transfer, Studs Lonigan, Call It Sleep, The Dollmaker, The Assistant, The Pawnbroker*, and *Mr. Sammler's Planet*. Proposing that in these works nature "is neither principal character nor mere backdrop, but an integral part of the setting, language, symbolism, and even characterization," Goldsmith focuses on (1) scenes set in parks and other pastoral islands of cities; (2) the wordscape of nature metaphor, simile, and analogy; (3) cityscape influenced by the natural elements of sunlight, moonlight, stars, clouds, and snow. Goldsmith's investigation of the rejection of the Arcadian myth by Dos Passos, Farrell, Roth, Arnow, Malamud, Wallant, and Bellow leads to insightful analyses of their fiction.

In *Sentimental Modernism* Suzanne Clark takes issue with the critical notion that sentimentalism is a feminized, debilitating element in American culture (as argued by Ann Douglas in *The Feminization of American Culture*). Confronting in this challenging work the modernists' aesthetic dismissal of the sentimental, Clark contends that "modernism developed its antisentimentality into a contemptuous treatment of women." Clark announces her intention to "problematize the sentimental, to open it up and to recall the variety of traditions, images, tropes, conventions, and ideological implications that modernism reduced to the single, gendered, and awful other, defining literature by its absence." In this light, she considers works by Emma Goldman, Edna St. Vincent Millay, Louise Bogan, Kay Boyle, Annie Dillard, and Alice Walker.

Joseph R. Urgo looks closely at representations of self in American postmodern fiction as a microcosmic mirror of the American self. In *Novel Frames* he contends that novels "provide the context for analyzing aspects of the culture which are not written about specifically in the literary texts themselves." Choosing novelists who represent a cross section of the American literary canon—Ralph Ellison, William Faulkner, and Willa Cather—Urgo juxtaposes works of fiction against pieces of journalistic writing: Ellison's *Invisible Man* is paired with a reading of Jesse Jackson's 1988 presidential campaign; Faulkner's *Sanctuary* is coupled with the October 1988 issue of *Glamour* magazine; and Cather's *A Lost Lady* is viewed in light of the spring 1988 edition of the Yippie publication *Overthrow.*

ii Proletarians

a. John Dos Passos and John Steinbeck Dos Passos scholars will welcome Melvin Landsberg's volume, *John Dos Passos' Correspondence with Arthur K. McComb, or, "Learn to sing the Carmagnole"* (Colorado, 1989).

As Landsberg points out in his introduction, both Dos Passos and McComb, before attending Harvard, had spent many of their early years in prewar Europe and were thus shocked by what they perceived as the decline in European civilization that followed World War I; consequently, "their different interpretations of and reactions to [this decline] are implicit in their letters." The letters span five decades (1916–1967) and include discussions of issues beyond World War I—the Spanish Civil War, and World War II, for instance. Importantly, Landsberg explains that even though Dos Passos's letters are charged with political rhetoric, he refused to let political differences undermine his friendship with McComb. Landsberg's narratives serve as inner chapters, contextualizing the correspondence biographically and historically.

Rediscovering Steinbeck: Revisionist Views of His Art, Politics and Intellect, ed. Cliff Lewis and Carroll Britch (Mellen, 1989), offers a broad range of critical approaches by a number of seasoned Steinbeck scholars. Britch in "Steinbeck's 'Breakfast': Godhead and Reflection" (pp. 7–32) argues that Steinbeck's narrator consciously reflects the unconscious protean godlikeness of the old man in the story. Britch identifies the "feeling" narrator and the "sensate" elder with Jung's description of the aesthetic and primitive states of the human psyche. Two sparkling essays on *East of Eden* extend our understanding both of the novel and of Steinbeck's inventive strategies. Robert DeMott's "Creative Reading/ Creative Writing: The Presence of Dr. Gunn's *New Family Physician* in Steinbeck's *East of Eden*" (pp. 35–57) points to Gunn's book as the source for specific contemporary medical information and details which amplified characterization and dramatic episodes in the novel. By analyzing references to Gunn in *Journal of a Novel* and noting Steinbeck's manipulation of the material through various stages of revision, DeMott proves that "Steinbeck created a symbolic context for Gunn's book rather than a merely referential one," a context which constituted an important connection between Steinbeck's family history and major themes of the novel. In "The Story of a Writing: Narrative Structure in *East of Eden*" (pp. 60–76) Louis Owens's close reading of the opening pages of *East of Eden* lays the foundation for his argument that "what Steinbeck may be beckoning us to in this great, rather unwieldy novel is the study of the creative process itself, with the focus being the mind of John Steinbeck." Owens's treatment of this problematic novel clarifies Steinbeck's motives for including the Hamilton family story and makes sense of Steinbeck's authorial intrusions. Marcia Yarmus in "The Picaresque Novel and John

Steinbeck" (pp. 79–103) documents Steinbeck's familiarity with two Spanish picaresque novels, Ibañez's *La Barraca* and Cervantes's *Don Quixote,* outlining the picaresque influences on *Tortilla Flat, Cannery Row,* and *Sweet Thursday.* By highlighting elements of the picaresque (social criticism, episodic structure, and championing of an antihero), Yarmus strongly supports the argument for Steinbeck's adaptation or "recreation of the picaresque tradition to suit his own purposes. John Ditsky offers yet another angle on literary influences on Steinbeck in "Steinbeck, Bourne, and Human Herd: A New/Old Gloss on *The Moon Is Down*" (pp. 177–91). Ditsky distinguishes between Randolph Bourne's notion of free men and herd men in time of war (which Steinbeck may have gotten directly from reading Bourne) to show how *The Moon Is Down* marks a significant turn in Steinbeck's abandonment of "scientific" thinking. Ditsky also asserts that Steinbeck's moralistic distinctions in the play marked a move away from the influences of Ed Ricketts toward an autonomous philosophical identity.

Two essays in *Rediscovering Steinbeck,* "Steinbeck's Uncollected Stories" (pp. 106–24) by Robert S. Hughes, Jr., and "The Journalist as Serious Writer: Steinbeck in the 1950s" by Judith Malcahy (pp. 241–59), contribute to our understanding of Steinbeck's multidimensional craft. Hughes evaluates the settings and themes in nine stories published during the 1940s and 1950s to show how they differ from the earlier stories collected in *The Long Valley.* Generally, the pieces discussed focus on domestic scenes with characters modeled after Steinbeck's own family members; in some, Steinbeck experiments with themes of divorce, nuclear holocaust, and childhood discovery of sexuality. Malcahy also focuses on Steinbeck's work in the '50s and takes issue with critics who have dismissed this era of Steinbeck's journalism as trivial. Two essays by Cliff Lewis take note of Steinbeck's political interests: "Steinbeck: The Artist As FDR Speechwriter" (pp. 194–217) and "A Peculiar Air" (pp. 218–37). The first establishes Steinbeck's "political acumen and political vision" by illustrating that specific elements in Roosevelt's social platform, such as jobs for veterans and a global economy, apparently came directly from Steinbeck's platform proposals. In the second, Lewis proposes that the diatribe against communism in the movie *Viva Zapata!* resulted from the political voices of director Elia Kazan and producer Darryl Zanuck rather than from the artistic voice of Steinbeck.

Britch and Lewis, in addition to editing this collection, also collaborate in "Shadow of *The* Indian on the Fiction of John Steinbeck" (pp. 127–54), claiming that Steinbeck never intended to treat Indians sociologically. Though they offer a number of examples (Kino, Pepe, Zapata, Juan Chico, Tularecito, and others) by way of proposing that "Steinbeck characterizes his Indian figures as members of a particular race, who act as they do because of some subconscious predisposition," the message remains vague throughout. In another collaborative effort, "*The Wayward Bus:* Steinbeck's Misogynistic Manifesto" (pp. 157–73), Bobbie Gonzales and Mimi Gladstein claim that in *The Wayward Bus* "Steinbeck's characterization of Everywoman, particularly Everywife, is done with a pen dipped in venom." Drawing on references to Gwyn Conger made by Steinbeck in letters after the bitter divorce, Gonzales and Gladstein illustrate parallels between Gwyn's behavior, Alice Chicoy's "illness," and Bernice Pritchard's headaches—behavior aimed at manipulating men and repressing sexual urges. Thom Tammaro in "Lost in America: Steinbeck's *Travels With Charley* and William Least Heat Moon's *Blue Highways* (pp. 260–77) discusses Moon's book as an artistic success to show how Steinbeck's book "fell short of its intention" artistically. As much an analysis of the American reader as a critique of the literature, Tammaro's essay is an interesting conclusion to this useful anthology.

Donald V. Coers's *John Steinbeck as Propagandist:* The Moon Is Down *Goes to War* (Alabama) presents a detailed report of how a skilled artist/propagandist's work captivated the imagination of oppressed peoples. For example, Coers draws on personal interviews and letters from those involved in the Swedish publication of a Norwegian-language edition of *The Moon Is Down* and the illegal shipments of the book into Norway. Through an interview with Jorgen Jacobson, the Danish translator for Steinbeck's war literature, Coers uncovers the book's significance as a spiritual contribution to anti-Nazi resistance groups. A responsible piece of New Historical criticism, *John Steinbeck as Propagandist* is a well-written, carefully researched account of what happened to *The Moon Is Down* in countries under German control.

The dozen essays edited by Tetsumaro Hayashi and introduced by Warren French in *Steinbeck's Short Stories in* The Long Valley: *Essays in Criticism* (Steinbeck Society) closely scrutinize the writer's best-known short fiction. In "'The Chrysanthemums': Steinbeck's Pygmalion" (pp. 1–9) Susan Shillinglaw compares Steinbeck's Elisa Allen to the women in both Ovid's and Shaw's versions of the Pygmalion legend. Most notably this comparison sheds light on Elisa's attraction to the tinker and her questions about the fights. Shillinglaw concludes that Steinbeck's treatment of the myth is bleaker than either Ovid's or Shaw's because Elisa is categorically denied the power of maleness which so fascinates her. Michael J. Meyer in "Pure and Corrupt: Agency and Communion in the Edenic Garden of 'The White Quail'" (pp. 10–17) makes use of David Bakan's terms "communion" (living for others) and "agency" (living for oneself) from *The Duality of Human Existence* to argue for Steinbeck's valley as a symbol "signifying humanity's constant struggle to cope with polar opposites and to create a balance or understanding of the duality of human existence." Meyer calls on Hawthorne's "Rappaccini's Daughter" as well to show that Mary Teller in "The White Quail" sets up absolute laws against freedom which might alter controlled perfection. Meyer also contributed essays on two other stories, "Breakfast" and "The Raid." In "'Symbols for Wordlessness': Steinbeck's Silent Message in 'Breakfast'" (pp. 32–35) he argues for the acceptance of paradoxical opposites throughout the vignette to highlight the moral ambiguity at the center of the piece—an ambiguity which requires symbolic representation because words provide inadequate expression. In "The Illusion of Eden" (pp. 38–44) Meyer continues his discussion of moral ambiguity in *The Long Valley* by focusing on Steinbeck's intention in "The Raid" to examine "the major dilemma in man in a postlapsarian world: how to cope with moral ambiguity." Meyer believes that Steinbeck uses this story to illustrate humankind's predilection for discovering absolutes and to argue that such absolutes do not exist. Robert M. Benton's "A Search for Meaning in 'Flight'" (pp. 18–25) and "'The Snake' and Its Anomalous Nature" (pp. 26–31) contribute to the usefulness of this monograph. In a brief discussion of Steinbeck's most acclaimed story, "Flight," Benton shows clearly that "too many problems become apparent if one assumes that Pepe achieves manhood when he kills." In his analysis of "The Snake" Benton argues that the story should not be dismissed as merely a practice story for a "Doc" character, but more reasonably considered as Steinbeck's interpretation of an event that actually occurred in Ed Ricketts's lab.

Steinbeck's Short Stories in The Long Valley also contains two essays by Louis Owens, author of *John Steinbeck's Re-Vision of America* (1985) and The Grapes of Wrath: *Trouble in the Promised Land* (1989). Owens's discussion in "'Bottom and Upland': The Balanced Man in Steinbeck's 'The Harness'" (pp. 44–48) echoes Meyer's comments on "The White Quail" as a study of the duality of human nature. Owens clarifies the central image of "The Harness" by explaining that "Peter Randall is Emma's garden, and with the harness and girdle that she forces him to wear, Emma attempts to assert an artificial control over time and change." The central irony of the story is Peter's essential goodness and his own inability to recognize that fully human beings may be imperfect without being totally evil. In " 'The Little Bit of a Story': Steinbeck's 'The Vigilante' " (pp. 49–53) Owens reminds us of the historical event which inspired the piece and of Steinbeck's multiple attempts at capturing the facts in a suitable fictional form. Owens proposes that Steinbeck altered the "facts" of the historical lynching to make the victim a black man and the crime implicitly sexual in order to create "a powerful sexual vortex in the story."

The two most unoriginal essays in the collection deal with "Johnny Bear" and "The Murder," two of the finest stories in *The Long Valley.* In "Chaos, Evil, and the Dredger Subplot in Steinbeck's 'Johnny Bear' " (pp. 54–62) Patricia Mandia makes connections between the metaphorical messages of the swamp dredging and the community tragedy of the Hawkins sisters. In "Sexism and Racism, or Irony? Steinbeck's 'The Murder' " (pp. 62–69), Mandia asserts that Steinbeck depicts sexism and racism ironically in the story, not intending to promote these ideas. To Thom M. Tammaro fell the dubious chore of discussing one of Steinbeck's most maligned works. In " 'Saint Katy the Virgin': The Key to Steinbeck's Secret Heart" (pp. 70–77) Tammaro suggests that we may learn what to make of the story better by examining the 1936 gift edition of it than by measuring it against the other *Long Valley* pieces. In this light, Tammaro sees "Saint Katy" as belonging to the chapbook tradition and concludes that "had the story remained in its original chapbook form and not been forced between the covers of *The Long Valley,* critics and readers alike would have received it more graciously and sympathetically." An informative, well-written overview of Steinbeck's short story canon, "Steinbeck, the Short Story Writer," by Robert S. Hughes, Jr. (pp. 78–89), provides a strong conclusion for the monograph. By discussing a number of uncollected and less well-known pieces, Hughes emphasizes Steinbeck's range as a story writer while admitting that Steinbeck "was not an innovator in the short-story form itself." A table charting the dates of composition and first publication for *The Long Valley* stories is a handy reference tool.

Tetsumaro Hayashi has also produced *Steinbeck's Literary Dimension: A Guide to Comparative Studies,* Series II (Scarecrow). This sequel to his

1973 *Guide* is a collection of 15 previously published comparative essays on Steinbeck and such authors as Blake, Faulkner, Hardy, Hemingway, Twain, and Jung. Reloy Garcia's introduction stresses the variety and complexity of the essays and compares reading them to having one's eyes examined: seeing all of the essays together results in a clearer vision of Steinbeck's work. Another reprinted essay appears in Hayashi's Steinbeck Essay Series, "Steinbeck's *Cannery Row:* A Reconsideration" by Jackson J. Benson (Steinbeck Society), originally published in *Western American Literature* in 1977. Benson issues an important critical corrective: "I would suggest that too often we have approached the novel backwards: we have tried to apply literature where we should be looking to see how the book, as a work of literature, has captured life."

Hayashi may also be given credit for bringing out several new essays through the International John Steinbeck Society. Joseph Dewey in " 'There Was a Seedy Grandeur about the Man': Rebirth and Recovery in *Travels With Charley*" (*StQ* 24, i–ii:22–30) draws parallels between *Travels with Charley* and Thoreau's *Walden* to offer a reading of Steinbeck's trip across America as a "metaphor of a journey inward." Dewey's analysis of Steinbeck's character/persona as an entity separate from the author leads to the conclusion that "the persona's recovery is not complete until he recognizes also the revitalization of his nation. . . . America is not rediscovered but rather recovered, shifting the emphasis from the persona to the country itself." Mimi R. Gladstein in "The Strong Female Principle of Good or Evil: The Women of *East of Eden*" (*StQ* 24, i–ii:30–40) asserts that Steinbeck's symbolic depiction of women as temptresses or ideals includes not only the Eve of Genesis, but with the creation of Abra "incorporates a Lilith figure in a redemptive role." Gladstein's insightful analysis of the various mothers in the novel indicates that women in the Trask narrative of *East of Eden* suffer incredible ills, while women in the Hamilton family are portrayed with "humor, nostalgia, family pride, and affection." "Steinbeck's Statement on the Inner Chapters of *The Grapes of Wrath*" by Phyllis T. Dircks (*StQ* 24, iii–iv:86–94) includes a copy of Steinbeck's letter to a Columbia University undergraduate explaining the purpose and design of the inner chapters and Dircks's assessment of how critical commentary on them measures up to Steinbeck's pronouncement. Hayashi himself contributes "John Steinbeck and Adlai E. Stevenson: Their Moral and Political Vision" (*StQ* 24, iii–iv:94–107). In this informative essay Hayashi analyzes "the nature and extent of the moral and political vision" of the two "liberal Democrats." Drawing on Stevenson's letters and speeches of the 1950s and 1960s and Steinbeck's letters and fiction from that same period, Hayashi details their battle against McCarthyism and emphasizes Steinbeck's role as adviser and speechwriter for Stevenson.

The *Steinbeck Newsletter* (Summer 1991), ed. Susan Shillinglaw, carried several items of scholarly interest. Preston Beyer's report, "John Steinbeck and the Armed Services Edition" (p. 5), details the operations of the Council of Books in Wartime, which met first in June 1942 and set out "to achieve the widest possible use of books contributing to the war effort of the United Peoples." Seven Steinbeck titles were chosen for this project, which printed the books in a special format and delivered them free to servicemen. John Ditsky in "California Dreaming: Steinbeck and West" (pp. 6–7) identifies vivid descriptions and a satirical strain as parallels between Steinbeck's fiction and Nathanael West's. "In *Pippin,* the irruption of the satirical into the fabular, or vice versa, may well go back to Nathanael West," Ditsky asserts. In addition to a point/counterpoint discussion of Todd Johnson of *Pippin* and Todd Hackett of *The Day of the Locust,* Ditsky also suggests that Faye, the "perverse enchantress" of *Locust,* may be "an ironic inversion of Steinbeck's Clotilde."

b. Richard Wright, Ralph Ellison, James Baldwin Sure to stimulate critical commentary among Richard Wright scholars is the Library of America's unexpurgated edition of Wright's works *Lawd Today!, Uncle Tom's Children, Native Son, Black Boy,* and *The Outsider.* It restores passages which were censored or altered by editors in the original publications and annotates them. Basing the texts on Wright's original typescripts and proofs, the Library of America editors offer this two-volume set as authoritative. A noteworthy essay by B. Eugene McCarthy, "Models of History in Richard Wright's *Uncle Tom's Children*" (*BALF* 25:729–43), analyzes the relationship among the stories, centering on the war/history motif. McCarthy sees the work as "a fictional representation of the world of black Americans at several stages of history from the 1910s to the 1930s—illustrating history, creating models of what history was like, what it might have evolved toward in final violence, what the promises held out to black people meant, and how to respond with power to contemporary crises."

Richard Kostelanetz includes essays on Wright and Ellison in the previously published work collected into *Politics in the African-American Novel.* Tracing Wright's political awareness through his canon, Kostelanetz notes that "themes for collective action that are suggested in his earlier writing are modified or even repudiated in later fiction, and character-types portrayed as saviours in youthful works become false messiahs in mature ones." Kostelanetz deals with Wright's treatment of generational differences, religion, his critique of the "monopoly of violence as power" practiced by whites against blacks, and the African nationalist and Communist influences on African Americans. In his treatment of Ellison, Kostelanetz convincingly argues for *Invisible Man* as "the most comprehensive one-volume fictional—symbolic—treatment of the history of African-Americans in the twentieth century." According to Kostelanetz, most major scenes in the novel embody symbolic dimensions that complement the literal action while underscoring the various political impulses at work: Jim Crowism, radical communism, black nationalism, and expatriation.

In *From Harlem to Paris* Michel Fabre examines the history of black intellectuals, including detailed accounts of the French experiences of both Wright and Baldwin and an analysis of French influences on their work. In "Richard Wright: An Intellectual in Exile" (pp. 175–94) Fabre describes Wright's first impressions of Paris in 1946, the move to Paris with his family in 1947, his relationship with Sartre, and his involvement with French-speaking African intellectuals who were concerned about France's colonial politics. In "James Baldwin in Paris: Love and Self-Discovery" (pp. 195–214) he contrasts Baldwin's French experiences with Wright's. Because Baldwin was much younger than Wright, knew little French, and had not established himself as an author, their circle of friends rarely intersected. Fabre reports that "Baldwin found himself very much on his own, associating mostly with white American students and artists and only occasionally with French friends and lovers." Fabre draws a detailed sketch of Baldwin's dedication to his craft and the young writer's realization that he was, indeed, an American most interested in pursuing American subjects and themes in his work.

Fabre also makes a contribution to *James Baldwin*, ed. Jakob Köllhofer (Peter Lang), which includes 10 selections, some categorized as personal remembrances, others as critical commentary. His "James Baldwin in Paris: Hardship and Romance" (pp. 45–56) covers the same territory as *From Harlem to Paris*. Baldwin's search for identity in Paris is explained by James Oliver Horton ("In Search of Identity: James Baldwin and the Black American Intellectual Tradition," pp. 95–108) in these terms: "Baldwin felt more American in Europe, in part because Europeans saw him as an American." Peter Freese analyzes problems with German translations of Baldwin's works in "Some Remarks on the Reception of James Baldwin's Work in the Federal Republic of Germany" (pp. 11–32). Friederike Hajek's "Historical Aspects of the Reception of James Baldwin in the German Democratic Republic" (pp. 33–43) is a discussion of the German fascination with Baldwin's style and unease with the content of his work. Hélène Christol considers the issue of white power and sexual dominance in "Whose Power? Baldwin and the 'American Legend of Masculinity' " (pp. 79–88), and Fletcher DuBois "bears witness" to a homosexual's responses to Baldwin's fiction in the '50s and '60s in "With Only the Rain As a Witness" (pp. 89–93). Roberto Marquez in "One Boricua's Baldwin" (pp. 57–78) offers a moving personal tribute to the author, adding insightful commentary on the impact that *Notes of a Native Son* had on a "streetwise Puerto Rican of looming intellectual ambition but very doubtful prospects." Maria Diedrich reviews obituaries in "James A. Baldwin—Obituaries for a Black Ishmael" (pp. 129–40).

James Campbell in *Talking at the Gates: A Life of James Baldwin* (Viking) strikes a healthy balance between portraying significant events in Baldwin's life and analyzing his works. In the opening chapters Campbell discusses the early influences of religion, music, and art on Baldwin's aesthetics, the master-pupil relationship with Richard Wright, Baldwin's declaration of his homosexuality, and his first move to Paris. The account of Wright's angry reaction to Baldwin's 1949 essay, "Everybody's Protest Novel," is enlightening, as is Campbell's analysis of the declining friendship between Wright and Baldwin, a relationship that in Baldwin's estimation moved from hero-worship to pity. The split between the two authors, according to Campbell, centered on a disagreement over "the social and artistic responsibilities of the writer." As Campbell shows in the second half of *Talking at the Gates,* consciousness of responsibility to humanity is a recurring theme in Baldwin's work and life and also is basic to his criticism of the Black Muslims, whom Baldwin considered racist. Though the portrait of Baldwin the man is never overshadowed by the literary criticism woven through the study, Campbell makes a good case for his observation that most of Baldwin's life was consumed by his work and that much of his work was influenced by his life-style.

Baldwin scholars should also look at "The Critical Reception of James Baldwin in Japan: An Annotated Bibliography," compiled by Yoshinobu Hakutani and Toru Kiuchi (*BALF* 25:753–79), covering every journal article, book chapter, and review on Baldwin published in Japan from 1960 through 1989.

iii Southerners

a. Margaret Walker and Zora Neale Hurston An outstanding achievement in feminist criticism this year is Melissa Walker's *Down from the Mountaintop: Black Women's Novels in the Wake of the Civil Rights Movement, 1966–1989* (Yale). As the subtitle indicates, this probing critical study addresses relevant questions about the past, the present, and the future of the African-American community as it is reflected in fictional narratives ranging from Margaret Walker's *Jubilee* to Alice Walker's *The Temple of My Familiar.* Melissa Walker's revisionist treatment of *Jubilee* serves as a solid introduction to this excellent book. After detailing the history of its composition, she focuses on the novel not as the story of a conventional romantic past, but of "the past as the recognition of the present." In *Down from the Mountaintop,* Walker concisely juxtaposes what was going on in the United States at the time of the composition of each stage of *Jubilee* with what goes on in the novel to show with what historical accuracy scenes set in the 1860s reflect the political mood of the 1960s.

Three new essays on Zora Neale Hurston are worth looking at: Janice Daniel's " 'De understandin' to go 'long wid it': Realism and Romance in *Their Eyes Were Watching God*" (*SLJ* 24, i:66–76), Joseph R. Urgo's " 'The Tune is the Unity of the Thing': Power and Vulnerability in Zora Neale Hurston's *Their Eyes Were Watching God*" (*SLJ* 23, ii:40–54), and Marion Thomas's "Reflections on the Sanctified Church as Portrayed by Zora Neale Hurston" (*BALF* 25:35–41). Daniel identifies parallels between Hurston's novel and the traditional literary romance, emphasizing psychological realism as the element which adds to the book's complexity and richness. Using the terminology of Northrop Frye's *The Secular Scripture,* Daniel points out elements of the romantic quest motif in Janie Crawford's search for self. Also focusing on Janie's self-realizations, Urgo discusses variations on the theme of power and weakness in *Their Eyes Were Watching God,* asserting that "autonomy, in the novel, flows not from overcoming vulnerability but from locating strength within it." Thomas, in a more general essay, validates Hurston's study of the African-American institution known as the sanctified church, tying the visionary experiences of the religious context to the "lying" sessions in *Mules and Men* and *Their Eyes Were Watching God.*

A valuable anthology, *Zora in Florida,* ed. Steve Glassman and Kathryn Lee Seidel (Central Florida), treats each major phase of Hurston's career related to Florida, with special attention to lesser-known material such as *Jonah's Gourd Vine.* In "Flora and Fauna in Hurston's Florida Novels" (pp. 1–12) Ann R. Morris and Margaret M. Dunn discuss central symbols derived from the natural elements of the region for each of three novels: *Jonah's Gourd Vine, Their Eyes Were Watching God,* and *Dust Tracks on a Road.* Alan Brown's " 'De Beast' Within: The Role of Nature in *Jonah's Gourd Vine*" (pp. 76–85) is a more sophisticated chronicle of Hurston's use of nature to externalize the internal struggle of John Pearson, the central character. Brown draws references from Hurston's other works to establish the natural dangers of the region—snakes, hurricanes, alligators, etc.—and centers his argument on the snake/serpent references as symbolic of John's struggle with sexual promiscuity. In "Voodoo as Symbol in *Jonah's Gourd Vine*" (pp. 86–93) Barbara Speisman offers a provocative discussion of Hurston's understanding of the influence of African voodoo ceremony on black culture in the American South. Speisman illustrates this influence on Hurston's fiction, specifically in the use of three symbols of voodoo: the snake, the drum, and the sermon. On the other hand, Beulah S. Hemmingway in "Through the Prism of Africanity: A Preliminary Investigation of Zora Neale Hurston's *Mules and Men*" (pp. 38–45) claims not that Hurston's folklore originated in Africa, but that her *use* of folklore serves an African function. In *Mules and Men* language becomes symbolic action, and through oral tradition blacks redefine their world in accordance with their needs. Hemmingway discusses Hurston's trickster figures and their employment of wish fulfillment and role inversion, activities which "promoted group cohesiveness, strengthened black resolve, and fueled the will to survive." Two other essays deal specifically with *Mules and Men:* Dana McKinnon Preu's "A Literary Reading of *Mules and Men,* Part I" (pp. 46–61) and Mary Katherine Wainwright's "Subversive Female Folk Tellers in *Mules and Men*" (pp. 62–75). Asserting that orality makes *Mules* the work of art that it is, Preu illustrates how an oral culture and literature use a different set of mental processes and behavioral patterns than does a world of literacy. Preu praises Hurston's oral epic style of physical action and congratulates the author "for providing not artifacts to be dissected, but a means whereby we may positively experience orality." Wainwright is also interested in Hurston's orality and in demonstrating how the politics of gender undermine male authority in *Mules and Men.* She examines Hurston's own folkloric voice as well as structure, theme, and female storytellers as instruments of liberation for black women.

"Excursions into Zora Neale Hurston's Eatonville" by Anna Lillios (pp. 13–27) features interviews with several women who recall Hurston's life in Eatonville and identify two potentially alienating factors surrounding the author in her hometown: her education at Barnard and her sometimes harsh portrayal of Eatonville folks. Also focusing on Hurston's biography is Kevin M. McCarthy's report, "Three Legal Entanglements of Zora Neale Hurston" (pp. 174–82). "Adaptation of the Source: Ethnocentricity and 'The Florida Negro'" by Christopher D. Felker (pp. 146–58) examines how working on "The Florida Negro" for the Florida guide, part of the Federal Writers' Project, enabled Hurston to concentrate on black culture and to moderate her association with the dominant white culture. According to Felker, "Folklore and music held ethnocentric messages that Hurston sought to apprehend and then inscribe within the cultural patternings of the state as a whole." Warren J. Carson in "Hurston as Dramatist: The Florida Connection" (pp. 121–29) catalogs Hurston's dramatic creations and summarizes the plot of *Color Struck.* "Zora Neale Hurston at Rollins College" by Maurice J. O'Sullivan, Jr., and Jack C. Lane (pp. 130–37) is a biographical piece detailing Hurston's involvement with Bob Wunsch and Wunsch's effort to broaden his English students' experiences with black folklore and black performance art. "Text and Personality in Disguise and in the Open: Zora Neale Hurston's *Dust Tracks on a Road*" by Kathleen Hassall (pp. 159–73) points to Hurston's omission from *Dust Tracks* of comments concerned with the impact of racism on her life. Hassall proposes that Hurston's seeming powerlessness and nonconfrontational poses are merely disguises, performances by a character adept at participating in lying contests. Hassall views whole sections of *Dust Tracks* as "unannounced performances."

"'Beginning to See Things Really': The Politics of Zora Neale Hurston" by David Headon (pp. 28–37) examines the conventional notion that Hurston's work did not reflect the growing politicization of the black community. Headon claims that Hurston's work from 1924 to 1950 shows an "evolving political consciousness" demonstrated by her recognition of the quality of black communal life, her suspicion of cultural appropriation by Western civilization, and her celebration of a self-identity which also embraces an emergent feminist aesthetic. Rosalie Murphy Baum's "The Shape of Hurston's Fiction" (pp. 94–109), however, calls for more critical attention to the aesthetic achievement of Hurston's early work and more careful consideration of pieces which do not necessarily set forth statements on issues of race or gender. Baum discusses three stories ("Isis," "Sweat," and "The Gilded Six-Bits") in light of their realistic elements, their structure, and Hurston's ability to "tantalize the reader with realism highlighted by framed moments." In fact, Kathryn Lee Seidel, with "The Artist in the Kitchen: The Economics of Creativity in Hurston's 'Sweat'" (pp. 110–20), offers the very kind of critical view called for by Baum. Admitting the naturalistic elements of the story, Seidel goes on to show how Hurston employs a dual narrative focus through the naturalistic narrator and the oral commentary of the townspeople; these add the dimension of self-knowledge and highlight Delia's ability to impose an order on her world.

b. Eudora Welty and Katherine Anne Porter Welty's narrative technique received skillful treatment from several sources. Gerda Seaman and Ellen L. Walker render a perceptive reading of Welty's *The Ponder Heart* in their essay, "'It's All in a Way of Speaking': A Discussion of *The Ponder Heart*" (*SLJ* 23, ii:65–76). According to Seaman and Walker, "Edna Earle practices a narrative sleight-of-hand that points at one thing, usually an object or a physical detail of setting, in order to obscure another." Though the narrator never falsifies action, she short-circuits the reader's understanding of events by manipulating chronology and imposing her own assumptions about characters on the reader. In a skillfully orchestrated discussion, "Recovering Otherness in *The Golden Apples*" (*AL* 63:489–506), Susan V. Donaldson applies Bakhtin's theory of the carnivalesque to analyze a "two-fold revelation" in *The Golden Apples.* Donaldson reveals a complex narrative plan in which Welty uses parody and subversion of monologic discourse to celebrate transgression and broken boundaries. Also applying discourse analysis to Welty's fiction, Suzan Harrison in "'The Other Way to Live': Gender and Selfhood in *Delta Wedding* and *The Golden Apples*" (*MissQ* 44:49–67) asserts that "Welty decenters the patriarchal discourse, reducing it to merely one of the many voices she incorporates into her fiction." By featuring Shelley Fairchild's diary and Ellen Fairchild's dreams, for example, Welty disrupts the unity and linearity of the narrative with traditionally feminine genres. Welty goes even further with this disruptive strategy in *The Golden Apples,* with female characters who "openly rather than covertly insist on alternative visions and who voice their own feminine pleasure."

The Winter issue of *Studies in Short Fiction* offers essays devoted to two of Katherine Anne Porter's most celebrated stories. In " 'Flowering Judas' and the Failure of 'Amour Courtois' " (*SSF* 28:77–82) Norman Lavers draws the tentative conclusion that Laura's "No" at the end of the story "seems to be a denial of her former denials." Lavers argues that Laura's death dream forces her to realize her incompleteness and the barrenness of her self-denials. In "The Jilting of (Hetero)Sexist Criticism: Porter's Ellen Weatherall and Hapsy" (*SSF* 28:9–20) Roseanne L. Hoefel argues that the most important relationship in Ellen Weatherall's life was neither with jilting George nor steady husband John, but with another woman, the lost Hapsy. Close readings of certain passages certainly support Hoefel's claim, but the entire discussion hinges on our acceptance of Hapsy as Ellen's closest friend rather than her child.

James T. F. Tanner in *The Texas Legacy of Katherine Anne Porter* (North Texas, 1990) claims that in Porter's fiction compulsive preoccupation with gender roles, depiction of children in a hostile environment, and the pervasiveness of evil are the result of the author's early life in Texas. Tanner's analysis of Porter's motives for presenting a Texas South, not as she knew it to be, "but as she consciously created or invented it for literary purposes," merits attention, but much of the discussion is simply a gloss on Joan Givner's 1982 biography of Porter; Tanner does, however, offer insightful analysis concerning the problems that critics have with Porter as a "Texas" writer. Several essays also look at the importance of place in Porter's fiction: "Texas and Berlin: Images of Germany in Katherine Anne Porter's Prose" (*SLJ* 24, i:77–87) by Diana Hinze, and "The 'Booby Trap' of Love: Artist and Sadist in Katherine Anne Porter's Mexico Fiction" (*JML* 16:617–34) by Mary E. Titus. Hinze juxtaposes the depiction of German characters from two stories representing opposite ends of Porter's career—"Holiday" and "Leaning Tower"—to compare views of the artist. Both protagonists undergo experiences which help them break down their misconceptions about themselves and about reality. The sentimentally romantic view of the artist in "Holiday" is replaced by a wholesome idyllic reality in "Leaning Tower"; however, the artist's sentimental romanticism is displaced by the "reality of ugly oppressions." Titus, in a convincing, well-written essay, examines

Porter's desire to expose the sadomasochism fueling the "transformation of women into symbolic and erotic objects" in four stories set in Mexico: "Flowering Judas," "Virgin Violeta," "The Martyr," and the unpublished "The Lonely Legend." Titus identifies several male artists (poets and painters with whom Porter became involved) as models for the men in these stories—men who interpret the actions of silent, passive women and claim those actions for their own pleasures. According to Titus, the women are "seduced by the romantic love tradition and often find their own objectification exciting."

Porter's Texas origin is the organizing principle for the critical anthology *Katherine Anne Porter and Texas: An Uneasy Relationship,* ed. Clinton Machann and William Bedford Clark (Texas A & M, 1990). Sylvia Ann Grider's introduction to the anthology, "A Folklorist Looks at Katherine Anne Porter" (pp. xiii–xxiii), reiterates the feud between Porter and her home state that Tanner deals with at length in *The Texas Legacy of Katherine Anne Porter.* Sally Dee Wade in "The Homeless One Home Again" (pp. 115–23) also dwells on the issue of Porter versus Texas literati. The first part of the collection features personal recollections by Willene Hendrick, Cleanth Brooks, and Paul Porter. The second part, "Katherine Anne Porter and the Transfiguring Imagination," includes five essays. In "Problems of Personal Identity in Texas' 'First Writer'" (pp. 41–57) Joan Givner, Porter's biographer, discusses the writer's fascination with two historical figures, Joan of Arc and Mary Queen of Scots. Don Graham in "A Southern Writer in Texas: Porter and the Texas Literary Tradition" (pp. 58–71) comments on Porter's creation of her professional persona, particularly her habit of casting herself as a daughter of the southern plantation culture. Thomas F. Walsh reviews Porter's earliest and previously unknown Mexican writing to set the stage for a discussion of paradise lost in better-known stories in "From Texas to Mexico to Texas" (pp. 72–85). Janis P. Stout in "Estranging Texas: Porter and the Distance from Home" (pp. 86–101) points out not only that Porter's Texas is more distinctly southern than western, but also that the greater part of her work is set in regions other than Texas. Stout sees the conscious fictional choices on Porter's part as a means of distancing herself from her childhood home, a consciousness that accounts for Porter's distinct fictive voice. Claiming that "Porter's assimilation of her sources made it possible for her to meet her own literary standards," Darlene Harbour Unrue in "Porter's Sources and Influences" (pp. 102–

12) details biographical influences on the writer and scrutinizes critics' claims for the influence of particular writers on her work. *Katherine Anne Porter and Texas* concludes with a Texas bibliography of Porter.

c. Carson McCullers, Flannery O'Connor, Harper Lee, and Margaret Mitchell A single article each for Carson McCullers and Harper Lee deserve attention. A brief but perceptive essay by Laurie Champion considers race and religion in McCullers's best-known work. In "Black and White Christs in Carson McCullers's *The Heart Is a Lonely Hunter*" (*SLJ* 24, i:47–52) Champion interprets Willie's imprisonment and torture as a black crucifixion which, like southern Christianity for blacks, is not redemptive. Though Champion acknowledges Singer as a Christ symbol, she points out important differences between Singer's death and Willie's persecution: Singer executes his own symbolic crucifixion, whereas "Willie as Christ demonstrates humanity's persecution and betrayal of the Negro race." Claudia Johnson's "Code and Law in Harper Lee's *To Kill a Mockingbird*" (*SAF* 19:129–39) focuses on the legal codes which permeate relationships in the story and on its major subplots. As Johnson shows, finally even Atticus must succumb to the limitations of law and allow the primitive, hidden force of Boo Radley to deliver justice via the slaying of Bob Ewell.

"Flannery O'Connor's Attacks on Omniscience" by Marshall Bruce Gentry (*SoQ* 29, iii:53–61) takes issue with modernist interpretations of O'Connor's work and suggests that a closer look at her treatment of omniscience reveals narrators who are "constantly projecting meanings we can question." Gentry asserts that O'Connor promotes a worldview more feminist than modernist by creating male narrators "whose power, authority, and omniscience are overthrown." Jean W. Cash in "O'Connor as Distinguished Alumna: Wit and Wisdom" (*ELN* 29, i:67–70) reviews O'Connor's "two pages of thanksgiving" prepared in response to an alumnae award bestowed by Georgia State College for Women in Milledgeville in 1957. In "O'Connor's Ancient Comedy: Form in 'A Good Man Is Hard to Find' " (*JSSE* 16:29–40), Robert Donahoo retraces the journey that many other critics have already taken with the Dante/O'Connor parallel. The most original portion of the discussion comes in the final section of the essay, which compares the intense dialogue of the Misfit and the Grandmother to the comic debates in Aristophanes' plays between the Agonist and the Antagonist. Michael Clark's note, "Flannery O'Connor's 'A Good Man Is Hard to Find': The Moment of Grace"

(*ELN* 29, ii:66–69), reviews recent critical statements about O'Connor's most discussed short story and calls for further examination of the Grandmother's achievement of spiritual insight. Also this year Miles Orvell reissued his 1972 study, *Invisible Parade,* under the title *Flannery O'Connor: An Introduction* (Miss.), adding a new preface which surveys critical responses to O'Connor's work over the past two decades.

Darden Asbury Pyron's *Southern Daughter: The Life of Margaret Mitchell* (Oxford) is a monumental accomplishment of historical record, detailing (sometimes to the point of tedium) the family history and private and public life of Margaret Mitchell from birth to death. The reader who gets bogged down in Pyron's devoted descriptions of Mitchell's myriad illnesses, real and imagined, might be forewarned that Mitchell herself was often paralyzed by preoccupation with her health. This whole line of inquiry pays off when Pyron reports that Mitchell began *Gone With the Wind* in 1926 after months of confinement because her foot had "given out." Pyron makes a convincing argument for Mitchell's associations of writing with pain and illness. Letters to friends and family after 1926 reveal her belief in her own inadequacies, along with the conviction that digging into her memory, her childhood, produced childish results (the novel). "She never thought of writing without pain" sums up perfectly Pyron's portrayal. He effectively supports his argument for the psychological overtones of Mitchell's epic work with an analysis of the mother/daughter relationship, concluding that in *Gone With the Wind* "while mothers fail their children, motherhood is also fatal to the mothers themselves." Pyron's analysis highlights the theme of Social Darwinism in the novel and its structure as women's history. The final chapters of *Southern Daughter* lead toward the conclusion that Mitchell did not produce another work of fiction after *Gone With the Wind* because she spent so much creative energy making up fictions about the fiction itself and about herself as a writer.

"The Book, The Movie, The Dream" (*MissQ* 44:183–92), a personal essay by Robert Drake (author of "Tara Twenty Years After," the first essay on the novel to appear in an academic journal, the *Georgia Review,* Summer 1958), cleverly captures his own involvement with *Gone With the Wind* while discussing the impact the work made on American life and letters. Drake praises Mitchell's talents as a storyteller, but he also insists that timing was an important factor in the *Gone With the Wind* phenomenon: the survival theme which emerges most strongly in the book proved irresistible to readers who were striving to survive the Great Depression. Elizabeth I. Hanson in her study *Margaret Mitchell* (TUSAS) claims that the phenomenal popular success of *Gone With the Wind* is to blame for the critical neglect of Mitchell's work. Like Pyron, Hanson emphasizes the importance of Mitchell's Atlanta family experiences and the author's efforts to adapt her family's credo of business success to her own ambitions for literary achievement. In this slim volume Hanson highlights pivotal events in Mitchell's life and presents their connections to the writer's career. By zooming in on Mitchell's *Atlanta Journal* experiences, for example, Hanson neatly juxtaposes Mitchell's marital woes with Red Upshaw, the young bride's journalistic abilities, and her professional and private relationship with John Marsh, whom she later married. Appropriately, Hanson devotes half of her study to discussion of *Gone With the Wind*—its creation, popular and critical reception, and Hanson's own thoughtful analysis.

d. Erskine Caldwell, Thomas Wolfe, and William Styron Sylvia Jenkins Cook's *Erskine Caldwell and the Fiction of Poverty: The Flesh and the Spirit* (LSU), which contains a chronological consideration of all of Caldwell's novels, short stories, and nonfiction, methodically reveals how Caldwell "created a grotesque universe from his imagination and his native South, and then proved himself the most enigmatic part of it." Cook examines Caldwell's experiences as a journalist and book reviewer, as well as the early stylistic experiments which were later refined in the more successful works, *Tobacco Road* and *God's Little Acre.* Discussion of the short stories reveals much about the personality of the writer, his methods, and his program of action—or, as Cook calls it, "the mechanics of getting into print." Paying close attention throughout this study to Caldwell's theme of poverty, Cook provides enough sociohistorical detail to justify her assertion that despite his claims that he was *not* a social critic, "he did in fact concede in many specific instances that his stories and novels had originated in his observations of social and economic inequities."

A number of biographical pieces on Thomas Wolfe, reviews of recent scholarship, and notes about several of his short stories appear in the *Thomas Wolfe Review* (15, i, ii). The best work on Wolfe this year, however, can be found in the extensive introduction by Suzanne Stutman to the previously unpublished novel, *The Good Child's River* (No. Car.), which describes the process of establishing a definitive text for the work. In addition to editing the manuscript, Stutman pieces together the complex history of the composition from Wolfe's letters, notebooks, published stories, letters from Aline Bernstein (model for Esther Jack of the Esther stories), and details in Bernstein's autobiography, *An Actor's Daughter.* Stutman substantiates the claim that "all that [Wolfe] wrote was part of a gigantic work in progress, and as its actor and sole owner, he felt no restrictions in using any of this text whenever and wherever the purpose suited him." In this well-written essay Stutman also offers some sensible speculation as to why Wolfe's writing became increasingly disoriented as he "traveled further into the world of *The Good Child's River.*"

Samuel Coale in *William Styron Revisited* (TUSAS) examines the various critical stances that critics have taken with Styron, then introduces a new category of observation involving the "encapsulated self" which Coale sees at the center of Styron's fiction. Coale concentrates on *The Confessions of Nat Turner* and *Sophie's Choice* to develop his claim that "Styron's fiction seems most successful when he is able to link the self at the center of it . . . to a wider pattern or event." The source of unevenness in Styron's canon, according to Coale, is the tendency to allow one character's Christian beliefs to act as a structural pattern for the novels, a point which is illustrated most clearly in the chapter, *"Set This House on Fire:* A Puddle of Self." The chapter on *Sophie's Choice,* "Styron's Heart of Darkness," clinches his argument: through close reading and careful character analysis Coale makes a strong case for this novel as Styron's most successful because the narrator, Stingo, acknowledges his past and the influence of that past on his present and future.

e. Robert Penn Warren Warren scholars have several new pieces of criticism to ponder: *The American Vision of Robert Penn Warren* by William Bedford Clark (Kentucky) and two essays, Will Fridy's "The Author and the Ballplayer: An Imprint of Memory in the Writings of Robert Penn Warren" (*MissQ* 44:159–66) and Mark Jancovich's "Robert Penn Warren as New Critic: Against Propaganda and Irresponsibility" (*SLJ* 24, i:53–65). Clark's full-length study surveys Warren's entire career, but concentrates on the years from 1925 through 1955, the period in which Bedford believes that Warren's vision "assumed its clearest focus and sharpest definition." Clark documents Warren's fight against "barren homogeneity" in America, against an "uncritical faith in the rightness of a cause," and his promotion of participation in the wider world. A perspective which yields rich critical insight is Clark's identification of Warren's first three published novels (*Night Rider, At Heaven's Gate,* and

All the King's Men) as the author's vision of democratic process. In an informative, New Historical analysis of Warren's use of childhood memories, Fridy works from interviews with Warren and an early friend, Kent Greenfield, a New York Giants' pitcher in the 1920s who left baseball because of problems with alcohol. The discussion details several touching exchanges of letters between the two grown men and reveals Greenfield as the real-life Goodwood in "Goodwood Comes Back" and as "K" in "American Portrait: Old Style." Jancovich analyzes Warren's discussion of literature as social engagement to argue against Richard Ohmann's claim in *English in America* that New Criticism was concerned only with literature as artifact, caring nothing for sociocultural or historical concepts.

iv **Easterners**

a. Saul Bellow M. A. Quayam's "Adopting Emerson's Vision of Equilibrium: Citrine and the Two Opposite Poles of Twentieth-Century Consciousness in *Humboldt's Gift*" (*SAJL* 10:8–23) clarifies common misconceptions about Emerson's Transcendentalism as it is manifest in Bellow's fiction, distinguishing between Emerson's vision of equilibrium and the one-sided optimism that is often attributed to him. According to Quayam, Humboldt, reacting against materialism and intellectualism, goes to another extreme—wild romanticism; however, the two extremes are reconciled in Citrine and symbolically in Humboldt when Citrine arranges for Humboldt's reburial. Liela H. Goldman's " 'Shuffling Out of My Vulgar Origins': The Masculinist-Elitist Language of Saul Bellow's Fiction" (*MELUS* 16 [1989–90]:33–42) is a clearly supported discussion of Bellow's use of Yiddish to perpetuate the East European sex/class bias. Goldman asserts that Bellow's protagonists speak an intellectual, refined Yiddish colored with biblical allusions, while women and secondary characters speak a vernacular Yiddish.

A major contribution to Bellow studies this year is *Saul Bellow at Seventy-five: A Collection of Critical Essays*, ed. Gerhard Bach (Gunter Narr), which includes 14 essays developed from papers originally presented at the International Symposium "Saul Bellow at 75," held in Heidelberg in July 1990. Bach contributes the lead essay, "Saul Bellow and the Dialectic of Being Contemporary" (pp. 17–31), which delves into the disparity of reactions among readers and critics over Bellow's position in the contemporary world of literature. Looking at the direction of Bellow's work as it plays out in various topics (the nature of reality, death, the vitality of language), Bach describes what he considers Bellow's code for representing the dialectic embedded in contemporary life. Malcolm Bradbury in "Saul Bellow's Intellectual Heroes" (pp. 33–39) likens Bellow to György Lukács, the Hungarian philosopher-critic who is one of the subjects of Claudio Magris' meditations in *Danube.* Bradbury argues that though Bellow's works are steeped in romanticism, the author insists that his heroes answer to "soft romanticism" by maintaining intellectual preconceptions and persistently searching for reality. Astrid Schmitt-v. Muhlenfels in "Novel into Opera: *Henderson the Rain King* and Leon Kirchner's *Lily*" (pp. 41–52) discusses the simultaneous use of different media in the opera and questions whether Henderson constitutes the center of orientation and consciousness in Kirchner's work. Michael Shiels in "Place, Space, and Pace: A Cinematic Reading of *Seize the Day*" (pp. 55–62) calls for a reading of Bellow's novella "in which thematic concerns are made visually congruent with the structure, dynamics, and aesthetics" of the narrative. Shiels disagrees with Bellow's choice of a "freeze-frame" conclusion to the novel.

Several of the essays in *Saul Bellow at Seventy-five* deal with Bellow's treatment of Jewishness, while others raise questions about his feminine perspectives. In "The End of Enlightenment: Bellow's Universal View of the Holocaust in *Mr. Sammler's Planet* (pp. 63–80) Kurt Dittmar argues that Bellow's vision transcends the Holocaust as a specifically Jewish tragedy. Dittmar develops his thesis by analyzing Bellow's dialectical manipulation of "explanation," "distinction," and "disinterestedness" as states of mind, particularly as they apply to Sammler as a survivor of the Holocaust. Judie Newman in "Saul Bellow and Social Anthropology" (pp. 137–49) proposes that "the question of cultural changes and creative adaptation has special relevance for [Bellow] as a Jew." Regine Rosenthal in "Memory and the Holocaust: *Mr. Sammler's Planet* and *The Bellarosa Connection*" (pp. 81–92) looks at Sammler and the first-person narrator of *Bellarosa* through the lens of Bruno Bettelheim, the psychoanalyst, child psychologist, and concentration-camp prisoner who did a study of reaction patterns in survivors of extreme trauma. On a lighter note, Steve Bloom in "Why Billy Rose? Bellow's Use-Misuse of the Real Billy Rose in *The Bellarosa Connection*" (pp. 189–200) argues against confusing Bellow with his narrator and promotes Bellow's assertion that American Jews behave the way they do, "not because they are Jewish, but because they are American." Gloria J. Cronin in "The Quest for the Feminine Poetic in *Humboldt's Gift*" (pp. 93–112) takes issue with critics who emphasize the assumed universality of Bellow's protagonists while overlooking such categories as gender. Cronin proposes that in *Humboldt's Gift* the hyper-masculine construct of destructive male egos competes with a " 'feminine poetic' construct [which] is symbolized almost exclusively in Jungian terms of the anima representing Eros, the soul, and the realm of the unconscious." In "The Authority of Representation and the Discourse of Post-Modernity: *Humboldt's Gift*" (pp. 113–23) Utz Riese draws on Derrida's description of the four layers of meaning that the term "representation" includes, and Riese adds a fifth dimension, the ethical (from J. Hillis Miller), to discuss *Humboldt's Gift* as a meditation and a farce. Riese concludes that the center of representativeness in the text "is in the feminine order of mourning, enacted in the ethical space of meditation."

Paul Levine contributes the only essay in *Saul Bellow at Seventy-five* that concentrates on *The Dean's December*—"*The Dean's December:* Between the Observatory and the Crematorium" (pp. 125–36). Placing Bellow in the context of the East European writers Kundera, Milosz, Kiš, Zinoviev, Konwicki, and Škvorecky, Levine discusses East and West as mirror images in the novel. According to Levine, in Bellow's work "the public question of how we collectively create a civil society is linked to the private question of how we individually face death." In "*A Theft:* Bellow's Clara between Anarchy and Utopia" (pp. 177–88) Marianne M. Friedrich looks at Bellow's ability to combine detective story with fairy tale for a new approach to mythic presentation. Friedrich contends that the Tristan and Hera myths contribute to characterization in the novel: "Clara moves from an anarchic, fragmented concept of the self and of love to a unified vision of 'wholeness,' whereby the two myths amalgamate." Dieter Schultz in " 'Family' in Bellow's *More Die of Heartbreak*" (pp. 151–62) reviews Bellow's previous fiction to point out revisions of the family theme that have occurred throughout Bellow's canon. Schultz's investigation leads to the sound conclusion that "Bellow's portraits of the modern family in various degrees of disintegration are counterpointed by nostalgic reminiscences of the old family" and "by a tentative though equally significant utopian vision of family connections projected by the narrator-protagonist into the future." On the other hand, Daniel Fuchs in "*More Die of Heartbreak:* The Question of Later Bellow" (pp. 163–76) proposes that "Bellow is trying to read meaning into love and family relations and into death as well, but these are more often than not themes for parody."

b. Bernard Malamud Malamud enthusiasts should welcome Kathleen G. Ochshorn's *The Heart's Essential Landscape: Bernard Malamud's Hero* (Peter Lang), a sensitive, straightforward overview which includes a chapter on each of Malamud's eight novels and three collections of short stories. Ochshorn's analysis centers on the Malamud hero as a mensch—"a term of approbation for someone possessing qualities of humaneness and responsibility." Seeking to separate Malamud from his contemporaries (Pynchon, Barth, Vonnegut, Italo Calvino, and others), Ochshorn delineates how Malamud's hero "suffers from what humankind has suffered from for thousands of years," and she insists that the author does not promote the notion that "modern life is somehow more absurd, unstructured or meaningless than it has ever been." Ochshorn admits in her discussion of an early Malamud hero, Roy Hobbs of *The Natural,* that not every Malamud hero evolves from a schlemiel to a mensch; however, while Roy remains distant and unreal, Malamud's later heroes "become less heroic, more fallible, more emotional, more believable, closer and closer to the natural human person."

In *Conversations with Bernard Malamud* (Miss.) Lawrence M. Lasher has collected 27 previously published Malamud interviews and a memorial essay by Evelyn Avery, "Remembrances of Malamud: 1972–1986" (pp. 145–52), a recollection of conversations with Malamud. Ranging chronologically from Joseph Wershba's interview "Not Horror but Sadness" (pp. 3–7), which appeared in the *New York Post* in 1958, to Joel Salzberg's "Malamud's Last Interview? A Memoir" (pp. 139–44), first published in *SAJL* in 1988, the interviews cover varied topics such as Malamud's advice to young writers, the complex connection between the writer and his Jewish experience, Malamud's interest in the short story as a form, and the writer's search for new and effective forms of expression.

Two other items of interest are *Bernard Malamud: A Descriptive Bibliography* by Rita N. Kosofsky (Greenwood) and "Bernard Malamud: Oregon as the Western Other" by Suzanne Clark (*Oregon English Journal* 13:24–27). Kosofsky's bibliography summarizes Malamud's career, includes a detailed chronology, and documents a large number of critical sources: chapters of books, scholarly articles, journalistic interviews, and newspaper reviews and articles. It should prove a valuable resource. In a brief essay aimed at reminding readers of the diversity of regional voices, Clark insists that Malamud's work contributes not only to the Oregonian ecological consciousness; in *A New Life,* which is set in Oregon, he also makes readers aware of the regional threats to cultural diversity.

c. J. D. Salinger John Wenke's *J. D. Salinger: A Study of the Short Fiction* (Twayne) examines the Salinger short-story canon, 22 uncollected stories and three collections. In his reading of the uncollected pieces (of which all but one were published in the 1940s), Wenke identifies typical Salinger concerns—the hypocrisy of social pretense and longing for a lost idyll. Wenke singles out seven of these stories to support his argument that Salinger "tried out" the character of Holden Caulfield for a decade before writing *The Catcher in the Rye.* Wenke questions New Critical readings of *Nine Stories* which view the collection as a story cycle or a novel. Likening Salinger's work to other modernist collections such as Joyce's *Dubliners,* Anderson's *Winesburg, Ohio,* Hemingway's *In Our Time,* Faulkner's *Go Down Moses,* and Welty's *The Golden Apples,* Wenke asserts that *Nine Stories* "suggests relationships but denies narrative completion." The study also includes reflections on Salinger's life and a collection of critical excerpts which deal largely with the "putative unity of *Nine Stories* and the religious preoccupations of the later fiction."

v Westerner D'Arcy McNickle

In "Trusting Story and Reading *The Surrounded*" (*SAIL* 3, ii:22–27) Bill Brown offers a brief but helpful discussion of the models of storytelling and accepting stories in D'Arcy McNickle's novel. Brown identifies what he calls "inset" stories focusing on the "Big Paul" tale, which presents "the sad inability of cultures to hear one another's stories." Brown contends that the stories Archilde hears at the feast do for him what stories are supposed to do—they move the character, they change him somehow, and affect his course of action thereafter.

vi Émigré Vladimir Nabokov

In *Social Semiotics as Praxis: Text, Social Meaning Making, and Nabokov's* Ada (Minnesota) Paul J. Thibault "theorizes the relations between dynamic contextual processes and their textual products in the making, maintaining, and changing of systems of social meaning making processes." He uses *Ada* to test his case, but the curious are hereby forewarned that the novel does not enter Thibault's highly theoretical discussion until page 50 and the semiotics jargon will surely baffle all but the anointed. *Ada* is not among the six major Nabokov novels that Vladimir E. Alexandrov considers in *Nabokov's Otherworld* (Princeton). Alexandrov accounts for this omission by deferring to Brian Boyd's *Nabokov's* Ada: *The Place of Consciousness* (1985), "a highly insightful and convincing book about the novel that approaches it from many of the same vantage points I would have liked to use." And what are Alexandrov's vantage points? Above all, he breaks with the majority of Nabokov's critics by claiming that what lies at the heart of Nabokov's work is not "the ironic manipulation of the devices and forms of narrative fiction," but a deep and consistent belief in a transcendent realm of being. Alexandrov reaches definitive conclusions about the relations between beauty, epiphany, and ethics in *The Defense, Invitation to a Beheading, The Gift, The Real Life of Sebastian Knight, Lolita,* and *Pale Fire.* Boyd himself steals the spotlight this year with his exhaustive critical biography, *Vladimir Nabokov: The American Years* (Princeton), the successor to his *Vladimir Nabokov: The Russian Years* (1990). With chapters on Nabokov's most famous novels, *Lolita* and *Pale Fire,* this volume will likely become the more popular of the two, at least among generalists.

Boyd looks at yet another Nabokov work in "Nabokov's *Bend Sinster*" (Shenandoah 41:12–28). According to Boyd, what Nabokov is after in this novel is not a political statement but a philosophical one—a declaration that the individual consciousness must question conventions and assumptions on every side. In "A Referential Reading of Nabokov's 'Signs and Symbols' " (*SSF* 28:129–75) Charles W. Mignon uses Piaget's theories of accommodation and assimilation to argue that "the mother and the father in Nabokov's story have reached some form of self-regulation by at least partial reversibilities, and that their son has not." By illustrating how these three characters assume the referential nature of language and symbols, Mignon sorts out two contrasting critical views of the story—one which finds meaning and one which sees significance in the difficulty of finding meaning.

Southern Oregon State College

15 Fiction: The 1960s to the Present

Jerome Klinkowitz

The metafictive impulse—fiction exploring the conditions of its own making—was once considered no more than a small part not just of contemporary writing but of innovative fiction itself. Yet as time passes, the formerly specific term spreads into a critical umbrella accommodating any type of fiction not predominantly realistic. On the one hand, such practice indicates a fresh rechanneling of the literary mainstream; on the other, it can provide an easy means for wholesale dismissal. In each case, readers must look past the label to see just what the critic includes.

i General Studies

By now, even the most provincial scholar of American literature should be familiar with deconstruction, an approach that identifies and interrogates the otherwise unspoken assumptions underlying any statement of fact. A certain amount of deconstruction is helpful in identifying two major critical surveys of the period, edited by Richard Kostelanetz and Emory Elliott. As a widely respected but academically unaffiliated scholar, Kostelanetz is able to employ a diverse range of critics in order to present a genuinely catholic appraisal of contemporary fiction and the theories behind it, without any of the hasty categorization (and attendant name-calling) that too often confuses such issues as metafiction, irrealism, and the avant-garde. In *American Writing Today* Kostelanetz uses his expertise with Gertrude Stein to lay a foundation for postmodernism upon which his assembled critics can build. Many are writers themselves with special insights to offer, such as Richard Burgin's understanding of Isaac Bashevis Singer as a fictionist who can be politically and socially pertinent while purging his work of any such direct statements,

Rochelle Ratner's belief that Sylvia Plath is much more a visionary writer than a confessional one, Sharon Spencer's debate over whether being told one "writes like a woman" is a compliment or a slur, and Calvin C. Hernton's appreciation of how James Baldwin disputes not just the rhetoric of racial division but how one treats one's self. Rather than slanting his volume's approach according to one school of criticism, Kostelanetz invites affiliated scholars of all persuasions, and he delights in arranging dialogues between such contrasting figures as John Simon and Ihab Hassan. Fiction as conservatively realistic as Irvin Faust's and as radically innovative as Raymond Federman's is given fair, unprejudiced treatment. As a result, *American Writing Today* quite uncontroversially lives up to its title.

Editor Emory Elliott's *The Columbia History of the American Novel* also reflects the key elements of its name. Restricted to coverage of novelists, it necessarily discounts the contribution of fictionists who invested larger proportions of their talents in shorter forms (such as Donald Barthelme), while it has to fully disregard others just as central to the fictive scene (such as Grace Paley). As a self-proclaimed "history," it assumes a mantle of authority with which neither Kostelanetz's book nor any survey of current work could be comfortable: indeed, when novelist Stephen Millhauser is discussed with the same canon-forming force as are Nathaniel Hawthorne and Herman Melville, one questions whether such claim-making projects should presume to extend themselves past literary epochs that have yet to run their course. Finally, the imprimatur of Columbia University is important not just in the volume's title but in the basis of its approach, for the critics who write on postmodern fiction are affiliated with elite private universities and the proportion of works studied, even as "avant-garde," is heavily weighted in favor of those published by prominent New York commercial houses. Not surprisingly, the picture painted by the editor's commentators on the contemporary is colored by the concerns of English departments (colonialism, imperialism, gender) rather than by writers of fiction, and therefore it bears far less pertinence to the state of the novel today than does the view offered in Kostelanetz's collection.

Too limited in space to challenge either Kostelanetz's or Elliott's surveys in terms of authority, Richard Ruland and Malcolm Bradbury's *From Puritanism to Postmodernism* (Viking) makes brilliant use of just 18 pages near its end to present a synthesis of current fictive trends that avoids calling all experimental work "metafictive" and instead incorporates irrealism as an important phase within the larger movement of postmodernism. History itself "has upset the coherence of any single vision," Ruland and Bradbury understand, and thus they appreciate how neither a comfortable realism nor modernistic anxiety can totalize experience in postmodern times. Rather than trying to discredit the innovations of the 1960s and 1970s by refashioning a neoconservative history of those decades, the authors distinguish between the "indeterminate, radical spirit" of fiction flourishing then and the "more conservative styles" that have followed—not a simple realism but an experimental or "dirty realism" that builds on the past rather than rejecting it.

A similarly helpful understanding of the period is provided by Aleid Fokkema in *Postmodern Characters* (Rodopi). Beginning with the "dense metafictionalism" of Thomas Pynchon and progressing through the reemergence of historical reference in work by Robert Coover and the parody of such concerns in novels by Gilbert Sorrentino and Donald Barthelme, Fokkema shows how an emphasis on the reality of language (as opposed to represented action) does not flatten character but privileges other semiotic elements in assembling a new set of conventions. Peter Stoicheff agrees: his "The Chaos of Metafiction," pp. 85–99, in N. Katherine Hayles, ed., *Chaos and Order: Complex Dynamics in Literature and Science* (Chicago), compares metafiction's properties with the scientific definition of chaos, concluding that such texts are complex systems not only of self-interrogations but of "self-generative readings"—and that such readings present in the text invite similar readings of the world. Eugene Goodheart devotes a chapter of his *Desire and Its Discontents* (Columbia) to comparing two writers not often linked: Don DeLillo and Philip Roth. Roth's *The Counterlife* presents fluid narrator/reader boundaries that erode completely in *The Facts,* a warning that "the risk-taking violence of the imagination, its acting out of desire, makes it therapeutically unsound," while DeLillo's *Players* steps beyond the techniques of metafiction into outright social criticism to fault desire's "imperial role in the cinematic consumerist culture in which we live."

Other important studies take unique views on current styles of fiction. Thomas Hill Schaub's *American Fiction in the Cold War* (Wisconsin) portrays the postmodern novel trying to be born but facing the severe restrictions of an academically imposed modernism; his readings of Norman Mailer's "The White Negro" and John Barth's *The End of the Road* reveal subversions "by the prevailing discourses of the liberal culture [Mailer] wished to repudiate" and by "the Europeanization of American literature" that Barth's second novel undertakes. Restructured male bonding in novels of the 1980s by Frederick Busch, John Irving, Larry Woiwode, and E. L. Doctorow (among others) is seen by Donald J. Greiner as a result of newly perceived gender relationships; his *Women Enter the Wilderness* (So. Car.) acknowledges the canonization of earlier male bonding but argues that recent novelists respond intertextually to Cooper, Twain, Faulkner, and Hemingway in refashioning male relationships for feminist times. (An interesting coda examines the refiguring of female bonding in Gloria Naylor's *The Women of Brewster Place* and Marianne Wiggins's *John Dollar*). Another intertextual response is traced by David Castronovo in *The American Gentleman: Social Prestige and the Modern Literary Mind* (Continuum). New World experiences certainly shaped American concepts of gentlemanliness, but in recent times Richard Yates has celebrated an unheroic gentility, John Cheever's fiction has disclosed the frightening anonymity within genteel systems (and fashioned counterstrategies for identity and power), Tom Wolfe has decried a false traditionalism, and Walker Percy has fashioned characters estranged from gentry values whose ideals become problematic and uncomfortable when related to larger issues.

The self-interrogation so characteristic of current fiction lends itself to issues in the gay community, where David Bergman finds self-examining writing an important part of life. His *Gaiety Transfigured: Gay Self-Representation in American Literature* (Wisconsin) charts changes in the categories of approval (otherness, genuineness of experience, quality of relationships) in relation to camp (disguise within intimacy, buoyant humor, and an exaggerated elaboration of style). AIDS provides a new death metaphor, a loss of control, and family desirability as hollow. Special attention is given to the resistance and discomfort among James Baldwin's bisexual characters, causalities of their author's virtues being firmly lodged within the Protestant ethic of individuality and volition.

Interrogation itself has become a scholarly device in the hands of interviewers. An issue of *Mississippi Review* (20, i–ii) is devoted to exceptionally probing interviews with Kathy Acker, Paul Auster, Eudora Welty, Jamaica Kincaid, Ishmael Reed, Robert Stone, Marianne Hauser, Kenneth Gangemi, and others; cogent advice on what makes a literary interview successful is given by critic Larry McCaffery in a talk with Lewis Shiner (pp. 155–67). As editor of *Storming the Reality Studio: A Casebook of Cyberpunk and Postmodern Fiction* (Duke), McCaffery marshals interviews, commentaries, and critical studies to suggest that once divergent trends in science fiction and innovative fiction have now combined, producing a style of narrative that uses artificial intelligence and new textures of communication. Just as postmodernism owes its existence to new understandings of linguistics, so does cyberpunk literature capitalize on philosophical readjustments prompted by technology.

ii Transnational Studies

In 1978—the distance now seems like light-years—Ishmael Reed and Al Young prefaced their *Yardbird Lives!* anthology (Grove) with the admonition that "by the early 1970s, it was no longer a secret among astute observers that what officially passed for literature in the United States was really only representative of a select monoculture." Dissatisfied that their own African-American writing might have its momentary periods of vogue for social and political reasons, the two figures organized a publishing house dedicated to discovering and disseminating a truly national literature by recognizing its component factors: not just Euro-American or even African-American but Asian-American and Hispanic-American as well. Today, such transnational interest has become common in literary studies.

One such work pioneered by the interest that Reed and Young describe is Margaret Bedrosian's *The Magical Pine Ring: Culture and the Imagination in Armenian-American Literature* (Wayne State). Drawing on the aesthetic of painter Arshile Gorky, Bedrosian finds that contemporary Armenian-American fiction shares much in common with mainstream postmodern fiction—for its subject, the country of Armenia, is something physically lost that must be repossessed in art. Like the work of other immigrant cultures, Armenian-American literature brings old traditions into a new world, transfiguring both; but in postmodern times ethnicity is reinvented and reinterpreted, becoming something as much created as inherited.

Diaspora is a new journal edited by Pynchon scholar Khachig Tölölyan and dedicated to transnational studies in all disciplines. Noteworthy from its inaugural number is "Heterogeneity, Hybridity, Multiplicity: Marking Asian American Differences" (1:24–44), in which Lisa Lowe finds more diversity and difference among the work of Asian-American fictionists than the simple binary oppositions that critics have fixed on; rather than "dominant" and "minority," Lowe suggests "heterogeneity, hybridity, and multiplicity" as characteristics more enabling of literary art—an approach that Reed and Young's *Yardbird Lives!* called for a decade and a half ago.

iii Women

"I ask some 'American' questions about history, traditions, and contradictions of American women's writing," Elaine Showalter admits at the start of *Sister's Choice,* but she immediately adds that "I also question the idea that in the multi-cultural reality of the present we can continue to assume a monolithic national identity with a given relation to gender and literary production." The answer to this question involves discovering how the "yearning for community and continuity" especially among contemporary American women fiction writers makes obsolete Harold Bloom's "Oedipal metaphors of murderous 'originality'" and makes irrelevant Virginia Woolf's "image of a room of one's own, so enabling for women modernists in England seeking privacy and autonomy." Showalter is especially adept at relating American women's fiction across centuries and other gaps, noting Joyce Carol Oates's refashioning of the themes and structures of *Little Women* to allow an exercise of possibilities rather than their frustration and repression, Sylvia Plath's adoption of Gothic techniques for "rejecting and exorcising the Mother" (whereby the Woman's House of the 1950s is a "suffocating equivalent of the Gothic castle"), Alice Walker's now-classic use of quilting as a metaphor for reconciliation and connection, and Bobbie Ann Mason's way of dealing with "women's self-destructive commemoration of the patriarchal traditions in which their own freedoms have been thwarted."

As consulting editor, Elaine Showalter also leads the impressive masthead responsible for *Modern American Women Writers* (Scribner's), where a similarly broad range of subjects distinguishes her philosophy of inclusion: Joan Didion, Maxine Hong Kingston, Toni Morrison, Joyce Carol Oates, Grace Paley, Sylvia Plath, Susan Sontag, Anne Tyler, and Alice Walker. An indication of the volume's strength is Anne Hiemstra's essay on Paley (pp. 389–96), where the writer is seen to transcend the narrower categorizations of "Jewish American, woman, wife, mother, political activist, [and] storyteller," for every one becomes a virtually metafictive component in her work. More socially inclined are Virginia Blain et al., whose *The Feminist Companion to Literature in English* reads Ann Beattie's stories for their "Diane Arbus-like grotesques" (seen as attributes of character rather than as artistic fashionings), Grace Paley's for their daily-life material (with no sense of that material's metafictive use), and Louise Erdrich's for their narrators who "endure"; only with Erdrich's fiction do the authors credit literary technique, and here it is seen as a result of social stress.

With so much attention going to social and political issues, it does become a struggle for critics to address matters of literary art. The most successful studies are those that begin with a technical interest, such as Suzanne Clark's *Sentimental Modernism.* Feminism "denaturalizes the monological discourse, making the dialogic visible," Clark finds, and she uses Alice Walker's *The Color Purple* to show how the traditional slave narrative can be recast by taking sentimental love as a theme and epistolary form as a mode. Editor Florence Howe's *Tradition and the Talents of Women* is distinguished by Deborah Silverton Rosenfelt's "Feminism, 'Postfeminism,' and Contemporary Women's Fiction" (pp. 268–91), where feminist texts of the 1970s such as *Sula, The Color Purple,* and *Woman on the Edge of Time,* motivated by a concern for the indicators of power with respect to women's lives, are contrasted with a postfeminist text, Louise Erdrich's *Love Medicine,* that is less clear about its program and "more likely to grieve and worry than to rage and hope." The earlier works decode the dynamic of oppression and resistance, marking progress toward awakening and empowerment (in the process privileging women's bonding and marginalizing heterosexual love); Erdrich's novel reinstates heterosexual passion and love, restores familial relationships (especially with the father), and is more skeptical than optimistic.

Sexuality, more than just a theme, can become a technical device in fiction, as understood by Judith Roof in *A Lure of Knowledge: Lesbian Sexuality and Theory* (Columbia). It is "the desire for desire" that generates fictive action, especially when "the absence of a biological mother in a remarkable number of lesbian novels" works against the "nostalgic wish and maternal fulfillment" that theorists such as Chodorow and Kristeva say motivates much narrative action. Even when a mother is present in the narrative strategy, the results can be technically complex, as editors Brenda O. Daly and Maureen T. Reddy show in *Narrating Mothers: Theorizing Maternal Subjectivities* (Tennessee); among the volume's essays are Judith Arcana's treatment of the interrelationships of mothers in Grace Paley's stories (where children become more important than husbands as the community of mothers writes its history), Hertha D. Wong's charting of the correspondences between "female" and "Indian" as part of the "intricate interrelatedness" of Louise Erdrich's characters, and Daly's own contribution on "civil rights according to mothers" evident in Alice Walker's *Meridian* (where both men and women must strive for transformation beyond monological thought). A third possibility exists in editor Laura L. Doan's *Old Maids to Radical Spinsters: Unmarried Women in Twentieth-Century Novels* (Illinois); as Gayle Greene explains in "An 'Old' Story: Gail Godwin's *The Odd Woman*" (pp. 169–92), by defining herself against the image of women in Gissing's text, the protagonist adapts conservative conventions to serve an unconventional view of women. Even subgenres offer uniquely intertextual possibilities. *Haunting the House of Fiction* presents essays by Gayle K. Fujita Sato on Maxine Hong Kingston (who has a ghost play a role in writing by placing identity not in a divisive mix of races but in an integral Chinese America), Ruth Rosenberg on Cynthia Ozick (whose "The Pagan Rabbi" subordinates reality to the priority of "truth demands" in the clash of Greek and Hebraic epic cultures), and Barbara Hill Rigney on Toni Morrison (in whose *Beloved* a spirit demands retribution for the break that slavery makes between the continuity of earth mother and child); Wendy K. Kolmar, one of the editors of the volume, writes about the epistemology evident in works by Toni Cade Bambara, Sandra Cisneros, Judy Grahn, and Louise Erdrich, suggesting a challenge to the conventional ghost story routine of a dualistic world contrasting present and past, the living and the dead, and natural and supernatural. *Where No Man Has Gone Before: Women and Science Fiction* (Routledge), ed. Lucie Armitt, includes Susan Bassnett's "Remaking the Old World: Ursula Le Guin and the American Tradition" (pp. 50–66), an essay that credits Le Guin for her attention to marginalized activity, her refusal to distinguish between science fiction and fantasy (an important boundary within the subgenre), and for her awareness of what other traditions remain unsettled within larger cultural history. Native American mythology is a developing line in Le Guin's novels, making them more lyrical in their use of oral tradition, song, and storytelling.

Virtually every aspect of Marge Piercy's increasingly complex body of work is attended to in editors Sue Walker and Eugenie Hamner's *Ways of Knowing: Essays on Marge Piercy* (Negative Capability). For Piercy the word is indeed a weapon, as Madonne Miner clarifies in her study of *Small Changes;* and just as *Woman on the Edge of Time* accommodates the utopian vision so important to the feminist program, "personal preoccupations" are always evident among this writer's politics. There is an exhaustive bibliography as well as an interview with Piercy undertaken by the editors that draws her out on such subjects as not seeing herself in the tradition of Virginia Woolf (a writer who fears overt act and drama) but rather in the mode of working-class women whose fiction emphasizes action and event. Especially valuable is Walker's "Marge Piercy: An Overview" (pp. 132–47), a model of incorporating history and critical biography with an astute sense of artistic development.

iv Toni Morrison and Other African Americans

As noted in *ALS 1990* (p. 305), the current decade, at least in critical terms, is that of African-American women. This year no less than five important books address the subject, all of them capitalizing on recent breakthroughs in theory to explain the complexities in their texts. For Jacqueline de Weever, mythmaking underlies the narrative strategies of contemporary fictionists; although her *Mythmaking and Metaphor in Black Women's Fiction* (St. Martin's) is more traditional in its use of metaphor as a critical tool, the readings of Toni Cade Bambara and Paule Marshall are especially insightful. Less reductive about Toni Morrison is Missy Dehn Kubitschek, whose *Claiming the Heritage* recognizes how matrilineal roots yield empowerment through their discovery; Octavia Butler's *Kindred* uses time travel between past and present to establish a contemporary identity, and Paule Marshall's novels mark distinct stages in the historical quest—but in Morrison's *Beloved* the dangers of such historical passage are not only admitted but employed as part of the narrative action. Such action's relation to larger historical contexts is the subject of Melissa Walker's *Down from the Mountaintop: Black Women's Novels in the Wake of the Civil Rights Movement, 1966–1989* (Yale), where contemporary novels and their distant historical topic are compared. Thus, the "black feminist essentialism" of Sherley Anne Williams's *Dessa Rose* emerges in the context of "private victories" within the post-civil rights era, while Morrison's *Beloved* reads more conservatively than a nonhistorical view would imply; Celie's private emotions and attachments are subtly evident in *The Color Purple,* where Alice Walker empowers Shug's behavior and voice with more overt authority. In *Engendering the Subject: Gender and Self-Representation in Contemporary Women's Fiction* (SUNY) Sally Robinson uses *Corregidora* and *Eva's Man* by Gayl Jones to "dismantle the social structures and discourses" that position the black female subject's identity; Jones's protagonists oscillate between interior and exterior selves, in the process "dismantling the representational and social structures that enforce the marginalities of minority subjectivities"—a tactic that counters humanistic "identity politics," a politics that is nothing more than a colonialist strategy for containing the other. French theory, especially the Bachelardian symmetry of opposition within that thinker's notion of space, informs Houston A. Baker, Jr.'s *The Workings of the Spirit;* within an imagistic field womanly values can be associated and attached, liberating one's vision from the dialectics of order—an approach that values the spirit work and mythomanic performance of the conjurer (a "taking care of business" attitude prevalent among Toni Morrison's women characters, whose sense of place allows space to generate time).

Toni Morrison draws the most attention for single author studies. In *Fiction and Folklore: The Novels of Toni Morrison* (Tennessee) Trudier Harris describes the author's alternative universe in which thesis changes place with antithesis—a style of magic realism much as practiced by folk culture and empowered by community participation. Morrison is unique in her ability to work both within and above the folklore tradition, using it and critiquing it, making it alter reality and then turn back to be altered itself. Morrison's challenge, Harris believes, is to see women other than witches or scapegoats and to find something other than masculinity as the driving force in her novels. Barbara Hill Rigney's *The Voices of Toni Morrison* (Ohio State) focuses on those techniques that form a language beyond established literary conventions: silence, music, and conjure. Using the terminology of French feminist thought, Rigney discusses this fiction's marginality and "blackness" as symbolic of "radical dissonance and linguistic revolution," even though (as Harris would agree) Morrison moves beyond the limits of language while continuing to work through it. There is a *jouissance* (Roland Barthes's term for sexual bliss) to black women's speech—a musical, erotic "truth in timbre" that encourages a controlled disorder and allows a "serious anarchy." More socially inclined is a resource-based study by Doreatha Drummond Mbalia, *Toni Morrison's Developing Class Consciousness* (Susquehanna), which finds the roots for Morrison's commitment in "environment, family background, historical events, her Random House [editorial] experience, and the writing process itself." Of special importance is the impact of the African writer Chinweizu and appreciation of traditional African life-style as opposed to capitalistic oppression.

That Morrison is not a postmodern fabulist but rather abolishes old narrative limits to make room for previously excluded voices is demonstrated by Eileen T. Bender, whose "Repossessing Uncle Tom's Cabin: Toni Morrison's *Beloved*" (pp. 129–42) appears in *Cultural Power/Cultural Literacy.* Written against the mythology of Stowe's representation, Morrison's narrative revoices the slave's own agony and emancipates culture from false impressions, refocusing a previously distorted chapter of African-American history. The psychological aspects of this same struggle are detailed by Barbara Schapiro in "The Bonds of Love and the Boundaries of Self in Toni Morrison's *Beloved*" (*ConL* 32:194–210), while exposing and eradicating "the sin of innocence"—naive assumptions of one's ability to know the truth—becomes the key to Morrison's authorial identity, according to Catherine Rainwater's "Worthy Messengers: Narrative Voices in Toni Morrison's Novels" (*TSLL* 33:96–113).

Readers of James Campbell's *Talking at the Gates: A Life of James Baldwin* (Viking) may be surprised at the harsh view this editor of the *Times Literary Supplement* takes of Baldwin's work from the 1960s onward. Involvement with the civil rights movement is, for Campbell, the culprit. For biographical details, however, this study is a worthwhile addition. Welcome attention to fictionists too infrequently studied is given by Jeffrey J. Folkes in "Ernest Gaines and the New South" (*SLJ* 24, i:32–46) and by Ashraf H. A. Rushdy in "Fraternal Blues: John Edgar Wideman's Homewood Trilogy" (*ConL* 32:312–45). As editor of the collection *African American Writers,* Valerie Smith has commissioned essays on both Gaines and Wideman; other contemporary fictionists covered include Gayl Jones, Paule Marshall, Toni Morrison, Gloria Naylor, and Ishmael Reed. Henry Louis Gates, Jr.'s chapter on Reed (pp. 361–77) is an especially important contribution to scholarship in that it accounts for Reed's activities as an experimentalist. Another writer emerging from the innovative atmosphere of the 1960s and 1970s to become a genuinely mainstream artist is given thorough treatment in two essays appearing in *BALF* 25. "Something to Serve: Constructs of the Feminine in Charles Johnson's *Oxherding Tale*" (pp. 689–703) by Jennifer Hayward argues that the text's richness is due to "cross-fertilization" from Buddhism as well as the feminine; and "The Liberation of Perception: Charles Johnson's *Oxherding Tale*" (pp. 705–28) by William Gleason notes that a "whole series of literary fathers," from St. Augustine to Herman Melville and James Weldon Johnson, provide models for Charles Johnson's complex view. Finally, *The LeRoi Jones/Amiri Baraka Reader* (Thunder's Mouth) is of special use because of editor William J. Harris's introduction and chronology, both of which make eminent sense of Baraka's profound transformations of literary identity.

v Cynthia Ozick, Philip Roth, Woody Allen, and Other Jewish Americans

General editor Matthew J. Bruccoli's series, "Understanding Contemporary Literature," continues to publish volumes far more substantial than their introductory nature would imply. *Understanding Cynthia Ozick* (So. Car.) allows Lawrence S. Friedman to analyze Ozick's fiction as a judgment of the world; Ozick speaks out against assimilation as a form of aping and argues in her work for history over romance, where Jewish solidarity complements the moral seriousness of modernism.

Philip Roth combines two previous interests to break new ground, according to " 'This Obsessive Reinvention of the Real': Speculative Narrative in Philip Roth's *The Counterlife*" (*MFS* 37:197–215) by Debra Shostak; fiction about fiction and speculations regarding the relationship between art and life work together in this novel to "fully explore the theoretical implications that exist for the *structure* of fiction," a process that shatters conventions and deconstructs the unitary self while creating a profitable tension between metafictive authority and the "realistic texture of the speculative episodes." That *The Counterlife* is a breakthrough may be implied by Sanford Pinsker's view of the Zuckerman novels; whereas Roth had earlier maintained an autobiographical fidelity toward his fiction's generative conditions, here he seems beleaguered by postmodernism. Also central to Pinsker's *The Schlemiel as Metaphor: Studies in Yiddish and American Jewish Fiction* (So. Ill.) are interpretations of Isaac Bashevis Singer as an author dedicated to creating a subject matter that cannot otherwise be imagined (because of the changed circumstances of Jewish life in the post-World War II world) and of Woody Allen as a metaphysician of the persona whose "mused juxtapositions" offer a multidimensional view of character.

That Woody Allen merits sustained attention as a fictionist is established by Maurice Yacowar, whose *Loser Take All: The Comic Art of Woody Allen* (Continuum) suggests that a reinforcement of characterization by narrative strategy makes Allen more than a simple parodist. True, Allen's stories rely for part of their effect on the familiar comic image of a loser in a hostile world; but that loser's improbable dreams contribute to his often hilarious defeats, all of which are overlaid by the technique of the narrator's own inability to deal with subject matter as it contradicts itself and deconstructs.

vi Rolando Hinojosa, Ana Castillo, Thomas McGuane, and Others from the Southwest and West

Three important books mark the year as important for Chicano fiction. In *Chicano Satire: A Study in Literary Culture* (Texas) Guillermo E. Hernández studies the novelistic project of Rolando Hinojosa, whose interconnected series finds unity in a people's collective search for truth. Presented from a vernacular point of view, these narratives seek fragments of a traditional culture in the oral community, where mnemonic procedures maintain history and identity. The important role of personal narrative is analyzed by Alvina E. Quintana in "Ana Castillo's *The Mixquiahuala Letters: The Novelist as Ethnographer*" (pp. 72–83), a contribution to editors Héctor Calderón and José David Saldívar's *Criticism in the Borderlands: Studies in Chicano Literature, Culture, and Ideology* (Duke); ethnographies are now understood to be "written in the interest of the dominant culture," but in Castillo's "postmodern, Chicana feminist novel" newer techniques are employed to demarginalize narrative. Ethnological and other concerns motivate José David Saldívar's *The Dialectics of Our America: Genealogy, Cultural Critique, and Literary History* (Duke), where border narratives are seen as a cultural critique too often denied attention for prejudicial reasons. "U.S. Border history is clearly a serious contest of codes and representations," Saldívar notes, "and Hinojosa's chronicle necessarily involves the re-historicizing of the mythic subject and a historical account of its making" in addition to the linguistic transformations already credited in his work. A text excluded from the canon for majority-determined theoretical motives, Saldívar believes, is Arturo Islas's *The Rain God*, a novel that defies the Anglo-American New Critical stricture that "international literature [be] independent of all socio-temporal determinants."

Thomas McGuane's fiction likewise fights its way through critical limits traditionally placed on western novels. In "How Ambivalence Won the West: Thomas McGuane and the Fiction of the New West" (*Crit* 32:180–89) Gregory L. Morris cites McGuane's belief that "to accept the new West . . . we must first deny the complete, continued existence of the old"; this strategy yields a style of work that combines both affection and disdain for the region. Another writer "straying across the boundaries" and thereby modifying western fiction is studied by Jonah Raskin in *James D. Houston* (BSWWS); Houston's psychological and sociological view surveys society rather than the landscape and accepts tighter forms than western writers customarily favor. On the other hand, a more formulaic western (and at times romantic) approach can drive away critical attention, as Judy Alter finds in *Jeanne Williams* (BSWWS), an undeserved fate, given Williams's ability to fashion compelling narratives on a level with James Michener. An even more popular novelist dismissed too easily is given a second chance by Hal W. Hall in *The Works of Louis L'Amour* (Borgo). Already appreciated for his themes of family and the tradition of stories passed down through generations, L'Amour merits study for his increasingly complex view of Native Americans and for his almost postmodern mix of fact and fiction, a "cultural history lesson" that at the same time shows great imaginative invention.

vii Walker Percy, Cormac McCarthy, and Other Southerners

Long known as an apocalyptic writer, Walker Percy benefits from a distinction made by Gary M. Cuiba in *Walker Percy: Books of Revelations* (Georgia) that his eschatology proposes the demise of outer but not inner worlds. There is a way to live foreseen in the vision of one's own end, a path that avoids the temptations lurking in what Percy's work presents as typically modern and postmodern recourses. His protagonists benefit from a coming to consciousness that frees them from self-absorption and allows an attentiveness to the world that makes selfhood more evident as a part of larger being. This catastrophe is transformed into a "crisis of consciousness" that challenges these visionaries "when they have exhausted all their strategies to create a supposedly new world." A different view is taken in one of two important essays in editors Jan Nordby Gretlund and Karl-Heinz Westarp's *Walker Percy: Novelist and Philosopher* (Miss.), Elzbieta H. Oleksy's "Walker Percy's Demonic Vision" (pp. 199–209); here, *Launcelot* parallels *Moby-Dick* in its marriage of black and white and the sanity of controlled madness in a biblical vision that Oleksy sees as a blend of maternal and bridal vision. "Will Barrett Redux?" (pp. 42–51) lets Joseph Schwartz prove that "there is a completeness about *The Last Gentleman* that argues against the kind of sequel Percy wrote" in *The Second Coming:* "The work is successfully enclosed within its form, each element in harmony with every other." *The Second Coming* is better seen as a success on its own terms, for as a sequel it lessens Will's crucial discovery. Percy's own collection of essays, *Signpost in a Strange Land* (Farrar), is of special value to scholars for the author's "Questions They Never Asked Me" (pp. 397–423), including comments on artistic as opposed to scientific explorations of reality, and "An Interview with Zoltán Abádi-Nagy" (pp. 373–96).

Attention to an increasingly prominent author continues with Terri Witek's " 'He's Well When He's Well': Cormac McCarthy's Rhyming Dictions" (*Shenandoah* 41:51–66) and Andrew Bartlett's "From Voyeurism to Archaeology: Cormac McCarthy's *Child of God*" (*SLJ* 24, i:3–15). The "furthest reaches of both educated and rustic dictions" contribute to McCarthy's "single narrative," Witek shows—in a close, sensitive reading that appreciates how "things can be both syntactically equal yet always relentlessly individual." In similar manner Bartlett finds that the powerful attraction of McCarthy's antagonist comes not from his grotesque character but from "the play of positions taken by the narrator" through which we see him. Another novelist worthy of note speaks his own piece in editor Jefferson Humphries's *Conversations with Reynolds Price* (Miss.), a collection of interviews dating from 1966 through 1989. One special value of this fine series of "Conversations" books has been a uniform diligence in seeking out early, often fugitive pieces; another is the individual editor's ability to undertake a new, comprehensive interview that benefits from all the rest, which Humphries does in a crucially important talk with Price that includes cogent analysis of the women's voice in *Kate Vaiden* as the autobiographical memoir of an imagined character in which the imaginative demands of both death itself (the ultimately unverifiable experience) combines with the emotional task of imagining motherhood (for a man another unverifiable experience) to create an uncommonly convincing narrative.

Another triumph of the fictive imagination, in which life and death, madness and sanity, and health and sickness are made organic and not distinct is outlined by Elsa Nettels in "Elizabeth Spencer" (pp. 70–96), a contribution to editor Tonette Bond Inge's *Southern Women Writers: The New Generation* (Alabama); also in that book is Jean Haskell Speer's "Montani Semper Liberi: Mary Lee Settle and the Myths of Appalachia" (pp. 20–45), an essay establishing how Settle is less interested in nostalgia than in meaning (specifically the "dendritic patterns of taproots and growth"). In *Mary Lee Settle's Beulah Quintet* (LSU) Brian Rosenberg argues in similar fashion that these novels are less "historical fiction" than a carefully constructed, continuous narrative action, and that they are not romances but rather contributions to the mainstream of American literature. What history there is is deconstructed through the oppositions of empowerment and powerlessness, dispossession and being dispossessed, governing and being governed, Anglo-Saxon and non-Anglo-Saxon, and ultimately male and female. A use of the present tense maintains Settle's characters in the narrative stream, yielding a form of apprehension akin to that of the *nouveau roman.* Another writer whose work can be much more than it seems is given able treatment by Alice Hall Petry, whose *Understanding Anne Tyler* (So. Car., 1990) places her subject in the Russian tradition of defining characters through their relationships. Whether self and community, self and family, or selves themselves, Tyler's people are often distinguished as figures who do not quite fit where they are; their potential includes the chance to grow beyond such debilities.

As for new trends in the criticism of contemporary southern fiction, two books stand out: Elizabeth Jane Harrison's *Female Pastoral: Women Writers Re-Visioning the American South* (Tennessee) and Fred Hobson's *The Southern Writer and the Postmodern World* (Georgia). Harrison is noteworthy for her progression of subjects: Ellen Glasgow, Margaret Mitchell, Willa Cather, Harriette Arnow, and then not the predictable figures of earlier studies of the contemporary South but Alice Walker and Sherley Anne Williams. Walker's *The Color Purple* is studied for its re-visioning of the rural community, a process that alters the male pastoral vision by neither having to escape from nor flee to "the southern garden." Sexism and racism are handled sequentially rather than simultaneously in this novel, allowing black male power to share the same roots as white supremacy: "the desire for ownership and control over others' lives." Williams's *Dessa Rose* "imagines a different world from Alice Walker's *The Color Purple*" but is only superficially "plantation fiction" thanks to its dismantling of worlds and questioning of archetypes. Postmodernism is another contemporary feature only now making its critical impact on southern fiction, but Fred Hobson traces changes in southern assumptions back to the transformation of social reality in the 1960s. Definitely not postmodernist was Walker Percy, whose work accepts the world rather than fantasies and does not question the conventions of narrative or the nature of fiction itself. How are postmodern influences being expressed? Hobson cites the minimalism of Bobbie Ann Mason (as opposed to the more common historical approach), the reversals against folk society apparent in the fiction of Lee Smith, Barry Hannah's freedom from other influences in favor of a fabulative interest in tall tales, Richard Ford's culturing of the role of southern expatriate, and Josephine Humphreys's effective satire of the Percy novel of ideas.

viii Norman Mailer, Sylvia Plath, Joyce Carol Oates, and Others in the Realistic Tradition

For Mailer and Plath, biography sets the tone for this year's scholarship. Carl Rollyson's *The Lives of Norman Mailer* (Paragon) sees its subject from the perspective of his involvements in the literary world: organizing the PEN Congress (which many women writers found infamous), attempting to rehabilitate the murderer Jack Abbott, being involved with wives on an increasingly literary-world level (much is made of Norris Church being the close friend of Jill Krementz, who is the wife of Kurt Vonnegut), and so forth. Slanted as it is toward the Mailer who has striven to dominate the literary scene in New York, Rollyson's book is valuable simply because such personal advertisements and dramatic posturings in the world of literary politics have indeed consumed several decades of Mailer's career. In *The Death and Life of Sylvia Plath* (Carol) Ronald Hayman faces the same obstacle as Paul Alexander in *Rough Magic: A Biography of Sylvia Plath* (Viking): Olwyn Hughes's alleged management of Plath's literary estate in the interest of Ted Hughes. Hayman attempts to correct Olwyn Hughes's influence on previous biographical writings (such as those by Anne Stevenson and Dido Merwin) and centers his interpretation on Plath's death and its interpenetration with her writing. While less interpretive, Alexander's account becomes almost pryingly intrusive, including candid details from Plath's psychotherapy. The common new ground for both studies is that walked by Plath and her dates at college, the sometimes salacious nature of which may have been a factor in their commercial publication. Literary analysis is stronger in Pat McPherson's *Reflecting on the Bell Jar* (Routledge), where Plath's life is seen against a backdrop of mid-1950s conformity (which included an official cultural language, Red-baiting paranoia, anxiety over the Rosenberg executions, and a climate of surveillance and exposure that fostered tensions between the secret and public aspects of life). The Rosenbergs were an important influence on Plath's literary vision, McPherson believes, as were the claustrophobia and breakdown of suburban home life and the self-betrayal of alien mothers.

Joyce Carol Oates's fascination with boxing is an important part of

The Culture of Pain (Calif.); David B. Morris shows how, for Oates, tragedy has changed since Aristotle's definition, with boxing unable to provide a catharsis of pity and fear but existing nevertheless as something "darker and fiercer than we know" and functioning thus as a remnant of tragedy. E. L. Doctorow's clever use of apparent realism prompts Christopher D. Morris to study his methods in *Models of Misrepresentation: On the Fiction of E. L. Doctorow* (Miss.); these methods "eventually disclose the artifice that created this false impression." Representing America is both an imperative and an impossibility, Doctorow finds, and therefore he turns to a Nietzchean concept of "eternal return" as a way of showing how repetition is inherent in the act of narrative itself, with death occurring only when linguistic representation (necessarily) fails. Astute use of theories promulgated by Paul de Man and Jacques Derrida shows the author's distrust of hermeneutics and employment of misinterpretation as a fictive strategy (in which "mistaking the arbitrary for the real" leads to a correction that is in fact a "new figuration"). A more traditional reliance on voice is credited by J. K. Van Dover in *Understanding William Kennedy* (So. Car.); location is important in Kennedy's work, but even more so are alienations and dislocations, the activity of which both generates and anchors Kennedy's narratives. In *Understanding John Irving* (So. Car.) Edward C. Reilly draws on interviews and book-business notes to picture his subject as an author moralistically involved with his own characters' happiness. Granted, Irving's fiction has grown increasingly affirmative. Reilly notes that his later novels are strong on plot and short on most other techniques, beyond being expansively Victorian—but without fully explaining how this trend grows from (or contradicts) Irving's earlier work.

Garrison Keillor: A Voice of America (Miss.) by Judith Yaross Lee corrects the popular image of Keillor as a genial yarn-spinner from the great white North. Instead, he is a self-consciously fictive performer, whose conflicting feelings about Minnesota are managed by dramatizing them as a love/hate relationship. *Lake Woebegon Days* harbors a deep distrust beneath its gestures toward the idyllic, just as a darkness lurks within the humor of Keillor's short stories. These tall tales deflate rural innocence and sentimentality, and while sounding mildly condescending when told to radio audiences become scornful as published fiction. Yet, as George H. Douglas notes in *The Smart Magazines* (Archon), the *New Yorker* prints Keillor as another practitioner in its long and distinguished line of writers who purvey "superior humor and light material," an important factor in the magazine's ability to "renew its readership appeal year after year."

Realism in its minimalistic variety is studied by David Wyatt in "Ann Beattie" (*SoR* 28:145–59) and Kirk Nesset in " 'This Word Love': Sexual Politics and Silence in Early Raymond Carver" (*AL* 63:292–313). It is "the possessiveness of love" that motivates Beattie's fiction, a process that leads her to abandon "irony for ambiguity, coolness for arousal," and to discard the understated manner of minimalism in her later work. Love and its absence, however, are strong themes in Carver's earliest fiction and anticipate his strongest work, much of which strives to see that little can be made of a diminished thing.

A counterforce to the Beattie-Carver minimalism has been the more exuberantly thematic work of novelists such as Tom Wolfe, Bret Easton Ellis, and Jay McInerney, the commercial dynamics of which are played against literary theory by David Kaufmann in "Yuppie Postmodernism" (*ArQ* 47, ii:93–116). Nicki Sahlin's " 'But This Road Doesn't Go Anywhere': The Existential Dilemma in *Less Than Zero*" (*Crit* 33:23–42) reads Ellis's novel as an endorsement of survival over its world's nihilistic alternatives. George Plimpton draws out Tom Wolfe on *The Bonfire of the Vanities* in "The Art of Fiction CXXII: Tom Wolfe" (*ParisR* 118:92–121), a conversation that touches on Wolfe's growth from personal journalism.

ix The Mannerists: John Updike and John Cheever

Autobiography is the major contribution to this year's shelf of Updike and Cheever materials, although a John Updike issue of *Modern Fiction Studies* (37) provides a thorough updating, both bibliographically and interpretationally, since the journal's last number devoted to this author in 1974. That a contemporary writer merits two issues says a great deal, although the range of critical essays offered holds a clue. Updike is capable of fiction both unique (*The Coup*) and accumulative (the Rabbit tetralogy, the trilogy responding to sexual structures in *The Scarlet Letter*, and his pair of Henry Bech volumes), and these are the books *MFS* surveys. Three essays deal with Updike's treatment of Harry "Rabbit" Angstrom: Derek Wright's study of form and space in *Rabbit, Run* (where gestures toward love struggle against the clutter and constriction of a limiting world), Stacey Olster's careful reading of *Rabbit at Rest* as a re-visioning of Harry's life (accomplished by a rerun of its formative popular culture elements), and Matthew Wilson's survey of the full tetralogy (where predetermined forms are embraced rather than rejected). For Barbara Leckie, *Marry Me* dramatizes the tension between the privacy of adultery and our culture's trend to go public on the issue; John N. Duvall finds *Roger's Version* to be generated by an opposition between deviance and normality, "the play of difference in the theological (heresy/orthodoxy)" mapping "the realm of desire (pornography/erotica)." Henry Bech is an image of Saul Bellow's "distracted writer writ large, Jewish, and befuddled," Sanford Pinsker suggests, while Malini Schueller regards *The Coup* as "simultaneously an attempt to contain anticolonial and anti-imperialist resistance," a text that "simultaneously empowers the norms of middle-class America and works to contain the threat of revolution and Otherness that the Third World poses." In the issue's most valuable essay, "Updike's New Versions of Myth in America" (pp. 25–33), Basem L. Ra'ad draws on the autobiographical *Self-Consciousness* to explain apparent contradictions in the author's fiction and criticism of it; present conditions in the world make myth more difficult to fashion even as it is more desperately needed, and therefore Updike "presents us with forms of fetishes and myths that are distinctly modern and American rather than with anything that has much to do with the mythic creations of the past," diagramming "the un-natural but formative landscapes which generate such new private and public forms of myth." *Self-Consciousness* also interests Peter J. Bailey, whose " 'Why Not Tell the Truth?': The Autobiographies of Three Fiction Writers" (*Crit* 32:211–23) contrasts Updike's work with Philip Roth's *The Facts* and Tobias Wolff's *This Boy's Life* as "staunchly Modernist" in its insistence "on the absolute divisibility of literature and life and in [its] assumption that the former represents an improvement upon, or refinement of, the latter."

John Cheever's life becomes increasingly fascinating, as the years following his death have been filled with numerous revelations of and commentaries on his alcoholism (and recovery), adulteries, and bisexual preferences. The contradictions implied by this Brooks Brothers-attired country gentleman are evident in his own *The Journals of John Cheever* (Knopf), the pages of which range from the later 1940s to his death in 1982. Scholars will wish to compare Cheever's musings on God and Nature, home and sexuality, with his daughter Susan's *Treetops* (Bantam), a memoir that suggests her mother was repressed by John Cheever's artistry and expresses embarrassment at his fictive use of family events.

One more reminder that from this troubled life Cheever could produce "a minor masterpiece" comes from Robert A. Hipkiss in " 'The Country Husband'—A Model Cheever Achievement" (*SSF* 27:577–85); dependent less on plot than images, this story "creates the richness of emotional awareness for the reader" by mixing images in a dramatics of epistemology.

x Kurt Vonnegut, Donald Barthelme, and Other Innovators

Two more especially sound books in Bruccoli's "Understanding Contemporary American Literature" series provide firm grounding for the innovations in American fiction so prevalent since *Cat's Cradle* and *Catch-22*. William Rodney Allen's *Understanding Kurt Vonnegut* (So. Car.) centers on the author's most experimental period, reading *Mother Night* as a tautly structured and tightly focused narrative confession, *Cat's Cradle* as an exuberant test of such limits, *God Bless You, Mr. Rosewater* as a significant shift to realism, and *Slaughterhouse-Five* as a masterful transposition of time and space. Among the later works, Allen prefers *Jailbird* and *Bluebeard* for their apt renderings of important cultural, social, and political issues. In *Understanding Joseph Heller* (So. Car.) Sanford Pinsker probes the disorder Heller seeks at the "anxious edge" of existence; far beyond thematic referentiality, Heller's language functions as a story in itself by means of use and misuse. Heller's continuing appeal lies in his persistence of comic dialogue with the insanities of life—even the relentless medical challenge to this antic spirit in *No Laughing Matter* cannot keep the satirist down.

Despite the controversy over alleged plagiarism that dogged the last decade of his life, Jerzy Kosinski continues to merit first-class scholarly attention. Especially wide-reaching is Gloria L. Cronin and Blaine H. Hall's *Jerzy Kosinski: An Annotated Bibliography* (Greenwood), which tracks down virtually everything by and about this fascinating author. Virtually, but not literally—missing is any reference to a late essay that Kosinski considered one of his most important, but which was rejected by all his customary markets and appeared as journalism in the *Boston Globe's* "Focus" section (pp. A1, A19) on 4 November 1990: "The Second Holocaust," which argued "American Jews are so obsessed with the Nazi killings that they're destroying their own culture and character." The finest single study yet is by Welch D. Everman; his *Jerzy Kosinski: The Literature of Violation* (Borgo) tracks protagonists so free that even terms such as "self" and "individual" have no interpretive bearing, a circumstance that forces the critic to devise uniquely postmodern strategies of comprehending the consequent narrative force.

Another lull in Barth and Hawkes scholarship puts two important studies into higher profile. In "Practicing Post-Modernism: The Example of John Hawkes" (*ConL* 32:29–57) John M. Unsworth examines several creative and critical texts to show how "first generation postmodernism" has been safely institutionalized within the influential walls of the university. Thomas Schaub contributes "Allusion and Intertext: History in *The End of the Road,*" pp. 181–203 in *Influence and Intertextuality*. John Barth's novel, Schaub indicates, is based on history and readings of earlier works, with "a multitude of cultural discourses traversing the text." The character's voice that produces this text is repudiated, as experience eclipses reason's ability to track it (a case of the descriptive taking precedence over the prescriptive).

William H. Gass flourishes as the subject of an issue of *Review of Contemporary Fiction* (11, iii) guest-edited by Arthur M. Saltzman. Saltzman's interview with Gass sets the tone by capturing the author's thoughts on the bland predictability of minimalism ("When I've read about two sentences of Ray Carver, I know the whole sense of the story") as compared to the extraordinary surprise of more innovative work (which rejects the commercial junkiness so popular among the MFA-trained new realists). Saltzman also selects letters from the Gass archive at Washington University's Olin Library and presents important essays on Gass's relation to reality (by Philip Stevick), his Emersonian transcendence (by Richard J. Schneider), and a number of pieces on the author's short fiction. Another leading critic, Marc Chénetier, conducts "A Conversation with William H. Gass" (*RFEA* 51:89–94) on issues spatial and musical, including textual strategies for distancing the narrative voice from the authorial voice. Gass himself undertakes revealing critical responses to a wide variety of texts in *Fifty Literary Pillars* (Olin Library, Washington University), an important document that establishes his fundamentally classical position toward literary art.

By a combination of coincidence and cooperation Pynchon scholars this year have focused on their subject's second (and by far the shortest) novel. Editor Patrick O'Donnell's *New Essays on* The Crying of Lot 49 (Cambridge) features essays by various hands, most notably Bernard Duyfhuizen's "'Hushing Sick Transmissions': Disrupting Story in *The Crying of Lot 49*" (pp. 79–95), where patterns of cultural transmission occur in texts beyond the visible, often in silence. Manfred Pütz probes "The Art of the Acronym in Thomas Pynchon" (*SNNTS* 23:371–82) to decode the cryptograms of this same novel; as multidimensional signifiers, they are both intertextual and thematically referential, challenging the heroine to bring structure and meaning "to the chaotic phenomena of a given world that precisely refuses to yield forms of order and meaningful structure." *Pynchon Notes* 24–25 (1989) approaches the novel from two perspectives: Vivienne Rundle's "The Double Bind of Metafiction: Implicating Narrative in *The Crying of Lot 49* and Travesty" (pp. 31–44) and Mark Conroy's "The American Way and Its Double in *The Crying of Lot 49*" (pp. 45–70); instability of narrative voice creates a fruitful readerly oscillation between acceptance and rejection that allows the novel to explore "the limits of its own existence," while its detective-novel qualities allow the failure of Oedpia's quest to reveal important facts and attitudes about the American consumerist society in which she searches.

An interesting correspondence between Pynchon and Robert Coover is drawn by Christopher Ames in *The Life of the Party: Festive Vision in Modern Fiction* (Georgia). In *Gravity's Rainbow* one finds "a carnivalized consciousness," an encyclopedic mix of discourses that transposes highs and lows, reverses roles, plays form against content, and contrasts festivity's preservation of order with its more apparent subversion of it. Coover's novel *Gerald's Party* uses carnival for both thematic and formal purposes; like the text itself, the party runs out of control, different novelistic elements colliding as phantasmagoric possibilities grow in the festive setting. Coover thus expands the possibilities of fictive form by intersecting conflicting codes, much in the manner of carnival.

Donald Barthelme joins the party in an extremely important book by Paul Maltby, *Dissident Postmodernists: Barthelme, Coover, Pynchon* (Penn.). The three are chosen for their representative responses to the social history and politics of their times. Rather than dismissing the world as irrational, Barthelme studies its "late-capitalist culture" in order to question postmodern America's definition of the political. Coover's critique is of a "technocratic culture" that generates its own meaning system. Pynchon's view is the most cautionary, that humanism is "a precarious cultural construct that, under certain historical conditions, may disappear." Especially notable for its revealingly close readings, Maltby's study establishes what other theorists have suggested may be the essentially conservative nature of Barthelme's, Coover's, and Pynchon's fiction.

Yet there remains a radical dimension to Barthelme's work that qualifies it as at least transitional to the outright surfictionality of authors such as Ronald Sukenick, Raymond Federman, and Walter Abish. Stanley Trachtenberg's *Understanding Donald Barthelme* (So. Car., 1990) describes the writer "straining, at least in part, toward the world," with the sometimes apparent agony (and more often comedy) of that effort yielding patently metafictive effects. My own *Donald Barthelme: An Exhibition* (Duke) traces a progression from linguistic distancing to textual involvement with *The Dead Father* as the center of Barthelme's canon. Two special issues devoted to his full range of fiction and literary activities, *Review of Contemporary Fiction* (11, ii) and *Gulf Coast* (4, i) (the latter published by the late author's writing program at the University of Houston), confirm this dual nature of Barthelme's quest: to be both in the world and in the text generated from that world. As Guy Davenport notes in the title to his *RCF* essay, "Style as Protagonist in Donald Barthelme" (pp. 69–74), Barthelme succeeds Hemingway just as Hemingway succeeds Kipling, Hemingway having declared Kipling the world's worst writer—such are the motivations for style becoming a voice in itself. (Both journals are also replete with biographical commentaries on how Barthelme's presence in the literary world was just such a voice in itself.)

Gilbert Sorrentino's presence is attested to by William McPheron, whose *Gilbert Sorrentino: A Descriptive Bibliography* (Dalkey Archive) includes such pertinent and extensive annotations of the history of this author's publications as to qualify as historical analysis. *Mulligan Stew* is reviewed in M. Keith Booker's *Techniques of Subversion in Modern Literature* (Florida); Sorrentino's masterwork undertakes a subversive dialogue with itself, Booker states, the novel using parody and outright undercutting to be "continually different from itself."

Two pieces of work by the British critic David Seed are worth seeking out: "Raymond Federman," an interview published in Hull (*Bête Noir* 10–11:180–86) and *Rudolph Wurlitzer, American Novelist and Screenwriter* (Mellen). Samuel Beckett's influence on each writer is important, and just as Federman calls for a new understanding of how such formal experimentation still has referential pertinence, so Wurlitzer's fiction strives to fill a referential gap (the American West of postmodern times, where the novelist sees empty space waiting to be defined by movement through it).

Scholars of the innovative turn increasingly to the work of Don DeLillo. The issue of *South Atlantic Quarterly* (89, ii [1990]) devoted to analysis of his fiction (see *ALS 1990*, p. 326) has been enlarged as *Introducing Don DeLillo* (Duke), in which editor Frank Lentricchia includes his "*Libra* as Postmodern Critique" (pp. 193–215), an essay that finds Lee Harvey Oswald becoming a postmodern figure when he enters the world's televised aura (movie voices speak through him, and his experience is received as if Watergate and Iran-Contra had already happened). Lentricchia also edits *New Essays on White Noise* (Cambridge), where ground is broken by Paul A. Cantor's "Adolf, We Hardly Knew You" (pp. 39–62), a study of how Hitler is defended and even admired because his enormity lies beyond the range of rational discourse (in postmodernism, everything is equally available, causing DeLillo to get stuck in his materials).

xi Fiction at War and in Sport

In an age when fiction sometimes plays a touch-and-go game with the referentiality of subject matter, warfare and sports offer chances to measure the fictive against observable standards. Editor Nancy Anisfield's *The Nightmare Considered: Critical Essays on Nuclear War Literature* (Bowling Green) includes Lee Schweinger's thoughts on Tim O'Brien's novel, *The Nuclear Age*, Tom Hearron's study of various guilt-inspired cataclysms in Kurt Vonnegut's novels, and my own appraisal of how Vonnegut's career consists of one long duty-dance with the looming possibility of mass destruction. If nuclear warfare is a challenge to the imagination, so was Vietnam, a war that refused to follow either conventional military strategies or literary stereotypes. In *Re-Writing America: Vietnam Authors and Their Generation* (Georgia) Philip D. Beidler traces the "new and creative alliances between literature and the work of cultural revision," a process that includes Tim O'Brien's new morality based on cultural myths, James Webb's renewal of older soldierly virtues, Philip Caputo's neotraditionalist way of dealing with posttraumatic stress, Robert Olen Butler's archetypal view of the outsider, and most significantly Larry Heinemann's rewriting of memory as an "ongoing revisionary encounter with the sundry mythologies of the national culture at large." Good analyses of a key domestic novel are found in David Booth's "Sam's Quest, Emmett's Wound: Grail Motifs in Bobbie Ann Mason's Portrait of America After Vietnam" (*SLJ* 23, ii:98–109) and in Katherine Kinney's "'Humping the Boonies': Sex, Combat, and the Female in Bobbie Ann Mason's *In Country*," pp. 38–48 in editor

Philip K. Jason's *Fourteen Landing Zones: Approaches to Vietnam War Literature* (Iowa), a volume that also features Maria S. Bonn's "The Vietnam Veteran Novel Comes Home" (pp. 1–16), an insightful look at what happens to idyllic visions in the face of contrary new mythologies. Joan Didion's more generalized approach to war as defined by husbands and families is treated by Lynne Hanley in *Writing War: Fiction, Gender and Memory* (Mass.).

Several volumes attest to the growing importance of sports as a critical topic in literature. In *Sporting with the Gods* Michael Oriard speaks of the dualism in American culture that indulges in play while worrying that such play should be repressed. In contemporary fiction this trend remains evident in the ways that Barth and Pynchon use sports as a vehicle for alienation from society rather than for integration with it, just as Kosinski often uses athletic endeavors for victimization rather than achievement. Among the innovators, Gilbert Sorrentino and Ronald Sukenick are described as using "chance" rather than formalism or experiment in their work. In my own *Writing Baseball* (Illinois) and "Structuring *Short Season*" (*Short Story* 2, i:46–60) I address the idea that baseball in particular avoids metafictional problems with representation because it is already something made up (with actions and characters already devised and meaning nothing other than themselves).

Christian K. Messenger, whose *Sport and the Spirit of Play in Contemporary American Fiction* (*ALS 1990*, p. 300) helped start this trend, continues it with "Expansion Draft: Baseball Fiction of the 1980s," pp. 62–79, in editor Wiley Lee Umphlett's *The Achievement of American Sport in Literature* (Fairleigh Dickinson). Citing the 1919 Black Sox scandal as baseball's "primal cautionary tale," Messenger goes on to analyze the magic and fantasticism evident in James McManus's *Chin Music* and W. P. Kinsella's *The Iowa Baseball Confederacy* and the lyricism of Nancy Willard's *Things Invisible to See*. That an entire industry for such products exists is evident from editor Alvin L. Hall's *Cooperstown Symposium on Baseball and the American Culture: 1989* (Meckler), a volume containing four good essays on baseball fiction, chief among them Peter C. Bjarkman's "Baseball Novels from Gil Gamesh to Babe Ragland to Sidd Finch" (pp. 32–59). No critic knows this area of fiction better than Bjarkman, and his exhaustive bibliographical survey is prefaced with an excellent synthesis of the form's development and virtual renaissance in recent years.

University of Northern Iowa

16 Poetry: The 1940s to the Present

Richard J. Calhoun

This year was one of collections of essays by critics—M. L. Rosenthal, Peter Davison, Marjorie Perloff—who have profoundly contributed to our understanding of contemporary poetry and have reviewed most of the modern poets prominent during 20th-century literature's postmodernist phase. Comprehensive studies of contemporary poetry appeared, both a survey and a "profile." There was even an award-winning book on postmodernism, but its concerns were loftier than business with a single genre like poetry. There was interest in how traditional issues have fared in the postmodernist period, such as the "sublime" or the feasibility of the long poem. Ongoing interest in southern literature expanded a bit to include poetry. Even more momentous than "overviews" is the continuing literary "market value" of some poets, the up-and-down fluctuation of others, and efforts to discover new poets and rediscover neglected ones. Interest in women poets continues to flourish, notably Sylvia Plath and Anne Sexton, with another good year for Elizabeth Bishop. Feminism is a force, but there is now more emphasis on craft and less on feminist politics and thematics. There was an explosion of interest by critics and ecologists alike in Gary Snyder and an ongoing interest in James Wright and James Dickey. Tribute is still being paid to the fallen poet laureate, Robert Penn Warren. Robert Lowell is still held in critical regard, as is Theodore Roethke, and interest in John Berryman multiplies.

For research on African-American poetry, I am again indebted to the work and expertise of my colleague at Clemson, Abasi Malik.

i Overviews, Collections

Gertrude Stein warned Ernest Hemingway against writing anything that was *inaccrochable,* by which she meant the prose equivalent of a picture that cannot be hung. The question about a general survey like Richard Gray's *American Poetry of the Twentieth Century* (Longman) is where it can be useful, given what it is. Gray's book was not designed to offer new insights or to be a thesis-oriented study of the relationships of modernism and postmodernism; it is described forthrightly as an introduction to individual American poets of our century and their relationship to the idea of the poem in America, with a special interest in charting the move from modernism to postmodernism. Gray does rather well in meeting all of his objectives, but he is at his best in capsule surveys of individual writers. He offers a concise but necessarily oversimplified view of the movements surveyed—including the modernist experiment, the traditions of Whitman, formalists and confessionals, Beats, prophets, and aesthetes. An appendix even includes a brief consideration of the problem of literary analogy with England, using T. S. Eliot as the case study. The bibliographies are brief and fairly up-to-date. There is little danger of this survey being *inaccrochable,* since nothing else except David Perkins's more theoretical two-volume *History of Anglo-American Modern Poetry* is current on the market. The new *Columbia Literary History* provides better critical insights into the limited number of poets that it includes, but it excludes too much to be a useful survey. Gray has a long-term interest in southern literature, which would help explain a separate chapter devoted to "the fugitive movement." Overall, his survey has a dominant fairness, a welcome nonpartisanship as to literary movements and directions, perhaps because of the objectivity of an English critic who teaches American literature abroad.

In yet another survey, this time designated "a profile," Jack Myers and David Wojahn have edited *A Profile of Twentieth-Century American Poetry* (So. Ill.), announced as an attempt to fill the need for a comprehensive history of its subject. The collection of essays is not intended to ride any particular thesis hard but to avoid narrow perspectives and to "restore an eclectic, comprehensive, and humanistic overview of American poetry." Ed Folsom was invited to give a scholarly and critical overview, and the rest of the contributors, all working poets, to provide a perspective from his or her own "cultural, historical, craft aesthetic." Folsom's overview is advertised as being different because it includes more than the official literary tradition, incorporating commentary on popular, ethnic, politically radical, and gender literature—in short, offering "political correctness." The overview specifies "continual interreflections" among "periods of upheaval and critical assessments." This means affinities are found among the modernist revolt against its Victorian heritage, the revolt of the left in the '30s against modernism, and the postmodernist revolt of the '50s and '60s against modernism and the New Critical formalism. Changes detected include a decline in Eliot's stature and a dismissal of New Critical views, a turning away from poetry of social and political protest to an advocacy of the feminist movement, suspicion of the New Academics, and a growing restlessness and dissatisfaction among the confessional, surrealist, and Deep Image modes of poetry. The chapters relevant to poetry are decade studies: Mark Doty, "The 'Forbidden Planet' of Character: The Revolutions of the 1950s" (pp. 102–30); Leslie Ullman, "American Poetry in the 1960s" (pp. 190–224); Jonathan Holden, "American Poetry: 1970–1990" (pp. 254–76). There are ethnic and gender studies: Timothy Seibles, "A Quilt in Stages of Black: The Black Aesthetic in Twentieth-Century African American Poetry" (pp. 158–89); Kate Daniels, "The Demise of the 'Delicate': The Women's Movement in Twentieth-Century American Poetry" (pp. 224–53). I especially enjoyed Doty's account of the "domestication of modernism" faced by poets in the 1950s. He provides a fresh view of an important moment in the history of American poetry, one in which poets felt the imperative to reinvent colloquial language. The title comes from one of the best science-fiction movies of the '50s, *Forbidden Planet,* in which "voyagers in an unknown territory in outer space encounter 'beasts from the id' which are projections of their own psyches." What poets did in poetry then was to push "at the boundaries of formal canons to make room for personal vision." The poets discussed are those practicing "open forms"—Charles Olson, Robert Creeley, Robert Duncan, Denise Levertov, and a rediscovery, Weldon Kees; the Beats—Allen Ginsberg, Gregory Corso; the "New York School"—Frank O'Hara and John Ashbery. There is something of value, if not new, in the discussion of the contributions made in later poetry by "exploring the possibility of the self as narrator"—Berryman, Roethke, Bishop. Lowell provided an individual voice, "the individual mode of perception enacted in language," which became "the driving force for new American poetry." Ullman's survey of the '60s is at its best in his account of the Deep Imagists.

Anthony Easthope and John O. Thompson have edited *Contemporary Poetry Meets Modern Theory* (Toronto) with the intention of contrasting two relationships: the one between current practice in poetry and a deconstructive critical theory that denies the text as existing apart from the way it is read in a context of interpretation. A second contrast exists between the New Criticism, which presumed that the literary text was given as a verbal icon "in which the imaginative and sympathetic could participate on the basis of shared human values," and the poetry of its time. In the context of deconstruction, the poem is no longer the point of origin but exists only in the process of its reading. Nevertheless, there are possible benefits: Derridean deconstruction not only has made it possible to enjoy the poetry of a poet who writes in as challenging a manner as Ashbery, but it has influenced the way in which poets think about their poems. The essay exemplary for what deconstruction can do for our understanding of poetry is Steve Connor's analysis in "Points of Departure: Deconstruction and John Ashbery's 'Sortes Vergilianae' " (pp. 5–18). The problem with this Ashbery poem, as with others, Connor believes, is that it seems in its own terms "deconstructive." That Ashbery is the poet for deconstruction is hardly a discovery; what is fresh is a reading of a poem that requires finding a narrative and then requiring a deconstruction of that narrative through interruption of the very time-scale and sequence of the life journey that the poem seems to imply. Richard Rand ("Sortes Vergilianae," pp. 19–33) explores the same poem, raising a question about the cost of attempting to read an Ashbery poem against the profit that finally comes from the act. He is hardly the first to have wondered. Rand effectively explores the poem's possible topics, maxims, struggles, victories, origins, duplications, revelations, and concealments. The compensation may be that, even if the poem says nothing at all, it does entertain us with an analogy. Jerome McGann reads another difficult poem, "Charles Bernstein's 'The Simply' " (pp. 34–39), more briefly and less complexly, managing to place it as the opening poem of *The Sophist.* I also would commend Harriet Davidson's " 'In the Wake of Home': Adrienne Rich's Politics and Poetics of Location" (pp. 166–93) as a welcome shift from a preoccupation with Rich's feminist poetry to her political poetry. In the 1960s Rich pioneered not only in feminist poetry but in political concerns with matters of "race, class, ethnicity, and sexual preference." Davidson's informative analysis of the ambivalences in the 1983 poem "In the Wake of Home" identifies it as "a site of contradiction in a politics of location." I also should mention Helen M. Dennis's "Adrienne Rich: Consciousness-Raising as Poetic Method" (pp. 177–94), written from an Anglo-American "gynocentric" point of view. Rich has "confronted and resolved" as both poet and feminist critic the conflict of where her allegiances lie, "with literary theory or with women's lives." Her poetry is informed "strategic feminist analysis and conceptualization"; her prose uses the strategies of the confessional mode "to make connections between the autobiographical or 'personal' and the public, cultural arena, i.e. the 'political.'" Rich has kept an "accurate register" of her own intellectual development, creating a record of "the changes in consciousness which have occurred for WASP women in the past forty years." Dennis discerns stages in this consciousness-raising, from an awareness of working in a formalist, masculinist tradition, to reinventing a woman's feminist rhetoric, to a confrontation with other issues beyond what the public persona has allowed.

Marjorie Perloff's *Radical Artifice: Writing Poetry in the Age of Media* (Chicago) engages a major problem of current poetry: rather than the old neo-Romantic bohemian one of the alienated poet and a hostile mass media, a portrait of a poetic medium, contaminated by mass media, which actively makes use of the communication models of everyday discourse. Perloff targets the modernist concern, not only with speech rhythms and diction, but with the "natural speech" of television talk shows, with the visual impact of billboards, and the sound bites of advertising. More meets the eye here than can be summarized verbally; the medium is clearly the message, and the book is almost as full of visual devices as the poetry and the media discourse that it describes. It is an attempt to answer a question that a student from Eastern Europe asked her: why current writers cannot face a confusing world and still write as lucidly as Kafka did. She views postmodernism as signaling the breakdown between high art and mass culture, and as featuring a criticism that scrutinizes popular art with the care once reserved for the high art of Donne or Flaubert. Nevertheless, academic criticism and classroom practice continue to treat the literary text as an object detachable from its context in an electronic culture. Central to her analysis are the poetry and music and silences of the late John Cage. The book contains a great deal of theory and far more of popular culture than of contemporary poetry; but brief attention is profitably given to Ashbery, George Oppen, Clark Coolidge, Creeley, Susan Howe, Philip Levine, Steve McCaffery, Ron Silliman, Louis Zukofsky, concrete poetry, and language poetry. The breadth of coverage is more impressive than the depth.

Perloff's *Poetic License: Essays on Modernist and Postmodernist Lyric* (Northwestern, 1990) was not received for review last year. Certainly the postmodernist dimension of this book deserves comment; and even though the essays were previously published, they were revised variously for republication here. Among these, "The Two Ariels: The (RE)Making of the Sylvia Plath Canon" (as devastatingly fair an account of Ted Hughes's role as there is) and "Apocalypse Then: W. S. Merwin and the Sorrows of Literary History" have been previously reviewed and recommended. The 1986 essay " 'Howl' and Its Enemies" has been combined with a 1985 review of Ginsberg's *Collected Poems,* then revised and made into an admirable essay, "A Lion in Our Living Room: Reading Allen Ginsberg in the Eighties" (pp. 199–230). The result is the best brief assessment of Ginsberg. Also reprinted with revisions are three reviews: "On the Other Side of the Field: The Collected Poems of Paul Blackburn" (pp. 251–66); " 'Voice Whisht through Thither Flood': Steven McCaffery's 'Panopticon and North of Intention' " (pp. 285–96); and " 'Collision or Collusion with History': Susan Howe's *Articulation of Sound Forms in Time*" (pp. 297–310). Another item, "Barthes, Ashbery and the Zero Degree of Genre" (pp. 267–84), is a revision of a 1985 article perceptively comparing key terms in Roland Barthes with significant passages in Ashbery. The common element in Perloff's readings of poets is her stress on "license" in the double sense as permission that permits the work to be done and as defiance of authority.

If it is beneficial to have a collection of essays like Perloff's from a choice critic of the '80s, it is fitting to have a collection of essays and reviews, *Our Life in Poetry* (Persea), constituting the collected works covering nearly half a century, from one of the most influential critics of contemporary American poetry, M. L. Rosenthal. Rosenthal had the distinction of naming one of the significant movements, Confessional Poetry, even though he had his doubts about its importance. No one has had a say on more poets. Included among contemporary poets Rosenthal has reviewed or commented critically on are all the great modernists, and, among middle and younger generations—Richard Wilbur, Randall Jarrell, Ginsberg, Lowell, Warren, Roethke, Imamu Amiri Baraka, Plath, Olson, Blackburn, Galway Kinnell, A. R. Ammons, Creeley. The initiatory essay on the confessional mode, "Poetry as Confession," is included as well as two lesser-known essays that detect the divided poetic landscape of that time as well as any I can recall, "Poets of Academe" and "Poets of the Dangerous Way" (the dangerous way is that of Lowell, *For the Union Dead,* and Plath, *Ariel*). In truth, Rosenthal has never been a welcomer of new directions in poetry, but he usually has had a clear vision of what is going on.

As a Fulbright lecturer in Eastern Europe I was told (and I found it to be largely true) that the teaching of contemporary poetry in what were then Marxist countries was neglected because it did not "have enough social and political content." Literary theory and other genres, drama, and fiction were much more highly regarded. I am reminded of this experience because I had to conclude, on examining Fredric Jameson's James Russell Lowell prize book, *Postmodernism, or, The Cultural Logic of Late Capitalism* (Duke), that poetry still is not worth considering in the value theory of a leading self-professed Marxist critic. This book with considerable justification has been acclaimed as the most important for anyone hoping to understand "not just the cultural but the political and social implications of postmodernism." Jameson tours, learnedly and provocatively, contemporary architecture, film, video, economics, and even fiction, but not enough contemporary poetry to earn extended treatment here.

In his *American Sublime: The Genealogy of a Poetic Genre* (Wisconsin) Rob Wilson makes central Wallace Stevens's metaphysical question: "How does one stand / to behold the sublime?" Wilson's version is: "How does one stand to behold the *Americanization* of the sublime?" The last two chapters of his book—"Postmodern Sublime" and "Towards the Nuclear Sublime"—are rather negative about the prospects of the sublime in a nuclear world. In the first of these chapters I was bothered a bit by the faulty geographic perspective of his opening hyperbolic analogy of the sublime in the postmodern landscape to the (unlikely) confrontation of "drifting along Michigan Avenue" against the "horizon-dominating hyperspace of Sears Tower." What Wilson is trying to determine is a sense of the current stage in the American transformation of the sublime. Traditionally, the presentation of the American landscape has involved a "sacralization of power." Writing post-Hiroshima and within a nuclear technological age that has exhausted the earth of sublimity, postmodern poets (Hart Crane is an early prototype) have had to relocate the sublime in a world dominated by main frames, space rocketry, and speculations about some vast "vacant space." Wilson seems more concerned with cultural theorists than with poets in maintaining that Emersonian nature has been supplanted by "postindustrial imageries and the phasings-in of cybernetic/robotic technologies which threaten to make Romantic 'man' obsolete." But he does find the older preoccupations persisting in the "discourse of natural correspondences," evident in poets like William Stafford, Kinnell, Dave

Smith, or Bruce Weigl. These poets are unfortunately outside the province of Wilson's thesis, and the only contemporary poet of import is Ashbery with his urban wrecking ball in "Down by the Station Early One Morning," signifying with "the stigmata of massive energy and mass image" the "technological sublime." It is suggested, rather than substantiated, that poets like Kinnell and Louis Simpson, in poems that attempt pastoral correspondences, or Lowell in an occasional poem like "The Mouth of the Hudson," cannot escape registering "the shock of the nuclear horizon." In his last chapter, on "the nuclear sublime," Wilson appends the final terror of our fatal technological determinism; his poetic resources for that contemplation include Edward Dorn, Creeley, Ginsberg, Kinnell ("The Fundamental Project of Technology"), Robert Haas, Marc Kiminsky, Lowell ("For the Union Dead"), and Robert Pinsky. Wilson's final reference on the necessary confrontations with technology in a poetry of the nuclear sublime is Martin Heidegger. Struggling through much theory, extensive jargon, and very little consideration of specific poems may be worth it for some, but not for one interested principally in contemporary poetry.

In *Points of Departure: International Writers on Writing and Politics* (Michigan) David Montenegro introduces his interviews with writers on politics by noting the good news that a playwright very much concerned with politics, Vaclav Havel, had just been elected president of Czechoslovakia. From this later perspective, we know that Havel's tenure did not last long; the influence of the writer on politics may be only ephemeral. Nevertheless, Montenegro has edited 10 interviews with international writers on politics, adding follow-ups in November 1990 on what had transpired since the interviews. Among the Americans interviewed are Rich, Carolyn Forché, Derek Walcott, Joseph Brodsky (recently our poet laureate), and Seamus Heaney (Irish but part-time Harvard-based). Montenegro finds in his subjects a reluctance to speak out solely on political issues. It is not their politics but their "lyric instinct and spontaneity of their art that guide these writers from image to provocative insight." For their art to be "genuine" it must be spontaneous and unforced. These interviews testify that poets have a certain measure of resistance to social and political responsibility being forced on them, but they come to recognize that their poetry must be "informed by a knowledge of the world and of people." This dual view is hardly surprising, but what is perhaps unexpected is that poets we have regarded as dominantly political, Rich and Forché, also share this reluctance.

Joseph M. Conte in *Unending Design: The Forms of Postmodern Poetry* (Cornell) raises the question of whether postmodernism is merely a critical term or actually identifies a poetic movement. He attempts to establish what he considers as a systematic typology of modern poetry forms. This goal requires more than the usual discussion of "open" and "closed" forms, or a simple identification of formalist and antiformalist poets, or dialogue on a "new content, or subject matter," such as that introduced by Lowell, Sexton, and Berryman. Since "revolutions" have always been of style and content, what is consequential is "the emergence among postmodernist poets of a new perception of poetic form," which Conte distinguishes as either "serial" or "procedural." Serial form is an alternative to the "organic sequence" of romanticism through accommodating in poetry "the rapidly shifting contexts and the overwhelming diversity of messages that we now experience as part of our daily routine." As a complement to serial form, procedural form "consists of predetermined and arbitrary constraints that are relied upon to generate the context and direction of the poem during composition." This is an appropriate form for a time when we no longer are able to suppose "a grand order in the world" and the poet must enact a personal order in terms of his poem. If serial form offers an alternative to "the organic sequence of romanticism," procedural form provides an alternative to the "well-made, metaphorical lyric whose practitioners were the subject of new critical explication." Periods in literary history are noted for identifiable forms and distinctions in structure, such as the Neoclassical couplet, the great Romantic lyric, the Modernist fragment, and now seriality and proceduralism. To Conte, postmodernist forms are a bit more difficult to grasp. He admits that there are other postmodernist forms he does not include, such as concrete poems, minimalist poems, and talk poems. Conte's paradigms are also regrettably not the best-known poets, since he wishes to make a case for some who have not yet received the critical recognition he believes to be their due. Duncan, Creeley, Jack Spicer, Oppen, Zukofsky, and Lorine Niedecker are proposed as poets who use serial form; Ashbery, Kees, Harry Mathews, William Bronk, and Cage are the exemplars of users of procedural form, but Creeley and Zukofsky reappear here. There are agreeable brief discussions of the academic poetry and closed forms of the '40s and '50s, the Beat, bohemian, and open-form poetics of the '60s and '70s, and the appropriateness of both directions, open and closed, in poetry to the society and politics of these decades. Although Conte believes that the importance of a poetic form depends on the scope and diversity of its use and in the importance of the poets he considers, he has to admit that no "truly dominant poet" has emerged in the past two decades, leaving his reader with the impression of factions, like New Formalism and Language Poetry, rather than viable movements in contemporary poetry. He also makes it clear that it is the language poets he values because of their more innovative and less retrogressive attitude toward form. This book requires often painful going.

Robert McDowell in *Poetry After Modernism* (Story Line) has edited a series of essays (most of them commissioned) representing diverse perspectives but a shared belief that Modernism as a literary movement ended "long ago." Regrettably, the book has no editor's overview. Frederick Pollack's "Poetry and Politics" (pp. 5–55) argues that some of the distinctions current two decades previously between Beat, Black Mountain, Deep Image, confessionalism, New York School are not as substantive as they appeared to be. He believes that in the '80s only the Deep Image movement of Robert Bly, James Wright, and W. S. Merwin "retains an extensive following." Language Poetry is still viable as a movement, but his interest is in the illogical stances of Ashbery and the New Formalism and in an even more vital movement of Neo-Narrative Poets. The key Modernist figure is no longer Eliot but Wallace Stevens, and his successor is Ashbery, aptly described as a poet whose narration is incoherent and who equates "life with society, society with media, and art with entertainment, and insisting on his role as epicure spectator." The Neo-Narrative Poets believe that a poetry "reoriented towards storytelling and authorial impersonality may regain, and may deserve to regain, a reputation for wisdom." It is that wisdom that Pollack is concerned with from a Marxist perspective. What lyricism had rejected and Neo-Narrative Poetry may uncover is "the collective nature of experience." Just when it seemed that Marxist views of American poetry were extinct, Pollack almost makes them interesting again. Dick Allen's "The Emperor's New Clothes" (pp. 71–99) identifies a cultural context in which a nation has turned to journalists and politicians and poetry has been trivialized. The good news was, at first, a golden age of lyric poetry; the bad news has been a poetry for later generations lacking in emotion, idea, and social meaning. In "Poetry and the University" (pp. 56–70) Bruce Bawer takes the view that if poetry is to become more than it is at the present, it will have to be a narrative and dramatic poetry, "stressing meaning." Mark Jarman, "Poetry and Religion" (pp. 134–74), finds religion still necessary in poetry, even if the poets appear in the guise of "forest Christians" in a turn to nature (he gives several examples including James Dickey), or write more personal religious poems, like Berryman or Paul Mariani. His point is that the religious impulse in poetry compels many poets who would not call themselves religious to try to link their experience to a transcendent reality. Carole Oles and Hilda Raz in "The Feminist Literary Movement: 1960–1986" (pp. 175–210) contend that feminist poets, such as Marge Piercy, Rich, Maxime Kumin, have ended cooperation with others and turned inward; if there is to be a truly feminist movement, they need to collaborate in mutual interest. There are still poems stressing women's connections to each other by Carolyn Kizer, Alice Walker, Marilyn Hacker, Michelle Cliff. Other bonds are being found in collections of lesbian poetry, or the poetry of racial and ethnic groups. There are also poems in which poets of the present create connections with women of the past. Marilyn Nelson Waniek and Rita Dove provide, in "A Black Rainbow: Modern Afro-American Poetry" (pp. 217–75), support for a view of black poets as having created their own tradition from older folk sources that "have nurtured the race since slavery." This poetry is audience-directed in a sense that most modern lyrics are not. The presence of a black audience has permitted black poetry two tongues, standard English and/or dialect. Black music has been a rich source of influence. In two subsections to this brief history of black poetry, "The Poetry of Rage," on Bob Kaufman, LeRoi Jones/Imamu Amiri Baraka, Etheridge Knight, and "The Seventies and Beyond: Black Poetry into the Present," the two authors conduct an interesting dialogue in what is unquestionably one of the book's best chapters. Lynn Emanuel surveys Language Poets and New Formalists in "Language Poets, New Formalists, the Techniquization of Poetry" (pp. 276–99), assessing the poems discussed as neglected but now being recognized. A point worth making is that the poems themselves—even the actual versification of many of these poets—is at times at odds with their reputation for reactionary politics. Individual poets in this movement have just not been carefully enough read. In Robert McPhillips's "The New Formalists" (pp. 300–328) Brad Leithauser, Timothy Steele, Charles Martin, Gjertrud Schnackenberg, Dana Gioia are poets "read" or "reread" to demonstrate that there is now a recovery of what a tradition of free verse had almost lost to poetry. The book also includes several previously published essays.

Peter Baker in *Obdurate Brilliance: Exteriority and the Modern Long*

Poem (Florida) offers what he believes to be a new interpretation of the long poem, working with a concept that is far from new—"exteriority." His concern is with exteriority in the sense of having to disregard the Romantic "I" of 19th-century poetry or the anticipated speaker of the lyric. His reading finds that both modern and postmodern poetry turn outward from the "I" to the experiences of others, deemphasizing the poet's personal, or inner, life. Baker's thesis would seem to fit modernist poetry better than postmodernist. There is a chapter on "Poetic Subjectivity in Olson's *Maximus Poems*"; an obligatory one on Ashbery, "Humor, Irony, and Exteriority in Ashbery's 'Fragment' "; brief notice of feminist poetry and language theory, "Language Theory and the Languages of Feminism"; his best chapter, on three current poets, "Language, Poetry, and Marginality: Coolidge, Palmer, and Mayer"; and half a chapter on Louis Zukofsky, " 'They tell me it's difficult': Stein/Zukofsky." The afterword makes clear an implicit thesis that the exteriority on which these modern long poems are based is "an aspect of the ethics of the literary practice they represent," a shift from a phenomenological view to a deconstructive one.

Roger Gilbert in *Walks in the World: Representative Experience in Modern American Poetry* (Princeton) provides some good reading from a topic that might not seem promising but turns out to be as significant as we should have known it would be. His focus is the walk poem, specifically the physical and metaphorical landscapes of poets in the act of taking walks. I was enlightened and entertained enough to wish I had thought of the idea myself. Among contemporary poets singled out are O'Hara, Snyder, and Ashbery. Obviously, more poets could be extensively treated. But Gilbert does carefully define an interesting sort of drama explored more in English poetry than in American and, consequently, a drama open for further exploration. The walk poem genre emulates the lyric itself in that it is "a brief excursion . . . purely for the pleasures of movement, reflection, and aesthetic perception." It also promotes erasing "the difference between text and experience." Poets take walks, not just for exercise, but in order to make poems. Poems in this genre are fruitful for pondering the relationship between the poetry of craft and the poetry of experience. Subgenres can be established—rural and urban walks, mountain and seaside, etc. I recommend this book as an excursion from too much critical jargon.

Peter Davison has edited his previously published reviews as a poetry critic for the collection in the University of Michigan "Poets on Poetry" series—*One of the Dangerous Trades: Essays on the Work and Workings of Poetry.* He finds in his own experience, and in his friendships with poets, an uneasiness at the center of personal relationships; it is the poetry that brings poets, and poets and readers, together. Davison has not felt it proper to include for critical comment the poets he has published during four decades of editing. He does reprint his fine early contrast of James Dickey and Lowell, "The Great Grassy World from Both Sides: The Poetry of Robert Lowell and James Dickey at Mid-Career" (pp. 37–53) and his personal comments on Plath, whom he knew early, as well as reviews of Bishop, Merwin, Mark Strand, Ammons, Kinnell, James Wright, Robert Haas, Charles Simic, Walcott, and Hayden Carruth, available previously only in their originally published versions in the *Atlantic Monthly.* The review-essays are short but generally perceptive. An update on Plath would have proved intriguing, but Davison chooses silence on those he knew personally.

Amy Clampitt has collected her own comments on predecessors and contemporaries in another volume in the same series—*Predecessors, Et Cetera Essays* (Michigan). The essays are short. Those on Thomas McGrath, Berryman, James Merrill, Howard Moss, Julia Bucenz, and Ashbery were previously published in magazines and newspapers and are more readily available here. "Made Things: Burrowings, Borrowings, and Anthony Hecht" (pp. 154–57) is apparently a new essay, commenting on a poet's memories of better-forgotten things as almost a badge identifying the poetry of Anthony Hecht, who, she shows, can be very humorous. As a poet Clampitt is fascinated with odd words she has used and found, to her surprise, in other poets, especially in Hecht.

Richard Kostelanetz's *American Writing Today* requires mention only because it contains interviews with Allen Ginsberg and Kenneth Koch and a brief literary self-portrait of Donald Hall. It is wide in scope and shows its origins as Voice of America radio talks edited for the U.S. Information Agency. Appropriately, Hispanic-American literature is included, but the most interesting contributions are accounts of the kind of experimental poetry that interests Kostelanetz as critic and as a poet writing "concrete poetry."

Hardly a big book but worth mentioning for the critical approach it takes to regional literature is Parks Lanier's *The Poetics of Appalachian Space.* The interest comes not from what it says about poetry of Appalachia; Lanier's concern is mostly with fiction, and the treatment of Fred Chappell as a regional poet is the only recommendation I would make for reading it. But the application of Gaston Bachelard's critical theories on poetry and space leads to one of the clearest depictions of the mountainous South as a different geographical and literary landscape.

Albert Cook's collection of essays in *Soundings: On Shakespeare, Modern Poetry, Plato, and Other Subjects* (Wayne State) is almost as wide-ranging as the title purports—Sartrean idealism, Derridean deconstruction, Foucault, Lacan. After all, this is a collection of essays. The view of poetry in these speculations is limited primarily to Ezra Pound and William Carlos Williams, and, even more briefly, to their contemporary manifestations in Olson and Creeley in a demonstration that "measure" leads to "vision."

I recommend Robert Bechtold Heilman's *The Southern Connection: Essays* (LSU, 1990) as reminiscences (he calls them "recollections" and "impressions"). The more recent essays among the 17 here are the interesting and well-written recollections of LSU in the 1930s and 1940s, of Huey Long, the *Southern Review,* of Warren, and Cleanth Brooks. They are, as he calls the essay on Brooks, "selected snapshots" but by one who contributed significantly to literature in the South and to the New Criticism. The rest of the book reprints reviews and essays on Brooks and *The Well Wrought Urn,* Welty, Katherine Anne Porter; but the only poet is Warren, and even there Heilman's attention is directed to the fiction. Poets who appeared in the *Southern Review,* like Berryman, are briefly mentioned; but (disappointingly) practically nothing is said about a former graduate student, Lowell.

ii Women Poets

a. Collections Suzanne Clark's *Sentimental Modernism* is concerned with a problem not new but old, the need for women writers in the 20th century, if they were to be modernist, to escape from the sentimental traditions with which women writers had been associated. The fiction of Annie Dillard and Alice Walker is examined, but no contemporary poet is included. The only writer whose work extends into the postmodernist period is poet Louise Bogan, more properly treated in the earlier period.

Suzanne W. Jones's *Writing the Woman Artist: Essays on Poetics, Politics, and Portraiture* (Penn.) earns notice as another collection of essays by women on women writers taking a feminist approach to writers they consider feminist. There is the usual delineation of the search for a feminist voice that effectively repudiates the sentimentalized conventions associated with women writers, as well as the struggle to be freed from paternalistic conventions in a literary world where "men write poems and women inhabit them." I credit Suzanne Jones for grouping the essays under the rubrics of feminist criticism and explaining their contributions there. Among poets, Bishop (Kathleen Brogan, "Lyric Voice and Sexual Difference in Elizabeth Bishop," pp. 60–80) and Rich (Lynda K. Bundzen, "Power and Poetic Vocation in Adrienne Rich's *The Dream of a Common Language*," pp. 43–59) are dutifully included. What is said about Bishop seems a bit fresher and more interesting than usual, but the essay on Rich has the advantage of focusing on one work. Otherwise, this is another collection of feminist criticism using the familiar formulas, always of value but hardly news. The origins, in papers selected and not selected for a South Atlantic Modern Language Association conference but considered worthy of publication, are evident.

Southern Women Writers, ed. Tonette Bond Inge (Alabama), appeared late in 1990; I did not include it then on the misperception that it included only fiction writers. However, this collection of essays does give some note to the neglected genre for southern writers—poetry. Carol E. Neubauer provides attention to the poetry of Maya Angelou in "Maya Angelou: Self and a Song of Freedom in the Southern Tradition" (pp. 114–42), Joanne Veal Gabbin turns needed attention to "The Southern Imagination of Sonia Sanchez" (pp. 180–203), and Martha Cook treats "Nikki Giovanni: Place and Sense of Place in Her Poetry" (pp. 279–300). The collection's purpose is to stress the importance, and even predominance, of women writers in a third generation of southern writers. With the current valuation of the writings of Flannery O'Connor and Eudora Welty, it seems a bit amiss to contend that this predominance began only with this third generation. Nevertheless, it is helpful to show another predominance, that of black women writers, and to stress their southernness, albeit with the danger of overstating it. The value of this collection is that it clearly demonstrates the increasing importance of women in southern literature and suggests that traditional southern themes may be present in writers actually more concerned with the problems of women and of black writers. It should be noted that these essays were papers given at conferences in 1982 and 1983.

Elizabeth Jane Harrison's *Female Pastoral: Women Writers Re-Visioning the American South* (Tennessee) focuses more specifically on how southern women writers had to "re-vision" the pastoral, and it includes poet Sherley Anne Williams but examines only her first novel *Dessa Rose.*

b. Sexton That Diane Wood Middlebrook has written a biography on Anne Sexton is hardly news by this time. I have never commented on a book that is better known, more famous or infamous, than *Anne Sexton: A Biography* (Houghton Mifflin). What more can be said? Certainly, reviewers expected a book about a poet known for her apparently intimate poetry to deal with intimate matters. Yet no one apparently anticipated the ethical and legal problems resulting from the complete cooperation from the estate that Middlebrook received, unrestricted access to the private papers of a poet who had committed suicide, as well as to the papers of family members, and, surprisingly, even approval of the opening of her psychiatric records by her psychiatrist, which included audiotapes of more than 300 sessions. Controversy materialized only after Sexton's family and other psychiatrists read what was published. The appropriate questions postcontroversy are what this book does for Sexton's reputation as a poet. How profoundly does it become a study of poetic genius and madness? Does it help explain the late flowering of creativity after Sexton's self-proclaimed "rebirth at 29?" Is this biography a significant addition to a fast-growing field of feminist studies of women's literature? And the answer is "more or less." Middlebrook's thesis is satisfactorily demonstrated. Sexton's writing was verifiably about the only success she had in dealing with a set of conditions she could not control otherwise. Her psychiatrist, Dr. Martin T. Orne, justified his release of the tapes on the grounds that Sexton wanted to share the process of her life as a troubled poet so that other patients, therapists, and readers could learn from reading her life very much as she wanted them to realize through her poetry. The tapes are arguably her last contribution to the confessional mode. They are much less a part of this reading of the life of a troubled poet than the controversy would lead one to expect. They have helped, but less than the rereading of the poems. Middlebrook realizes, as she hopes her readers will, that Sexton's suicide should not be viewed as another feminist-interpreted story of a female victim but rather as an existential choice providing closure to a life and career in which Sexton had done all she could do, living and writing. Middlebrook judges the success of her biography in terms of its popular acceptance rather than the reception of literary critics or the disclaimers of psychiatrists. It has the value of being an authorized biography with the appeal of a popular biography, a psychological biography but not a work of psychological criticism. It is not so satisfactory, judged as a literary biography, in using the life to elucidate the poetry, as William Pritchard's contributions to that genre on Robert Frost and Randall Jarrell. Recent critical studies stressing Sexton's considerable craft as a poet have made the greatest contribution to her reputation as a poet.

Judith Nichols-Orians in " 'Sexton's 'The Farmer's Wife' " (*Expl* 49:190–93) evidences how Sexton imparts this poem's content emotionally and intellectually to the reader by a "skillful use of narrative voice, metaphor, simile, diction, rhythm, and sound-play."

c. Plath Steven Axelrod's *Sylvia Plath: The Wound and the Cure of Words* (Hopkins, 1990), based on the closest readings yet of Plath's available journals, is advertised as a "biography of the imagination." It owes something to Barthes's criticism in tracking "the body's journey through language," but it is especially noteworthy for stressing the importance in Plath's life and in her poetry of her increased skills in the use of language and the ordering processes of form. Axelrod's approach is appropriately feminist in the examination of the roles of "all the fathers" in both life and poetry in constructive and deleterious ways. But it is equally effective in stressing the power of "all the mothers," Auriel Plath and her literary surrogates, Woolf and Dickinson. I especially liked the brief focus on a possible link between doubling in Plath's narratives and in her life; Axelrod owes something to John Irwin and his fine studies of this feature. This is a good, well-documented study, demonstrating critical sense without resorting to critical jargon.

Paul Alexander's *Rough Magic: A Biography of Sylvia Plath* (Viking) contrasts effectively with an earlier biography, Anne Stevenson's *Bitter Fame* (reviewed in *ALS* 1989). To Alexander, Ted Hughes is not the victim he was for Stevenson, but is restored to the role of villain in which feminist critics have seen him. Alexander is an admirer of Plath's poetry, especially of the late poetry, and perceives her as important beyond any narrow feminist advocacy. For her personal tragedy Alexander blames Hughes, going beyond culpability in the affair with Assia Gutmann Wevill to such matters as threatened physical violence, recounting Ted's choking her on the ship to America when he learned she was pregnant. Subsequently, this is another book that must make its case without permissions from Olwyn Hughes, effectively barring any efforts to make it a literary biography. What virtues there are come from a bonus—the most complete account of what has happened to Plath's family since her death. To get a full and balanced treatment that the life and poetry of this poet require, we must await the kind of cooperation on Plath that Diane Middlebrook got from Sexton's family.

Bruce Bawer certainly eschews a balanced view of Plath's poetry. In "Sylvia Plath and the Poetry of Confession" (*NewC* 9, vi:18–27) he places Plath's poetry in the context of the rise to popularity of confessional poetry after the publication of Lowell's *Life Studies.* He agrees now with some of the criticism then that the sensationalism of confessional poems detracts from their literary merit, leading poets and critics to judge poems by their apparent "candor" rather than by the degree of their "artistry." He concedes that "the best confessional poetry is marked by balance, control, a sense of form and rhythm, and even a degree of detachment," but he fails to find these virtues in most of Plath's poems. Her *Ariel* poems are identified as "the quintessence of confessional poetry," based on a life that is "fascinating . . . as a study in the nexus among art, ambition, and abnormal psychology"; but he finds them less interesting than her life, offering "little possibility of enlightenment, of discovery," with a professed goal of "not self-knowledge but self-display." The self-knowledge that Bawer faults Plath for not having arrived at was recognition that "she is in fact her own destroyer, her own victim." I do not doubt that this would have added a further dimension to her poetry, but remember Plath's own stated reservations about valuing confessional poetry "as a cry of the heart" while stressing the importance of controlling and manipulating her poems. He scorns Plath's "devotees" as either feminists who find her work "extremely useful to the women's movement" or like "many a young person in the throes of adolescent torment," with neither group cherishing "her work chiefly for its literary merit." Bawer on the confessional mode is comparable to Yvor Winters on American Romanticism. Both disdain unbridled emotion in poetry. Bawer, like Winters, the neohumanist, requires both self-knowledge, thematically arrived at, and structural evidence of control of emotions in proper poetry. If Winters found the "Maule's curse" romanticism of Emerson and Whitman a danger to later poets like Hart Crane, Bawer finds the "Maule's curse" of confessionalism a similar danger to contemporary poets.

Timothy Materer's "Occultism as Source and Symptom in Sylvia Plath's 'Dialogue over a Ouija Board' " (*TCL* 37:131–47) identifies Plath's and Ted Hughes's personal fascination with the occult as the source of inspiration for the poem "Dialogue," which was mentioned in Plath's notebooks but never shown to anyone before her death. Plath's occultism grew out of her desire to "find new ground for writers beyond the traditions represented by Oedipus and Christ." Rather than criticizing Christianity, as some have contended she does, Plath was seeking a "religious stance of her own," trying like one of her poetic fathers, Yeats, "to express compelling and universal emotions through their highly personal mythologies." Materer maintains that Plath's ventures into the occult were not a result of mental instability but "a stage in her poetic development." He follows his examination of Plath's occult connections with an analysis of the poem. The main characters, Leroy and Sybil, are based on Hughes and Plath, while "the spirit of the board" is the child they hoped to have. The letters on the board stand for language itself, and the players are poets trying to make sense of language. Plath's personal life plays a part throughout this poem; eye-catching among the examples Materer uses, the sardonic reference to her father's death. "Do you know how my father is? ROTTING. . . ."

Plath's mirrors as structural devices come up again in Donna Richardson's "Plath's 'Mirror' " (*Expl* 49:193–95). Richardson explains that Plath's mirror is an adjustable one, physically and thematically, whereby the "mirror adjusts to the viewer and becomes what she makes of it." Richardson believes that this poem reveals the fallacy of "committing one's identity to the shallow truth of physical appearance" and, consequently, being "dehumanized" in the process. Kella Gerrisa Svetich in "Plath's 'the Disquieting Muses' " (*Expl* 49:131–32) makes a minimal point about a substantial poem, noting only that it expresses what I would say is a Dickinsonian theme, "how overwhelming hypersensitivity to the complexities of life can be."

d. Bishop In *Elizabeth Bishop: Questions of Mastery* (Harvard) Bonnie Costello's focus is profitably on Bishop's way of seeing things, especially on her use of multiple perspectives in an endeavor to realize in poetry "the condition of the visual arts." The usefulness of Costello's approach is that it leads to careful readings of many of Bishop's poems, with fine attention to detail, culminating in rich readings of "The Map" and "Sonnet." Costello provides convincing evidence of Bishop's mastery of the particular forms she uses but wisely questions the success of her attempts to master reality. This is a valuable study, focused on Bishop's craft, one that helps to establish what Robert Lowell came to realize about his friend: she was one of the most accomplished poets of their generation.

Renee R. Curry's "Augury and Autobiography: Bishop's 'Crusoe in England'" (*ArQ* 47, iii:71–91) uses one of Bishop's most frequently explicated poems to establish her use of augury "as an archaic form of interrogation to delicately unmask a muted lesbian identity." Curry focuses on the poem's use of "a layered complexity requiring answers, speaker, self, and the augural imagination" in order to probe Bishop's relationship with Lota de Macedo Soares and the effect of the latter's suicide on Bishop and her poetry. Although Curry gainfully examines instances of masking, encoded language as well as Bishop's use of "goats and turtles, typical oracular animals," she is more interested in the poem's "exploration of marginality, particularly the kind Bishop experienced as a woman writer and as a lesbian." Consequently, augury is treated simply as a loose binding for Curry's explication of "Crusoe" as it "reveals the endless alienation that has gone on since the days of Sappho." With such narrow blinders, little enlightenment is offered on the more oracular moments of a rich poem.

Thomas Travisano in "Heavenly Dragons: A Newly Discovered Poem by Elizabeth Bishop" (*WHR* 45:28–33) appraises "The Ballad of the Subway Train," which appeared in the high school literary magazine from Bishop's only year in attendance at North Shore Country School in Beverley, Massachusetts, plausibly Bishop's "first poem published anywhere." Travisano judges that this poem surpasses those published later at Walnut Hill School and finds that it "foreshadows the freshness and surprise, complexity of tone, and firm command of a poem's shape that characterized Bishop's mature work." "Ballad" is compared with "The Man-Moth" (1936), since "both poems feature as protagonists strange, invented creatures touched by mythic overtones," and "counterpoint a life of freedom and mobility above with a constrained life below." Travisano hails "Ballad" as Bishop's "first fully realized work of art" and declares that "the delicacy and accuracy of the observation, the musical subtlety and dramatic visual contrasts wedded here, predict genius." The case made here seems not just to predict but to confirm precocious talent.

Bishop's talent for locating the universal human experience in the particulars of the simplest daily experiences is the subject of Victoria Harrison's "The Dailiness of Her Center: Elizabeth Bishop's Late Poetry" (*TCL* 37:253–72). Harrison uses "Santarem," "In the Waiting Room," "Crusoe in England," and "12 O'Clock News" to explore Bishop's talent for elevating the trivialities of daily life to central experience. Although Bishop seemed to tire of a rather simplistic view of the world, Harrison finds that "Bishop's late poetry, especially, makes central the difficulty, the pain, and the rewards of our relationships in all their dailiness." It is precisely in the simple daily experiences of people that Bishop best reveals the complexity of human experience. Bishop's poem "Sonnet" is added to the discussion without being made clearly relevant.

e. Levertov Diane C. LeBlanc in "Pilgrimage, Duality, and Quest in Denise Levertov's 'Pig Dreams'" (*ELWIU* 18:106–21) wishes to reclaim Levertov's *Pig Dreams* as an important part of the Levertov canon, despite reviews which have consistently relegated the book to a secondary status as "children's literature." LeBlanc's intent is to "concentrate on the theme, the structure, and the politics of gender important to 'Pig Dreams,'" in the immediate context of "Candles in Babylon" and in the larger context of Levertov's work as a whole. By analyzing the poems as a sequence, LeBlanc shows that the life of Sylvia, the pig, may be seen as a "pilgrimage" and even suggests "how Levertov urges women to transcend patriarchal dualism in order to achieve social and spiritual freedom." This article is another worthy recent attempt (Richard Flynn's book on Jarrell [see *ALS 1990*] is an outstanding example) to include what has been regarded as children's literature in the poet's canon.

Also out this year is Linda Wagner-Martin's *Critical Essays on Denise Levertov* (Hall), reprinting a score of reviews and a dozen or so articles. This volume contains fewer new essays than is usual for this series, only Jerome Mazzaro's "Denise Levertov's Political Poetry" (pp. 172–87) and Wagner-Martin's "Levertov: Poetry and the Spiritual" (pp. 196–204). Both essays ably cover important topics. Mazzaro's treatment of "lyrical poetical poetry" is thorough, up-to-date, and well-documented; but there are so many brief quotations that the text becomes a little hard to follow. A good case is made not only for the poetry but for Levertov as exemplary of a way to revive political poetry. Wagner-Martin complements Mazzaro's study, offering a good application of existential angst and especially Martin Buber's *I and Thou* as routes to an understanding of Levertov's politics as poet. My only complaint is that this essay is too short; more could be done. The editor's introduction, "Levertov as Poet" (pp. 1–14), briefly and adequately surveys the critical reception of Levertov's work and the contributions of the essays included here.

f. Garrigue Lee Upton has compiled a brief study, *Jean Garrigue: A Poetics of Plenitude* (Fairleigh Dickinson), of a neglected and almost forgotten poet whose work feminist critics have yet to revive. Garrigue began her career promisingly in the *Kenyon Review,* received praise from Jarrell, Roethke, and Lowell, and wrote eight volumes of poetry. Upton makes a case for a renewed interest in her poetry on women and her erotic poems on loving. The final chapter focuses on the use of imagery for walks by the water as a mirror for the process of assuming a "desirous imaginative identity." Everything is too briefly discussed, and the slim book is filled out with an appendix of five selected poems.

iii Middle Generation Poets and the Confessional Mode

a. Roethke Don Bogen's *A Necessary Order: Theodore Roethke and the Writing Process* (Ohio) is neither the best nor the worst of books on Roethke. It is simply a chronological study, as the title suggests, of an evolution of the writing process that paralleled his personal development toward self-discovery. Not much is added to our knowledge of the journey, but there is something of value in the account of Roethke's progression in his use of images, in growth of voice, and in changes in style. The reader gets a better idea of changes in groups of poems but little in the way of extended explications of individual poems. Since Roethke's development as an artist is integral to the life journey toward self-discovery, biography effectively serves explication here. This is another well-researched study, showing close examination of the Roethke materials at the University of Washington and benefiting from interviews with friends, students, and colleagues.

Mary Floyd-Wilson's "Poetic Empathy: Theodore Roethke's Conception of Woman in the Love Poems" (*SoAR* 56, i:61–79) attempts to find a "personalized" view of "woman" in the love poems in Roethke's posthumous collection, *The Far Field.* Floyd-Wilson concedes that Roethke's earlier love poems in *Words for the Wind* are chiefly concerned with conflicts from within himself and treat "woman" more or less as an abstraction; but in his last poems Roethke, happily married, achieved the emotional maturity to portray women concretely and objectively. There is a helpful review of the literature on "woman" in Roethke, beginning with Kenneth Burke's classic, "The Vegetable Radicalism of Theodore Roethke." Floyd-Wilson's stance is that Roethke's fear of losing his "identity" to his lover had kept him from a mature and objective view of women. She demonstrates rather convincingly that Roethke's progression in the final love poems led to a recognition of "the other's reality as equal to his own"—"an important step," Floyd-Wilson forcefully argues, "in Roethke's journey out of the self."

b. Berryman *The Gettysburg Review* offers a significant issue devoted to John Berryman, the man and the poet. Philip Levine in "Mine Own John Berryman" (4:533–52) has crafted the best tribute to Berryman as a teacher that I have read. It is a portrait of hero as teacher as he salvages the autumn 1953 Iowa workshop for poets by following Lowell's seminar disaster with a brilliant class. (Levine's memories are hard on Lowell, who did better at Boston University a few years later and who apparently was beginning the serious breakdown that struck him soon after his leaving Iowa for Cincinnati.) This is also a narrative of one of the more talented creative writing classes ever assembled—Levine, W. D. Snodgrass, Donald Justice, William Dickey, and others—with a teacher, not without his own personal problems, effectively at work. Levine sympathetically gets across contradictions in Berryman as a teacher, seemingly without plan but actually with everything carefully planned, open to students but always aware that they were the students and he the teacher. The important relationship of Berryman and Jarrell is briefly but effectively treated in Mark Jarman's review-essay, "John & Randall, Randall & John" (pp. 565–79). The main part of the issue contains reviews of collected poems and biographies, William Pritchard's of Jarrell and Paul Mariani's of Berryman, but Jarman makes telling comments on the talent and tragedy of these two poets and friends. Paul Mariani's "Lowell on Berryman on Lowell" (pp. 581–92) draws on his research to recount Berryman's feeling of betrayal over Lowell's not-too-favorable review of his *77 Dream Songs* in the *New York Review of Books.* Berryman even suspected jealousy on Lowell's part to keep him out of the No. 1 spot in American poetry, now that Frost and Williams were dead. We are told that at 5 A.M., 11 May 1964, Berryman sat down to work out his feelings about Lowell in "Dream Song 177," where, unbeknown to most readers, Lowell figures as Addison. What Berryman did not know, and Mariani reveals, is that Lowell wrote as he did to stave off the powerful effect that Berryman's poems had on him. The friendship was renewed after a meeting in 1962 and continued, chronicled here, until Berryman's death.

c. Lowell Brent Garner in "Anxious Odes of Tate and Lowell" (*JASAT* 25, iv:93–99) ostensibly is concerned with a comparison of two famous odes, that of teacher Allen Tate, "Ode to the Confederate Dead," and that of sometime pupil Lowell, "For the Union Dead." To some extent, but with little largess, Garner demonstrates that the New Englander does a better job of bringing the past into the present than the southerner. But Garner's real intention is to target a critical work that might have been considered a basis for ferreting out such influence, Harold Bloom's *The Anxiety of Influence.* Garner strays from his announced subject to comment on Bloom's own anxiety, caught between the opposing influences of New Criticism and deconstruction. An influence study becomes an attack on a major study of influence.

Henry Hart's "Robert Lowell and the Psychopathology of the Sublime" (*ConL* 32:496–519) is more rewarding. The "sublime" here is filtered through the Oedipal psychology of Freud. Lowell's "sublime personae are doggedly Oedipal," the product of his obsessions on "overthrowing powerful father figures," but not without "brief, illusory apotheoses from which they inevitably crash." This is one of the best short treatments of Lowell and the influence of Freud, as suggested by Lowell's own writings. According to Hart, Freud is central to Lowell's understanding of America with "all its violent contradictions and competing factions." Freud, the Oedipal, and the concept of the sublime were all crucial for Lowell as a means of working out his own frustrations, alternating between "leaps" toward the sublime and "descents" to the depths, following his "guilty recognitions" of his own antic behavior. The concept of Lowell's "pathology of the sublime" works for understanding both poet and poetry.

John Whalen-Bridge in "Lowell's Presentation of Violence in 'Water,' 'Florence,' and 'The Neo-Classical Urn'" (*NConL* 21, iii:5–7) not only finds violent imagery but calls attention to the violent structure of the poems, including "clipped lines and jagged rhythms." Whalen-Bridge compares this imagery to similar imagery in poems by Warren, Frost, and Robinson Jeffers. Lowell is mindful that even the Creation was an act of violence.

iv Formalists and Old Establishment

a. Wilbur I am pleased to welcome Bruce Michelson's new study, *Wilbur's Poetry: Music in a Scattering Time* (Mass.), as an overdue reevaluation of Richard Wilbur. When Delmore Schwartz, Jarrell, and Lowell commented on the great skill that poets had achieved by the 1950s, the best of Wilbur was always exemplary. There has been a critical hiatus of 25 years about a poet who was once our most honored. Michelson wisely avoids rehashing the old arguments about formalism versus experimentation, closed and open forms, academic poetry and postmodernism, where Wilbur always came across as a "reactionary," if not a "heavy," and goes directly to the poems themselves to argue not only for the stylistic range and achievements of Wilbur's artistry but also for a sensitivity to the major moral and aesthetic crises of his times. Wilbur is presented as not only the still-acknowledged master of light poems but also of some neglected darker meditative ones. This poet is not only a brilliant translator of the language of Molière and Racine into English but a master of language himself. Through close readings of the poems, Michelson makes a convincing case for complexities in style and in thought that recent critics have failed to recognize. I am not sure that those who will take the trouble to reread the poems as Michelson carefully does will be fully convinced of the "skeptical virtuosity" that he touts there, but this study may lead to a fairer assessment of Wilbur's considerable achievement as a critic, translator, and, especially, as a poet. Michelson deals well with Wilbur as an individual poet; importantly, however, he fails to establish Wilbur's place and importance among his current contemporaries. Read this book and return to a rereading of Wilbur to form your own judgment.

b. Warren: New Critic as Poet William Bedford Clark's book, *The American Vision of Robert Penn Warren* (Kentucky) is the latest of several books on the late poet laureate. Central is Warren's troubled "love affair" with America. This study merits mention for showing Warren's interest in literature and history and especially for noting the play in his imagination between both, but that is of more concern to those approaching Warren as fiction and prose writer than as poet. There are comments on the most relevant poem, *Brother to Dragons,* but there is, regrettably, no detailed reading.

Will Fridy, "The Author and the Ballplayer: An Imprint of Memory in the Writings of Robert Penn Warren" (*MissQ* 44:159–66), uses interviews he conducted with Kent Greenfield and others to show how Warren translated experiences from his childhood friendship with Greenfield into the short story "Goodwood Comes Back" and into the poem "American Portrait: Old Style." Warren visited Greenfield during most of his returns to Guthrie, Kentucky, and during those visits the two men talked about their shared childhood experiences. Since Warren "yearned all his life for the home of his youth," he often uses memories of Guthrie in his writing. Fridy demonstrates that "Goodwood" was based on the negative side of Greenfield, while the character "K" in "American Portrait" represents his friend's positive side.

c. Hecht Henry Taylor's "Forms of Conviction" (*SoR* 27:235–42) traces the development of Anthony Hecht's poetry as revealed in *The Collected Earlier Poems.* Taylor reviews the poems as they were grouped in their original publication, tracking changes in thematic content while noting the intricate craftsmanship evident in most of Hecht's poetry. Whether dealing powerfully with "mortality and torture" or with "momentary and illusory pleasures," Hecht is able to create beautiful poetry. Taylor reckons that "no other poet of our time has been able to find such beautiful language for our peculiar joys and horrors." Taylor's essay does not delve too deeply into the thematics of individual poems but offers a good account of Hecht's style, too often disregarded as merely crafted formalism.

v Beats and Open Forms

a. Ginsberg, Corso It is useful to have an assessment, in Edward Halsey Foster's *Understanding the Beats* (So. Car.), from the perspective of the '90s of the four most prominent Beat poets. Foster's treatment of Ginsberg cannot match Thomas Merrill's superb introduction in Twayne's United States Authors Series, but then, of the writers included here, Ginsberg needs reintroduction least of all in the wake of Barry Miles's recent biography (see *ALS 1988*). I endorse Foster's thesis that "Ginsberg is preeminently an elegiac poet" and ascribe to his acknowledgment of William Carlos Williams as well as of "a great range of poets" (and the painter Cézanne) as providing Ginsberg with new traditions. I also appreciate the stress on the feeling of loneliness and solitude that comes across from Ginsberg's best poems, especially the attention given to his two stellar elegies for his father. There is little proof of development and change in Ginsberg's poetry. The chapter on Gregory Corso explores an apparent paradox in returning the poet to the poem: Corso's poetry is so "deeply personal" it becomes "at times hermetic and obscure." The precursors of his poetry are properly identified as Poe and André Breton and Surrealism. Although Ginsberg and the other Beats emphasized the spontaneous character of Corso's poetry, Foster persuades that his poems are "the product of careful revision and craft" and never merely imitative. The friendship and aid of Randall Jarrell are, for the first time, properly credited. Foster chronicles but does not explain the falling off in Corso's productivity after 1962 following abundant productivity during the preceding seven years. He does examine several of the later poems which have been mostly neglected. There are, of course, chapters on Kerouac and Burroughs, not relevant here. The introductory chapter, "Hipsters, Beats, and the True Frontier," is adequate, identifying writers Foster might have included if his emphasis had been other than literary. This is, at best, a serviceable introduction with a startlingly brief account of Neal Cassady, whose time may have gone. There is a commendable but too cursory attempt to relate the Beat movement to American expressionism.

b. Rexroth In his survey *American Poetry in the Twentieth Century* (reviewed above) Richard Gray judges Kenneth Rexroth to have been the finest of the American radical poets. With slightly less conviction, I welcome any book that furthers this poet's reputation. Linda Hamalian's *A Life of Kenneth Rexroth* (Norton) should make an important contribution to reevaluation in that it manifests Rexroth's life and poetry as integral to what happened to writers and literature in the movement from modernism to postmodernism. An honest biography requires facing matters concerning Rexroth that have turned some critics off. The picture that emerges is of a man with whom, for all his flaws and malfeasances, a reader can empathize. Rexroth appears from this well-written and often dramatic account as a bawdy and generous mentor to others, still a good poet, nearly a cultural icon. This biography of a writer opens up important aspects of an age.

I would slip in here for additional mention a complementary volume, Lee Bartlett's well-edited and informative *Kenneth Rexroth and James Laughlin: Selected Letters* (Norton). This collection is important for what it reveals of Rexroth and tells us of many other writers, Ginsberg, Duncan, Snyder, Lawrence Ferlinghetti, and the whole New Directions benevolent enterprise that Rexroth was continually in contact with.

c. Beats and San Francisco Warren French's *The San Francisco Poetry Renaissance* (Twayne), though narrow in coverage, is a better book than *Understanding the Beats.* It is much more limited in time, chronicling only five years of the renaissance in San Francisco, from Ginsberg's first reading of *Howl* at the Six Gallery in October 1955 to the final issue of

Beatitude in May 1960, but much more comprehensive in that French has reexamined all of the original documents he could find. He attests that this was the most important postwar literary movement on the West Coast as well as the "last important counterculture movement to express itself principally through traditional literary genres." He also establishes that the Beats were never themselves organized enough to be a calculated movement but rather gained their identity from a mass media attempt to impose a group identity on resolutely individualistic writers; the media attention publicized their writings but helped to bring an end to any real renaissance in the Bay Area. French's study is estimable because he carefully identifies not only similarities between individual Beats, like Ginsberg and Jack Kerouac, Snyder and Whalen, but also because he brings out dissimilarities in the movement. He recognizes women writers, Lenore Kandel (who wrote a feminist "Howl" in "First They Slaughtered the Angels") and Diane Di Prima ("Memoirs of a Beatnik"), both of whom contributed to the renaissance without much scholarly acknowledgment. French details the renaissance's foreground and aftermath as well. He agrees with Kingsley Widmer that the real importance of a San Francisco Renaissance or Beat movement was primarily as a populist cultural phenomenon rather than as a literary movement. French goes beyond the usual introductory territory of a Twayne study to produce an interesting original work.

d. Beats and Venice If you want to read about the life-style but not about any lasting art that came out of it, there is John Arthur Maynard's *Venice West: The Beat Generation in Southern California* (Rutgers), an account of the least productive and by far the least-known segment of the Beat movement, the colony located in a beachfront slum in "Venice West." In case you did not know, the two most significant writers were Larry Lipton, author of *The Holy Barbarians,* and Stuart Perkoff, Venice's leading poet. If interested, read and learn—but more about eccentric life than about art.

e. Olson Tom Clark's *Charles Olson: The Allegory of a Poet's Life* (Norton) is a year-by-year account of the private man whose inner struggles and tortures have long been hidden behind the public face of the founder of projective verse and the advocate of open forms. Olson was, as detailed here, a man both driven and guilt-obsessed. Despite his own impressive physical size and eventual literary stature, he had doubts of measuring up to "fathers," both actual and literary. His competitive drives and his brooding doubts led to a private life of overwork at one extreme and escapes from work at the other. His fascination with Melville became a lifetime concern with the meanings possible in myth and tragedy which he found revealed in that great writer. Olson's own public self was the kind of which myths of leader and father for other writers and for a literary movement could be created. His private self was his own tragedy. But out of both his personal struggles and his learned knowledge of myth, tragedy, and poetry came his major work, begun in 1953 at the age of 43, the *Maximus* poems.

f. Creeley David L. Elliott discusses the relationship of poetry and jazz in "An Interview with Robert Creeley" (*Sagetrieb* 10, i–ii:45–65). This discussion of jazz "beat" leads to a discussion of the Williams poetic line as Creeley read it himself and heard Williams read it, contrasted with his own line endings. Creeley gauges his closeness with fellow poets, a brotherhood in the arts, with the late Robert Duncan (not surprisingly) and (more surprisingly) with Ashbery. He denies that his admiration of Ashbery's *Self-Portrait in a Convex Mirror* constituted in any way a betrayal of his earlier principles. In the same issue, Vincent Prestianni provides "Robert Creeley: An Analytic Bibliography of Bibliographies" (*Sagetrieb* 10:209–13).

g. Dorn Christopher Beach, "Migrating Voices in the Poetry of Edward Dorn" (*ConL* 32:211–28), attempts to assess Dorn's place in modern poetry. He begins by noting that Dorn, while a contemporary of Creeley and Ginsberg, has little in common with these poets. Dorn's dissatisfaction with the "modernist mode of observation" led him to seek a new mode of poetic expression, complete with a new locale. In an effort to depart from the European mode of Pound and the still too East American mode of his Black Mountain mentor Charles Olson, Dorn turned to the West for geographical distinction. Beach finds that Dorn took Olson's "critique of historical poetry" a step further by "effecting a negation of history except as 'space'—that is, except as reflected in a physical and intellectual movement through that space." Through his own revisions Dorn came to a "radically altered understanding of the ontological and linguistic processes of poetry itself." Beach concludes that what is important in the world of Dorn's anti-epic *Slinger* is no longer "what things 'mean' but where one has been and when one has been there." The message of this essay is simple, reasonable, and not especially new; but the style is, unfortunately, circuitous and stiff.

vi The New Establishment and New York Poets

a. Merwin Edward H. Brunner in *Poetry as Labor and Privilege: The Writings of W. S. Merwin* (Illinois) reminds us that Merwin is more than a poet, even a veritable man of letters. This book is an examination of the total canon of Merwin's work—poetry, fiction, essays, translations. I credit Brunner for careful research in primary materials, including the manuscripts and relevant materials in the Merwin archives at Illinois-Urbana. He relates Merwin's concern with family to his poetry, disclosing that Merwin was another poet affected by the death of parents, especially of his father. He also does a commendable job of covering the reception of Merwin's work, both favorable reviews and unfavorable. The extended notes on the literary works and the bibliography are useful. I do fault Brunner for not viewing Merwin's work meaningfully in the context of his literary contemporaries or evaluating his poetry in literary context. Mine is not the only review that adds a complaint about the writing. It is stylistically undistinguished, sometimes unclear, and, as is often the case today, prone to critical jargon.

b. Ashbery Sara L. Lundquist's *"Legerete et Richesse:* John Ashbery's English 'French Poems' " (*ConL* 32:403–21) explains Ashbery's "French Poems," both French and English versions, as a revelation of the nature of language as "abundant in resources ultimately incapable of an absolute mimesis." Because Ashbery wrote the poems in French and then translated them into English, the two existing versions "invite their readers to investigate the points of difference and points of sameness" between the languages. Lundquist tries the obvious approach to a comparison—seeing one version "serv[ing] an explanatory role to the other"—but soon finds this too simple an arrangement. The nearly complete lack of idiom from either language, the extensive use of cognates, and even the similar syntax all point to the interrelatedness of the languages. Not surprisingly for Ashbery's poetics, the poems begin with Babel and return to Babel as he explores this connection in relation to the need to communicate.

Lundquist compares the French and English texts in each of the four poems, correlating the use of language with the apparent themes. This essay is useful for anyone interested in the complexities of language, in the complexity of poetry, and, of course, in the complexities of Ashbery.

Ned B. Williams, "Ashbery's 'The Grapevine'" (*Expl* 49:251–55), discusses speaker, "the stereotypical Roman soldier of B movies"; the three distinctions signaled by *we, you,* and *they;* and the event, the Crucifixion of Christ. The rest is paraphrase of key words, illuminating how the poem deals with levels of faith achieved because of the Crucifixion contrasted with the soldier's failure to comprehend the significance of what he has observed.

c. Ammons Elizabeth McGeachy Mills (*Expl* 49:187–90) presents a surprisingly detailed account, for an *Explicator* note, of how A. R. Ammons uses "carefully chosen signs" in "Singing & Doubling Together" to create "a complex, nonrational experience of union." The seven "claims" of the poem are signaled with distinctive punctuation (five colons and one dash). The number "seven" signifies "the unity of heaven and earth." Diction signals the complex experience of the poem. "Indexical signs" of relationships signal "doubleness," both intimacy and difference. Word repetition signals "the complex, often paradoxical, tension that the event arouses." Death is not an end but a transformation. If an *Explicator* note can be a little tedious, this essay qualifies.

vii Nature: Realism, Surrealism, Metaphysics

a. Bly In *The Incorporative Consciousness of Robert Bly* (So. Ill.) Victoria Frenkel Harris tries to establish the "incorporative nature of Bly's poetic journey by concentrating upon [the] assimilative, yet selective consciousness" of the poet over 25 years, from 1962 to 1987. By "incorporative" Harris means a superior awareness that integrates everything it encounters through its intuitive and subjective powers. The focus is on Bly's "aesthetic consciousness," primarily in two significant books, *Silence in the Snowy Fields* and *This Tree Will Be Here for a Thousand Years.* This is hardly an introductory survey, but it does contribute fundamentally to an understanding of the poetic intentions of one of our most significant poets of the last 30 years. The extensive bibliographies of primary and secondary material should be useful.

b. Wright Andrew Elkins in *The Poetry of James Wright* (Alabama) assigns a chapter each to Wright's seven volumes of poetry and stresses his total work as "one epic poem, a continuing quest . . . for the poet's self, his identity." Not surprisingly, Wright's most valuable works are identified as his later journeys along the road he travels during this search. Wright was clearly a modern Romantic, a poet who, at his best, "dramatizes the central problems of the creative individual in a late industrial society as he tries to turn his life into art." Elkins effectively uses previous criticism of Wright and adds further testimony to Wright's importance as an American poet. This introduction reads as a clearly written, intelligently articulated account.

c. Snyder If you want to write a book about an American poet, applying the theories of French critic and psychoanalyst Jacques Lacan, Gary Snyder is a good choice. Tim Dean in *Gary Snyder and the American Unconscious: Inhabiting the Ground* (St. Martin's) attempts that and more. The problem for the reader is that the treatment of Snyder as poet gets lost in the discussion of the existential problems he has in "inhabiting the ground." Snyder's extra-American interests, Japanese culture and Zen Buddhism, are in this book put aside to see him as "quintessentially a poet of America." With this reemphasis, Snyder becomes not marginal to American culture and poetry but central. He has not only been influenced by our culture and poetry, but he has strongly influenced them. What Snyder has helped to bring out of his and our unconscious is the concept of the "land," which, as Robert Frost has poeticized, America was before it was anything else. Americans do not consciously know the American land. Snyder has, however, been conscious "as few other cultural representatives are of what is at stake in the effort to 'inhabit the ground.' " Even Snyder cannot quite speak the unconscious meaning; but, analogous to a psychologist, he has been a means of "bringing to the consciousness elements which would have otherwise remained unknown." The first part of Dean's book ranges too far in too brief a space into literary history, cultural history, and American history, necessitating multitudinous footnotes to clarify the text. It is at its best when Dean focuses on the landscape of specific poems. As a study of Snyder, it attempts too much in setting up its thesis and accomplishes too little in its analysis of specific poems.

Patrick D. Murphy's *Critical Essays on Gary Snyder* is one of the more valuable volumes in the G. K. Hall Critical Essays series, reprinting some of the best past essays and commissioning new ones. The book contains a fuller than usual introduction and five new or revised essays. Thomas J. Lyon in "Twenty Years Later—A Coda" (pp. 44–48) briefly updates his reprinted article. Katsunori Yamazato looks currently at *Turtle Island* in "How to Be in This Crisis: Gary Snyder's Cross-Cultural Vision in *Turtle Island*" (pp. 230–47). Jack Hicks valuably rereads an interesting poem, in "Poetic Composting in Gary Snyder's 'Left Out in the Rain' " (pp. 247–57). David Robinson delivers an unpublished interview (1989) in "Practicing the Wild—Present and Future Plans: An Interview with Gary Snyder" (257–62), bringing the reader up-to-date on Snyder's activities. In his introduction Murphy informs the reader of the importance of the reprints and of the updates, but he does not undertake an introductory survey of the poet.

There is almost an embarrassment of riches. Jon Halper has edited *Gary Snyder: Dimensions of a Life* (Sierra Club), reminiscences and appreciations, including just about everyone willing to write about Snyder. The reminiscences are arranged chronologically, according to periods in Snyder's life from 1930 to the present. The appreciations are arranged according to subjects—poetics, Dharma, and culture and politics. Visual artists have supplied illustrations, some of them very beautiful. The contributors to this extensive project are, fortunately, all identified. Among them are Wendell Berry, Dan Ellsberg, Clayton Eshleman, Ginsberg, Paul Hansen, Laughlin, Michael McClure, Tim McNulty, Jerome Rothenberg, Gioia Timpanelli, Whalen, Alan Williamson—people from "all walks of life," who share interests in poetry and in ecology.

Julia Martin in "Speaking for the Green of the Leaf: Gary Snyder Writes Nature's Literature" (*CEA* 54:98–109) admits, with considerable understatement, that "it should be clear that my reading of Snyder's position is generally sympathetic." Martin is an advocate not only of Snyder's poetry but of his staunch environmentalism. The focus is on the poems of *Turtle Island* (1974). In the first of four sections Martin examines Snyder's monistic rejection of the basically dualistic thinking of Western culture. Using "generalization and caricature," Snyder attacks the Judaeo-Christian tradition that has "assumed that a feminized 'nature' is something from which we are (or should be) distinct." Snyder condemns this view, delivering a "strong polemic against capitalist America's acquisitive devastation of the wilderness." In the second section Martin examines Snyder's identification with the "marginalized voices" in nature in the culture of women through the use of "metaphors of descent and a reevaluation of the quotidian" and the recalling of "traditions that model this very world as being sacramental, rather than as something to be transcended." The third section focuses on Snyder's use of goddess mythology and Buddhism as a source for metaphors which "emphasize the arbitrariness of binary dichotomies." Dualism is rejected for a view that "the life of each is . . . bound up with that of others." In the last section Martin answers some questions about Snyder's message, recognizing that by giving voice to the marginalized "other," Snyder sets up a "reversal of the current [dualistic] model." This essay is a good acknowledgment of Snyder's monistic advocacy and identification with the "other," without going heavily into Zen and "the Buddha nature." But it is not exactly easy reading.

d. Dickey There is more to James Dickey this year than appears in the *James Dickey Newsletter.* Ernest Suarez's "Emerson in Vietnam: Dickey, Bly, and the New Left" (*SLJ* 23, ii:77–97) begins with a reassessment of the ostensible moral "failure" of Dickey's poetry as charged by Robert Bly in the heat of anti-Vietnam war protests. Suarez uses three Dickey war poems that infuriated Bly because they made no conspicuous antiwar statement—"The Performance," "Between Two Prisoners," and "The Firebombing"—to illustrate Dickey's appropriate place in a tradition of "American visionary poets" that began with Emersonian transcendentalism. Dickey does not advocate "concrete changes in the social and political sphere" but rather "transformations of the self." Dickey does not condemn the violence of war but in the Emersonian tradition stresses perceptions that come from violent situations that may transform the self. I do not know that Dickey currently needs defense from Bly's attack, but it is good to have a reading of three fine poems that relates him to yet another literary tradition.

That violence is central to Dickey is recognized by Marion Hodge in "James Dickey's Natural Heaven" (*SoAR* 56, iv:57–70), and I suppose by everyone who reads him. This article is commentary on Dickey's nontraditional concept of heaven, most evident in "The Heaven of Animals" but less plainly in "Falling" and "For the Last Wolverine." In Dickey's scheme, heaven is a state reached through "the way instinctive beings live their lives right now in the natural world." Hodge retells Dickey's view as testimony that "we are not like animals, we are animals. . . . we must accept the natural world as it is." In Dickey's heaven there is hunting and killing without death and consequent guilt and birth without pain. We must accept the fact that we are part of the violent cycle of life on the planet; survival of the species depends on it. The truth, as Dickey tells it, is such that he must assume what some critics judge an amoral stance.

In the more interesting of two articles, "James Dickey Rex: The Murder of the Father" (*JDN* 8, i:2–8), Marion Hodge considers Dickey's rejection of reason as denoted by the actual and symbolic deaths of father figures in several of Dickey's earlier poems. Fathers represent "repression and authority," characteristics that emanate from reason. Hodge demonstrates in "Cherrylog Road" that the two lovers "kill" the father symbolically, an act which results in a renewal of nature. Hodge analyzes "Dover: Believing in Kings" to show that the father-murdering son achieves the freedom to "abandon himself to the joys of choice, sex, and fatherhood." In "Approaching Prayer," Dickey is concerned with a son's freedom from the strictures of reason. "For the Last Wolverine" and "May Day Sermon" are concerned with a symbolic "father-murdering" conflict that Hodge describes as "murdered" repression. Hodge's different slant on violence and fathers in Dickey's poetry is well worth reading.

Gina D. Peterman also takes a new approach in "The Clothing Metaphor in James Dickey's 'Springer Mountain' and 'Falling' " (*JDN* 7, ii:12–18), discussing the use of clothing in these substantial Dickey poems as it relates to his view of the inhibitions of "modern man." Dickey believes in the need of humans to renew themselves through heightened awareness of the natural world. Our concepts of time represent a major setback in achieving such an awareness. As the deer hunter in "Springer Mountain" and the stewardess in "Falling" shed their clothes, they also lose touch with time and space in order to permit themselves to experience the fullness of life. As a symbol for the trappings of civilization, clothing in each case is discarded so that nature may be experienced "unencumbered—spiritually naked." This article identifies a symbol but makes nominal use of it.

C. Hines Edwards, Jr., "Initiation Ritual in Dickey's 'The Shark's Parlor' " (*JDN* 7, ii:19–23), begins with Robert Kirschten's analysis of the form of the poem, and then adds his own thoughts on the symbolism. Kirschten (see *ALS 1988*) found that the form supported Dickey's theme, the rite of passage; Edwards demonstrates that the symbolism in the poem fits better into the scheme of initiation mythology. The narrator/boy is the initiate, his beer-drinking constitutes a time of preparation, the men who help the boy serve as guides in the initiation, and the shark is a sacrificial animal necessary to complete the ritual. The text is read closely, but the mythos seems rather obvious.

viii African American

a. Brooks Henry Taylor in "Gwendolyn Brooks: An Essential Sanity" (*KR* 13, iv:115–31) uses examples from each published collection of Brooks's poetry in an attempt to find unity in the canon, despite the "conventional divisions of her career." Noting the "traditional technical virtuosity of her early works," Taylor points to the social issues evident. That her work became more stridently critical of those "aspects of the Black experience which are imposed by white society" after which she gained notoriety is not a surprise to Taylor. But he is nonplused that recognition of the increased anger apparent in many of these poems from the middle years of her career would lead critics to discount the social criticism of her earlier work and lament a presumed "change" in her poetry. A further change in Brooks's technique, principally departures from traditional white male forms, which occurred in the late 1960s, has led critics to see a sharp division in the Brooks canon. Conscious of the need to make black literature for black readers, Brooks experimented with new forms, but maintained above all a consistent commitment to write poetry about the black experience in America.

b. Dove In "Rita Dove: Crossing Boundaries" (*Callaloo* 14:419–33) Ekaterini Georgoudaki noteworthily distinguishes how Rita Dove's style differs from that of other contemporary black poets and helps explain why, though acclaimed by the critics, she is not known to many black readers. A conspicuous reason is that she has not been a political writer. Dove "does not adopt the polemical voice of either a black nationalist or a feminist poet." Influenced by her residence in Europe, in her second book, *Museum,* Dove "crosses socio-political, literary and other boundaries and divisions." It is only in her fourth book, *Thomas and Beulah,* that her poetry focuses specifically on the racial conflicts blacks face in the United States. Georgoudaki argues convincingly that this book should have engaged the audience that her previous books had not reached. An additional item, Bonnie Costello's "Scars and Wings: Rita Dove's *Grace Notes*" (*Callaloo* 14:434–38), proclaims the craft of Dove's writings—her "descriptive precision, tonal control, metaphoric reach"—

all as functional in conveying her "uncompromising realism." The analysis of *Grace Notes* effectively discloses the autobiographical dimensions of her work, from the "ontological dimensions of origin and destiny" to "beautiful poems of motherhood."

c. Lorde In contrast to Dove's involved indirectness, Audre Lorde openly proclaims her political involvement to Charles H. Rowell in "Above the Winds/An Interview with Audre Lorde" (*Callaloo* 14:83–95): "I am a Black, Lesbian, Feminist, warrior, poet, mother doing my work." One of the questions posed for Lorde is why she recently moved from a center of political involvement, New York City, to her island "retreat" in St. Croix. Her reasons are personal, health and relaxation; her conviction is that her poetry can now explore meaningfully the poor livelihood of blacks in the islands, the terrible effects on the poor of disasters like Hurricane Hugo, the lack of concern of those on the mainland with their condition, and the exploitation of black natives by oil companies. *Callaloo* also includes short interviews with Lorde, discussing the devastation of Hurricane Hugo in a letter, "Of Generators and Survival—Hugo Letter" (*Callaloo* 14:72–82); and her continuing concern with the fate of lesbian and gay publishing, "What Is at Stake in Lesbian and Gay Publishing Today" (*Callaloo* 14:65–66).

d. Jay Wright Isodore Okpewho in "From a Goat Path in Africa: An Approach to the Poetry of Jay Wright" (*Callaloo* 14:692–726) identifies a poet who has been concerned with Africanism in his own poetry. Okpewho meticulously indicates the older tradition (W. E. B. Du Bois, Langston Hughes, Countee Cullen) into which Wright's concern fits, and he offers an enlightening discussion of specific African images based on rituals from the ancient Dogon and Bambara mythologies of Mali that flourish in Wright's poetry. Wright's poetry is as African as the poetry of Wole Soyinka, but his regard has been for American problems.

e. Hughes The reprint of the late Larry Neal's "Langston Hughes: Black America's Poet Laureate" in Richard Kostelanetz's *American Writing Today* (pp. 61–72) makes a case for Hughes as "the poet laureate" of his people from the 1920s through the '40s and '50s until his death in 1967. On a more general issue, James Sullivan's "Real Cool Pages: The Broadside Press Broadside Series" (*ConL* 32:553–72) is the first in-depth study of 20th-century African broadsides, whose graphics and poetry promoted until 1975 a Black Arts Movement and demonstrated how art "was useful in the struggles of racial politics rather than art that simply attained traditional standards of beauty."

ix Others; Conclusion

I will provide notice for Michael Burns's edited collection *Miller Williams and the Poetry of the Particular* (Missouri) as the first collection of essays on a poet who only recently has been getting the notice he deserves. The 13 essays reveal the versatility of Williams, who has been variously an editor of anthologies and textbooks, the author of short stories, a translator, and a poet who won no prizes until the Poets' Prize for 1990. Respect from his fellow poets is indicated by very brief essays contributed by the late Howard Nemerov and by William Stafford, John Frederick Nims, Maxine Kumin, Fred Chappell, James Whitehead, C. D. Wright, Robert Wallace, and Lewis Turco.

Because this year was the first time that the MLA *Bibliography* was unavailable on Knowledge Index and available on CD-ROM, a few worthy items may not have been recorded. Amendments will be made next year.

Clemson University

17 Drama

Peter A. Davis

The publication drought of last year has abated. Although the publication of new material is still below the high levels of only two or three years ago, there still is much to celebrate. A number of excellent histories and critical studies highlight the offerings. In several important ways theater scholarship is finally displaying an originality not often found before. Much of this exploration is taking place in criticism and feminist theory. But even theater history has shown an awakening to important trends in historiography. Whether this is the start of an updating of American theater scholarship with an eye toward current worldwide movements in parallel fields is impossible to predict. At the same time, however, areas such as African-American theater, which have benefited from several productive and innovative years, have recently been weak.

This year sees the arrival of yet another journal, *Theatre Topics,* devoted to research in dramaturgy, performance studies, and theater pedagogy—three appropriately amorphous subject headings that ought to produce an interesting variety of material. The journal is the second cooperative venture between the Association for Theatre in Higher Education and the Johns Hopkins University Press, which also publishes *Theatre Journal* for the ATHE.

Sadly missing from the list this year are substantial works in Hispanic theater, which with a number of important studies in both history and criticism had lately developed into one of the more interesting fields. Another casualty is the demise of UMI's "Theater and Dramatic Studies" series, which had gained an uneven reputation for publishing moderately revised doctoral dissertations.

Theater scholarship continues to operate largely in isolation, seemingly unaware of most new theories and ideas in complementary fields. The pervasiveness of Foucault, Derrida, and Lacan notwithstanding, it lags far behind trends in history, comparative literature, anthropology, English, philosophy, and psychology. A great deal must be done to catch up.

i Reference Works and Anthologies

Until the past few years theater scholars could usually count on a fresh and bountiful annual crop of reference texts to pique their interests and refresh their courses. The trend has leveled off as the field has become saturated. Nonetheless, a few offerings provide new and valuable sources of information, although not necessarily in traditional areas.

Irene Shaland's *American Theater and Drama Research: An Annotated Guide to Information Sources, 1945–1990* (McFarland) is a useful addition to the standard bibliographical references and provides a thorough updating of sources since 1965. Shaland has wisely avoided including plays and anthologies as well as acting and directing texts. Instead, she focuses on "information sources dealing with the historical and aesthetical development of American theater and drama." The book contains 536 entries; the annotations are for the most part useful, although sometimes a bit glib and awkward.

One of the more unusual references to appear in recent years is *Stage Deaths: A Biographical Guide to International Theatrical Obituaries, 1850 to 1990*, 2 vols. (Greenwood), comp. George B. Bryan. Not exclusively American in coverage, it contains hundreds of relevant entries spanning the past 140 years. The book's concept and execution are simple: major performers, their birth and death dates, and citations of obituaries are listed. Yet it is an exhaustive source, providing invaluable information for biographical researchers. The two volumes contain more than 26,000 entries, culled from nine major American and English newspapers, including the *New York Times*, the *Times* of London, the *Los Angeles Times*, *Variety*, and the *New York Dramatic Mirror*. Such a short list is arguably of limited value, offering only the obituaries of popular figures while ignoring lesser-known people. But the sheer number of people covered more than compensates for the book's lack of depth. Although it may not end up on many scholars' personal bookshelves, it will certainly become a fixture in the reference library.

The consummate American theater bibliographer, Don B. Wilmeth, has provided another in a long and distinguished list of bibliographies in his "Popular Entertainment: A Checklist of Representative Books Published Primarily in the United States Since 1977" (*THStud* 9:151–65). Besides restricting the list to books published in the United States and Canada, Wilmeth omits serial essays and wisely limits offerings in musical theater; as he points out, these topics are adequately covered elsewhere. The list, as it stands, is the most comprehensive compilation on popular entertainment since Myron Matlaw's *American Popular Entertainment* (1979), which it intends to augment. Wilmeth highlights several dozen works he considers of special significance. Such a source has been long overdue in this expanding field, and Wilmeth's work will once again serve as the primary offering.

Edward Harrigan was among the most popular performers of the 19th century. Recognizing that no substantial bibliography had been published on him, Alicia Kae Koger has compiled the first major list of Harrigan material in a two-part series, "An Edward Harrigan Bibliography" (*NCTR* 19:29–44, 105–29). Included are plays, songs, songsters, recordings, nondramatic works, scrapbooks, set renderings, and costumes, all demonstrating Harrigan's enormous range and productivity. Fans of 19th-century performance will find this useful.

Several anthologies of note were published this year, countering a steady and unfortunate decline of late. It is significant that these books represent recent or contemporary writers and have little to do with the mainstream. Eileen Joyce Ostrow's *Center Stage: An Anthology of Twenty-one Contemporary Black-American Plays* (Illinois) is a paperback reprint of the 1981 edition, but it is worth mentioning for its extraordinary collection of African-American plays from a most formative era—the 1970s. While some of the themes and dialogue appear dated, the collection's overwhelming power is undeniable. In its paperback edition this anthology continues to be one of the most important assemblages of recent years. The University of Pittsburgh Press has produced the first collection of August Wilson's plays, *August Wilson: Three Plays.* And a most impressive collection it is: *Ma Rainey's Black Bottom, Fences,* and *Joe Turner's Come and Gone.* All three plays received New York Drama Critics' Circle awards, and *Fences* was the 1987 recipient of the Pulitzer Prize for Drama. The prologue is Wilson's commentary on his life and influences, interesting for its condensed account of his early years but with little that is surprising. Paul Carter Harrison supplies a critically detailed afterword that places Wilson within the cultural context of the last three decades. In a similar vein is *The LeRoi Jones/Amiri Baraka Reader* (Thunder's Mouth), ed. William J. Harris. While most of the collection focuses on Baraka's poetry and prose, it contains three plays considered to be hallmarks of modern American theater, *Dutchman, Great Goodness of Life,* and *What Was the Relationship of the Lone Ranger to the Means of Production?* Harris's introduction divides Baraka's life into three major periods, providing a critical survey suitable for undergraduate digestion.

ii Theater History

This year produced a rare abundance of work on the history of theatrical performance in the United States, with a variety of approaches and topics. I have selected for inclusion here works that reflect the traditions and changes in American theater history, both to point out weaknesses and to encourage the field to break from its dated methodology by using current trends in historiography.

The most innovative work this year is a landmark study of interdisciplinary scope that incorporates literary and political history, sociology, anthropology, and religion in a comprehensive examination of the theatrical metaphor in colonial America. Jeffrey H. Richards's *Theatre Enough: American Culture and the Metaphor of the World Stage, 1607–1789* (Duke) may not appear to be a work of theater history, but its understanding of the colonial American mind and the infusion of theatrical images and allusions makes this an essential work for anyone interested in the founding of this nation's dramatic and aesthetic principles. It is a remarkable work, richly detailed and annotated, well-written, and cleverly organized. The work is much more than simply an exhaustive culling of every known theatrical allusion and reference in colonial American literature. Richards has guided the study into a detailed exploration of colonial life and values using the theater as the unifying force. Not all is perfect about the book, of course. Some important factual errors occur. One is Richards's use of the Moral Dialogues bill of 1761, which has been shown to be fraudulent. And in places he relies too heavily on secondary and outdated sources. Historians of the 18th century would certainly find fault with his vague application of the term "puritan," which remains a contentious issue. But on the whole the book is of great importance and should alter current perceptions of America's theatrical and cultural origins.

The rise of popular culture as a serious academic pursuit has finally taken hold among theater historians. Minstrelsy, vaudeville, pageants, parades, musicals, and even wild West shows and sporting events have received much attention. Lagging behind, surprisingly, has been the one obvious form of 19th-century amusement, the burlesque, which often incorporates much from the other forms. Robert C. Allen's *Horrible Prettiness: Burlesque and the American Culture* (No. Car.) attempts to address this deficit. Allen has surveyed most of the major works on American theater history and assembled a chronological narrative of the long history of burlesque on the American stage. The only problem is that he draws almost entirely from secondary sources, with little that is original apart from gathering the material under one cover. The book is amply illustrated and is the most complete study of the subject to date; but it falls short on original research, making it more suitable as a textbook.

One of the most intriguing studies in recent years is Albert Furtwangler's *Assassin on Stage: Brutus, Hamlet, and the Death of Lincoln* (Illinois). Combining historical research with critical theory, Furtwangler has juxtaposed Lincoln's murder with the theatrical life of his assassin. He offers credible literary evidence that John Wilkes Booth was acting out a Shakespearean tragedy. *Hamlet* and *Julius Caesar* become not just convenient metaphors for comprehending Booth's actions, but authentic manifestations for an obsessed actor who readily compares himself to Brutus in the days surrounding the assassination. Furtwangler also draws in Booth's brother Edwin to complete the study of a theatrical family caught up in a real-life tragedy. *Assassin on Stage* is an admirable work that demonstrates how often theater and history are the same.

Funny Woman: The Life and Times of Fanny Brice (Indiana), by Barbara W. Grossman, a revised dissertation, is a thoroughly documented study of Fanny Brice's life. This revision is readable and should be reasonably popular with the nonacademic public. It is essentially a traditional, nonfeminist biography that follows a predictable chronology. Little new or unusual will be found in the text, but it offers another perspective on popular entertainment during the first half of this century and captures the essence of Brice's life.

Among the most innovative and controversial theater companies of the 1960s was Richard Schechner's The Performance Group. Apart from Schechner's own account-cum-manifesto, *Environmental Theatre* (1973), little writing of substance has been published on this short-lived yet influential theater. A fascinating account by the leading actor in the group's most famous production, *Dionysus in '69,* William Hunter Shephard's *The Dionysus Group* (Peter Lang) is an accessible yet scholarly assessment of the group's growth and process. Analytical and personal, Shephard draws heavily on his experiences. Although some may find his approach too direct and private, especially when he explores his own motivations and feelings, his account is viable primary material.

Similarly, Janet Coleman's *The Compass: The Improvisational Theatre that Revolutionized American Comedy* (Chicago) documents the story of America's premier comedy company, which served as the home for such improvisational performers as Mike Nichols and Elaine May, Viola Spolin, Shelly Berman, Alan Arkin, and Barbara Harris, and was the inspiration for most of the major groups that emerged in the '60s and '70s, including the Committee and Second City. Its preeminence is undeniable, yet virtually nothing has been published on the company and thus its position in American theater history has been largely ignored. Coleman's approach is more traditional and objective than Shephard's, but no less interesting. The subject alone makes this book worthy, but the research and intelligent writing elevate it to required reading.

Instructors of modern theater history will be pleased to learn that Oscar G. Brockett and Robert Findlay have issued a second edition of their popular text *Century of Innovation: A History of European and American Theatre and Drama Since the Late Nineteenth Century* (Allyn and Bacon). This edition is considerably shorter than the first: the 19 chapters of the first edition have been pared to 15, and its 800 pages to 520. The production values also are noticeably thinner: photographs are not so clear, the typesetting is less consistent, and in places the printing is faded and blurred. Nonetheless, most will find this an excellent revision. The authors have not merely appended an updated final chapter but have rewritten substantial portions, incorporating current theories and historiographical trends.

Steve Vineberg has written a weighty text on *Method Actors: Three Generations of an American Acting Style* (Schirmer). Not merely a survey of "the Method," the book is more a performance history, tracing the acting theory on stage and in cinema from the arrival in the United States of its first proponent, Russian émigré Richard Boleslavsky, in 1923 to Rip Torn, Blythe Danner, and Jack Nicholson. True to cinema texts generally, this one has black-and-white stills illustrating great moments in American acting. The book's effort to integrate the entire chronology and evolution of this pervasive acting style, incorporating the Group Theatre, the Actors Studio, the Neighborhood Playhouse, and beyond into a cohesive narrative with detailed critical observation must be commended. Performance historians will find this an indispensable interpretation of a vital aspect of 20th-century aesthetics.

Director, producer, and scholar Norris Houghton has written his autobiography, *Entrances and Exits: A Life In and Out of the Theatre* (Limelight). From his early days with Josh Logan at Princeton University and with the University Club Players on Cape Cod, Houghton traces his experiences in commercial theater, Broadway, Off-Broadway, and academia. Judging by this account, his was certainly a full and colorful life. And like most books of this genre it is rich with anecdote and ruminations of numerous celebrities and productions. Clearly its most interesting contribution is Houghton's description of the founding and growth of the Phoenix Theatre between 1953 and 1962, forging and defining the essence of what would become identified as Off-Broadway.

In "Out of the Kitchen and into the Marketplace: Normalizing *Uncle Tom's Cabin* for the Antebellum Stage" (*JADT* 3, i:5–28) Bruce McConachie examines the ways in which the two most popular stage adaptations of Harriet Beecher Stowe's novel (by Aiken and Conroy) altered its perceived interpretation as a challenge to "the secular, masculine, and capitalist society of the antebellum North." McConachie uses Thomas Haskell's 1985 article "Capitalism and the Origins of the Humanitarian Sensibility" as a philosophical foundation from which to argue that the two staged versions, while representing a diluted version of Stowe's abolitionist position, reveal an implied reinforcement of northern market capitalism, contrary to the novel. It is a convincing argument, well-stated and amply supported.

Walter J. Meserve surveys dramatic interpretations of the American frontier in "The American West of the 1870s and 1880s as Viewed from the Stage" (*JADT* 3, i:48–63). He demonstrates his immense knowledge of American dramatic literature, setting the plays of Bartley Campbell, James J. McCloskey, Augustin Daly, Steele Mackaye, Fred G. Maeder, Howard Hill, and Clay Greene within the context of growing American fascination with all things western. Among the more interesting points is how Maeder's 1872 production of Ned Buntline's story *Buffalo Bill, King of the Bordermen* eventually convinced William Cody to take to the stage himself, giving rise to a new genre of wild West shows and paratheatricals. Another 19th-century study worth reading is Pat M. Ryan's "The Horse Drama, with Supernumeraries: Bronson Howard's Semi-Historical *Shenandoah*" (*JADT* 3, ii:42–69), a good example of critical analysis and production history in which the play becomes a social, political, and cultural revelation of postbellum attitudes toward the South and the recently freed slaves. The article is expertly researched and constructed.

Patty S. Derrick amplifies the work and life of one of America's premier performers in "Julia Marlowe: An Actress Caught Between Traditions" (*TS* 32:85–105). Marlowe, it seems, attempted to perpetuate a romantic idealism against the tide of realism. For her efforts she was initially revered and inevitably reviled, as the American taste for more contemporary interpretations of Shakespeare and the classics led her to retire in 1924. Like William Winter, her critical champion and himself a romantic idealist, Marlowe represented the remnants of a failed 19th-century movement to elevate American theater to European standards. Her work, although often overlooked, is a crucial link to our aesthetic past and exemplifies the extent of change in American theatrical taste.

The theatrical life of one of Marlowe's younger contemporaries is profiled by Margaret Loftus Ranald in "When They Weren't Playing O'Neill: The Antithetical Career of Carlotta Monterey" (*THStud* 11:81–106). Although she is best remembered as Eugene O'Neill's second wife, Monterey had an active and reasonably popular acting career. Ranald points out, however, that Monterey's flamboyant and vampish professional style starkly contrasted to that of O'Neill's brooding seriousness. In fact, "her career epitomized the theater against which he rebelled." With this underlying principle, Ranald examines Monterey's theatrical life as it leads up to her years with O'Neill.

Dean Howd attempts to resurrect the career of one of America's most popular scene designers in "Joseph Urban and American Scene Design" (*TS* 32, ii:173–86). Howd reveals Urban's extensive influence and capacities, while appropriately lamenting his profoundly obscure position in American theater history. In part, Urban's relative lack of visibility in theater texts results from the breadth of his skill and accomplishment: apart from designing more than 160 plays and 40 films, he was a renowned architect and industrial designer. Howd serves Urban's memory and reputation well, surveying his life and highlighting his major accomplishments as a reminder to theater students that many great artists have gone unnoticed or remain poorly studied.

iii Criticism and Theory

Critical studies in American theater rebounded this year with several notable works displaying the range of approaches now starting to affect dramatic scholarship. *From Class to Caste in American Drama: Political and Social Themes Since the 1930s* (Greenwood), by Richard G. Scharine, is a sweeping study of American drama's development through the essential filter of political and social change. Scharine does a remarkable job of defining and evaluating the distinctions between political and traditional forms of theater. With this theoretical basis, he follows a chronological history, employing political and social themes to understand how American drama reflected or altered the realities of American life. The study's scope is commendable, moving from WPA productions and the labor-oriented theater of the '30s through the cold war and Vietnam war periods, the civil rights movement, and concluding with the current gay rights movement. For each period Scharine extracts apt and provocative examples of dramatic literature to illustrate his themes. Some are plays rarely included in such analyses, including *Johnny Johnson, Deep Are the Roots, Darkness at Noon, China Gate, The Gentleman Caller, The Mighty Gents, Los Dos Caras del Patroncito, Black Elk Speaks,* and *As Is.* The superb blending of criticism and history makes this required reading for any contemporary student of American theater and culture.

Versions of Heroism in Modern American Drama: Redefinitions by Miller, Williams, O'Neill and Anderson (St. Martin's), by Julie Adam, critically evaluates the changing nature of the "hero" in American dramatic literature through the works of the writers listed in the title. Although reading much like a dissertation, the book offers a convincing argument about the shaping of heroism in recent drama as an aspect of individualism. Adam concentrates on the four variations that heroism takes: idealism, martyrdom, self-reflection, and survival. It is a succinct and well-reasoned study, although somewhat predictable.

The role of professional critics and their influence on contemporary theater is the subject of John E. Booth's *The Critic, Power, and the Performing Arts* (Columbia). Booth assesses the impact of critics on theater, dance, and music; the world of the critic; and the philosophy of criticism. As one of only a handful of such studies, the book is a vital addition to theatrical scholarship. The extensive list of interviews indicates the degree to which Booth sought a comprehensive overview of the profession. But the effect is less scholarly than practical; indeed, the book's title might read, "How to Be a Critic." Too few theater students study the critic's role; with Booth's book, perhaps more of them will pursue the subject.

Sue-Ellen Case and Janelle Reinelt have assembled an equally impressive array of articles, *The Performance of Power: Theatrical Discourse and Politics* (Iowa). One of the initial offerings of the new "Studies in Theatre History" Series, ed. Thomas Postlewait, the collection features a list of authors who represent some of the more active minds in theater history and theory. But the initial promise of the text falters on close reading. Almost all of the articles are revised papers from 1989 conferences of the Association of Theatre in Higher Education and the American Society for Theatre Research. The editors saw the need to anthologize what they perceived as an emerging debate in theater studies "regarding the borders of its territory, its methodologies, its subject matter, and its scholars' perspectives. The nature of this debate, one might even say struggle, is political. It concerns the 'performance of power'—the struggle over power relations embedded in texts, methodologies, and the academy." The idea is important and certainly needs to be addressed. The editors have organized the collection into materialist semiotics, deconstruction, revealing surveillance strategies, constructing utopia, and the academic institution and the production of knowledge. But the headings are only marginally appropriate to the articles in each section, and the articles themselves are inconsistent in quality. Those worth reading are "The Politics of *Metamora*" (pp. 92–110) by Jeffrey D. Mason, "The Artificial Eye: Augustan Theater and the Empire of the Visible" (pp. 131–45) by Joseph Roach, "The Playhouse and the Committee" (pp. 146–62) by Barry Witham, "Charlie Chaplin, Soviet Icon" (pp. 199–220) by Spencer Golub, "Conferring Power in the Theater" (pp. 256–65) by Gay Gibson Cima, and "The Theory of History" (pp. 272–80) by Marvin Carlson. These entries alone make the text an appropriate selection for a graduate course in theater historiography and theory. But the forceful argument made by the editors in their introduction is not fully realized in the articles.

Michael Vanden Heuvel's *Performing Drama/Dramatizing Performance* (Michigan) takes a historical/critical view of the American avant-garde, positing a blend of mainstream and alternative drama as the source of contemporary performance art. Vanden Heuvel examines the recent history of American avant-garde performance, the formulative effects of Samuel Beckett, and the functional application of new forms by the Wooster Group, Robert Wilson, and Sam Shepard. The book is well-written, and the author does a creditable job of sorting out difficult contemporary theories and practices. In a similar vein, *Contemporary American Theatre* (St. Martin's), ed. Bruce King, attempts to articulate the shape and direction of American drama in the 1980s through essays by prominent scholars. Most of them focus on better-known artists. Barbara Kachur surveys the state of "Women Playwrights on Broadway: Henley, Howe, Norman, and Wasserstein" (pp. 15–40), and Dennis Carroll focuses on "Not-Quite Mainstream Male Playwrights: Guare, Durang, and Rabe" (pp. 114–36). There are also articles on David Hwang, the Wooster Group, recent performance artists, and the obligatory article on Peter Sellars. The breadth of material is noteworthy.

Sellars is featured again in Tom Mikotowicz's "Director Peter Sellars: Bridging the Modern & Postmodern" (*Theatre Topics* 1, i:87–98). This brief survey of Sellars's career is a good introduction for the uninitiated. More interesting is Andrea J. Nouryeh's critical assessment, "JoAnne Akalaitis: Post-Modern Director or Socio-Sexual Critic" (*Theatre Topics* 1, ii:177–91). Nouryeh does what Mikotowicz fails to do; she substantively evaluates the director's major work. The article contextualizes Akalaitis as a postmodern director through a play-by-play analysis of her technique.

iv Feminist Theater

Two excellent books survey women's contributions to the American theater before 1900. Mary M. Turner's *Forgotten Leading Ladies of the American Theatre* (McFarland) looks at eight influential women, comparing them in pairs beginning with Susanna Haswell Rowson and Anna Cora Mowatt in "Playwrights"; each woman is covered thoroughly with a brief biography and critical assessment. The other chapters include "Actresses" (Sophia Turner and Charlotte Cushman), "Managers" (Laura Keene and Mrs. John Drew), and "Activists" (Fanny Kemble and Minnie Maddern Fiske). Although the book contains no new information, it is good to have this sort of introductory survey available.

Similarly, Mary Anne Schofield and Cecilia Macheski have edited a worthwhile collection of new essays on Restoration and 18th-century women in the theater, *Curtain Calls: British and American Women and the*

Theater, 1660–1820 (Ohio). The text is organized conceptually into seven sections with 22 essays by notable scholars. Much attention is devoted to English women, but in "Set Change: The Colonial Scene," three essays evaluate the American side. Doreen Alvarez Saar adds a new perspective on the works of "Susanna Rowson: Feminist and Democrat" (pp. 231–46), focusing on *The Slaves of Algiers* (1794) as symbolic of "the female as metaphor of the spirit of the nation." It is well-argued and effectively written, perhaps the best critical essay on the play. Less effective, although no less interesting, is Jean B. Kern's brief overview of "Mercy Otis Warren: Dramatist of the American Revolution" (pp. 247–59). Each of Warren's five major works is covered, but brevity of treatment results in some unfortunate oversights, including a discussion of the disputed authorship of *The Blockheads* that ignores scholarship in *Theatre Survey* (see Krystan V. Douglas, "A Question of Authorship: Mercy Otis Warren and *The Blockheads*" [*TS* 30:85–92]). The final offering is Mary Anne Schofield's "'Quitting the Loom and Distaff': Eighteenth-Century American Women Dramatists" (pp. 260–73), which attempts to revive the histories of several forgotten women playwrights after the Revolution. The article mainly deals with Judith Sargent Murray, but Schofield manages some references to Mrs. Marriot of the Old American Company, Margaretta V. Bleeker Faugeres, and Madame Gardie. Clearly more work needs to be done on these early writers.

Perhaps the best example of American feminist theater history in the past few years is Barbara Melosh's richly detailed and exquisitely written study, *Engendering Culture: Manhood and Womanhood in New Deal Public Art and Theater* (Smithsonian). Its glossy production values, rare in academic publishing today, highlight the study's interdisciplinary nature and its adherence to the best in feminist scholarship and art history. Melosh's conceptualization of feminine and masculine imagery in American art and theater redefines the aesthetic norms of pre-World War II culture. Balanced approach, impeccable research, and interdisciplinary historiography make this a model of feminist history.

A short critical survey of recent women playwrights and feminist topics on stage is provided in Janet Brown's *Taking Center Stage: Feminism in Contemporary U.S. Drama* (Scarecrow). Included are chapters on Darrah Cloud's *The Stick Wife*, Ntozake Shange's *For Colored Girls Who Have Considered Suicide When the Rainbow was Enuf*, Kathleen Collin's *The Brothers*, Marsha Norman's *Getting Out* and *'Night, Mother*, David Rabe's *In the Boom Boom Room* and *Hurlyburly*, and Caryl Churchill's

Top Girls. Its critical observations are neat if somewhat predictable. And the selection of plays will appeal to a popular audience.

Drama by Women to 1900: A Bibliography of American and British Writers (Toronto), comp. Gwenn Davis and Beverly A. Joyce, might be more appropriately listed among reference texts. But I choose to highlight it here since it represents the only such source book now available and indicates another aspect of feminist studies rarely pursued. The third volume in the series "Bibliographies of Writings by American and British Women to 1900," it offers appendixes of chronological listings and actresses in addition to subject, adaptation, and translation indexes. This carefully prepared source should prove useful.

v African-American and Hispanic Theater

Most research in African-American and Hispanic theater this year resulted in studies of individual playwrights; these are discussed below in the appropriate sections. General critical and historical studies are represented by relatively few articles.

Of special note is an issue of *Black American Literature Forum* devoted entirely to "The Black Church and The Black Theatre." Several articles are of particular interest in their innovative use of methodology to examine the changing nature of African-American theater. Rhett S. Jones combines sociological perspectives with popular culture to deconstruct black audiences in "Orderly and Disorderly Structures: Why Church and Sports Appeal to Black Americans and Theatre Does Not" (25:43–52); his conclusions are a fascinating comment on popular aesthetics and values. Anthony D. Hill looks at the proliferation of religious elements within the black theatrical experience in "The Pulpit and Grease Paint: The Influence of Black Church Ritual on Black Theatre" (25:113–20). Contemporary literature is examined in Leslie Catherine Sanders's " 'I've wrestled with them all my life': Langston Hughes's *Tambourines to Glory*" (25:63–72) and Sandra G. Shannon's "The Long Wait: August Wilson's *Ma Rainey's Black Bottom*" (25:133–46). The collection is well edited and thoughtfully conceived.

vi The American Musical

Demand for published accounts of the American musical remains high, despite declines in musical productions on Broadway and elsewhere.

Americans revere this homebred hybrid melodrama, although the form has apparently exhausted itself aesthetically and financially. Close reading suggests that even in scholarly circles the musical is nearing its nadir as a critical subject as well as a reflector of American culture.

Perhaps the best single resource on the subject is Gerald Bordman's revision of his *American Musical Theatre: A Chronicle* (Oxford). When the first edition appeared in 1978 it was hailed as the most complete source to date and immediately became the standard text for countless undergraduate courses. As a chronicle of the American musical, the second edition is unparalleled, extending the chronology through the 1990 season. Bordman also has made a number of corrections and several important additions in the light of recent scholarship. While the text lacks much substantial or modern evaluation, it is not intended to be a critical assessment as much as a linear narrative of major musical moments. A hefty 800 pages at a hefty price, it is nevertheless a valuable and timely record.

Following in the footsteps of countless sycophantic chroniclers before him, Thomas S. Hischak has written *Word Crazy: Broadway Lyricists from Cohan to Sondheim* (Praeger), a brief formulaic paean to the writers of American musicals. The book comprises short chapters on various lyricists in rough chronological order, detailing their unique contributions. Hischak covers all of the usual names and adds a few lesser-known writers. There is little detailed analysis and what can only be described as a deliberate lack of critical perspective; the author is a "fan," and his enthusiasm clearly shows. Unfortunately, this makes for thin scholarship, a problem common among studies of the American musical.

A refreshing exception to this rule, however, is Susan L. Porter's *With an Air Debonair: Musical Theatre in America, 1785–1815* (Smithsonian). Despite the musical's popularity among spectator and scholar alike, studies of its early development have been scarce. Julian Mates's *The American Musical Stage Before 1800* (1962) added only slightly to O. G. Sonneck's *Early Opera in America* (1915). But with Porter's study the history of the form in postrevolutionary America takes on greater significance, and its place in the growth of a national drama is more clearly defined. This is an impressive work. Porter embellishes her conceptual approach with fresh and detailed sources. By focusing on this thirty-year period she reveals a startling complexity of primary references. Her thorough knowledge of musical history never overwhelms the essential theatrical nature of the study, making this lengthy and readable book invaluable for the musicologist and scholar. Two appendixes offer an extensive list of musical productions before 1815. A masterful work, it should redefine the history of the American theater in the late 18th and early 19th centuries.

vii O'Neill

Thanks to such publications as the *Eugene O'Neill Review* there is never a shortage of scholarly material on America's most studied playwright. This year's offerings are as rich and varied as always, although no substantial monograph was produced. *Eugene O'Neill's Century: Centennial Views on America's Foremost Tragic Dramatist* (Greenwood), ed. Richard F. Moorton, presents one of the more diverse collections of essays on O'Neill in recent years. As a product of the O'Neill centennial celebrations of 1988, the anthology assembles an array of papers presented at the Collaborations III festival in New London, Connecticut. The purpose of the festival was to commemorate the anniversary by inviting an unusual variety of scholars to comment on O'Neill, presumably to demonstrate his broad appeal and interdisciplinary reach. The book clearly reflects this purpose. Apart from the usual complement of English and drama professors, there are pieces by two psychology professors, two classicists, a German scholar, a philosophy professor, and a theater arts administrator. The breadth alone should be commended. And indeed, there is a richness in the collection not normally found in such thematic anthologies. But although the individual essays are interesting reading, the overall organization reflects the awkwardness of trying to combine disparate views. Perhaps out of the need to simply break the table of contents into manageable chunks, the editor has organized the work into three unequal, amorphously titled sections, "O'Neill's Tragic Art," "Art and Life—The Wellspring of Genius," and "O'Neill Onstage." Constraints on space allow me to note only a few highlights. Spencer Golub draws on his impressive knowledge of Russian literature and cultural history to examine the pervasive thread of European symbolism and "how strange is the seemingly familiar" in "O'Neill and the Poetics of Modernist Strangeness" (pp. 17–39). Conventional Freudian analysis is applied to *Mourning Becomes Electra* in S. Georgia Nugent's "Masking Becomes Electra: O'Neill, Freud, and the Feminine" (pp. 55–71); while the mask-behind-the-mask idea has become a dated symbol of sexual displacement, it is actually refreshing to see the well-worn methodology applied again with such vigor. Taking a different tack, although equally interesting, Richard F. Moorton, Jr., employs a classics background to deconstruct O'Neill's sexual imagery in "The Author as Oedipus in *Mourning Becomes Electra* and *Long Day's Journey into Night*" (pp. 170–88). Other pieces worth reading include Roger Brown's "Causality in O'Neill's Late Masterpieces" (pp. 41–54), Rita Terras's "A Spokesman for America: O'Neill in Translation" (pp. 87–104), and Kristin Pfefferkorn's "Searching for Home in O'Neill's America" (pp. 119–43). The text is indexed and contains a useful list of works cited.

The usual complement of articles in the *Eugene O'Neill Review* range from the profound to the peculiar. The spring issue includes Edward L. Shaughnessy's "O'Neill's Catholic Dilemma in *Days Without End*" (pp. 5–26); Marc Simon's "Eugene O'Neill's Introduction to Hart Crane's *White Buildings:* Why he 'would have done it in a minute but . . .' " (pp. 41–58); Egil Törnqvist's "Strindberg, O'Neill, Norén: A Swedish-American Triangle" (pp. 65–78); Julie M. Gram's " 'Tomorrow': From Whence *The Iceman Cometh*" (pp. 79–92); and Bruce J. Mann's curious but fascinating discovery, "An FBI Memorandum on O'Neill" (pp. 59–64). The autumn issue, on the other hand, has only one substantial article, Edward L. Shaughnessy's extended family biography, "Ella, James, and Jamie O'Neill" (pp. 5–92), as well as several items on documents.

Those interested in O'Neill's early influence abroad will find Marjorie L. Hoover's "Three O'Neill Plays in 1920s Productions by Tairov's Kamerny Theater" (*THStud* 11:123–28) most illuminating. While short on evaluation, it provides invaluable information on the presentation of O'Neill's dramas in the early Soviet Union. Other articles worth considering are Normand Berlin's "O'Neill the 'Novelist' " (*MD* 34:49–58) and Kurt Eisen's " 'The Writing on the Wall': Novelization and the Critique of History in *The Iceman Cometh*" (*MD* 34:59–73).

viii Odets, Anderson, Saroyan, Hansberry, Williams

Clifford Odets receives unusual attention this year in two major works that add substantially to understanding his position in American theater. William W. Demastes has edited the first of what promises to be a series of bibliographies on major American playwrights by Greenwood Press. *Clifford Odets: A Research and Production Sourcebook* contains a chronology, brief biography, critical assessments and plot summaries of the plays, production histories, an exhaustive annotated bibliography, and production credits. In short, it is a definitive literary and critical resource. If the rest of the series is as thorough, Greenwood will have made a substantial contribution to theater scholarship.

As part of the "Critical Essays on American Literature" series published by G. K. Hall, *Critical Essays on Clifford Odets,* ed. Gabriel Miller, follows the standard outline by piecing together an assortment of reviews, interviews, and reprinted essays. An attempt is made to cover the range of material, from Joseph Wood Krutch's 1935 reviews of *Waiting for Lefty* and *Till the Day I Die* to Brooks Atkinson's 1954 review of *The Flowering Peach.* In between are reviews by Burns Mantle, John Mason Brown, Richard Watts, Jr., and William Hawkins. Among the essays are critical perspectives by George L. Groman, Harold Cantor, Gerald Weales, C. W. E. Bigsby, Margaret Brenman-Gibson, and Edward Murray. Inevitably, however, such compendia usually come up short, managing only to highlight selected moments in the writer's career, augmented by dated critical summaries of his work.

Overshadowed by the O'Neill centennial in 1988 was the centennial celebration of Maxwell Anderson. Nancy J. Doran and Kenneth Krauss have edited the only anthology to commemorate the event, *Maxwell Anderson and the New York Stage* (Library Research Associates). Sadly, the collection is not impressive; the seven scholarly essays and one interview are largely cursory examinations of Anderson's life and work. Two articles are notable, however: Perry D. Luckett examines Anderson's worldview and how it affected his use of honor and heroism in "Maxwell Anderson's Skepticism and the Making of His Plays" (pp. 81–95) and Ron Engle inventories "The Critical Reception of Maxwell Anderson's Plays in Foreign Language Translations on the European Stage" (pp. 113–48). Of particular interest too is Engle's 13-page appendix of Anderson productions abroad, 1929–88.

William Saroyan has received scant attention since his death in 1981. But Warsaw Visitor; Tales from the Vienna Streets: *The Last Two Plays of William Saroyan* (CSU-Fresno), ed. Dickran Kouymjian, offers an introduction documenting Saroyan's final years and illustrating the process that produced these last plays, the playscripts themselves, and a number of photographs completing this belated tribute. It is by no means sufficient recognition, but given the scarcity of material it helps.

In *Hansberry's Drama: Commitment Amid Complexity* (Illinois)

Steven R. Carter presents the most complete study of the playwright and her work to date. Granted access to the estate papers and manuscripts, Carter unearths important information on Hansberry's influences and views. The book contains a critical summary followed by detailed analyses of specific plays and writings. Remarkable for its discovery of Hansberry's unusual diversity of interests and unfulfilled projects, this study enhances our understanding of her acknowledged contribution, her great promise, and the extraordinary loss as a result of her death at age 34.

Drewey Wayne Gunn has produced a second edition of his 1980 resource, *Tennessee Williams: A Bibliography* (Scarecrow). In addition to a decade of updating, the text is better-organized and the index is more complete. The chronology is particularly helpful and probably the most comprehensive available. In a year surprisingly short of Williams material, this revision is most welcome. Philip C. Kolin has written a fascinating study of "The First Critical Assessments of *A Streetcar Named Desire:* The *Streetcar* Tryouts and the Reviewers" (*JDTC* 6, i:45–68). Drawing on previously unpublished material from the Williams estate and a healthy dose of long-forgotten reviews, Kolin documents the month of tryouts and rehearsals preceding the play's opening on Broadway in December 1947, tracing the development of Williams's reputation and the controversy evoked by the play even before it reached Broadway.

ix Current Dramatists

Ruby Cohn has revised and updated her 1982 survey of contemporary theater, *New American Dramatists, 1960–1990* (St. Martin's). Like the highly successful first edition, the revision offers a concise overview of the major writers and their most popular works. The book touches on most of the big names, including Simon, Kopit, McNally, Wilson, Rabe, Guare, Hwang, Howe, Henley, Norman, Gelber, Fornès, Valdez, Baraka, Childress, Mamet, and Shepard.

The existential angst of theatrical characters in the nuclear age is revived in a compact but intriguing comparative study, *Tragicomedy and Contemporary Culture* (Michigan), by John Orr. Beginning with a redefinition of modernism and tragedy, the book traces the concept of tragicomedy from Synge and O'Neill through Albee, Orton, and Fugard. Orr devotes a chapter to Beckett's seminal writings, followed by two chapters on Pinter, and he concludes by relating the tragicomedy to the mythic elements in three detailed chapters on Sam Shepard. His thesis is well-crafted and reasonably argued, although it covers well-worn territory.

Melissa E. Biggs, the founding editor of the undergraduate literary and arts journal *The Yale Vernacular,* has compiled a collection of interviews published between 1987 and 1990, *In the* Vernacular: *Interviews at Yale with Sculptors of Culture* (McFarland). Most of the interviews are with nontheater people, but several provide wonderfully disarming insights into some of the better-known American playwrights and directors. Peter Sellars, for example, admits that he is "tired of having to reduce material so that somebody who isn't interested in it anyway can understand it." And the interview with Ntozake Shange concludes with "M.B.: How do you pronounce your first name? Shange: EN-toe-zah-kay." Other interviews, with Jules Feiffer, Arthur Miller, Spalding Gray, and Wendy Wasserstein, are equally amusing.

Katherine Arens addresses the unanswerable in "Robert Wilson: Is Postmodern Performance Possible?" (*TJ* 43, i:14–40). Despite the subject, this is probably the best and most accessible assessment of Wilson's performance aesthetic. Arens offers a good critical overview of the canon and places Wilson's difficult work in a comprehensible context. A thoughtful and detailed structural comparison is made by Sheila Rabillard in "Destabilizing Plot, Displacing the Status of Narrative: Local Order in the Plays of Pinter and Shepard" (*TJ* 43, i:41–58). Using Pinter's *Old Times* and Shepard's *A Lie of the Mind,* Rabillard argues that "the pattern of a traditional storied plot cannot wholly dominate and is destabilized, to some extent displaced, by principles of order derived instead from what seems a local, smaller-scale pattern." Her thesis both effectively reevaluates the uses of rhetorical structures in plotting and designs a new basis for understanding structure in Shepard's plays.

University of Illinois, Urbana-Champaign

18 Themes, Topics, Criticism

Michael Fischer

It is difficult to generalize about the diverse books discussed here. Many of them, however, focus on what may be the central assumption of current literary theory, namely, that facts, values, reason, and the self are social constructs, not unchanging, objective realities. In addition to arguing for or against this assumption, many writers explore its consequences. Does a historical approach to knowledge underwrite political activism or lead to an uncritical relativism? This is the kind of question that many theorists today are struggling with, often in productive ways.

i Literary Theory

One of the most important books published this year—James L. Battersby's *Paradigms Regained: Pluralism and the Practice of Criticism* (Penn.)—argues for a philosophically defensible pluralism, "a relativism with muscle, with standards of rightness." According to Battersby, we can support these standards without resurrecting the metaphysical foundationalism that recent theorists have rightly discredited: "when the Foundation is dropped, everything stays in place; everything stays pretty much the same. We continue to do pretty much as we had been doing." Battersby is impatient with theorists who hope to disrupt business as usual—too impatient, in my opinion. But this is a lively, rigorously argued book—the best apology for pluralism since Wayne C. Booth's *Critical Understanding* (1979).

If Battersby is impatient with what he sees as the anything-goes relativism supposedly sponsored by recent theory, Harold Fromm is livid. His *Academic Capitalism and Literary Value* (Georgia) is a wholesale assault on the pretentiousness, careerism, and exaggerated political claims that for Fromm characterize contemporary theory. Fromm's targets are many: everyone from Jacques Derrida, Fredric Jameson, and Henry Louis Gates, Jr., to feminists who for political reasons elevate "inept, third-rate performances like *Frankenstein*" into masterpieces. Fromm is right to challenge theorists to earn their radical political claims. And I share his concern over the costly separation of much academic criticism from nonspecialist lay readers. But *Academic Capitalism and Literary Value* is finally an embittered, defensive book, warped by Fromm's suspicion that all, or at least most, academic criticism is just plain phony. According to Fromm, "the real aim [of politically minded academic theorists] is personal success and power, not genuine ethical reform in the world." In statements like these Fromm's healthy questioning of contemporary theory degenerates into reductive cynicism.

A more nuanced but still critical discussion of recent theory informs Patrick Colm Hogan's *The Politics of Interpretation: Ideology, Professionalism, and the Study of Literature* (Oxford, 1990). Hogan criticizes much academic criticism, especially deconstruction and French feminism, for engaging in ineffectual shadow-boxing and aiming rhetorical blows at abstractions like phallogocentricism while leaving untouched "the political concerns of real human life." Hogan grounds his own leftist politics in "ordinary principles of rational inference and empirical investigation," for him "the basis not only of natural science but of political action—including political interpretation—as well." While I agree that many academic political critics—some deconstructionists and French feminists included—promise more than they deliver, I question Hogan's positivist-sounding alternative. At the very least, he needs to explain why many would-be activist critics have felt compelled to challenge the empiricist guidelines by which he measures them.

In *Theory, (Post)Modernity, Opposition: An "Other" Introduction to Literary and Cultural Theory* (Maisonneuve) Mas'ud Zavarzadeh and Donald Morton also attack deconstruction from a leftist perspective, criticizing the apparent complicity of "ludic (post)modernism" with a repressive status quo. This is a repetitive, often crudely polemical book that delights in smoking out affinities between would-be radical theorists and the conservatives they claim to be criticizing. A particularly egregious example: Barbara Johnson and Paul de Man get linked to Jerry Falwell. In opposition to deconstruction, Zavarzadeh and Morton advocate a "resistance (post)modernism" that aims "not simply to change the means and relations of signification (to obscure ready-made cultural obviousnesses), but to change the relations of production and end economic exploitation." How "resistance (post)modernism" will achieve this goal is never made clear.

In *Canons and Contexts* (Oxford) Paul Lauter also has some harsh words for theory, claiming that it "has primarily succeeded in reestablishing academic privilege—ironically, not for the study of literature in the academy, but for those who practice theory within the literary profession." Despite its aura of activism, "much poststructuralist theorizing has often turned out to be politically paralyzing." According to Lauter, a comparative approach to American literature can be more politically effective than theory. A comparative approach juxtaposes mainstream canonical texts with marginalized ones and takes note of how they illuminate one another. *Canons and Contexts* is a convincing answer to the many questions that still dog critics interested in enlarging the canon, especially questions that belittle the allegedly parochial subject matter, unsophisticated audience, and inferior aesthetic value of excluded texts. Lauter astutely links curricular change to transforming some familiar institutional practices, for example, peer review of job applicants and tenure and promotion candidates ("But who are one's 'peers'?" he asks. "This is no more an idle question in academia than it is in the courtroom"). Although I think theory can contribute to the changes that Lauter seeks, he is right to wonder "what, beyond reinforcing status, is the function of criticism?"

Offered as a sequel to Lauter and Louis Kampf's *The Politics of Literature: Dissenting Essays on the Teaching of English* (1971), *Left Politics and the Literary Profession,* ed. Lennard J. Davis and M. Bella Mirabella (Columbia, 1990), offers a sophisticated account of the strengths and weaknesses of activist literary criticism. In fact, anyone interested in the politics of contemporary literary study will find this collection of essays indispensable. It features an excellent introduction by the editors and provocative contributions on a wide range of topics important to politically motivated critics: the omnipresence of theory in current criticism (Gerald Graff), the function of English studies at the present time (Richard Ohmann), the significance of feminist criticism (Catharine R. Stimpson, Nellie Y. McKay, Kate Ellis), the opening of the canon (Paul Lauter, Lillian S. Robinson, Constance Coiner, Barbara Harlow), and the value of noncanonical literary traditions (Héctor Calderón on Chicano literary studies, Pancho Savery on African-American literature, and

Julie Abraham on lesbian writing). The book concludes with some personal reflections on literary study by Robert C. Rosen, Robert Rich, Lillian S. Robinson, Susan Gushee O'Malley, and Louis Kampf.

Three other impressive collections of essays dealing with the social ramifications of literary study deserve mentioning. *Intellectuals: Aesthetics, Politics, Academics,* ed. Bruce Robbins (Minnesota, 1990), features solid discussions of specific cases (among them, Robbins on Raymond Williams, R. Radhakrishnan on Michel Foucault, Christopher Prendergast on Paul de Man), and general issues (for example, Barbara Ehrenreich on the professional-managerial class revisited and Edward Said on American intellectuals and Middle East politics). Other highlights include David Simpson's insightful recounting of the Colin McCabe debacle at Cambridge and Elizabeth Gross's interview with Gayatri Chakravorty Spivak. In the latter, some excellent questions—for instance, "how is it possible to avoid a politics of representation, speaking for or on behalf of other women, retaining their specificity, their difference, while not giving up our own?"—unfortunately net some cryptic answers.

Subject to History, ed. David Simpson (Cornell), is subtitled "Ideology, Class, and Gender," appropriately called by Simpson "the most emphatic concepts in the lexicon of state-of-the-art cultural criticism." The volume's essays interrogate these terms (along with "subject" and "history") from a materialist perspective that is not so much applied as ceaselessly developed and reworked. Contributors include Mary Poovey ("Domesticity and Class Formation: Chadwick's 1842 *Sanitary Report,*" pp. 65–83), Catherine Gallagher ("The Bioeconomics of *Our Mutual Friend,*" pp. 47–64), Frank Lentricchia ("Lyric in the Culture of Capital," pp. 191–216), and R. Jackson Wilson ("Emerson's *Nature:* A Materialist Reading," pp. 119–42).

Finally, *Consequences of Theory,* ed. Jonathan Arac and Barbara Johnson (Hopkins), offers several essays examining the sometimes uneasy alliance between theory and political activism. Of special note: Bruce Robbins's "Oppositional Professionals: Theory and the Narratives of Professionalization" (pp. 1–21), Cornel West's "Theory, Pragmatisms, and Politics" (pp. 22–38), and Nancy Fraser's stirring critique of Richard Rorty, "Solidarity or Singularity? Richard Rorty between Romanticism and Technocracy" (pp. 39–62).

Dubbed by Harold Bloom "the most interesting philosopher in the world," Rorty certainly is interesting to many literary theorists. Some of his work most relevant to literary theory is reprinted in *Essays on Heidegger and Others* (Cambridge), the second volume of his philosophical papers. "Others" include Derrida, Foucault, and de Man, along with Milan Kundera and Charles Dickens. Several essays unfold an important—and controversial—view of deconstruction that concedes its lack of argumentative rigor and political importance while valuing Derrida's originality as "a great *comic* writer—perhaps the funniest writer on philosophical topics since Kierkegaard." This book should be required reading for students of contemporary literary theory.

As should be clear from these examples, deconstruction and Derrida still command the attention, if not always the adulation, of most critical theorists. Several new books take a philosophical rather than political approach to Derrida's work. J. Claude Evans's *Strategies of Deconstruction* (Minnesota) is a sharp critique of Derrida's treatment of Husserl in *Speech and Phenomena* and *Of Grammatology*. Matthew H. Kramer's *Legal Theory, Critical Theory, and Deconstruction* (Indiana) is a more sympathetic, often turgid deconstructive critique of legal and political theory. Christopher Norris's *Spinoza and the Origins of Modern Critical Theory* (Blackwell) is a much more readable analysis of modern critical theory. Against those advocates and assailants of deconstruction who associate it with no-holds-barred, hedonistic free play, Norris argues that Derrida exemplifies as well as complicates argument and logical rigor. From Norris's point of view, deconstruction can coherently "invoke standards of truth and falsehood." Despite Norris's skillful application of Spinoza to current theoretical debates, I remain unpersuaded that "the current 'situation' of literary theory is one that can only be understood by going back to Spinoza and examining his role at a crucial point in its formative prehistory"—a claim that even Norris suspects may be overstated. Finally, J. Hillis Miller's *Theory Now and Then* (Duke) brings together Miller's influential essays published between 1966 and 1989, among them "Tradition and Difference" (the review of *Natural Supernaturalism* that sparked his ongoing debate over deconstruction with M. H. Abrams) and "The Critic as Host" (his contribution to *Deconstruction and Criticism*). This volume will be valuable to anyone interested in the still-embattled reception of deconstruction in the United States.

Although not explicitly engaged with deconstruction, several other books look at contemporary criticism from a philosophical vantage point. *The Interpretive Turn: Philosophy, Science, Culture*, ed. David R.

Hiley et al. (Cornell), is a solid collection of essays, primarily by philosophers, on several important topics, among them the concern of the human and natural sciences with interpretive and epistemological questions. *The Question of Humanism: Challenges and Possibilities,* ed. David Goicoecha et al. (Prometheus), offers workmanlike essays by several philosophers exploring the history and dilemmas of humanism. In *Literature and Rationality: Ideas of Agency in Theory and Fiction* (Cambridge) Paisley Livingston carefully analyzes how theories of rationality that have been developed in the human sciences and philosophy can shed light on our understanding of literature. I especially like how Livingston does not simply apply concepts of rationality to literature but asks, "in what ways can the reading of literary texts lead to the refinement of contemporary hypotheses about rationality, irrationality, and the framework of intentional explanations?" In *Philosophical Hermeneutics and Literary Theory* (Yale) Joel Weinsheimer tries to demonstrate the relevance of Hans-Georg Gadamer's thought to various interpretive questions, including a question that Weinsheimer thinks should be central to the debate on the canon: "in regard to the classic, how do we maintain the dialogue between the work and its reader without silencing either?" Leonard Jackson in *The Poverty of Structuralism* (Longman) argues that the scientific intent and explanatory power of Saussure's thought get sabotaged by Derrida and other poststructuralists, who inexplicably opt for irrationalism and give up all hope of arriving at a scientific basis for the study of language. Jackson's analysis is marred by his inability to understand what motivates contemporary theorists: "why is there," he irritably asks, "this absurd campaign to show that there is something nasty in the idea of formulating objective scientific theories about human beings?" From Jackson's point of view, Marx, Freud, and Saussure would be appalled by the poststructuralist perversion of their thought: "When a modern Lacanian gives a presentation, the ghost of Freud protests: 'This is unscientific gibberish.' And whenever I read Derrida's book, *Of Grammatology,* I hear the ghost of Saussure howling 'Liar!' "

An unusually large number of books this year probe the relationship between literary criticism and still another discipline: psychology. Three of the best tackle the always elusive Jacques Lacan: Mikkel Borch-Jacobsen's *Lacan: The Absolute Master,* trans. Douglas Brick (Stanford), surveys Lacan's major writings and plumbs their philosophical significance; Samuel Weber's *Return to Freud: Jacques Lacan's Dislocation of*

Psychoanalysis, trans. Michael Levine (Cambridge), is a scrupulous introduction to Lacan's thought and its antecedents in structural linguistics; and John Forrester's *The Seductions of Psychoanalysis: Freud, Lacan, and Derrida* (Cambridge) unfolds the history of psychoanalysis from Freud through Lacan and Derrida. *Lacan and the Human Sciences,* ed. Alexandre Leupin (Nebraska), includes essays on important aspects of Lacan's work, among them Jean-Claude Milner on "Lacan and the Ideal of Science" and Jane Gallop on Juliet Mitchell, one of many feminist writers indebted to Lacan. Finally, Peter L. Rudnytsky takes a more skeptical view of Lacan in *The Psychoanalytic Vocation: Rank, Winnicott, and the Legacy of Freud* (Yale), arguing that D. W. Winnicott and British object relations theory provide a basis for criticizing Lacan's postmodernism. Sheldon Brivic's *The Veil of Signs* (Illinois) is a significant, if sometimes murky, contribution to the growing number of Lacanian studies of Joyce.

Several other books apply psychoanalytic theory to the interpretation of literary texts. Among the best of these I would place Zachary Leader's *Writer's Block* (Hopkins). The first part of the book lucidly surveys psychoanalytic theory from Freudian psychology through British object relations theory, zeroing in on psychoanalytic analyses of writer's block. The rest of the volume looks at several writers who at various times feel unable to write, paralyzed by something within them (like Wordsworth at the outset of *The Prelude*) or by social obstacles (several women writers are Leader's examples here). Leader is especially interested in what he calls the "great paradox of creative impairment: that it can be a necessary precursor to health, that blockage and breakthrough often go together."

Drawing on French feminist revisions of psychoanalytic theory, Katherine Cummings in *Telling Tales: The Hysteric's Seduction in Fiction and Theory* (Stanford) looks at seduction from the point of view of the woman being seduced. Seduction narratives in Freud's writings, *Clarissa, Bleak House,* and *Tender is the Night* help Cummings describe seduction "doubly as both an instrument of patriarchal domination and a potential vehicle for challenging male hegemony." Sarah Kofman's *Freud and Fiction,* trans. Sarah Wykes (Northeastern), makes available in translation Kofman's 1974 *Quatre romans analytiques,* an influential investigation of several motifs in Freud. An introduction would make this book more accessible.

Lacan and Derrida are only two of several Continental writers who continue to interest literary theorists. *Re-Reading Levinas,* ed. Robert

Bernasconi and Simon Critchley (Indiana), brings together essays responding to Emmanuel Levinas's difficult work. The volume includes contributions by Derrida (entitled "At this very moment in this work here I am," pp. 11–48) and Luce Irigaray ("Questions to Emmanuel Levinas: On the Divinity of Love," pp. 109–18). Still another important French writer, Jean-Luc Nancy, presents in *The Inoperative Community*, ed. Peter Connor and trans. Peter Connor et al. (Minnesota), a challenging meditation on the fate of community in postmetaphysical thought. *Community at Loose Ends*, ed. Miami Theory Collective (Minnesota), also includes an essay by Nancy ("Of Being-in-Common") and extends his attempt to redefine community without grounding it in a shared human nature. The introduction puts the problem this way: "To think community no longer as a foundational or immanent *comunus* but as inaugurated and sustained in difference is thus no idle complication but a determined way to raise new questions and chart alternative possibilities about what it is for us to be together, about what it means for us to have in common above all the commonality of our difference."

In *Heidegger and "the Jews"*, trans. Andreas Michel and Mark Roberts (Minnesota, 1990), Jean-François Lyotard strains to do justice to the complexity of Heidegger's thought without excusing its political irresponsibility. As David Carroll concedes in his foreword, complicating what Nazism means or problematizing what Heidegger says—a characteristic poststructuralist move—can disarm criticism of ideas that are all too painfully clear to their victims: hence, Lyotard's ambivalence toward deconstruction. Nevertheless, Carroll optimistically holds that in Lyotard's case investigating "critically what some already pretend to *know* does not necessarily lead to apologetics." Still another attempt to rethink community without succumbing to liberalism or fascism takes place in György Lukács's *The Process of Democratization*, trans. Susanne Bernhardt and Norman Levine (SUNY), an interesting addition to Lukács's important oeuvre. Lukács is a seminal figure in Peter Uwe Hohendahl's *Reappraisals: Shifting Alignments in Postwar Critical Theory* (Cornell), a lucid overview of Frankfurt School critical theory from Lukács and Adorno through Habermas. Finally, in *Freedom, Foucault, and the Subject of America* (Northeastern) Lee Quinby uses Foucault's work on normalization to study how several texts—among them Jefferson's *Notes on the State of Virginia*, Thoreau's *Walden*, Maxine Hong Kingston's *The Woman Warrior*, and June Jordan's *On Call: Political Essays*—fashion an aesthetics of liberty in opposition to bureaucratic, technological, and state control. I am not sure that Quinby needs Foucault to argue his case, but this clear book sympathetically discusses several American writers who argue that "ethical-political problems of freedom require more than a revolution to solve them. They require an ethos of everyday life—whereby individuals engage in practices of liberty."

Although Continental theorists dominate contemporary criticism in the United States, some theoretically engaged work still trickles over from England. Frank Kermode's *The Uses of Error* (Harvard) reprints 44 of his reviews from the *London Review of Books* and other publications. The Paul de Man scandal, the New Historicism, Shakespeare, and St. Augustine are only a few of his subjects in this refreshingly unpretentious, wide-ranging collection. Kermode sides with writers who feel that some of their best writing occurs in reviews, perhaps because reviewers for the popular press are reminded "that they have a duty, easily neglected, to make themselves intelligible to non-professors. Talking among themselves they may feel some need to be impressively arcane, but when addressing intelligent non-professors they need to remember one of the less offensive precepts of Lord Chesterfield: 'Speak the language of the company you are in; and speak it purely, and unlarded with any other.'" *Addressing Frank Kermode: Essays in Criticism and Interpretation,* ed. Margaret Tudeau-Clayton and Martin Warner (Illinois), is a rather uneven collection of essays on Kermode's work, along with a wry response by Kermode to his readers. Bernard Bergonzi's *Exploding English: Criticism, Theory, Culture* (Clarendon, 1990) is a readable, anecdotal collection of Bergonzi's pieces on literary study in modern England. F. R. Leavis, the Colin McCabe affair, and the continuing resistance of the English to theory are all dealt with.

What Bergonzi describes as the "bursting canon" is one of the many developments exploding English as a discipline in the United States and England. Several new studies advocate diversifying the texts that we teach and the approaches that we take. D. Emily Hicks's *Border Writing: The Multidimensional Text* (Minnesota) examines several Latin American and Chicano/a writers in light of Deleuze and Guattari's work on deterritorialization. In *The Dialectics of Our America: Genealogy, Cultural Critique, and Literary History* (Duke), José David Saldívar takes a more eclectic approach to several American writers of color (Rolando Hinojosa, Gloria Anzaldúa, and others) as well as Latin American authors (José Martí, Gabriel García Márquez, and others). A long chapter on "Chicano Border Narratives as Cultural Critique" persuasively argues that this writing challenges "not only the canon of American literature (as it is usually understood in the Anglocentric model prevalent in our normal curricula) but the notion of America itself." *Criticism in the Borderlands: Studies in Chicano Literature, Culture, and Ideology*, ed. Héctor Calderón and José David Saldívar (Duke), is a ground-breaking collection of essays exploring many dimensions of Chicano/a literature; its importance to the redefinition of American literature; its treatment of race, class, and gender; and its political aspirations. Contributors include Norma Alarcón, Genaro Padilla, Héctor Calderón, and Renato Rosaldo; texts discussed include *This Bridge Called My Back, Life Span,* and *The Mixquiahuala Letters,* among many others. A useful annotated bibliography of contemporary Chicano/a literary criticism concludes the volume.

Lucy Maddox's *Removals* argues that 19th-century debates on the "Indian question" prefigure current quarrels on the status of Native American literature in the canon. Maddox discusses Melville, Hawthorne, Thoreau, Catharine Maria Sedgwick, and other writers, showing how they were influenced by the civilization-or-extinction predicament facing Indians. This provocative book uses recent theory while keeping a critical eye on that theory's shortcomings. Maddox goes so far as to assert that "contemporary criticism, even with its emphasis on demythologizing literary discourse and politicizing critical discourse, is still essentially replicating nineteenth-century criticism when it comes to the subject of Indians. Either the Indian presence is ignored or the Indians are *re*-mythologized by the critic." Maddox concludes that "most of us who teach and write about American literature still do not believe that it is necessary, or even important, to know much about American Indians or about the history and politics of Indian affairs in order to do our teaching and writing confidently and authoritatively." *Removals* is a major attempt to correct our myopia.

Other books on cross-cultural understanding deserve mentioning. Sander L. Gilman's *Inscribing the Other* (Nebraska) focuses on German literature but confronts questions that matter to many contemporary theorists: "how stereotypes are generated, how they are embedded in cultural artifacts (texts, in the widest sense of the word), and, most important, how once sanctioned in this arena they form the basis for action." Also concerned with the problem of constructing "otherness," Lisa Lowe's *Critical Terrains: French and British Orientalisms* (Cornell) deals with representations of non-Europeans, starting with Lady Mary Wortley Montagu's *Turkish Embassy Letters* and concluding with the treatment of the Chinese Revolution and the People's Republic of China during the early 1970s by Julia Kristeva, Roland Barthes, and the writers associated with *Tel quel. The Bounds of Race: Perspectives on Hegemony and Resistance,* ed. Dominick LaCapra (Cornell), presents first-rate essays, many of them previously published, on such topics as African and South African fiction, colonial literature, the African-American sermon, and the politics and epistemology of white supremacy in America.

Also focusing on postcolonialism and the construction of difference, John Tomlinson's *Cultural Imperialism* (Hopkins) rigorously analyzes many current arguments against one culture, usually contemporary American culture, imposing its way of life on others. Tomlinson prefers describing cultural imperialism as the global spread of modernity. His problem becomes criticizing modernization while appreciating its complexity and power—criticizing it as a resistible process. Anyone interested in the critique of cultural imperialism will find this an important book.

Several other books draw on literary theory in analyzing two often marginalized fields in the culture of English departments: textual editing and composition. *Devils and Angels: Textual Editing and Literary Theory,* ed. Philip Cohen (Virginia), features several essays arguing for a mutually beneficial dialogue between textual editors and literary theorists. Contributors include textual scholars (Paul Eggert, Hans Walter Gabler, and others), critics with a foot in both camps (most notably Jerome J. McGann), and theoretically minded critics interested in what theorists and editors can learn from one another (William E. Cain and Steven Mailloux). *Representing Modernist Texts* includes several distinguished editors reflecting on the problems that attend editing modernist writers (for example, Richard J. Finneran on Yeats, A. Walton Litz and Christopher MacGowan on William Carlos Williams, Ronald Bush on Pound) as well as a helpful concluding essay by Michael Groden on "Contemporary Textual and Literary Theory" (pp. 259–86).

In *Textual Carnivals: The Politics of Composition* (So. Ill.) Susan Miller applies feminist and cultural studies of marginalization to the analysis of composition: "Descriptions of the historical workings of patriarchy, of the sociology of stigmatized groups, and leftist political critiques offer useful analogues for comprehending the simultaneous separation and regulation that situate the theme park that composition now occupies." This curious book promises more than it delivers. Empirical research (for instance, a survey of professional composition specialists and a look at early catalog descriptions of English departments) oscillates with abstract theoretical pronouncements "on how composition is an element in, and an active symbol of, hegemonic cultural maintenance." Along similar lines, *Textual Dynamics of the Professions: Historical and Contemporary Studies of Writing in Professional Communities,* ed. Charles Bazerman and James Paradis (Wisconsin), includes a useful analysis by Jeanne Fahnestock and Marie Secor of the rhetoric of literary criticism based largely on a survey of journal articles published from 1978 through 1982.

(Inter)views: Cross-Disciplinary Perspectives on Rhetoric and Literacy, ed. Gary A. Olson and Irene Gale (So. Ill.), reprints interviews and responses first published in the *Journal of Advanced Composition.* Interviews are conducted with Jacques Derrida, Noam Chomsky, Richard Rorty, Gayatri Chakravorty Spivak, Clifford Geertz, and other major figures from outside rhetoric and composition whose work has influenced the field. It is fascinating to see these luminaries address—and sometimes evade—the down-to-earth questions of their interviewers: to hear Derrida commenting on what university department he thinks should teach writing ("I would not rely on a model in which composition instructors are confined simply within one discipline; nor would I rely on a model in which they are simply dispersed, scattered among a variety of disciplines. There should be a specificity and also a crossing of boundaries. So, it's a very difficult question"); Geertz speculating on a possible similarity between anthropology and composition, a field he admits he knows nothing about (like composition and rhetoric, anthropology does not have a distinct subject matter or a real method, creating "a great deal of anxiety over what it is": "I think that if you don't like that kind of anxiety, you should go into organic chemistry"); and Rorty curtly rejecting the notion that freshman English instructors should teach students the discourse of the field that interests them rather than the traditional generic academic essay ("It strikes me as a terrible idea. I think the idea of freshman English, mostly, is just to get them to write complete sentences, get the commas in the right place, and stuff like that—the stuff that we would like to think the high schools do and, in fact, they don't").

I can only briefly mention several other books that will interest literary theorists. The seventh volume of René Wellek's magisterial history of modern criticism has appeared: *German, Russian, and Eastern European Criticism, 1900–1950* (Yale), covering everyone from Friedrich Gundolf and Ernst Bertram to György Lukács and Leon Trotsky. *Theorizing American Literature* tries to establish the importance of Hegel to American literature and criticism. Gregory S. Jay's "Hegel and the Dialectics of American Literary Historiography: From Parrington to Trilling and Beyond" (pp. 83–122) is one of the more convincing essays. Gale H. Carrithers, Jr., *Mumford, Tate, Eiseley: Watchers in the Night* (LSU) sympathetically discusses three critics of American culture. It is interesting to think about Allen Tate in this context, especially at a time when the New Criticism is still faulted for being apolitical (or only inadvertently political). Finally, *Northrop Frye: A World in a Grain of Sand*, ed. Robert D. Denham (Peter Lang), makes available 22 interviews with Frye on a remarkable range of topics, from "Literary Theory in the Classroom" to "The Hypnotic Gaze of the Bible."

ii Gender Studies

The most controversial book published this year in feminist theory has to be Elizabeth Fox-Genovese's *Feminism Without Illusions: A Critique of Individualism* (No. Car.). Fox-Genovese criticizes feminist critics' commitment to individualism, not because she opposes feminism but because she wants to "convince the majority of American women of its relevance to their lives." According to her, individualism shortchanges the political causes that feminists think it supports. I am not always sure what Fox-Genovese means by "individualism." She seems to regard it as the (mistaken) claim that women, like all people, have innate rights as individuals, a claim that has freed women from arbitrary restrictions, only to deprive them of what Fox-Genovese often calls "protection." By insisting on their rights, women, she reluctantly concedes, have made progress, "if to be treated as an independent, self-accountable individual is regarded as progress. But if married and single women can now cast votes, hold property, claim their own wages, keep their maiden names, and generally behave like independent individuals, they have also lost the host of protections that, in theory and to some extent in practice, sheltered their dependent status." Fox-Genovese's remedy for this problem—if loss of "protection" is in fact a problem—remains unclear to me. She admits that her book "does not offer a political program," which is to say that in my view she does not answer her overriding question: "How do we protect women, as women, without restricting their opportunities for individualism, notably the ability to support themselves?" Still, despite the fuzziness of Fox-Genovese's answers, I admire her willingness to address specific issues; family relations, maternity leave, affirmative action, abortion, pornography, and the makeup of the canon all receive thoughtful analysis in her book.

Carol J. Adams's *The Sexual Politics of Meat: A Feminist-Vegetarian Critical Theory* (Continuum) is another certain-to-be-debated book. According to Adams, feminist theory is incomplete without vegetarianism; vegetarianism similarly needs feminist theory to bring out what is at stake in eating meat—for Adams, nothing less than patriarchal control of women and animals. "How do we overthrow patriarchal power," she asks, "while eating its symbol?" Her answer: we cannot. "Autonomous, antipatriarchal being is clearly vegetarian. To destabilize patriarchal consumption we must interrupt patriarchal meals of meat." Some of Adams's connections—for instance, between meat eating, male control, violence against women, and war—seem strained to me, and I am intrigued rather than convinced by her argument. Whereas she sees the oppression of women and animals as interdependent, I am inclined to differentiate between the two. Nevertheless, this book challenges the wrongheaded assumption that feminism goes too far or has done all that it can do. For Adams, it has not yet gone far enough. Literary critics will be especially interested in her chapter on how vegetarian impulses shape *Frankenstein.*

Ethical concerns also motivate Kathryn Pyne Addelson's *Impure Thoughts: Essays on Philosophy, Feminism, and Ethics* (Temple). Drawing on Carol Gilligan's work and other sources, Addelson wonders what an ethics would be like that takes women seriously as moral agents. Such an ethics would not pretend "that a single individual can decide what is just or right for all of us by reasoning all by himself." A feminist ethics, by contrast, would favor "nonhierarchical modes of decision making": forming collectives, rotating offices, working things out by consensus. Although Adams claims that far-reaching consequences follow from taking women seriously in ethics, I am not sure what she thinks these consequences are, especially when she disavows wanting to run great nations nonhierarchically or longing for a "low-tech, pastoral utopia," for her "a dream suited for the well fed who lack responsibility for children, the elderly, the poor, and the sick."

Jennifer Ring's *Modern Political Theory and Contemporary Feminism* (SUNY) is an important contribution to the growing body of work committed to fleshing out the implications of feminism for political theory. Ring cautions against clinging to the differences between men and women: "Thinking in those terms, even if carefully done, leads inevitably to a theory of nature, and I do not think it is possible to establish once and for all a theory of immutable human, feminine, or masculine nature. It makes more sense to me to focus on the possible similarities between men and women if the relationship between the sexes is to change significantly from what it has been." She is also leery of deconstruction: "it offers no basis, indeed, it self-consciously denies the very *possibility* of a solidly grounded alternative to the past. It surrenders too much." Eschewing liberal empiricism as well as deconstruction, she advocates a "minimalist" (as opposed to Marxist) dialectics that does not eliminate knowledge but makes it the always provisional, unforeseeable outcome of conflict. Chapters on contemporary feminist epistemology, John Stuart Mill's *The Subjection of Women* and *A System of Logic,* and Marxist and Hegelian dialectics spell out why minimalist dialectics provides the epistemology most compatible with feminist political goals. This is a serious attempt to answer an urgent question for feminist literary theorists: "what is the structure of knowledge that will most effectively encourage political change?"

Several other books deal more directly with literary questions. *Feminism, Bakhtin, and the Dialogic,* ed. Dale M. Bauer and S. Jaret McKinstry (SUNY), brings together essays arguing for the usefulness of Bakhtin's work to feminist criticism. As the introduction puts it, a "feminist dialogics" responsive to Bakhtin's concerns "becomes a way of recognizing competing voices without making any single voice normative." Contributors include Josephine Donovan ("Style and Power," pp. 85–94), Suzanne Kehde ("Voices from the Margin: Bag Ladies and Others," pp. 25–38), and Sheryl Stevenson ("Language and Gender in Transit: Feminist Extensions of Bakhtin," pp. 181–98).

Elaine Showalter's *Sister's Choice* originated as Showalter's Clarendon Lectures at Oxford University in May 1989. Applying what Showalter calls gynocriticism to a wide range of American texts—from *Little Women* to contemporary American Gothic writing—she clearly addresses key feminist concerns: "Does a 'muted' culture have a literature of its own, or must it always revise the conventions of the dominant? Can there be an 'authentic' and separate language, theory, and culture expressive of the soul of any group living within a hybrid culture? What is the relationship between contemporary literary theory and a noncanonical literature?" Her concluding chapter, "Common Threads," favors replacing the melting pot with the patchwork quilt as a metaphor for American cultural identity—a metaphor that acknowledges "ethnic difference, heterogeneity, and multiplicity." Showalter is drawn to it because it originates in women's culture yet is adaptable to the needs of various groups: hence, the importance of the AIDS Quilt, for Showalter a sign of "the continued vitality of the quilt metaphor, its powers of change and renewal, and its potential to unify and to heal."

Shari Benstock's *Textualizing the Feminine: On the Limits of Genre* (Okla.) is an exercise in "psychogrammanalysis," a reading practice "which investigates the sexual organization of textuality and the textual structuring of the psyche." "Psychogrammanalysis" receives theoretical support from Derrida, Kristeva, and Lacan; texts psychogrammanalyzed include Derrida's *The Post Card,* H.D.'s *Helen in Egypt,* Joyce's *Ulysses* and *Finnegans Wake,* and Woolf's *Three Guineas.* This book will be heavy going for noninitiates put off by sentences like the following: "My approach to the question of gender/genre is from within dialectical, either/or structures: from within the slash (/) or the apostrophic mark of inclusion-exclusion (') that transforms itself into an elliptical curve (. . .) as it deconstructs the literary genre of 'letters' or the letter's status as alphabetic symbol and turns translation back on the residue of meaning that escapes or resists its efforts." Benstock's often provocative insights get lost in her convoluted prose.

Also indebted to Kristeva and Lacan, Patricia Elliot's *From Mastery to Analysis: Theories of Gender in Psychoanalytic Feminism* (Cornell) is an intelligent defense of feminist psychoanalytic discourse. Major writers contributing to the development of this discourse—among them, Juliet Mitchell, Dorothy Dinnerstein, Nancy Chodorow, and Luce Irigaray—are carefully studied. While acknowledging the shortcomings of the various theories which she studies, Elliot argues that psychoanalytic feminism can help "develop a theory of gender that escapes ahistoricism, idealism, and determinism, and that accounts for both gender oppression and resistance."

One of the Continental feminist theorists cited by Benstock—Hélène Cixous—has two important books appearing in translation: *The Book of Promethea,* trans. Betsy Wing (Nebraska), and *Readings: The Poetics of Blanchot, Joyce, Kafka, Kleist, Lispector, and Tsvetayeva,* trans. Verena Andermatt Conley (Minnesota). Less well-known to American readers may be Christina Thurmer-Rohr's *Vagabonding: Feminist Thinking Cut Loose,* trans. Lise Weil (Beacon), a collection of essays bent on directing "a fury of questions" to feminists and the male culture that they criticize.

iii Modernism and Postmodernism

Fredric Jameson's massive *Postmodernism, or, The Cultural Logic of Late Capitalism* (Duke) opens with his influential 1984 essay "The Cultural Logic of Late Capitalism," then explores four themes that Jameson thinks postmodernism resonates with: interpretation, utopia, survivals of the modern, and " 'returns of the repressed' of historicity." Disclaiming any wish to survey postmodernism or even provide any examples of it, Jameson nevertheless offers as "exhibits" an extraordinary range of postmodernist phenomena, among them the videotext, the *nouveau roman,* current architecture, contemporary photography, film, installation art, and theoretical discourse (in particular, deconstruction and the New Historicism). Anyone interested in postmodernism will need to come to terms with this ground-breaking book.

Stanley Aronowitz and Henry A. Giroux's *Postmodern Education: Politics, Culture, and Social Criticism* (Minnesota) takes a self-described "postmodern" approach to many of the controversies unsettling high school and higher education: for instance, the politics of literacy, teachers as public intellectuals, and classroom responsiveness to student experience. By "postmodernism," Aronowitz and Giroux mean the critique of "all claims to universal reason and impartial competence": in postmodernist thought, "general abstractions that deny the specificity and particularity of everyday life, that generalize out of existence the particular and the local, that smother difference under the banner of universalizing categories are rejected as totalitarian and terroristic." So defined, postmodernism has reactionary as well as progressive potential: "some versions of postmodern discourse want to recognize and privilege the marginal without engaging the important issue of what social conditions need to exist before such groups can actually exercise forms of self- and social empowerment." Aronowitz and Giroux want to supplement postmodernism with respect for such "modernist" democratic values as justice, equality, and liberty: "when linked with the modernist language of public life, the notions of difference, power, and specificity can be understood as part of a public philosophy that broadens and deepens [rather than deconstructs] individual liberties and rights *through rather than against* a radical notion of democracy." I am skeptical about "combining the best insights of modernism and postmodernism," but I appreciate the political needs behind the quest for such a synthesis. Like many contemporary critics, Aronowitz and Giroux seek "ethical and epistemological grounds for a politics of solidarity within difference."

Whereas Aronowitz and Giroux keep in view specific educational and political problems, several other recent studies treat postmodernism in a more abstract, theoretical way. Steven Best and Douglas Kellner's *Postmodern Theory: Critical Interrogations* (Guilford) is a useful, balanced introduction to some of the major commentators on postmodernism: Foucault, Deleuze and Guattari, Baudrillard, Lyotard, Jameson, and Habermas among them. Like Aronowitz and Giroux, Best and Kellner worry that "an extreme postmodern theory can occlude important common interests and provides no basis for a politics of alliance. . . . Political struggle can become little more than single-issue politics that only accomplishes short-term gains for different groups while failing to organize various groups into alliances fighting for more general social transformation." Julian Pefanis's *Heterology and the Postmodern: Bataille, Baudrillard, and Lyotard* (Duke) also delves into the origins of postmodernism by looking closely at three inaugural French theorists. In *Prefaces to the Diaphora: Rhetorics, Allegory, and the Interpretation of Postmodernity* (Purdue) Peter Carravetta studies some postmodern perspectives on several topics, including the quarrel between poetry and philosophy. A cryptic opening section entitled "Irrgarten" unfortunately sets the tone for what follows. Colin Falck's *Myth, Truth, Literature* (Cambridge), subtitled "towards a true postmodernism," attacks the "ludic charm" and "abolition of reality" presumably sponsored by postmodernism. Falck wants "to restore the concepts of truth or vision to our discussions of literature," because literature "gives us our purest and most essential way of grasping reality or truth." Falck too often lets assertion and citation (especially of the Romantic poets) substitute for argument. Turning from philosophy and literary criticism to the performing arts, Johannes Birringer in *Theatre, Theory, Postmodernism* (Indiana) explores how the body appears not only in contemporary theater but in new postmodernist forms of performance art and multimedia performance such as video.

Two helpful collections of essays treat many of the issues raised by the books I have been discussing. *Image and Ideology in Modern-Postmodern Discourse,* ed. David B. Downing and Susan Bazargan (SUNY), grows out of the postmodernist concern with images, simulacra, and representation. Numerous writers (Conrad, Woolf, Pound, Faulkner, O'Connor, Fowles, and others), critics (Benjamin, Baudrillard, Panofsky, Althusser), and issues (among them, feminist politics and postmodernist style, the politics of representation) are dealt with. *Zeitgeist in Babel: The Postmodernist Controversy,* ed. Ingeborg Hoesterey (Indiana), also ranges over several key topics: characterizing postmodernism in music, architecture, film, theater, and the visual arts; sorting out the relationship between feminism and postmodernism; and responding to the political and philosophical critiques postmodernism has triggered. Contributors include such important commentators as Charles Jencks ("Postmodern vs. Late-Modern," pp. 4–21), Richard Rorty ("Habermas and Lyotard on Postmodernity," pp. 84–97), and Martin Jay ("Habermas and Postmodernism," pp. 98–110).

Modernism is the subject of several new books. In *Modernism as a Philosophical Problem: On the Dissatisfactions of European High Culture* (Blackwell) Robert B. Pippin discusses many of the philosophical figures who helped define modernity, chiefly Kant, Hegel, Nietzsche, and Heidegger. Herbert N. Schneidau's *Waking Giants* competently studies various modernist writers' preoccupation with the past. Joyce's *Ulysses,* Hardy's poetry, Forster's *Howards End,* Conrad's *Secret Agent,* Anderson's *Winesburg, Ohio,* and Pound's *Cantos* are Schneidau's primary examples. In *Modernity and Self-Identity: Self and Society in the Late Modern Age* (Stanford) Anthony Giddens sketches the problems and opportunities attending self-development in the "risk culture" that for Giddens defines modernity. Finally, Zygmunt Bauman's *Modernity and Ambivalence* (Cornell) analyzes how modernity breeds an ambivalence that some modern states (most notably Nazi Germany) have tried to eliminate in totalitarian ways. The political implications of modernism as well as postmodernism are thus still being sorted out.

University of New Mexico

19 Foreign Scholarship

i East European Contributions—1990: F. Lyra

Efforts to establish an efficient system for the dissemination of critical work on American literary culture (I think, for instance, of the Laboratoire Orléans-Tours de Littérature Américaine—LOLiTA for short) have yet to reach a scope and level that would make eliciting material for the task at hand independent of chance or sporadic manifestations of colleagues' goodwill. As long as the international flow of information (and goods) remains at a trickle, because of the chronic distribution deficiency in this part of the world, the term "East Europe" is bound to stand as synecdoche for the former Soviet Union (Russia) and Poland, as is the case this year.

Once again, centrifugal forces have given fresh substance to the curse of the Tower of Babel. With due respect for the national aspirations of the republics and regions which made up the Soviet Union, I dare presume that Americanists in the newly independent states, in the spirit of intellectual ecumenism, will continue to publish their works in Russian or, preferably, English, and that such well-established sources of information on current literary life as *Knizhnaya letopis* and *Letopis zhurnal'nykh statei* will not restrict the coverage to Russia.

In the Soviet Union the sustained ideological liberalization continues to affect literary study. The tenets of Socialist Realism have ceased to function as the ultimate measure of artistic achievement; supportive references to Marx, Engels, Lenin, and party congresses have markedly declined, although some publications on American literature still manifest vestiges of dialectical materialism, Soviet-style. To be sure, belief that literature is a reflection of life continues to dominate interpretation, as does critical realism in the evaluation of artistic work; but there was a diversification of scholarly interests. Occasionally the title of a scholarly book signals interest in unconventional literature, but on closer examination it reveals traditional topics of investigation, not attempts at studying how American writers exceed realism. Such is the case, for instance, with *Traditsii i novatorstvo v literaturakh stran Zapadnoi Evropy i Ameriki XIX–XX vv.* [Tradition and innovation in the literatures of Western European countries and America of the 19th–20th centuries] (Gorki, 1989). The collection offers the following contributions on American literature: "Roman E. Dzh. Geinsa *Avtobiografiya Miss Dzhein Pittman* v kontekste negritanskoi literatury i istorii SSHA" [Ernest J. Gaines's novel *The Autobiography of Miss Jane Pittman* in the context of black literature and American history] by L. A. Mishina (pp. 24–34); "Tvorchestvo Dzh. K. Outs v otsenke sovettskogo i amerikanskogo literaturovedeniya" [Joyce Carol Oates's work in Soviet and American criticism] by N. N. Nartyev (pp. 17–24); and T. L. Selitrina's "K probleme stanovleniya realizma v literature SSHA" [Toward the problem of the formation of realism in American literature] (pp. 85–94).

a. General Studies One of the most impressive literary enterprises in recent years is *Istoriya vsemirnoi literatury w devyati tomakh* [A history of world literature in nine volumes] (Moscow: Nauka), which began to appear in 1983. Russian scholars have managed to bring out seven monumental volumes (although the seventh at the time of this report was not available for comment). The widespread skepticism toward such gigantic projects notwithstanding, the *Istoriya* serves a useful educational goal; for one thing, it provides the widest possible historiographical context for specific national literatures. Constructed in chronological order along broadly conceived traditional epochs of cultural history, it provides both a diachronic and synchronic perspective for them. In such a framework American literature enters late; it starts in volume 4 (1987). In the context of world literature, the beginnings of American letters appear inauspiciously indeed, presented by F. M. Dvoitsenko-Markova as "Literatura rannykh angliiskikh poselenii v Severnoi Amerike" [The literature of early English settlements in North America] (pp. 559–63). In approach and coverage her contribution reflects the state of American literary historiography in the late '40s, although she deals with the material judiciously. By contrast, Maiya Koreneva's chapter "Literatura severoamerikanskikh kolonii i SSHA" [The literature of the North American colonies and the United States] (vol. 6 [1988], pp. 425–41), which covers the 18th century to Hugh Henry Brackenridge and Charles

Brockden Brown, reviews the period with a firm grasp of the material and in a well-organized narrative. At several points she breaks with traditional Soviet as well as American historiography—for instance, opening her detailed presentation with a separate section on Jonathan Edwards, the only figure thus distinguished in the chapter, stressing the literary qualities of his writings and pointedly discussing his achievements; or when she opens the section on the poetry of the Revolution with a succinct discussion of popular folk songs. Laudable as her extensive treatment of Jefferson, Paine, Franklin, and Freneau is, comprehensiveness and versatility would have called for at least brief mention of the beginnings of the American novel, the drama, or Crèvecoeur. The chapter on the romantic period in the sixth volume has been supplied by Yu. V. Kovalev (pp. 551–82). After a general characterization of the era, which he periodicizes into three stages, he chooses to apply the representational approach, describing the work of Irving, Cooper, Hawthorne, Poe, and Melville. No such distinction is bestowed on Emerson or Thoreau. Contrary to long-held expectations, the contributors have not broken with the bad customs of citing only Russian versions of titles and identifying American authors in Cyrillic transcription only; in addition, most of the time only the first and middle initials are provided, which obscures both name and gender. For example, Kovalev mentions an author by the name of "S. Rouson"; a Russian unfamiliar with early American literature will not know that this is Susanna Rowson.

In Poland the bulkiest work for both 1989 and 1990 has been furnished by Elzbieta Oleksy, *Theistic Existentialism in American Letters: Hawthorne and Percy* (Lodz: Wydawnictwo Uniwersytetu Lodzkiego, 1989) published as a habilitation dissertation. It offers a telling illustration of Nina Baym's observation about "the remarkable 'openness' of Hawthorne, his adaptability to an enormous range of critical modes" (see *ALS 1970*, p. 21). Oleksy's work is a feat in scholarly dexterity that occasionally comes close to intellectual jugglery. The structure of *Theistic Existentialism* encloses a triadic set of existential ideas that are applied to three alternating pairs of Hawthorne's and Walker Percy's novels: "Renunciation" to *The Scarlet Letter* and *The Moviegoer;* "Catharsis" to *The House of the Seven Gables* and *Lancelot;* "Intersubjectivity" to *The Marble Faun* and *The Second Coming.* Her multiple approaches to both writers produce interpretations based on various shades of existentialism. Thus, *The Scarlet Letter* and *The Moviegoer* are analyzed as manifestations of Kierkegaard's existential pathos; *The House of the Seven Gables* and

Lancelot are subjected "to a biblical exegesis, à la [Northrop] Frye," as "apocalyptic" and "demonic visions"; *The Marble Faun* and *The Second Coming* are filtered through some basic tenets of Gabriel Marcel's "personalist theory." In actuality, Oleksy has applied her theory only to an analysis of Hawthorne's romance in the light of Marcel's "Broken—Unbroken World," while Percy's is mainly read through Pascal, only marginally through Marcel. The study's most important aim—"to elucidate parallel developments of Hawthorne's and Percy's fictional interests"—is fulfilled mostly through a comparison of both writers' biographies and through Oleksy's reading those biographies into their texts—a questionable procedure. By proposing to approach Hawthorne as "a trailblazer" of American existentialism, Oleksy just escapes the fallacy of using a writer's work as evidence for his philosophical views, and then only because she is aware of the liquefied meaning of existentialism, which prompts her to doubt "the validity of my approach." She quells her doubts, though, and she then wants to read *The Marble Faun* "as Hawthorne's anticipation of several personalistic theories." We learn from her that there are two groups of existentialists, "theistic" and "atheistic." But the qualifiers are not strictly antonymous; Oleksy seems to know it intuitively, perhaps, for throughout her work she avoids using the term "theistic," appropriately replacing it with "religious."

Judging from the titles, several contributions purport to address general issues, but they turn out to be illustrative rather than comprehensive or synthetic. Thus, Jim B. Philip's essay "Toward a Philosophy of American Writing" (*Discourses/Texts/Contexts,* pp. 9–17) takes the concept of American individualism as a criterion for assessing the quality of American literature. Starting with a polemic discussion of Jeffrey Meyer's views, Philip proposes to look at "the more secret and more traumatic processes of original formation. Or, to put it another way, we have to pass on from that kind of analysis of the present that is possible for the social scientist, towards that kind of remembering of the past that is more available in literary texts." By way of illustration he draws on a passage from E. L. Doctorow's *Loon Lake,* which in his view reveals "those external and internal processes that have gone into the making of an American individual." Doctorow's work, however, is "excessively negative" about American life. Philip finds Charles Olson's "Maximus to Glouster, Letter 27 [Withheld]" an example of a work that would use "dissatisfaction . . . as the moment in which new kinds of subjectivity, a new kind of relationship to the world, are glimpsed." The poem "projects the emergence of a wider critical force in American culture in which poetry and philosophy might work in tandem to explore the limitations of the constructed world and its ideological underpinnings."

Marek Wilczynski's "Beyond Totality—Postmodernism and American Fiction" (*Discourses/Texts/Contexts,* pp. 18–29) might be considered an extension of Philip's essay were it not for its peculiar style of exposition, which is the opposite of Philip's lucidity. Wilczynski's cacophonic and disjointed presentation reflects his murky concept of postmodernism. What his forays into the thought of Habermas, Lyotard, and Wittgenstein seem to suggest is that a certain convergence occurred of typically postmodern (whatever that means) and minimalist characteristics complemented by a revival of realism.

In "Setting Golems in Motion: Postmodern Inter/Textual Figures (John Gardner, Joseph Heller, Robert Nye)" (*Discourses/Texts/Contexts,* pp. 30–42) Piotr Siemion seriously considers a postmodern game played, among others, by the writers in his title. The similarity of narrators-protagonists in many postmodern novels induces Siemion to take the original concept of the golem as a generalized model of such artificial narrators "brought to fictive life whenever an author tells a story which was originally someone else's, using a first-person narrator also borrowed from the author of the initial text."

The collection of articles *Amerikanskaya literature: Problemy razvitiya metodov i zhanrov* [American literature: the problem of the development of methods and genres] (Krasnodar: Kuban. Gos. Universitet) could not be procured for review.

b. Pre-20th-Century Literature In view of the transformation of Soviet reality, Maiya Koreneva's latecomer *Avtobiografiya B. Franklina* [Benjamin Franklin's *Autobiography*] (Moscow: Moskovskii Robochii, 1988) acquires symbolic meaning. It appears that through this booklet, consisting of selected extracts from Franklin's work interspersed with her own comments, Koreneva wants to remind her compatriots of some fundamental social and moral values indispensable to constructing a new society in a way that Enlightenment values exemplified in Franklin shaped the rise of the American republic as a civic, democratic society. With an eye on the special class of readers (the book was published by a firm whose name is self-explanatory—"The Moscow Worker"), Koreneva is less concerned with the *Autobiography* as a work of art than as a document revealing the life of a person worthy of imitation.

Vladimir V. Sogrin's *Dzhefferson, chelovek, myslitel', politik* [Jefferson: man, thinker, politician] (Moscow: Nauka, 1989) is to my knowledge the first Russian book on Jefferson. Although issued by the publishing organ of the Academy of Sciences, the monograph has little scholarly value; still, its narrative style makes pleasant educational reading for the uninitiated. With literary èclat and an empathic attitude toward the subject, Sogrin has captured the complex quality of Jefferson's life and work; yet he fails to critically evaluate Jefferson's writings. I might add that on the reverse of the book's title page, which—following Russian publishing tradition—contains a characterization of the contents, the reader will be surprised to note that Jefferson was "the fourth president of the United States."

In her biography *Aleksander Hamilton* (Wroclaw: Ossolineum) Izabella Rusinowa passes up the opportunity to say something about her subject's literary skills, and her discussion of *The Federalist Papers* amounts to little more than a description.

Among 19th-century authors, Hawthorne attracted several scholars in Poland. Taking the lead from various American interpretations, Elzbieta Foeller-Pituch offers an excellent study of his last romance, "Arcadia in Ruins: Mythology in Hawthorne's *The Marble Faun*" (*American Studies* [Warsaw] 8 [1989]:139–51). She integrates the mythological elements with those carrying the idea of *felix culpa* present not just in Donatello but in the other three protagonists. Her dexterous description of their relationships, however, is not matched by an adequate consideration of the different roles that Hawthorne assigned them. In "Anguish and Exhaustion: Fowles's and Hawthorne's Studies in Scarlet" (*Discourse and Character,* pp. 76–84) Piotr Dziedzic meditates eloquently, though somewhat fancifully, on the rebellious Hester Prynne and Sara Woodruff of *The French Lieutenant's Woman* to conclude that "*The Scarlet Letter* belongs in the literature of anguish; *The French Lieutenant's Woman*—in that of exhaustion." Miroslawa Ziaja surveyed several groups of Polish students to investigate whether their "misreadings" of "The Minister's Black Veil" were a manifestation of "intolerance or generation gap." Her findings have predictably yielded ambivalent results (*"We Are All Indians,"* pp. 112–25).

I was unable to procure G. D. Pulatova's "Persidsko-tadzhikskie motivy v tvorchestve Ral'fa Ualdo Emersona" [Persian-Tadzhik motives in Ralph Waldo Emerson's work] (*Izvestiya Akademii Nauk Tadzh. SSR Seriya Vostokovedenie, Istoriya, Filologiya* 1:10–16) to comment on the

Soviet scholar's contribution to Emerson criticism. I can say only that its publication is another proof of growing interest in Emerson in Russia.

A 19th-century favorite was the subject of only one brief publication. In "Huck Finn—Boy or Man?" (*Discourse and Character,* pp. 85–95) Warren Staebler ponders Huck's evolution from boyhood to manhood as stimulated and shaped by Jim's personality. Although the essay is of little value to Twain scholars, it makes an excellent introduction to *Adventures of Huckleberry Finn.*

c. 20th-Century Literature Vladimir N. Bogoslovskii's "Literatura Soedinennykh Shtatov Ameriki" ["The literature of the United States"] in *Istoriya zarubezhnoi literatury XX veka 1917–1945* [The history of 20th-century foreign literature, 1917–1945] (Moscow: Prosveshchenie, pp. 221–79) manifests the lingering Soviet Marxist interpretation of literature, the more disturbing in that it is—like its earlier editions (1963, 1973, 1984)—a handbook for students at pedagogical institutes. In comparison with other recent Russian publications on American literature, the piece is a historiographical curiosity doomed to the lumber room.

No approach to the study of literature could be more different from that between Bogoslovskii's and Tadeusz Slawek's *The Dark Glory: Robinson Jeffers and His Philosophy of Earth and Time* (Katowice: Uniwersytet Slaski). Slawek considers his study "a meditation on earth, time and things" as reflected in Jeffers's longer poems, and he divests himself of the scholar's duty to be critical. Approval, of course, does not preclude perceptive cognition, but *The Dark Glory* is so thoroughly tinted by the ontologies of Nietzsche, Spengler, and especially Heidegger that Slawek even strips Jeffers of both his American and California identity, insisting instead on "regional" identity, which consists in a special relationship with the poet's topographic location. Following Heidegger, Slawek reads Jeffers's work as radical criticism of the traditional humanism rooted in the belief in man's centrality in the universe. Jeffers wanted to "unhumanize" man, "to rediscover *his thingly nature,*" to recognize that he is not "the measure of all things." Slawek complements his illuminating study with an analysis of Jeffers's poem "The Humanist's Tragedy" read through Nietzsche's concept of "philosophising with a hammer" in "A Hammer of Philosophy: The Scene of Violence in Nietzsche and Jeffers" (*"We Are All Indians,"* pp. 20–33).

Jerzy Sobieraj's "The Grotesque in the Fiction of Carson McCullers and Truman Capote" (*Discourse and Character,* pp. 132–44) demonstrates how both writers use the various forms and meanings of the mode to convey characters' moral degradation. Interestingly, Sobieraj links McCullers's grotesque elements with the paintings of Bosch and Brueghel, but he does not elaborate. Capote, according to Sobieraj, intensifies the grotesque to such a degree that his characters resemble figures from fairy tales.

In a nicely construed but logically shaky argument, Anna Machinek maintains in "That Troubling Presence: Female Characters of William Faulkner's Fictional World" (*Discourse and Character,* pp. 145–58) that Caddy, Emily, and Lena, taken together, constitute a composite image that comes close to representing ideal womanhood. Men are unable to understand their "otherness," which is derived from values that differ from men's. This difference accounts for the "troubling presence" of these women, which threatens the general order.

In the Soviet Union the year 1990 saw a hiatus in scholars' preoccupation with Faulkner; I found only one publication of merit devoted to a single novel, *As I Lay Dying,* analyzed by A. K. Savurenok in "Izderzki obrotennogo masterstva: roman U. Folknera *Kogda nastal moi smertnyi chas*" [The price of gained mastership: William Faulkner's *As I Lay Dying*] (*Vestnik Leningradskogo Universiteta,* series 2, no. 3:44–54). Savurenok maintains that both Soviet and foreign students of Faulkner's novel have failed to perceive the "ironic coloring" that results from the specific nature of correlation between the title and the plot, both derived from the Eleventh Book of *The Odyssey* where the spectral Agamemnon relates to Odysseus the scornful refusal of Clytemnestra "to administer to her husband as he lay dying." As with so many of Faulkner's admirers, Savurenok is captivated by *The Sound and the Fury,* which becomes the yardstick by which to measure the worth of his other works. Consequently, of every book that Faulkner wrote, Russian critics consider it inferior to the story of the Compson family. For Savurenok, the creative defect of *As I Lay Dying* lies in Faulkner's failure to "sustain the feeling of harmonious unity which constitutes the criterion of high art."

O. B. Sabinina's perceptive though excessively hasty review of the ideological characteristics of "Zhanr antiutopii v angliskoi i amerikanskoi literature 30–50kh godov XX v." [The anti-utopian genre in English and American literature of the 1930s–1950s] (*Vestnik Moskovskogo Universiteta,* series 9, Filologiya, 2:51–57) invites close readings of anti-utopian novels. Only Aldous Huxley's *Brave New World* and George Orwell's *1984* receive fleeting comments; American practitioners of the genre, such as

Kurt Vonnegut and Ray Bradbury, are not even identified by their initials, while the first initial of Asimov appears as "A" instead of "I[saac]."

O. Yu. Surova's " 'Chernyi eksistentsializm' i ego mesto v negritanskoi literature SSHA XX v." ['Black existentialism' and its place in 20th-century Negro literature] (*Vestnik Moskovskogo Universiteta,* series 9, Filologiya 4:19–27) stands out as an exception in the Russian scholars' preoccupation with mainstream American literature. Surova sets the origin and development of "black existentialism" against the background of American blacks' dual consciousness, determined by their identity as blacks and as Americans. Surova follows the shifts in emphasis on either identity and points out the ideological circumstances accounting for the embrace of European existentialism by black American writers. Substituting history for analysis, she presents a schematic characterization of the differences and affinities in the works of the first generation of black existentialists (Richard Wright and Chester Himes) and those of the second (Ralph Ellison and James Baldwin), concluding with a few remarks on "postexistentialist" novelists (Ishmael Reed and Toni Morrison).

d. Miscellaneous Regretfully, a study that promises substance—L. K. Zemlyanova's *Sovremennoe literaturovedenie v SSHA: Teoreticheski napravleniya i konfrontatsii 1920–1980* [Contemporary literary scholarship in the United States: theoretical trends and confrontations, 1920–1980] (Moscow: Izdatel'stvo Moskovskogo Gosudarstvennogo Universiteta) was not available for review.

As in past years, 1990 yielded a crop of contributions on literary relations—*Literaturnye svyazi i traditsii v tvorchestve pisatelei Zapadnoi Evropy i Ameriki XIX–XX vv.* [Literary connections and traditions in the works of Western European and American writers of the 19th and 20th centuries] (Gorki: Gorkii Gosudarstvennyi Universitet), which contains four articles on a variety of "relation" topics. A. F. Golovenchenko writes on Italian-American connections, using the example of *The Marble Faun;* N. V. Kireeva presents Maksim Gorky as a reader of Sherwood Anderson; N. A. Kubanev traces the influence of classical Russian writers on 20th-century American novelists; and V. V. Khorolskii compares the use of the eclogue by Robert Frost and Thomas Hardy.

This review would be incomplete without paying attention to *Amerikanskaya literatura v russkoi kritike. Bibliograficheskii ukazatel' 1981–1985* [American literature in Russian criticism: a bibliographical list, 1981–

1985] (Moscow: Institut Nauchnoi Informatsii po Obshchestvennym Naukam, 1989), compiled by V. A. Libman and I. N. Isaeva—an indispensable source for anyone interested in the Soviet reception of American literature. The bibliography is a follow-up to Valentina Libman's *Amerikanskaya literatura v russkikh perevodakh i kritike* (see *ALS 1977*, pp. 463–64) as well as Libman and Isaeva's *Bibliographical List* covering criticism from 1976 through 1980 (1984). Unless a reform reduces the length of the publishing process, a list of Russian criticism for 1986–90 is to be expected in 1994. The bibliography at hand is proof of the intense and extensive Russian interest in American letters, although the impressive quantity of information does not correlate entirely with scholarly quality. Still, just a listing of American authors who elicited widest attention shown by the number of publications entries for each one is revealing. I have arranged them in diminishing order, including only writers who drew more than 10 publications during 1981–85: Hemingway 69, Faulkner 61, Poe 36, London 34, Henry James 31, Twain 29, Fitzgerald 27, Tennessee Williams 22, Mailer 22, Hawthorne 20, Steinbeck 20, Cooper 19, Whitman 19, Vonnegut 19, Dreiser 18, Emerson 18, Melville 16, Thornton Wilder 16, O'Neill 15, John Gardner 15, Frost 14, Flannery O'Connor 14, Robert Penn Warren 13, Irwin Shaw 12, Updike 12, Saroyan 12, Albee 12, Longfellow 11, Sherwood Anderson 11, Styron 11, Capote 11.

University of Warsaw

ii East European Contributions—1991: F. Lyra

Studies in this year's survey, on the whole, continue to deal with traditional subjects, although some Hungarian publications offer interesting new perspectives, and most Russian scholars maintain the course away from past dogmatic constraints. Nothing substantial has appeared in Poland except for two American contributions in *American Studies* (Warsaw). Czech, Slovak, Bulgarian, and Romanian Americanists failed to submit any publications. Russian material is even harder to come by now than during the Soviet era because of the turbulent reorganization of life in the Russian Federal Republic that has affected production and distribution of books and periodicals, including such basic bibliographical sources as *Knizhnaya letopis* and *Letopis zhurnal'nykh statei*. The present review incorporates a few leftovers from one and even two years ago.

Grateful acknowledgment is due Zoltán Abádi-Nagy for his generous assistance in procuring the Hungarian contributions, and to E. P. Khanzhina for several collections of articles on literary topics, among which are studies of American letters, published by Perm' State University.

a. Pre-20th-Century Studies Bálint Rozsnyai's "'Reader! I Am No Poet': The Author, the Book, and the Reader in Early American Literature" (*HSE* 21 [1990]:7–15) takes Perry Miller and Karl Keller to task for their teleological approach to early American poetry, studying it "from within" and ignoring the meiotic masks assumed by the poets. He argues instead that behind the poets' protestations that they were only versifiers, they longed for recognition as artists, although they realized that poetic recognition carried socially discriminating associations. In "Nativizm i problemy poetiki v amerikanskoi lirike epokhi romantizma" [Nativism and the Problems of Poetics in American Lyrical Poetry in the Romantic Period], pp. 41–52 in *Problemy metoda i poetiki v zarubezhnykh literaturakh XIX–XX vekov* [Problems of Method and Poetics in Foreign Literatures of the 19th and 20th Centuries] (Perm', 1989) E. P. Khanzhina unintentionally follows up on Rozsnyai's postulate to regard early American poetry within the emergence of a native poetical theory that the Russian scholar finds rooted in the poets' attention to American nature. She demonstrates how Bryant, Richard Henry Wilde, Whittier, and Longfellow expressed their conceptions of nature in an American-English lexicon and American Indian onomastic forms, thus initiating an American poetics codified by Emerson, Thoreau, Whitman, and Emily Dickinson. In another study, "Zhivopisnoe nachalo v lirike amerikanskikh romantikov (Uitt'er, Braiant, Longfello)" [The Picturesque Elements in Lyrical American Romantic Poetry: Whittier, Bryant, Longfellow], pp. 9–25 in *Traditsii i vzaimodeistviya v zarubezhnoi literature XIX–XX vekov* [Traditions and Interrelations in Foreign Literature of the 19th and 20th Centuries] (Perm', 1990), Khanzhina envelops her subject in the aesthetic theories of F. W. I. Schelling and H. E. Toliver, and following Coleridge's "spiritual optics" she argues for the superiority of the poet over the painter in the depiction of landscape. She considers the spiritualization of landscape painting and poetry as a basic attribute of American romantic poetry. To her credit, she reaches beyond traditional coverage of the subject within the limits of the Hudson River School. Khanzhina has confirmed her interest in the lesser Romantics with a close reading of Whittier's "Snow-Bound" in "Khudozhestvennyi mir poemy Dz. G. Uitt'era 'Zanasennye snegom'" [The Artistic World in

J. G. Whittier's "Snow-Bound"], pp. 40–56 in *Problemy metoda i poetiki v zarubezhnoi literature XIX–XX vekov* [Problems of Method and Poetics in Foreign Literature of the 19th and 20th Centuries] (Perm', 1990). Falling back on Bakhtin's concept of the idyl, she identifies the poem as a uniquely American pastoral, its poetic reality constructed on the Hegelian principle of dialectic opposites, the chief one obviously being man vs. nature; man himself is further dichotomized into individual and social man, and only social man is capable of facing the might of nature. This allows Khanzhina to associate Whittier with Hawthorne and Melville rather than with the Transcendentalists.

The year's most significant contribution to pre-20th-century studies is El'vira Filippovna Osipova's *Ral'f Uoldo Emerson: Pisatel' i vremya* [Ralph Waldo Emerson: The Writer and His Times] (Leningrad: Izdatel'stvo Leningradskogo Universiteta). Osipova's book may be regarded as a peak in the renaissance of Russian reception of Emerson that began in the late 1970s after almost total neglect throughout the Soviet epoch. (Indeed, his name does not even appear in the index of Deming Brown's *Soviet Attitudes Toward American Writing* [1962]). Some Emersonians might question the pivotal status that the Russian scholar has assigned to *The Conduct of Life,* imputing to her a desire to read Emerson pragmatically; after all, its chapters "Wealth" and "Power" have attracted wide audiences. The imputation might be justified, but it should be balanced against her comprehensive treatment of the more abstract components of Emerson's philosophy. Actually, her admission that Emerson "cannot be fully comprehended rationally" may be regarded as both an expression of humility toward a genius and a tribute to the transcendental quality of his thinking. Osipova is not blind to the flaws of Emerson's moral system, which she brings into relief by comparing it with Dostoyevsky's. Neither does she uncritically embrace Emerson's historiosophy, but she censures it mildly through reference to Ortega y Gasset, and she rejects V. R. Skrypnik's opinion of it as "antihistorical," as she also does T. L. Morozova's characterization of his values as a manifestation of "moral relativism"—opinions shared by not a few Western intellectuals in their reading of "Self-Reliance" as an indication of bourgeois morality. She makes a strong case for Emerson as a social thinker and explains his late, reluctant commitment to social causes. She closely follows the evolution of his thinking about slavery and sees his engagement in the cause of abolition as a manifestation of bravery. A separate chapter on Emerson's poetics, preceded by one (the longest in her book) polemically directed against Poe's theory of art and his notorious aversions to the Transcendentalists, bespeaks her deep interest in Emerson as an artist. For good reason, Osipova grounds Emerson's philosophy in New England theology and social history as well as in Kant's philosophy, but one feels almost grateful to her for not harping on the Transcendental movement in America beyond the necessary range. Her fortuitous treatment of *Nature* (1836) in preference to "Nature" (1844) strikes me as a flaw that does not diminish the optimistic message which the book carries to her countrymen.

Osipova also discusses Poe's critical attitude toward the Transcendentalists in her excellent "Rasskaz Edgara Po 'Ligeiya' (Problemy interpretatsii)" [Poe's "Ligeia": Problems of Interpretation] (*Filologicheskie Nauki* 4 [1990]:102–09). In contrast to earlier Soviet critics who concentrated on the social significance of Poe's work, Osipova examines "Ligeia" in light of Schlegel's theory of Romantic irony and Kant's aesthetics. She focuses on its antiromantic attributes and finds them directed against the Transcendentalists. In turn, I. V. Golovacheva scrutinizes an instance of the uneasy literary relationship between Henry James and Poe in "Literaturnyi istochnik *Svyashchennego istochnika* (Detektivnaya traditsiya E. A. Po v povesti G. Dzhemsa)" [The Literary Source of Henry James's *The Sacred Fount:* Poe's Detective Tradition] (*Traditsii i vzaimodeistviya,* pp. 91–99). Looking at the deeper levels of the texts, Golovacheva maintains that the countless imitators and epigones of Dupin's inductive thinking "degraded" his "detective ideology" rooted in "critical pure reason." The incompetence of James's detective, his inability to unlock the secret, and the structural open-endedness of the novel induce her to regard *The Sacred Fount* as a parody of Poe's detective method.

In view of the absence of studies on other American romantics Elzbieta Foeller-Pituch's modest contribution "Subversive Allusions: Classical Myth in Melville's 'The Paradise of Bachelors and the Tartarus of Maids' " (*American Studies* [Warsaw] 11:35–39) deserves at least brief comment. The article flounders on the claim that the tale "is one of Melville's most subversive texts." Besides classical allusions, Foeller-Pituch also identifies sexual ones and finds in them "the author's misanthropic message of the destructive side of women's biological destiny, motherhood."

A sense of fairness compels me to involve myself in an instance of unfortunate double, or even triple, criticism in connection with Aladár Sarbu's "The Topicality of *The Scarlet Letter*" (*Americana & Hungarica,* pp. 35–55), which Frederick Newberry (*ALS 1989*, p. 26) briefly commented on as raising "familiar issues, mostly in dialogue with critics two or more decades ago." In fact, Sarbu's dialogue is mostly with Jonathan Arac (*ALS 1986*, pp. 29–30) and Zelda Bronstein (*ALS 1987*, p. 25) and is cogently constructive and not just polemical as Newberry implies.

b. 20th-Century Literature Instead of commenting on Zsolt K. Virágos's "The Hazards of Interpretive Overkill: The Myths of Gatsby" (*HSE* 22:49–68), I suggest that it be distributed to critics and scholars engaged in the heated production of publications on American literature, to students in advanced graduate courses, and to the various university boards that oversee faculty hiring, firing, and promotion, with the proposition that a temporary moratorium be adopted on publish or perish. The Hungarian scholar's work sounds eloquent warning against both the decline of the critical ethos and the deterioration of standards in the pursuit of American literary scholarship. Using *The Great Gatsby* as an exemplary text, Virágos demonstrates the distortions that have resulted from excessive application of analogical and paradigmatic readings within just one school of interpretation, myth criticism.

With two exceptions, all contributions on 20th-century literature are devoted to individual writers. One exception is M. P. Kizima's "Esteticheskaya platforma poetov f'yudzhitivistov" [The Aesthetic Platform of the Fugitive Poets] (*Filologicheskie Nauki* 4 [1990]:36–46), which replaces the Soviet ideological prejudices against the movement with such favorable revision that it invites critical reaction, at least of the kind that characterized most of the Fugitives' own reevaluation of their views after the group's demise. The other exception, provided by Kathleen A. Bagley, is no less complimentary to its subject, although presented with greater discretion. In "Writing the Body: Female Creative Imagination in Black American Women's Fiction" (*American Studies* [Warsaw] 11:19–34) Bagley briskly explores color, nature, song, and caretaking ritual as motifs in the novels of Toni Morrison, Alice Walker, Toni Cade Bambara, and Zora Neale Hurston, "the lately discovered grandmother" of them all. Her profusely illustrated exposition is illuminating but insufficiently substantiated to reserve for black women "the center of the American literary scene." Christopher J. Knight would be inclined to expand the center space for all contemporary female authors when in "Kathryn Davis's *Labrador* and a Feminist Poetic: Or Kathleen Liked Willie" (*American Studies* [Warsaw] 11:7–17) he observes that "women participate actively in the production of Anglo-American fiction but they might almost be said to rule the field." He sees Davis's first novel as fulfillment of Virginia Woolf's vision of an epoch wherein "women artists, confident in their talents and significant in the number, would not conceive of men as 'the opposing faction.'" According to Knight, however, this fulfillment remains hidden in Davis's story and by extension in all women's stories. They affirm a feminine ethic and a poetics never announced: "What this ethic and what this poetic are we do not exactly know." In "Black Saga and White Language in Toni Morrison's *Song of Solomon* and Alice Walker's *The Color Purple*" (*Americana & Hungarica,* pp. 153–57) Éva Federmayer uses Virginia Woolf's views on the unique attributes of male and female language as one of a series of referential categories—others being "bildungsroman," "magic realism," "language as palimpsest," and "inverse prototypical white middle class saga"—to point out the feminist characteristics of two leading black women authors in synchronic and diachronic contexts in the American literary tradition. The tantalizing hint at "the markedly different ideologies of both novels," however, Federmayer leaves unexplored. In style, her essay reads almost like entries to a "biographia literaria" of Morrison and Walker; if expanded, it might make an original contribution to black feminist scholarship. Originality need not be a sole measure of critical or cognitive value, of course, as can be seen in Sarolta Marinovich's "The Divided Self: Women in the Mirror" (*Americana & Hungarica,* pp. 79–88), which provides a charming glimpse into the meaning of one of the oldest motifs in the imagination of Shirley Jackson, Anaïs Nin, Flannery O'Connor, and, incidentally, Angela Carter. Feminism also serves I. N. Klepatskaya as a pretext for presenting Anne Tyler's *Earthly Possessions* in the context of "contemporary feminist prose of the United States" in "Roman E. Tailer *Blaga zemnye* i traditsii sovremennoi feminintskoi prozy SSHA" (*Traditsii i vzaimodeistviya,* pp. 135–43). Klepatskaya's understanding of feminism is not limited to women writers but includes female protagonists in the work of male writers as well. With the exception of Erica Jong she neglects to compare Tyler's heroine with those of other authors and pays only cursory attention to Tyler's distinctiveness in the group.

Among today's literary critics only a few seem capable of reading a female author's work without measuring it against feminist ideology. This preoccupation has reached a point at which surprise greets a piece of criticism about a woman author who is treated outside this framework. With this feeling, I read Charlotte Kretzoi's article about the author of *Tender Buttons*, "An American in Paris (Gertrude Stein)" (*Americana & Hungarica*, pp. 97–107). Kretzoi successfully argues that Stein "possessed a greater share of earlier and near-contemporary American tradition than was supposed when she first became known." In the light of Kretzoi's argument Stein proves to be an illustration of Emerson's famous dictum about his countrymen going abroad to be Americanized. As Kretzoi points out, Stein's attitude toward the United States remained ambiguous, often contradictory, but ultimately resolved itself in her statement, "America is my country and Paris is my home." Stein's aesthetic antipode, Theodore Dreiser, is the subject of E. A. Morozkina's "Roman T. Dreizera *Oplot* i evropeiskii pozitivizm (Ob evolutsii filosofsko-eticheskikh vzglyadov T. Dreizera)" [Dreiser's *The Bulwark* and European Positivism: The Evolution of Dreiser's Ethical Views] (*Traditsii i vzaimodeistviya*, pp. 99–107). While chafing at earlier Soviet disregard of the novel's religious and ethical aspects, Morozkina does not succeed in fully accounting for Dreiser's long struggle over it, but she manages to convey its complex quality, determined by "religious consciousness in conflict with capitalist reality: the influence of family on the shaping of character; individual will and man's responsibility for his actions." She acknowledges the complex nature of Dreiser's aesthetics, the evolution of his views from a mechanistic philosophy toward a recognition of the importance of the individual in the struggle for justice. In pointing to his joining the Communist party as the peak of this evolution, however, and by omitting the direct circumstances of his act, Morozkina does not break completely with earlier Soviet critics' erroneous evaluations of the act.

Turning to publications on present-day prose writers, Zsuzanna Griga's "Negative Initiation: A Change in the American Developmental Novel" (*Americana & Hungarica*, pp. 109–24) offers a close reading of Joseph Heller's *Something Happened* and a quick look at William Styron's *Lie Down in Darkness* as well as E. L. Doctorow's *Loon Lake* within a rambling presentation of the American variation of the bildungsroman. Ferenc Takács's "Self-Reflexivity and Metafiction: The Instance of Robert Coover" (*Americana & Hungarica*, pp. 125–43) consists of an illuminating discussion of the titular concepts treated as functionally independent yet "loosely synonymous" notions, perspicacious commentary on the key issues in Coover's art corroborated and expanded on by Coover himself in an interview that is a meditation on the emergence of the sixties movement, and a profession of adherence to traditional forms of novelistic art modified by magic realism. In contrast to Coover, Robert Pirsig rarely makes it into *ALS*, perhaps because his best-known opus challenges traditional taxonomy. His long absence is interrupted by Zsófia Bán's "Deconstruction and Its Easy Rider (On Robert Pirsig's *Zen and the Art of Motorcycle Maintenance*" (*Americana & Hungarica*, pp. 145–53). Bán identifies Pirsig's work as a "culture-bearing book," "an intellectual detective story whose author has ventured upon a quest for Quality (the subject proper of *Zen*) and a deconstructionist work par excellence because it questions the basic truths of Western culture."

c. Drama In the number of publications devoted to one author no other American figures more prominently this year than Eugene O'Neill. The five studies I was able to elicit for review in all probability do not fully represent the surge of critical interest initiated by his hundredth birthday. In Hungary Péter Egri celebrated the event with a weighty book (see *ALS 1988*, pp. 179–81), in the Soviet Union S. M. Pinaev with a monograph that I know only by title (see *ALS 1988*, p. 479). Two years later the Moscow publisher Nauka brought out Maiya Koreneva's *Tvorchestvo Iudzhina O'Nila i puti amerikanskoi dramy* [Eugene O'Neill's Work and the Development of American Drama], a copy of which she generously submitted for review. The book constitutes the summation of her long interest in O'Neill, exhibited in several past studies of his plays; and it is an impressive achievement in both generic and analytical historiography of a playwright's output. Koreneva has ordered her study in two parts: one deals with O'Neill's plays chronologically within a traditional interpretive framework, "The Social-Philosophical Quest: The Discovery of American Reality" (pp. 49–214); the other presents "O'Neill's Dramaturgical Aesthetics" (pp. 215–82), including chapters on his quest for form for modern tragedy and on the "poetics of O'Neill's theater." The first part is preceded by a succinct survey of the antecedents of the American drama and a chapter, "The American Drama at the Turn of the 19th and 20th Centuries." The second part is followed by a retrospective view of O'Neill's legacy in the work of a host of 20th-century playwrights, from Paul Green to Edward Albee. The value of Koreneva's book is in the thoughtful integration of every major play's thematic and formal components with those of O'Neill's other works, which she relates to the currents of European philosophical thought and art, notably Nietzsche, Ibsen, and Strindberg, and thus brings into relief

O'Neill's great variety of dramaturgical forms. She discusses his "dialogue" with critics concerning his notion of tragedy, staging experiments, the protagonists' idiolects, and his replies to accusations that he concentrated too much on the dark side of human nature. Koreneva herself attenuates the dramatist's ironic vision of man in favor of the tragic. Writing about his humor, she chooses not to analyze *Ah, Wilderness!,* his only performed comedy. She examines at length some of his unfinished plays and points out their importance for a better understanding of his known dramas. She draws attention to his weak plays to indicate that they stimulated his creative energies. Koreneva's penetrating interpretation of the plays, however, appears to me as slightly biased in favor of their realistic properties and their Americanness, although she fully accounts for O'Neill's innovations and experiments as well as for their nonrealistic qualities. She also avails herself of the opportunity to bring in various Russian motifs connected with both literary and theatrical matters, which enhance the cognitive value of the book, although many of them have been dealt with earlier, notably those referring to Chekhov, Gorky, Dostoyevsky, Tolstoy, and Tairov's staging of O'Neill in the Kamiernyi Theater in 1926 (which O'Neill saw in Paris four years later).

Two short contributions by L. N. Vysotskii may be considered complements to Koreneva's book. In "Obshchennyi obraz sovremennika v drame Yudzhina O'Nila 'Prodavets l'da gryadet' " [The General Image of the Contemporary in O'Neill's *The Iceman Cometh*] (*Problemy metoda i poetiki,* pp. 99–110) she offers a diffuse reading of the play that Koreneva sees primarily as a philosophic parable, prompted by the dramatist's comparison of it to a symphony. In turn, Vysotskii's "Traditsii romantizma i poetika dramy Yudzhina O'Nila 'Velikii bog Braun' " [The Romantic Tradition and the Poetics of O'Neill's *The Great God Brown*] (*Problemy metoda* [1989], pp. 60–72) demonstrates a fine analysis of the ideological and artistic complexity of the play supported by extensive scholarship. Critics and sophisticated readers alike will savor Péter Egri's intellectually delightful "The Psychology of Alienation, or What Parodies Are Good for: A Note on O'Neill's Modernity" (*Americana & Hungarica,* pp. 89–95). Egri provides scholarly substance to the dramatist's repeated insistence that his plays, especially *Strange Interlude* and *Mourning Becomes Electra,* should be read as illustrations of psychoanalytical tenets.

A. V. Otchman's "L. Khellman i Chekhov: Traditsii poetiki 'novoi dramy' " [Lillian Hellman and Chekhov: The Tradition of the "New Drama" Poetics] (*Traditsii i vzaimodeistviya,* pp. 65–77) reveals less concern with the poetics of the new drama than with the generic similarities between the Russian and American playwrights, especially between *The Autumn Garden* and *Toys in the Attic.* The article also draws attention to the resemblance of *The Little Foxes* to Gorky's *Egor Bulychov.* Zoltán Szilassy's "Sam Shepard and Some Other Dramatists of the Unheroic 1970s" (*HSE* 21 [1990]: 59–66) is a rambling presentation that can be adequately appreciated only by qualified drama connoisseurs.

d. General Zsolt Virágos contributes a richly documented article in Hungarian with a summary in English, "An 'American' in Paris: Thomas Paine and the French Revolution," to a collection of essays *Tanulmányok a Francia Forradalomról* (Debrecen: Kossuth Lajos Tudományegyetem, pp. 41–49), in which he follows Paine's political career during the French Revolution and suggests that "it may have been Gouverneur Morris . . . rather than Robespierre, who was indirectly responsible for Paine's ten-month incarceration."

Virágos's highly compact "Myth, Ideology, and the American Writer" (*HSE* 21 [1990]:29–44) is an incisive commentary on John Updike's description of the cultural situation of the American writer (see *ALS 1977,* p. 304) who, in Updike's words, "has suffered loss both in the dignity assigned to it by non-writers, and in the sense of purpose that shapes a profession from within." Against the background of a set of selected American cultural myths Virágos shows how transformations in that background have brought inevitable changes in the American writer's "sense of purpose," which in Virágos's opinion depends on the existence of "broad ideological myth systems" that would generate centripetal forces capable of creating a social consciousness, a central ideology that existed in the past but does not in the present, having been broken into pieces. Consequently, "a new center must be defined. Till this happens, the American writer has to content himself with the broken pieces. The question is whether he is going to be in the position to integrate the broken pieces."

The American "mission" topos that constitutes a key component in Virágos's discussion figures prominently in Kurt Vonnegut's views of the United States as he meditates on his country's relation to the world and her place in the universe, in " 'Serenity,' 'Courage,' 'Wisdom': A Talk with Kurt Vonnegut" (*HSE* 22:23–37). Assuming the role of a conversationalist rather than that of a conventional interviewer, Zoltán Abádi-Nagy manages to draw the writer into a series of monologues and comments on a wide range of philosophical, political, and literary issues, including revealing remarks on a work in progress, even personal matters as well as life experiences that have shaped Vonnegut's largely pessimistic worldview. Little is said about American literature at large, though, which is just as well, for Abádi-Nagy seems to know that questions addressed to writers on that issue usually produce little more than a handful of bromides, unless the interviewed subject happens to be a critic. The conversation promises nonetheless to be of significant value to Vonnegut criticism—and it provides a fitting finis to this year's survey.

University of Warsaw

iii German Contributions—1990: Rolf Meyn

The year 1990 was one of joint ventures in German scholarship. The output was unbalanced, however, since the majority of essays and monographs were again devoted to 20th-century literature. With the exception of Benjamin Franklin's autobiography, colonial literature was not dealt with. Ethnic literature—black, Native American, Hispanic, and Asian-American—seems to attract more and more German scholars. Thanks to a special issue of *Amerikastudien,* binational publications were more frequent than in the recent past.

a. Literary Criticism and Theory: Comparative Studies In this section Heinz Tschachler's habilitation dissertation, *Ökologie und Arkadien. Natur und nordamerikanische Kultur der siebziger Jahre* (Frankfurt: Lang) should be mentioned first. By focusing on the terms "ecology" and "arcadia," Tschachler attempts to show to what extent the concept of nature was ideologized during the 1970s. He analyzes discourses critical of progress and growth: James Dickey's *Deliverance,* Margaret Atwood's *Surfacing,* Ursula Le Guin's *The Dispossessed,* Ernest Callenbach's *Ecotopia,* Charles Reich's *The Greening of America,* and Marge Piercy's *Women on the Edge of Time.* His discussion is embedded in critical theories that range through Marxism, neo-Marxism in the critical theories of Adorno and Habermas, John Gardner's vision of a "moral nature," and the ideas of the intellectual guru of the 1960s and 1970s—Herbert Marcuse. It is impossible here to give even a crude overview of the philosophical and sociological debates from Rousseau and Hegel to Bataille and Jameson that Tschachler's study incorporates. Sometimes it appears more a historical and philosophical treatise than a discussion of literary texts, but the novels are by no means neglected. Tschachler interprets Atwood's *Surfacing* and Dickey's *Deliverance* as "neoprimitivistic, mythicizing novels" in which a flight from liberated subjectivity to new authoritarian leanings, in Atwood's case on Canadian nationalism, in Dickey's on Yukio Mishima's "philosophy of sun and steel," is obvious. Le Guin's *The Dispossessed* does not solve the antagonism between individual and society, Tschachler claims; rather, the novel presents "an ambiguous utopia" because it simultaneously reflects a utopian and a retrospective mentality. Piercy's *Women on the Edge of Time* also deals with an "endangered utopia" since it remains unclear whether the female protagonist suffers from hallucinations or really travels through time and space. Furthermore, Piercy clearly doubts the possibility of the narratability of any historical progress. Tschachler sees Callenbach and Reich as representatives of a liberal nonconformism in the tradition of Emerson and Thoreau, although in his eyes Callenbach transcends the "without-me attitude of the neo-Transcendentalist counterculture." Yet even Callenbach, Tschachler astutely observes, retains his anthropocentric view, for his Ecotopians reduce nature to an object that is hedonistically enjoyed, even exploited. Although not always easy reading, *Ökologie und Arkadien* is a stimulating discussion.

Another remarkable book is devoted to only one poet. Balz Engler's *Poetry and Community* (Tübingen: Stauffenberg) begins with a general discussion of the orality of literature. Engler reminds us that literate culture may be dominant in urban centers "with their so-called 'High Culture,'" but that oral elements have survived not only in distant regions, such as Ireland and Wales, but in the United States—in ethnic minorities and in the folk-song tradition. Engler then defines an interpretive community. Building on the theories of Stanley Fish, Emile Durkheim, Victor Turner, Joseph R. Gusfield, and Mary Douglas, he develops a model of a reading community that is differentiated by a system of shared and private classifications and by an ego controlling other people or controlled by the pressure exerted by other people. The search for community symbols leads him to the question of what constitutes a classic, which he sees arising in three forms, as representative of certain patterns of experience, as figures of certain types of personality and behavior, and as commonly used phrases and passages. Two chapters on cultural symbolism and on rituals and reading conclude the first, theoretical part of the study.

The second part bears the title "The Scandal of Vachel Lindsay" and is a passionate endeavor to resurrect Lindsay from his current lowly regard. Engler holds that Lindsay is the product of a changing relationship between poet and community in the English-speaking world. The "high modernists" were bent on writing revolutionary manifestoes and on establishing social and cultural elites, whereas the Georgian poets and the poets of the Chicago Renaissance stressed the social function of poetry. In Engler's opinion, Lindsay went beyond all of them, since he took a position that was acceptable as late as the 1980s, when postmodern poets and ethnopoetics emphasized performance and group experience. Like Sinclair Lewis and Sherwood Anderson in their later careers, Lindsay celebrated American small towns and the spiritual life of their inhabitants. Yet he departed from traditional, post-Romantic poetics by firmly taking the side of orality. According to Engler, Lindsay's poetic performances can be divided into three groups: (1) the poems of the "Higher Vaudeville," created to evoke a feeling of community in the audience (e.g., "The Congo"); (2) the poems that share private visions with the audience; and (3) poems on visionaries like Lincoln and Poe who are able to serve as models. Ultimately, Engler concludes, Lindsay is an American Dreamer and a transitional figure because he realized earlier than his fellow poets that the reading public was fragmented.

Gerd Lauten's dissertation, *Kommunikation und Literarizität im Erzähltext. Roman Jakobson und die Narrativik. Eine Untersuchung anhand englischer und amerikanischer Romane* (Frankfurt: Lang), starts out from Roman Jakobson's model of communication, which, however, is modified into separate elocutionary and referential categories. Referential orientation, furthermore, is augmented by a procedure that gets hold of the narrative structure. In addition, the "modernized" model of communication is seen in the light of Charles S. Peirce's semiotics with its distinction between textual sign and narrative sign. The combination of Jakobson's model of communication and Peirce's semiotics, Lauten claims, transcends on the basis of connotative semiotics a purely object-oriented, solely linguistic foundation of the narrative text as well as the one-sided concept of an abstract narrative sign. Lauten also develops a model of "discoursivity," under which he subsumes the foregroundings and manipulations of the "object horizon." Although Lauten's study seems to place too much emphasis on theory rather than texts, his modified model of communication works, as his analyses amply testify.

Hans-Christoph Ramm's *Modell für eine literarische Amerikakunde. Zugänge zum modernen schwarzamerikanischen Roman am Beispiel von Ann Petrys* The Street, *James Baldwins* Go Tell It On the Mountain *und Ralph Ellisons* Invisible Man (Frankfurt: Lang, 1989) is a didactic enterprise that explores the three novels for classroom teaching. That requires both a concise theoretical framework and the inclusion of literary, sociological, historical, and ethnic resources. Ramm succeeds in incorporating all of them. For instance, he discusses Ann Petry's *The Street* not only as the female counterpart of Richard Wright's *Native Son,* but also as a forerunner of many novels written by black women after 1945 in which the key element is the unfolding of a complex female personality under pressure from a racist, patriarchal society. Ramm's interpretation of *Go Tell It On the Mountain* concisely describes black Pentecostalism as a vital part of black culture and its role in the novel. The discussion of Ellison's *Invisible Man* starts with a chapter on the dialectics of autonomy and obedience as the novel's structural center. Diagrams, maps, comic strips, and chapter-by-chapter analyses complete a book that will be helpful for teachers and students.

A few articles contained in a festschrift, *Modes of Narrative: Approaches to American, Canadian, and British Fiction, Presented to Helmut Bonheim,* ed. Reingard M. Nischik and Barbara Korte (Würzburg: Königshausen & Neumann), deserve mention. Lothar Hönnighausen's "Metaphor in the Twentieth-Century Novel" (pp. 3–19) touches on Conrad's *Lord Jim,* Woolf's *To the Lighthouse,* Joyce's *Ulysses,* and Faulkner's *The Sound and the Fury* and *Light in August* to plead for a more flexible approach to metaphor, since all these works contain a "creative rendering of the tension between the permanence of flux and the stasis of the aesthetic moment." Franz K. Stanzel in his "Textual Power in (Short) Short Story and Poem" (pp. 20–30) notices a growing similarity between modern poetry and the (short) short story after 1900, the only difference being typographical arrangement. Stanzel claims that this partly stems from many writers starting out as poets and later turning to the short story. He even surmises that modern narrative discourse may turn toward the condition of poetry because it seems to move away from authorial explication toward figural empathy. Waldemar Zacharasiewicz in his essay, "The Search for Autonomous Voices: Intertextuality and Revision in Modern Fiction" (pp. 31–44), assesses the first novels of William

Styron and the Canadian writer Jack Hodgins, who were both heavily indebted to Faulkner. Styron's *Lie Down in Darkness* (1951) and Hodgins's *The Invention of the World* (1977), Zacharasiewicz holds, reveal the precarious balance between the influence of a "towering genius" and the dynamics of liberating creative resources within the young writers themselves. Jon Erickson's "Fairytale Features in Kate Chopin's 'Désirée's Baby': A Case Study in Genre Cross-Reference" (pp. 57–67) is also comparative since it discusses two frames of reference in Chopin's story, namely, the fairy-tale feature and the potential of a realistic short story embedded in a rigid social context. The opposition between these reference frames results from the tension between appearance and reality and is responsible for the deeply ironic effect that the "anti-fairy-tale" ending creates. Peter Freese in "Bret Easton Ellis, *Less Than Zero:* Entropy in the 'MTV Novel'?" (pp. 68–87), argues that Ellis's novel, besides being a cultural document, by its heavy reliance on sensational films and videos may point toward future literary developments.

Another highlight of the 1990 harvest was again a joint endeavor—Günter H. Lenz et al., eds., *Reconstructing American Literary and Historical Studies* (Frankfurt: Campus Verlag), which in its theoretical aspects deserves discussion here. These collected essays are organized into four chapters: "The Problem of Synthesis," with the exception of Hans-Joachim Lang's "From the Old Cambridge History to the New *Columbia Literary History of the United States*" (pp. 110–27) concerned with purely historical studies; "Gender, Race, and Canon Formation"; "History and Fiction"; and "Postmodernism, History, New Historicism." Lenz provides a concise overview of recent trends in American literary studies, ranging from deconstructionism and New Historicism to black and feminist criticism. He focuses on the debate over pluralism and synthesis, which he believes is by no means over. In one way or another, most of the contributors add something to this discussion. Hans-Joachim Lang thinks it next to impossible for this problem to be solved in any literary history. Hartwig Isernhagen in his " 'American Studies' and 'New Literatures in English': (Literary-) Historical Paradigms in Conflict" (pp. 145–68) points to Native American and ethnic literature in other English-speaking countries and questions the terms "national" and "America" from an ideological point of view. He envisions an "American" literature characterized by "discourses of difference" that allow minorities to voice their separate identities. Renate Hof insists on otherness and difference in her "Writing Women into (Literary) History: Toward a Poetics of

Gender?" (pp. 211–24). She is convinced that a poetics of gender will offer insights into the ways that power relations structure fictions as well as theories. Sabine Bröck-Sallah follows the same line in her "Women Writing: Plotting against HIStory" (pp. 225–37). Focusing on black women's fiction and black feminist criticism, she chides male black literary historians like Houston Baker and Henry Louis Gates, Jr., for their neglect of black feminist writing, which laid the foundation for their own methodological approaches. Furthermore, she holds, women writers like Toni Morrison, Margaret Walker, and Alice Walker rewrote history as female experience and deconstruction of patriarchal heritage.

The other festschrift contributions are specialized studies. Alfred Hornung's "Autobiography and Democracy: The Case of Lincoln Steffens and Ida Tarbell" (pp. 238–53) discovers nostalgia for a past, simple life, which runs counter to the authors' earlier belief in the progress of human nature and democracy. Maria Diedrich turns to a special form of autobiography in "Mastering American Destiny: The Ante-Bellum Slave Narrative" (pp. 254–67) and concludes that in spite of censorship black authors were able to launch effective attacks on the racist white consensus approach to American history because they possessed sophisticated rhetorical skills. Arno Heller's essay is a short version of his book on fantasies of violence (to be discussed below), "Fictions of Violence in American Literature: A Probing into Psycho-Historical Criticism" (pp. 268–84). A different theme is assessed in Ursula Lehmkuhl's "The Historical Value and Historiographic Significance of Jane Addams' Autobiographies *Twenty Years at Hull House* and *Second Twenty Years at Hull House*" (pp. 285–97). Lehmkuhl argues that the two autobiographies are historiography combining three important aspects of Progressivism—the concept of social settlement, the woman suffrage movement, and pacifism. Juliane Mikoletzky in "Fiction as a Source for Social History: The Example of German Immigrant Experience" (pp. 298–307) is uncertain whether the "preservationists" or the "assimilationists" prevail in German-American immigrant literature. What she is sure of, however, is that emphasis on German moral and intellectual superiority is a frequent literary topic.

Two essays in the volume dealing with E. L. Doctorow testify to the high regard in which he is held among German scholars. In "Doctorow's 'Criminals of Perception,' or What Has Happened to the Historical Novel" (pp. 345–71) Peter Freese, after pondering the customary argument of the "epistemological crisis of the traditional historical novel," concludes that in recent American narratives from Mailer's *The Armies of the Night* to Coover's *The Public Burning* the protagonist-narrator's character and voice, and not so much the action, are at the center of the story. Rüdiger Kunow deals with the same writers in "Without Telos or Subject? Coover's and Doctorow's Presentations of History" (pp. 372–90). His essay contains important remarks on tendencies at work in relatively recent historical narratives. For example, he singles out Coover's *The Public Burning* as a "deconstructive . . . narrativization of history" and opposes it to Doctorow's *The Book of Daniel,* which in his opinion attempts to recover historical reality to convey a sense of suffering and pain inflicted on average people. Bernd Klähn adds a concise summary of entropy and chaos theories in "From Entropy to Chaos Theories: Thermodynamic Models of Historical Evolution in the Novels of Thomas Pynchon and Robert Coover" (pp. 418–31). The focus is on Coover's novel *Gerald's Party,* which reads like an enlargement of Pynchon's short story "Entropy." Klähn discovers in Coover's novel a constant movement back and forth between instances of chaos and patterns of ordering elements. This leads Klähn to believe that chaos is but a refined variant of an ordered universe.

It is fitting that Gerhard Hoffmann's "Pluralism, the Proliferation of Aesthetics and Postmodern Literary History" (pp. 391–417) concludes this enterprise. Hoffmann adheres to his customary approach of looking at literature from an all-inclusive viewpoint. After touching on problems such as reader response, deconstruction of categories, time, newness, and periods, he concludes that a new "comprehensive aesthetic worldview" is necessary, one that allows for "playful rationality."

b. Literary History One of the most memorable achievements produced on the theme of violence in American literature over the past few years is Arno Heller's *Gewaltphantasien. Untersuchungen zu einem amerikanischen Phänomen des amerikanischen Gegenwartsromans* (Gunter Narr). Heller's investigation of violence fantasies begins with a historical overview of violence in the United States and its treatment by the mass media. A synopsis of violence then covers literature from Charles Brockden Brown's *Edgar Huntley* to the present. Heller draws four basic conclusions. (1) From the beginning, representations of violence have been individual or collective, all types of them pushed back into the unconscious. To be fought more efficiently, they become demonized and ideologized scapegoat-objects. According to Heller, in the novels of

Brown, Cooper, and Simms and in popular culture even today, Native Americans are embodiments of untamed savagery, dangerous unpredictability, and animal primitiveness, targets for fantasies of violence and projections of the dominant culture's destructive impulses. In the 20th century blacks, communists, Nazis, Japanese, Vietnamese, all kinds of foreigners and outsiders, even women serve this scapegoat function. (2) Committing acts of violence is rarely the expression of a sadistic impulse, but far more often it is a kind of psychic transformation or regeneration. The journey into the heart of darkness leads to identification with or rejection of evil and becomes—as in novels by Hawthorne, Melville, Twain, Crane, Faulkner, Hemingway, and Warren—*the* decisive initiation experience. (3) The polarization of good and evil turns into something cosmic-philosophical, archetypal. Violence becomes a realm of the exploration of the self, a threat to one's psychic depth, but also a desperate tool of existential self-defense. (4) From the 1960s on, authors such as William Burroughs, John Hawkes, Jerzy Kosinski, Joseph Heller, and Kurt Vonnegut reduce reality to destructive scenarios of structural violence, the product of an ever more perfect bureaucracy and technocracy. The world seems to be a senseless mechanism in which violence is resorted to as the last means of psychophysical survival.

Heller tests these conclusions in his discussion of Norman Mailer, Joyce Carol Oates, Hubert Selby, James Dickey, Walker Percy, Ken Kesey, Thomas Pynchon, Robert Coover, and women writers including Judith Rossner, Margaret Atwood, Diane Johnson, and Lois Gould. He agrees with Kate Millett's verdict that "no one has done so much to explain yet justify violence" as Mailer has. Heller interprets Oates's early works and the psychic situations of her protagonists as symptoms of illness in a competitive culture. Selby's novels are posited as Oedipal fantasies of revenge against the victimizing authority of a society whose exact structure is never revealed. Dickey's *Deliverance* and Percy's *Lancelot* are classified as retrogressions to earlier and historically anachronistic ways of life, in which women play only marginal roles (Dickey) or are part of the civilization under attack. Heller analyzes Pynchon's *The Crying of Lot 49*, Kesey's *One Flew Over the Cuckoo's Nest*, and Coover's *The Public Burning* under "structural violence." The female body, he convincingly holds, becomes a victim of male concepts of reality in which the body is reified and exploited in the service of an abstract ideological will to power. This "patriarchal-sadomasochistic" ideology is bitterly fought by recent women writers, who express their longing for a world in which an androgynous spirituality has overcome the deeply disturbed relationship between the sexes. I find Heller's study one of the most stimulating books done on this subject. It should be translated into English as soon as possible.

Hardly any year passes without publication of a book-length study of postmodern literature in Germany. In 1990 Joseph C. Schöpp's habilitation dissertation, *Ausbruch aus der Mimesis. Der amerikanische Roman im Zeichen der Postmoderne* (Munich: Fink), stands out as the major contribution. The first part of the German title is telling, since the word "Ausbruch" (breaking away, escape from) has a decidedly positive connotation here. Schöpp reviews the poetic concept of mimesis as it was outlined by Plato and Aristotle, redefined by Schlegel and Humboldt, and developed further by Nietzsche, Henry James, and Erich Auerbach. Schöpp is aware that American romancers such as Brown, Poe, Hawthorne, and Melville already doubted mimetic representation. Yet Schöpp's chief interest is the 1960s, "those apocalyptic and emancipatory years," which he approaches by looking at Lionel Trilling's sensibilities for cultural change and Saul Bellow's depictions of "cultural debris" in the '50s. Schöpp then turns to Heller and Pynchon and their presentations of highly entropic systems. He touches briefly on Vonnegut's *Slaughterhouse-Five,* in which he discovers, as in Pynchon's *Gravity's Rainbow,* "anecdotal stories" lacking coherence. The rest of his study analyzes novels by Raymond Federman, Donald Barthelme, Ronald Sukenick, and Walter Abish, through whose works he explores the next decade as well. Schöpp's book is highly selective (neither Robert Coover nor John Barth is dealt with), yet it admirably fulfills his intention to show that even the seemingly realistic texts of postmodern literature are "unusual architectonic arrangements of relics from different periods and styles." Schöpp makes no scientific or philosophic explanations for the preference of "discourse" to "story" in so much postmodern writing. His emphasis is on what Henry James once called "the house of fiction," which, as Schöpp claims, has mostly become a carefully planned set of literary games.

A new publication of the series "Erträge der Forschung" (harvests of research) should be mentioned. Waldemar Zacharasiewicz's *Die Erzählkunst des amerikanischen Südens* (Darmstadt: Wissenschaftliche Buchgesellschaft) truly keeps up the high standard of all studies in this series, each combining overviews of the critical reception of works of specific regions or literary periods with astute evaluations of the authors.

Zacharasiewicz treats southern writers—Ellen Glasgow, Katherine Anne Porter, Thomas Wolfe, Erskine Caldwell, Margaret Mitchell, Robert Penn Warren, Carson McCullers, Eudora Welty, James Agee, Elizabeth Spencer, William Styron, Flannery O'Connor, Walker Percy, and Ernest Gaines. He is aware that several of them have become marginal figures in literary history and that others—to name only Caroline Gordon, Alice Walker, and James Dickey—could have been included. Yet given his limited space, he has done an impressive job. Of great merit also is his competent discussion of Spencer, Agee, and Gaines, who in Germany have received scant attention.

Studies in apocalyptic literature in the United States have increased since 1960, as the bibliography to Joseph G. Böck's dissertation, *Die Kontinuität der Geschichte im amerikanischen apokalyptischen Roman* (Frankfurt: Lang), demonstrates. The title is slightly misleading since Böck makes no attempt to interpret the apocalyptic novels under consideration as personal or collective reactions to real or imagined historical crises. For him, continuity is provided by the pre-text of the biblical Apocalypse, as found in Genesis and Revelation, and by the emergence of three different types of apocalyptic discourse. The first comprises apocalypses as universal events. Here, Böck discusses Walter M. Miller's *A Canticle for Leibowitz,* Kurt Vonnegut's *Cat's Cradle,* and Bernard Malamud's *God's Grace.* The second type of novel treats apocalypses as "particular events," that is, the settings are local, yet are microcosms in which events attain universal dimensions, as in Melville's *Moby-Dick,* Twain's *A Connecticut Yankee in King Arthur's Court,* Nathanael West's *The Day of the Locust,* and Ralph Ellison's *Invisible Man.* Finally, Böck discovers a third type of discourse—the apocalypse as event in one's own consciousness or fantasy, as in Coover's *The Universal Baseball Association* and Twain's "No. 44, The Mysterious Stranger." In both texts the external, fictional world loses most of its significance in favor of processes unfolding within the protagonist's consciousness. According to Böck, there is also a growing emphasis on metafiction. He adds to his study a list of American novels from 1715 to the present that, for one reason or another, critics have called apocalyptic.

Klaus Benesch's dissertation, *The Threat of History. Geschichte und Erzählung im afro-amerikanischen Roman der Gegenwart* (Essen: Die Blaue Eule), explores a border country where novel-writing, autobiographical storytelling, and the desire to rewrite the history of one's own racial group meet. Benesch selects Gaines's *The Autobiography of Miss*

Jane Pittman, Ishmael Reed's *Flight to Canada,* David Bradley's *The Chaneysville Incident,* and Charles Johnson's *The Oxherding Tale,* all of them novels or fictional autobiographies in which rewriting of history is paramount. Benesch comes up with some valuable insights, although I do not go along with his thesis that a chief impetus in all of these books is "the telling of stories as a means of ego-boost."

Problems concerning the meaning of the "American Dream" (whatever that may be) will probably never lose attraction for German scholars. In 1990 it was Peter Freese's *'America': Dream or Nightmare?* (Essen: Die Blaue Eule). Although it is mainly addressed to German students and teachers, the book should be of interest for American readers. Freese begins with a highly personal chapter, his discovery of the United States after World War II when, for him and millions of other Germans, the friendly GI, freely sharing his chewing gum, cigarettes, and chocolate with hungry young Germans, became the symbolic figure of a benevolent nation whose leadership ensured a better future for the world. Freese turns to the specter of German anti-Americanism, which he sees as a result of vague stereotypes and diffuse emotions, but also resulting from the dichotomy between the American way of life (which most Germans passionately cling to) and certain aggressive aspects of American foreign politics (which they as deeply reject). Freese leaves these harsh facts (that is, as they existed before the reunification of Germany) behind and turns to America as a place of the mind, which has too often turned out to be a utopia on which Germans since Goethe's time have projected their unfulfilled desires. Freese's survey of the American Dream, as it was dreamed by the first American settlers, and its more recent variants, as well as its opposite, the American Nightmare, is highly selective, but it provides the reader with a great deal of information. Brief but substantial chapters on different forms of the Frontier, Manifest Destiny, the melting pot, and multiethnicity investigate important aspects of the Dream. The book's second part consists of chapters on growing up ethnic in American short stories, on the portrait of the American businessman in short stories, and on revisionist interpretations of the myth of the West, as exemplified in E. L. Doctorow's *Welcome to Hard Times* and Bernard Malamud's *A New Life.*

Vital aspects of American literary history are also covered in an issue of *Amerikastudien* (35, iii), "Autobiography and Democracy in America," ed. Alfred Hornung. Horst Dippel in "Autobiographies of American Presidents: The Ambiguity of the Franklin Tradition" (pp. 253–66) asserts that in the second half of his autobiography Franklin stressed the importance of an active life in a democratic society, a life in the service of public benefit and personal improvement. Many American presidents—Dippel points to John Adams, Jefferson, Monroe, Van Buren, Lincoln, Grant, and Theodore Roosevelt—wrote autobiographies that followed this line, but above all these presidents reflected the political and economic changes of their lifetimes because they felt themselves to be the legitimate interpreters of their nation's history. Anne Koenen in her "Democracy and Women's Autobiographies" (pp. 321–36) understands the autobiographies of Gertrude Stein, Lillian Hellman, Maya Angelou, Maxine Hong Kingston, and Minnie Bruce Pratt as documents of marginalization. With the exception of Gertrude Stein, these women refused to accept male values. In addition, Angelou and Kingston attack sexism and racism from the viewpoint of a strong group consciousness. My own "Reform Work and Autobiography" (pp. 337–53) examines three autobiographies of the 1930s—Lincoln Steffens's *The Autobiography of Lincoln Steffens,* Joseph Freeman's *An American Testament,* and Claude McKay's *A Long Way from Home.* I hold that all of these texts dramatize the tension between the individual and a fully envisioned ideology and as such are a rarity among American autobiographies. Manfred Pütz scrutinizes two very different presidential autobiographies in his "Democratic Versus Autocratic Autobiography: McGovern's *Grassroots* and Nixon's *Memoirs*" (pp. 355–70). To Pütz, McGovern is a "democratic" autobiographer because he seems to enter a dialogue with his readers, offering them a variety of aims and orientations. In contrast, Nixon resorts to an autocratic self, which either excludes or manipulates outside perspectives. Alfred Hornung's excellent "American Autobiographies and Autobiography Criticism: Review Essay" (pp. 371–407) concludes this collection. These essays, together with some American contributions for which I lack space, will certainly enrich the theoretical work done on autobiography as a specific genre.

This section should fittingly close with an interesting document bearing on the process of reorientation of scholars who until two years ago voiced opinions that were deeply imbedded in a seemingly untouchable, monolithic system of literary Marxism. Utz Riese's essay "Avantgarde als Zitat. Postmoderne Epochenzäsur in den Vereinigten Staaten (*Weimarer Beiträge* 36:1701–28) considers literary modernism, which for him began in the 1890s, as a program or "project" of social emancipation, yet one that allowed a spectrum of literary strategies. In Riese's opinion these strategies entered a "cumulative phase" in the 1930s, and it was mainly the "left discourse," the debates about proletarian literature, that fertilized literary modernism. Yet this "left discourse" ended abruptly when the Hitler-Stalin agreement of 23 August 1939 became known. From that moment many American intellectuals felt that modernism as a vital part of history had ended in catastrophe. Riese cautiously surmises that they realized they were living in a postmodern world, a world threatened by totalitarianism, the nuclear holocaust, and an encroaching technocratization.

c. 19th-Century Literature An issue of *Amerikastudien* (35, i), the fruit of a research program at the northern German university of Göttingen, is devoted mainly to German translations of 19th-century American writers. Daniel Göske's " 'Kindred Spirits'? The Question of America's Literary Independence as Reflected in Early German Anthologies of British and American Poetry" (pp. 35–51) surveys a number of 19th-century German anthologies of British and American poetry. As Göske shows, American poetry was for most of the century considered an annex. Only at the turn of the 20th century were the works of Poe, Bryant, Lowell, Longfellow, Taylor, Whitman, and Whittier, among others, seen as distinctively national achievements. Harald Kittel turns to a single author in "An Innovative Mode of Literary Self-Revelation: Free Indirect Discourse in Charles Brockden Brown's *Edgar Huntly* and Its German Translation" (pp. 53–66) and claims that Brown's contribution to fictional first-person narratives was the extensive use of free, indirect discourse. Kittel finds that Brown's German translator was partly aware of this narrative device, although there were no precedents in either English or German literature. Klaus Martens's "The Art Nouveau Poe: Notes on the Inception, Transmission, and Reception of the First Poe Edition in German Translation" (pp. 81–93) thinks it significant that the first of four large Poe editions coincided with the rise of German literary modernism. Martens even suspects that the publication of the Poe edition was prompted by that development. Baudelaire's French translations of Poe also deeply influenced the German reception of Poe, leading to the inclusion of his poems and stories, which until then had not been translated. Baudelaire-inspired modernism, "art nouveau," also opened new channels for the interpretation of Poe's works. In her " 'Daisy Miller' als Tragödie einer impressionistischen Sehweise" (pp. 67–80) Eva Hulpke notices important differences between James's novella and two fairly recent German translations (1959 and 1983). James endowed the fictive character of Winterbourne with a style of mind that imitated the idiosyncrasies of French literary impressionism. James's dislike of Winterbourne and hence of literary impressionism is clear in the foregrounding of this style. The German translators, however, failed to convey these peculiarities.

Daniel Göske's excellent dissertation, *Herman Melville in deutscher Sprache* (Frankfurt: Lang), is without doubt the climax of the Göttingen project. Göske thinks that any translation of a literary work is an artistic reproduction bordering on creative art. He focuses on "Benito Cereno" and *Billy Budd,* but he also comments on the translations of other works by Melville, and he even incorporates recent literary criticism. The German translations are analyzed against the historical backgrounds of their times, those done in the Hitler years being of special interest. Göske shows that Melville's reception in Germany improved more slowly than in France and Italy because Germany lacked a great mediator like Cesare Pavese, whose translation of *Moby-Dick* (1932) has remained the standard Italian text. Ironically, it was the French writer and Melville translator Jean Giono and his biographical essay *Pour saluer Melville* (1941; translated into German in 1944) that became trailblazers for the Melville reception in Germany. Göske has done an admirable job not only in pointing out shortcomings and merits of different translations and their indebtedness to earlier versions, but in fully placing them in a historical context.

Most of the remaining contributions to 19th-century literature are found in Klaus Lubbers, ed., *Die englische und amerikanische Kurzgeschichte* (Darmstadt: Wissenschaftliche Buchgesellschaft). Jochen Achilles's "Washington Irving: 'The Legend of Sleepy Hollow' " (pp. 1–11) is a solid attempt to explore the stature of this story within the framework of Irving's *The Sketch Book of Geoffrey Crayon.* Peter Freese provides us with a concise discussion of the different interpretations of one of Hawthorne's most ambiguous stories in "Robin und seine vielen Verwandten: Zur Rezeptionsgeschichte von Nathaniel Hawthornes 'My Kinsman, Major Molineux' " (pp. 12–27). Freese conjectures that the strangely irrelative "My" of the title forces the reader to see himself as Robin's relative and to interpret the story within the context of his own problems. Manfred Markus's "Nathaniel Hawthorne: 'Wakefield' " (pp. 28–39) presents this story as a poetological and personal self-reflection of Hawthorne himself. The artist's cosmic journey into nothingness is the theme of Herwig Friedl's "Edgar Allan Poe: 'MS. Found in a Bottle' " (pp. 40–51). Ulrich Martzinek's "William Gilmore Simms: 'The Snake of the Cabin' " (pp. 70–78) stresses Simms's qualities as a regional frontier writer whose stories make ample use of biblical symbolism and allegories.

Late 19th-century literature is also tackled in Lubbers's collection. In "Ambrose Bierce: 'Parker Addison, Philosopher' " (pp. 89–99) Arno Heller defines the story as a parable of the absurdity of all forms of escapism in the face of death's finality. Yet in this text Bierce also outlines a positive attitude toward death that transcends his usual sardonic view. Carmen Birkle's "Kate Chopin: 'The Storm'—Die Geburt der 'New Woman' aus dem Geist des Regionalismus" (pp. 110–19) centers on the story's sexuality and sees it as an expression of subjective morality and a deliberate transgression of the moral confinements of a specific region.

d. 20th-Century Literature Early 20th-century literature is almost exclusively covered by Lubbers's *Die englische und amerikanische Kurzgeschichte.* Claus Gadau dissects O. Henry's most acclaimed story in "O. Henry: 'The Gift of the Magi' " (pp. 100–109) and points to the author's ironic distance from the short-story conventions of his time. O. Henry, Gadau posits, wanted to break away from the concomitant gender prescriptions. Walter Pache's "Jack London: 'The Pearls of Parley' " (pp. 196–208) treats London's story as a text that refutes the common accusation that his later works are of inferior quality. London succeeded in creating a moment of revelation in which the physical and moral endangering of human existence is forcibly laid bare.

Sherwood Anderson continues to have a small band of faithful scholarly followers, as a booklet edited by Jürgen Dierking entitled *Sherwood Anderson—Erzähler des amerikanischen Traums* (Gulliver 28) demonstrates. It begins with a number of evaluations of Anderson's works, partly by writers such as Hart Crane, Gertrude Stein, and Edmund Wilson, and partly by German writers like Bertolt Brecht and Hans-Magnus Enzensberger. A series of essays by American and German scholars follows. Of the German contributors, Wolfgang Karrer in his "Modernismus und Realismus in Sherwood Anderson's *Dark Laughter*" (pp. 71–77) calls this novel Anderson's "black *Ulysses.*" He believes that Anderson must have known *Ulysses* when he embarked on his own work. Joyce's formal experiments encouraged Anderson to try similar things, although he felt too restricted to create a sexually daring monologue such as Molly Bloom's. In my " 'In a time like this, when there is so much depression'—Sherwood Anderson's schriftstellerische Karriere in den dreissiger Jahren" (pp. 78–89) I claim that Anderson from the beginning of his writing career envisioned the industrialization sweeping over a hitherto agrarian Midwest as a social force that would dramatically change the lives of many of his literary figures. He felt deep compassion for the sufferings of men and women in the depression-ridden textile towns of Virginia and North Carolina, and for a while he was sympathetic to communism, although he was never interested in communist ideology. Toward the end of his life, however, he idealized the American small town, whose neighborliness and "healing intimacy" he praised as a counterforce to the rapid urbanization of even the Midwest. Jürgen Dierking's "Sherwood Anderson: Der amerikanische Mann und vielleicht die Frauen" (pp. 118–24) sets Anderson in contrast to most of his male colleagues as sensitive enough not only to register, but to probe into, the tensions between the sexes. A selective binational bibliography concludes this fine short book.

Klaus Lubbers's *Die englische und amerikanische Kurzgeschichte* also contains an essay on Anderson. Lubbers's "Sherwood Anderson: 'The Egg' " (pp. 207–21) discusses the story as a subtle, ironic attack on the American ideology of progress and advertising jargon. Lubbers adds astute remarks on Anderson as a short-story writer in general. Heinz Ickstadt's "F. Scott Fitzgerald: 'May Day' " (pp. 255–64) underlines the story's experimental character and its depiction of urban nervousness, exhaustion, and confusion. Gerhard and Gisela Hoffmann examine one of Faulkner's lesser-known stories in "William Faulkner: 'Red Leaves' " (pp. 231–54). To them it is a typically Faulknerian story ending in "frozen moments," which are not related to plot, character, or social environment, but to a state of being, in this case, the fact of death. In "Ernest Hemingway: 'A Very Short Story' und 'The Killers' " (pp. 265–78) Klaus P. Hansen singles out what he calls a "neglected jewel" and one of Hemingway's best-known stories to demonstrate that the writer's philosophical position can be defined only if one keeps in mind the discrepancy between contemporary theory and its textual realization. A modern ghost story combining the powerful death wish of an individual with the decline of a segment of the American middle class is discovered in Bettina Friedl's "Edith Wharton: 'Pomegranate Seed' " (pp. 120–33).

An important summary and commentary on many aspects of American literary modernism as discussed in Lubbers's collection is contained in Heinz Ickstadt's "Modernisierung und die Tradition des Neuen: Aspekte der amerikanischen Moderne 1900–1920" (*Amst* 35:175–87). For Ickstadt the period between 1890 and 1920 is marked by confrontations between classes, ethnic groups, the sexes, and tradition and innovation, but also by real and symbolic acts of crossing boundaries. Reform institutions on the one hand and consumerism and urban culture on the other contributed to the erosion of existing hierarchies. Therefore, Ickstadt holds, order is redefined as process in American modernism. A truly modernist novel is analyzed in Carin Freywald's "Henry Roth: *Call It Sleep*" (*Amst* 35:443–59). Although she agrees with a number of critics who interpret the novel as a chaotic record of a sensitive soul's progress to maturity, comparable to Joyce's *Portrait of the Artist as a Young Man*, Freywald's main thesis is that Roth by combining the story of Jesus Christ with that of David wanted to reconcile the Old Testament with the New.

American literature after 1945 is assessed in a number of essays and dissertations, and by no means confined only to prose. In her dissertation, *Die Darstellung der Familie im modernen amerikanischen Drama* (Frankfurt: Lang), Andrea Kallenberg-Schröder deals with Arthur Miller's *All My Sons* and *Death of a Salesman*, Tennessee Williams's *The Glass Menagerie*, and Edward Albee's *The Sandbox* and *The American Dream*. She is convinced that modern American drama is family drama, and the plays she chooses seem to support her conviction. Time and again the audience is confronted with destruction of families in scenes in which the individual must either escape or accept oppression. The nuclear family is unable to function as an agent of civilization in our times; family life becomes a battleground, which symbolizes life at large.

Two good contributions to criticism of recent American poetry appeared this year. Michael Meyer's dissertation, *Struktur, Funktion und Vermittlung der Wahrnehmung in Charles Tomlinsons Lyrik* (Frankfurt: Lang), is a highly theoretical enterprise that addresses Charles Tomlinson's poetry, which has often been criticized for its seemingly contradictory sensual perceptions. Meyer holds that this was no accident since Tomlinson conceived of poetry as aesthetically transformed and structured perception. Meyer's theoretical concept is based on Jurij Lotman's structuralism and Maurice Merleau-Ponty's phenomenology of perception. Using their concepts, Meyer asserts that Tomlinson's poetry is characterized by multiperspective and expressive introspection, by which he means that Tomlinson does not look for a direct, personal expression of feelings, but for images that in combination with meditative reflections convey melancholy or sadness. Although Meyer is indebted to the theories of Merleau-Ponty and discovers striking parallels between him and Tomlinson, he does not believe a direct influence exists. In Meyer's opinion, Tomlinson's poetry is rooted in romantic aestheticism. Coleridge's differentiation between "primary" and "secondary" imagination resembles Tomlinson's understanding of perception and poetry, that is, the primary imagination corresponds to the perception that organizes sensual phenomena, whereas the poetry equals the aesthetic transformation of this experience. John Ashbery, Tomlinson's contemporary, is confronted in Ulf Reichardt's "Umgangssprache und Alltagsmythen in John Ashberys Dichtung: Spiel oder Kritik?" (*ArAA* 15:39–50). Reichardt contradicts those critics who accuse Ashbery of solipsism and playing games with language; for him, Ashbery is a poet of everyday life, which is described from within and marked by indefiniteness and ambiguity.

Toni Morrison remains the most compelling black woman writer to German scholars, as two essays prove. Aribert Schroeder's "An Afro-American Woman Writer and Her Reviewers/Critics: Some Ideological Aspects in Current Criticism of Toni Morrison's Fiction" (*ArAA* 15:109–25) focuses on two approaches dominating Morrison criticism—the assimilationist and the feminist. Schroeder finds fault with both. After presenting a spectrum of assimilationist criticism, he concludes that these critics, for the most part white, are too caught up in their notion of a mainstream literature as the expression of a "larger society." In their eyes, Morrison's novels are just protest literature. Feminist critics are of no great help either, since they tend to overlook that Morrison's main strategy has been to dramatize the impact of white racism from various social perspectives. Walter Göbel in "Canonizing Toni Morrison" (*ArAA* 15:127–37) tries to situate Morrison solely in the context of the African-American novel. Göbel takes into account Calvin Hernton's opinion, voiced in 1984, that a black feminist perspective permeates contemporary African-American literature. Yet he is sure this cannot be applied to most of Morrison's novels, since they move from latent feminism and pan-African "escapism" to outright protest, as in *Beloved.* A white woman writer's novel is examined in Mario Klarer's "The Gender of Orality and Literacy in Margaret Atwood's *The Handmaid's Tale*" (*ArAA* 15:151–70). Beginning with the observation that the banning of books and the forcing of the population (or parts of it) into orality is a common topos in dystopian novels, Klarer thinks that in Atwood's novel it has further implications. Writing as a part of the male power structure becomes a leitmotiv in the novel; yet overlapping it are other themes, such as orality, implying political stability, and the feminist poetic concept of "writing the body."

This overview ends with another collective enterprise. In Wolfgang Karrer and Hartmut Lutz, eds., *Minority Literatures in North America. Contemporary Perspectives* (Frankfurt: Lang), Asian American, black, Chicano, and Native American writers are assessed. The collection begins with a substantial introduction by the editors outlining such essentials as intracultural attitudes, the problem of time and relatedness, identity and alienation, cultural nationalism, and cross-cultural coalitions in politics and publishing. Michael Staub grapples with Hispanic and Chinese immigrant biographies in "Contradicting Memories: The Autobiographical Writing of Kingston and Rodriguez" (pp. 65–76) to demonstrate how both works deal with the difficulty of constructing an identity that is both American and ethnic. Karin Meissenburg's "An Undivided Self? The Case of Asian-American Groups in the USA (An Evaluation of Sojourner I–IV)" (pp. 77–96) ponders a text written in the final years of the Vietnam war, when an Asian-American consciousness developed out of Asian immigrant cultures. Maria Diedrich focuses on black experience in " 'When You Kill the Ancestor You Kill Herself'—Africa and the Modern Black Identity in Toni Morrison's Novels" (pp. 97–113). In Diedrich's opinion, all of Morrison's novels emphasize that neglect of the spiritual resources of a black folk tradition, which reaches beyond the American experience, makes black communities unfit for the painful struggle with the American present.

Chicano literature is treated by two German experts. In "Chicano Literature of Memory: Sandra Cisneros, *The House on Mango Street* (1984), and Gary Soto, *Living Up the Street: Narrative Recollections* (1985)" (pp. 129–42), Heiner Bus scrutinizes two autobiographical narratives and claims they share circular structures and reject an artificial concept of reality. More embracing is the late Dieter Herms's "Developments in the Chicana Cultural Movement and Two Works of Chicana Prose Fiction in 1986: Estela Portillo's *Trini* and Ana Castillo's *Mixquiahuala Letters*" (pp. 143–57). Herms begins with an overview of the Chicana movement, in terms of literary history as well as scholarship, before he deals with the two novels at some length. His thesis is that *Trini* is a Chicana bildungsroman, whereas *Mixquiahuala Letters,* as the title suggests, is an epistolary novel moving freely within metropolitan areas, from New York and Chicago to Los Angeles, Acapulco, and San Juan.

The other contributions study Native American writers and their works. Brigitte Georgi-Findlay's "Concepts of History in Contemporary Native American Fiction" (pp. 159–74) contains the stock-taking that is still typical of many German discussions of this subject. Georgi-Findlay touches on novels by N. Scott Momaday, Leslie Marmon Silko, James Welch, Louise Erdrich, and Michael Dorris and discovers that history in all of them appears as essentially fragmented, a fact she attributes to oral traditions of knowledge and the pressure of U.S. federal Indian policies. In her " 'Academic Squaws': Some Aspects of Culture Contacts in the Literature and Criticism of Paula Gunn Allen and Wendy Rose" (pp. 175–91) Elisabeth Hermann points to Rose's poetry collection *Lost Copper* and Allen's novel *The Woman Who Owned the Shadows* as works of academic teachers and writers who derive a new self-assurance from their intercultural backgrounds. Hermann also believes that these two writers are bent on saving important elements of oral culture from oblivion by integrating them into their own literary culture. The last two essays, Wolfgang Klooss's "Fictional and Non-Fictional Autobiographies by Métis Women" (pp. 205–25) and Manfred Mossmann's "Louis Riel's Lyrical Self-Images as Métis Author and Activist" (pp. 227–40), are concerned with native Canadian literature. This collection should greatly interest all scholars working in the field of American minority literature.

Universität Hamburg

iv German Contributions—1991: Rolf Meyn

The year's scholarly output in Germany is truly impressive. It covers all periods of American literature, from the beginnings to the present. Theoretical discussions of postmodern literature and the application of poststructural theories to contemporary literature, which have often dominated German scholarship in the last decade, are going out of fashion. A historical perspective on literature is definitely gaining ground. Joint endeavors are increasing, although there is still a balance between such works and monographs.

a. Literary Criticism and Theory: Comparative Studies A comparative study in its own right is Therese Fischer-Seidel, ed., *Frauen und Frauen-*

darstellung in der englischen und amerikanischen Literatur (Gunter Narr). In her preface the editor stresses that the collection differs from many American enterprises of the kind in that half of the contributors are male. Joint venture of this kind, Fischer-Seidel argues, will prevent academic marginalization; this is even more so, because studies of female characters have always attracted male interpreters. American literature is assessed in five of 15 essays. Fischer-Seidel's " 'But simple I according to my skill': Amerikanisches Selbstverständnis und Frauenrolle in der Dichtung Anne Bradstreets" (pp. 33–43) celebrates Bradstreet as a poet who does not have to be called an early feminist, but who by her sheer existence as a female artist rendered the cause of women the greatest service. Gisela Ecker in her " 'I master pieces of it': Das literarische Experiment von Gertrude Stein, Hilda Doolittle (H.D.) und Djuna Barnes" (pp. 141–60) lumps three divergent female artists together, but in my opinion succeeds in pointing out that these modernist avant-garde writers were skeptical of bringing both sense and dehierarchization into modern literature at the same time. Herbert Grabes in " 'If it can be done why do it'—Gertrude Steins unmögliche Dramenästhetik" (pp. 161–80) turns to a largely neglected chapter of Stein criticism. He strongly believes that Stein employed the modernist collage technique when she wrote plays like *Tender Buttons* and *Byron a play*. Bettina Friedl's "Die Inszenierung im Spiegel: Aspekte pikarischen Erzählens bei Theodore Dreiser und Edith Wharton" (pp. 217–33) is to me the collection's most important essay. Friedl notices that in Dreiser's *Sister Carrie* as well as in Wharton's *The Custom of the Country* the self-staging of the two female protagonists in the form of playing a special part becomes a dominant theme. Both are repeatedly shown acting in front of a mirror. In Carrie Meeber's case this means she imagines dramatic scenes in order to provide herself with social mimicry and become a "reflector of the world." Wharton's Undine Spragg, in contrast, is driven to seek self-assurance there; her self-centeredness borders on pathology. Friedl sees Carrie and Undine as typical "picaras," deviating from the behavioral norms of a world to which they must nevertheless adapt. Yet where Dreiser tries to protect his heroine from the attacks of general readers, Wharton dissociates herself from hers by way of satire; Undine Spragg is the representative of a new society that Wharton detested. Bernfried Nugel's "Von Elektra zu Lavinia: Eugene O'Neills Konzeption der Titelfigur in *Mourning Becomes Electra*" (pp. 295–318) concerns the character of Lavinia, who, Nugel claims, is occasionally ironized because of her extreme obedience to her father.

A mixture of comparative study and literary history is Winfried Herget, ed., *Sentimentality in Modern Literature and Popular Culture* (Gunter Narr). This collection begins with a concise introduction by the editor, who explains the unbroken continuity of sentimental texts as response to a world that for many readers is devoid of feeling, tenderness, harmony, and union. A person able to respond to a sentimental text becomes part of a "pathetic community" sharing "suffering as the *conditio humana*." Winfried Fluck's "Sentimentality and the Changing Functions of Fiction" (pp. 15–33) covers a wide range of sentimental American literature in which the motif of seduction is central. Fluck points to Susanna Rowson's *Charlotte Temple* (1791) as the first American novel dealing with this theme. Yet combined with it there is a bundle of other elements belonging to the realm of sentimental fiction, for example, affirmation of the family, violation of the moral order, painful separation and tearful reunion, and the moral redemption of a fallen heroine. *Charlotte Temple,* however, offers one special solution—the "reinforcement of the idea of true and truthful guardianship." Fluck holds that the sentimental domestic novel had no room left for the 18th-century seduction story, since it focused on problems of courtship and marriage, which meant that the guardian and suitor, often combined in one person, replaced the suitor. Yet even the guardian's position is eventually undermined or abolished, as Henry James's *The Portrait of a Lady* and some of his later novels demonstrate. In Dreiser's *Sister Carrie* this process is carried further, because temptation and seduction emerge as unpredictable events; the "unstable self" becomes the true hero. In her "Suspicious Harmony: Kitsch, Sentimentality, and the Cult of Distance" (pp. 35–57) Dagmar Buchwald defines kitsch as "the world of happy moods" that "can be bought and manipulated according to the consumer's need," whereas the sentimental mode is "a kind of art encouraging the sentimental attitude in its consumer." Brigitte Finkbeiner's essay "Becoming God's Child: *The Wide, Wide World* of Susan Warner" (pp. 93–108) centers on two areas that are highly emotionalized—that of the family (epitomized in the mother/daughter relationship) and that of religion, the basis of the heroine's spiritual growth. Udo J. Hebel takes on a Fitzgerald novel in his "'Platitudes and Prejudices and Sentimentalisms': F. Scott Fitzgerald's *This Side of Paradise* and Sentimental Popular

Culture" (pp. 139–53). He points to the fact that the author alludes to more than 60 best-sellers written between 1895 and 1900 and the six most popular authors between 1900 and 1925 and to at least 14 popular songs of that time. He did so, Hebel claims, for pejorative reasons, since he had joined intellectuals like Van Wyck Brooks and Harold Stearns in their attacks on the sentimentality of American popular culture. Hans-Ulrich Mohr turns to poetry in his "Configurations of a Sudden Authenticity: Sensibility and Sentimentality in the Poetry of Robert Creeley and Denise Levertov" (pp. 205–23), but in my opinion he misses the theme of the collection, since his essay is more concerned with poetic sensibility than with sentimentality. In a second essay, "Alice Walker's 'Womanist' Novel *The Color Purple:* Sensibility, Sentimentality, or What?" (pp. 225–40), Mohr again examines a novel which, as he admits, can hardly be discussed within the traditional categories of sensibility and sentimentality. But he is right in maintaining that the novel's plot is "unreal and romance-like" and contains elements of popular culture, including an emotional appeal. The German contributions end with a selected bibliography of critical studies on sentimentality, compiled by Winfried Herget and Udo J. Hebel. This collection is doubtlessly useful.

Also comparative, but devoted more to British literature, is Bernd Engler and Franz Link, eds., *Zwischen Dogma und säkularisierter Welt. Zur Erzählliteratur englischsprachiger katholischer Literatur* (Paderborn: Ferdinand Schöningh). In his introduction Engler concedes that it is not easy to say how exactly the Catholicism of a writer shows in his or her work. But he believes that all Catholic authors are concerned with their own religious convictions and their applicability to a secular world and its temptations, especially because many of them are converts. Waldemar Zacharasiewicz's " 'Unter der unbarmherzigen Sonne der Gnade': Flannery O'Connors 'Good Country People' and 'Revelation' " (pp. 101–12) explores "the merciless sun of grace," which is seen as O'Connor's favorite theme. Alfred Hornung's " 'In hoc signo vinces': Religion und Fiktion in Walker Percys postmodernen Welt" (pp. 113–23) deals with two of Percy's novels—*Love in the Ruins* (1971) and *The Thanatos Syndrome* (1987). Hornung detects in both works a hopeful, death-conquering vision of postmodern life, but he also reads them as symbolic representations of philosophical and social changes within American society. In *Love in the Ruins* the balance between body and soul is lost. In both novels responsible human acting is sadly lacking. In *The Thanatos Syndrome* the doctor is able to diagnose, but unable to offer a treatment;

the scientist is only interested in observing phenomena; the reduction of language is heavily ironized when a speaking female gorilla cures a psychiatrist suffering from a speech impediment. According to Hornung, Percy's intention is to reestablish the religious feeling as a radical bond, which helps to rediscover a sense of community. Percy also looms large in Franz Link's "'The unsubsumable minority': Euthanasie und Genozid bei Raymond Federman und Walker Percy" (pp. 124–34). Link begins with Federman's *The Voice in the Closet* (1979), a short text dealing with the Holocaust and Federman's childhood experiences, but he dwells largely on his next novel, *The Twofold Vibration* (1982), a science-fiction novel in which space colonies become places to which "undesirable elements" deviating from any kind of norm are sent—in other words, deportation into space becomes a kind of "final solution." Link discovers in *Love in the Ruins* and *The Thanatos Syndrome* related themes. In the first novel a geriatric center becomes an institution where people unfit for regaining their creativity by electric shock are selected by euthanasists and deported to a "Happy Island" where they are driven to "peaceful suicide." In *The Thanatos Syndrome* the protagonist finds out that a colleague is trying to make mankind happier by reducing the human mind to the simplest acts of communication in order to deliver them from all forms of aggression, although this means that they cease to belong to the species Homo sapiens. Link sees Federman and Percy, the Jew and the Catholic, as spiritual brothers, for both affirm the rights of minorities in a world of genocide and euthanasia. Bernd Engler concludes the American section with "'In Search of a Spiritual Shelter': Mary Gordons *The Company of Women*" (pp. 135–44). For Engler, the question whether Gordon wanted to satirize Father Cyprian, the stereotype of a self-righteous patriarch, is of no great importance. He is certain, however, that Gordon wanted to encourage her female readers to emancipate from the male authority of clerical institutions. Engler also notices that at the end of the novel the feminist perspective recedes in favor of the mere desire to realize in the here and now a life of "ordinary human happiness" under the auspices of a disciplined "prosperous love."

The most important contribution to the field of binational projects this year is Walter Grünzweig's *Walt Whitman. Die deutschsprachige Rezeption als interkulturelles Phänomen* (Munich: Fink). Grünzweig does not approach his subject with the help of a complicated methodological apparatus that often blurs the real issues. Instead, he prefers a plain historical approach that considers the problem of Whitman's technique and its transferability into German poetic language, literary periods (especially naturalism and modernism), and political systems and their attempts to make use of Whitman. Grünzweig cogently shows that it was Karl Marx's contemporary Ferdinand Freiligrath and some German-American mediators who paved the way for Whitman's early reputation in Germany. They interpreted Whitman's poetry politically—as a passionate plea for unconditional democracy in the face of the Prussian police state. Grünzweig then examines the reception of Whitman in the transitional period between naturalism and impressionism, emphasizing the role played by the poet Johannes Schlaf, founder of the first Whitman cult in Germany. Through Schlaf's translations, Whitman's poetry won a German audience aware of the dichotomy between life-denying decadence and his life-asserting celebration of physical prowess. Grünzweig also notices that Whitman was hailed at the turn of the century partly as a Rousseauistic poet advocating a return to nature and partly as a bard of modern technology. Whitman was also compared to Nietzsche, since both assumed the role of quasi-oriental prophet and seer. The image of the bardic "good gray poet" also suited the hymnic, messianic expressionists of 1910–15, for whose transcendental homelessness Whitman could provide some cure. The German left between 1900 and 1933 also took hold of him, although the Social Democrats, in compliance with their ambiguous attitude toward World War I, referred to him both as the "wound-dresser" and the war poet. The Nazis had a harder time integrating him, in contrast to the German emigrants, as Klaus Mann's article "The Present Greatness of Walt Whitman" well proves. Grünzweig has only a few things to say about Whitman's reception in West Germany and Austria after World War II, but he discovers that young East German poets were sometimes quite "Whitmanesque."

After this general survey, Grünzweig turns to more specific case studies of writers and poets he believes to be shaped by Whitman. Starting with Johannes Schlaf and his rival Arno Holz, he moves on to the expressionists Franz Werfel, Johannes R. Becher, and Armin T. Wegner. A concise chapter is also devoted to the "worker poets" Karl Bröger, Heinrich Lersch, and Gerrit Engelke, this last killed in action in World War I. Engelke's world-embracing war poetry, free of any chauvinism, clearly shows Whitman's influence. A brief excursion into musical compositions based on Whitman's poetry, written in cooperation with Grünzweig's brother, as well as some suggestions concerning future research on

Whitman's reception in Germany, concludes a book that in many respects is an exemplary intercultural study.

African-American literature was by no means neglected. Thomas Huke's *Jazz und Blues im afroamerikanischen Roman von der Jahrhundertwende bis zur Gegenwart* (Würzburg: Könighausen and Neumann, 1990) covers a wide range of African-American literature, from James Weldon Johnson's *The Autobiography of an Ex-Coloured Man* (1912) to the post-Baldwin era and Alice Walker's *The Color Purple* (1982). The treatment of 22 novels in one monograph must leave some questions open; on the whole, however, this is a good introduction to two comparative aspects, because it describes the way in which these writers incorporate the world of jazz and blues as a black experience into their novels, and it undertakes to show the impact of musical forms on the structure of the novels. It is regrettable, however, that Huke barely tries to identify differences and similarities in the novels under consideration.

Jakon Köhler, ed., *James Baldwin: His Place in American Literary History and His Reception in Europe* (Frankfurt: Peter Lang), the fruit of a symposium at the University of Heidelberg in 1990, is another comparative and multinational enterprise and at the same time a homage to James Baldwin. Peter Freese's "Some Remarks on the Reception of James Baldwin's Work in the Federal Republic of Germany" (pp. 11–32) is a concise report in which Freese shows that the German literary establishment dismissed Baldwin because in its eyes his initial promise remained unfulfilled. Ironically, some of his early works have become standard texts in German classrooms. Friederike Hajek follows with "Historical Aspects of the Reception of James Baldwin in the German Democratic Republic" (pp. 33–43). Hajek uncovers two phases of Baldwin reception in the former East Germany. After Baldwin's belated publication in the late 1960s, he became one of the most important contemporary black writers, although his style was dismissed as being decadent. In the second phase, under the impact of new literary theories and a broader inclusion of social history, Baldwin gained new prominence as a fierce opponent of all forms of racial suppression. Wolfgang Karrer's "Discursive Strategies in James Baldwin's Essays" (pp. 113–28) carefully maps the ideological shifts and changes that are obvious in the essays. Karrer notices a shift from hatred, contempt, and pity for the national scene of racial discrimination in his earlier works to universal history in his later career, accompanied by a growing ambivalence of love and hatred, even self-hatred.

Karrer is surely right in claiming that this basic ambivalence must be attributed to the "strains and tensions of a black middle class writer, trying to maintain a dialogue with whites and blacks at the same time." Maria Diedrich's "James A. Baldwin—Obituaries for a Black Ishmael" (pp. 129–38) is a moving eulogy to a writer whose alienation and uprootedness have been overlooked too often.

b. Literary History A collection of essays on 19th- and 20th-century writers that in itself is a literary history of cultural criticism is Hartmut Heuermann, ed., *Classics in Cultural Criticism, Vol. II: U.S.A.* (Frankfurt: Peter Lang, 1990), which I did not have time to read last year. Among the German contributors, Fritz Fleischmann begins with "Margaret Fuller (1810–1850)" (pp. 39–68), an astute evaluation of Fuller's position as a critical observer of American and Italian scenes in the age of Transcendentalism and of her heroic attempts at self-culture. Hans-Peter Rodenberg's "Henry David Thoreau (1817–1862)" (pp. 69–99) treats Thoreau as an early ecologist, but also as a cultural critic moving from his early ideal of the "anarchic disobedience of those spiritually cleansed and reborn" to the "dictatorship of saints" (John Brown), to a "New Jerusalem with an openly totalitarian strain," and, shortly before his death, back to the mysticism of his early years. Rosita Becke assesses the next generation of cultural critics in her "Henry Adams (1838–1918)" (pp. 101–29). She discusses Adams as a man of letters whose criticism was kindled by his disappointment with a post-Civil War America that had moved too far away from the moral standards of the early republic. This disappointment even turned into gloom and catastrophic pessimism in his last years. Klaus P. Hansen in his "Thorstein Veblen (1857–1929)" (pp. 131–72) praises Veblen's work as original, especially his insight that relics of archaic behavior are a hindrance to economic progress. Hansen also thinks that Veblen's system of epochs, although not intended to replace historiography, is a successful model of laying bare basic structures that are components of what is understood as "historical reality." The exploration of 20th-century cultural criticism begins with Hartmut Heuermann's "Henry Louis Mencken (1880–1956)" (pp. 195–226). In Heuermann's opinion, Mencken deserves praise for helping to establish an American audience for European writers such as Shaw, Ibsen, Joyce, and Maugham, and for preparing the ground for the acceptance of a generation of younger American writers such as Lewis, O'Neill, Fitzgerald, Anderson, and others. Mencken's unceasing attacks on American genteel culture, which had degraded to a bloodless philistinism, and on scandals in politics and legislation also make him a cultural critic without disciples who were urgently needed in later decades. Yet Heuermann is also aware of Mencken's weaknesses—his vulgarity, his simplistic borrowings from original thinkers such as Nietzsche, Darwin, and T. H. Huxley, and his ambivalent attitude toward social reform. After essays on Paul Elmer More and Van Wyck Brooks by American scholars, Heinz Tschachler's "Lewis Mumford (1895–1990)" (pp. 287–315) features a versatile thinker who, despite his affinity with Horkheimer, Marcuse, and the Frankfurt School and despite his being a forerunner of F. O. Matthiessen with his book *The Golden Day,* was neglected throughout his career. Probably Tschachler is right in surmising that this neglect occurred because of the decline in the number of broadly educated readers in favor of a "fragmented, specialized, jargon-ridden world." Hans-Joachim Lang's "Lionel Trilling (1905–1975)" (pp. 385–419) highlights a man of letters who was shaped by the decade of the Great Depression and the lure of communism, but under the influence of Max Eastman soon learned to reject Stalin's totalitarianism. To Lang, the main thrust of Trilling's criticism is characterized by his embracing Matthew Arnold and E. M. Forster as two variants of a "liberal" and by his elevating of Freud to mythic dimensions. Peter Ludes's "Marshall McLuhan (1911–1980)" (pp. 421–47) concludes a collection that, together with additional essays by American scholars on Alexis de Tocqueville, W. E. B. Du Bois, Edmund Wilson, and Kenneth Burke, is nothing less than a comprehensive history of cultural criticism in the United States.

An interesting contribution to the history of the sentimental novel in America is Klaus P. Hansen's "Realism and Myth: The Sentimental Tradition in American Literature" (*Amst* 36:15–24). After discussing Richardson's *Pamela* as the first full-fledged sentimental novel and *Clarissa* as the prototype of the novel of victimization, Hansen tackles Susanna Rowson's *Charlotte Temple* (1791) and *Trials of the Human Heart* (1795), arguing that as the first sentimental novels in the United States they are nonetheless completely dependent on English models, in the case of *Trials of the Human Heart* the novel of victimization. The transition from Victorianism to "aesthetic modernity" is the theme of Utz Riese's "Universality and Differentiation: The Functional Context of Hamlin Garland's 'Veritism'" (*Amst* 36:43–53). Riese demonstrates this transition mainly with the help of Garland's novel *The Rose of Dutcher's*

Coolly, in which he discovers a clash between feminine domesticity and "masculine aesthetic universality," the latter a result of "automatization and the masculinization of art and realism." Günther Klotz also dissects a transitional novel in his "Pudd'nhead Mark Twain: A Curious Perspective on Victorianism" (*Amst* 36:55–61). Mark Twain's *Pudd'nhead Wilson,* he holds, should not be criticized for its weakness of structure and lack of guidance to the reader. Instead, the novel should be seen as a text with a deliberately decentered plot, willfully devoid of moral signification. The novel foreshadows the end of the 19th-century novel and a new literary era marked by nonmoral, subjective, and multiple-discourse experiments. Hans Bak in his "Between Romance and Modernity: The Ambiguous Realism of Harold Frederic" (*Amst* 36:63–70) argues that Harold Frederic, especially in his later novels *Seth's Brother's Wife* and *The Damnation of Theron Ware,* must be placed between the romance tradition as defined by Hawthorne and the modern mode of symbolic realism as practiced by Fitzgerald. Winfried Fluck's "The Marginalization of American Realism" (*Amst* 36:71–76) continues and enlarges the thesis of a "masculine realism" brought up by Utz Riese. According to Fluck, the masculinization of American realism that many American critics, from Santayana to Trachtenberg, have favorably commented on and even supported is part of a broader cultural phenomenon that still has to be explored in detail. Dietmar Schloss in his "Culture and Criticism in Matthew Arnold and Henry James" (*Amst* 36:77–87) sees striking parallels between Arnold and James and surmises that James's attitude toward American life and culture was shaped by the British tradition of cultural criticism. In contrast to Arnold, however, who blamed the French Revolution for a rupture in the process of civilization, James believed modern American civilization to be a chaos that could no longer be grasped in its full implication by the human mind.

Concerned with a more recent aspect of literary history is Ulfried Reichardt's "Poststrukturalismus und der New Historicism: Geschichte(n) und Pluralität" (*ArAA* 16:205–23). Reichardt thinks that the New Historicism is an offspring of poststructuralism, since, like poststructuralism, it retains a strong text-centeredness, although it is now seen in close connection with politics, social life, and culture. But in contrast to traditional history, literature is understood as cultural work, which is historically determined. As such, it not only reacts but acts itself by "social constructions." This means that there is no difference between all manifestations of culture, for example, witch-hunts, sexual practices, consumer mechanisms, and literary texts. The text is part of the historical context; it is not a mirror or reflector, but a register or seismograph. Furthermore, the New Historicists do not write history as a sequence of events, but as a history of structures. Reichardt, however, is highly critical of the "arbitrary connectedness," that is, the way in which many historicists put literary and nonliterary texts on the same level, thereby dissolving the foreground-background opposition.

c. Colonial Literature This section will be devoted to only two volumes and one work—the late Hans Galinsky's *Geschichte amerikanischer Kolonialliteratur: Multinationale Wurzeln einer Weltliteratur in Entwicklungslinien und Werkinterpretationen (1542–1722), Vol. 1: Literatur der Erforschung und Besiedlung einer Neuen Welt: Spanische Anfänge bis Gründungsphase Neuenglands (1542–1676)—Vol. 1.1 Spanische Anfänge bis Grundlegung der Versdichtung Neuenglands, Vol. 1.2 Grundlegung der Prosa Neuenglands* (Darmstadt: Wissenschaftliche Buchgesellschaft). As the long title indicates, Galinsky had planned a five-volume enterprise. However, only the first volume could be published (in two parts) before his death. Although he incorporates the findings of scholars in this field, from Perry Miller and Sacvan Bercovitch to lesser-known colleagues, his two books represent a unique approach. Galinsky gives less emphasis to philosophical and religious traditions and controversies than to the form of the texts under consideration. Each subgenre is elucidated by exemplary interpretations. Thus, in his initial chapter on records of expeditions and explorations, he deals with texts by Castañeda, Champlain, and Harriot and ends with a concise evaluation of this genre as a whole. The same procedure is applied to the literature of permanent settlement in different regions of North America, to literature to promote immigration, political treatises, descriptions of nature and wilderness, royalist narratives of immigration and repatriation, autobiographies, diaries, satires, and poetry. More than any American scholar, Galinsky is interested in illuminating transatlantic connections and crosscurrents. To him, the literatures of the Old and the New World share the same stylistic criteria, because both are products of the same baroque epoch. But at the same time he emphasizes that American colonial literature had multinational origins. One of the great merits of Galinsky's two books is that they deal with European writers other than English who had lived in the New World.

Galinsky carefully differentiates between intentional prose and fiction. He singles out Thomas Shepard's diary as an example of didactic prose with providential, "soul-leading" intentions. Conversion stories written by clergymen are discussed within the framework of spiritual autobiography. Criticism of colonial recklessness, religious intolerance, and dubious jurisdiction written by disappointed returnees to England receives the same treatment as antinomian and internal Puritan controversies. Of special interest is Galinsky's comparative analysis of Catholic and Protestant "mission prose" in the Southwest, Maryland, French Canada, and New England, and the various portraits of Native Americans as "convertible heathens."

Probably the most important chapters of Galinsky's study concern the transition from intentional prose to fiction and poetry. Galinsky regards William Bradford's *Of Plimoth Plantation* as one of the best examples of this transition contained in a single work. Edward Johnson's *Wonder-Working Providence* (1654) is hailed as the first printed history of New England, designed as millenarian history of foundation to give religious support in a time of crisis. According to Galinsky, its central metaphors are the war against Satan, the Antichrist, who threatens the settlers through the Indians, the antinomians, and the Cambridge synod, the lack of food in the wilderness, and blackmailing by evil opponents like Thomas Morton in England. The highly subjective character of Johnson's work is ultimately a result of the biblical typology related to the Apocalypse, although Greek mythology also functions as a storehouse of figures of reference.

d. 19th-Century Literature Charles Brockden Brown has been frequently dealt with over the last decade, but to my knowledge never as a literary critic. This is the sole aim of Wolfgang Schäfer's *Charles Brockden Brown als Literaturkritiker* (Frankfurt: Peter Lang). Schäfer starts with an examination of the "Belles Lettres Club" and "The Friendly Club" in New York, two literary clubs that provided Brown with the encouragement and the congenial response he needed to develop his projects. Schäfer maintains that it was largely owing to the literary clubs that a reading community deeply interested in high literature came into existence, because the clubs helped to distribute books, mediated between literary works and their readers, and conveyed impulses and suggestions. One of the most prominent members of the "Friendly Club," Elihu H. Smith, helped Brown to plan the short-lived *Monthly Magazine*. Schäfer discovers in Brown's essay "Walston's School of History" a strong emphasis on the didactic function of historiography and the outline of an ideal form as the synthesis of "factual historiography and elements of narrative fiction, a kind of historical romance." The form of the literary romance is defined by the dichotomy "Hisory versus Romance." According to Schäfer, Brown links a historian's job to the task of a scientist, that is, to record facts and phenomena, whereas a romancer has to point out connections as well as causes and effects. Schäfer also analyzes Brown's important essay "Distinction Between Poetry and Prose" at some length and reminds us that he rejected this opposition and recommended "verse versus prose" and "poetry versus philosophy" instead. As Schäfer convincingly points out, Brown throughout his literary career wavered between the two poles of fact-oriented narrative and ingenious and fantastic romance. At the center of his literary theory looms the reader, whom literature must teach basic moral and social values. According to Schäfer, Brown's book reviews center on stylistic and methodological problems and on questions of usefulness for a young national culture. Schäfer's book will not be the last word on Charles Brockden Brown as a literary critic, but it is a solid study of an earlier American writer who has rarely been seen in this light.

The aim of Liliane Weissberg's *Edgar Allan Poe* (Stuttgart: J. B. Metzler) is to provide an introduction that puts Poe in an American context, but at the same time presents him as an intermediary between European romanticism and the modernism of a Charles Baudelaire. This is an ambitious undertaking for an introductory work, but Weissberg succeeds. She broadly outlines social and cultural conditions in Poe's America, then proceeds to Poe's art forms—his burlesques and satires, his contribution to the Gothic tradition, his concept of the arabesque, his poetic landscapes, his poetry, and his detective stories. Of special interest are brief chapters on Poe's influence on British, Irish, French, Russian, South American, and German literature.

Bernd Engler's book *Fiktion und Wirklichkeit. Zur narrativen Vermittlung erkenntnisskeptischer Positionen bei Hawthorne und Melville* (Berlin: Duncker and Humblot) is another remarkable product of the 1991 harvest. Engler starts from the hypothesis that both writers created romances not only because they wanted to remain within a tradition that their hoped-for audience was accustomed to, but because it suited their epistemological skepticism. Engler is anxious not to give the impression that the book is another attempt to present 19th-century writers as forerunners of today's metafictional practitioners. To him, Melville and

Hawthorne were "metaphysically disoriented" and unable to find religious support in the Transcendentalism of their time. Their religious uncertainty was the source of their epistemological skepticism. Their "quarrel with fiction" was not the result of their dissatisfaction with concomitant literary traditions, but a conflict that originated in their refusal to differentiate between concepts of everyday reality and the fictional reality of literature. Hawthorne's *The Scarlet Letter* is not a traditional novel, since neither plot nor characters seem to be of primary interest, but the unfolding of epistemological problems. It is a text, Engler claims, on the inadequacies of cosmologies, on deception and errors, and hence on the necessity of a permanent skeptical scrutiny of reality. Hawthorne's moralizing is nothing but a smoke screen hiding his aversion to all forms of didactic literature. After discussing all the novels and some of the most important tales, Engler concludes that Hawthorne was primarily interested in the changes of reality concepts and world models from Puritan times to the mid-19th century. In contrast to Melville, however, he felt uneasy about the consequences of epistemological skepticism.

Engler devotes half of his pages on Melville to *Moby-Dick.* He finds that the narrator, although permanently engaged in unmasking illusions and misrepresentations of reality, is incapable of finding a convincing explanation of human existence that incorporates his own fate and his entanglement with what happens on the *Pequod* as something necessary and meaningful. Ultimately, *Moby-Dick* remains a work of unreconciled contradictions. This is also the case with *Pierre,* in which Melville finally recognizes the "everlasting elusiveness of Truth." Engler then turns to "Bartleby, the Scrivener," "Benito Cereno," and *Billy Budd* and posits that for Melville authenticity and "models of plausibility" never existed; he even deliberately introduced errors that turn *Billy Budd* into a virtual confidence game. Where Hawthorne still propagated the fiction of a "consensus reality" that members of society can live by, Melville's works tell us time and again that concepts of the world and human existence, after becoming norms, can have only negative consequences on society in general. This happens because human experience of phenomena must always remain subjective, limited, and ultimately be as fictitious as literary fiction itself. Engler's book is certainly indebted to Nina Baym, Harrison Hayford, and Hershel Parker. Nevertheless, it is a highly original and inspiring study that should receive a timely translation into English.

Engler's view of Hawthorne is partly shared by Dietmar Schloss, who in "The Art of Experience in Hawthorne's *The Blithedale Romance*" (*Amst* 36:303–16) considers the novel "a jeremiad of experience in modern times." The Blithedale radicals, he posits, learn to distrust appearance, but at the same time all reality becomes appearance for them. Melville is also the subject of a substantial essay, Rolf Lessenich's " 'Die Geisterwelt ist nicht verschlossen.' Herman Melville and European Romanticism" (*Arcadia* 26:246–64), which comments on the affinities between Melville and European romanticism. Lessenich believes *Moby-Dick* and "Bartleby, the Scrivener" to be influenced by Goethe and Carlyle and their creations of "demoniacal dark power(s) of life negation" in Mephistopheles and the "Everlasting No." But he also points to Melville's Pacific islands and "Encantadas" as typical romantic landscapes, poised between goodness/innocence and evil. Lessenich is also sure that Coleridge's "Rime of the Ancient Mariner" partly inspired Melville to create the "white phantom Moby Dick." The influence of Ann Radcliffe's Gothic novel *Mysteries of Udolpho,* Lessenich argues, had the strongest impact on "Benito Cereno."

e. 20th-Century Literature Several decades of city novels are assessed in Gerd Hurm's *Fragmented Urban Images: The American City in Modern Fiction from Stephen Crane to Thomas Pynchon* (Frankfurt: Peter Lang). Hurm sticks to the traditional canon, Stephen Crane's *Maggie, A Girl of the Streets,* Theodore Dreiser's *Sister Carrie,* Upton Sinclair's *The Jungle,* F. Scott Fitzgerald's *The Great Gatsby,* John Dos Passos's *Manhattan Transfer,* Richard Wright's *Native Son,* Hubert Selby's *Last Exit to Brooklyn,* and Thomas Pynchon's *The Crying of Lot 49.* Urbanism, Hurm elaborates, often has been seen as an inevitable development but too often has been interpreted in the Sodom and Gomorrah tradition. Yet sociologists and writers like Crane, Dreiser, and Dos Passos were able to encounter city life as detached observers. All in all, American culture developed a persistent set of city metaphors reaching back to the beginnings of Western civilization. Antiurbanism, often in the form of a mourning over the loss of nature and agrarian values, or, as in the case of Henry James, as complaint about the coarseness and lack of civilization in American cities, has often been in competition with the myth of traditional community, in recent decades embodied in the images of a suburban Arcadia. In any case, all approaches to urban experience, whether in sociological or literary studies, have been informed by a "sociology of fragmented experience." Hurm's book incorporates the three approaches that underlie American urban fiction, the psychological-archetypal, the aesthetic-thematic, and the sociological-historical. In my opinion his most original interpretation is that of Pynchon's *The Crying of Lot 49*. According to Hurm, the "grid, as connectedness and closure, appears in numerable forms and contexts in the novel." San Narciso, as part of a vast Californian megalopolis, stands for an urbanized-suburbanized America. Its spatial forms express cultural and political conditions—suburban conformity, urban entropy, and the '60s underground. Oedipa Maass, the "slumming suburbanite as detective," is a representative of the consumer society, dominated by mass media and mass commodities. Hurm summarizes that in modern city novels the concern for craft and form achieves paramount significance.

Marie-Louise Wolff's book *Fiktionalität in der Textkonstituierung. Lesewirkung in den Romanen von Sinclair Lewis* (Frankfurt: Peter Lang) is predominantly addressed to teachers of literature and is concerned with the question of what constitutes the fictionality of a literary text, using Sinclair Lewis's novels as examples. Wolff's thesis is that fictional texts provide language signals that help readers recognize them as fictions. Yet she goes along with Wolfgang Iser's thesis that fiction is also a contract between reader and author, who constructs acts of border-crossing from the real to the imaginary. Wolff argues that Lewis's novels present themselves more emphatically as nonfictions than as fictions.

Upton Sinclair has never been neglected in post-World War II scholarship in Germany—neither in the former GDR, where his earlier works always were part of "progressive literature," nor in the Federal Republic, where he also had ardent proponents. A collection of essays by the late Dieter Herms, *Upton Sinclair: Literature and Social Reform* (Frankfurt: Peter Lang, 1990), the fruit of a symposium at the University of Bremen in 1988, testifies to that interest. Utz Riese in his "Upton Sinclair's Contribution to a Proletarian Aesthetic" (pp. 11–23) stresses that Sinclair appropriated "mass-cultural effects" such as sensationalism in close connection with the "authority of proletarian discourse." Riese singles out Sinclair's novel *Jimmy Higgins* (1919) to demonstrate how the author conceived a representative of the socialist movement and invested him with all the glory of a proletarian weltanschauung. Alfred Hornung in "Literary Conventions and the Political Unconscious in Upton Sinclair's Work" (pp. 24–38) applies Fredric Jameson's theory of the "political unconscious" to four of Sinclair's novels, each of them belonging to a different narrative genre—the historical romance, *Manassas* (1904); the naturalistic novel, *The Jungle* (1906); the factual narrative, *The Brass Check* (1920); and the autobiography, *American Outpost* (1932). Hornung seems to contradict Riese. Apart from the fact that Sinclair's early work demonstrates a nostalgia for a southern aristocratic past and the author's repressed sexual desires, Hornung insists, it should be obvious that even after Jurgis's conversion to socialism the protagonist remains part of the "corporate reality of America." Jurgis joins a labor corporation to fight the big trusts. But this does not end his deindividualization. Wolfgang Karrer in his "World's End? Upton Sinclair and World War I" (pp. 39–51) holds that Sinclair's World War I novel *World's End* (1940) is an antiwar novel, but restricted to the criticism of the armaments industries and the ideologies of the upper classes. It also illustrates the ambivalence of the middle-class intellectual Sinclair, who was incapable of dealing with a national war and class war at the same time. Renate von Bardeleben in her "Upton Sinclair and the Art of Autobiography" (pp. 114–30) emphasizes that Sinclair not only knew and admired Mark Twain's autobiography, but shared his uneasiness about autobiographical conventions. Like Twain, he wavered between an elevated and a colloquial style, with a preference for the colloquial. *American Outpost* is not faulty in construction and balance, however. If there is a change between forms after the first half, it stems from his growing loss of interest in story. Ingrid Kerkhoff turns to female characters in Sinclair's novels. Her "Wives, Blue Blood Ladies, and Rebel Girls: A Closer Look at Upton Sinclair's Females" (pp. 176–94) largely attempts to demonstrate how hard Sinclair labored to make his more or less autobiographical figures part of a fictitious world.

The last three contributions concern Sinclair's reception in Germany. Gerhard Probst's "Erwin Piscator and Upton Sinclair" (pp. 234–41) illustrates how deep an influence the American writer had on one of the greatest German stage directors of the 1920s, who wrote stage adaptations of the Lanny Budd novel *The Presidential Agent* and the short novel *Our Lady* (1948). Dieter Herms's "The German Reception of Upton Sinclair" (pp. 242–51) sketches Sinclair's popularity in Germany from the enthusiastically received translation of *The Jungle* in 1906 to the three German writers of today who claim to be under his spell, Max von der Grün, Erich Fried, and Günter Wallraff. Marion Schulze's combination of overview and bibliography, "German Reception of Upton Sinclair: A Bibliography" (pp. 249–71), concludes a collection that, together with the essays of American and European scholars for which I lack space, is a valuable addition to Upton Sinclair scholarship.

The same can be said of a collection of papers from an international symposium held on Saul Bellow at the University of Heidelberg in 1990. Again, I can focus only on the German contributions. In Gerhard Bach, ed., *Saul Bellow at Seventy-five: A Collection of Critical Essays* (Gunter Narr), the editor offers "Saul Bellow and the Dialectic of Being Contemporary" (pp. 17–31). Bach scrutinizes Bellow's three major concerns: his concept of reality and experience, the relationship of language to art, and death. Astrid Schmitt von Mühlenfels's "Novel into Opera: *Henderson the Rain King* and Leon Kirchner's *Lily*" (pp. 41–53) tackles a so-called "Literaturoper," that is, Leon Kirchner's opera *Lily,* which is based on Bellow's novel. Kurt Dittmar in his "The End of Enlightenment: Bellow's Universal View of the Holocaust in *Mr. Sammler's Planet*" (pp. 63–80) defends Bellow against the reproach of having evaded treatment of the Holocaust. Dittmar convincingly argues that the novel deals with the "dialectical forces of the Enlightenment," that is, the destructiveness of a "purely rational organization," which ultimately resulted in the organization of concentration camps and the "reduction of human existence into mere corporality." Regine Rosenthal's "Memory and the Holocaust: *Mr. Sammler's Planet* and *The Bellarosa Connection*" (pp. 81–92) adds some important aspects to Dittmar's conclusions. Rosenthal holds that in both works the memory of the Holocaust years is kept alive by a subtle analysis of the relationship of benefactor to beneficiary, victim to oppressor. Utz Riese attends to a different theme in "The Authority of Representation and the Discourse of Post-Modernity: *Humboldt's Gift*" (pp. 113–23). Making use of Derrida's "layers of meaning" included in the term "representation" and adding the dimension of ethics, Riese detects the novel's center in the "feminine order of mourning," in the deep understanding and sympathy of the protagonist. Dieter Schulz's " 'Family' in Bellow's *More Die of Heartbreak*" (pp. 151–62) assumes that the family in all of Bellow's novels is in bad shape. That at the end of *More Die of Heartbreak* the family man is literally exiled to the Arctic, the very region where Mary Shelley's Frankenstein's monster perishes miserably, is Bellow's harshest verdict on modern society, according to Schulz. To Marianne M. Friedrich, "*A Theft:* Bellow's Clara Between Anarchy and Utopia" (pp. 177–88), the text is a sure indication of Bellow's final shift to myth, fairy tale, and romance.

The Jewish-American writer Cynthia Ozick has not aroused much interest among German scholars. This deficit has largely been made up by Beate Rzadtki's *Jüdische Tradition in der amerikanischen Diaspora. Das Erzählwerk Cynthia Ozicks* (Frankfurt: Peter Lang). As the title signals, Rzadtki discusses Ozick's prose as the result of Jewish particularism and the attempt to establish a Jewish tradition as a bulwark against assimilation in the United States. Rzadtki begins with a lengthy introduction, ranging from a summary of Ozick criticism, the debate on a distinctly Jewish-American literary tradition and the history of Jewish immigration to America, to literary history. The main part of the study focuses on Ozick's dominant themes: rejection of assimilation and the search for a Jewish identity, the necessity of remembering the Holocaust, Jewish religion in a secular world, and the problem of Jewish religion in a diaspora. Rzadtki sees Ozick as a predominantly realistic writer, in spite of some surrealistic and even postmodern elements in her novels. She also shows that Ozick in most cases constructs a timeless American setting in combination with parts of Jewish history and religion. In Rzadtki's opinion, this explains why Ozick seems close to the tradition of Hawthorne's and Hardy's moralistic parables.

Feminist criticism is the basis of Margaret Keulen's *Radical Imagination: Feminist Conceptions of the Future in Ursula Le Guin, Marge Piercy, and Sally Miller Gearhart* (Frankfurt: Peter Lang). The title is a bit pretentious, since Keulen analyzes only three novels, Le Guin's *The Left Hand of Darkness,* Piercy's *Woman on the Edge of Time,* and Gearhart's *The Wanderground: Stories of the Hill Women.* But this restricted selection is a good one because it illustrates three different thrusts of utopian writing by women—in Le Guin's novel the thesis that the full enactment of androgyny will improve society, in Piercy's the message that Mattapoisett as an extension of contemporary society is a practicable alternative to a deficient present, in Gearhart's the call for a radical lesbian separatism. All three novels imply a critique of the contemporary belief in unlimited progress and technology; they all propagate gender equality, ecology, a holistic worldview, and the return to a simpler life-style. In this respect they are part of a retrospective mentality, which Keulen explains as the endeavor to reach back to the roots of the patriarchal system.

Discussions of postmodernism in contemporary literature have decreased, but they are still an essential part of German scholarship, as Ulfried Reichardt's *Innenansichten der Postmoderne. Zur Dichtung John Ashberys, A. R. Ammons', Denise Levertovs und Adrienne Richs* (Würzburg: Königshausen and Neumann) amply proves. Reichardt encounters poets who were born in the 1920s and reached their poetic maturity through a confrontation with the dominating modernism of the 1950s. His selection enables him to set two representatives of postmodern, aesthetically innovative, and epistemologically skeptical poetry against two proponents of politically engaged but otherwise traditional poetry. Reichardt is interested neither in an overtly ideological approach nor in the fact that the latter are women and therefore might be creators of different forms and styles. But he definitely succeeds in working out the uniqueness and typicality of these four poets. For Ashbery, Reichardt finds, no final truth exists that allows a decision between alternatives; man thinks and feels according to a structured way of experience from which he cannot escape. This explains why Ashbery refuses to evaluate ethical and social problems. In Ammons's opinion, man is determined by the laws and processes of nature. Both he and Ashbery accept the social conditions of contemporary society and share a nonteleological worldview. Levertov and Rich comprehend time as a linear movement and the present as a moment on the way to fulfillment. This process can be sped up by conscious decisions and acts of will. For both women, experience is paramount, more important than message and reflection. Rich's central experience is that of community and solidarity without patriarchal dominance. Levertov's emphasis on the "heart" as the agent of change in society is rooted in her religiosity. These findings, together with painstaking analyses of form and imagery in the poetry under consideration, make Reichardt's book an excellent study.

Three more essays are worth introducing. Monika Fludernik's "The Illusion of Truth in Eugene O'Neill's *A Touch of the Poet:* Dynamics and Reversals" (*Amst* 36:317–35) treats a much-neglected play that thematizes the enigma of the protagonist's real identity. Fludernik lucidly illustrates O'Neill's masterful evasion of clear-cut binary oppositions when dealing with the problem of truth and falsehood in Con Melody's various roles. Peter Freese's "Natural Selection with a Vengeance: Kurt Vonnegut's *Galápagos*" (*Amst* 36:337–60) stresses the novel's "characteristic mixture of serious intellectual concerns and hilarious popular techniques." To Freese, the novel's concern is a reversal of the law of natural selection and the message often pronounced in science fiction that mankind can survive only by a steady growth of human intelligence. Instead, it suggests that only by retrogression can our planet's survival be secured. Udo J. Hebel's "Breaking Through the 'Suburban Wasteland': Transgression as Affirmation of the Self in Joyce Carol Oates's *Expensive People*"

(*ArAA* 16:13–29) considers a novel that cuts mercilessly through the thin veneer of seemingly arcadian suburban happiness and exposes suburban life as one of conformity, boredom, and hollowness. Hebel interprets the protagonist, Richard Everett, as a rebel who refuses to be taken in by the uniformity and emotional indifference of American suburbia.

Universität Hamburg

v Italian Contributions: Algerina Neri

Last year Massimo Bacigalupo, whose five-year collaboration will be hard to equal, commented that his contribution looked more like a catalog than a survey because of the number of items reviewed. The situation has not changed this year. American studies in Italy are thriving, although university positions are scarce and the situation shows no signs of improving. Italian scholars prefer certain areas. Colonial literature and 19th-century poetry have received no attention, and drama, as usual, has been the Cinderella, while the privileged fields are travel and ethnic literature, Ezra Pound and modernism. Besides the usual output of books and articles, several collections of essays were published, nearly always as the result of international conferences.

a. General Work, Literary History, Criticism, Theory, and Reference Works "A Classic is a book which has never finished saying what it has to say," Italo Calvino suggests in *Perché leggere i classici* (Milan: Mondadori). Introductory essays on Mark Twain's "The Man That Corrupted Hadleyburg" and on Henry James's *Daisy Miller,* together with other illuminating contributions, such as one on Hemingway's importance for Calvino's generation, have been chosen by Calvino's widow for this collection on writers he particularly admired. Whereas Calvino in discussing a book hints at the greatness of its author ("like the sentences in which James seems always on the point of saying what he does not say"), the poet Attilio Bertolucci employs small biographical incidents to offer enlightening, unexpected critical shortcuts on his favorite authors in *Aritmie* (Milan: Garzanti), a literary autobiography built on collected newspaper articles. The timeless, precise, ambiguous poetic prose that Bertolucci uses to voice a sudden arrhythmia, as when he encounters Edith Wharton at Salsomaggiore or reads Robert Lowell's biography or Flannery O'Connor's letters, completely dissolved my initial fastidiousness at not being able to determine the exact dates of entries.

Fifty years after the publication of the famous anthology *Americana* by Elio Vittorini, the writer Franco Cordelli has prepared *La mia America: Antologia della Letteratura Americana dal 1945 a oggi* (Milan: Leonardo). Neither author has visited the United States, as Cordelli proudly confesses in the introduction in which he interviews himself; this is the only point that the two anthologies have in common. Vittorini's provocative and pioneering work followed a historical pattern, providing excellent translations and informative introductions, whereas Cordelli's ambition is to build a literary continent through imagination. His idiosyncratic two-volume anthology is constructed from 15 themes, illustrated by brief narrative extracts. By contrast, direct experience is the basis of Alessandro Portelli's *Taccuini Americani* (Rome: Manifestolibri), a carefully and ingeniously organized book made up of articles first published mainly in *Il manifesto.* Portelli explores his relationship with the United States over the past 10 years in an effort "not to explain and interpret America, but in order to try at least to see it." Through the opening and closing notes and his observations on religion, music, and politics, Portelli builds an alternative, real, endearing image of the United States.

Two translations of histories of American literature appeared in 1990, and a much-awaited Italian history has emerged this year, although its publication has been something of a detective story. The mysterious disappearance of chapters on poetry prompted the publisher to reissue the book. Guido Fink, Mario Maffi, Franco Minganti, and Bianca Tarozzi's *Storia della letteratura americana* (Florence: Sansoni) is therefore not a "new edition," as stated on the front cover, but a "complete edition." The superhuman effort to reduce the material into a manageable book and unresolved doubts about structural presentation and even about the enterprise itself are ironically discussed in the introduction. Fink, the mainstay of this team, finally decided to divide the book into five periods, confining the years up to the Civil War to 130 pages, while giving 423 pages to late 19th- and 20th-century literature. The latest cultural trends are discussed, sometimes to the detriment of neglected or underestimated fields.

Following Francesco Binni's *Modernismo letterario angloamericano* (see *ALS 1978,* p. 470), Giovanni Cianci has edited a sound, weighty, scholarly contribution, *Modernismo/Modernismi: dall'avanguardia storica agli anni trenta e oltre* (Milan: Principato). It is a well-balanced and comprehensive study of English modernism, with full bibliographies for each essay. After a general introduction by Cianci, the second part analyzes "the forerunners," with essays by Carlo Pagetti, Marialuisa Bignami, and Franco Marenco. The book expands on numerous questions, aspects, and problems concerning language, tradition, World War I, the classical revival, the recovery of mythology, the modernist metropolis, and feminine writings, with essays by Ruggero Bianchi on Imagism and Massimo Bacigalupo and Silvano Sabatini on Pound and Eliot, to mention a few essays more directly related to American literature. Another contribution on modernism is Sergio Perosa's "Browning e le forme del modernismo," pp. 21–35 in Sergio Perosa, ed., *Browning a Venezia* (Florence: Olschki), in which the critic examines the importance of Browning for Eliot, Pound, and James. A more general work is Tommaso Pisanti's *Le Muse erranti: cultura e poesia in America* (Naples: Liguori), which offers an informative overview of American poetry from the Puritans to the present.

American critical theory is discussed in "Heidegger e Derrida nella critica americana" (*Il Ponte* 47, iii:91–106), where Giuseppe Patella tentatively investigates the present position of American literary criticism. He explores the debates that Derrida's theories have provoked in the United States, giving particular attention to Jonathan Culler's book *On Deconstruction,* and he confronts them with destructionism, largely influenced by Martin Heidegger's philosophy. In "Fredric Jameson e il dibattito modernismo-postmodernismo negli U.S.A." (*Malavoglia* 8/9:18–20) Federico Siniscalco argues Jameson's position in the modernism and postmodernism debate, showing that Jameson has deconstructed some postmodernist axioms through a rigorously logical exercise only to reaffirm them in an optimistic, conclusive note. Among the useful aids available to Italian scholars is the newly published *Bibliografia dei soci A.I.A.: Members' Publications, 1984–1990,* ed. Giovanna Mochi and Guy Aston (Bologna: CLUEB), the bibliography of the Italian Association of English Studies, which lists numerous titles connected with American literature from a 1984 edition by Donatella Abbaste Badin of Arthur Miller's *The Crucible* to the article by Erina Siciliani on Kate Chopin. Addresses of scholars are provided, thus suggesting an easy way to obtain offprints.

b. Travel Literature The approach of 1992 explains the publication of at least two books in this section: *Nuovo Mondo: gli Inglesi,* ed. Franco Marenco (Turin: Einaudi), and Washington Irving's *Approdo di Colombo al Mondo Nuovo,* ed. Rosella Mamoli Zorzi (Venice: Marsilio). Marenco's beautiful book (the first of three volumes by different authors on the English, Italians, and Spaniards in America during the same period), brings together the documentation of English exploration and colonization from 1480 to 1640, with a cogent introduction, maps, beautiful reproductions, useful notes, and a list of geographical names. Leonardo Buonomo's careful translation of the fourth book of Irving's *The Life and Voyages of Christopher Columbus* is presented as a typical and successful 19th-century idealization of the Italian navigator, which Mamoli Zorzi skillfully contrasts to the 20th-century negative vision in Alejo Carpentier's *El arpa y la sombra.*

The conference proceedings, mainly by European and American historians, of the First European Interdisciplinary Symposium of the Southern Studies Forum, held in Genoa in 1990, have been collected in *The United States South: Regionalism and Identity,* ed. Valeria Gennaro Lerda and Tjebbe Westendorp (Rome: Bulzoni). Collecting plants, seeds, bulbs, and roots was the specific aim of William Bartram's journey to the South in 1772. In "The South as a Garden: The *Travels* of William Bartram" (pp. 107–21) Bonalda Stringher shows how Bartram's book of travel becomes a garden of words. Travel, even in a metaphorical sense, can either be a form of self-enrichment or gradual self-destruction, as Claudio Magris suggests in his foreword to *L'Altrove Narrato: Forme del viaggio in letteratura,* ed. Renzo Crivelli (Novara: De Agostini, 1990). Certainly in Fedora Giordano's "Mary Austin: la terra alla fine del viaggio" (pp. 69–75) Indians taught Austin to see the "earth horizon which is the nurture of the spiritual life" at the end of her journey to the West. In her "America: fine del viaggio?" (pp. 89–98) Barbara Lanati subtly explores the image of America as a mythical "elsewhere" in early European culture and then as a never-ending land of possibilities up to the beginning of our century, when American writers turned back either to Europe or more recently to their own lost cultures. In "Viaggio senza ritorno: dallo 'shtetl' russo al ghetto americano" (pp. 103–10) Giordano De Biasio examines Russian Jewish culture in the United States from 1881 to the 1930s.

"Americans in Italy" is the subtitle of a special issue of the *Bollettino* (8, i–ii [1987, but published 1991]) of the Centro Interuniversitario di Studi sul Viaggio in Italia, which puts together some general articles (Marilla Battilana's "Venice and Its Region in American Literature," Giuseppe Pasquale's "Thomas Jefferson in Italy," Franco Meregalli's "George Ticknor in Italy," Margaretta Lovell's "John S. Sargent's Venice," and Rita

Severi's "I 'Beats,' il viaggio, l'Italia") and reviews of recent work on Americans in Italy. There are some pages of Harriet Beecher Stowe's unpublished Italian journal and Alessandra Pinto Surdi's bibliography, "Americans in Rome, 1764–1870." Americans in Rome also are the subject of Andrea Mariani's "Artisti e scrittori americani a Roma" (*Rivista di Studi Romani* 43 [1990]:485–97), which reviews William Vance's *America's Rome* and *The Italian Presence in American Art: 1760–1860,* ed. Irma B. Jaffe. Julia Ward Howe's Roman poems are presented in Leonardo Buonomo's "Julia Ward Howe's 'Italian' Poems in *Passion Flowers* (1854)" (*Annali di Ca' Foscari* 30, i–ii:27–35).

c. 19th Century The formation of different nations in America was the subject of the 1989 conference of the Department of American Studies, University of Rome, the proceedings of which have been published in *Nascità di una identità: la formazione delle nazionalità americane,* ed. Vanni Blengino (Rome: Edizioni Associate, 1990). In "Sui 'Vangeli' di Thomas Jefferson" (pp. 257–67) Cristina Giorcelli brilliantly examines Jefferson's use of collage art in the preparation of his two recently published works, *The Philosophy of Jesus* and *The Life and Morals of Jesus,* as edifying, true, and real versions of the Gospels, composed in a rational, logical language for the new American nation. The social and cultural importance of language is the subject of Maria Anita Stefanelli's "Il rapporto tra lingua e territorio nell'opera di Timothy Dwight" (pp. 298–309). Language again provides the vantage point in Caterina Ricciardi's " 'In the language of the country': J. F. Cooper e le origini del Susquehanna" (pp. 83–99), a reading of the stratifications of cultures reflected in the naming of the American frontier, a unifying and disruptive territory in the Leatherstocking series. One of the last contributions of Caterina Gullì, whose untimely death has deprived American studies of a fine and perceptive scholar, is "Un'ipotesi di presenza: la figura femminile e la frontiera in *The Pioneers*" (pp. 334–43). Centering on Elizabeth Temple of Cooper's *The Pioneers,* Gullì, contrary to current critical stands, shows how women, because of their inferior position, have, like the Indians and Natty Bumppo, a distinct perception of the frontier and a desire for a better frontier society. Concentrating on Charles Brockden Brown's *Alcuin,* in "Charles Brockden Brown e l'identità americana" (pp. 276–83), Annalisa Goldoni discusses Brown's search for the true American identity.

The present interest in Emerson in Italian culture is shown by another translation of Emerson's essays, *Teologia e Natura* (Genoa: Marietti). In his afterword Pier Cesare Bori argues that Emerson had not yet arrived at a philosophical religious eclectism, but was taking his ideas from sapiental books. In *Cittadini di un assurdo universo* (Milan: Editrice Nord, 1989), a collection of six previously published articles, Carlo Pagetti presents the absurd universe, an unstable and disrupted land, where dreams of a rational and orderly science clash with distinctive physical and natural forces, through his analysis of Poe's short stories, Twain's *A Connecticut Yankee,* Lovecraft's many stories, and *Swastika Night* by the English writer Katherine Burdekin.

Hawthorne received particular attention this year with two book-length studies. Gordon Poole's *Taking Hawthorne's Coverdale at His Word: On* Blithedale *and Other Writings* (Sorrento: Franco Di Mauro Editore) attempts, on the basis of the distinction between Coverdale as narrator and Coverdale as protagonist, to invert the critical distrust of his telling of events, the other parts being dedicated to narratological analysis of *The House of the Seven Gables,* "Alice Doane's Appeal," and "The May-Pole of Merry Mount." Paola Russo's more ambitious book, *Il Bosco delle Ninfe: Nathaniel Hawthorne e la classicità* (Rome: Bulzoni), offers light on the classical mythological element present since Hawthorne's first stories. Classical mythology and its connection with historical and Puritan themes is also a starting point for an analysis of its relation to the new American mythology.

Melville scholarship has been much in evidence. Besides an international conference organized in Rome by AISNA at the end of 1990 to commemorate the centenary, several new translations have come out. Massimo Bacigalupo edited a good selection of Melville's work in *Opere* (Milan: Mondadori). New or thoroughly revised translations, carefully annotated texts, a chronology, maps, a good bibliography, a stimulating introduction, and the pleasant surprise of seeing Ahab called by his real name instead of the harder Achab make these two volumes an essential introduction to Melville's world. The first volume covers the prose works from *Typee* (1846) to *Billy Budd,* "Daniel Orme," and "Rip Van Winkle's Lilac," with a complete translation of *Piazza Tales;* the second volume is mostly made up of a revised translation of *Moby-Dick,* a selection of letters, and an ample presentation of poems. Some of the poems, mostly those in *John Marr and Other Sailors,* completely translated for the first time, also have been presented by Bacigalupo in "Il recitativo rauco di Herman Melville" (*Poesia* 40:42–49). Exemplary though this collection may be, Melville's more complex allegorical works, *Mardi* or *Clarel,* for example, have been left out, as Mario Materassi points out in "Melville lo scrivano" (*Il Giornale,* 22 September). Luckily for the Italian reader, Ruggero Bianchi is publishing Melville's complete narrative works in several volumes, the sixth volume, *Racconti della veranda, il truffatore di fiducia* (Milan: Mursia), appearing this year. As usual, Bianchi provides an extensive and scholarly introduction, "Il Narratore come attore dialettico" (pp. 11–85). He reconstructs the period (1849–56) during which these works were written, linking them to past and future developments, and he tries to explain Melville's relative silence in his later years. The competent translations are by Enzo Giachino (a new version of *The Confidence-Man* with a new Italian title), Bianchi (reprinting his 1971 translation of "Bartleby" and "Benito Cereno"), and Alessandro Monti (all the other *Piazza Tales*). *Mardi*'s complexity attracts Paola Russo's inquisitive mind; she explores the novel's different departures with no return in "Mardi: cinque partenze senza ritorno" (*RSAJ* 2:3–19).

Barbara Lanati's long fascination with Emily Dickinson's work and art has prompted her to publish *Lettere 1845–1886* (Turin: Einaudi), an expanded edition of her 1982 volume. This new book, which has an informative introduction, photographs, and useful notes, shows the favor and interest that Dickinson persistently elicits from Italian readers. Leo Marchetti is also intrigued by Dickinson's letters, which he examines in "Emily Dickinson e i giocattoli dell'Amplitudine" (*Merope* 2 [1990]:69–83).

Henry James has not received the usual amount of attention this year. His Italian novels, a much-beaten path, have been collected in *I racconti italiani* (Turin: Einaudi). However, unreliable notes, understandable omissions (*Daisy Miller, The Aspern Papers*), and old and dated texts mar an otherwise fascinating enterprise. In contrast, Sergio Perosa sensitively investigates James's fascination with Venice and his intriguing, masterly skill in the introduction to *Il carteggio Aspern* (Venice: Marsilio), competently translated by Gilberto Sacerdoti. In her attractive and excellent close examination of *The Turn of the Screw* in "Che cosa è veramente successo a Bly? Memoria e affidabilità in *The Turn of the Screw* di Henry James" (*Strumenti Critici* 4, i [1989]:1–48) Paola Pugliatti carefully puts forward her convincing and credible interpretation of the story, although she does refrain from clearly stating it, honoring the lesson of James. An unusually intimate portrait of James can be read in Ford Madox Ford's *C'erano uomini porti* (Parma: Pratiche Editrice), a translation of *Portraits from Life* with a foreword by Giovanna Mochi. Stephen Crane, another of Ford's subjects, is the focus of Giorgio Mariani's "The Horrors of War: *The Red Badge of Courage,* the Spectacle of Ideology, and the Ideology of Spectacle" (*Igitur* 2, ii [1990]:23–53). In Mariani's view, *Red Badge* becomes an accomplice of that martial ideology that it would seemingly want to deconstruct. Mariani's "Ambrose Bierce's Civil War Stories and the Critique of the Martial Spirit" (*SAF* 19, ii:221–28) is on a similar theme.

d. 20th-Century Prose The year 1925 was crucial, Guido Fink suggests in "'Inesprimere l'esprimibile': tre romanzi americani del 1925" (*RSAJ* 2:37–52), because it saw the publication of such different works as *An American Tragedy, The Great Gatsby,* and *Manhattan Transfer.* Although they have contrasting narrative strategies, which Fink subtly assesses to throw light on the relationship between American writers and modernism, the three books share common themes and techniques, seeming to follow Roland Barthes's prescription "not to express that [which] could be easily expressed." An unusual and interesting analysis comes from Palmira De Angelis, "L'interpunzione contraddetta: voci dal Novecento letterario," pp. 57–85 in *Interpunzioni: Punti, virgole e altro ancora . . . ,* ed. Mariantonia Liborio (I.U.O.). De Angelis follows the evolution in punctuation use from 19th- to 20th-century writers, giving special attention to Gertrude Stein's comments in *Poetry and Grammar* and to E. E. Cummings's attempt to unite poetry and painting to recover the semantic comprehension of primordial pictographic signs. Intellectuals of the 1930s are examined in Gabriella Ferruggia's "Organizing the 'Ivory Tower': The Communist Party and the United Front of Intellectuals During the Late Thirties" (*Storia Nordamericana* 6, i–ii [1989, but published 1991]:31–59). Ferruggia's contribution thoroughly peruses the fact that by the mid-1930s the American Communist party's line on literary matters was completely dropped. Using three examples, she shows that the party not only made no attempt at regimenting and controlling intellectuals, but it also fell short of meeting their demands for a coherent cultural and political line. The writer's position in the '30s is also the starting point of an interview with Tillie Olsen ("Tillie Olsen, An Interview with Mario Materassi," *RSAJ* 2:85–98), a rambling, almost hypnotic wander through her life and work.

The proceedings of an international Faulkner conference held in Rome in 1989 are published in *The Artist and His Masks.* The papers examine Faulkner's achievement from the point of view of metafiction, filling a gap in Faulkner studies and enriching the vision of his art. Contributions by American, European, and Japanese scholars make this excellent book an invaluable tool for the Faulkner scholar. Mamoli Zorzi, Lombardo, Fink, Materassi, Rubeo, Portelli, Boitani, and Ricciardi knowledgeably investigate Faulkner's works in brief but sound essays. In "Per non Finire: l'arte di contar storie in *The Sot-weed Factor* di John Barth," pp. 51–69 in *La Fine del racconto,* ed. Monique Streiff Moretti (Naples: E.S.I.), Clara Bartocci discusses Barth's novel in relation to contemporary fiction, suggesting that reality is perpetuated through fiction and that since life is fiction, narrative fiction is life. In her other contribution, "L'ambiguità fatta mestiere: *The Sot-Weed Factor* di John Barth," pp. 191–221 in *Sei tipi di ambiguità III* (Naples: E.S.I.), Bartocci analyzes Barth's novel as an open structure in which the main plot is continually modified and ambiguously reshaped by the other minor but necessary 25 subplots. Philip Dick has always received enthusiastic attention from some Italian scholars. Most of his books have been translated, and in 1988 his works were the feature of a section of the National Conference of Science Fiction. The conference proceedings, together with introductions to Dick's books and a complete bibliography of Italian translations and contributions, has been gathered and published by Carlo Pagetti and Gianfranco Viviani in *Philip K. Dick: Il sogno dei simulacri* (Milan: Editrice Nord, 1989). Science fiction is also the topic of Oriana Palusci, *Terra di lei: l'immaginario femminile tra utopia e fantascienza* (Pescara: Tracce, 1990). Palusci's clever survey of women's utopias and science fiction in English is the first of its kind in Italy. Tracing the roots of feminist utopianism from the 18th and 19th centuries to the development of science fiction, it focuses on feminist fabulation, paying special attention to Judith Merril, Doris Lessing, Joanna Russ, and Suzy McKee Charnas. In her well-informed "Finzioni extraordinarie: la scrittura di genere" (*DWF* 13–14:47–61) Liana Borghi stimulatingly expands on recent American trends in utopian feminist novels from Joanna Russ onward.

Il racconto delle donne: voci autobiografie figurazioni, ed. Angiolina Arru and Maria Teresa Chialant (Naples: Ligori), is an interesting collection on the theory and range of women's autobiographical writing. Three excellent essays deal more or less directly with American literature: Paola Splendore, "La difficoltà di dire 'io': l'autobiografia come scrittura del limite" (pp. 71–88), shows the postmodern developments of the genre through the work of Gertrude Stein, Mary McCarthy, Susan Sontag, and Kate Millett, among others; Daniela Daniele, "L'autoritratto come macabro strip-tease: *The Bell Jar* di Sylvia Plath" (pp. 161–74), reads Plath's fiction as an attempt to turn the pornographic bent of self-revelation into an act of self-possession; in "Senso, nonsenso, desiderio: 'The Yellow Wallpaper' di Charlotte Perkins Gilman" (pp. 233–44) Eleonora Rao shows how a diary may break with the syntax of patriarchy. Autobiography is also the subject of Maria Parrino's "Breaking the Silence: Autobiographies of Italian Immigrant Women" (*Storia Nordamericana* 5, ii [1988 but published 1991]:137–58), part of an issue on American women's history edited by Elizabetta Vezzosi. Parrino presents three women's autobiographies to conclude that "the vision of the self and of the world is not only filtered by the act of writing, but is also interwoven and mediated by archaic and modern myths, stereotypical constructions and cultural influences of various origins." Guido Fink too is fascinated by autobiography. He has published Mary McCarthy's last book, *Una giovinezza americana* (Bologna: Il Mulino). In his lively and perceptive "Una parte del corpo alla volta," Fink outlines McCarthy's method in the book of building her personality and its transformation.

e. Ethnic Literature Until this year Charles Chesnutt's work has not been translated into Italian. Alessandro Portelli, a long-time expert in African-American studies, has published three short stories under the title *La sposa della giovinezza* (Venice: Marsilio), a bilingual translation by Cristina Mattiello. In his fine introduction Portelli discusses Chesnutt's "color line" theme, the satirical, tragic, comic intermingling of black and white and the attentive, disruptive search for identity. In "Zora Neale Hurston, the Black Woman, the Black Woman Writer in the Thirties and Forties" (*Annali della Facoltà di Economia e Commercio* [Cagliari], pp. 297–308) Luisanna Fodde places Hurston's life and realistic works in the black literature of the 1930s and 1940s. An old hand at the subject, Stefania Piccinato dedicates her work this year to Jean Toomer and Ralph Ellison. In her fine "Le Metafore del Dissidio: Paesaggi naturali e immaginario urbano in *Cane* di Jean Toomer" (*LAmer* 39 [1989]:57–90) Piccinato subtly explores the internal contrast through which the natural and urban landscapes can be read in a circular symbolic journey from South to North and back to the South to achieve a full identity. A similar circular movement is used, she claims, in Ellison's *Invisible Man*. In " 'The End was in the Beginning': un epilogo," pp. 125–37 in *La Fine del racconto,* ed. Monique Streiff Moretti (Naples: E.S.I.), Piccinato presents an interesting examination of the circular structure of Ellison's novel, the prologue and epilogue framing its 25 chapters in a blueslike sequence. Ishmael Reed's first book to be translated into Italian, *Mumbo Jumbo* (Milan: Rizzoli), has provoked publicity in newspapers and an interesting interview by Franco Minganti, "Per una nuova estetica nera: Ishmael Reed" (*Leggere* 35:56–60). Serena Anderlini interviews Ntozake Shange in "Drama or Performance Art? An Interview with Ntozake Shange" (*Journal of Dramatic Theory and Criticism* 6, i:85–97). Shange's choral drama is the subject of Anderlini's " 'Colored Girls': A Reaction to Black Machismo, or Hues of Erotic Tension in New Feminist Solidarity?" (*JADT* 2, ii:33–54).

Native American studies is a flourishing field in Italy. Laura Coltelli, a well-known scholar, has edited an issue of *Storia Nordamericana* (5, i [1988 but published 1991]) on "The American Indian Today." Ten good contributions by American studies scholars, mainly historians and anthropologists, conclude with Coltelli's fine article on "Native American Literature and Mainstream American Literature, 1968–1988: A Bibliographical Evaluation" (pp. 185–211). An anthology of contemporary Native American poets has been edited by Franco Meli in *Parole nel sangue* (Milan: Mondadori). After an informative introduction to major themes, he presents several poems by each of 19 poets in alphabetical order, giving special place to Momaday, Ortiz, and Silko, in his view the best writers. Wendy Rose, a poet represented in this collection, is the subject of Fedora Giordano's "Wendy Rose: le parole dell'assenza" (*RSAJ* 2:73–84). Giordano connects the development of Rose's poetic language with her estrangement from her family's multiethnic traditions. Navajo traditions are of paramount importance in the work of Tony Hillerman, not a Native American but a best-selling detective-story writer. Most of Hillerman's novels take place on a Navajo reservation, and Mario Materassi interviewed him while Materassi was in Albuquerque ("Giallo nella riserva dei Navajo," *Il Ponte* 47, ii:106–18). Materassi also provides the Italian reader with two interesting translations: Cynthia Ozick's *Il Messia di Stoccolma* (Milan: Garzanti) and Hugh Nissenson's *L'elefante e la mia questione ebraica* (Florence: Giuntina). Both works have common Jewish themes; Ozick seems to feel that exposing problems is a transgression, while in writing Nissenson finds that world order he is persistently and painfully seeking. The translation of Harold Brodkey's *Stories in an Almost Classical Mode* (*Storie in modo quasi classico* [Milan: Mondadori]) and Brodkey's presence at the Mondello Award, given this year to Kurt Vonnegut for foreign fiction, stimulated Marisa Bulgheroni to ask him interesting questions about his work and art, "La memoria del Proust americano" (*L'Indice* 10:9).

In 1982 the "Appalachian Project," a research, teaching, and cultural program, was formed within the English department of the University of Rome; it has been growing ever since with conferences and international exchanges, prompting the publication of a book. Annalucia Accardo, Cristina Mattiello, Alessandro Portelli, and Anna Scannavini, principal members of the group and editors of *Un'altra America: Letteratura e cultura degli Appalachi meridionali* (Rome: Bulzoni), state that their concern is not just a marginal and backward part of America, but the condition and experience of modernity. Society and history, literature, and music form the patchwork through which we observe and appreciate this special American place. The literary essays (Accardo on Gurney Norman, Scannavini on James Still, Portelli on Appalachia as the setting for science fiction works, Igina Tattoni on Thomas Wolfe, Federica Tecchiani on theater and common essays on women's stories) are the book's core. Accardo and Scannavini also present Jo Carson's work in "Mi chiamo narratrice" (*Linea d'Umbra* 63:59–65).

f. 20th-Century Poetry Ezra Pound is still the most studied American writer in Italy. Besides two reprints, *Lo spirito romanzo,* ed. Sergio Baldi (Milan: SE) and *Guida alla cultura* (see *ALS 1986,* p. 469), Caterina Ricciardi has published two fine contributions. In *Idee Fondamentali* (Rome: Lucarini) she has collected a selection (40 out of 90) of the articles that Pound wrote for the weekly Fascist literary magazine *Il Meridiano di Roma* from 1939 to 1943. In her introduction Ricciardi neither dwells on the regime's use of this great poet nor discusses Pound's "fascism" and anti-Semitism; instead, she prefers to confront various topics in the articles (literature, economics, music, historiography, religion, philosophy, and architecture) with Pound's poetry. Pound's contributions to another fortnightly literary magazine, *L'Indice,* is the subject of Laura Barile's "Un paradosso culturale: Ezra Pound e 'L'Indice' di Genova," pp. 104–22 in her fine *Elite e divulgazione nell'editoria italiana dall'unità al fascimo* (Bologna: CLUEB). Barile examines the equivocal relation between the narrow-minded politics of this short-lived (1930–31) magazine and its director, Gino Saviotti, and Pound's two successive columns, "Appunti" and "Affari Esteri," in which the poet, assuming his cherished role as cultural talent scout, introduced foreign writers (see also *ALS 1980*, p. 575).

A more ambitious work is Ricciardi's excellent *Eikones: Ezra Pound e il rinascimento* (Naples: Liguori), the fruit of long and careful research. Ricciardi reads the Cantos as a great Italian Renaissance fresco, where Humanism and Classicism intermingle with Florentine Neoplatonism and the Hermetic philosophy of Marsilio Ficino to generate the rebirth of symbolic icons. She attentively traces Pound's interest in imagery and its poetic rendering in Victorian and Pre-Raphaelite culture (mainly Walter Pater and Robert Browning) and especially his appreciation of the paintings of Piero della Francesca, Pisanello, Titian, Tintoretto, and others, but above all Botticelli. Botticelli's Venus, as a symbol of creation, of beauty, of rebirth, is chosen as the Cantos' propellent and patronizing symbol, as it was in Renaissance culture. Massimo Bacigalupo's long familiarity with Pound's oeuvre is shown in his "La scrittura dei Cantos" (*Lingua e letteratura* 16:56–77), a revised and extended Italian version of the first section of "L'ecriture des Cantos" (see *ALS 1989*, pp. 435–36). Bacigalupo's continuous interest in primary sources is shown by his frequent trips to Pound archives (see "Gli archivi di New Haven," *Il Verri* 1:171–73).

The 1989 T. S. Eliot centenary elicited a Sardinian seminar, the proceedings of which have been gathered into *"The Spectre of a Rose": Intersections*, ed. Mario Domenichelli and Romana Zacchi (Rome: Bulzoni). The articles' critical standpoints offer various perspectives on different themes in this stimulating and scholarly book. Francesco Binni dwells on Eliot and Modernism and Vita Fortunati on Eliot as a forerunner of the "Yale Critics"; Viola Papetti compares Eliot and Hopkins, while Cristina Giorcelli thoroughly discusses Eliot and William Carlos Williams's "Portrait of the Lady." In the fourth and last section (Readings) Eliot's works are discussed. Eliot's biographical and poetical similarities with the Italian poet Clemente Rebora are examined by Enrico Grandesso in "La sensazione e la parola: il vociano Rebora e il primo T. S. Eliot" (*Otto/Novecento* 6:179–85).

Andrea Mariani has collected and translated some of James Merrill's finest poems in *La Divine Commedie e altre poesie* (Caltanisetta: Sciascia Editore). After a brief biographical introduction Mariani presents bilingual samples of Merrill's poems, which cover his entire output, followed by a vivacious but sound afterword on his poetry. Women poets have fared worse this year. Besides the highly regarded translation of

Marianne Moore's *The Complete Poems* by Lina Angioletti and Gilberto Forti, *Le Poesie* (Milan: Adelphi), a bilingual reprint of the 1972–74 edition, there is Bianca Tarozzi, who presents Elizabeth Bishop's work in "Elizabeth Bishop: Diario della vertigine" (*Leggere* 34:20–31). Also, Maria Carmela Coco Davani perceptively investigates Anne Sexton's use of literary communication as a transgression of norms and conventions in "Anne Sexton: the Scene of the Disordered Senses" (*RSAJ* 2:53–72).

University of Pisa

vi Japanese Contributions: Keiko Beppu

The centennial year of Melville's death has become, as expected, "the Year of Herman Melville" for Japanese scholars of American literature. The publication of two book-length studies, Katsutoshi Hoshino's *Herman Melville: Naraku to Hoshi* [Herman Melville: The abyss and the star] (Liber) and Koichi Nakamura's *Melville no Katarite-tachi* [Melville's narrators] (Kyoto: Rinsen Shoten), is a major event on our academic calendar. Another is the special number of *Eigo Seinen,* which features eight articles by Melville scholars. And finally a collection of essays in English by Japanese Melvilleans is being prepared (to be published by Greenwood Press). Yet to say that Japanese scholarship on American literature for 1991 is dominated by the author of *Moby-Dick* would be misleading. The year registers well-balanced academic activity; the scholarly output covers fairly equally all phases of American literature, with the exception of the colonial period and the 18th century, which rarely receive extended critical attention from Japanese scholars despite the popularity of Sacvan Bercovitch's work.

Another significant feature this year is the introduction of clearly cross-cultural perspectives into American literary studies. Whether dealing with the writers of the '20s or with contemporary novelists, arguments are invariably made in relation to their Japanese counterparts or in cross-cultural context. Noteworthy in this regard are Katsuji Niki's *Ushinawareta Sedai to Showa Shoki* [The Lost Generation and the early years of Showa] (Bunkashobo Hakubunsha), Sachiko Nakada's *Fuso-tachi no Kamigami: Jack London, Upton Sinclair to Nihonjin* [Gods of our fathers: Jack London and Upton Sinclair in Japan (Kokusho Kankokai), and Hideyo Sengoku's *Airon o Kakeru Seinen: Murakami Haruki to America* [Cultural leveling-off: Haruki Murakami's America] (Sairyusha). Different in focus and methodology, these interesting explorations constitute (1) a group portrait of the writers of the Lost Generation; (2) a comprehensive reception study of two American writers with a socialist penchant; and (3) a readable cross-cultural analysis of our own time.

As is the custom in this review, articles surveyed are restricted to those published in our major academic journals, *SALit, SELit,* and *EigoS,* and in a few cases chapters in books. Unless otherwise indicated, all books have been published in Tokyo.

a. The Colonial Period and the 18th Century A sensible general survey of early American literature is found in Muneyuki Kato's *America Bungaku: Dasshutsu to Saisei eno Shodo* [American literature: rejecting the past and making it new] (Kaibunsha), an extended sociocultural history of the United States from its beginning to its intellectual independence proclaimed in Emerson's "The American Scholar." Drawing on colonial histories and early Puritan literature, the book traces the period of America's "long apprenticeship to the learning of other lands," but an obvious omission is recent scholarship on the subject—Robert Spiller, Randall Stewart, and Norman Pearson are major sources of Kato's information—and the book leaves much to be desired.

b. 19th-Century Fiction and Poetry Toshio Watanabe's "Re-examining the Reconstructed American Literary Canon" (*EigoS* 137:130–42) seems to represent the silent majority of Japanese academics in the controversy over the literary canon reported in *ALS 1989.* Watanabe acknowledges the canonical "reconstruction" reflected in *The Columbia Literary History of the United States* (1988) and in *The Heath Anthology of American Literature* (1990). At the same time he has a few strong reservations to the selection of authors in the *Heath Anthology* (both excluded and included), on the ground that many of them are irrelevant to foreign readers. Hence, the major (and our favorite) 19th-century American writers such as Emerson, Hawthorne, and Melville continue to be the object and subject of scholarly investigation.

Worth mentioning first is Toshihiko Ogata's *Uorudo Emasun* [Waldo Emerson] (Kyoto: Apollon-sha), a culmination of Ogata's research on the "representative American man of letters." Ogata's solid scholarship and familiarity with Emerson's prose and poetry make this book of nearly 600 pages a treasure to take in hand and a delight to peruse. The book consists of six chapters followed by a chronology, a "Tentative Family Tree," and a selected bibliography (pp. 565–77): (1) general introduction;

(2) the early trilogy—"Nature," "The American Scholar," and "The Divinity School Address"; (3) the Emersonian cosmos—"Self-Reliance," "The Over-Soul," "Circles," and other essays; (4) Emerson the writer; (5) Emerson as poet; (6) the collapse of the Emersonian cosmos. The chapter on "Emerson as Poet" (pp. 327–504), the longest in the book, includes Ogata's translations of the poems and an assessment of Emerson's poetics. Most illuminating (to this reviewer) is Ogata's summation of "the sage of Concord"; here, Ogata unveils the intellectual and psychic complexity of the great American romantic idealist, whose idealism lost its magical hold on Americans on the eve of the Civil War. *Waldo Emerson* is a definitive critical biography of "the giant star of American literature" and a valuable addition to Emerson scholarship in Japan.

Another significant achievement this year is Yoshitaka Aoyama's *Hawthorne Kenkyu: Jikan to Kukan to Shumatsuron-teki Sozoryoku* [Nathaniel Hawthorne: time, space, and apocalyptic imagination] (Eihosha). Like a few other books reviewed here, *Nathaniel Hawthorne* is a collection of essays that appeared in *SALit, SELit,* or other academic organs; most essays in the collection have gone through extensive revision and are expertly edited to enhance one consistent theme of the book—Hawthorne and typology. Aoyama considers Hawthorne's major novels and stories as unequivocal illustrations of the orthodox Christian view of history, which Aoyama claims is Hawthorne's own view. The thesis that Hawthorne's novels and stories exemplify *the* Christian view of history is fully articulated, and his reading of *The Scarlet Letter, The House of the Seven Gables, The Blithedale Romance, The Marble Faun,* "The Birthmark," and "The Artist of the Beautiful" is supported by a thorough investigation of Judaeo-Christian tradition and by extensive reading in biblical literature and its relevant scholarship. Aoyama's expertise becomes an effective tool for unraveling the hidden meaning, for example, of Maule's curse on Judge Pyncheon; "God will give him blood to drink!" is an echo, Aoyama argues, from Revelation that underscores the Apocalypse. Aoyama's knowledge of Christian theology is best-employed in his chapter on *The Marble Faun,* where he clarifies once and for all the meaning of "the fortunate fall"; a careless and erroneous application of this Christian concept often yields, he contends, a fatal misreading of Hawthorne's denouement. *Nathaniel Hawthorne* is a fully documented vindication of Hawthorne's oeuvre as a self-evident dramatization of "history as Providence"; for Aoyama, the critical talisman, "the ambiguity of Hawthorne," frequently exploited to explain the "unnatural" endings of his novels and stories, has no potency. Credit should go to Aoyama's incisive execution of this problematic issue in Hawthorne scholarship here and abroad.

A few words on Masahiko Narita's article in English on Hawthorne's romance, "The Semiotic Arcadia: Hawthorne's *The Blithedale Romance*" (*SALit* 28:1–17), are necessary. Using Julia Kristeva's theory of revolutionary poetic language that "there is a close connection between radical discourse and female sexual drives," Narita tries to clarify the nature of Hawthorne's radical discourse in this romance. The essay is a passable example of feminist criticism, which has now gained its place in Japanese scholarship on American literature.

As mentioned, Melville monopolizes Japanese scholarship on 19th-century fiction this year. *Herman Melville: The Abyss and the Star* collects Katsutoshi Hoshino's essays written over 15 years; to most readers the book will present a unified whole of the author's judicious reading of Melville's works from *Typee* to *Clarel.* The study consists of four sections, each divided into three short chapters. Hoshino's sensible general examination of Melville's ideological and intellectual construct places him in the social and intellectual context of his time. The second section discusses *Typee, Moby-Dick,* and *The Confidence-Man;* the third takes up short fiction—"The Bell-Tower," "Cock-A-Doodle-Doo!" and "Bartleby"; the fourth deals with selected poems from *Battle Pieces* and *John Marr,* and with *Clarel.* The reader may be disappointed that no radically new interpretations of Melville's works appear here; yet, based on a close reading of the texts, Hoshino's discussions of the interactions between Emersonian Transcendentalism and a Melvillean worldview are informative, persuasive, and cautious. And the message ("the Abyss and the Star") of Hoshino's conclusion recapitulates the ultimate vision to which John Marr, a Melvillean sailor, is a trustworthy witness.

If Hoshino's book attempts to come to grips with "the truth" of the Melvillean world, Koichi Nakamura's *Melville's Narrators* concerns itself with "the art" of telling that truth; the focus of Nakamura's scholarly work is the question of Melvillean rhetoric and language. Published in various academic journals over the past 20 years, the 18 essays that make up *Melville's Narrators* are arranged not in order of their publication, but in the chronology of Melville's texts: *Typee, Omoo, Mardi, Redburn, White Jacket, Moby-Dick* (three chapters), *Pierre* (two chapters), *Israel*

Potter, "The Paradise of Bachelors and the Tartarus of Maids," "Benito Cereno," "Bartleby," *The Confidence-Man, Battle Pieces, Clarel,* and "Billy Budd."

The first chapter, "Spinning a Yarn—to *Typee,*" is the keynote, with the clear-cut thesis that the creation of Tommo, the narrator, makes Melville's first romance more than an adventure story. Structurally, *Typee* is well-equipped with Melvillean "narratology," which is employed over and over in *Moby-Dick* and *Pierre;* the famous "cetology" chapter in *Moby-Dick,* according to Nakamura, is a natural development of Tommo's "digressions" in which Melville's narrator shows off an expertise on the anthropology and ethnography of the South Sea Islands and the Polynesian tribes. Another excellent discussion of a Melvillean narrator is "The Three 'Benito Cerenos'" (pp. 225–39). Here, Nakamura deals with the form that the story takes, comparing it with Robert Lowell's treatment of the same story as verse play; Melville's ambiguous equation of evil with Babo, the black, is clearly nullified in Lowell's *The Stars and the Stripes* (pp. 236–39). The title of Nakamura's book is perhaps deceptive because he admits in his afterword that the application of "narratology" per se does not interest him, since that approach will make his discussion mechanically uniform and impersonal. Indeed, the strategy he chooses makes *Melville's Narrators* extremely readable to non-Melville scholars as well as experts.

As for "narratology," a few words on Masaki Horiuchi's essay seem appropriate. In "*Billy Budd* Between 'Allegory' and 'Facts'" (*SALit* 28:19–23) Horiuchi takes up the issue of two irreconcilable modes, "allegory" and "narrative of facts," in *Billy Budd.* Horiuchi's contention is that Melville makes Captain Vere bridge the gap between the two through his act of reading—reading the allegory enacted by Budd and Claggart, but in vain; and the futility of such dissociation explains the nature of Melville's dichotomy.

Other articles on Melville worthy of note appear in the special number of *EigoS* (137), prefaced by a brief survey of recent Melville studies in the United States (p. 44). To show the diversity and scope of our Melvilleans' interest, it will suffice to list the titles of various centenary tributes: "Melville and Politics" by Ginsaku Sugiura; "Melville and the Reader—A Dialogic Relation" by Kazuko Fukuoka; "Melville in Japan—Hisama Jyugi's Prize-winning Story (1990)" by Kenzaburo Ohashi; "Melville and Madness" by Toshio Yagi; "Some Thoughts on *Clarel*" by Hideyo Sengoku; "Melvillean World and Love" by Takeshi Morita; and

"Melville and the Riddle" by Takuya Nishitani. The articles represent a good sample of the scope and depth of Japanese scholarship on Melville; the contributors likewise represent a good index of the cross-generational (but hardly mixed in terms of gender) community of Melville scholars. Indeed, Melville studies for 1991 constitute a remarkably comprehensive enterprise.

Both Hoshino and Nakamura in their books give considerable space to Melville's poetical works, which have received scant critical attention here; similarly, much of Ogata's book on Emerson is devoted to his poetry and poetics. Which brings this review to Walt Whitman. Shiro Tsuneda's *Musono Tensai no Hikari to Kage: Whitman no "Kusa no Ha" (I)* [The light and shadow of the visionary poet: Whitman's "Leaves of Grass" (I)] (Aratake Shuppan) is a lengthy critical biography of the American bard. As the subtitle indicates, the book is the first part of Tsuneda's detailed examination of the three editions of *Leaves of Grass.* Interwoven with his explications of the poems are detailed biographical materials. Tsuneda's story of Whitman's early years is enthralling; in this respect the book is a readable account of the poet's life reconstructed from Tsuneda's avid readings in the journals and prose works as well as the poems. Whitman's exposure to urban crime, degradation in the city and in villages alike, the deplorable state of impoverished people he encountered, and the misery of his own family all went into making his poetry. Tsuneda's "narrative" of Whitman's factual biography is read into the discussion of the poetry. The 90-year-old devotee's wholehearted commitment to Whitman's life and the writings is readily felt. But the book suffers from redundancy.

Quite different in approach is Morito Uemura's article, " 'A Voice from the Sea': Whitman's 'A Word Out of the Sea' and Swinburne's 'Thalassius' and 'On the Cliffs' " (*SELit* 68:75–87). This article in English is a good example of intertextual study; Uemura shows that Whitman's poem is one source for two important Swinburne poems.

The current volume of *SALit* includes one essay on Emily Dickinson: Hiroyuki Koguchi's "Emily Dickinson and Pastoralism" (*SALit* 28:35–51), also written in English, in which he successfully demonstrates that pastoralism, which more often than not remains unnoticed but "lucidly present" in Dickinson's poetry, "constitutes a basic network of her poetic ideas and imageries" and that American pastoralism is not solely Whitman's province.

Two other 19th-century writers, Henry James and Edith Wharton, received some critical attention. Shinichi Nakamura's *Shosetsuka Henry James* [Henry James the novelist] (Shueisha) is a collection of the editorial prefaces that Nakamura wrote for the Japanese edition of *The Collected Works of Henry James* (Kokusho Kankokai, 1983–85) as well as his literary essays from 1986 through 1990. Although the book is not a "scholarly" exploration of James's novels and stories, even so Nakamura's familiarity with James's texts is long, intimate, and professionally thoroughgoing—he has read all of James's novels and 50 of some 100 stories and *novelle* in translation and in the original. A unique study on "the art of the novel," à la Blackmur, Nakamura's book concentrates on the act of writing and reveals the evolution of James as a modern novelist as well as his own development as one of the foremost Japanese critics. Of special significance is the last chapter, "On the Writing of the Novel" (pp. 277–90), which examines James's literary criticism; it is a concise yet comprehensive assessment of the Jamesian aesthetic of fiction.

In contrast to the growth of Wharton scholarship in the United States in recent years, Japanese writings on Wharton are sparse. Therefore, Noriko Kato's essay, in English, "Doubling in Edith Wharton's Postwar Fictions" (*SALit* 28:53–76), deserves professional moral support. Kato mainly discusses doubling in *The Age of Innocence,* with some references to other "postwar fictions"—"The Old Maid" and *The Mother's Recompense.* Kato's concluding remark that these three fictions are more of "an autopsy" of Wharton's divided selves needs clarification.

c. 20th-Century Fiction and Poetry Two significant book-length studies are Sachiko Nakada's *Gods of Our Fathers: Jack London and Upton Sinclair in Japan* and Katsuji Niki's *The Lost Generation and the Early Years of Showa,* both cross-cultural comparative studies. Nakada's book is one of the year's most valuable scholarly accomplishments. It is a remarkably well-documented reception study of two American writers whose indelible influence on Japanese society at the turn of the century has been slighted or obliterated until recently. The volume consists of three parts, corresponding to the three phases of the Japanese reception of London and Sinclair: (1) The Beginning: 1903–1917, (2) The Golden Years: 1918–30, (3) After the Deluge: the Post-World War II period. Nakada has done an amazing amount of research in relevant materials, which include *The Call of the Wild, The Jungle,* journal and newspaper articles written about and by London and Sinclair, and all Japanese translations of their works. These documents appear in order in "the notes" and "the list of translations" in the appendix (pp. 371–410). More important is the list of the Japanese who had direct or indirect contacts with the two writers. The index is well-prepared. *Gods of Our Fathers* is an absorbingly rich documentary history of how London's and Sinclair's ideas and writings have influenced Japanese writers and leaders. In addition to being an invaluable comparative literary study, the book satisfies a reader's personal need—the pleasure of reading itself. Together with *Jack London: Essays* (see *ALS 1989*), Nakada's study offers a revisionist distribution map of the American literary canon in this country.

This year no book-length study was published on any single one of our favorite 20th-century novelists—Hemingway, Fitzgerald, or Faulkner. Instead, the three writers are the subject of a modest group portrait in Niki's *The Lost Generation and the Early Years of Showa.* The book is a kind of decade study, like Larzer Ziff's *The American 1890's* or Frederick Hoffman's *The Twenties,* and a reception study of these writers in the early years of "Showa," the decade 1925–35. A companion volume to *Gods of Our Fathers,* Niki's book is much lighter in scope and objective. Even so, it provides sufficient supporting material to show the far-reaching influences that modernist poetry and aesthetics have exercised on Japanese poets such as Junzaburo Nishiwaki and Tatsuji Miyoshi. In an informative chapter Niki examines the founding of the poetry magazine *Poetry and Poetics,* which became the major instrument for introducing the three writers to Japanese scholars and readers. Niki's book abounds in literary episodes that may seem to contradict the popularity these American writers enjoy today, for example, the poor reception of Hemingway's *A Farewell to Arms* when it first appeared in translation, or of Faulkner, whose first story translated into Japanese was "A Rose for Emily." A finishing touch to Niki's group portrait is his inclusion of Gertrude Stein, who is given the book's most extensive treatment (pp. 43–118). Whatever the critical reception of these writers between 1925 and 1935, Niki clearly shows that the decade was a significant initiation for Japanese readers.

Publication of a revised edition of the same scholar's 1988 book on Faulkner, *Faulkner no Seikimatsu to Girisha no Tsubo* [William Faulkner's "fin de siècle" and the Grecian urn] (Bunkashobo Hakubunsha), offers an exploration of Faulkner's romanticism and traces the influence of Keats and the English fin de siècle poets on his works. A similar publication is the revised edition of the 1988 *Steinbeck's Tampen Shosetsu Kenkyu* (A study of Steinbeck's short stories] (Yashio Shuppan), ed. Hisashi

Egusa, in which the bibliography of Japanese scholarship on Steinbeck (pp. 258–78) has been updated.

Among articles on 20th-century fiction, the following deserve brief comment: Naomi Imaoka's "William Faulkner's *Light in August:* Its Thematic and Structural Analysis" (*SELit* 68:121–36) and Makoto Igakura's "'Shapin Words t Fit M Soul': Reading Jean Toomer, 1923–1991" (*SALit* 28:111–25). Using Michael Millgate, Regina K. Fadiman, and others, Imaoka demonstrates how Faulkner synthesizes the three separate stories—Hightower's, Christmas's, and the romance of Lena and Byron—into a "composite novel." Igakura offers an intriguing discussion, in English, on the artistic difficulties that Toomer faced in writing *Cane;* Toomer is treated as an avant-garde poet who sensed "the radical problems inherent in Afro-American literary expression." Igakura's article is a welcome addition to African-American studies, which have attracted an increasing number of scholars in recent years.

Niki's *The Lost Generation and the Early Years of Showa* records the significant influences of Gertrude Stein and the Imagist movement on modern Japanese poetry; surely, 20th-century American poetry is one of the challenging fields of study for Japanese scholars. Akiko Miyake's *Ezra Pound and the Mysteries of Love: A Plan for "The Cantos"* (Duke) is a highlight in that research. The book crowns Miyake's long scholarly engagement with Pound studies, which began with her doctoral dissertation at Duke in 1970. Unlike any other 20th-century American poet, Pound—the Pound of *The Cantos,* in particular—seems to defy most Japanese critics. However, *The Cantos* provides Miyake with inexhaustible resources for her tireless scholarly investigation, which sometimes verges on intellectual narcissism. Making use of her knowledge in several languages (classical and modern), of her expertise in Chinese poetry and Japanese Noh drama, and of her avid reading in classical literature, Miyake unveils an intricate "figure in the carpet" hidden within the texture of *The Cantos,* which she calls "a plan for *The Cantos,*" a deliberate design that informs Pound's masterpiece.

Miyake's book is a brilliant source study, placing *The Cantos* in the Christian mystical tradition; in her expert handling of relevant scholarship and abundant sources, including a superb selection of illustrations, she forges a strong case for *The Cantos* as religious literature. It is impossible to do full justice here to Miyake's intellectual energy and scholarship, completed, as she acknowledges, by the collaboration of "the international community of scholars." The book is a monumental achievement, crowning earlier Pound scholarship in this country, and should be welcomed by Poundians abroad.

The following are some noteworthy articles written on 20th-century American poets. Keiko Wells's "The Development of Images in Pound's Poetry" (*EigoS* 137:2–6) is a lyrical sketch of the poet's obsession with words as images: for example, of how the image cluster flame/woman/song in Pound's early poem "Vena" changes through the poet's Imagist years and period of Vorticism, finally forming the cluster tree/petals/pale faces/female, symbolizing a mystical experience, in *The Cantos.* Kayoko Hashimoto's chapter, "Greek Myth and Modern American Poetry," pp. 242–69 in *Girisha Shinwa to Eibeibunka* [Greek myth and Anglo-American culture] ed. Akira Arai et al. (Taishukan), presents a quick survey on the uses of Greek myth in American poetry from Whitman through Pound and Eliot. Of special note is Hashimoto's discussion of H.D., which introduces a feminist reading of that tradition; H.D.'s *Helen in Egypt* is the first epic written by an American woman poet, and women in Greek myth—Helen for H.D.—become a vital means for them to unleash their emotional needs and establish their autonomy as artists.

Two articles on T. S. Eliot deserve brief comment: Keiko Saeki's " 'After Such Knowledge, What Forgiveness?'—Parting from the Kurtzian World in 'The Hollow Men' " (*SELit* 68:257–71) and Miyuki Nagaoka's "In the Beginning Was Drive/Affect/Rhythm: A Reading of *Sweeney Agonistes*" (*SELit* 68:273–86). The first is a nicely written essay on "The Hollow Men," which anticipates the poet's affirmation of his belief that complete knowledge (self-knowledge) leads to salvation of one's soul in *The Waste Land;* a detailed reading of the text explains Eliot's use of the epigraph taken from Conrad's *Heart of Darkness.* Nagaoka's is a provocative examination of the creative process from the semiotic to the symbolic in Eliot's poem. The critic's implementation of the Kristevan theory of language and of the theory of "drive" and artistic expression expounded by Keiichiro Maruyama (a much-quoted Japanese linguist) ably shows the mysterious shift from the nonverbal—drive/affect/rhythm—into the verbal in *Sweeney Agonistes.*

d. Contemporary Fiction The large number of translations produced in this country each year partly depend on the popularity of various contemporary American writers among Japanese readers—students and scholars as well as the general audience. To list some of the favored

American writers among Japanese readers: (1) Jewish American writers—Bernard Malamud and Philip Roth; (2) postmodernists—Raymond Carver, Richard Brautigan, Thomas Pynchon, and John Irving; (3) women writers—Bobbie Ann Mason, Mary Morris, and Anne Beaty, as well as African-American women, with Alice Walker, Toni Morrison, Paule Marshall, and Gloria Naylor the leading voices. As with 20th-century fiction, no book-length study was published on an individual contemporary novelist this year, but the three books reviewed here clearly indicate which American writers enjoy critical acceptance in Japan: Tateo Imamura's *Gendai America Bungaku: Seishun no Kiseki* [Contemporary American literature: the fates of adolescent heroes] (Kenkyusha); Tsunehiko Kato's *America Kokujin Josei Sakka Ron: Alice Walker, Toni Morrison, Gloria Naylor* [A study of black American women writers: Alice Walker, Toni Morrison, and Gloria Naylor] (Ochanomizu Shobo); and Sengoku's *Cultural Leveling-Off: Haruki Murakami's America* (Sairyusha).

Contemporary American Literature: The Fates of Adolescent Heroes collects 12 essays published in academic and literary journals. These essays are lacking in uniformity of approach and methodology—some no more than charming literary chit-chats, while others, the three chapters on Raymond Federman, for example, constitute a substantial discussion of the writer's major works. Yet the essays have one consistent leitmotiv in the theme of "adolescence" and "the adolescent hero." Imamura traces the literary genealogy of Salinger's Holden Caulfield (whose brother is Hemingway's Nick Adams), which includes protagonists in novels by Malamud, Roth, Federman, Truman Capote, Brautigan, Carver, Irving, and Jay McInerney. Curiously, the genealogy of adolescent heroes in Imamura's study ends with veterans of the Vietnam war and their female companions in novels about the Vietnam experience by women writers like Mason, Phillips, and Morris. In view of the cross-gender perspective in today's life and culture, the conclusion to Imamura's explorations seems appropriate, especially since the shrewd critic provides a stepping-stone in his discussion of Salinger that capitalizes on the presence, however marginal, of Holden's "little sisters" in Salinger's early stories. Those little sisters are given center stage in novels by women in the 1980s: Sam Hughes is the female adolescent narrator of Mason's *In Country* and Zoe, Badger's sister, is made a point-of-view character in Morris's *The Waiting Room.* Despite its unevenness, Imamura's book is a readable guide to contemporary American literature on the theme of "the trauma of adolescent experience"—which, to echo Russell Banks, might be the one and the only story worth writing about.

Kato's *A Study of Black American Women Writers* is a sequel to *The World of Black American Women Writers: Alice Walker, Toni Morrison, and Paule Marshall* (1986). The present volume reflects Kato's partiality to Naylor, who receives half the space. Since among Japanese readers Naylor is the least-known of the three writers, Kato's remarks on her major novels—*The Women of Brewster Place, Linden Hills,* and *Mama Day*—are helpful to general readers. Similarly, Alice Walker is well-represented by discussions of her major works, including *The Temple of My Familiar* (1989), whereas Morrison, who has a higher standing than either of the other two, is treated in one slim chapter dealing with *Tar Baby;* today, it would seem, any discussion of Morrison is terribly deficient without reference to *Beloved.* Better editorial judgment would have made Kato's discussion more satisfactory. Further, Kato uses "feminism" or "feminist interest" in analyzing these works without defining the term or clarifying the nature of the writers' "feminist interest." Thus, more often than not, Kato's discussions fail as extended treatments.

Gods of Our Fathers and *The Lost Generation and the Early Years of Showa* are records of viable interactions, heavily one-sided, to be sure, between American literature and Japanese culture. Hideyo Sengoku's *Cultural Leveling-Off: Haruki Murakami's America* is an astute cross-cultural analysis of these two multicultural societies. Sengoku's book starts, curiously enough, with a clever review of *Norwegian Wood,* the best-selling novel by Haruki Murakami, which (like his earlier *Wild Sheep Chase*) has been translated into English; the critic presents Murakami, probably the most popular Japanese writer today, as cultural leveler for both American and Japanese society. Known also as the translator of works by Fitzgerald and Carver, the Japanese novelist assimilates these writers and their culture and transmits what he perceives as "America" to young Japanese readers. The characters in Murakami's novel talk like those in Fitzgerald's *The Great Gatsby*—and at times like Salinger's Holden Caulfield or a Hemingway hero for that matter—and he attempts to duplicate the style of Carver's stories.

Cultural Leveling-Off is another collection of previously published essays and articles. The chapters entitled "Literary Criticisms in America and American Poetry" (pp. 97–144), "The Future of New Fiction" (pp. 146–68), and "After Minimalism, What Then?" (pp. 170–84) read very much like lecture notes jotted down in graduate courses at an

American university. Nonetheless, they are readable and informative "conversation pieces" on each subject; of special interest are Sengoku's remarks on David Ignatow's poems from *Selected Poems* (1975), perhaps one of the few discussions of this poet by a Japanese scholar.

Another enjoyable discussion is Sengoku's unique comparison of Carver and Brautigan in "Carver's Salmon and Brautigan's Trout" (pp. 207–29). Those two writers are chosen because they are the Americans most avidly read by Murakami and, in Murakami's translations, by young Japanese. As the book's subtitle indicates, it is "American graffiti" painted in and on Murakami's writings and serves as a cultural leveler for American and Japanese society today. Ironically, Sengoku's commentary provides a breakthrough for the political and economic deadlock that has confronted the two countries. It appears so much easier for one culture to reach across to another than for political and economic representatives to agree in international trade negotiations.

The following three articles on contemporary fiction deserve brief comment: Yo Tabayashi's "The Magic of 'Narratives' in Philip Roth's *Zuckerman Bound*" (*SALit* 28:95–110); Keiko Misugi's "Yasha Mazur's Flight from Life: Isaac Bashevis Singer's *The Magician of Lublin*" (*SALit* 28:141–56); and Takayuki Tatsumi's "Greek Myth and the American Novel" in *Greek Myth and Anglo-American Culture* (pp. 272–94). The first essay discusses Nathan's struggle in *Zuckerman Bound* to create new "narratives" that transcend those of Wolfe, James, Joyce, Aeschylus, and Shelley. Misugi's article deals with the dilemma of Yasha Mazur, Singer's failed Jewish patriarch, a dilemma that Misugi regards as a "prevailing phenomenon in modern Jewish fiction." Tatsumi's chapter is a succinct survey, like Hashimoto's similar discussion on Greek myth and American poetry in the same volume, on the uses of Greek myth from Puritan literature through postmodern fiction. Drawing on earlier studies, Tatsumi clearly demonstrates how euhemerism helped American writers create America's own myth-history out of the Bible—"Manifest Destiny" and its secular version, the American success story. The strength of the chapter, however, lies in Tatsumi's shrewd analysis of the way in which Greek myth transforms itself in the metafiction of John Barth's *Chimera* or Thomas Pynchon's *Vineyard,* a viable Pygmalion myth for our time.

e. American Studies To conclude this review, some remarks on two important books in American studies are necessary: Koji Oi's *Bitoku no Kyowakoku: Jiden to Denki no nakano America* [The republic of virtue:

America in autobiography and biography] (Kaibunsha) and *America Bungaku no Hero* [The hero in American literature] ed. Yoshiaki Koshikawa (Seibido). Oi's *The Republic of Virtue*—the last of his trilogy that includes *The Frontier Closed* (1985) and *The Gilded Age* (1988)—deals with the republican ideal and its failure through the republic's history. Oi's primary concern is evaluation and reevaluation of the virtues that make up republican ideology—honesty, diligence, sincerity, cleanliness, conscience, and resolute mind, or the frontier spirit; Oi argues that these values find their best articulation in the autobiographies and biographies of U.S. leaders.

The Republic of Virtue consists of seven compact chapters whose headings speak for themselves: (1) autobiographies of Franklin and Jefferson provide the pillar and cornerstone of republican ideology; (2) Mason Weems's *The Life of Washington* is recommended as a guideline that teaches republican virtues; (3) Francis Parkman's *Vassall Morton* is a "Garden of Eden" myth; (4) William Dean Howells's campaign biographies for presidential candidates envision the future of the republic; (5) Howells's *A Boy's Town* is a nostalgic recollection of a lost "paradise"; (6) Henry Adams's *Life of Albert Gallatin* records the failure of republicanism; (7) and Carry Nation and Jane Addams are remembered. *The Republic of Virtue* is a valuable study on "the founding spirit" of American society in its sociohistorical context. With an exhaustive bibliography of relevant scholarship (pp. 182–95), Oi's completed trilogy significantly adds to American studies in Japan.

The Hero in American Literature is similar, exploring different faces of the American hero in sociocultural context. The American hero is indeed the republican virtues made flesh in both canonical and noncanonical literature. The book collects 20 explorations, including a contribution by Ihab Hassan; most of the essays were originally written to commemorate the retirement of Professor Iwamoto, one of our distinguished scholars of American literature. Koshikawa's introduction provides a framework for the ensuing case studies, which are arranged in three parts. The six chapters in the first part discuss the prototype of the American hero and its variations in the writings of Cooper, Hawthorne, Brown, Stowe, Poe, Parkman, Fitzgerald, Wolfe, and Hemingway. In the second section, 19th- and 20th-century American writers provide still more varied faces of the American hero; the list includes Melville, Hawthorne, James, Twain, Hemingway, Faulkner, and O'Neill. The last part considers the American hero or antihero in contemporary American writings by

Singer, Bellow, Malamud, West, Heller, Vonnegut, Barthelme, Nabokov, Tennessee Williams, Albee, Shepard, Barth, Pynchon, Carver, and Le Guin. The great number of writers considered in the discussion of the American hero make *The Hero in American Literature* a comprehensive survey on the theme, for the changing faces of American heroes through history are reflections and refractions of changing values in American society. The multiplicity and scope of materials are also good indicators of recent trends observed in Japanese literary studies: less rigid demarcation among literary genres, with the inclusion of theater, popular fiction, and science fiction in the last section serving as examples.

In support of this assumption, reference should be made to the final installment of Shunsuke Kamei's series in *EigoS,* "The Genealogy of the American Hero," which has been serialized over two and a half years and concludes in the current issue. As usual, Kamei's explorations range far and wide in search of avatars of the American hero in literary works, films, popular fiction, science fiction, and cartoons. Prophetically coincidental is his summation, which accords with that of Yoko Imaizumi's chapter in *The Hero in American Literature,* "Neither Male nor Female, the Hero in Le Guin's Science Fiction" (pp. 226–35). Interestingly, Hiroko Sato's interdisciplinary study on "The Making of the American Girl," another series that continues in *EigoS,* may reveal still more different faces of "the American hero."

Kobe College

vii Scandinavian Contributions: Jan Nordby Gretlund, Elisabeth Herion-Sarafidis, and Hans Skei

Scandinavian work on American literature shows a leaning this year toward contemporary poetry and fiction. But Emily Dickinson, as so often before, fares well in the hands of Scandinavian scholars, with three essays: one on the poet and Christianity, one considering Dickinson in the light of Virginia Woolf's *A Room of One's Own,* and one discussing Dickinson the reader. Rationality and utopia in Edgar Allan Poe's work is the subject of another book. Henry James's concern with American culture is explored, as are the antebellum diaries of southerner Sarah Morgan Dawson, and two stories by Stephen Crane are subjected to a metaphoric reading. Arriving, then, at the work devoted to the fiction and poetry of the 20th century, the harvest includes an essay on T. S. Eliot, a book on Sylvia Plath's *Ariel,* a discussion of Robert Haas's sensuous imagery, one essay on Bob Dylan, and one on the experimental feminist poet Beverly Dahlen. The "postmodern" nature of modernism is the subject of one ambitious study. Work also has been done on southerners Faulkner, O'Connor, Percy, and Welty and on Norwegian travelogues from the Midwest. Two essays concern themselves with minimalists like Raymond Carver, and one discusses American popular fiction translated into Norwegian.

a. 19th-Century Poetry In his "Gud er bestemt en skinsyg Gud: Om Emily Dickinsons religiøse digtning" ["God is indeed a jealous God": On Emily Dickinson's religious poetry] (*Fyens Stiftsbog* [Odense: Fyens Stift], pp. 85–97) Niels Kjaer continues his work on Dickinson's poetry (see *ALS 1989*, pp. 452–53) in a consideration of the poet and Christianity. Her poems express facets of faith ranging from blasphemy to sincere devotion, and it is this drama of her constant quest for religious certainty that makes her a great poet. Kjaer argues that the peculiar mixture of Puritanism and Romanticism of Dickinson's poetry is what makes it an expression of the American Soul even today. Dickinson's mental development mirrors in several ways the traditional Puritan progression toward Truth. Although she was for a time impressed with Emerson's happy idealism, she finally rejected the notion that nature is divine; only God is unknowable and divine. In accordance with her Puritan heritage her interest was not in Christ, but in Old Testament figures like David and Job who questioned the ways of God. Kjaer compares their angry, disappointed, and powerless questioning of God to Dickinson's religious poetry and finds obvious parallels. She protested God's apparent cruelty to man, but, Kjaer postulates somewhat surprisingly (even in terms of his own essay), Dickinson never wavered in her faith. This is simply not true as regards all her poetry. Kjaer is closer to the truth when he concludes that although Dickinson was not a Christian in any orthodox sense, her poetry is based on a profound experience of the Divine.

Lene Olufsen's "Tekstuelle rum og rumlige visioner" [Textual room and spatial vision] (*Egne rum: En antologi om køn, skrift og rum* [Rooms of their own: An anthology on gender, text and room], ed. Eva Lous and Lis W. Pape [Aarhus: KLIM], pp. 13–40), considers Dickinson's poetry in the light of Woolf's *A Room of One's Own*. Dickinson was, according to Olufsen, nourished by a specific women's tradition that Woolf later wrote about. Dickinson used her foremothers' example to create her own room and her consciousness of herself as one belonging to "Races—nurtured in the Dark," and Dickinson's staging of herself as "the woman in white" may be seen as an expression of a demonstrative alienation in a world that restricts women's possibilities. Olufsen shows convincingly that Dickinson's ideas of the father and the father's house, the spoken versus the unspoken, "myself" versus "me," marriage, isolation, madness, and her desire to break down psychological barriers and experiment with language and states of consciousness anticipate essential elements in Woolf's fiction and Plath's poetry.

In her "Emily Dickinson: Poetic Consumption, or the Poet as Reader" (*Consumption and American Culture,* ed. David Nye and Carl Pedersen [Amsterdam: VU University Press], pp. 99–117), Lis Møller argues that Dickinson participated fully in the culture of her day through her reading, which included journals, magazines, and newspapers. She consumed Gothic tales, sentimental verse, and much else meant for the general market. Møller joins the old discussion on the originality of Dickinson's themes and images and finds her "less original than we have been inclined to believe." Møller then goes on to offer examples of poems with images Dickinson is supposed to have appropriated, but not all the supposed parallels are equally obvious. The essay points out, however, that what Dickinson read is not so important as how the poet read, and how she used her reading. Through her indiscriminate absorption of very different cultural voices Dickinson broke down literary hierarchies, reading "for parts rather than for wholes." The use of the consumed reading is also fragmentary, disjunctive, and broken. The modernity of her oeuvre, Møller concludes, is that the poems do not add up to a whole. Fragmentation is seen as Dickinson's strength and "a clue to the specific modernity of her poetry."

b. 19th-Century Fiction In *Kirke og Kultur* (95 [1990]:566–68) Øyvind Gulliksen reviews Harold P. Simonson's *Prairies Within: The Tragic Trilogy of Ole Rølvaag,* and by and large accepts Simonson's understanding that Beret "is the key" to the work as a whole, and that her mental landscapes, the "prairies within," are more important than the soil on which Per Hansa toils to eke out a living. The key to an understanding of Beret is her strong heritage of religious feeling, definitely linking her to Norway, and thus we have a rising conflict with those who tend to become Americans almost too easily. Gulliksen's only critical remark is that Simonson moves too quickly from his analysis of Beret to the author himself, although Rølvaag most certainly put many of his beliefs into this female character.

Henning Goldbaek's *Graensens Filosofi: Rationalitet og utopi hos Edgar Allan Poe* [The philosophy of limits: rationality and utopia in Edgar Allan Poe] (Copenhagen: Akademisk) discusses the development of Poe's reputation from the neglected romantic poet and gothic storyteller to the ever-present "modern" truth-teller who anticipated much of 20th-century reality. Goldbaek praises Poe for treating such issues as idealism, progress, the American Dream, optimism, materialism, mass culture, reification versus freedom, and democracy versus truth, that is, most of what makes up the identity of modern Western civilization. He claims that "Poe expresses the fear and fragmentation of a post-idealistic reality, which his work tries to master." The chapter on Poe's detective stories has been published separately (see *ALS 1990*, p. 465). The best chapters detail Poe's reception in France, Germany, and the United States. Goldbaek criticizes American scholars for their failure to see that Poe was rooted in history, in his contemporary society and popular culture, and more critical of what he saw than were other writers of the American Renaissance. Goldbaek is disappointed with Poe's final book, concluding that in spite of himself Poe was finally caught up in the dynamics of progress. Goldbaek seems unaware that the German idealism which Poe absorbed was actually Coleridge's version. Goldbaek ignores Poe's study of Coleridge's prose works, which sold well in the United States in the 1830s. If the value of Coleridge's philosophy for Poe had been noted, Goldbaek would not have been puzzled by the mixture of epistemology, aesthetics, and religion that Poe created in *Eureka*. It is also a surprise that the author of a book based on the theories of Benjamin and Adorno fails to realize that the issues considered particularly modern in Poe were also subjects of debate in the antebellum South. Goldbaek sees Poe as rooted in his contemporary society and popular culture, and yet he does not mention Poe the editor and finds no space to consider him in his everyday life. But it is through his journalism, particularly for the *Southern Literary Messenger*, that Poe's life in his particular society is best understood. Although Poe in history is supposedly his primary concern, Goldbaek's apparent ignorance about him as a southerner engenders readings of "The Fall of the House of Usher" and *Pym* that are oblivious of antebellum ideology and culture. Goldbaek is at his best when he suggests that it would be worth examining "the connection between recent Poe research and the change in ideology in American Studies." It would also be helpful, he adds, if Poe's European critics would realize that mass society and alienation are also European phenomena. It is time for Poe criticism to steer away from purely ideological reactions, so that Poe does not forever remain adrift in his balloon between the continents. Goldbaek's "Poe in Progress: A Reappraisal" (*AmerSS* 23:105–20) is a useful summary of *Graensens Filosofi*.

With her "Behind Confederate Lines: Sarah Morgan Dawson" (*SoQ* 30, i:7–18) Clara Juncker continues her work on antebellum Southern women diarists (see *ALS 1989*, pp. 451–52). *A Confederate Girl's Diary* is a journal begun in Baton Rouge in 1862 and concluded three years later with a mention of Lincoln's assassination (at least in the printed version). According to Juncker, the diary reveals that Dawson was more than "just the dutiful daughter of the Confederacy." "Imprisoned by history," she continued to relish her caste and class, but by writing a diary added "a feminine space" where she could oscillate "between respectability and rebellion" and question her assigned role and traditional gender distinctions. Although she tried to be a southern lady, she describes her efforts with self-irony and humor. At the end of three years, after the forced move to New Orleans and the death of two brothers, Dawson was, Juncker claims, "a newly-born woman and a budding Louisiana reconstructionist."

Helle Porsdam's "The 'Question of Europe': Henry James and the Debate Concerning American Culture in the Early Twentieth Century" (*Consumption and American Culture*, pp. 210–22) argues that James anticipated the main elements of the debate of the 1910s and '20s about the United States as a spiritual and cultural wasteland. Although Van Wyck Brooks, Lewis Mumford, H. L. Mencken, Harold Stearns, and others failed to see his concern with American culture, "James did not for a moment forget his native country and its cultural problems"; on the contrary, the United States "took precedence in his works over almost any other theme." In an argument deserving more space, the essay postulates that James in *The American Scene* wrote "a critique of modern America that was explicitly linked to the modern crisis in Western thought as a whole." Furthermore, James saw that the question of America called for a consideration of Europe, "its contrary and cultural ancestor." The last part of *The American Scene* sounds a note of hope for America, Porsdam concludes, for James believed that "his native country—as opposed to Europe—was freed from the burden of history."

In his interdisciplinary enterprise *Meaning by Metaphor: An Explora-*

tion of Metaphor with a Metaphoric Reading of Two Short Stories by Stephen Crane (Almqvist and Wiksell) Gunnar Backman endeavors to "unite current views of metaphor in linguistic theory with text interpretation in literary critcism." Backman's basic contention is that metaphor is essential in human communication, "that meaning is created through metaphor," that literature is a metaphoric statement. His study consists of one linguistic part and one literary part, the theoretical exploration of the role of metaphor in the first part serving as a base for a metaphoric reading in the second of Crane's "The Bride Comes to Yellow Sky" and "The Blue Hotel"—a reading that attempts to uncover Crane's metaphoric strategies, to lay bare the metaphoric conceptions behind the texts, and thus enhance our understanding of Crane's vision and intention. After an initial survey of different theories of metaphor, Backman establishes a model of his own based on componential analysis. Such a procedure, he argues, focuses on intended meaning, breaking down constructions into features, studying their patterns to determine how a writer delivers his message, "in what words [he] shapes his thoughts." Backman moves on to put his model to work, to analyze the narrative metaphoric strategies of a randomly chosen writer, deciding on Crane because of the accessibility of the plots and because the language is "plain and clear." The reading of Crane's two short stories is perceptive and illuminating; *this* reader would have liked to have seen the method applied to more texts, something that would have redressed the imbalance between the historical and theoretical part of the book and the actual investigation of a writer's language. As it is, Backman makes no claim to any radically new interpretation, merely to have found "a tool to make Crane's outlook on life explicit by drawing on semantic evidence," in itself no insignificant feat.

c. 20th-Century Poetry In "Arnold Bennett and T. S. Eliot: What Happened to *Sweeney Agonistes*?" (*T. S. Eliot Annual No. 1,* ed. Shymal Bagchee [Macmillan], pp. 145–52) Hans Hauge raises the question of whether Bennett read an almost-finished version of *Sweeney Agonistes* before it was published. "Is it likely," Hauge asks, "that Bennett's role in connection with *Sweeney Agonistes* is comparable to Pound's in connection with *The Waste Land*?" Hauge shows that there is no reason to be surprised that the poet asked the successful novelist for advice, since Eliot did not share Pound's negative view of Bennett. The essay establishes that the result of Eliot's visit to Bennett in September 1924 was probably *not* the unfinished poem, but rather "On the Eve: A Dialogue," which is "a forerunner of *The Cocktail Party*." Hauge concludes that "Bennett influenced Eliot more than is generally assumed," adding that "the story of Eliot's start as a dramatist" may need some revision.

Jennifer Draskau's *The Liberation of Sylvia Plath's* Ariel: *Psychosemantics and a Glass Sarcophagus* (Copenhagen: POET) discusses some of the classic themes in Plath scholarship: the nymph form of Ariel, the "glass" and mirror themes, the parent-child relationship, and the quest for female identity; but the book also raises the idea of a "psychosemantic illness" and language as a cure. Having treated these topics, Draskau quotes Anne Sexton on Plath: "What matters is her poems"—an unexpected quotation, since the argument in the book is based almost exclusively on journals, letters, biographical and critical statements, and Plath's only novel. In this study there is too little on the poems; even the *Ariel* poems of the book's title are not read in any detail. It is refreshing, however, that Draskau refuses to see Plath as simply a victim of her social situation and the sexism of her age. Without ignoring that the "bell jar of social and material inequity" was an obstacle to a search for identity, the book details the cultural, economic, and social environment, and Draskau concludes that Plath's social situation was better than has been supposed by some critics. The book does not ignore the poet's mental illness, arguing that it was only when her "sensibilities were stretched to the breaking point" that Plath could write the disturbing and unique poetry that shatters complacency. Draskau offers an illuminating comparison of Plath's thoughts on the art of suicide and Sheila MacLeod's thoughts on anorexics in *The Art of Starvation* (1981), showing why both, as artists, regarded their female destiny as "problematic." For Draskau, Plath's greatness, in spite of her limited range, resides in the integrity and craftsmanship of her treatment of her chosen theme. Draskau concludes, "In her mirror we may not like what we see, but the image still takes our breath away by its precision, its boldness and the sheer voltage of the emotion that charges it."

Exploring Robert Haas's aesthetic consciousness, Gunilla Florby in "Holding Out Against Loss and Jacques Lacan: Some Reflections on Robert Haas's Sensuous Line" (*SN* 63:189–95) describes the poet as a man who, in a triumphant celebration of sensuousness, holds on to and finds a kind of affirmation in "concrete sensory experience." In his poetry Haas is concerned with a tangible reality, with the magic of the senses—but he is also convinced of the numinous quality of words. Florby considers

Haas's strategy of naming to be something of a defense mechanism, a way of recapturing history and claiming a world that is known, convinced as this poet is of the "power of poetry to transcend abstraction."

The poetry of Bob Dylan, "songs that pierce morally and glow poetically," is the subject of Johan Svedjedal's "Röstens litteratur [The literature of voice] (*Bonniers Litterära Magasin* 60:25–31). Part of the essay is a consideration of the influence of Dylan's texts on Swedish writers and poets, the rest an overview of themes and major considerations in Dylan's poetry. Svedjedal argues that Dylan can be said to have guarded not only the legacy of modernism, but that of Romanticism, since more than most writers he has assumed the roles of the Romantic artist as visionary and prophet.

The poetic strategies of Beverly Dahlen, an experimental feminist poet associated with writers described as "language centered," is the subject of Alan Shima's "Metonymy and the Promiscuous Text: Beverly Dahlen's *A Reading*" (*Consumption and American Culture,* pp. 134–48). Dahlen is a poet striving to escape the confines of patriarchal language, who through formal innovations—such as fractured narratives, inversion of literary conventions, and abandonment of genre distinctions—attempts to "subvert masculine literary values and forms." Shima argues that one of Dahlen's main concerns is "to write that which has not been fully thought" in an attempt to embody a future "where the very form of the writing becomes the corporeal space of that which is not fully clear." He demonstrates how *A Reading,* a blend of verse and prose narrative, uses metonymy as structuring strategy.

d. 20th-Century Fiction Øyvind Gulliksen uses the title of one of Thomas Wolfe's novels for his article on Norwegian travelogues from the Midwest, " 'You Can't Go Home Again'—Norwegian-American Travel Accounts" (*AmerSS* 23:95–104). Gulliksen singles out five travel accounts, published in the Midwest between 1900 and 1930, and discusses them in relation to the particular American version of the genre, insisting at the same time that they should be discussed as "a genuine literary genre." This is a very important point; we have used literary works more than enough as source material for history, sociology, and the like. Gulliksen bases his discussion on a very early review of some of these travel books by Waldemar Ager (in *Norden,* 1929). Ager's main point is that the writer of a travel book seems to insist that he is of more interest than the places and people he observes. Even in the better of the books under scrutiny in Gulliksen's essay, this proves to be true. The first book discussed by Ager—and by Gulliksen—is N. N. Rønning's *A Summer in Telemarken* (1903), a romantic description of rural life in Norway. Such a way of life seems basically to have remained static, at least if compared to the changing circumstances of life in the New World. Rønning displays a nostalgia for a past that is irrevocably lost, although he only wants this past to be a part of his readers' life in the New World—he did not want them to go home again, and he himself never went back after his one and only return trip eastward.

Wilhelm Pettersen, *Fra bjørkeskog og granholt* (1911), J. A. Berven, *Reisebreve og digte* (1916), Anton A. Nybroten, *Fra en Norgestur i 1919* (1922), and Kristian Prestegaard, *En sommer i Norge* (2 vols., 1928) are the other books discussed briefly by Gulliksen. Only Rønning's book seems to have reached more than a very limited audience, and some travel books were even printed privately and distributed in a few hundred copies to a clearly defined audience of Norwegian-born Americans. Gulliksen finally compares these books, or the trend they set, to recent attempts in the genre such as Patricia Hampl's award-winning *A Romantic Education of 1981* (1981), in which Hampl describes her journey back to Prague in search of a "usable past." The longing for a lost culture, and none to replace it, seems to send new Americans off on new journeys and to lead them to report from them, perhaps in the hope of creating a livable present?

Tom Sandqvist's *Vid Gränsen: En essä kring det postmoderna avantgardet i 10-talets New York* [At the border: An essay about the postmodern avant-garde in New York in the 1910s] (Stockholm: Carlssons Förlag) is a challenging and occasionally frustrating book, a mixture of social analysis, cultural reportage, and theoretical essay. Sandqvist's point of departure is the nature of the relationship between the modern and the postmodern, "between the modern as dawn and the postmodern as dusk? Or the modern as dusk?" He questions Habermas's frequently discussed suggestion that the "meltdown" of differences and contradictions today has become so complete that it is no longer possible for criticism to supply either contrasts or ambivalent nuances in a "totally discharged, calculated, and impotent world's flat and ash-gray landscape." Sandqvist, however, believes there is reason to highlight the fact that ambivalence is inscribed in the very notion of modernity, "the paradoxical weave of criticism and noncriticism, rebellion and distance, by means of the art and literature that make themselves legitimate precisely in the nonmeasurable." Are the modern and the postmodern caught perhaps in a circular motion of eternal return?

Seeking to establish the hotbed out of which new art erupts, to isolate the avant-garde impulse where the postmodern consciousness is announced, Sandqvist starts off with a portrait of New York City in the 1910s, then blends biographical data and anecdotes about political radicals, writers, poets, and painters with theoretical discussions. In an attempt to get at the zeitgeist, he seeks and demonstrates connections between these artists and their fates, identifying the reality of the borderline personality, the reality in which "fellow human beings rotate around the objectified, fragmented subject like more or less shadowy and always exchangeable objects and pawns." The text itself, the run-on sentences and collagelike structure, seems to bear witness to the themes it is trying to identify. And so does the attitude of the author toward his text, his purposely practiced lack of distance; he flows with the text, incorporating contradictions as well as inconsistencies, fragments well as totality.

In the growing field of biographical and bibliographical studies the Norwegian Faulkner scholar Hans H. Skei gives a complete survey of Faulkner's short-story career in *American Short-Story Writers, 1910–1945* (*DLB* 102:75–102). The essay includes a brief biographical sketch, but it is otherwise an account of the writing, publication, and collection of Faulkner's more than 120 short stories written over more than 40 years.

Skei's contribution to the International Faulkner Symposium in Rome in 1989, "The Function of Metafictional Elements in William Faulkner's Fiction," is included in *The Artist and His Masks* (pp. 147–58). Using Linda Hutcheon's *Narcissistic Narrative,* Peter Brooks's *Reading for the Plot,* and Brian McHale's *Postmodernist Fiction* as a theoretical basis, Skei discusses portions of *As I Lay Dying* and *Absalom, Absalom!* as well as short-story material, demonstrating that care is recommended in the search for "metafictional aspects" of Faulkner's fiction. Of course, the artist can be found, as well as an abundance of implicit comments on the pains of creative work. But we should never presume to think that we have unmasked the writer, Skei states, concluding that "even after our struggle with Faulkner's metafictions, we should linger on in the twilight zone of the magic of his fictions—a textual world in which wonders never cease."

Erik Nielsen's "Sexualiteten som motiv i Flannery O'Connors roman *Wise Blood*" [Sexuality as motive in Flannery O'Connor's novel *Wise*

Blood] (*Edda* 308–21) notes that even though sex and lust are not among O'Connor's favorite topics, a number of erotic situations do occur in her fiction. Although these instances have been generally ignored, they are, according to Nielsen, essential for an understanding of her work. The erotic situations, included in the fiction not because O'Connor wanted to dwell on romantic love or the pleasures of the flesh but as parts of a metaphysical argument, demand interpretation. Why does Hazel Motes go straight from the train to the whore Leora Watts's bed? Nielsen demonstrates Hazel's conviction that sin and evil in himself reside in the soul and that he equates sex with the nonexistence of the soul. It is the chance to prove his soullessness that urges Hazel to visit Leora, and whoring is his proof that Jesus never existed. After an entertaining mini-excursion on the meaning of morning erections in the modern southern novel, and with detailed reference to O'Connor's reading of Thomas Aquinas (see *ALS 1990,* pp. 471–72), Nielsen finds that O'Connor in depicting Hazel's vain attempts at secularizing his existence through sexual encounters sought to dramatize a universal battle between atheistic nihilism and religious faith.

In "Flannery O'Connor's Displaced Persons" and "Lost in the Cosmos: Place in Walker Percy" (*Where?: Place in Recent North American Fictions,* ed. Karl-Heinz Westarp [Aarhus], pp. 89–98, 108–17), Westarp shows how O'Connor and Percy used a southern setting as "a gateway to reality." They both show postlapsarian man as alienated or displaced physically as well as spiritually. The essay on O'Connor focuses on "The Displaced Person," in which "everybody is afraid of the otherness of newcomers." O'Connor addresses a concrete social reality in the story, but the displacement that all her characters finally experience is not just from their material possessions but also a "metaphysical displacement." The essay on Percy shows his protagonists on a quest for their true selves as wayfarers in a concrete reality. Westarp focuses on the discussion of man's place in the world in Percy's linguistic-philosophical essays. Percy assists us in our self-finding process by helping us focus on our self-deception. His message, the essay concludes, is that man can only hope to avoid despair and reach self-knowledge by listening to God-sent messages. In the same volume is Jan Nordby Gretlund's "A Neighborhood Voice: Eudora Welty's Sense of Place" (pp. 99–107), on Welty's use of her native Jackson in "Where Is the Voice Coming From?" Gretlund argues that the civil rights leader's assassination in the story is committed by a man not only a part of Jackson, but a part of all of us. His voice is not unknown to us, Gretlund concludes: "it is universal in its inhumanity to others and we all run the risk of falling victim to it." Gretlund has also written "On the Porch with Marcus Aurelius: Walker Percy's Stoicism" (*Walker Percy: Novelist and Philosopher,* ed. Gretlund and Karl-Heinz Westarp [Miss.], pp. 74–83), arguing that Percy's stoicism merits more critical attention because the stoic southern heritage (through William Alexander Percy) is essential in his fiction. After considering the battle between stoicism and Christianity in the individual novels, Gretlund concludes that Percy did not finally see them as antithetical, adding "what Percy shows us about his ethical Stoic heritage is *not* that there is something wrong with it, but that Stoicism is not enough."

Traditionally, the short story has been assigned a decidedly obscure position in Sweden, where writers seem to regard it more as a failed novel than an accomplished piece of prose on its own. There is, however, a considerable and growing public interest in contemporary American fiction, as shown by the many stories translated into Swedish almost simultaneously with their American publication. Fredrik Thurfjell's essay "Amerikanska novellister" [American short story writers] (*Bonniers Litterära Magasin* 60:40–45) attempts to sum up the state of the short story in the United States today, discussing major influences, trends, and tendencies. Thurfjell considers Raymond Carver, Richard Ford, Bobbie Ann Mason, and Tess Gallagher, and stresses the extent to which they are responsible for the impressive revitalization of American prose in the 1980s.

These minimalists, or "dirty realists," are the subject of another essay. In "Stranger than Fiction: Postmodernity and the Recent American Novel" (*Moderna Språk* 85:12–18) Peter Nicholls discusses the main features of Fredric Jameson's account of postmodernity as found in his 1984 essay, "Postmodernism, or, The Cultural Logic of Late Capitalism." Considering the relevance of these ideas to contemporary American fiction, Nicholls argues that the work of Jayne Anne Phillips, Carver, Mason, and others is troubling to Jameson's briefly outlined postmodern "schizophrenic" fiction. These texts are cognizant of the many images and simulacra of a postmodern "history," but they strive to reckon the effects of the characters' loss and displacement through a high degree of awareness of local experience, a realism that both appraises the reader, in the postmodern fashion, "of the constructedness of our world (forever mediated through signs and images) and yet remind us too of a sociality which postmodernity may occlude but not completely efface."

In "Amerikansk populaerlitteratur i Norge—noen betraktninger" [American popular literature in Norway: some comments] (*Skriftserie for litteraturvitenskap* 1) Hans H. Skei discusses the creation of a canon and whether or not it is possible to establish one for popular fiction since Norway lacks most institutions that keep watch over such a process. He borrows categories for classification of popular literature from Cawelti's *Adventure, Mystery and Romance* and from Eco's *The Role of the Reader,* and he tries to find the criteria used by Norwegian publishers when selecting popular American books for translation and publication. Apparently, fame, high sales, and book club publication are important criteria; yet one has to look carefully at the very different treatment of subgenres such as mystery fiction, science fiction, and the like. Skei has had his fill of Sidney Sheldon and Mary Higgins Clark while researching the field, but he knows that he will return to Elmore Leonard and Ed McBain as often as time allows.

Odense, Uppsala, Oslo Universities

20 General Reference Works

David J. Nordloh

The year's production of bibliographies, guides, literary dictionaries, and checklists reflects in broad ways the same mix of traditional and more contemporary concerns as permeates work in the field at large. But then the reference shelf is an unlikely site for dramatic revisionism. Comprehensive author and genre regional-literature studies retain their usual place, and publications on women writers and African-American and Latino writers reflect the solidity with which these newer concerns have fixed themselves in the enterprise. The quality of work in all of these areas is high. That it remains so despite the dramatic incursions of electronic technology into the library demonstrates how insistent is our need for thoughtfully selected and organized information rather than for indiscriminate, high-speed data.

If anything marks the difference between the old dispensation and the new in both the central interests of American literary scholarship and in methodology, it is *Bibliography of American Literature.* With the publication of volume 9 by Yale University Press, covering 14 authors (Edward Noyes Westcott to Elinor Wylie, with Walt Whitman, John Greenleaf Whittier, Augusta Jane Evans Wilson, and Constance Fenimore Woolson among them), this massive initiative at last concludes under the supervision of Michael Winship, 50 years after originally conceived by the late Jacob Blanck. Although fundamentally a first-edition bibliography, *BAL* also records the complexities of transatlantic publication, notes ephemera and subsidiary publications, and even provides selected lists of related secondary items. The final entry is numbered 23539, but that number disguises the actual number of separate items referred to—I would estimate a minimum of 75,000—as well as the multiple copies examined in preparing the full descriptions of the primary items. Blanck and his assistants and institutional collaborators probably handled half a million books in the making of this monument. Monument it is, with all the ambiguity that word invokes in the present age: a triumphant production of that great moment of canonical American culture that also produced *Literary History of the United States,* a lifetime labor of love of the kind that computers and on-line library catalogs seem to make obsolete. But *BAL* gives us the kind of skillful judgment of the record that these newer resources do not—as anyone who studies the findings concerning intercallations, variant states, and hidden printings in the history of Whitman's *Leaves of Grass* in volume 9, for instance, soon discovers.

Facts on File Bibliography of American Fiction 1919–1988 (Facts on File), ed. Matthew J. Bruccoli and Judith S. Baughman, is the first published part of a planned three-part series; the other two will cover fiction to 1865 and from 1866 to 1918. Presented in a single alphabetical series over this two-volume set are more than 200 authors, from James Agee to Roger Zelazny. Entries, signed by their contributors, consist of the briefest biographical-critical headnotes and uniformly organized lists of primary and selected significant secondary materials, along the model of the *New Cambridge Bibliography of English Literature* (1972). Authors are placed in the series according to the dates of their first major work rather than simply their earliest publications; Sinclair Lewis, for instance, appears in this part of the series because of *Main Street* (1920). The primary listings are heavily indebted to such sources as *Bibliography of American Literature* and *DLB;* the secondary ones are up-to-date selections of major scholarly work. The set also includes "A Vade Mecum for Students of American Literature," identifying 100 basic reference works, and a more comprehensive "General Bibliography: Reference and Research Works." Even though I am an advisor to the project, I have to admit that it is thoughtfully designed and well-executed. A critical project also focused on fiction is *The Columbia History of the American Novel* (Columbia), under the general editorship of Emory Elliott, a companion volume to the *Columbia Literary History of the United States* (1988). Its four major sections, five introductions, and 31 chapters constitute a coordination of essays rather than anything so definitive as a history; the essays are devoid of documentation, and the appended biographies of American authors and selected bibliography of critical works—the latter uncategorized and unannotated—do not particularly enhance the usefulness of the whole for reference purposes.

A 10-volume supplement to "The Schomburg Library of Nineteenth-

Century Black Women Writers" (Oxford), ed. Henry Louis Gates, Jr., adds both more texts and an impressive bibliography to this series, the first 30 volumes of which were published in 1988. Each of the text volumes, reproducing in facsimile where feasible, begins with prefatory comments by Gates and a scholarly introduction. Seven of these deal with single authors: *The Collected Works of Olivia Ward Bush-Banks, The Collected Works of Effie Waller Smith, Selected Works of Ida B. Wells-Barnett, Narrative of Soujourner Truth, Selected Works of Angelina Weld Grimké, The Works of Katherine Davis Chapman Tillman,* and *A Hairdresser's Experience in High Life* by Eliza Potter. One reprints two biographies: Josephine Brown's *Biography of an American Bondman* and Frances Rollin's *Life and Public Services of Martin R. Delaney.* Another, *Short Fiction by Black Women, 1900–1920,* prepared by Elizabeth Ammons, reprints in the order of original publication 46 stories by more than 30 different writers selected from the periodicals *Colored American Magazine* and *Crisis.* The bibliography volume, comp. Jean Fagan Yellin and Cynthia D. Bond and bearing the exhaustive title *The Pen Is Ours: A Listing of Writings By and About African-American Women Before 1910, with Secondary Bibliography to the Present,* is even more impressive than the title suggests. Its five sections inventory writings by and about women who produced separate publications, by and about women who had been held in slavery and whose narrative or biographies were written by others, by and about women whose work appeared in periodicals and collections, about notable women not writers but written about, and selected contemporary publications dealing with women of the period covered. The artificiality of the distinctions between women who published books and those who only wrote is one of the major awkwardnesses of the arrangement, but an index of all the names mentioned in the volume compensates. And the value of the material also compensates for the ugliness of the design of this series, with its small, squat pages, tight binding, and black-cloth covers stamped crudely in gold.

Three self-standing publications survey biographies. The most satisfying of them is *St. James Guide to Biography* (St. James), ed. Paul E. Schellinger, which takes the world and not just England or the United States as its field. The succinctness of the editor's prefatory description of the project is indicative of the clarity of the whole work: "We do not supply biographical data on the entrants, but rather bibliographical and critical analysis of biographies already available." The list is arranged alphabetically by the names of persons biographized, with each entry consisting in turn of a selective list of the most important or current biographies and a signed essay evaluating them. Some entries are perfunctory (see, for example, the description of Washington Irving's *History of the Life and Voyages of Christopher Columbus* under "Columbus"), but on the whole the guide is both informative and sensible. Similar in organization to the *St. James Guide* is *Biographies of Creative Artists: An Annotated Bibliography* (Garland), comp. Susan M. Stievater, which may suffer from its being a one-person project. Here too the record is selective, emphasizing significant book-length works; thus, some major artists are missing because no such work exists, and some very minor ones are present because the biographies are so good. The conception is not necessarily faulty, but the execution is, with annotation both unfocused and badly written. Besides a comprehensive author index, there are indexes listing the entrants by art form and by country of origin, and another listing women creative artists (I suppose we figure out who the men are by a process of elimination). And then there is *Literary Exile in the Twentieth Century: An Analysis and Biographical Dictionary* (Greenwood), ed. Martin Tucker. The 20 pages of preface and introduction do not begin to make sense of this project, much less put its findings to use. There are alphabetically arranged sections of "Group Entries" (e.g., American Expatriates in Europe, 1900–1990) and "Writers in Exile." Exile is a controlling feature in the essays describing the groups; it seems coincidental in the author biographies. Appendixes of waves of exile (from where to where), flight and expulsion (identifying points of departure and who left from there when), refuge and haven, and exile by category (cultural, political, and so on) support the whole, and no doubt will enhance its value to exile specialists.

Meanwhile, new volumes expand several continuing biographical series. Supplement III of *American Writers: A Collection of Literary Biographies* (Scribner's), ed. Lea Baechler and A. Walton Litz, in two volumes, forms the latest continuation of *American Writers: A Collection of Literary Biographies* (1974). But whereas the first edition of this work simply gathered together essays originally published separately in the series of Minnesota Pamphlets on American Writers, the supplements to it have presented original essays, with increasing emphasis on the contemporary, the female, and the ethnic and racial. The essays are printed in alphabetical order, John Ashbery to Walker Percy in volume one, Philip Roth to Louis Zukovsky in volume two. A cumulative index to the entire project is appended.

The cumulative index is also an essential feature of the three most recent additions to *Dictionary of Literary Biography*, a series with so many volumes now that it overwhelms the rest of the American literature reference collection on the shelves. One is *American Short-Story Writers, 1910–1945: Second Series* (*DLB* 102), ed. Bobby Ellen Kimbel, with essays on 37 authors, among them Dreiser, Faulkner, Hemingway, Sinclair Lewis, J. D. Salinger, and Welty. The essays do their best to focus on the stories as stories; unfortunately, the introductory bibliographies, adhering to the *DLB* pattern, concentrate on their appearance in book collections. *American Literary Biographers, First Series* (*DLB* 103) and *American Literary Biographers, Second Series* (*DLB* 111), ed. Steven Serafin, survey between them a total of 34 authors; included in the group are such of our distinguished professional colleagues as Matthew J. Bruccoli, Carlos Baker, Edwin H. Cady, Joseph Blotner, Scott Donaldson, and Madeleine B. Stern. Although these two volumes were published in the same year, they are not alphabetically sequential. Back to that cumulative index again.

An essential contribution to women's studies is *Women in the West: A Guide to Manuscript Sources* (Garland), by Susan Armitage et al. A project growing out of Andrea Hinding's *Women's History Sources* (1979), this inventory of primary materials is organized by state, city, and archive name (including, very helpfully, address, telephone number, and contact person), and provides in each instance a list of kinds but not numbers of documents, including diaries, reminiscences, photographs, and oral histories. Even in this raw catalog the recovered record is impressive. Almost as sizable is the more strictly literary canon of more than 6,000 items identified in *Poetry by Women to 1900: A Bibliography of American and British Writers* (Toronto), comp. Gwenn Davis and Beverly A. Joyce, the second volume in the series "Bibliographies of Writings by American and British Women to 1900." Writers are grouped alphabetically within 50-year periods, and authors' names are accompanied by bibliographical information on their published works. No effort is made to ascribe nationality. A subject index, including such categories as affection, bereavement, sunshine, and religious thoughts, tends to stress the least satisfactory aspect of gendered history of the genre. Also adding to bibliographical information about women in genre is Carol Farley Kessler's "Bibliography of Utopian Fiction by United States Women, 1836–1988" (*Utopian Studies* 1 [1990]:1–58), listing 262 titles of stories and novels, arranged by period, year, and author; and Kathleen L. Nichols's

"Earlier American Women Dramatists: From National to Sexual Politics" (*THStud* 11:129–50), which demonstrates that there was indeed a feminist theater before Rachel Crothers and Susan Glaspell by offering a survey essay about earlier work and a selected bibliography of authors, titles, and dates and places of first production.

Besides the bibliography in the Schomburg supplement, mentioned above, there were three lesser contributions on African-American topics. James Edward Newby has compiled *Black Authors: A Selected Annotated Bibliography* (Garland) "of works written, coauthored or edited *by* black Americans." The attempt to cover all possible occupations, from sports to science, necessarily means thinness. Chapter 7, "Language and Literature," records 834 entries, some of them annotated, some not, one of them assigning Charles Chesnutt's *The Marrow of Tradition* to Donald Chesley. Information relevant to literature also dots *African-American Traditions in Song, Sermon, Tale, and Dance, 1600s–1920: An Annotated Bibliography of Literature, Collections, and Artworks* (Greenwood), comp. Eileen Southern and Josephine Wright. Broadly surveying relevant materials both primary and secondary—collections of African-American poems and stories as well as George Washington Cable's 1886 essay describing slaves in New Orleans performing "The Dance in Place Congo," for example—which deal in the kinds of performance listed in its title, the volume treats literature as the first category in its four chronological sections. A fifth section inventories the WPA Slave Narrative Collection. All items are annotated, and the tables of contents of printed collections are listed in full. And James V. Hatch's "Anthologies of African-American Plays" (*BALF* 25:183–92) lists the contents of some 30 collections composed solely or predominantly of this work; his article is part of a special issue on "The Black Church and the Black Theatre," ed. Hatch and Michael S. Weaver. (With its first 1992 issue, incidentally, *BALF* becomes *African American Review*.)

The literature of other culture groups also gets some attention. *Jewish American Fiction Writers: An Annotated Bibliography* (Garland), ed. Gloria L. Cronin et al., is massive and useful and yet less comprehensive than the title might suggest. More than 60 authors, among them Stanley Elkin, Howard Fast, and Tillie Olsen, are represented by complete primary and fairly exhaustive secondary records. But even with that and more than 1,200 pages, the book makes "no attempt to add to the current debates among Jewish writers and critics . . . as to what constitutes a Jewish American author or work of fiction." I suppose the implication of that remark is that some writers considered marginally Jewish American are not included; it does not explain, however, why such central figures as Bellow, Malamud, and Philip Roth are also missing, and by what process of discrimination *Jewish American Fiction Writers* selects instead "the 'vast penumbra' of lesser but not unimportant lights" in the Jewish-American tradition. A more modest and satisfactory enterprise is María Teresa Márquez's "A Selected Bibliography of New Mexican Hispanic Literature," pp. 297–316 in Erlinda Gonzales-Berry, ed., *Pasó por Aquí: Critical Essays on the New Mexican Literary Tradition, 1542–1988* (New Mexico, 1989), noting primary and secondary sources, including such writers as Sabine Ulibarrí and Rudolfo Anaya as well as such genres as contemporary Chicano poetry.

The lure of place explains several bibliographies of region. Tom Lewis has compiled *Storied New Mexico: An Annotated Bibliography of Novels with New Mexico Settings* (New Mexico). Lewis is cautious in his claims about the volume, noting that in content and format it "falls between an amateur's checklist and a scholar's study." Organizing alphabetically by author, from Edward Abbey to Eva Zumwalt, he offers some 1,200 entries, supplying for each work first-edition information and a statement of theme full enough to justify its inclusion. Concerned that there might be later attempts to remap the territory, Lewis marks some items as marginal but records them nonetheless to "save someone future disappointment" and then offers a separate list of works he has been told fit his criterion but which he has not seen. Appropriate indexes support a nicely modest but effective project. Less well-designed and executed is Donald W. Maxwell's *Literature of the Great Lakes Region: An Annotated Bibliography* (Garland). Unlike Lewis's compilation, which resulted from reading the books, this one is derived from other lists. Maxwell's standard of selection is that works must, "to some extent, be preoccupied with the region or a locality within it. Furthermore, the author should have had the intention of writing about the area while creating the work." He organizes alphabetically by author, then title, and offers perfunctory annotation that is sometimes irrelevant to his focus and sometimes just wrong (for example, that Howells's *A Hazard of New Fortunes* should be included because of its "being based, in part, on the Haymarket Riot of 1886 and its aftermath").

Vincent Prestianni's "From Porter to O'Connor: Modern Southern Writers of Fiction: Seven Bibliographies of Bibliographies" (*BB* 48:137–51) treats Katherine Anne Porter, Andrew Lytle, Eudora Welty, Walker

Percy, Carson McCullers, Peter Taylor, and Flannery O'Connor to a record so elaborately annotated and cross-referenced that the titles of the bibliographies get lost in the maze.

Useful for special aspects of literary and cultural history are Madeleine B. Stern and Daniel Shealy's "The No Name Series, with a Bibliography" (*SAR:* 375–402), which identifies the authors of the anonymous items in this three-series late-19th-century publishing enterprise whose most famous participant was Emily Dickinson, that epitome of anonymity; and Stephen P. Hidalgo's "A Selected Bibliography of Vietnam War Poetry" (*BB* 48:12–24), whose record by year of first publication of items in journals, author collections, and general anthologies packs a great deal in a small space.

I will conclude with a grabbag of useful resources. One is *Twentieth-Century Literary Movements Index* (Omnigraphics), ed. Laurie Lanzen Harris and Helene Henderson. The first section of the volume identifies movements, artists associated with them, and the crucial reference sources in which the movements are discussed; the second section does the same for authors, identifying them with movements and noting reference sources. Another, of continuing value, is the *DLB Yearbook*. In addition to regular essays on the year's work in the novel, short story, poetry, drama, literary biography, and book reviewing, each volume covers the winner of the Nobel Prize in Literature, discusses new literary periodicals, offers symposia on critical topics, obituaries, and much else. There is even a list of the major literary awards and honors announced during the year. For strictly bibliographical purposes I should also mention the "Bibliography: A Checklist of Scholarship on Southern Literature," supplied by George C. Longest and his colleagues in *Mississippi Quarterly*. Since 1988 this listing, which had appeared quarterly in the journal, has been consolidated into a separate annual supplement volume. Although only a southern record, it is nonetheless an increasingly vital resource as the MLA *Bibliography* gets ever shakier.

Indiana University

Author Index

Subject Index